Sustainable Development

Studies in Environmental Anthropology and Ethnobiology

General Editor: **Roy Ellen**, FBA

Professor of Anthropology, University of Kent at Canterbury

Interest in environmental anthropology has grown steadily in recent years, reflecting national and international concern about the environment and developing research priorities. This major new international series, which continues a series first published by Harwood and Routledge, is a vehicle for publishing up-to-date monographs and edited works on particular issues, themes, places or peoples which focus on the interrelationship between society, culture and environment. Relevant areas include human ecology, the perception and representation of the environment, ethno-ecological knowledge, the human dimension of biodiversity conservation and the ethnography of environmental problems. While the underlying ethos of the series will be anthropological, the approach is interdisciplinary.

Sustainable Development

An Appraisal from the Gulf Region

Edited by
Paul Sillitoe

berghahn
NEW YORK · OXFORD
www.berghahnbooks.com

Published by

Berghahn Books

www.berghahnbooks.com

Library of Congress Cataloging-in-Publication Data

Sustainable development : an appraisal from the Gulf Region / edited by
  Paul Sillitoe. — First edition.
      pages cm — (Environmental anthropology and ethnobiology ; volume 19)
  Includes bibliographical references and index.
    ISBN 978-1-78238-371-0 (hardback : alk. paper) — ISBN 978-1-78238-372-7
    (ebook)
    1. Sustainable development—Persian Gulf Region. 2. Sustainable
  development—Government policy—Persian Gulf Region. 3. Economic
  development—Environmental aspects—Persian Gulf States. 4. Environmental
  policy—Persian Gulf States. I. Sillitoe, Paul, 1949– , author, editor of compilation.
    HC415.3.Z9E578 2014
    338.9536'07—dc23

                                                                    2014000990

British Library Cataloguing in Publication Data

A catalogue record for this book is available from the British Library

Printed on acid-free paper

ISBN 978-1-78238-371-0 hardback
ISBN 978-1-78238-372-7 ebook

Contents

Illustrations

Figures

Tables

Boxes

Foreword

Sheikha Al-Misnad

It is my privilege to introduce this timely book which challenges us all, in the academic realm and beyond, with the question: how can sustainable development be achieved by a country – and indeed a region – so heavily reliant on hydrocarbon resources and on an accelerated trajectory of economic and urban development? This question has occupied policymakers in Qatar for several years now, and the State of Qatar has made great strides in positioning sustainable development as a cornerstone of its future outlook in both the *Qatar National Vision 2030* and the *National Development Strategy 2011–2016*.

The book begins by exploring the definition of *sustainable development*, which has been used in a wide variety of contexts. For some, sustainability refers to environmental sustainability and the concern over practices that deplete irreplaceable natural resources. For others, the main feature of sustainability is financial sustainability, meaning the ability of an organization or even a project to maintain itself and provide for its future needs given a limited set of financial resources. Others still are concerned about sustaining local culture and traditional ways of life in the midst of fast-paced changes. The different emphases are certainly not mutually exclusive, and they share an underlying concern. The concern is over maintaining present gains while considering their future costs. It is a concern over what we leave behind for the coming generations and the type of burdens they will inherit.

Any discussion of sustainability is therefore necessarily a discussion of roles that need to be defined clearly and of responsibilities to be shared. It is a discussion that touches us all in our different walks of life. The themes of the book: energy and economics, urban issues, environmental issues and social and cultural development all point to the complex and interrelated nature of sustainable development.

The book draws on work undertaken as part of the sustainable development initiative at Qatar University in partnership with Qatar Shell GTL, which rightly points out that there is urgent need for education and discussion of sustainable development in our region. Indeed as the primary units of socialization, the place where values are shaped and visions of the future are nurtured, educational institutions, like Qatar University, have a natural role and even a moral obligation to lead the intellectual and values debate about sustainability.

There have been several initiatives around the world to integrate the concept of sustainability into education. They have ranged from adjustments of the academic curriculum to changes in the physical environment and infrastructure of educational institutions. There is much that remains to be explored and learned from those initiatives. However, we do know some facts. We know that the issue of integrating sustainable development into education involves building a knowledge base that may necessitate modifications to the curricula. However, the more difficult battle is that of values that would facilitate teaching and practicing sustainability. What is needed is fundamentally a shift in long-held beliefs, behaviors and values, and, as we all know, this is the most difficult part of any effort to change. The upcoming generation in this region has known nothing but abundance and wealth. It is not easy for such a generation to consider the impact of their lifestyles and to think seriously about how to change them. With all the tools of globalization at their disposal, this generation, perhaps more than any other, has been bombarded with all kinds of messages about the ideal way of life, the meaning of success and their right to pursue them. How educators can impart a sense of responsibility towards the future and towards other people who share this planet is a challenge that we all need to think about.

We also know that we have made much progress in methodologies and technologies of teaching and learning. How then can we put these pedagogic advancements in the service of integrating sustainability into education? This is a challenge indeed, but it is not an insurmountable one for the creative and motivated educator. This book will also add to the much-needed conversation on methodologies in researching sustainable development, and it is the hope that this research will then find its way into practical applications.

Effective and strategic partnerships between institutions of higher education and their local communities are crucial. The days of universities as isolated ivory towers are long gone. Universities are now enmeshed in society's problems and must be part of producing solutions with cooperative and creative strategies. Similarly, industries, whether energy or otherwise, cannot afford to operate in disregard of the impact of their actions on the environment and on people. The visionary companies are those that realize that sustainability and consideration of human impact is in their best interest, whether measured by the financial profit margin or any other measure. The gap between academic discourse and industry practices is an important one to bridge, and I am glad to see that this book has included the input and perspectives of professionals and academics of diverse backgrounds. Without this holistic perspective and joint discussion, progress is unlikely to occur.

In conclusion, sustainability is simply a concept that we can ill afford to ignore. We must acknowledge the difficulty of teaching its meaning and implications to a generation that has known nothing but prosperity as well as the challenge of changing values and established mindsets. This book is a welcome voice in that conversation.

Sustainable Development in the Gulf

Paul Sillitoe

Sustainable development has emerged as a prominent issue in the twenty-first century. Indeed, it is arguably going to be *the* issue with growing evidence of unsustainable use of the world's resources, such as its fossil fuel reserves, and related environmental pollution, for instance alarmingly evident in climate-change predictions (Adams 2001; Baker 2006; Robertson 2014). The column inches, research resources and teaching time devoted to sustainable development and associated topics the world over since the late 1980s are colossal. They contrast with the position in the Gulf and Middle East region where, until recently, regardless of environmental concerns plain to see with harsh climate and scarcity of water, countries have shown little interest in sustainable development. The goal was economic growth with scant regard to environmental issues. They sought rapid industrialization and urbanization, often featuring environmentally unfriendly technology, without apparently considering the negative consequences, such as destruction of natural resources and pollution. There is increasing realization that secure long-term development cannot be achieved at the expense of the environment.

There is an urgent need for awareness and discussion of sustainable development in the region. It is on a doubly unsustainable trajectory: first, in supplying non-renewable oil and gas to the rest of the world to meet current unsustainable global energy demands, worryingly polluting the atmosphere further with CO_2 laden gases; second, in using the enormous revenues it receives from these energy exports to develop large urban conurbations that will prove unsustainable on the region's resources when non-renewable fossil fuels are exhausted, as is already evident with water supplies dependent on energy-hungry desalination plants and the pumping of groundwater from deep aquifers at rates way beyond natural replenishment.

The United Arab Emirates and Qatar currently have the largest ecological footprints of any nations in the world. They are also the unenviable holders of world-record carbon footprints, with Kuwait coming in third place in that league table and Saudi Arabia eleventh (Ewing et al. 2010: 19). The ecological footprint indicates our impact on the planet; it is a global carrying capacity calculation that tells us the land area needed to provide us with what we consume (food, goods, energy etc.) and to absorb our waste (Wackernagel and Rees 1996). It may be expressed in global hectares (1.9 ha per person is the world's carrying capacity) or number of planets required if everyone were to enjoy the same standard of living (it would require more than five planet Earths for all of us to live like Gulf citizens, which is clearly out of the question).

The idea for this book originated when I accepted a post to teach and research sustainable development at Qatar University, funded by Shell, one of the multinational energy companies that have a large stake in the country's liquid gas developments.[1] Few can resist commenting on the post's irony when told about it. But it indicates something hopeful, I believe, namely a widespread wish for us to get back onto a sustainable pathway, all of us (energy company employee or green activist) inhabiting the one planet. Or maybe for the cynical it just so happens that capitalist economic interests coincide with environmentalist concerns. No one denies that fossil fuel reserves are finite and will probably run out in a few decades (even with newly discovered sources such as 'frackable' gas containing shales). Consequently, we must find alternative sources of energy, and renewable ones are logically the more secure and have become a priority with mounting evidence of the environmental damage caused by non-renewable ones.

The magnitude of the challenge of establishing a sustainable development programme at the University soon became evident. No ecological footprint calculation is necessary to tell the visitor to the Gulf that the energy-profligate lifestyle is unsustainable. However, awareness of sustainable development or 'green' issues more generally proved to be hazy at best among Qatar University students. They were not alone. Tenure of the chair, for instance, required membership of Shell's 'Sustainable Development Committee' where the subjects discussed ranged from the excellent safety record at a gigantic liquid-gas-processing-plant construction site (a health and safety issue) and the funding of a garment-factory project for women in a town affected by the plant's construction (a community outreach issue).[2] When I turned to the daunting task of teaching sustainable development, I found that while the best way to engage students' interest was to address familiar issues that feature in their lives, there is little written on the topic in a Gulf context, or even a Middle East one. So the idea of this book was born to introduce sustainable development, both to encourage students to ask what the implications are for their region and to have the confidence to draw on their cultural heritage in thinking about the issues (Ansari 1992; Foltz, Denny and Baharuddin 2003). [3]

The book aims to give a wide-ranging introduction to the field of sustainable development focusing on the Gulf region generally, although not exclusively. It innovatively teams university faculty and government personnel from the Gulf and wider Middle East region with colleagues from Europe and North America whose research interests focus on sustainable development. In this way, the volume ties together a well-informed regional focus with an in-depth understanding of sustainable development issues and research, drawing on experience from various regions of the world, including Africa, Pacific, Asia and Latin America. It outlines the context, contemporary and historical, local and global, of the sustainability debate. It is structured according to key themes. Each contributor outlines principal concepts and foci that their respective field brings to bear on sustainable development (such as the environment, health, urbanism etc.), before reviewing and discussing current problems and debates, and proposing areas for future research and policy analysis. In this way, each chapter deals with cutting-edge issues central to the Gulf in the context of global development initiatives and dilemmas and overarching concerns central to sustainable development.

The volume is designed to be useful to those teaching and studying sustainable development, particularly in the Gulf and wider Middle East region, and also beyond. It is aimed at a general audience interested in the issues and seeks to inform discussion central to development and sustainability, both within educational (school and university) contexts and beyond, between interested parties in government and industry and wider public. What does it mean to be sustainable in a region reliant on oil revenues and in the throes of an economic development boom? What are the challenges faced? What needs to happen now and in the future to enable the Gulf region to achieve sustainability? How are obstacles to the creation of a more sustainable lifestyle being tackled? It is such questions that are the focus of this book.

The Gulf

The Gulf, or *Khaleej* in Arabic, comprises a shallow body of water extending from the Shatt al-Arab delta in the northwest to the narrow Strait of Hormuz in the southeast.[4] It is surrounded by Saudi Arabia, United Arab Emirates, Qatar, Kuwait, Bahrain, Oman, Iraq and Iran; the former six countries comprise the Gulf Cooperation Council, which is a political and economic union (figure 0.1). It is a hot subtropical desert region. Rainfall is low (approximately 80 mm per annum) and temperature high (reaching 50°C and beyond in the summer). Rocky hills, gravel plains and sand dunes (figure 0.2) are common features with saline mudflats and some beaches along coasts (Osborne 1996). Vegetation is sparse in this harsh arid environment, comprising a few drought-tolerant trees and perennial grasses together with some dwarf perennials and annuals, some of which bloom after rains; it includes salt-tolerant halophytes on the coast (Batanouny 2001). Wild animals include rodents (jerboa, gerbils), antelope (oryx, sand gazelle), goats (ibex, tahr), lizards and snakes and many migratory and local birds (pelicans, cranes, flamingos etc.). Wildlife is vulnerable in this fragile and austere natural environment (Gross 1987). There is also a rich marine fauna including dugong, dolphins and turtles, with

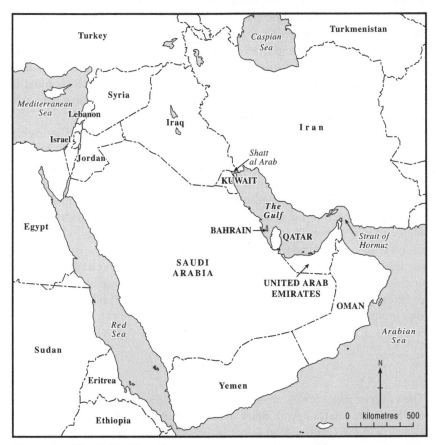

Figure 0.1. The Gulf region.

Figure 0.2. Desert environment at Khor al Udayd, S. Qatar.

extensive areas of coral reef and mangrove swamp (figure 0.3) supporting a range of fish and crustaceans. Some of these are at risk with the destruction and pollution of habitats, notably the major oil spillages occurring in recent wars.

The Gulf has good fishing grounds exploited by dhow fleets. The pearl oyster was also previously important to the local economy but diving largely ceased in the 1930s with production of the cultured pearl. The herding of camels, goats and sheep by nomadic Bedouin was also significant with some farming around oases of dates, alfalfa, beans and other vegetables. Today the Gulf States derive most of their income from oil and gas (Kubursi 1984). The region is the world's largest source of crude oil and gas with over 50 per cent of global oil reserves and some 40 per cent of gas reserves, and related petrochemical industries are the mainstay of the economy such as petrol refining and liquefied natural gas production. They are funding a development boom with numerous infrastructure and other construction projects. The regional economy depends on large numbers of migrant workers to supply the necessary labour, largely from South and Southeast Asia with some from neighbouring Arab and North African countries, Europe and America. The influx of migrant labour, greatly outnumbering Gulf citizens, gives rise to an 'us and them' attitude

Figure 0.3. Mangroves at Qurm, Oman.

that promotes loyalty to current political arrangements that 'keep them in their place'. The per capita incomes of citizens are among the highest in the world. The state is also seeking to invest the returns on oil and gas to build up an economy that will be able to support the current standard of living when these non-renewable resources run out or the world switches to more sustainable energy sources, with considerable investment, for instance, in education and also foreign capital assets, including land acquisitions elsewhere (notably parts of Africa) in an attempt to ensure future food security.

The southern Gulf States speak the same Arabic dialect and have a regional culture. They are culturally conservative Muslim nations. The Gulf Cooperation Council comprises hereditary monarchies with limited formal but considerable informal political representation. The rulers comport themselves as benevolent leaders who use traditional tribal consultation channels in making decisions, their administrations adhering strictly to Islamic *shari'a* law, ensuring security for all (Gause 1994). They distribute the oil and gas revenues so as to bolster their hold on power, particularly seeing that they keep influential families and tribal sheiks content, and further cement allegiances with appointments to powerful posts in the state administration and through marriage. A small elite of mostly related persons holds political power; prime ministers and many cabinet ministers belong to ruling families, which invariably control foreign affairs, defence and interior portfolios. It is a continuation of the tribal tradition of buying loyalty and alliances, and skilfully manipulating relations between internal factions and external enemies to counterbalance one another (Eickelman 1981: 361–363; Netton 1986; Zahlan 1998: 21; Abdulla 2000).

While the Gulf States are experimenting with forms of popularly elected advisory councils and representative legislatures, the ruling families retain control of the majority of seats, ensuring that their central autocratic authority remains intact with all decision making in their hands (Peterson 1988; Nonneman 2007). To the outsider they may look like fragile political arrangements, particularly in view of the recent 'Arab Spring', but they have proved surprisingly resilient so far. And all citizens share in the petroleum-derived wealth with, for instance, free health care, welfare services and education, and free utilities (water and electricity), no taxation, low fuel costs and subsidized goods, massive investment in infrastructure shared by all and employment for those who seek it, much in the expanded state bureaucracy. In short, the state, as the owner of most national assets and the main employer, encourages dependency. They are not arrangements likely to foster the frugality necessary for sustainable lifestyles that are within, and represent equitable consumption of, the planet's limited resources long term.

From the Past to the Present

It is informative to set contemporary concerns about sustainable development within an archaeological context, with the Middle East region witnessing the collapse of several unsustainable civilizations in the past. In the first chapter, Mark Manuel, Robin Coningham, Gavin Gillmore and Hassan Fazeli remind us that concern with sustainability, while currently a hot topic – particularly with dire warnings about human-induced climate change – is not new. Looking at sustainable development issues from an archaeological viewpoint is noteworthy given the short-term focus of most writing on development. Rather than repeatedly make the same mistakes, we have lessons to learn from the past.

The early kingdoms of Mesopotamia and the eastern Mediterranean broke down in the Late Bronze Age about 4,200 years ago. There was political instability, central authorities collapsed with violent struggles for power, depopulation occurred notably in urban areas and disruption of long-distance trade led to shortages of certain goods. The reasons for all of this are unclear. Some think that sudden climate change led to the collapse, with a drop in rainfall resulting in extended drought, crop failure and famine (Fagan 2004: 127–146; Rosen 2007). The shortages resulted in overpopulation crises (Babylonian seals from 1600 BC mention problems of overpopulation; Cohen 1995). Others note migration or possibly invasion by Indo-European populations, such as Dorian, Thracian and Macedonian peoples, movements perhaps triggered by environmental change (Yoffee 2005: 131–160). Yet others cite increased warfare featuring new weapons and tactics, perhaps exacerbated by environmental problems and associated socio-economic stresses and shortages of goods. The disturbance of maritime trade by 'Sea People' pirates would have increased the pressure on these fragile civilizations.

While archaeologists have previously approached the issue of sustainability in the idiom of the collapse of civilizations, which they long attributed to single momentous events such as natural catastrophes or foreign invasions, they are critical of such rather simplistic 'crash of society' interpretations today and argue that several factors more likely contributed to the crashes with complex social, economic and environmental interactions. A combination of factors was perhaps more likely behind the disruption experienced by Late Bronze Age states, the socio-political complexity of which – political centralization and economic specialization – proved a weakness and contributed to a 'general systems collapse' (a response to complexity that features recourse to simpler arrangements, in this case a return to small city states; Tainter 1988). The complex societies proved fragile in the face of social unrest occurring between states, with citizen revolts and wars, inflamed by fickle mercenaries.

The archaeological evidence (figure 0.4) also suggests that some civilizations evinced long-term sustainability, constantly adapting to changing environmental and political-economic conditions. Manuel, Coningham, Gillmore and Fazeli, for instance, argue that archaeological evidence from the Chalcolithic communities of the Central Plateau of Iran, dating from 7,000 years ago, shows that they sustainably adapted to the marginal semi-arid environment over extended periods of time, moving their settlements as water courses shifted, skilfully using irrigation channels to manage water supplies. The evidence of pottery wheels and ceramic kilns point to craft specialization in places such as Tepe Pardis, where large deposits of suitable clay occurred, with inhabitants producing pottery that could be traded elsewhere, showing how appropriate use of resources and technology allowed for craft specialization and long-term sustainable settlement. It is an early example of how trade, exploiting local natural advantages in raw materials, can sustain communities, so long as the exploitation remains within sustainable limits.

Figure 0.4. Archaeological dig at Zubara, N. Qatar

The archaeological evidence of communities in the Middle East relying on craft specialization and trade to overcome arid region environmental constraints is a forerunner of today's Gulf arrangements, where over 90 per cent of food stuffs are imports exchanged for gas and oil exports. Commerce is a central theme in both capitalist- and socialist-informed economic development discourse. But can we learn to manage it and avoid the unsustainable booms and busts, as experienced in calls for regulation and then deregulation of markets (recently manifest in development as 'structural adjustment' with crippling effects on many Third World economies), and consequent deleterious impacts on economic activity as one interest group or another – banks, companies, unions – gets the upper hand and ruthlessly exploits its advantage to profit from others?

Economic and social arrangements are clearly an aspect of the sustainability or otherwise of current developments, as shown by the growth mentality of market economics thwarting any prospect of a sustainable equilibrium state, as I will discuss in this book's conclusion. Rodney Wilson asks in chapter 8 if Islamic economics could offer a resolution to the conflict between growth and sustainability. The application of Islamic principles to finance has proved successful and this could potentially contribute further to the promotion of sustainability. The performance of

Islamic banks during the recent global financial crisis was more reliable than other institutions that engaged in the unsustainable trade of dubious and ultimately toxic financial assets. Islam promotes a more cautious approach to finance, avoiding speculative dealings and sharing risk fairly (Wilson 2008). It could be argued that Islamic finance is better suited to funding long-term sustainable development projects. The principles of *shari'a* compliance parallel those of ethical or socially responsible investment, which aim to invest in ecologically friendly activities and eschew those that damage the environment. Islamic institutions have developed screening methods to distinguish between acceptable and unacceptable activities that have the potential to promote sustainability by persuading businesses to change their practices. Furthermore, Islamic views on the custodianship of natural resources (Ansari 1992; Foltz, Denny and Baharuddin 2003) chime with financial mechanisms designed to promote environmentally responsible practices, such as trade in carbon credits. We should not however have unrealistic expectations for Islamic financial institutions managed by fallible human beings, some of which were involved in Dubai's speculative property crash, which posed questions about how compliant their practices were with *shari'a* law.

What is Development?

Before proceeding further, it is perhaps as well to have some idea of what we understand by the term *sustainable development*, which for many is synonymous with *economic development*, although how the two could be squared is a mystery. Development is not working like those who advocate it suggest it should be, and apparently it never has – or to put it more charitably, the returns on the considerable resources invested in it have been disappointing, not to mention the less charitable view that the funds have been used for dubious imperial purposes or to promote corruption. Since its inception after the 1939–45 war with the founding of the Bretton Woods institutions – when development replaced colonialism as the way in which the 'civilized' (or as it now became, the 'developed') world was going to advance the interests of those it thought less fortunate – we have seen promise after promise broken and goal after goal missed. The failure of development to deliver has resulted in it becoming one of the most fashion driven of pursuits, as those involved go from one 'solution' to another in the hope of hitting upon the 'right' one – modernization and trickle-down to structural adjustment and trade liberalization, women in development to gender and development, basic needs to poverty alleviation, integrated rural development to participation in its many acronymic forms, delivery via multilateral versus bilateral versus non-governmental organizations – to mention a few.

Sustainable development is one of the approaches currently much in favour (Roorda 2012; Robertson 2014). Is it going to deliver where the others have failed? Some will argue that it cannot afford to fail if life as we know it on this planet is to continue for many more decades. While the perceived needs of so-called underdeveloped nations drive the push for sustainable development to a considerable extent, equally evident is the growing sense of an impending global environmental crisis. Public opinion is increasingly supportive of action to promote sustainability, with reports of growing problems such as global warming and ozone depletion due to atmospheric pollution, increasing toxic contamination of the world's oceans, deforestation and land degradation on unprecedented scales, problematic disposal of dangerous radioactive waste, increasing levels of electromagnetic radiation with unknown health implications, and concerns about genetically modified organisms getting into ecosystems with unforeseen possibly disastrous consequences.

The idea of sustainable development is, like that of development generally, highly contested with many competing versions to demonstrate that they have the 'solution' (Adams 2001: 4–6; Grainger 2004: 20; Baker 2006: 25–27). According to some pundits there are almost as many definitions of sustainable development as there are commentators on the topic (Redclift 2002: 275).[5] It suggests some confusion, to say the least, if we cannot agree on what it means, as we potentially have people talking past one another, making debate on a difficult issue considerably more difficult, if not impossible. I do not wish to engage in a dry discussion about definition as such, but rather to ask what might be at the root of this confusion and lack of consensus, which suggests some profound contradictions, over what comprises sustainable development (Pezzey 1989).

We encounter problems at the outset with the noun *development* (Adams 2001: 6–9), which clearly augurs problems when we discuss sustainable development. It is strange that while those responsible for effecting development have passed from one fashionable 'solution' to another, they have remained stubbornly convinced that their aims and assumptions are correct. They seem to think that it is simply a case of finding the right recipe or method to achieve development as *they* conceive it. No one questions the fundamental idea of development itself; whereas the many failed half-baked-recipe approaches suggest that something is awry here.

The discrimination between developed and underdeveloped regions or nations is a manifestation of the problems that we face in defining development. We use vague terms such as First World and Third World countries or those of the North and South. If we take the latter discrimination, while there are some poor nations in the southern hemisphere (such as Tanzania and Mozambique), there are obviously wealthy ones too (such as Australia and New Zealand). The Middle East, classified as a developing region, further illustrates this point. While we do find some desperately poor countries there – war-torn nations such as Palestine, Syria and Iraq – we also find some affluent ones such as Qatar, the United Arab Emirates and Kuwait; to speak of these as undeveloped regions compared to Europe and the United States makes little sense.

Development implies progress of a sort that we can assess, or better measure, largely technologically driven change. It also assumes a certain political-economic order, predominantly the capitalist market, to effect the efficient production and distribution of the fruits of progress. At root, these assumptions rest on the theory of evolution, applied not to the fitness of biological organisms but to the material conditions of human communities (Hinterberger 1994). When talking about development, many have such a quasi-biological or material-related perspective in mind (Reid 1995: 139–142), which current development discourse expresses according to economic measures targeted at reducing poverty. The present aim of development, if we can believe the Millennium Development Goals and if we can agree how to measure poverty (which is notoriously difficult to assess), is to halve poverty globally by 2015.[6] In elementary terms, the aim in this materialistic view is to ensure that people enjoy 'food security', that is have sufficient food to eat, and 'basic health rights', that is do not suffer and die from preventable illnesses. These are goals to which I assume most humans can sign up for whatever their culture, as few of us likes to go hungry or fall ill. In other words, our biology is universal, whatever our religion, politics, social order etc.

Planning for Development

The development-as-evolution view informs the activities of national and international agencies as they seek to intervene and promote what they consider to be positive change. It commonly takes the form of so-called top-down interventions, such as have characterized these activities since colonial times and continue to this day, albeit often under participatory guises. These are interventions planned and implemented by agencies outside, and in political terms above, the communities subject to them, spoken of as the beneficiaries. These top-down interventions are associated with the theory of modernization (box 0.1)–which assumes that lesser-developed regions will imitate the West when the conditions are right for so-called take-off to self-sustained economic growth (Shepherd 1998: 1–10).

As several of the contributions to this book will show, the Gulf States illustrate the centralized planning approach well, as it is popular with the region's governments, perhaps predictably in view of their autocratic constitutional arrangements. The chapter by Trudy Tan, Aziza Al-Khalaqi and Najla Al-Khulaifi, all development planners, introduces this approach in the context of a discussion of the Qatari governments' development strategy – as set out in the *Qatar National Vision 2030* and the country's *National Development Strategy, 2010–2016* – which address issues of sustainable development from a general policy perspective. These documents define long-term national development goals, outline strategies to achieve them and provide a framework for their implementation. The plans build on the principles of sustainable development and rest on four so-called development pillars: Human, Social, Economic and Environmental Development. They identify the challenges the country has to address to prevent uncontrolled expansion, balancing between economic growth, social needs and environmental stewardship, modernizing while preserving Arab traditions, managing the size and skills of the expatriate labour force, and, with a nod to the UN's definition of sustainable development, overseeing growth so as to meet the needs of the current generation without compromising the ability of future generations to meet theirs. The plans set out the route that Qatar needs to follow to become an 'advanced, just and caring society' able to sustain prosperous development and provide all with a high standard of living, and also contribute to global development.

Box 0.1. Materialistic (Modernization) Approach

Classic examples of top-down projects include the cotton programme of Sudan, the groundnut scheme in Tanzania, lower Indus irrigation projects in Pakistan and the flood defences across Bangladesh. The Gezira Scheme in the Sudan, started a century ago, set out to establish cotton as a cash crop (Gaitskell 1959; Barnett 1977a). It invested heavily in agronomic research to improve crop yields, devising complex crop rotations featuring cotton, sorghum, hyacinth beans, wheat, groundnuts and fallows to manage soil fertility, particularly nitrogen, which is deficient in the region's difficult-to-manage dark cracking clays (vertisols). It devised crop-management regimes featuring spraying with biocides, as cotton is susceptible to pests and diseases such as boll worms, bacterial blights and viruses. It also engaged in considerable engineering work, notably on the Sennar and Al Roseires dams and associated canal networks to supply water for crop irrigation. All of this work was undertaken without consultation of the local population. The Scheme divided the irrigated region, extending to almost one million hectares, into standard plots let to individual tenants and employed advisors to direct their activities – when to cultivate, how, what crops to plant – all farmers having to follow an eight-course rotation. It supplied seed, fertilizers and hired machinery, and controlled the irrigation regime and cotton marketing arrangements, deducting the costs from tenants' earnings.

While the scientific research was sound, there was little interaction between the technical advisers and local people, which led to problems when tenants encountered difficulties with the cultivation regime. They came to resent the scheme for several reasons. They sensed that the heavy demands cotton made on the soil were environmentally unsound and they railed against not being able to grow the crops they wanted. The demand that they pay for irrigation water for cotton further exacerbated resentment of the crop altogether. Regardless of the scientific research, the heavy machinery used in cultivation badly compacted the heavy soil, making it increasingly difficult to work. The silting up of canals reduced the efficiency of the irrigation system, and pests and diseases increased, spreading rapidly with the mono-cropping of cotton. Delays in payments for cotton as a result of bureaucratic complexities and inefficiencies further frustrated the tenant farmers, as did the unpredictability of cotton earnings compounded with fluctuations in its market price.

The farmers rebelled against the scientific rotation scheme, inserting crops that would sell on the local market. Soil fertility declined with the rotation disruption, notably where farmers increased cultivation of nitrogen-demanding sorghum to feed an increasing population. With the decrease in their incomes, they could not afford inorganic fertilizer nor could they afford herbicides to control the increased weed infestation. The standard of people's diets declined along with their health, exacerbated by a drop in water quality as a result of biocide pollution and irrigation-system failures that led to increased waterborne disease (such as snail-borne bilharzias). The weakened labour force took less care of cultivations. The growing population added to these problems, with the government succumbing to demands from tenants to divide their holdings between children, resulting in a fall in their average size from forty acres to fifteen, which was not economically viable. Many younger persons left the region, depleting families of workers and obliging some tenants to employ day labourers, thus undermining the scheme's capitalist logic of harnessing individual interests through the profit motive, these workers having no long-term investment in holdings (Barnett 1977b, 1978; Barnett and Abdelkarim 1991).

In addition, there are political problems that further show the scheme's insensitivity to local arrangements (see also Castro 1998). Armed guards were employed to keep out cattle pastoralists who traditionally graze their animals in the Gezira region, only to find out that these nomads were accustomed to fighting over pasture access. Periodic political upheaval in the Sudan added to these local problems, notably tensions between the north and south, with a long, drawn-out and highly disruptive civil war. The Gezira Scheme illustrates how a top-down programme has trouble planning for the intricacies of real life, finding itself in a self-reinforcing downward spiral involving a complex combination of environmental, agricultural, economic, social, political and health issues. Experts have suggested various measures to reverse the decline, such as constructing a new dam, pumping underground water, new cropping rotations, revised tenancy agreements and new roads to reduce transport costs, which largely amount to more of the same, overriding on local concerns.

Any national sustainable-development policy demands supporting environmental legislation to make it a reality, as Wesam Al Othman and Sarah Clarke point out in chapter 5, drawing on several key legal environmental cases. Until recently, such legislation was lacking in Gulf Cooperation Council countries, as is evident in Qatar, which has only had a Ministry of the Environment since June 2008 focusing on policy-making and implementation. But in the last decade or so, the amount of environmentally related legislation and associated regulations has increased markedly. Governments have also demonstrated their increased commitment to such developments as signatories to key international environment treaties. But they also need to address the lack of reliable data on the environment, against which to assess progress in protecting it from damaging development, which implies a robust research process to strengthen the legislative programme. And they have to promote necessary environmental management skills among those responsible for the implementation of legislation.

Predictably, the grand-plan approach to development is subject to considerable criticism. In his chapter, Bahaa Darwish focuses on the 2nd National Human Development Report commissioned by the Qatari government to assess challenges facing the *National Vision 2030*'s implementation. The report identifies three particular challenges that demand attention: water security, climate change and the marine environment. But its assessment of the obstacles facing sustainable development as envisioned in terms of balancing economic growth, social needs and environmental management are bland given the magnitude of these challenges. Words are fine, he argues, but action is necessary to make them reality. And action implies awareness among citizens and others of the stakes involved in advancing the sustainable agenda, which relates to the challenges of participatory approaches discussed below. Furthermore, the various plans of the Gulf are too insular, defining long-term national development goals and strategies only, which is not enough. Sustainable development demands a transnational approach to tackle the problems that face today's interconnected globalized world or the best-laid plans at home to achieve economic development while ensuring local environmental and social sustainability are likely to unravel under external pressures.

Whatever the criticisms and problems of development approached in this planned or 'biological' material-informed way – and they are many, as discussed here in several chapters – it is the only way that we can legitimately talk about development in terms of objective progress. We can, for example, objectively measure improvements to communications, and if speed of communication is thought to be an improvement – from fork-stick runner and smoke signals to telegraph, video-conferencing and mobile phones – then we can talk of development in the sense of progress, or faster communication. It is also arguably the only way that we might morally be able to interfere in the lives of others. In other words, if we think that we have the wherewithal, the technology, to assist in the alleviation of chronic poverty – namely ensure 'food security' and 'basic health rights' – and people wish to avail themselves of such assistance, we surely have a moral obligation to help. If we have nothing to offer in this biological-material sense, what are we doing interfering in their lives in the name of development, unless it is, as some left-wing commentators suggest, the reverse of humane assistance, cynically to further exploitative relations (Middleton and O'Keefe 2001)?

Urban Sustainability

An issue that has attracted considerable planning attention is the rapid growth of urban areas. The unprecedented rate of urbanization, epitomized in Dubai's rapid expansion, has become a prominent issue with respect to sustainable development in the affluent Gulf region. The Qatari government, for instance, has invested heavily in drawing up plans to guide future development of Doha, the capital city. In his chapter, Khondker Rahman describes how the Qatar National Master Plan seeks to manage future expansion of urban infrastructure, and commercial, industrial and private real estate, given projections of continued astronomical rates of population growth. It is an insightful introduction into the planning process. The plan gives policies and strategies to guide urban development sustainably up until 2032 together with the monitoring and evaluation criteria to ensure goals are met.

Cities feature prominently on the sustainable development agenda, as Andrew Gardner points out, with the urban sustainability movement promoting initiatives and arguing that urban densities of settlement lead to economic and environmental efficiencies (Newman and Jennings 2008). He identifies a number of challenges to sustainability in the rapid urbanization occurring in the nations of the Arabian Peninsula, notably that political stability is linked to burgeoning urban expansion. The growth of cities relates to the legitimacy and authority of the Gulf States' ruling families, with mega-urbanization a way for them to share petroleum-derived wealth with their citizens. They cannot afford calls for sustainability to stunt urbanization projects, by which they distribute a substantial part of their rentier economy incomes. The importance of urbanization to current political-economic arrangements relates to the fixation on centralized master planning, as discussed here by Tan, Al-Khalaqi and Al-Khulaifi, Rahman, and Darwish. The prominence of 'super-modernism' in the urban planning discourse of the Gulf region, while it deploys contemporary sustainable development rhetoric, may nonetheless exacerbate current unsustainable trends.

The master planning of the 'sustainable' Gulf city plays to a national imagination that is keen to be modern, as Gardner point out, subscribing to foreign criteria of modernity that have globally unsustainable implications, which combined with political imperatives, inhibit the region using its extraordinary wealth to be a world leader in sustainable urban design. Instead, Gulf cities are competing to build the highest (figure 0.5), largest and most avant-garde developments on the planet. In a couple of decades they have become global hubs served by their burgeoning national airlines. The surprising cities of the Gulf such as Dubai, Doha and Manama are designed and built, as Ali Alraouf and Sarah Clarke point out, with little regard for local and global environment. The call for sustainable building design and urban planning has gone largely unheeded to date. The residents of the ever sprawling and pedestrian-unfriendly cities drive everywhere, often in large 'gas-guzzling' vehicles. Alraouf and Clarke argue that

Figure 0.5. The world's tallest building: Burj Khalifa in Dubai.

sustainable approaches are necessary to guarantee the future of these cities with their futuristic buildings. They advocate adoption of a 'smart' low-carbon compact city model (Hinte, Neelen and Vollaard 2003) that re-interprets traditional elements using new technologies and is sympathetic to local cultural context and endorses sustainability. Furthermore, they argue, there is a need to plan contemporary cosmopolitan Gulf cities with all residents in mind, which adequately accommodate everyone.

A crucial issue with respect to urban sustainability that attracts insufficient attention is waste disposal, a topic that many prefer to brush under the proverbial carpet. But waste is something that we cannot ignore without monumental environmental costs and health risks, as Sarah Clarke and Salah Almannai argue in their chapter. They point out that the higher the annual income – and Gulf citizens have some of the highest in the world – the larger the volume of municipal waste generated per capita, underlining the need for comprehensive integrated waste-management systems in the region. All nations face the challenge of how to deal with the waste resulting from everyday life, but as they move along the 'development path', with increasing industrialization and urbanization, casual disposal of waste – such as typified Gulf society half a century ago – is no longer tenable with the environmental and health hazards. Rapidly growing populations and increasing materialism and consumption threaten a crisis. According to Clarke and Almannai, waste disposal in the Gulf region, which until recently relied on landfill, courts serious negative environmental impacts. They recount how the authorities are beginning to adopt an integrated approach to waste management, necessary in any move towards more sustainable lifestyles. They discuss things that promote or hinder best practice, noting that a lack of accurate information hampers planning and organization of sustainable waste management.

Effective waste management is a public health issue, which brings us to another issue sometimes overlooked in discussions of sustainable development, namely health. Any change that fails to improve the health status of a population scarcely merits being described as sustainable. According to one authority, health includes a capacity to cope with change: 'the ability to adapt to one's environment ... [it] is not a fixed entity' (*The Lancet* 2009: 781). It is a topic that Mylène Riva, Catherine Panter-Brick and Mark Eggerman take up in chapter 16, pointing out that the promotion of human health has social, economic and environmental benefits. A healthy population, they argue, is both a prerequisite and a product of sustainable development. Research shows that investing in human health, for instance clean water programmes, reduces poverty by encouraging economic growth, and furthers protection of the natural environment. They see parallels in the international agenda regarding rights to health and moves towards sustainable development, and highlight the need for integrated local, national and global action to achieve both goals. They explore the contribution to sustainable development of 'health impact assessment', another central planning tool used to gauge the outcomes of policies and interventions on a population's health. They examine the health priorities and strategies of the Gulf Cooperation Council and WHO's Eastern Mediterranean Regional Office, two planning bodies that seek to reduce the disease burden of the Arab world, addressing social and environmental factors, and they look at partnerships forged internationally to achieve the Millennium Development Goals in health. They identify some crucial issues regarding inter- and intragenerational equity and sustainability, which demand wider political and research attention, notably to tackle the strains resulting from rapid population growth, skewed economic development and disturbing health profiles, locally and globally.

What is Sustainability?

Returning to definitional issues again, we encounter further problems when we consider the qualifying adjective *sustainable*, which as Fadwa El Guindi points out in her chapter has a myriad of meanings. It more obviously has biological roots, specifically in ecology, and assumes systemic balance. A system is sustainable for the foreseeable future so long as the relationships between components, such as their cycling around the system, remain in equilibrium; that is, the system will continue as it is without structural change due to depletion or degradation of resources. This biological or environmental perspective (box 0.2) is the one that comes to most people's minds when they talk about sustainable development (Marten 2001; Raynaut et al. 2007: 22). It again relates to phenomena 'out there' that we can measure, having decided what are the critical factors concerning sustainability in any system.

Box 0.2. Ecological Sustainability

A well-known example of sustainability in the ecological sense concerns the management of soil nutrients in farming. We see this in shifting cultivation where people manage soil fertility not by rotating crops on the land or using fertilizer inputs but by rotating their use of the land (Nye and Greenland 1960). After cultivating an area for a limited period – with yields declining through a possible combination of decreasing available nutrients, build up of disease and pests, and weed infestation – they abandon it to fallow for many years and so that secondary forest may establish itself. Perhaps a generation later, descendants may clear the rejuvenated site again, burning the natural vegetation to release stored nutrients for crop uptake, the ash acting as a fertilizer. Extensive shifting is not inevitable under such regimes; where soil conditions permit, people may evolve sustainable cropping regimes that allow them to practice near sedentary farming, as on volcanic ash soils in the New Guinea highlands with staple sweet potato cultivation (Sillitoe 1996). So long as the population remains in balance with land resources, this farming regime, which has long had a maligned reputation in development circles, can go on indefinitely in long-term balance with the cycling of the natural ecosystem. The demographic-resource-balance caveat applies to any farming system; however, a shifting one can only support limited numbers compared to others, and its destruction of forest is obvious whereas that of sedentary regimes is in the past and overlooked.

Farmers have devised other ways to manage soil fertility where regimes are sedentary. The Celtic field system of Britain, for instance, involved more-or-less concentrically arranged in-fields and out-fields (Grey 1959). The in-field adjacent to homestead was under continuous cultivation, fertilized with cattle dung from the byre. Crops were rotated with pasture in the nearby out-field, and beyond was an area largely for grazing animals that imported nutrients to the centre. Farmers improved the land with rig and furrow drainage and by using lime to manage soil acidity. They developed various systems of crop rotation. The Romans introduced legume and cereal rotations, in addition to the mouldboard plough. The Medieval period saw the introduction of the three-field system, with two plots under crops at any time and the other fallow; the fields again surrounded by common pasture that supplied some nutrients via manure of grazed animals spread on cultivations. While some argue that the communal land tenure system, where villages redistributed arable plots between families each year in an attempt to ensure equitable use of resources, militated against long-term land improvement, the farming regime was, broadly speaking, in environmental balance. The seventeenth century saw the emergence of sophisticated rotations in England, such as the Norfolk four-course that featured the cycling of wheat, grass and clover (pasture), oats (horse fodder) and turnips, together with fertility maintenance through the application of manure and night soil (the law prohibited tenants selling manure, tantamount to stealing nutrients off the land). It is from these farming regimes that today's organic farming descends with its emphasis on the sustainable management of land resources by the appropriate organic management of nutrient cycling and soil structure, as certified in the UK through the Soil Association.

The implications for sustainable development are intriguing: namely, sustainable implies a relatively steady state, whereas development implies extensive change. While change inevitably occurs, whatever your cultural perspective (as the entropy postulate of the second law of thermodynamics predicts; Reid 1995: 26–27), the point is that from a sustainable perspective it is gradual, not suddenly disrupting the complex relations that characterize any ecological or social system. We face another contradiction. Such gradual change is the process that drives evolution, organisms slowly altering and causing changes in their surrounding environment, including changes in other organisms. But development, unlike evolution, is a rapid process that aims to promote speedy change (e.g. halve global poverty in a mere fifteen years). So is the idea of sustainable development an oxymoron? If so, it explains much about the confusion that surrounds the concept.

The biological or ecological view of sustainability is the one commonly adopted in development contexts. It is the standpoint that descends directly from the Brundtland Commission (1987: 43), which many cite as the juncture that unmistakably put sustainability on the official development agenda. According to the commission, it is 'development that meets the needs of the present without compromising the ability of future generations to meet their own needs'. But this seems disconcertingly out of step with the above ideas and goals that inform development, which prioritize economic growth, use of resources and rapid change now.

In chapter 12, Nobuyuki Yamaguchi further questions, as a biologist, what comprises a sustainable state, querying the widely assumed synonymity of sustainability with biodiversity conservation. From a biological perspective these may be mutually exclusive, albeit sometimes complementary. The word *sustainability* as used in 'sustainable development', which concerns the continuation of activities that meet human demands, differs from how it is used in 'biodiversity conservation' contexts, which concerns the preservation of natural species and ecosystems. Biodiversity relates to variety among organisms connected in complex ecosystems and assumes a wide range of genetic information both within and between species. Whereas the sustainable use of renewable natural resources concerns not genetic variety but numbers of individuals (or biomass). The population of any species is conserved so long as harvested such that it is able to reproduce in sufficient numbers to avoid extinction – albeit possibly with a greatly reduced gene pool if heavily harvested and with probable negative impact on other creatures and the wider ecosystem. And a previously heavily harvested species that has suffered a large population decline may be sustainably exploited from a simple population size (or total biomass) perspective, as sustainability is ironically achievable regardless of population size or biomass so long as the harvest does not exceed the maximum sustainable yield for the current (and not previous) population (Cowlishaw, Mendelson and Rowcliffe 2005). Used in this way, the sustainability view fails to draw attention to ongoing erosion of nature's riches. Such sustainability at a 'low' resource level may be used disingenuously as a positive point to hide the extent of the damage that human activities are doing to the planet's biodiversity.

The lack of reliable quantitative data makes it difficult either to assess biodiversity or monitor sustainable use of renewable natural resources, further allowing some parties to create the 'comfortable illusion' of sustainability. Moreover, sustainable yields of biota useful to humans may be more achievable with a reduction in biodiversity or even extermination of certain species – such as killing off pests that reduce crop yields – that interfere with what we seek to harvest (Margoluis 2001). Modern farming methods, for instance, are not in the interests of some organisms (in controlling pests they arguably try to exterminate them), which does not concern the sustainability of farming, unless they inadvertently destroy resources necessary to their continuance – such knock-on changes occur in highly complex ecosystems and have unforeseen adverse effects (for example reducing the numbers of insects needed to pollinate crops). While the extinction of some species due to human activities may not concern the sustainability of those activities, it is of central concern to those who argue that we need to protect the planet's biodiversity.

Environmental Sustainability

A feature of the rapid economic growth of the Gulf region is a large migrant labour population. Workers from around the world – Europe, South Asia, North America and Southeast Asia – are present in large numbers, many working in the construction industry on infrastructure and building projects. The terms and conditions of the region's migrant workers provoke considerable interest, notably those from poorer countries such as Pakistan, India, Nepal, Bangladesh and the Philippines, whose employment circumstances reflect current exploitative global economic arrangements (Longva 1997; Kapiszewski 2001; Gardner 2010). In chapter 9, Ben Campbell looks at migrant labour from a novel angle, arguing that employment of Nepali persons in the Gulf contributes significantly to the well-being of Himalayan forests and the poor communities that depend on them. He points out that not only may economic growth damage the environment but also that lack of economic growth may push the poor to overuse often-diminishing natural resources, particularly with population growth. Sustainable development programmes often seek to protect threatened environments by reducing local pressure on resources, for instance by declaring conservation areas and requiring people to adapt their livelihoods accordingly or find alternative ones. Even where local people continue to have access to such areas, controls on levels of harvesting to protect the environment often oblige them to meet their consumption needs via the market purchase of commodities. In this event, poor villagers, such as those in the Nepal Himalayas, need access to non-local income-earning opportunities such as the Gulf offers. The sustainability of these arrangements depends on the interlinking of the local and the global. The bio-diverse mountain forests of Nepal can continue in a healthy state only if some of the population can earn cash incomes elsewhere and remit some of their earnings back home.

In view of the ecological assumptions that inform the idea of sustainability, the status of human relations with the natural environment is predictably a central issue with respect to discussions of sustainable development. Conservation features prominently here. The migrant labour remittances view is an interesting take on the topic. The establishment of conservation areas to protect nature and preserve biodiversity, in at least limited selected regions, is a popular response to humanity's unsustainable use of natural resources and consequent degradation, even destruction of the environment. The Qatari government, confronted by the environmental consequences of oil and gas extraction and rapid urban development, strongly supports this approach, having designated about one-tenth of the country a conservation area. In the west of the peninsula, it is the Al Reem Reserve, subsequently declared a UNESCO Biosphere. It is the subject of my chapter with Ali Alshawi; other biosphere conservation reserves in the region are Marawah in the United Arab Emirates and Dana in Jordan.

Marine and terrestrial environments are under threat in the Gulf, as elsewhere, from rapid development. It frequently happens that when we consider protection of the natural world we overlook, as a terrestrial species, the marine environment, for degradation of land resources is so much more obvious to us. James Howard seeks to rectify this oversight, pointing out that protection of marine ecosystems poses particular problems, demanding international cooperation. The world's oceans are not only global in extent but also largely comprise an intercontinental commons, any nations' territorial waters being limited in area such that governments have limited powers. And the oceans are so large, covering some two-thirds of the planet, that we have until recently treated them as bottomless sinks for waste, as Clarke and Almannai discuss in chapter 15, causing increasingly evident pollution, threatening some entire oceanic ecosystems. The health of marine resources is of particular importance to coastal nations, contributing significantly to their economies. This is the case in the Gulf region, where some globally unique marine zones occur, featuring ecosystems adapted to high temperatures and salinities. But they are under

Figure 0.6. A dhow coming into Al Ruwais harbour, N. Qatar.

threat not only from the sizeable and largely unregulated dhow fishing fleets (figure 0.6), but also the construction of extensive infrastructure on the coast, such as the gigantic liquid gas processing facility at Ras Laffan on the Qatar peninsula. These short-term industrial complexes threaten long-term, even irreparable degradation of the marine environment with considerable local and regional consequences, and indeed global ones with the oceans playing a part in regulating the world's climate.

In contrast to seawater, availability of fresh water is markedly limited in the Gulf – a key sustainability issue, as several chapters make clear. Among the driest and most barren regions on earth, largely comprising desert, natural water sources are inadequate to meet the needs of today's burgeoning population. One solution is to use readily available seawater, large desalination plants supplying a considerable part of the water used in the region. In Qatar, for instance, desalinated seawater supplies 41 per cent of water for domestic, agricultural and industrial use, and 99 per cent of drinking water. Another 50 per cent comes from groundwater sources, and the remainder from treated wastewater (Hashim 2009: 112). Regarding sustainable development, both groundwater and desalinated sources are unsustainable. Extraction rates from groundwater sources exceed rates of natural recharge by 70 per cent or so,[7] predictably where rainfall is negligible; falling in short, occasionally heavy storms in winter months, sometimes flooding otherwise dry wadis. Whereas the desalination process is energy demanding relative to natural sources, and currently dependant on non-renewable fossil fuels (although research is underway to use abundantly available solar power). In addition, the process produces highly concentrated brine effluent (with added anti-scaling chemicals), which is usually pumped back into the sea, increasing salinity in the vicinity of plants, which is naturally high to start with in the Gulf, to the detriment of marine life (Dawoud and Mulla 2012).

Energy Issues

The changes occurring in the world's climate (so-called global warming due to CO_2 emissions) have brought energy issues to the top of the sustainable development agenda; for not only do we have to contend with global dependence on non-renewable fossil fuels and what to do when these inevitably start to run out (so-called peak oil, when supply fails to meet demand), but we also face the problem that their use may lead to catastrophic human-induced climate change and of how we can reduce our emissions of greenhouse gases responsibly. In this context, the development trajectory in the Gulf is doubly unsustainable. Not only are current developments locally unsupportable in the longer term, given the region's dependence on non-renewable oil and gas exports (figure 0.7), but they are also unstable globally in the shorter term, given increasingly urgent

Figure 0.7. Oil refinery at Qasasil, Qatar.

calls for the world to turn to renewable energy sources and break its reliance on hydrocarbons linked to increasing CO_2 levels in the atmosphere.

The need to switch to sustainable energy is a pressing global environmental concern, as Thomas Henfrey reminds us in chapter 6. He discusses three strategies that seek to advance the transition: reduction of carbon emissions from conventional fossil fuel use, development of renewable sources of energy and attempts to reduce energy demand. He points out that current technical limitations regarding efforts both to reduce carbon emissions (such as CO_2 capture and storage) and develop renewable sources (such as wind farms and solar arrays) oblige radical shifts in energy demand, particularly in the wealthiest nations (Fauset 2008). He questions the assumption that our technical ingenuity will solve the problems, in the short term anyway, as it has previously in our history; for instance as evident in the technological changes seen in the archaeological record – such as those in irrigation procedures recounted by Manuel, Coningham, Gillmore and Fazeli – show our ancestors overcame environmental constraints. Furthermore, he argues it will exacerbate our present problems if we think that the inventiveness that has enabled humans to address resource constraints before will allow economic growth to continue blazing away (Heinberg 2011: 156–174). Although we may soon have the technical means to cost-effectively change to renewable energy, this is of little help if it perpetuates a growth-led model of development instead of making this redundant in the long term, as all of the world's resources are finite. The prospects for managing demand are forbidding; the indefinite growth mentality of economics (of any school – capitalism, socialism or whatever) promotes an ever-increasing demand for energy that stymies any efforts to keep it within sustainable limits. It is necessary, Henfrey argues, that newer nations seeking to increase their citizens' prosperity avoid this unrealistic and ultimately disastrous growth mentality and find other ways to develop economies compatible with the world's finite resources (Abramsky 2010; Teske 2010). With this reality in mind, his chapter envisions possible future sustainable energy scenarios in the Gulf region.

The proposition that depending on non-renewable fossil fuel reserves to fund development is an insecure strategy has prompted some to argue that an abundance of such resources can be a liability rather than an asset. This is the reverse of the widespread assumption that plentiful natural resources will equate with economic growth and development. In chapter 7, Emma Gilberthorpe, Sarah Clarke and I explore a popular version of this argument: the resource curse thesis (Auty 1993; Humphreys, Sachs and Stiglitz 2007; Watts 2008). By definition, exploitation of non-renewable resources is, as Henfrey makes clear, unsustainable in the long term, but the resource curse thesis suggests that it may also be unsustainable in the short term by setting off unsound economic growth. It appears that curse-afflicted resource-rich nations experience less economic development than nations with fewer such resources. It is thought that this happens for several interrelated reasons, including a decline in economic competitiveness due to resource-revenue-stimulated currency exchange rate appreciation, exposure to volatile global commodity markets resulting in unpredictable swings in natural resource revenues, mismanagement of assets by governments and poor investment of wealth nationally, and unstable or corrupt institutions siphoning off resource revenues, with the entrenchment of a wealthy minority and impoverished majority.

The challenge posed by the resource curse thesis is how to convert what is an unsustainable wealth windfall into a sustainable future by investing appropriately and not being cursed and 'blowing it'. In chapter 7, we compare the relevance of the thesis to the Gulf and South West Pacific regions to make the point that the economic and social consequences of resource endowments can vary widely. The resource curse affects these regions in different ways. It more applies to Papua New Guinea, for instance, than Qatar where awareness of some of the pitfalls has the authorities searching for ways to invest hydrocarbon income to ensure a sustainable future, as evidenced by the plethora of strategy documents and plans discussed by Tan, Al-Khalaqi and Al-Khulaifi (chapter 2), Rahman (chapter 3) and Darwish (chapter 4). Also, the curse thesis focuses too much on economic issues, when social ones are relevant too. We can anticipate that different societies will react differently to having abundant natural resources. While the wealth coming from oil and gas royalties in Papua New Guinea is leading to a breakdown in social and political relations, this is not currently evident in Qatar, where social relations are nonetheless undergoing considerable change with urbanization, consumerism and so on.

Cultural Sustainability

Social issues are central to sustainable development, which touches upon a wide gamut of communal issues, wherever the community. International development policy and practice consequently has to address the cultural, as well as economic and technical, aspects of sustainability. It is now widely accepted that development is not, as once thought, solely the preserve of one social science, namely economics, but involves wider socio-cultural issues and all social sciences. A common criticism of the modernization approach, with its top-down economically driven planning, is that it often features little or no local consultation or involvement of the wider population, omitting those who are going to be subject to any intervention. There are wider issues of sustainability here, relating to the sustaining of development initiatives themselves, as Gina Porter points out in chapter 17. It is argued that those impacted by development plans will surely have a view and relevant knowledge and that involving them should help avoid project failure and further waste of scarce resources (Baker 2006: 1–5). The participatory approach to development emerged from such criticism.

While those involved in central planning increasingly acknowledge the need to involve people, they find it difficult to do so and retain control of the process, so necessary in the Gulf with its aforementioned political connotations. The planners responsible for the Qatar National Master Plan, for instance, realize that the successful achievement of sustainable urban development will depend on local ownership of the process, as Rahman describes, and recommend ways to achieve stakeholder buy-in. But they seem to overlook that involving the local population in drawing up the plan from the start would be more likely to ensure such buy-in. The reaction of Qatar University students during a workshop where the plan was presented and discussed show what may happen otherwise. They dismissed it, directing particular ire at the recommendation that everyone should use public transport more, which they thought demeaning, particularly for females. Clarke and Almannai, in chapter 15, also highlight the significance of public consultation and participation in establishing successful waste-management programmes, suggesting ways to improve communication between the relevant ministries and other stakeholders, including the wider public, whose engagement is essential if a sustainable waste-disposal system featuring recycling is going to be successful.

In chapter 18, Serena Heckler argues that we need to go further in recognizing the centrality of cultural issues to achieve genuinely sustainable development, both environmental and social. It is necessary to consider culture if local stakeholders are going to participate meaningfully in decision making and ensure that local, often sustainable values shape policy and practice. She points out, drawing on her work in Latin America and with UNESCO, how there are many ways culturally to be in the world and that Western-framed economic development may be detrimental to certain cultures, and may even represent an imposition of alien values on people who have quite different views. This relates to a human-rights approach to development and sustainability, notably the universal right to live according to one's own cultural values. It is important to realize the part that culture plays in identity and well-being, and the need to sustain socio-cultural distinctiveness and diversity; for instance to include indicators of cultural integrity in assessing the sustainability of any development. Heckler argues that we should use the 'cultural turn', with its championing of the understanding of other socio-cultural perspectives, to critically review current development practice with the aim of extending to local people more autonomy to promote development as they conceive it.

In chapter 19, Fadwa El Guindi picks up on the cultural theme in Arab contexts. She criticizes as shallow approaches to development and growth that rely on bland and tired management-speak slogans, which blithely overlook the complexity of related cultural issues. This is evident, she argues, in Qatar's Development Strategy, which while it acknowledges the distinctive part that the family plays in Gulf society, makes some questionable planning assumptions; for instance about limiting cousin marriage, which is common in the region and features unacknowledged aspects that are analogous to the incest taboo such as milk kinship. She argues for the inclusion of culture in the broad (holistic) sense in sustainability discourse. She points out that other culturally informed ways of being in the world can teach the capitalist order something about sustainability, contrasting the relations between humans and animals in the United States and Arab world. The Arabians have particular relations with falcons, camels and even their goats, which, kin-like, have their own genealogies. Egyptians have close relations with cats, which mummified feline remains suggest possibly date back to Pharaonic times. And the Turks have idiosyncratic relations with birds, their cities featuring numerous, sometimes mini-palatial, birdhouses. In discussing 'humanistic relations' with animals, she highlights harmony and balance as two prominent Arab cultural themes, which resonate strongly with the sustainability discourse and local knowledge advocacy. The implication is that other cultural ways and expressions of associated values may promote sustainable lifestyles.

Local knowledge may have something valuable to contribute to sustainable development by drawing on such sustainable cultural roots (Sillitoe, Bicker and Pottier 2002; Sillitoe, Dixon and Barr 2005). By turning to their cultural heritage, might the peoples of the Gulf region advance a unique approach to sustainable development? For instance, in chapter 13 Alraouf and Clarke point out that the Arab architectural tradition (Mortada 2003), which evolved over millennia to cope with hot arid climate – coming up with some ingenious solutions such as wind towers that are iconic features of the Middle Eastern architectural heritage (figure 0.8) – may have something to teach the emerging sustainable architectural movement, with its green designs and energy-conservation aims. They discuss Masdar City, the futuristic carbon-neutral urban project in the desert adjacent to Abu Dhabi, which deploys some traditional architectural techniques and town designs (Reiche 2009). Such consideration of

Figure 0.8. Wind tower architecture, Qatar University campus.

local building traditions may also contribute to the aesthetics of the built environment, being more culturally appropriate than the globalized steel and glass towers that currently dominate skylines across the region. They contend that truly 'smart' solutions designed specifically for the Gulf will draw on vernacular architecture, combining lessons from the past with designs and technology of the future.

But indigenous knowledge, culture and traditions are disappearing across the Gulf in the name of progress, things which for centuries have enabled the people to survive in a harsh climate while ostensibly preserving the natural environment (Mundy and Musallam 2000). This is something that exercises Kaltham Al-Ghanim in chapter 20 where she explores what local environmental knowledge might contribute to sustainable development and the conservation of natural resources, pointing out that rapid change may erode such knowledge and lead to resource destruction. She argues for the rediscovery of the local environmental heritage of the Gulf region and Qatar in particular – some of which she briefly documents – arguing that its revival will help communities follow more environmentally friendly ways (such as Lancaster and Lancaster 1997 detail).

The loss of such knowledge poses problems in conservation contexts, where participatory co-management is currently popular, involving local populations and superseding reserves that excluded them to protect nature. Local people, it is argued, are more likely to abide by restrictions on access and resource use if they are party to devising these and understand what they aim to achieve. Furthermore they also have much knowledge of the local environment, their activities often contributing to the ecology seen today, which has led recently to the idea of bio-cultural diversity and ensuring its continuance (Maffi 2001; Stepp, Wyndham and Zarger 2002). However, these assumptions may not hold where rapid social and cultural change occurs, such as in the Gulf region, as Ali Alshawi and I explore in chapter 10. The impracticability of the co-management approach seems to imply, paradoxically to us as strong advocates of local participation, turning the clock back to centrally managed arrangements that seek to control human access and local activities, even the prohibition of some to protect plants and animals.

Participating in Sustainability

The participatory approach to development poses further challenges (Kumar 2002; Cooke and Kothari 2001; Hickey and Mohan 2004). Political arrangements in Gulf Co-operation Council (GCC) States, as Gardner points out in chapter 14, make it difficult to see how they can square sustainable urban development – with its democratic emphasis on participatory and grassroots approaches to planning and implementation – with their centralized top-down decision making and management. Furthermore, people need to understand the issues to participate. One response is to advocate education, as several contributors to this volume do. For instance, Al-Ghanim envisages training programmes based on the local environmental heritage of the Gulf to promote ecological awareness and a more sustainable future. In this respect, Darwish argues that it is necessary to raise awareness among Qataris and others of the need to advance the sustainable agenda or else no amount of central planning will achieve such development, echoing the point made above about the Qatar National Master Plan and the need to secure people's buy-in from the start. In the course of their discussion of key legislation aimed at protecting the Qatari environment – the processes that enabled its formation and the administrative arrangements instituted to enforce it – Al Othman and Clarke argue in chapter 5 that lack of awareness obstructs its implementation. In order to make progress, the authorities need to give more attention to increasing public awareness and environmental understanding, so that all sections of society can collaborate in achieving sustainable development objectives. For instance, inadequate waste-disposal arrangements, as Clarke and Al-mannai argue in chapter 15, reflect limited public knowledge of issues such as recycling and scant appreciation of the consequences of disposing of refuse in environmentally unsound ways.

Meaningful participation involves collaboration between all partners, encompassing local community members, government representatives and non-governmental organizations together with researchers to shape and inform enquiries. Planning and managing such research is difficult, as Gina Porter illustrates in chapter 17 drawing on her experiences with a Ghanaian irrigation project and comparable research conducted in the Middle East region. They reflect the considerable methodological challenges surrounding research into sustainable development. Supplying and analyzing reliable data to inform and support such development requires inputs from and cooperation between a range of disciplines in both the natural and social sciences. In this respect, Porter distinguishes between multidisciplinary and interdisciplinary research – the first featuring disciplinary experts working in parallel and the second having them interacting continuously throughout the research. She argues that the interdisciplinary approach is necessary to further the sustainable development agenda, which requiring cooperation between several fields to further understanding of problems is particularly complex (Klein 1990; Lyall et al. 2011). James Howard, in chapter 11, illustrates the complexity in discussing the challenges that face sustainable development with conservation of marine resources; there are not only the complex interactions between the many stakeholders and sectors involved in developing and protecting coastal regions but also the marine environments themselves comprise complex and often poorly understood ecosystems. And such research, as Fadwa El Guindi points out, is time consuming and cannot be hurried without jeopardizing the results.

The book itself takes an interdisciplinary approach in its in-depth presentation of sustainable development issues in the context of the Gulf and Middle East, framed within a global perspective. It brings together, in a unique association for the Gulf region, a combination of specialists to introduce and discuss sustainable development, including social and natural scientists, architects and planners, economists and health specialists, environmentalists and biologists, ministry personnel and university academics, development specialists and archaeologists, to consider such topics as nature and environment, society and culture, industry and technology, economy and politics, history and geography as these relate to sustainable development.

Following on from the exploration of the concepts of 'development' and 'sustainability' in this introduction, the conclusion explores, in the light of the following chapters, the implications of joining these concepts together in 'sustainable development'. It discusses some contradictions at the heart of the idea, starting with the conflict between capitalist ideas of economic growth and environmentalist ideas of an ecologically steady state, which relate to the sustainability of development itself. Viewing development as a culturally relative concept affords one way of tackling such contradictions. Other perspectives on what comprises the good life, as exemplified in endogenous or indigenous knowledge approaches, suggest a way beyond the inconsistencies of capitalist informed development. The lifeways of hunter-gatherers, ironically considered the least economically developed, illustrate such regard for sustainability. While these perspectives suggest that genuinely participatory approaches should promote sustainable development, there are political obstacles, as pointed out, with powerful authorities that control resources reluctant to relinquish control. Also, not all local communities necessarily subscribe, as noted, to worldviews that may promote sustainable interventions, with the possibility of environmentally unsustainable participation. While we may promote local knowledge for ecologically and culturally sustainable development, we have to exercise caution – one policy does not fit all when it comes to sustainable development.

Notes

1. I gratefully acknowledge Shell's generous funding of the Chair in Sustainable Development that afforded me the opportunity to extend my work into the Gulf region (Fadwa El Guindi, this volume, endnote 1, comments further).
2. It is perhaps to be expected that a company supplying the global economy's addiction to fossil fuels (which is the responsibility of us all) will find the

questions that sustainable development brings up awkward; more relevant attempts to address these included research to sequester CO_2 resulting from the production of liquid gas (which itself is less environmentally polluting than oil per joule of energy produced) and sponsorship of a race between cars powered by renewable energy built by various university engineering departments.

3. I thank Jackie Sillitoe, Fadwa El Guindi, Ursula Koch-Bagley, Mariam Abdel-Hafiz, Sarah Clarke and Hind Al Sulaiti for their invaluable contributions to the sustainable development initiative, and helping to bring about this volume.
4. There is a dispute over whether this body of water should be called the Persian Gulf or the Arabian Gulf and in this book we refer simply to the Gulf.
5. According to Latouch (1995), there are some sixty definitions of sustainable development (cited by Raynaut et al. 2007). Some writers seek to make a virtue of this, such as Reid (1995: xvi) and Adams (2001: 20), who argues that 'far from making the phrase useless, it is precisely because of its ability to host divergent ideas that sustainable development has proved so useful, and has become so dominant'.
6. Poverty is a relative concept; as Jean Cocteau observes in *Les enfants terribles:* 'Wealth is an aptitude, poverty the same. A poor person who becomes rich will display a luxurious poverty' (1961: 91). For example, on joining some closed orders nuns and monks renounce all worldly possessions and consider themselves blessed. There is a large literature on poverty in the 'developing world'.
7. In 2003–2004, total groundwater consumption was 220.829 million m^3 and total aquifer recharge was 67.130 m^3 (Hashim 2009: 115).

References

Abdulla, A. 2000. *The Arab Gulf States: Old Approaches and New Realities.* Abu Dhabi: Emirates Center for Strategic Studies and Research.

Abramsky, K. 2010. *Sparking a Worldwide Energy Revolution.* Edinburgh: AK Press.

Adams, W. M. 2001. *Green Development: Environment and Sustainability in the Third World.* London: Routledge.

Ansari, M. I. 1992. 'Islamic Perspectives on Sustainable Development.' *American Journal of Islamic Social Sciences* 8 (4): 394–402.

Auty, R. 1993. *Sustaining Development in Mineral Economies: The Resource-Curse Thesis.* London: Routledge.

Baker, S. 2006. *Sustainable Development.* London: Routledge.

Barnett, T. 1977a. *The Gezira Scheme: An Illusion of Development.* London: Frank Cass.

———. 1977b. 'The Gezira Scheme: Black Box or Pandora's Box?' University of East Anglia Development Studies Discussion Paper No. 45.

Barnett, T., and A. Abdelkarim. 1991. *Sudan: The Gezira Scheme and Agricultural Transition.* London: Frank Cass.

Batanouny, K. H. 2001. *Plants in the Deserts of the Middle East.* Berlin: Springer.

Brundtland Commission (World Commission on Environment and Development). 1987. *Our Common Future.* Oxford: Oxford University Press.

Castro, A. P. 1998. 'Sustainable Agriculture or Sustained Error? The Case of Cotton in Kirinyaga, Kenya.' *World Development* 26 (9): 1719–1731.

Cocteau, J. 1961. *Les enfants terribles.* Paris: Le Livre de Poche.

Cohen, J. E. 1995. *How Many People Can the Earth Support?* New York: W.W. Norton and Company.

Cooke, B., and U. Kothari (eds.). 2001. *Participation: The New Tyranny?* London: Zed Books.

Cowlishaw, G., S. Mendelson and J. R. Rowcliffe. 2005. 'Evidence for Post-Depletion Sustainability in a Mature Bushmeat Market.' *Journal of Applied Ecology* 42: 460–468.

Dawoud, M. A., and M. M. Al Mulla. 2012. 'Environmental Impacts of Seawater Desalination: Arabian Gulf Case Study.' *International Journal of Environment and Sustainability* 1 (3): 22–37.

Eickelman, D. F. 1981. *The Middle East: An Anthropological Approach.* Englewood Cliffs, NJ: Prentice-Hall.

Ewing, B., et al. 2010. *The Ecological Footprint Atlas.* Oakland, CA: Global Footprint Network.

Fagan, Brian M. 2004. *The Long Summer: How Climate Changed Civilization.* London: Granta Books.

Fauset, C. 2008. *Techno-Fixes: A Critical Guide to Climate Change Technologies.* London: Corporate Watch.

Foltz, R., F. M. Denny and A. Baharuddin (eds.). 2003. *Islam and Ecology: A Bestowed Trust.* Cambridge, MA: Harvard University Press.

Gaitskell, A. 1959. *Gezira: A Story of Development in the Sudan.* London: Faber and Faber.

Gardner, A. M. 2010. *City of Strangers: Gulf Migration and the Indian Community in Bahrain.* Ithaca, NY: ILR/Cornell University Press.

Gause, F. G., III. 1994. *Oil Monarchies: Domestic and Security Challenges in the Arab Gulf States.* New York: Council on Foreign Relations Press.

Grainger, A. 2004. 'Introduction.' In *Exploring Sustainable Development: Geographical Perspectives,* eds. M. Purvis and A. Grainger, 1–32. London: Earthscan.

Gray, H. L. 1959. *English Field Systems.* London: Merlin Press.

Gross, C. 1987. *Mammals of the Southern Gulf.* Dubai: Motivate Publishing.

Hashim, M. A. 2009. *Water, Agriculture and Environment in Arid Lands: Water and Agricultural Vision for Qatar by 2020.* Doha: Friends of Environment Centre.

Heinberg, R. 2011. *The End of Growth: Adapting to Our New Economic Reality.* Gabriola Island: New Society Pubs.

Hickey, S., and G. Mohan (eds.). 2004. *Participation – from Tyranny to Transformation? Exploring New Approaches to Participation in Development.* London: Zed Books.

Hinte, van E., M. Neelen and J. V. P. Vollaard. 2003. *Smart Architecture.* Rotterdam: 010 Publishers.

Hinterberger, F. 1994. 'Biological, Cultural and Economic Evolution and the Economy-Ecology Relationship.' In *Toward Sustainable Development: Concepts, Meth-*

ods, and Policy, eds. J. C. J. M. van den Bergh and J. van der Straaten, 57–81. Washington, DC: Island Press.

Humphreys, M., J. D. Sachs and J. E. Stiglitz (eds.). 2007. *Escaping the Resource Curse.* New York: Columbia University Press.

Kapiszewski, A. 2001. *Nationals and Expatriates: Population and Labour Dilemmas of the Gulf Cooperation Council States.* Reading: Ithaca Press.

Klein, J. T. 1990. *Interdisciplinarity: History, Theory and Practice.* Detroit: Wayne State University Press.

Kubursi, A. A. 1984. *Oil, Industrialization and Development in the Arab Gulf States.* London: Croom Helm.

Kumar, S. 2002. *Methods for Community Participation: A Complete Guide for Practitioners.* London: ITDG.

Lancaster, W. and F. Lancaster. 1997. 'Indigenous Resource Management Systems in the Bâdia of the Bilâd ash-Shâm.' *Journal of Arid Environments* 35: 367–378.

The Lancet. 2009. 'Editorial: What is Health? The Ability to Adapt.' *The Lancet* 373 (9666): 781.

Latouch, S. 1995. *La mégamachine. Raison scientifique, raison économique et mythe du progrès.* Paris: La Découverte.

Longva, A. N. 1997. *Walls Built on Sand: Migration, Exclusion and Society in Kuwait.* Boulder CO: Westview.

Lyall, C., et al. 2011. *Interdisciplinary Research Journeys: Practical Strategies of Capturing Creativity.* London: Bloomsbury Academic.

Maffi, L. (ed.). 2001. *On Biocultural Diversity: Linking Language, Knowledge and the Environment.* Washington and London: Smithsonian Institution Press.

Margoluis, R. 2001. *Maximum Yield? Sustainable Agriculture as a Tool for Conservation.* Washington, DC: Biodiversity Support Program.

Marten, G. G. 2001. *Human Ecology: Basic Concepts for Sustainable Development.* London: Earthscan.

Middleton, N., and P. O'Keefe. 2001. *Redefining Sustainable Development.* London: Pluto Press.

Mortada, H. 2003. *Traditional Islamic Principles of Built Environment.* London: Routledge Curzon.

Mundy, M., and B. Musallam (eds.). 2000. *The Transformation of Nomadic Society in the Arab East.* Cambridge: Cambridge University Press.

Netton, I. R. (ed.). 1986. *Arabia and the Gulf: From Traditional Society to Modern States.* London: Croom Helm.

Newman, P., and I. Jennings. 2008. *Cities as Sustainable Ecosystems: Principles and Practices.* Washington, DC: Island Press.

Nonneman, G. 2007. 'Political Reform in the Gulf Monarchies: From Liberalisation to Democratisation?' In *Reform in the Middle East Oil Monarchies,* eds. A. Ehteshami and S. Wright, 3–45. Reading: Ithaca Press.

Nye, P. H., and D. J. Greenland. 1960. *The Soil Under Shifting Cultivation.* Harpenden: Commonwealth Bureau of Soils Technical Bulletin No. 51.

Osborne, P. (ed.). 1996. *Desert Ecology of Abu Dhabi.* Newbury: Pisces Publications.

Peterson, J. E. 1988. *The Arab Gulf States: Steps Toward Political Participation.* London: Praeger.

Pezzey, J. 1989. *Definitions of Sustainability.* London: C.E.E.D.

Raynaut, C., et al. 2007. 'Sustainability: Where, When, for Whom? Past, Present and Future of a Local Rural Population in a Protected Natural Area (Guaraqueçaba, Brazil).' In *Sustainability and communities of place,* ed. C. A. Maida, 21–40. New York and Oxford: Berghahn Books.

Redclift, M. 2002. 'Discourses of Sustainable Development.' In *The Companion to Development Studies,* eds. V. Deasi and R. B. Potter, 275–278. London: Arnold.

Reiche, Danyel. 2009. 'Renewable Energy Policies in the Gulf Countries: A Case Study of the Carbon-Neutral "Masdar City" in Abu Dhabi.' *Energy Policy* 38: 378–382.

Reid, D. 1995 *Sustainable Development: An Introductory Guide.* London: Earthscan.

Robertson, M. 2014. *Sustainability principles and practice.* London: Earthscan from Routledge.

Roorda, N. with P. B. Corcoran and J. P. Weakland. 2012. *Fundamentals of sustainable development.* London: Earthscan from Routledge

Rosen, A. M. 2007. *Civilizing Climate: The Social Impact of Climate Change in the Ancient Near East.* Lanham, MD: Altamira Press.

Shepherd, A. 1998 *Sustainable Rural Development.* London: Macmillan Press.

Sillitoe, P. 1996. *A Place Against Time: Land and Environment in the Papua New Guinea Highlands.* Amsterdam: Harwood Academic.

Sillitoe, P., A. Bicker and J. Pottier (eds.). 2002. *'Participating in Development': Approaches to Indigenous Knowledge.* London: Routledge.

Sillitoe, P., P. Dixon and J. Barr. 2005. *Indigenous Knowledge Inquiries: A Methodologies Manual for Development.* London: ITDG.

Stepp, J. R., F. S. Wyndham and R. K. Zarger (eds.). 2002. *Ethnobiology and Biocultural Diversity.* Athens: University of Georgia Press.

Tainter, J. A. 1988. *The Collapse of Complex Societies.* Cambridge: Cambridge University Press.

Teske, S. (ed.). 2010. *Energy Revolution.* Amsterdam: Greenpeace International.

Wackernagel, M., and W. Rees. 1996. *Our Ecological Footprint: Reducing Human Impact on the Earth.* Gabriola Island, BC: New Society Pubs.

Watts, M. 2008. *The Curse of the Black Gold.* New York: Powerhouse Press.

Wilson, R. 2008. 'Islamic Economics and Finance.' *World Economics* 9 (1): 177–195.

Yoffee, N. 2005. *Myths of the Archaic State: Evolution of the Earliest Cities, States, and Civilizations.* Cambridge: Cambridge University Press.

Zahlan, R. S. 1998. *The Making of the Modern Gulf States: Kuwait, Bahrain, Qatar, the United Arab Emirates and Oman.* Reading: Ithaca Press.

CHAPTER 1

Societal Change and Sustainability within the Central Plateau of Iran

An Archaeological Viewpoint

Mark Manuel, Robin Coningham, Gavin Gillmore
and Hassan Fazeli

Archaeologists and ancient historians have traditionally explained examples of societal collapse and cultural discontinuity, and engaged in more general discussions of the long-term viability of communities, with reference to external factors, be they invasions, migrations or natural disasters, rather than through attempts to identify continuity in populations, ideologies and technologies.

Perhaps the most famous example of a collapsed past civilization is that of the Roman Empire, whose demise was traditionally attributed to invasions of Visigoths, Vandals and Huns following a general decline in civic and military standards (Gibbon 1841). Subject to a heavy degree of romanticization by Victorian scholars, in reality the Roman Empire continued to flourish in the eastern portion of the Empire for many more centuries, albeit in a slightly different guise, and the western areas had already been overrun several times before they were finally lost (Tainter 1988: 11). Likewise, the palatial Bronze Age Minoan Civilization of the eastern Mediterranean was originally thought to have rapidly collapsed after a series of earthquakes, tsumanis and ash clouds associated with the eruption of Thera c. 1500 BCE, coupled with the expansion of the Myceneans to the Cyclades and Crete (Marinatos 1939). However, more recent scholars have stressed the effect of more complex environmental stresses which led to a decline in agriculture, the abandonment of major elite settlements, including the palaces (Antonopoulos 1992). As is clear from these earlier studies, the traditional focus of archaeologists and ancient historians has been identifying the point of collapse, attributing responsibility to single human or natural events with little focus on the adaptability or sustainability of the society or community under scrutiny.

These early studies were entirely in line with the dominant theoretical model in Anglo-American archaeology, the Cultural Historical, which promoted a concept that past cultures only changed through external stimuli, such as human or natural factors (Renfrew 1973). In contrast, the succeeding dominant model, known as New Archaeology or Processual Archaeology, concentrated far more on the impact of feedback, both negative and positive, on communities, which were themselves viewed as closed systems (Trigger 1989). This shift in focus from external to internal factors has, in turn, shifted academic focus to a consideration of continuity rather than change and an awareness of issues of longevity, resilience and sustainability.

This chapter will present a number of recent examples of how our understanding of sustainability within past communities is developing with reference to case studies from across the globe, before examining the Central Plateau of Iran in more detail and, in particular, the archaeological sites of Tepe Pardis in the Tehran Plain and Sialk in the Dasht-e Kashan. We will argue that rather than portraying past societies and civilizations as victims of environmental, political or societal collapse, we may instead trace how communities have managed their landscape, developed new technologies and, when necessary, moved in order to survive. Whilst less dramatic in terms of narrative, this chapter will highlight the ingenuity that characterizes humankind, and the instinct for survival. Finally, by viewing the past through the lens of sustainability, we can begin to approach present-day environmental challenges in the same manner and make lessons from the past relevant to the present.

Archaeology and Sustainability

The notion of sustainability has become more prominent in recent years within both the academic and public sphere. Climatic variability is becoming both more severe and more frequent, and questions are being asked over the continued reliance upon fossil fuels for generating power, and growing problems of access to reliable water supplies for much of the global population. This latter issue is not just restricted to developing countries, such as Sub-Saharan Africa, but is also of concern in developed countries such as the United States. The Colorado River, provider of water to many of the southwestern states is a prominent example in the United States, where projected water demand will soon exceed supply (Morrison,

Postel and Glock 1996). Further climate change will only exacerbate this situation, as well as have knock-on effects on wetlands and groundwater supply. However, such issues are often viewed as a symptom of modern lifestyles, a rapidly increasing global population and moves towards urbanization and industrialization, whereas archaeology teaches us that sustainability was equally important in the past.

Central here is the need to define exactly what we mean by sustainability when talking about past communities. Peter Bogucki states that 'why a ... community chose *not* to continue living in a particular location is as important as why that community chose to settle in that spot in the first place' (1996: 289). One of the most widely read volumes reviewing the issue of past sustainability is Jared Diamond's *Collapse* (2005), in which he argues that societies make conscious decisions as to their long-term viability and that, more often than not, societies within the past have chosen to fail. This book focuses primarily upon the issue of climate change and landscape manipulation in addressing the question of archaeological and historical sustainability. Diamond's critics have, amongst other things, focused on his categorization of societies as failures or successes (McAnany and Yoffee 2010: 5) and they suggest that ideas of collapse stem from notions of complete abandonment, that is: 'the complete end of those political systems and their accompanying civilisation framework' (Eisenstadt 1988: 242, cited in McAnany and Yoffee 2010: 5). Indeed, they come to the conclusion that the 'overriding human story is one of survival and regeneration' (McAnany and Yoffee 2010: 5).

For example, Diamond argues that the Mayan Civilization collapsed due to a combination of an increasing population stripping the landscape of resources with the resultant deforestation and landscape degradation leading to decreasing quantity and quality of farmland. This in turn led to increasing levels of internecine fighting as people compete for the diminishing space, all framed within a period of climate change leading to droughts and water scarcity further compounding the situation (Diamond 2005: 176f). However, Diamond crucially blames the short-sightedness of the Mayan rulers, 'their attention was evidently focused on their short-term concerns of enriching themselves, waging wars, erecting monuments, competing with each other, and extracting enough food from peasants to support all of these activities' (ibid.: 177). This is the classic example of Diamond's society, or at least those in power, that *chose* to fail through their inability to plan for long-term survival, and a focus upon short-term issues. But the Maya region did not witness widespread depopulation, population replacement or the introduction of new political or economic systems (McAnany and Negrón 2010). Instead, the Mayans appear to have adapted to the changing situations, which resulted from their own actions (i.e. deforestation) and those out of their hands (i.e. climate change). Maya society changed to cope with these problems, and with it – perhaps more crucially from a modern perspective – so did the archaeological signature of Mayan society.

Invariably, Diamond's reasoning behind collapse came down to environmental stress, either through climatic change or landscape degradation. What Diamond did not acknowledge is that in many cases, people and societies have thrived for long periods in subprime environmental conditions. In order to do so, they have both altered and managed, as well as adapted to, the landscapes around them. Archaeological and palaeoenvironmental investigations in the North Atlantic, namely the Faroe Islands, Iceland and Greenland, have traced the development of sustainable agricultural practices during the Norse colonization of them in the ninth and tenth centuries AD, before their eventual abandonment in the sixteenth century (Adderley and Simpson 2006: 1666–1667). Early settlements within Greenland were entirely dependent upon artificial irrigation for the creation of pasture lands, but this was not necessarily the case for early Iceland farms, where irrigation was used to enhance rather than create agricultural landscapes (ibid.: 1677). Landscape degradation within the North Atlantic Norse islands was often thought to have resulted from the overgrazing of domestic livestock by these early colonists (Simpson et al. 2001: 179). However, the abandonment of settlements on the islands appears to be linked to upland soil erosion during the eighteenth century (McGovern et al. 2007: 45–46). Mediaeval documentary evidence highlights the use of regulations to limit the amount of livestock allowed on the more environmentally fragile upland regions, and environmental reconstructions have demonstrated that there were sufficient resources available to support them (Simpson et al. 2001: 186f).

These early Norse settlements also survived the other classic cause of collapse – natural disasters – in this case volcanic eruptions at the beginning of the eleventh and thirteenth centuries AD (Dugmore et al. 2007). Indeed, climatic instability and the introduction of ocean-going vessels that could bypass these islands, and thus nullify their social and economic importance, are perhaps greater reasons for the stresses on and eventual abandonment of some of the settlements (McGovern et al. 2007: 45–46). This evidence suggests that, rather than conforming to Diamond's notion of societal collapse, the Norse island colonization presents a picture of long-term ecological sustainability through landscape and resource management in an environmentally fragile area, only to succumb at a later date to external social and technological changes.

The Central Plateau of Iran

The focus of this chapter is the Central Plateau of Iran, a semi-arid area flanked on the west and north by the Zagros and Alburz mountain ranges and the south and east by the upland areas of Baluchistan (figure 1.1). It incorporates the modern cities of Tehran and Isfahan, as well as major features such as the Dasht-i-Kavir, the large low-lying arid salt plains east of Kashan, formed by the evaporation of landlocked surface water. These inhospitable desert landscapes are fed by large volumes of meltwater from the mountainous edges of the Central Plateau. These fertile river valleys are home to most centres of modern occupation (Fisher 1968). Their true agricultural potential was realized with the introduction of *qanats* – subterranean irrigation channels – during the first millennium BCE. *Qanats* are artificial tunnels dug into sloping alluvium in order to transport subsurface water to areas without ready access to water. They are designed with a gently sloping tunnel directing water from the base of a 'mother' or head well to the mouth or end of the *qanat* tunnel, creating in effect an artificial spring (figures 1.2 and 1.13). They are constructed by digging a series of vertical shafts every 20–80 metres to allow access for the initial digging of the tunnel and for later maintenance (Beaumont 1968: 171). The use of *qanats* allows for the supply of water all year round to areas with little or

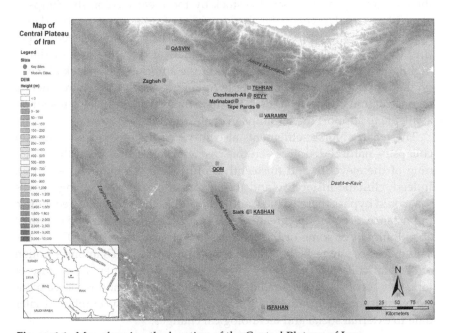

Figure 1.1. Map showing the location of the Central Plateau of Iran.

no access to natural water. However, the discharge of *qanats* is related to the height of the water table at its source, and thus is greatest in winter when water is needed the least, and results in large volumes of water being unused during these months (Beaumont 1968: 172). *Qanats* are located primarily along large alluvial fans, such as the Jajrood, and can have mother wells that are 275 metres deep, as for example near Birjand, and tunnels extending as far as 70 kilometres, as near Kerman (Beaumont 1971: 42).

The first evidence of sedentary communities within Iran is found at sites such as Ganj Dareh, Ali Kosh and Choga Bonut, all located in the upland areas surrounding the Central Plateau and dating from 8000 BCE (Hole 2004). These sites are associated with the domestication of sheep and goat, and the increasing husbandry of crops, in particular wheat, barley and lentils. However, little is known about the later phases of the Neolithic within the Central Plateau itself with Late Neolithic occupation levels only identified at sites such as Sialk near Kashan (Ghirshman 1939), Cheshmeh Ali near Rayy (Fazeli, Coningham and Batt 2004; Schmidt 1935) and Tepe Ebrahim Abad and Charboneh in the Qazvin plain (Majidzadeh 1981; Malek 1977, Fazeli et al. 2009). These sites, dating to the sixth millennium BCE, have no evidence of Early Neolithic occupation. In order to rectify this, a series of joint British and Iranian archaeological investigations were initiated during the 1990s.

Motivated by the destruction of archaeological sites within the Tehran Plain by industrialization, intensive farming, artefact looting and the spread of residential occupation, this collaborative project between UK and Iranian universities was established to study a large area, both temporally and spatially, in order to trace the origins of sedentary communities and socioeconomic complexity (Coningham et al. 2004; Coningham et al. 2006; Fazeli et al. 2007). Work in the Tehran Plain began in 1997 with the excavation of Cheshmeh Ali (figure 1.2) in order to establish a chronological sequence for the plain, supported by radiocarbon dates. A single season of settlement survey (Fazeli, Coningham and Pollard 2001; Fazeli, Coningham and Batt 2004), allowed archaeologists to model the development of craft specialization, standardization and networks of exchange (Fazeli, Donahue and Coningham 2002). A more substantial program of archaeological survey between 2003 and 2007 followed on the plain southeast of Varamin, encompassing a number of environmental zones – upland and piedmont areas, the alluvial plain and arid desert areas. It aimed to determine whether prehistoric and historic settlement was located, as it is today, mainly within the agriculturally fertile river valleys, and less in the more environmentally marginal zones. The survey identified sites for further detailed studies and test excavations to recover additional radiocarbon dates.

Figure 1.2. General view of the spring at Cheshmeh Ali, Reyy, now a public park.

Sustainability within the Central Plateau of Iran

We look at the question of sustainability within the Central Plateau during the Late Neolithic and Transitional Chalcolithic period (c. 6200–4300 BCE), specifically at the Tehran and Kashan Plains, and two sites in particular – Tepe Pardis and Sialk (the former excavations were supplemented with an extensive archaeological survey of the Tehran Plain). The Tehran Plain is drained by the Jajerud River, which flows south from the Alburz Mountains forming an alluvial fan. Annual rainfall on the plain near Varamin is 150 mm (although variations from 54 to 230 mm have been recorded) and is concentrated in the winter months between December and April. Annual temperatures fluctuate between 3.7°C in January to 28.9°C in July, with extremes of –17°C and 47°C recorded (Beaumont 1968: 169). Dry winds from the southeast bring large volumes of dust from the Dasht-e-Kavir, which is dumped across the landscape. Along with this coarse sandy topsoil are thin layers of coarse gravel that lack organic material near the mouth of the river, and deep sandy and silty loams to the south of the alluvial cone. The former soils are poor agriculturally, whilst the latter is exceptionally good, although lack of perennial water supplies can lead to salination, and ephemeral surface vegetation makes them prone to wind erosion (ibid.). The low rainfall means that agriculture can only be carried out with the aid of irrigation, traditionally through the use of *qanats*, but more recently pumped from wells and then distributed through lined irrigation canals. The subprime nature of the environment was ably summarized by one of its earlier archaeological pioneers, Roman Ghirshman, who stated that: 'The physical aspects of the Plateau was harsh and austere. The oases were dispersed over difficult country, the population was sparse and scattered. As a result the urban revolution was retarded, and society continued in its prehistoric stage for centuries' (1954: 42).

A total of 193 archaeological sites were identified within the Tehran Plain during the three seasons of survey, a breakdown of which is in table 1.1. Both archaeological and modern sites were recorded during the course of the survey. The single Palaeolithic site, as well as the Neolithic and Chalcolithic sites, are concentrated in the eastern section of the survey zone at the well-watered junction between piedmont terraces and the plain itself, but there are some exceptions, particularly during the Chalcolithic period with sites such as Tepe Pardis (A006), Tepe Daoudabad (A050) and Deh Mohsen (A020), all substantial tepes or tells located on or close to the alluvial fan of the Jajerud River. Tepes or tells are large mounds of human material representing the repeated rebuilding of structures on top of

Table 1.1. The periodization of archaeological sites, and categorization of modern sites recorded during the Tehran Plains survey between 2003 and 2007. (The number is greater than 193 due to some multiperiod sites.)

Period	Number of sites
Archaeological Periods	
Palaeolithic	1
Neolithic (6000–5200 BC)	18
Chalcolithic (5200–3400 BC)	13
Iron Age (2000–550 BC)	2
Parthian (247 BC–AD 224)	1
Sasanian (AD 224–651)	3
Historic (500 BC–AD 650)	31
Islamic (AD 650–1700)	59
Modern Sites	
Landlord Villages	15
Ceramic Scatters	22
Evidence of modern pastoral communities	22
Undiagnostic sites	15
TOTAL	**202**

Table 1.2. Prehistoric chronology of the Central Plateau of Iran.

Period	Date BC	Qazvin Plain	Tehran Plain	Kashan Plain	Damghan / Shahrud
Early Bronze II (Kura-Araxes)	*2900–2000*	Shizar Doranabad	Arasto Tepe	?	Hissar III
Early Bronze I (Proto-Literate)	*3400–2900*	Shizar	Tepe Sofalin Chogali	Arisman C Sialk IV	Hissar IIB
Late Chalcolithic	*3700–3400*	Ghabristan III–IV Ismailabad Shizar	Cheshmeh-Ali Tepe Pardis Sofalin Chogali	Arisman B Sialk South 6–7	Hissar IIA
Middle Chalcolithic	*4000–3700*	Ghabristan II Shizar	Cheshmeh-Ali Tepe Pardis Chogali	Sialk South 4–5	Hissar IC
Early Chalcolithic	*4300–4000*	Ghabristan I	Cheshmeh-Ali Tepe Pardis Chogali	Sialk South 1–3	Hissar IA–IB
Transitional Chalcolithic	*Late* *4600–4300*	?	Cheshmeh Ali Ismailabad Kara Tepe Chogali	?	Shir Azhian Aq Tappeh
	Early *5200–4600*	Ebrahim Abad Zagheh	Cheshmeh-Ali Tepe Pardis Ismailabad	Sialk North Period II	'Cheshmeh Ali' Phase
Late Neolithic	*Late* *5600–5200*	Chahar Boneh Ebrahimabad	Cheshmeh-Ali Tepe Pardis	Sialk North Period I, 4–5	Sang-I Chakhmaq
	Early *6000–5600*	Chahar Boneh	?	Sialk North Period I, 1–3	'Djetun' Phase

each other over time. A number of other smaller tepes, namely Fakrabad (A031), Tepe Tar (B118), B027 and B028 are located within the plain proper. By the later historic periods, and onwards, there is much more substantial occupation, in number, size and function of the settlements, in this latter area.

In order to understand the changing settlement patterns of the Tehran Plain, and in particular its early occupation, it is helpful to consider the evidence from the site of Mafinabad (figure 1.3), a Chalcolithic tell west of Tehran. A large section of the tepe had been cut away in preparation for construction work, revealing a complex sequence of migratory and braided river channels sandwiched between layers of Chalcolithic pottery. This suggests some irregularity regarding water resources, and Fazeli (2001) suggested that the unreliability of water has constrained the development of settlement within the Tehran Plain during the Neolithic and Chalcolithic. This point is supported by the thoroughly documented site of Cheshmeh-Ali, near Rayy, which has a sequence stretching from the Late Neolithic to the Chalcolithic period and is located immediately next to the spring which gives the site its name (Fazeli, Coningham and Batt 2004). The distribution of sites revealed by the survey supports such a pattern as few sites appear to support more than a single phase of Neolithic or Chalcolithic settlement. This is a consequence of human communities moving as the watercourses shift, such that social complexity and the permanent occupation of locations was largely delayed. These early communities were sustainable through their ability to move across the landscape, as and when they needed. Indeed, it is only with the later advent of *qanat* technology that we find the growth and spread of substantial permanent occupation in the Tehran Plain during the Historic and Islamic periods.

Figure 1.3. General view of palaeochannels visible in the section of a building site close to Mufinabad.

Excavations at the site of Tepe Pardis have revealed an anomaly to this general pattern of early communities as it is a long-lived prehistoric settlement in this marginal zone. These excavations have revealed an unbroken sequence stretching from the Late Neolithic to the Late Chalcolithic, with later sporadic Iron Age, Parthian and Islamic occupation. Tepe Pardis was identified during the 2003 survey season and identified as a site that was in danger of being destroyed (Coningham et al. 2004). Located in the western outskirts of the city of Garchak, it had been very badly damaged by a road on its eastern side and on its other three sides by a quarry extracting clay for brick manufacturing (figure 1.4). The site consisted of a mound 7 metres in height above the surrounding ground level with an additional 3.5 metres of depth revealed where the quarry had cut into the tepe, giving a combined depth of occupation of 10.5 metres.

The initial excavation sought to establish a chronological sequence and, in the process, uncovered part of a hearth or kiln. Extending the trench revealed a large complex of ceramic kilns and ovens, as well as evidence of a potter's slow wheel (Fazeli et al. 2007; (figures 1.5 and 1.6). The three slightly later kilns in Trench IV (Kilns 5, 6 and 7) were single-chamber updraught kilns with domed roofs and measured between 1.30 and 2.08 square metres. Fireboxes were situated at the front of the structures and vessels were fired on the raised floors behind. The earlier kilns

Figure 1.4. General view of Tepe Pardis showing the modern brick quarry in the foreground, and the step trench excavated into the cut away section of the tell.

Figure 1.5. Detailed view of Transitional Chalcolithic kilns at Tepe Pardis. The kiln floors are visible on the right-hand side, whilst broken pots are scattered across the floor.

from Trench III (Kilns 1, 2 and 4) were much bigger with areas of at least 12 square metres each. Indeed, cubic capacity highlights this difference, as Kiln 4 was also at least 1.5 metres high. At a minimum capacity of 18 cubic metres, it was much greater than other known examples of a similar age, presaging the large installations which, in Hansen Striely's words, are 'generally connected in later periods with palace or temple economy' (2000: 80). Kilns 3 and 8 were smaller and less well preserved. The presence of a terracotta slow wheel, the world's oldest example, is particularly interesting as, before this discovery, the earliest known previous example was from Ur (Woolley 1956: 28), dating to c. 3250 BCE. The development of the potter's wheel has been seen to represent a shift towards the mass production of ceramics between the Ubaid and Uruk periods in Mesopotamia (Oates 1960: 39) dated to c. 4100 BCE, and roughly equating to the Chalcolithic-Early Bronze Age transition. Valentine Roux and Marie-Agnès Courty support this fourth-millennium BCE origin of wheel-thrown pottery and equate it with the rise of urbanism (1999: 747–748, 761). As such, Tepe Pardis hosted an intensive industrial area covering over 60 square metres dating to c. 5000 BCE and the investment in permanent terracotta slow wheels and large kiln structures is suggestive of significant

Figure 1.6. A terracotta slow wheel found at Tepe Pardis, the oldest known example in the world, dating to the fifth millennium BCE.

settlement specialization during the Transitional Chalcolithic (Fazeli et al. 2007: 268–270).

In addition to the ceramic vessels manufactured within the kilns of Tepe Pardis, a large number of other terracotta artefacts were recovered, including spindle whorls, slingshots and beads, indicating the presence of a substantial craft specialism based on one of the key resources available to the inhabitants of Tepe Pardis – the surrounding clay deposits. That the modern industries of Garchak also rely heavily upon the natural clays for brick manufacturing testifies to the importance of raw materials to human settlements both past and present. It also provides an indicator as to why the early inhabitants of Tepe Pardis elected to reside in what is today an environmentally subprime location. However, in order to do so they had to manipulate the landscape, and in particular the water resources, around them in order to be able to sustain the settlement.

Pollen analysis from the Late Neolithic levels at the site have yielded evidence of pine and olive species. However, crucially they also identified a plant fungus and soil fungus which are indicative of soil erosion (Gillmore et al. 2009: 294), indicating that the early inhabitants of the site faced soil-erosion problems. Also interesting is the identification of an artificial water channel at the site dating to the Late Neolithic. The channel's triangular profile (figure 1.7) differed significantly from several other natural channels identified at the site, and ran perpendicular to them. Radiocarbon dates taken from immediately above and below the channel date it to between 5220 and 4990 BCE. As such, it represents one of the earliest examples of artificial irrigation within Iran and the Near East. The deposits within its sedimentary sequence indicate alternating periods of shallow and relatively quiet flow and periods of drying out (ibid.: 298). The presence of irrigation technology points towards a substantial investment in infrastructure at the site, and demonstrates an attempt at informal landscape manipulation in order to ensure the prolonged sustainability of the site.

Further parallels can be drawn at the site of Sialk, located in the western suburbs of Kashan, 160 kilometres south of Tepe Pardis. It is another large tell site with Late Neolithic and Chalcolithic occupation. The site is situated on the Dasht-e-Kashan (figure 1.8), which forms part of the Central Plateau of Iran and is located to the west of the Dasht-e-Kavir, or Great

Figure 1.7. Detailed view of artificial water channel at Tepe Pardis. The triangular profile indicates that it is not naturally occurring.

Figure 1.8. General view of desert to the south of the Tehran Plain.

Salt Desert. It can be divided into three major environmental sectors, the western mountainous region, the plain and desert. Reaching a maximum height of 3,900 metres, the Karkas Mountains (figure 1.9) form the western boundary of the Dasht-e-Kashan. To the east is the plain or *dasht*, formed by a series of alluvial fans spreading out from the Karkas Mountains. With its semi-arid conditions and an elevation of between 1,200 and 1,000 metres, the plain is similar to the Tehran Plain to the north. It has a seasonal rainfall pattern, and modern cultivation is aided by both *qanat* systems and modern pumps. Settlements within the plain are located along *qanat* systems and close to natural springs (figure 1.10). The desert or *kavir*, forming most of Iran's Central Plateau, starts east of the town of Arun. Standing at c. 1,000 metres above sea level, it is characterized by mountain ridges, fans and marshy basins of mud and salt. Its lack of water, swift evaporation and high temperature extremes make it unsuitable for cultivation and it is sparsely settled.

The site of Sialk was initially excavated during the 1930s by a team of French archaeologists led by Roman Ghirshman, who famously stated of its sequence, spread across two separate tepes, that one 'follow almost without interruption the progress made by the inhabitants of the Iranian

Figure 1.9. General view of the Karkas Mountains, with the excavations at Sialk in the foreground.

Plateau' (Ghirshman 1954: 29). He opened three trenches on the North Mound or tepe (figure 1.11) which he dated to the Neolithic and Chalcolithic periods, and four trenches on the South Mound which he attributed to later Iron Age occupation at the site. Sialk has been central to any attempt to define the prehistoric chronology of the Central Plateau of Iran, partially due to the 12-metre-deep Late Neolithic deposit complete with mudbrick structures and objects of copper and marine shell. Ghirshman also demonstrated that the site developed slowly from a Late Neolithic village to a small Chalcolithic town, with cultural continuity demonstrated through ceramics and architecture (1939). Ghirshman suggested that the occupation at the two mounds was separated by an occupational hiatus, perhaps caused by natural disaster or environmental stress; a more recent scholar, Yusef Majidzadeh, proposed that the shift from the Northern Mound of Sialk to the Southern Mound was due to intrusive migrations of people into the Central Plateau of Iran – 'Plum-Ware people', so titled because the shift appeared to be associated with the introduction of a new form of ceramic at the base of the new settlement on the South Mound (1981: 142f).

Figure 1.10. General view of the *qanat* mouth at Bagh-e-Fin, Kashan. The water supplies the former royal pleasure gardens.

New excavations, undertaken by the same Iranian and British team who worked together at Tepe Pardis, focused on the North Mound with the aim of characterizing the social and economic transformations which enabled the early communities of the Dasht-e-Kashan to establish and

Figure 1.11. General view of the North Mound of Sialk.

develop one of the earliest nucleated settlements on the Central Plateau of Iran in the Neolithic period. This began with a deep excavation on the North Mound, cutting a 2.5- by 2-metre step trench (Trench 5) into the south section of Ghirshman's original Trench II, an eroded and partially filled cutting measuring some 20 × 8 metres. Trench 5 was excavated down to a depth of 11 metres, and was augmented by a second step trench, Trench 6, in the base of Trench II, excavated in order to sample and date the earliest occupation levels at the site (figure 1.12). This smaller trench measured 2 × 1 metres and was excavated to a depth of 4.5 metres, giving a combined total of 15.5 metres of continuous sequence – 1.5 metres deeper than Ghirshman's original excavations.

Geoarchaeological investigations within another deep trench, Trench B, situated between the North and South mounds at Sialk have identified a changing pattern of river management during the Chalcolithic. At the base of Trench B were natural alluvial deposits, typically gravels, sandy silt loams and silt loams. Above this, were alternating phases of cultural occupation and finer alluvial deposits, possibly representing phases of reduced river flow during which occupation is evident, punctuated by high-energy events, such as flooding (Ian Simpson, pers. comm.). Over time, these high-energy events become less evident, and were replaced

Figure 1.12. Detailed view of the excavations at the North Mound of Sialk, showing Trench Five cut into the section, and Trench Six cut into the floor of Ghirshman's old trench.

by the detritus of cultural activity, such as pottery and charcoal, and thin bands of silty clay sediments derived from irrigation activity. Again, like Tepe Pardis, this demonstrates that the Chalcolithic inhabitants of Sialk were managing and altering their landscape in order to achieve the long-term survival and sustainability of their settlement.

Radiocarbon dates indicate that the North Mound was occupied until 4900 BCE, at which point there was a large amount of sedimentation build up, possibly indicative of flooding. Occupation of the South Mound begins approximately 4100 BCE, and this shift from the North to the South Mound has traditionally been viewed as a hiatus in occupation, although the reasons behind the move are still debated. It may well be that the landscape became uninhabitable due to floodwaters, or the sedimentation may reflect a breakdown of water management in the region. However, whatever the reasons, people returned to the site ensuring occupation of the site from the Neolithic and Chalcolithic Periods, between the seventh and fifth millennia BCE, through to the Iron Age in the second millennium BCE.

Conclusion

The early communities within the Central Plateau were restricted in their choice of settlement location by access to water. It is clear that Ghirshman's hypothesis that the 'harsh and austere' physical aspects of the Plateau resulted in the settlement of human communities close to dispersed oases (1954: 42) was an accurate prediction of the archaeological signature of the early occupation of the Central Plateau. However, it appears that he was wrong in thinking that that population was sentenced by those physical aspects to continue in a 'prehistoric stage for centuries' (Ghirshman 1954:42). The survey work undertaken within the Tehran Plain shows a concentration in the early periods of sites on the fringes of alluvial fans or at the interface of plain and upland areas. The central plain and desert areas were sparsely occupied. This pattern changes significantly in the Historic and early Islamic periods with an expansion of settlements into these previously unoccupied areas facilitated by the introduction of *qanat* technology (figure 1.13).

Although the exact date of the adoption of *qanats* within the Tehran Plain is not known, it allowed the occupants of the plain to concentrate population in one area, cultivating larger tracts of land and increasing numbers of animals. The access to reliable, perennial water sources led to permanently settled locales, rather than the itinerant settlement patterns of prehistory influenced by a dependency on shifting watercourses. The Tepe Pardis and Sialk projects have helped archaeologists develop an understanding of how early sedentary societies within the Central Plateau of Iran have utilized and manipulated their landscape in order to ensure their long-term sustainability. Drawn by large deposits of clay, the inhabitants of Tepe Pardis developed craft specialization and began to

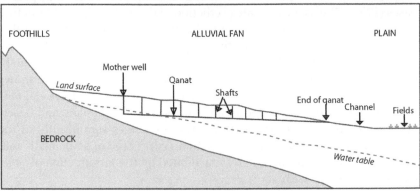

Figure 1.13. Top: General view of *qanats* on the Dasht-e-Kashan. Bottom: Overview of how *qanats* work (after Beaumont 1968: 171, figure 2).

adapt their marginal environment to meet their needs as indicated by the presence of early irrigation channels dating to the Late Neolithic (one of the earliest examples in Iran). This major investment in specialized pottery production and artificial irrigation indicates the sophisticated nature of settlement in the Tehran Plain during the Transitional Chalcolithic and demonstrates that human communities have often adapted and thrived on what may today be thought marginal or subprime environments through the development of technology.

Together, these two sites of Tepe Pardis and Sialk are helping archaeologists develop a new understanding of how past communities have attempted to ensure their long-term survival. Whilst stories of invasion, catastrophe and societal collapse may be more dramatic and exciting, the overriding narrative within archaeology is one of survival and development. From the icebound valleys of the North Atlantic islands, to the jungle cities of the Maya and the semi-arid deserts of the Central Plateau of Iran humans have adapted both themselves and their environment to ensure their survival. With environmental issues rising to the top of the modern global political agenda, such tales of localized sustainability rather than widespread collapse may provide a more positive vision for the future.

Acknowledgements

We would like to acknowledgement the support of the following institutions and individuals in undertaking the research discussed in this chapter: the British Institute of Persian Studies; the Iranian Cultural Heritage, Handicrafts and Tourism Organization (ICHHTO); the Iranian Centre for Archaeological Research (ICHHTO); the Sialk Archaeological Research Centre (ICHHTO); the British Academy; the Institute of Archaeology of the University of Tehran; Varamin, Garchak and Kashan City Councils. We are also very grateful to Professor Ian Simpson, Dr Ruth Young, Armineh Marghussian, Hingameh Ilkhani, Hossein Azizi, Dr Sayyed Taha Hasehmi, Dr Mohammad Gholam Nejad, Dr Seyed Mahdi Mousavi Koohpar, Dr Hassan Karimian, Dr Hayedeh Laleh, Dr Masoud Azarnoush, Mr Naser Pazouki, Dr Vesta Surkosh Curtis, Professor John Curtis, FBA, Dr Armin Schmidt, Dr Cathy Batt, Dr Randy Donahue and Mrs Sarakhani for their support and assistance. Finally, we would like to acknowledge the excellent help in the field and laboratories provided by staff and students from Durham University, the University of Tehran, the University of Bradford, the University of Leicester, the Azad University and the ICHHTO.

References

Adderley, W. P., and I. A. Simpson. 2006. 'Soils and Palaeo-Climate Based Evidence for Irrigation Requirements in Norse Greenland.' *Journal of Archaeological Science* 33: 1666–1679.

Antonopoulos, J. 1992. 'The Great Minoan Eruption of Thera Volcano and the Ensuing Tsunami in the Greek Archipelago.' *Natural Hazards* 5: 153–168.

Beaumont, P. 1968. 'Qanats on the Varamin Plain, Iran.' *Transactions of the Institute of British Geographers* 45: 169–179.

———. 1971. 'Qanat Systems in Iran.' *Hydrological Sciences Journal* 16 (1): 39–50.

Bogucki, P. 1996. 'Sustainable and Unsustainable Adaptations by Early Farming Communities of Northern Poland.' *Journal of Anthropological Archaeology* 15: 289–311.

Coningham, R. A. E., et al. 2004. 'Location, Location, Location: A Pilot Study of the Tehran Plain.' *Iran* 42: 1–12.

———. 2006. 'Socio-Economic Transformations: Settlement Survey in the Tehran Plain and Excavations at Tepe Pardis.' *Iran* 44: 33–62.

Diamond, J. 2005. *Collapse: How Societies Choose to Fail or Succeed*. Penguin: London.

Dugmore, A. J., et al. 2007. 'Abandoned Farms, Volcanic Impacts and Woodland Management: Revisiting Þjórsárdalur, the "Pompeii of Iceland".' *Arctic Anthropology* 44 (1): 1–11.

Eisenstadt, S. N. 1988. 'Beyond Collapse.' In *The Collapse of Ancient States and Civilisations*, eds. N. Yoffee and G. L. Cowgill, 236–243. Tucson: University of Arizona Press.

Fazeli, H. 2001. 'Social Complexity and Craft Specialisation in the Late Neolithic and Early Chalcolithic Period in the Central Plateau of Iran.' PhD thesis: University of Bradford, UK.

Fazeli H., R. A. E. Coningham and C. M. Batt. 2004. 'Cheshmeh-Ali Revisited: Towards an Absolute Dating of the Late Neolithic and Chalcolithic of Iran's Tehran Plain.' *Iran* 42: 13–23.

Fazeli, H., R. A. E. Coningham and A. M. Pollard. 2001. 'Chemical Characterisation of Late Neolithic and Chalcolithic Pottery from the Tehran Plain, Iran.' *Iran* 39: 55–72.

Fazeli, H., R. E. Donahue and R. A. E. Coningham. 2002. 'Stone Tool Production, Distribution and Use During the Late Neolithic and Chalcolithic on the Tehran Plain, Iran.' *Iran* 40: 1–14.

Fazeli, H., et al. 2007. 'Socio-Economic Transformations in the Tehran Plain: Final Season of Settlement Survey and Excavations at Tepe Pardis.' *Iran* 45: 267–286.

———. 2009. 'The Neolithic to Chalcolithic Transition in the Qazvin Plain, Iran: Chronology and Subsistence Strategies.' *Archaologische Mitteilungen Aus Iran und Turan* 41: 1–21.

Fisher, W. B. 1968. 'Physical Geography.' In *The Cambridge History of Iran, Volume 1: The Land of Iran*, ed. W. B. Fisher, 3–110. Cambridge: Cambridge University Press.

Ghirshman, R. 1939. *Fouilles de Sialk, prés de Kashan 1933, 1934, 1937*. Volume 1. Paris: Musée du Louvre, Department des Antiquités Orientales.

———. 1954. *Iran: From the Earliest Times to the Islamic Conquest*. London: Penguin.

Gibbon, E. 1841. *The History of the Decline and Fall of the Roman Empire*. Harper: New York.

Gillmore, G. K., et al. 2009. 'Irrigation on the Tehran Plain, Iran: Tepe Pardis – The Site of a Possible Neolithic Irrigation Feature?' *Catena* 78: 285–300.

Hansen Streily, A. 2000. 'Early Pottery Kilns in the Middle East.' *Paleorient* 26 (2): 69–81.

Hole, F. 2004. 'Neolithic Age in Iran.' *Encyclopaedia Iranica*, online edition, 20 July 2004, available at http://www.iranicaonline.org.

McAnany, P. A., and T. G. Negrón. 2010. 'Bellicose Rulers and Climatological Peril: Retrofitting Twenty-First Century Woes on Eighth Century Maya Society.' In *Questioning Collapse: Human Resilience, Ecological Vulnerability and the Aftermath of Empire,* eds. P. A. McAnany and N. Yoffee, 142–175. Cambridge: Cambridge University Press.

McAnany, P. A., and N. Yoffee. 2010. 'Why We Question Collapse and Study Human Resilience, Ecological Vulnerability and the Aftermath of Empire.' In *Questioning Collapse: Human Resilience, Ecological Vulnerability and the Aftermath of Empire,* eds. P. A. McAnany and N. Yoffee, 1–17. Cambridge: Cambridge University Press.

McGovern, T. H., et al. 2007. 'Landscapes of Settlement in Northern Iceland: Historical Ecology of Human Impact and Climate Fluctuation on the Millennial Scale.' *American Anthropologist* 109 (1): 27–51.

Majidzadeh, Y. 1981. 'Sialk III and the Pottery Sequence at Tepe Ghabristhan: The Coherence of the Cultures of the Central Iranian Plateau.' *Iran* 19: 141–146.

Malek, S. 1977. *Tepe Zagheh: A Sixth Millennium BC Village in the Qazvin Plain of the Central Iranian Plateau.* PhD thesis, University of Pennsylvania.

Marinatos, S. 1939. 'The Volcanic Destruction of Minoan Crete.' *Antiquity* 13 (52): 425–439.

Morrison, J. I., S. L. Postel and P. H. Glock. 1996. *The Sustainable Use of Water in the Lower Colorado River Basin.* Oakland, CA: Pacific Institute for Studies in Development, Environment, and Security.

Oates, J. 1960. 'Ur and Eridu, the Prehistory.' *Iraq* 22: 32–50.

Renfrew, A. C. 1973. *Before Civilisation: The Radiocarbon Revolution and Prehistoric Europe.* Harmondsworth: Penguin Books.

Roux, V., and M.-A. Courty. 1999. 'Identification of Wheel-Fashioning Methods: Technological Analysis of 4th–3rd Millennium BC Oriental Ceramics.' *Journal of Archaeological Science* 25: 747–763.

Schmidt, E. 1935. 'The Persian Expedition.' *Bulletin of the University Museum* 4 (5): 41–49.

Simpson, I. A., et al. 2001. 'Crossing the Thresholds: Human Ecology and Historical Patterns of Landscape Degradation.' *Catena* 42: 175–192.

Tainter, J. A. 1988. *The Collapse of Complex Societies.* Cambridge: Cambridge University Press.

Trigger, B. G. 1989. *A History of Archaeological Thought.* Cambridge: Cambridge University Press.

Wooley, C. L. 1956. *Ur Excavations: The Early Periods IV.* London: British Museum Press.

I

Planning Sustainable Development

CHAPTER 2

Qatar National Vision 2030

Advancing Sustainable Development

Trudy Tan, Aziza Al-Khalaqi and Najla Al-Khulaifi

Qatar seeks to build a vibrant and prosperous country in which there is economic and social justice for all, and in which humans and nature are in harmony (GSDP 2008). Its long-term development outcomes, as articulated in the Qatar National Vision 2030 (QNV 2030), are built on the principles of sustainable development, at the heart of which is the need to ensure intergenerational fairness.

Qatar has been enjoying a period of unparalleled prosperity, with exceptional economic progress evident in the increasing standard of living of its people. Foreign exchange revenues from the export of its hydrocarbon resources have provided the means for massive investments in cutting-edge infrastructure: in health, education and social protection. One result is that by 2007, Qatar had advanced to 33rd out of 182 countries in the United Nations Development Programme's Human Development Index, compared to a ranking of 57th a decade earlier (UNDP 2009). This is remarkable progress in less than a generation.

Qatar's advances in human development have been made possible by the prudent use of revenues from the country's abundant hydrocarbon resources, especially its vast gas reserves. Its increased wealth has created previously undreamt of opportunities. But the rights of future generations could be put at risk if this wealth is used inefficiently and/or economic development goes beyond the nation's carrying capacity. For many countries, natural resource abundance has become a 'curse' rather than a 'blessing', and has led to the so-called Dutch disease – a sharp inflow of foreign currency leading to excessive currency appreciation, thus making exports less competitive and imports cheaper, and resulting in deindustrialization apart from resource exploitation.

Given a development strategy that currently depends mainly on the exploitation of its oil and gas resources, Qatar is unable to avoid some adverse effects on its environment. The challenge is to make the transition from uncontrolled growth, which has real potential to stall or reverse Qatar's tremendous human development progress, to managed growth that is consistent with the principles of sustainable development.

Human and economic development and the protection of the environment are competing demands that must be reconciled with each other. The achievement of intergenerational equity with high human development necessitates the judicious use of Qatar's non-renewable resources. Returns from the current use of these resources need to continue to be invested wisely, especially in education, supportive infrastructure and research and development. This will help to ensure that future generations of Qataris can enjoy new sources of prosperity and sustain the prosperity enjoyed by the current generation.

QNV 2030 Premised on Sustainable Development

Achieving sustainable development in Qatar does not require a new or standalone sustainable development strategy. Qatar's long-term sustainable development goals and objectives are integral to QNV 2030. The vision commits the government to maintaining harmony between the three interdependent pillars of sustainable development – economic growth, social development and environmental management (GSDP 2008).

The QNV 2030 reflects national aspirations and enjoys the highest level of political commitment. It rests on four interdependent and mutually reinforcing pillars with clearly defined long-term outcomes (figure 2.1). Its goals and objectives will be operationalized through policies and programmes contained in a sequence of National Development Strategies, the first of which covers the period 2011–2016.

To achieve the QNV 2030 outcomes and remain true to its values, Qatar is endeavouring to balance five critical challenges:

(1) modernization and preservation of traditions;
(2) the needs of this generation and the needs of future generations;
(3) managed growth and uncontrolled expansion;
(4) the size and quality of the expatriate labour force and the selected path of development;
(5) economic growth, social development and environmental management (GSDP 2008).

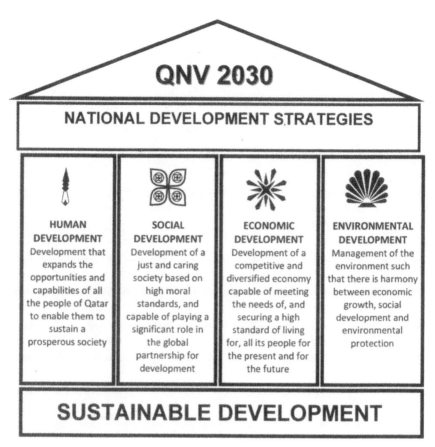

Figure 2.1. QNV 2030 built on principles of sustainable development.

Economic, social and environmental considerations are thus being integrated into the national planning processes. Where integration cannot be achieved, trade-offs are being negotiated based on a prioritization of needs and objectives, taking into account the impact of present decisions on future generations.

Sustainable Development in Qatar: Reconciling Competing Demands

Qatar's rapid development, as experienced from 2005 to 2008, is unsustainable. Negative environmental externalities include air pollution, diminishing water resources, excessive energy use, loss of biodiversity, and environmental degradation resulting from excessive urban development. These environmental concerns are a product of three factors: rapid population growth, increased consumption and production patterns and technological change.

The increase in manufacturing, infrastructure and commercial development in Qatar has resulted in massive inflows of predominantly unskilled male expatriate labour from South Asia. As a consequence, Qatar's population has grown at a phenomenal rate, averaging 15 per cent per year between 2005 and 2009 (figure 2.2). This exceptionally rapid rise is virtually unprecedented historically and globally. Even in the face of the global financial crisis, when the population in some neighbouring Gulf Cooperation Council countries declined, Qatar's population grew by some 10 per cent between 2008 and 2009.

Uncontrolled population growth is increasing consumption and the demand for services, threatening sustainability and adversely affecting Qatar's environment in terms of land use, water and energy resources, biodiversity, urban congestion, pollutions and emissions. It is also creating stresses on the nation's urban services such as housing and waste management, as well as on hospitals and schools.

Along with rapid population growth, Qatar's real GDP has been growing at a phenomenal pace (figure 2.3). Qatar's economic activity depends

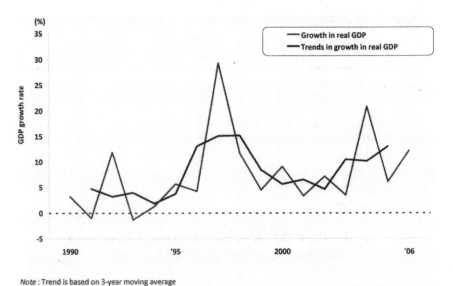

Note : Trend is based on 3-year moving average
Source : GSDP 2009

Figure 2.2. Qatar's population grew phenomenally between 2004 and 2008, reaching 1.6 million in 2009, compared with about 760,000 in 2004.

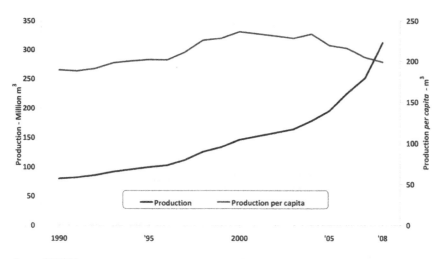

Source: GSDP 2009

Figure 2.3. Qatar's economic output grew 8 per cent annually with fluctuations around a long-term trend.

heavily on the increased exploitation of its natural resources. It has led to massive rises in per capita incomes, which in turn encourage greater consumption, and more energy-intensive lifestyles – lifestyles that also bring new health risks to the population.

Inevitably, such large increases in population and income per person are having a dramatic impact on Qatar's environment and are not sustainable. Human impact (I) on the environment comprises three aspects: the total population (P), income per person (A) and the environmental impact per dollar of income (T), the so-called I-PAT model, with the overall impact being the product of these three factors (Sachs 2008). To mitigate environmental damage from human activity, Qatar needs to produce high income per unit of environmental impact. The much-desired rise in income (A) needs to be offset with a stabilization of population (P) through better economic management and a reduction in the environmental impact per unit of income (T) through investments in sustainable 'green' technologies and increased productivity.

In line with this, Qatar is focusing on developing and utilizing sustainable technologies. For example, it is adopting 'green' standards in the construction of new buildings with plans to retrofit new technologies to existing buildings to lower CO_2 emissions. It is also adopting new technologies for improving emissions performance in its oil and gas industries and is exploring alternative energy sources, such as solar power and biofuels, to further reduce its carbon footprint.

Overall, Qatar requires a framework that includes three key complementary elements for improved sustainable development outcomes: pricing policy, technology policy and information policy. Pricing policies determine the distribution of costs, thus influencing behaviour and investment decisions of firms and individuals. Technology policies can support the development of a range of sustainable technologies that are urgently needed to lower the environmental impact of human activities. And information policies help build capacity of individuals and businesses to become environmental stewards and make informed decisions.

The choice and combination of policy tools to apply will of course depend on national circumstances, on the characteristics of particular sectors, and on the interaction between policies (Stern 2007). While there should be flexibility to adapt to changing circumstances, policies should build on national conditions and approaches to policy making, with strong links between current actions and long-term goals.

Achieving Sustainable Growth and Managed Expansion

Qatar is considering the extent to which it can sustain current levels of economic and population growth, and the broad policy framework for this reconsideration is outlined in QNV2030. It makes the case, inter alia, for managed economic growth, targeted expansion of the expatriate population and a transition to a knowledge economy.

One challenge facing Qatar is the determination of the balance between national workers and expatriate workers, that is aligning expatriates to the chosen development path. In recent years, labour-force growth has averaged more than 18 per cent annually. Current massive inflows of foreign workers are a manifestation of uncontrolled expansion. The economic benefits from such rapid increase in numbers of foreign workers entering Qatar must be weighed against the costs and pressures on the environment.

In line with the QNV 2030's aspirations for a diversified, knowledge-based economy, a more sustainable policy for labour-market strategy should focus on structural changes, including greater use of technology and automation. This would help limit the flows of low-skilled foreign workers, help develop local talent, and support the inflow of a higher proportion of higher-skilled expatriates. Sustainable growth will thus depend both on the extent to which public policies can push the transition towards a high productivity or high wage economy, and the extent to which national employees are willing and able to increase their skills and competitiveness.

Promoting Sustainable Production
and Consumption Patterns

A key challenge for Qatar is to ensure wise and sustainable use of resources through better management systems and investing in sustainable 'green' technologies. Achieving sustainable development necessitates a change in mindset, particularly concerning consumption and production patterns.

Qatar's natural resources are being used inefficiently and unsustainably, placing strains on the environment. Increased water demand and unsustainable levels of water extraction are exerting pressures on the nation's natural ecosystem. Despite the rapid expansion in annual production of desalinated water, production per capita has been declining in recent years due to the country's rapid development and exceptionally high population growth, leading to water stress (figure 2.4). Groundwater abstraction, which has been consistently above recharge levels, has also seriously depleted aquifer reserves (GSDP 2009). The quality of water remaining in the aquifers is of questionable quality and increasingly saline, thus decreasing agricultural productivity.

Ironically, while groundwater reserves throughout the country have been depleted, the water table under Doha is rising, saturating the ground under the most densely populated area in the country, increasing risk of flooding and damaging infrastructure. Inflows into the water table come from two main sources: leakage from the clean water distribution network

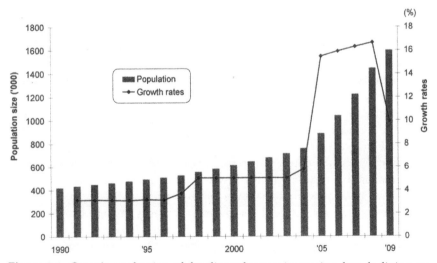

Figure 2.4. Qatar's production of desalinated water increasing, but declining on a per capita basis.

and leakage from the foul water collection network. In 2009, water leakage from the clean water distribution networks amounted to about 35 per cent of total production of desalinated water, whereas leakage from the foul water network is estimated between 5 and 10 per cent. The latter contaminates the water table, posing health and environmental risks. As some of the excess water is currently pumped directly into the sea along the country's most densely populated coastline, it also has implications for marine life and can cause harm to tourism and recreation.

The Qatari government, as a trustee for future generations, has an important role to play in managing and regulating resources to maximize resource efficiency and minimize environmental damage. There are two broad approaches that can be taken to protect Qatar's environment and resource base: regulations, such as legal restrictions and pollution permits, and taxation or subsidies. These policy instruments affect pricing and provide incentives or disincentives to reduce unsustainable behaviour and/or to encourage the adoption of sustainable technologies.

Regulations can correct negative externalities by making certain actions an offence or by establishing controls. For example, the cap and trade approach, common in European countries, places limits on the volume of greenhouse gases that an industry is allowed to produce. Governments enforce these limits by selling emissions credits up to a determined level while providing flexibility in compliance. As companies can buy and trade these credits among themselves, there is an incentive for them to reduce emissions to save costs or even make money by selling unused credits.

A robust regulatory framework is important to encourage sustainable water production and consumption in Qatar. Regulations can be used to address some of Qatar's water-related environmental problems, such as through the setting of quality standards for different uses of water and for the discharge of water to sea, into groundwater and into land. Legal frameworks are also important to support demand-side interventions which may include quota systems, tiered tariff systems, limitations on the use of groundwater or mandating improvements to irrigation technologies and technical standards for appliances.

Taxation may help reduce various forms of pollution and curb excessive consumption. For example, most European countries correct market failure from fuel use by imposing heavy taxes. This not only leads to more efficient resource use but also provides funds for other uses, such as for environmental clean-up and research and development of sustainable technologies.

Subsidies may have the opposite effect. They tend to encourage excessive and indiscriminate use of fuel, energy, water and other products, and discourage technological innovation. They tend to promote degradation without regard for the long-term consequences of short-term consumption.

Pricing strategies should reflect a fair value of resources so that governments do not end up subsidizing the depletion of an essential natural resource. In general, under-pricing or zero-pricing practices sustain overuse and do not reflect the scarcity value of natural resources, thus potentially compromising intergenerational equity.

Qatar currently provides water and electricity to Qatari residents for free and at heavily subsidized rates for non-Qatari residents. There is little awareness of the extreme scarcity of potable water or of the substantial cost of producing desalinated water, and so reduced incentive to curb use. Although farmers must pay pumping costs, groundwater, which is primarily used for agriculture, is free, and the prices of diesel and electricity are minimal, thus making the farming community relatively immune to the urgency of water conservation and management. This poses serious challenges for developing sustainable use of a scarce resource. While subsidies may be useful for attracting industry, it is at the expense of the environment, the health of citizens and ultimately at the expense of Qatar's future generations.

Qatar therefore needs to review its existing policies to ensure that present levels and patterns of consumption are sustainable and resource productivity is within the country's carrying capacity. Effective implementation of strategies and plans necessitates the development of an enabling environment through the use of legislation and fiscal measures. A major challenge is to encourage a participatory management approach that is capable of prioritizing among competing demands, utilizing appropriate technologies and regulating and expending the available supply of resources to meet justified demand. Qatar needs to improve its natural resource management strategy to be consistent with the sustainable development path of the QNV 2030.

In addition, policy decisions on how to finance public goods, such as water services, and how much revenue to collect from beneficiaries should take the following factors into consideration (UNESCO-WWAP 2006):

- *Financial sustainability*, requiring the collection of sufficient revenue to meet present and future financial obligations;
- *Economic efficiency*, requiring more efficient use of resources available and discouraging waste;
- *User pays principle*, requiring consumers to pay an amount equivalent to the burden that their consumption places on society and environment;
- *Security*, requiring adequate, reliable and affordable supply of public goods, regardless of how much people are able or willing to pay for them.

The global trend is to move away from a system where public goods are provided to all without charge and financed from public revenues, to one of full cost recovery based on the principles of fairness and sustainability. Exceptions can be made for low-income communities which can be charged according to ability to pay rather than the full costs.

Developing and Adopting Sustainable Technologies

The QNV 2030 recognizes that while economic progress incurs environmental costs, neither economic development nor protection of the environment should be sacrificed for the sake of the other. Qatar's future development path must be compatible with the requirements of protecting and conserving the environment, while allowing economic development to occur.

In order to achieve the objectives of high income, a stable population and environmental sustainability, Qatar is increasing its investments in the development of sustainable technologies. The nation's technology policy is progressively covering the full spectrum from research and development (for which it has pledged 2.8 per cent of GDP annually), to demonstration and early stage deployment. Such policy interventions generate incentives that affect which new technologies are developed and how rapidly and widely they spread.

Given its increasing affluence, Qatar is playing a leadership role in the quest for 'green' technologies, as evident through the establishment of the Qatar Science and Technology Park and the Qatar National Research Fund. Coupled with its huge investments in education, through the development of Qatar University and the network of elite universities within Education City, the country has established an enabling environment to encourage scientific research and development to support advancing sustainable development.

The private sector also plays a key role in research and development and technology diffusion. Partnerships and alliances between the government of Qatar and the multinational companies operating in the country will further stimulate the development of a broad portfolio of sustainable technologies and reduce costs.

Nevertheless, the development of environmentally sustainable technologies is only one aspect of the necessary change. Efforts are also required to encourage their widespread adoption by industry, and within households. The market prices of goods and services do not always reflect the environmental costs, that is the negative externalities resulting from the difference between private and communal costs. So while the extra cost of adopting sustainable technologies may be small relative to the large benefit to society, market prices do not send that signal to consumers (Sachs 2008).

Additionally, the adoption of new technologies is generally costly and the diffusion is typically gradual (Jaffe, Newell and Stavins 2005). Generally, users will be better off the more other people use the same technology. Besides economies of scale, there is greater information about the existence, characteristics and success of the new technology. This is particularly apparent where network benefits exist, that is when a product becomes technologically more valuable to an individual user as other users adopt a compatible product, such as with mobile phones and computer networks.

So, as noted above, appropriate public policies are needed to correct market failures and influence unsustainable consumption patterns. They should incentivize and spur technology adoption through, for example, subsidies for eco-friendly products, taxes on environmental harm or by setting limitations or conditions against operating permits. And where new technology may struggle to gain a foothold, supportive policies are critical (Stern 2007).

Qatar's transition to a low-carbon green economy, through the development and adoption of sustainable technologies, will be challenging. But if successful, it will increase competitiveness and growth. The global push for greater environmental stewardship will continue to open markets across a wide range of industries and services in emerging fields, such as emission-reduction approaches, energy-efficient technologies, green buildings, agricultural management in arid regions, and innovative financing of low-carbon activities. Qatar can position itself to take advantage of these opportunities.

Supportive policies and regulations that encourage innovation in the development and use of sustainable technologies will also have co-benefits on other national objectives, such as improvements in health and the preservation of biodiversity. They can help reduce existing inefficiencies and wastage, with positive implications for growth and cost savings. For example, incentives for the production and use of energy-efficient technologies may provide a platform for removing distorting energy subsidies.

Building Capacity and Environmental Stewardship

Achieving agreement on values, goals and actions to promote sustainable development is often difficult given the differing interests of stakeholders. Fostering a shared understanding of the QNV 2030's sustainable development goals will help shape supportive attitudes and behaviour, and underpin national and international action. A lack of reliable information, high adaptation and mitigation costs and limited incentives for behavioural change will limit the pace of progress. But building the capacity of people and organizations to recognize and address environmental issues will advance the sustainable development agenda.

Qatar currently has limited capacity in regulatory bodies and management agencies for effective implementation of coordinated sustainable development policies and programmes. Local scientific expertise and trained technical capacity are in short supply. Nevertheless, several public and private sector initiatives are already underway to build the country's scientific and technical capacity, through investments in people, research institutions and the overall regulatory and governance framework. For example, the Barwa and Qatari Diar Research Institute has established a performance-based rating system for 'green buildings' that aims to create sustainable urban development which reduces environmental impact while satisfying local community needs.

However, much more needs to be done to close existing capacity gaps, not just in identifying problems and solutions, but also in establishing monitoring and evaluation systems to track progress, capture key lessons and change strategic directions where necessary.

Further, as sustainable development has cross-sectoral implications, it concerns several areas of professional expertise, making it hard for any one ministry or department to address the issues adequately. For example, a sound water strategy must be informed by water management and hydrologic science, engineering, energy systems, ecology, agriculture, marine science, health science, economics, business and finance. In Qatar, as in many countries, the main responsibility for sustainable development policy lies with the Ministry of Environment. However, as elsewhere, the Ministry of Environment is under-resourced and insufficiently influential in government, thus hindering the necessary process of cross-sectoral policy integration. For Qatar, sustainable development issues, including longer-term, regional and global perspectives, need to be integrated into mainstream planning processes. Capacity enhancements and synergies could be further achieved through knowledge sharing and networking among stakeholders at the national, regional and international levels, such as through the creation of a central depository for scientific data and information.

To ensure commitment for sustainable development aspirations across ministries and agencies, there must be high-level political commitment. In some countries, coordination of sustainable development lies within the office of the prime minister, or through a Cabinet Committee on the

Environment, such as in the United Kingdom where each department designates a green minister to ensure sustainable development considerations are integrated into departmental strategies. In others, such as in New Zealand and Canada, long-term commitment is achieved by linking strategies to the country's fiscal framework.

Qatar should identify the stakeholders needed to progress an integrated sustainable development strategy, and outline their responsibilities, rights and relations. Broad participation from the private sector and civil society are important to maximize synergies and ensure ownership towards a common goal. Well-structured public-private partnerships, for example, can facilitate access to broader financing options, assist skill and knowledge development, and make possible sustainable delivery of basic services, particularly energy and water.

Building trust among stakeholders is fundamental for the success and ownership of strategies and programmes. Greater investments need to be made in long-term stakeholder engagement and communications strategies to bring about a shared understanding of sustainable development and its implications. This will involve information campaigns via the media, promoting constructive dialogues that are based on evidence, education, persuasion and discussion.

Sustainable development requires dramatic changes in the ways Qatari society manage the processes of production and consumption. Creating a national movement to raise public consciousness of sustainable development issues necessitates education and awareness programmes. Imperfect information can slow the adoption and diffusion of a new environmentally friendly policy or technology. Information policies, including labelling and the sharing of best practices, can promote increased understanding and acceptance of the importance of environmental stewardship for continued human progress. They can facilitate sound decision making by consumers and businesses, and stimulate competitive markets for low-carbon and high-efficiency goods and services. Where upfront costs of new measures or technologies are high, financing measures can also help overcome possible adoption constraints (Stern 2007).

As civil society becomes more empowered and knowledgeable, it can serve as a watchdog in ensuring that governments and the private sector abide by their national and international commitments to sustainable development. Civil society in Qatar is underdeveloped. Over time, as it matures, it can be expected to play a key role in monitoring for follow-through on the government's promises. Consumers informed about sustainable consumption practices can place pressure on the private sector to develop and adopt sustainable production mechanisms.

Creating a Regional and Global Platform for Cooperation

Qatar must increase momentum of its sustainable development initiatives. But its efforts alone will not be sufficient. Many problems faced by Qatar also confront other countries. Policy options and institutional reforms should identify links between national, regional and global concerns, with a view to regional and international alliances and partnerships continuing and expanding.

The Gulf region constitutes an ecological system that is affected by the practices and activities of every country in the region. Like Qatar, most of the region has, until the recent global financial crisis, experienced very high rates of economic growth due mainly to the exploitation of hydrocarbon reserves and increased trade and investment. The extensive resource exploitation, rapid urban development and increased consumption have led to major environmental degradation including, inter alia, severe coastal erosion, depletion of freshwater resources, air pollution and rising pollution of the Gulf waters. There is also an emerging recognition of potential natural disasters resulting from climate change.

The need for action is urgent and a shared regional and global perspective on long-term goals is essential to respond to the challenges of sustainable development, as well as build effective institutions to meet them. The Arab Green Economy Initiative, the UN Framework Convention on Climate Change, the Kyoto Protocol and a range of other bilateral and multilateral formal and informal partnerships and dialogues provide a framework that supports cooperation and collective action. The failure to reach a global consensus in Copenhagen in 2009 should not provide an excuse for national inertia or inaction in advancing the sustainable development agenda. Success for Qatar, as elsewhere, is dependent on having a clear objective, effective technologies, a clear implementation strategy, and adequate financing (Sachs 2008).

Policy frameworks should encompass the three complementary elements noted previously, namely: pricing policy, technology policy and information policy, with equitable distribution of effort across both developed and developing countries. Agreement on responsibilities should take into account costs and the ability to bear them, as well as starting points, prospects for growth and past histories (Stern 2007).

Qatar has the vision and financial resources to play a leadership role in spearheading best practices in sustainable development regionally and globally, especially in cutting-edge areas such as tackling climate change and biodiversity conservation where sustainable interventions are needed. The nation has been investing heavily in scientific assessments, and through public-private partnerships has the capacity to bring newly proven technologies to industrial scale. Transparency and information sharing, international research and development cooperation, international coordination of regulations and product standards, and the reduction of tariff and non-tariff barriers for low-carbon goods and services, are some cooperation issues that can help advance technological innovation and diffusion by pooling risks and rewards (Stern 2007).

Qatar also has the potential to play a significant role in supporting international finance initiatives to support cost-effective reduction of carbon emissions and provide momentum to global efforts in transitioning to a low-carbon economy. Given its efforts to become a regional financial and business hub, there are forward-looking opportunities for the country to pilot new approaches to carbon financing consistent with Islamic financing principles. Best practices and lessons learned from these projects can be extended to address other areas of environmental concern that are critical for achieving larger sustainable development objectives. The Al Shaheen Oilfield Gas Recovery and Utilization Project, as the first registered Clean Development Mechanism (CDM) project in Qatar, that captures and processes associated gas produced as a by-product of oil recovery activities at the Al Shaheen oil field is an example of a clean technology demonstration project that may stimulate development of similar projects throughout Qatar and the Middle East. Qatar could also support low-carbon investment in developing countries through the CDM or other bilateral or multilateral mechanisms.

Conclusion

The QNV 2030 provides a solid basis for new sustainable development policies and programmes, and for reducing unsustainable patterns of production and consumption. By bringing existing and new initiatives together under the broad umbrella of the QNV 2030, through the National Development Strategy 2011–2016 (NDS), Qatar will be able coherently to progress a range of cross-sectoral sustainable development initiatives. Further, it can rationalize existing policies and strategies, and take advantage of synergies stemming from collective action towards a common goal.

To advance sustainable development in Qatar, attention needs to be placed on increasing the well-being of Qatari society through sustained rates of economic growth; limiting population growth by rationalizing large-scale development projects and moving faster towards automation and a diversified knowledge-based economy; and developing and adopting sustainable technologies that can help lower the environmental impact per unit of income. Political will and national ownership, based on a shared understanding of these long-term goals, will be critical success factors.

The alignment of current actions to these long-term objectives should be at the forefront of initiatives emerging from the NDS. Pricing policies, technology policies and information policies will contribute towards a framework for sustainable development by influencing behavioural change and the adoption of best practices.

In an ever more globalized world, an effective strategy for sustainable development has to extend beyond Qatar's borders to regional and international players. Cooperation is essential at all levels, from within Qatari households to global platforms such as the United Nations, and across all interest groups.

Qatar must continue to play a proactive and significant role in efforts to promote sustainable development. Being able to afford 'the best' and being able to pay for responses to 'solve' problems in the short term, is not the same as investing in optimal and sustainable policies that provide a coherent, strategic long-term vision. Maintaining Qatar's significant advances in human development demands an agreed plan of action which identifies goals, objectives, expected outputs and the resources needed to support them, as well as a delineation of what should be monitored, by whom and when. Qatar's first NDS will serve this purpose and provide clear directions for advancing sustainable development.

Notes

The views expressed here are those of the authors and do not necessarily reflect the policies or positions of the General Secretariat for Development Planning.

References

Anand, S., and A. Sen. 2000. 'Human Development and Economic Sustainability.' *World Development* 28 (12): 2029–2049.

General Secretariat for Development Planning (GSDP). 2009. *Qatar Second Human Development Report: Advancing Sustainable Development*. Doha.

———. 2008. *Qatar National Vision 2030*. Doha.

———. In press. 'Population, Labour Force and Qatari Employment.' In *Qatar's Human and Social Development Profile*, chap. 2. Doha.

Jaffe, A., R. Newell and R. Stavins. 2005. 'A Tale of Two Market Failures: Technology and Environmental Policy.' *Ecological Economics* 54: 164–174.

Sachs, J. 2008. *Common Wealth: Economics for a Crowded Planet*. New York: Penguin Books.

Stern, N. 2007. *The Economics of Climate Change: The Stern Review.* Cambridge: Cambridge University Press.

United Nations Development Programme (UNDP). 2009. *Human Development Report 2009. Overcoming Barriers: Human Mobility and Development.* New York: Palgrave Macmillan.

———. 2006. *Human Development Report 2006. Beyond Scarcity: Power, Poverty and the Global Water Crisis.* New York: Palgrave Macmillan.

———. 2007. *Human Development Report 2007/2008. Fighting Climate Change: Human Solidarity in a Divided World.* New York: Palgrave Macmillan.

United Nations Educational, Cultural and Scientific Organization – World Water Assessment Programme. 2006. *Second UN World Water Development Report: Water, A Shared Responsibility.* Barcelona: UNESCO Publishing and Berghahn Books.

CHAPTER 3

The Qatar National Master Plan

Khondker Rahman

Qatar has experienced unprecedented development and economic growth in recent years, fuelled largely by exploitation of the country's vast reserves of hydrocarbon, mainly natural gas. Whilst this has placed Qatar at the top of GDP rankings, the growth has put significant stress on the natural and built environment. The increased economic activity has also led to a large rise in the expatriate population, both skilled and unskilled workers, with the population doubling in the last seven years, increasing demand for housing and accommodation. Qatar's winning bid to host the 2022 FIFA World Cup and also its ambition to submit bids to host Olympic Games entails commitments to build world-class sporting facilities (i.e. stadiums, training venues, athlete villages) and supporting infrastructure.

Lack of public transport, traffic congestion and urban sprawl, poor access to community services and utilities and negative impacts on the environment, businesses and everyday life are issues that the country needs to address as a matter of priority. The country is also facing a significant challenge to put in place an effective governance structure and regulatory regime with enforceable laws and policies to manage the growth in a sustainable manner (see Al Othman and Clarke, chapter 5, this volume). These are problems faced by many Gulf countries. This chapter discusses the Qatar National Master Plan, which is a tool for achieving sustainable urban planning and development that aims to meet these challenges. It outlines its objectives and describes the process by which the plan to manage urban growth was developed, which some contributors to this volume question (see chapters 4 and 14 by Darwish and Gardner). It includes several acronyms to give the reader a flavour of such development-planning exercises that are popular with governments and drive much top-down development.

The Qatar National Vision 2030 (QNV 2030) developed by the previous General Secretariat for Development and Planning (GSDP 2009a), now known as Ministry of Development Planning and Statistics, sets a national development strategy to address the above challenges (see Tan, Al-Khalaqi and Al-Khulaifi, chapter 2, and Darwish, chapter 4, this volume). It provides a framework to support the 'Millennium Development Goals', 'Principles of Advancing Sustainable Development' and 'Moving Beyond Carbon' scenarios (Qatar Statistical Authority 2008). It identifies five key challenges and four pillars of sustainable development.

The Ministry of Municipality and Urban Planning (MMUP) is developing the Qatar National Master Plan (QNMP), based on the principles and goals of QNV 2030 to regulate current and future land uses to cater for predicted population growth up to 2032. In essence, QNMP is a 'spatial' land-use plan that will guide development at strategic locations in the country focusing on transit-oriented development and equitable access to community and utility services. Figure 3.1 shows the broad challenges and principles that are central to the QNV 2030 and QNMP. The QNMP has two main parts: the Qatar National Development Framework (QNDF) and the Municipal Spatial Development Plans (MSDP) for cities, town centres and action areas. There are a number of companion documents that cover the details of urban design issues, place and zone codes, sectoral plans (e.g. National Transport Plans, National Environmental Management Plan, National Utilities Plans etc.). The QNDF sets the strategic framework for sustainable development and provides land-use plans for all seven of the country's municipalities. It has a development vision based on sustainability principles, objectives, policies and implementation actions, providing a disciplined framework for decision makers to assess land-use proposals in a sustainable manner.

Structure of the Qatar National Master Plan (QNMP)

The QNDF is the foundation of the QNMP, setting vision and strategic objectives to facilitate future sustainable development. It contains over sixty high-level policies and two hundred plus actions to be shared and led by a number of stakeholders impacted by land and infrastructure development. These actions have immediate (0–2 years), short–medium (2–5 years) and medium–long (5–15 years) term time horizons for completion. Assigning specific responsibilities and setting time frames is thought to indicate serious commitment by the decision makers to promote a sound land-use planning framework to deliver sustainable development outcomes.

The Municipal Spatial Development Plans (MSDPs), based on the policies and proposed spatial land-use structure plans couched within a 'Centres Hierarchy', describe in detail the role of urban centres, future

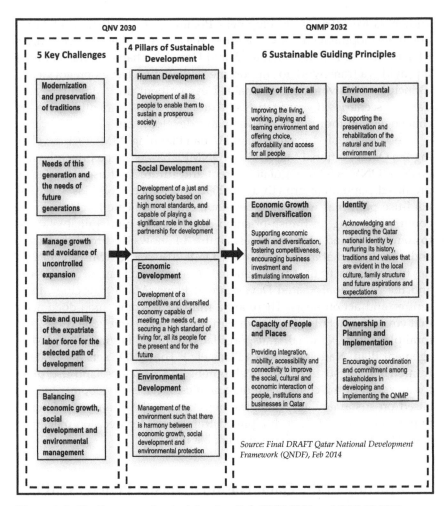

Figure 3.1. Challenges and principles that link QNV 2030 and QNMP 2032.

transit-oriented development patterns, associated infrastructure priorities and housing requirements based on anticipated population growth (MMUP 2008). Each plan has a 'Municipal Development Strategy' that includes an area-specific vision and a set of strategic planning objectives to address the specific development needs and issues within the municipal boundary. The MSDPs are also the key regulatory documents with specific development codes and action-area plans for community facilities, utility services and other necessary infrastructure. The development codes will incorporate, where applicable, relevant parts of the locally developed Global Sustainability Assessment System (GSAS; GORD 2011) to promote sustainable development.

Process for Developing the QNDF

The QNDF was developed by identifying the key planning issues followed by a set of strategic planning objectives and actions to address these issues. The process also aimed to set a clear 'vision' for delivering sustainable development in Qatar. Table 3.1 outlines the process (a similar framework was proposed to achieve sustainable energy use in Bangladesh; Rahman 2010).

Table 3.1. QNDF process.

Steps	Sustainable Development through Qatar National Development Framework (QNDF)
Step 1	Set the 'Vision'
Step 2	Identify planning challenges and issues
Step 3	Set the 'Strategic Planning Objectives' to address these issues
Step 4	Develop a set of actions and strategies to meet the strategic planning objectives
Step 5	Develop an assessment and evaluation framework to ensure achieving the vision for sustainable planning and development in Qatar

Table 3.2. QNDF vision.

Create a role model for sustainable urban living in the twenty-first century and the Gulf's most liveable cities and towns by:
Providing an attractive and liveable urban environment
Promoting economic and environmental sustainability
Creating a distinctive identity for Doha as an international cultural centre and dynamic knowledge hub
Providing a robust and innovative spatial and physical legislative planning framework

Source: Final DRAFT QNDF, Feb 2014.

The first step is setting the 'vision' (table 3.2) and the second step is 'identifying the planning challenges and issues'. Comprehensive data collection, including a community survey, was undertaken at the start of the project. This helped in identifying a number of key planning issues and challenges for the country. Table 3.3 gives a selection of major planning issues that featured in the development of the QNDF's policies and actions (note that these issues are categorized on the basis of the six 'Sustainability Principles' adopted for the QNMP).

Table 3.3. Issues and challenges to address in order to deliver a sustainable plan.

Sustainability Principles	Issues and Challenges
Quality of Life	• Adverse effects from roads and traffic (accidents, noise, air quality, time lost in congestion, etc.) • Existing dispersal of activities requires use of vehicles for all activities • Lack of public transport and pedestrian network • Qatari lifestyle requirements such as privacy not able to be accommodated by current planning requirements, resulting in marginalization from inner urban life • Lack of open space and basic community and cultural facilities outside greater Doha • Absence of a strong central core, leakage out to various sub-cores where maximum benefits of agglomeration not realized and cause dispersal and increased vehicle use
Identity	• Current land-use policies and development endangering Qatari cultural and family values • Lack of a definable downtown area resulting in dispersal and leakage of activity • Poor protection of heritage features and local landmarks resulting in a lost opportunity to promote local identity • Poorly integrated and dispersed mega projects further disperse and dilute the chances of creating an integrated and well-connected vibrant society • Existing patterns of subdivision are inconsistent with historical cultural practices of community building • Poor incorporation of traditional typologies and layouts in developments
Environmental Values	• Excessive and unsustainable water and energy usage • Deterioration of water quality • Sewerage network incomplete and poorly maintained, resulting in contamination of groundwater • Pollution and degradation of marine environment, loss of seagrass and other marine creatures • Very high GHG emission • Unconstrained development in areas subject to risk from sea level rise • Poor air quality from construction, industrial activities, extension of development into desert, vehicle emissions • High water table and the continuous need for dewatering into sensitive discharge locations

Connectivity of people and places	• Places and people are not connected • Lack of public transport and pedestrian and bicycle networks • Emphasis on private vehicle use, manifested through freeways and expressways segregates communities • Lack of appropriate sustainable traffic management, e.g. no signal phasing, ATM and median breaks • Incomplete and non-integrated network resulting into a higher number of vehicle kilometres • Existing land use and its distribution are not interlinked to support connectivity and sense of place • Segregation of communities through subdivision patterns and housing types, e.g. compounds
Economic growth and diversification	• High energy consumption impacts on economic development • Economic costs of traffic delays from inappropriately designed network and facilities • Lack of hierarchy of centres and urban structure has an impact on economic growth and diversification • Lack of real estate options for both commercial and residential developments constraining the development of a diversified economy • Historical emphasis on focussing growth into Doha, adversely affecting development and sustainability of other settlements • Spatial mismatch between demand and supply for real estate • Mega projects poorly bound into urban fabric, resulting in dispersal and duplication of activity, constraining economic development • Inconsistent land/property ownership regulation and administration, resulting in poor allocation outcomes
Ownership in planning and implementation	• Fragmentation and inconsistent delineation of responsibilities for the existing authorities and stakeholders result in a lack of ownership for implementing the planning outcomes • Poor sense of public ownership of public spaces • Lack of inter-agency coordination (internal and external; e.g. economic impact of Qatar Petroleum Zones and Mega Projects) • Inadequate capacity and knowledge (e.g. lack of technical expertise) and ill-informed developers • Lack of regulatory mechanisms for enforcement and implementation • Lack of public consultation and public awareness

The large growth in population (table 3.4) is an important factor in considering the planning challenges (GSDP 2009b).

Table 3.4. Population growth in Qatar (1986–2032).

	Year						
	1986	1997	2004	2008	2010	2017	2032*
Total Population	369,079	522,023	744,029	1,448,479	1,702,211	2,545,000	2,520,000
Growth Rate (pa)		3.8%	6.1%	23.7%	8.8%	7.1%	—0.1%

*Total population at 2032 extrapolated from 2030 forecast 'Beyond Carbon' scenario (i.e. knowledge based economy), which uses the year 2010 as the base year for forecasting purposes.
Sources: General Population and Housing Census 1986, 1997, 2004 and 2010 as reported in Annual Abstract, QSA (2012), 'Beyond Carbon' scenario, GSDP (2012).

The third step is 'setting the strategic planning objectives' to address the key planning issues and challenges, which identify sustainability principles (table 3.5). These objectives also aim to provide the spatial and physical development focus for achieving the 'vision'. Subsequently, a series of policy actions were also formulated to translate these objectives into implementable actions. The fourth step is 'developing a set of actions and strategies to meet the strategic objectives'. A key action in meeting the strategic planning objectives was to develop a 'National Spatial Strategy 2032' that provides for sustainable growth, balanced with economic activities. The strategy also provides an incentive for future investment in Qatar and guides government and private stakeholders in developing their own programs and business plans to ensure consistency for developers and investors.

Table 3.5. Strategic planning objectives linking the 'Sustainability Principles'.

Strategic Planning Objectives	Relevant Sustainability Principles
1. Promote a high-quality Capital City Precinct within inner Doha with a vibrant, attractive and sophisticated public realm where high-quality lifestyle choices are achieved	Quality of life for all
2. Develop a number of high-quality mixed-use, mixed density centres as transit-oriented development (TOD) based on the public transit system	Connectivity of people and places
3. Retain the cultural identity of rural/non-metropolitan communities and support enterprises that enhance the sustainability and liveability of these communities	Identity, Quality of life

4. Establish an integrated public transport network that results in a modal shift from private motor vehicles to public transport across Qatar	Connectivity of people and places
5. Ensure radial routes act primarily as transit corridors to reduce private motor vehicle usage and environmental costs and promote orbital routes to progressively accommodate a balanced growth and economic activities	Economic growth and diversification
6. Ensure mega projects and other large-scale developments are integrated into the wider community and contribute to the overall quality and sustainable living in Qatar	Connectivity of people and places
7. Promote equitable accessibility to community facilities and social amenities for all residents by co-locating them within key transit oriented mixed-use centres	Quality of life for all
8. Develop a unique and high-quality public realm which is equitably accessible and permeates throughout Qatar's urban areas	Connectivity of people and places
9. Plan and utilize urban block size, form and height to promote connectivity, a vibrant public realm and improve environmental and social conditions	Connectivity of people and places
10. Use density, building typology, connectivity and a vibrant public realm to promote a wide range of accommodation types and affordable housing for all residents	Quality of life for all
11. Develop a distinctive identity for Doha based upon Qatari values and supporting a Qatar brand and the future growth of the city as a cultural centre of the Gulf region	Identity
12. Protect and enhance the natural, built and cultural environment to avoid adverse impacts from urban land uses	Environmental values
13. Ensure risks from climate change impacts are evaluated and mitigation measures are developed and implemented for land-use planning and infrastructure development	Environmental values
14. Plan, coordinate, upgrade and deliver transport and utilities infrastructure services in a timely and cost-effective manner	Quality of life for all
15. Establish urban growth boundaries around metropolitan Doha and other urban areas to ensure the efficient use and timely release of land	Economic growth and diversification
16. Develop a policy and plan-led system that supports and manages development change processes through appropriate institutional governance frameworks	Ownership of planning and implementation

The QNMP team investigated a number of spatial distribution options, ranging from multi- or polycentric urban structures to rural growth opportunities, satellite cities around a central core to concentrated growth of one main urban agglomeration. However, the location of key centres and their anticipated future growth are largely already fixed by existing committed development in and around Doha and other emerging areas. A polycentric urban structure is identifiable, focusing on Doha as the capital city. The strategy concentrates on specific locations within Doha and the relationship between these in terms of service catchments, organized in a defined hierarchy and mix of uses. The hierarchy of centres was decided through an assessment involving five key criteria (final draft Qatar National Development Framework, QNDF, February 2014):

- Level of existing population and employment density, economic investment and infrastructure.
- Level of existing provision of government/municipality offices and community facilities.
- Potential accessibility to the future transportation network.
- Proximity of committed mega projects or other major government developments including Qatari national housing schemes.
- Level of vacant land and potential for regeneration or urban infill.

The National Spatial Strategy also recommends a 'Greenbelt' buffer around the greater Doha metropolitan boundary in order to contain development within it. The strategy suggests that this buffer would support the 'National Food Security Program' (i.e. necessary agricultural activities). It strongly recommends revising the 'Interim Land-Use Zoning' to introduce a land-use structure that supports mixed-use, mixed-density development in line with transit-facilitated development and the sustainable growth of key centres.

A total of 60 policies and approximately 210 actions were developed to address all the planning issues and challenges (table 3.3). Each policy comprises a heading, statement and set of actions and identifies relevant stakeholders to undertake these actions within a designated timeframe. The policies are grouped according to the following areas:

- economic prosperity;
- living in the community;
- the natural environment;
- the built environment;
- movement network; and
- the utilities.

Table 3.6 gives an example of a policy and associated actions related to environmental protection, without naming any stakeholders.[1]

Table 3.6. Example policy template.

Purpose
The purpose of this policy is to mitigate the effects of human activity to promote and protect the natural environment and resources for the benefit of current and future generations

Policy ENV1: Sustainable Planning and Development
Use the precautionary approach in the planning, assessing and construction of development and infrastructure to ensure impacts on the natural environment are minimized

Policy Actions	Time Frame	Relevant Stakeholders
In the absence of a defined sustainability assessment tool, a precautionary approach[1] will be used in consultation with relevant stakeholders to achieve sustainable development outcomes to prevent the risk of environmental degradation.	Immediate	Confidential
Progressively develop and implement a sustainability assessment tool for the planning, design and assessment of projects. This tool will include the preparation and implementation of guidelines (objectives, criteria, acceptable outcomes, best practice etc.) to monitor and report on the following impacts of change: (a) Water and energy usage (b) Greenhouse gas emissions (c) Air, water and noise pollution (d) Urban development and transport impacts (e) Biodiversity and habitat conservation (f) Climate hazards risk, coastal erosion, sea level rise and storm events (g) Scenic and landscape amenity (h) Open space and recreational amenities (i) Cultural and historical values and amenities	Short–Med	Confidential

[1]Precautionary Approach – Rio Declaration (1992, Principle #15): "Where there are threats of serious or irreversible environmental damage, lack of full scientific certainty should not be used as a reason for postponing cost-effective measures to prevent environmental degradation".

Municipal Spatial Development Plans (MSDP) address the strategic objectives at a local level. It is necessary to address locally relevant issues and needs through tailored urban plans supported by appropriate regulations that detail requirements necessary to delivering sustainable development outcomes for each municipality. These regulations will be developed on the basis of selected zones (residential, commercial, mixed-use etc.) and give the standards that will need to be met in these zones. The key focus in developing these regulations will be to translate the broader strategic planning objectives and the key 'sustainability principles' discussed above into actions that address the specific issues of the municipality.

The fifth and final stage in the QNDF development process is to 'undertake an assessment according to an evaluation framework'. The Qatar Ministry of Environment requires all major planning projects and master plans to undertake a 'Strategic Environmental Assessment (SEA)'. This is a systematic process for evaluating the environmental consequences of any proposed policy, plan or programme initiatives in order to ensure they are fully included and appropriately addressed at the earliest appropriate stage of decision making on a par with economic and social considerations (Sadler 1998). Such an assessment is necessary to ensure the sustainable outcome of any plan. The SEA process is divided into four tasks (table 3.7).

Table 3.7. Strategic Environmental Assessment (SEA).

Task	Task Details
Task 1: **Scoping**	• Review of relevant plans, policies and programmes; • Setting the context and establishing the baseline; • Identifying key environmental, social and economic issues; • Developing the draft SEA framework; • Stakeholder engagement and • Set out the programme for undertaking SEA in parallel with the planning process, and identify those responsible for carrying out the SEA process.
Task 2: **Assessment and Mitigation**	• Contributing to the development of the policy, plan or programme and appraising the relative effects of alternative options; • Predicting and evaluating the effects of the plan, policy or programme; • Identifying potential mitigation measures to improve the environmental outcomes of the plan, policy or programme; and • Suggesting appropriate systems and indicators to monitor the effects of implementing the plan, policy or programme.
Task 3: **Reporting and Consultation**	• Preparing a report on the assessment findings, mitigation measures and monitoring proposals; and • Carrying out consultation on the SEA.
Task 4: **Monitoring and Evaluation**	• Monitoring the effects of implementing the plan, policy or programme; and • Evaluating the effectiveness of the SEA process.

In Task 1 of the SEA process (table 3.7), approximately 17 SEA objectives and 55 assessment criteria were developed. Meeting each criterion would ensure the environmental/ sustainable outcome according to QNMP/ QNDP policy. Table 3.8 gives a snapshot of a couple of objectives, assessment criteria and specific questions that need to be evaluated in relation to energy issues, as an example. If a policy or planned activity fails to meet the SEA objectives/criteria, it is necessary to undertake a detailed risk assessment ('Fig Tree Risk Assessment' is the proposed method to assess the level of risk). After evaluating the risk, the SEA process suggests a set of mitigating options.

Table 3.8. SEA framework for assessment of energy issues.

SEA Framework		
SEA Objectives	**Assessment Criteria**	**Criteria Question(s) / SEA Requirement**
Objective 1 To promote clean and renewable energy technologies, and use energy more efficiently	Reduce the energy demands from residential, commercial and industrial sites	Does the plan require developments to reduce energy demands through adopting energy-efficiency measures?
	Support the development of sustainable energy technologies and infrastructure (i.e. solar or wind technologies)	Does the plan actively promote solar and wind energy opportunities and make provision in the land use?
	Plan for renewable energy sources to replace diminishing hydrocarbon reserves	Does the plan make provision to use renewable energy sources at a neighbourhood scale?
	Encourage sustainable transport (i.e. walking, cycling and public transport)	Does the plan make provisions for integrated public transport and access (through walking and cycling) and discourage vehicle use to reduce fuel consumption etc.?
Objective 2 To increase resilience to the potential effects of climate change	Avoid locating vulnerable land uses (such as residential development and water-supply infrastructure) in areas that may become vulnerable to flooding by rising sea levels	Does the plan delineate areas subject to sea level rise and restrict development (including utilities etc.) in those areas?
	Support development that increases resilience to the effects of climate change	Does the plan assess the risk posed by climate change?

In addition to the SEA evaluation required by the Ministry of Environment (MOE), the QNMP will deploy a robust sustainability assessment framework based on the six key 'QNDF Sustainability Criteria' to critically examine its policies and establish benchmarks for achieving sustainable planning outcomes. It will establish specific targets and sustainability indicators where applicable.

Implementation of the QNMP

Implementation of the QNDF spatial strategy and policies must ensure, as directed by the QNV2030, 'sustainable development outcomes'. Successful implementation of the QNDF will require cooperation from community stakeholders and the coordination and review of government ministries' and agencies' core business activities, infrastructure programs, plans and services. Policy actions are categorized into implementation timeframes to aid the ordered delivery of the plan and to assist future reviews. In addition to this, a much needed, upgraded and expanded planning governance structure will be proposed to better implement the QNDF and carry forward the program of planning and updating of regulatory control.

Obtaining stakeholder agreement to QNDF policies and actions will be a major challenge. A key step is to encourage stakeholder participation in implementing the plan. A comprehensive five-year 'Training and Capacity Building Program' is planned for decision makers and technical officers (engineers, planners, development assessment officers and others) not only to familiarize them with the plan and its policies, but also to enfranchise ownership. While awaiting government approval, the QNMP team has completed a comprehensive stakeholder engagement to encourage the 'buy-in' of agencies and adoption of policies as necessary in their business and strategic planning such that they will include the proposed actions in their work programs according to the proposed timeframe and take responsibility for them.

The Gulf Organization for Research and Development has developed the Global Sustainability Assessment System (GSAS), which is a green-building certification system that parallels others such as the LEED, BREEAM and ESTIDAMA sustainability assessment and rating systems. The primary objective of GSAS is to ensure a sustainable built environment that minimizes ecological impact while addressing Qatar's specific environmental needs (see Alraouf and Clarke, chapter 13, this volume). The rating system considers eight urban planning and design issues:

(1) urban connectivity,
(2) site considerations,
(3) energy,
(4) water,
(5) materials,
(6) indoor environment,
(7) cultural and economic value, and
(8) management and operations.

GSAS rates buildings on a neighbourhood scale for each phase of their lifespan. It can rate residential and commercial buildings, schools, mosques, hotels, light industry, sporting facilities and, importantly, neighbourhoods.

Direct adoption of GSAS in a spatial plan such as the QNMP, is a complex task as the system focuses on buildings and their immediate surroundings only, whereas the plan seeks sustainable outcomes at a much wider scale such as transport network, timely provision of necessary utility infrastructure, natural and built environment, community and recreational facilities etc. The Neighbourhood Scheme is the most relevant module of the GSAS that can address sustainability issues within neighbourhoods according to size and population density. The QMNP team is developing a set of sustainable planning requirements, from a large compound to a small urban centre, based on QNDF sustainability principles and strategic objectives. The adoption of this new GSAS Neighbourhood Scheme has the potential to feature as part of the Municipal Spatial Development Plans' regulatory tools to enhance the sustainable development outcomes for the municipalities. Regulatory provisions seek to ensure future growth occurs in the most appropriate areas and that land is utilized efficiently.

The QNMP and its companion documents give a new dimension to spatial planning and development in Qatar. They show a sound understanding of 'best planning principles' and adopt a holistic approach with serious commitments to deliver sustainable development outcomes. They recommend a set of sound planning objectives and locally relevant guiding principles to achieve these outcomes. The SEA evaluation and future sustainability assessment also provide a solid platform from which to undertake continuous checks and balances to ensure the plan delivers on its objectives. But it requires active participation of government and private sector investors to deliver the infrastructure and utility services necessary to the planned growth. The current governance framework and plan implementation process also require an overhaul to raise awareness of the new planning regime and to improvements to current land-use application and approval processes.[2]

Notes

1. At the time of finalizing this chapter the QNDF is awaiting government approval and official launching. Hence, information on the policy and the policy actions with assignment of relevant stakeholder are considered sensitive and 'strictly confidential'.
2. Disclaimer: Much of this chapter has been based on the Draft Qatar National Development Framework (QNDF) of the Qatar National Master Plan; the QNDF is currently going through final approval and launching. As such, comments and suggestions contained in this chapter do not necessarily represent the official position of the Ministry of Municipality and Urban Planning in Qatar.

References

General Secretariat for Development and Planning (GSDP). 2009a. *Advancing Sustainable Development – Qatar National Vision 2030.* Second National Human Development Report, Qatar.

———. 2009b. *General Population and Housing Census 1986, 1997 & 2004, Beyond Carbon Scenario.* Qatar.

Gulf Organization for Research and Development (GORD). 2011. Global Sustainability Assessment System (GSAS), Qatar.

Ministry of Municipality and Urban Planning (MMUP). 2008. Study Report 1, Qatar National Master Plan (QNMP), Qatar.

———. 2010. Draft Qatar National Development Framework (QNDF), part of the Qatar National Master Plan (QNMP), Qatar.

Qatar Statistical Authority. 2008. The Millennium Development Goals in the State of Qatar.

Rahman, K. 2010. 'Can Bangladesh Achieve a Sustainable Energy Future?' *Annual Publication of Energy and Power Magazine* 8 (1): 117–125.

Sadler, B. 1998. 'Strategic Environmental Assessment: Institutional Arrangements, Practical Experience and Future Directions.' Institute of Environmental Assessment International Workshop on Strategic Environmental Assessment, Organized by the Japan Environment Agency, Tokyo, 26–27 November 1998.

CHAPTER 4

The State of Qatar

Along the Way to Sustainable Development

Bahaa Darwish

The launch of the *Qatar National Vision Report 2030* (hereafter the QNV 2030) by the Qatari General Secretariat for Development Planning (GSDP) in October 2008 was a response to an increasing awareness of the necessity for a comprehensive view of the future development of the State of Qatar in all its dimensions. The QNV 2030 defines the long-term development outcomes for Qatar and provides a framework within which national strategies and implementation plans can be prepared (GSDP 2008: 2). In support of QNV 2030, the second National Human Development Report, *Advancing Sustainable Development* (hereafter the ASD Report), was issued in July 2009 by the GSDP. This report identifies three critical environmental challenges as the most important to be addressed: namely water security, marine environment and climate change. In addition, the report addresses issues surrounding the three interrelated pillars of sustainable development: economic growth, social development and environmental management, and assesses what has been achieved so far and future challenges. These two reports are often seen as representing the state's official vision of sustainable development. However, I argue that the issues these two reports mention are not enough for assessing the country's advance towards sustainable development; there are other challenges that can delay development that are not addressed in the reports, and the ASD Report identifies one obstacle to development with which I do not agree.

This chapter is a reflection on the State of Qatar's official vision of, and ways to advance, sustainable development mainly through reflecting on the two reports mentioned above. It starts by tracing the historical development of the concept of sustainable development to assess where Qatar stands in relation to it. Next, it gives an overview of the issues raised specifically in the ASD Report, explaining why these issues can help assess, though partially, the state's advance towards sustainable development. It finishes with a critical evaluation of the report and thus of Qatar's advance towards sustainable development by addressing the unmentioned issues that I think can also impede sustainable development in addition to an issue which the ASD Report sees, contrary to the my opinion, as inhibiting sustainability.

'Sustainable Development': The Developing Concept of Development

People in every period of human history have faced various problems and challenges. Their ability to deal with them determines the degree to which they develop. I think that the most difficult challenge of our time is human development, understood as achieving people's welfare. The obstacles to human development have been identified and strategies to overcome them have been formulated in what has become known as sustainable development.

During the 1960s,[1] development was understood as synonymous with economic growth and underdevelopment in some countries was due to lack of such growth and the application of modern scientific and technical knowledge. Only through the transfer of finance, technology and experience from the developed countries would the development problems of the underdeveloped world be solved quickly (Elliott 1999: 10).

Environmentalism, at that time, was a small movement concerned with the undesirable effects of industrial and economic development, considering ever-expanding population growth (particularly in the developing countries) and mounting demands on finite resources to be disastrous, exceeding the physical limits of the earth's resources. A concern for development and environment at this time were portrayed as incompatible: pollution and environmental degradation were considered inevitable consequences of industrial development (ibid.: 21).

In the 1970s, three important changes occurred in the development thinking: the idea that environment and development problems were incompatible was overthrown, the environmental movement 'came of age' and environmental issues were on the international political agenda, as evidenced by the participation of 113 countries in the 1972 UN conference on the Human Environment in Stockholm. There was also emerging recognition that a lack of development could cause environmental degradation (ibid.: 23). In summary, by the late 1970s, important changes in thinking led to the realization that environment and development are interdependent, with recognition of the interdependence of the developed and developing worlds (ibid.: 24).

In the 1980s, two reports prepared the way for the emergence of the concept of 'sustainable development' as a multidimensional issue that concerns intergenerational equity as well as equity within each generation. These were: the World Conservation Strategy (WCS), published by the International Union for the Conservation of Nature and Natural Resources (IUCN), which has been referred to as a 'launchpad' for the concept of sustainable development because it suggested that development could help achieve conservation rather than obstruct it (ibid.) and the third UN Development Decade of the 1980s, which saw 'development' as a multidimensional concept encompassing widespread improvements in the social as well as the material well-being of all in society (ibid.: 12). These two reports paved the way for the Brundtland Report which was issued by the World Commission on Environment and Development (WCED).

The WCED was charged explicitly with formulating proposals for dealing with global environmental and development issues, extending on the WCS. It gave greater attention to development concerns: to the challenge of overcoming poverty and meeting basic needs, and to integrating the environment into economic decision-making. It considered economic growth essential, but new forms of growth would be the key to sustainable development; growth must be less energy intensive and more equitably shared (ibid.: 25, 26). The report is unique in its emphasis on equity between generations, which logically implies equity within generations (United Nations Documents 1987). Since then, most definitions of sustainable development recognize the global nature of sustainable development and include 'the core ethic of intergenerational equity, emphasizing the current generation's moral obligation to ensure that future generations enjoy at least as good a quality of life as the current generation has now' (World Bank 2003:14), whether the current generation's moral obligation is to preserve the irreplaceable existing natural resources and services such as biodiversity and ecosystem stability, as proponents of the so-called strong sustainability claim, or to guarantee that the future generations can compensate for natural capital by equivalent amounts of human capital because human ingenuity is an infinite resource (Barry, Baxter and Dunphy 2004: 2).

In October 2008, the GSDP in Qatar issued the above-mentioned QNV 2030 meant to be based on the Guiding Principles of Qatar's Permanent Constitution (GSDP 2008: 10) and rested it on what it dubbed 'the four interrelated pillars': Human Development, defined as development of all the people of Qatar to enable them to live sustainably in a prosperous society; Social Development, or development of a just and caring society based on high moral standards, and capable of playing a significant role in the global partnership for development; Economic Development, which is development of a competitive and diversified economy capable of meeting the needs of, and securing a high standard of living for, all its people both for the present and in the future; and Environmental Development, the management of the environment such that there is harmony between economic growth, social development and environmental protection (ibid.: 11).

It is clear that these pillars were meant to show that the State of Qatar does not confine development to economic growth, but adopts the multidimensional concept of sustainable development which extends to increasing people's welfare. And welfare has other components that are not merely economic such as wealth distribution, leisure time, employment security, health, freedom and environmental goods and services (see Abaza and Baranzini 2002: 2). The pillars also show that Qatar recognizes the global and the intergenerational aspects of sustainable development, thus agreeing with the most recent definitions of sustainable development. However, the first pillar seems to be redundant. It is not clear what it adds to the concept of sustainable development beyond what the other three jointly give.

Progress Towards Sustainable Development: Critical Overview

In order for any nation to implement its vision of development, it needs a clear idea of what it has achieved so far and what it has still to achieve. This is what the State of Qatar has attempted to do through the GSDP. The aim of the ASD Report was to advance sustainable development as portrayed in the QNV 2030. It intended to designate, as mentioned above and as will now be overviewed, what Qatar has achieved and what challenges it faces in achieving the three goals of sustainable development: economic growth, social development and environmental management.

Economy in Qatar

Both the QNV 2030 and the ASD Report note that until the current global economic crisis, Qatar has enjoyed a period of unparalleled prosperity, with exceptional economic progress evident in high gross domestic product (GDP) and increasing standard of living of its people. In 2006, the GDP Index for Qatar and GCC countries increased sharply, exceeding the average of the five highest Human Development Index (HDI) countries, due largely to the sharp increase in oil prices (GSDP 2008: 1; 2009: 13).

Education in Qatar

Since the Dakar Framework for Action 2000, there is a worldwide consensus that education is not only a fundamental human right, but also a key to sustainable development, peace and stability within and among countries. It is indispensable for effective participation in societies in the twenty-first century caught up in rapid globalization (UNESCO 2000a: 8). In order for education to be responsive to people's needs, it should start in early childhood and extend through life, be of high quality, equitable and gender sensitive (United Nations Documents 2000).

The ASD Report mirrors Qatar's policy makers' commitment to such an educational mission. Qatar has invested heavily in education as one of the pillars of social progress: basic schooling is now universal in marked contrast to the situation a generation ago (GSDP 2009: 15). In 1995, the Qatar Foundation (QF) was established with a fund of US $2 billion to support education, research and capacity building. At Education City, QF supports elite international education institutions to provide world-class quality education to Qataris and non-Qataris, and to ensure skilled and knowledgeable human capital for present and future development (ibid.: 24). This educational policy shows recognition of the importance of investing in the population not just for raising productivity, but also for advancing sustainable development.

Investment in human capital can take the form of increased time in education (e.g. average years of schooling), increased quality of education, on-the-job training and work experience. It is reported that US cross-country evidence shows that 'the quality of schooling, as proxied by student scores on standardized international exams in science, has a stronger effect on growth than the quantity of schooling' (Crawford 2003: 50). The ASD Report acknowledges this is a problem in Qatar, where in spite of the economic growth, Qatar is lagging behind the five highest HDI countries in education as a result of relatively low enrolments in tertiary education (GSDP 2009: 13). It also mentions that the quality of education is not yet up to international standards, with Qatari students, especially boys, markedly lagging in mathematics and science subjects (ibid.: 15). It follows that significant advances in Qatar's HDI ranking will require achieving higher post-secondary enrolments, particularly of males, who have much lower enrolment rates than females (ibid.: 13).

Health in Qatar

Health, like education, is also commonly acknowledged to be a fundamental human right, since it is so defined in the well-known 1946 Constitution of WHO (WHO Basic Documents 2006: 1). It has also been seen as necessary for achieving sustainable development as expressed in the 1977 30th World Health Assembly resolution (Resolution WHA30.43). The 30th Assembly decided that the main goal of governments and WHO in the coming decades should be the attainment by all people of the world by the year 2000 of a level of health – primary health care – that would permit them to lead a socially and economically productive life. This goal is commonly known as Health-For-All by the Year 2000 and was reaffirmed in the 1998 fifty-first resolution (Resolution WHA51.7) known as 'Health-for-All for the Twenty-First Century', within which the commitment to primary health care was restated (UNESCO 2010a: 54).

The understanding that the attainment of primary health care for all is a necessary aspect of social development was reaffirmed in other international declarations. The International Conference on Primary Health Care, held in Alma-Ata, Kazakhstan, in 1978, for example, realized that improving health called for a comprehensive approach, whereby primary health care was seen as the key to achieving an acceptable level of health throughout the world in the foreseeable future as a part of social development and in the spirit of social justice. The Bangkok Charter, adopted at the WHO Sixth Conference on Global Health Promotion held in Thailand in August 2005 reaffirmed in its recommendations that health is a major determinant of socioeconomic and political development (UNESCO 2010a: 54, 55).

According to the ASD Report, health policy in Qatar does well to meet these international goals. The country is investing heavily in expanding its health services to improve the quality of life of its citizens. 'All health outcome indicators have improved markedly in the past two decades and child mortality levels have halved compared with a generation ago. Many diseases have been eradicated and health coverage is now nationwide' (GSDP 2009: 16). However, as the ASD report also notes, lifestyle diseases such as obesity, high blood pressure, diabetes and heart disease are on the rise, putting increased demand on health services. The death and injury toll from road accidents is also relatively high (ibid.).

The Environmental Pillar

The QNV 2030 identifies the environmental goals as increasingly important challenges (GSDP 2008: 34). It recognizes that while there are environmental costs for economic progress, neither development nor the environment should be sacrificed for the sake of the other. Qatar's future development path must be compatible with the requirements of protecting and conserving the environment (ibid.: 12).

The ASD Report mentions that increasing industrialization and infrastructure construction pose many challenges to Qatar's environment. Environmental concerns relate, inter alia, to water use, marine and land degradation and carbon emissions. There are also concerns about the exceptional population growth that has accompanied rapid industrialization and development (GSDP 2009: 16). The inflows of predominantly male expatriate workers are placing increased demands on infrastructure and services such as land for housing and recreation, on energy and water, waste disposal and sewage treatment (ibid.).

The report focuses on three environmental stresses that it sees as critical for Qatar and must be addressed: water security, the marine environment and climate change. If left unattended, the ASD Report notes, these could potentially halt or reverse the nation's significant development progress (ibid.: iv).

Water security. Throughout the ASD Report, there is an explanation of why there is a looming water crisis in the State of Qatar. It is an arid country that lacks many natural water resources, a feature shared with the other member states of the Gulf Cooperation Council (GCC) countries. With an average of less than 200,000 litres of natural water available per person per year, Qatar falls far below the internationally recognized 'water poverty line' of 1 million litres per person per year (ibid.: 39). Added to this are the heavy demands put on water resources by the country's rapid agricultural and industrial development and population growth due largely to inflows of expatriate labour (ibid.: 2). This unprecedented demand on water has already resulted in non-conventional water supplies (desalinated and treated wastewater) almost totally replacing conventional water supplies (from rainfall and groundwater) with agriculture rapidly depleting the remaining fossil water drawn from natural aquifers (ibid.: 17). The overexploitation of groundwater threatens the remaining reserves from saltwater intrusion, and its misuse in agriculture is resulting in soil salinization, threatening further desertification. There is heavy reliance on desalinated water, the production of which has grown markedly in recent years. It is energy intensive and costly, and efforts need to be made to curb damage to sensitive marine environments in addition to reducing consequent carbon emissions (ibid.). Water is supplied to Qatari citizens for free and at heavily subsidized rates to non-Qatari residents. This policy is encouraging the unsustainable use of an already scarce resource. It threatens the environment and the well-being of Qatar's future generations. Existing policies need review to ensure that present levels and patterns of water consumption are within the country's carrying capacity (ibid.: 21).

Marine environment. Marine environments are among the most productive, yet threatened, ecosystems in the world, and that of Qatar is no exception. The reasons behind these threats range from global climate change to the expansion of industrial activities in coastal areas and their related catchments, causing increasing degradation to marine environments. Changes to coastal habitats have resulted in the loss of ecosystem services and biodiversity with fisheries in decline globally, threatening food security and livelihoods (ibid.: 67; see Walther et al. 2002: 393). According to the ASD Report, the marine environment in Qatar faces the same threats for the same reasons. There are also the local effects of coastal reclamation projects, sea transport and overfishing (ibid.: 17). The report warns about adverse impacts or potential adverse impacts, that is, marine environment impacts have yet to be understood and quantified.

The report mentions that anthropogenic greenhouse gas emissions dissolve in the oceans, altering their acidity. If left unabated, ocean acidification may reduce the ability of marine organisms such as corals to build their skeletons, which in turn affects the reef topography that is home to local fish populations. The emissions also cause increases in temperature that may lead to decreases in plankton population, which would mean less food for fish, and consequently for seabirds too. Alteration in temperature will also change the salinity distribution and inundate mangroves. The ASD Report notes the importance of the maintenance of these coastal defence systems in Qatar for the health and survival of its marine environments, the sustainability of the local fishery, and for human development (ibid.: 80). Sea-surface temperatures are expected to reach marine organism thermal tolerance thresholds more frequently, possibly resulting in mass mortalities of key ecological species, although the mechanisms and outcomes are not yet fully understood (ibid.: 81).

Regarding the problem of water pollution, the ASD Report notes that the activities of the oil and gas industry could result in the Gulf sea becoming the most polluted in the world unless strict measures are implemented and enforced. The potential for operational and accidental oil spills exists and has serious implications for the environment, the credibility of companies and the reputation of the state. Oil tankers also frequently empty ballast and flush engines on the high seas, the oil residues ending up on the shore. Operational waste disposal is a serious problem requiring both the education of seafarers and the provision of adequate waste-reception facilities by ports and harbours, as mandated in regulations. Systematic waste management is needed within Qatar's waters and neighbouring regions given the large quantities of waste that wash up on the shorelines. This should include an efficient surveillance system for improved monitoring and enforcement (ibid.: 78, 79).

The ASD Report also notes that the growing fragmentation of the marine environment through habitat destruction, although difficult to determine, needs to be addressed. The loss of marine resources and the negative effects on biodiversity are insufficiently acknowledged. The lack of appreciation of the valuable functions of threatened habitats is a problem (ibid.: 81). Direct habitat loss occurs with land reclamation from shallow water and increased industrial and municipal pollution of the sea. The impact on marine biodiversity of the development of artificial islands, peninsulas and jetties along the coast of Qatar is yet to be quantified. This is difficult due to a lack of transparent and adequate baseline data. There are no proven techniques to restore the functionality of, for example, a seagrass bed or coral community although some marketed options purport such potential. The ASD Report advocates that while habitat restoration may be possible, it should only be considered as a last option in the implementation of coastal development projects (ibid.).

Overfishing also threatens the marine environment: the number of fishermen has increased steadily over the last twenty years, with landings in Qatar quadrupling since 1995 from 4,271 tonnes to 17,690 tonnes in 2008. The increased catch has generally been for all species, and most likely reflects an increase in all fisheries (ibid.: 76). The steady increase is largely due to increased productivity facilitated by new technology (ibid.: 77). There is also some illegal fishing and hunting with modern sporting weapons, with failure adequately to enforce existing national laws due to several factors including poor levels of national governance (ibid.: 78). Another significant and potential threat is the introduction of invasive species into Qatar's waters from the ballast tanks and hulls of ships, which may either outcompete local species or have no natural predators to keep them in check (ibid.).

The ASD Report notes the low prevalence of marine diseases in Qatar's waters, although this may be due to limited information and a lack of ongoing monitoring of key species. For instance, coral diseases not known in Qatar's waters are prevalent in those of neighbouring states. This needs to be addressed to identify potential risks, especially as the global incidence of marine diseases has increased dramatically. Diseases are more prevalent where organisms are stressed, suggesting that the Gulf waters around Qatar are a potential hotspot (ibid.: 81).

Climate change. As stated in UNESCO's *Report of The World Commission On the Ethics of Scientific Knowledge and Technology on the Ethical Implications of Global Climate Change*, 'global climate change is the defining issue of our era (because it) poses a severe threat to human welfare, biodiversity and ecosystem integrity, and possibly to life itself' (2010b: 7). This change concerns global warming which since the mid–twentieth century is 'very likely due to the observed increase in anthropogenic greenhouse gas concentrations' (IPCC 2007: 39). Both QNV 2030 and the ASD Report acknowledge the need to address the challenges of climate change. 'The environmental pillar will be increasingly important as Qatar is forced to deal with ... international environmental issues such as the potential impact of global warming on water levels in Qatar and thereby on coastal urban development' (GSDP 2008: 30). According to the ASD Report, Qatar's total carbon emissions from fossil fuels are on the rise. There are five climate change threats facing Qatar: losses in agricultural production and food security; increasing water stress and water insecurity; rising sea levels and exposure to floods; damage to ecosystems and biodiversity; and negative impacts on human health (GSDP 2009: 17, 102, 110). Necessary action can be summarized as 'climate change adaptation and mitigation', which in Qatar will involve reducing greenhouse gas (GHG) emissions, moving towards a low carbon economy and adapting to possible climate change impacts. Reducing GHG emissions is made easier with those responsible for high emissions concentrated geographically – at Doha, Ras Laffan and Mesaaid – facilitating optimisation of energy-use efficiency (ibid.: 119–121).

Managing the challenges of climate change and the transition to a low carbon economy, the report notes, require a high-quality educational system to prepare citizens to address the complex issues involved (ibid.: 122) – a step that the state of Qatar has already taken with the expansion of schools and universities (ibid.: 116). They also require a governmental strengthening of key features of the state's health systems to cope with health risks from a changing climate: 'Higher CO_2 concentrations and fiercer and more frequent sand storms in desert areas will possibly increase allergic reactions and pulmonary diseases all over the region' (AFED 2009: viii). The government is central in encouraging research, development and deployment of low-carbon technologies, providing information and, where necessary, creating incentives for achieving low carbon emissions (ibid.: 122). It has initiated steps in this direction investing in research and development through the establishment of the Qatar Science and Technology Park (QSTP), the Qatar National Research Fund (QNRF) and private-public partnerships (for example, between Qatar Petroleum, Shell and Imperial College London) to tackle environmental problems with a focus on water, energy and emissions, and also to promote medical sciences and education (ibid.: 116). The report also notes the importance of the private sector and civil society. Though the private sector so far does not generally have an economically or politically independent role in the Arab countries, it can, nonetheless, encourage the adoption of best available technology (ibid.: 123). The government remains the major player for many reasons. In the Gulf states, for instance, the ten largest listed companies are state-owned (e.g. SABIC, Emirates Bank Group, Qatar Telecom; Arab Human Development Report 2009: 72, 73).

The response to climate change has to be regionally and internationally integrated because the impacts recognize no national boundaries. The report notes that though the State of Qatar participates actively in the United Nations Framework Convention on Climate Change's Clean Development Mechanism (CDM) to reduce emissions and decarbonize energy-intensive industries (ASD: 123), the main challenge facing the country is how effectively to formulate, integrate and implement multi-sectoral sustainable development policies (ibid.: 26). The response to climate change has also to benefit from comprehensive analysis of problems and continuously monitor data, trends and technologies. But currently, as the report notes, knowledge of climate change and environmental management is rudimentary in Qatar (ibid.: 123). Another obstacle, according to the report, that not only hinders Qatar's attempts to tackle the problems of climate change, but also slows progress on implementing sustainable development plans, is the insufficiency of data on sustainable development. These remain partial and weak especially in relation to the environment. Sustainable development is generally difficult to measure because it is multidimensional in nature. More work is required to close existing data gaps, improve their timeliness, overcome lack of comparability and to develop indicators that better reflect the situation in Qatar (ibid.: 23).

Progress Towards Sustainable Development: Critical Evaluation

The launch of the QNV 2030, defining the long-term outcomes for the country to achieve as well as the framework by which national strategies can be implemented by the year 2030 is itself a governmental positive step towards sustainable development, because development starts with a vision for the future that can be translated into a plan. The ASD Report focuses on diagnosing the problems facing development, addressing the challenges that can hinder sustainability, thus showing transparency required for sustainable development. Transparency occurs mainly in designating obstacles in the field of education, health and environment

The economic situation outlined in the two reports shows that 'growth with equity' is a principle that Qatar recognizes and seeks to fulfil, that economic growth the country is enjoying is not accompanied by inequality amongst citizens as it is elsewhere, such as Brazil (Elliott 1999: 11) or in Nigeria, where the issue of distributive inequity is at the heart of the environmental crisis (Darkoh and Rwomire 2003: 9).

The ASD Report also reflects awareness of the principle that marked a turning point in our thinking about water and ecosystems in Agenda 21 of the United Nations Conference on Environment and Development (Rio, 1992). This principle is that the lives of people and the environment are profoundly interlinked and that ecological processes keep the planet fit for life, providing our food, air to breathe, medicines and much of what we call 'quality of life'. It recognizes that 'since water sustains all life, effective management of water resources demands a holistic approach, linking social and economic development with protection of natural ecosystems' (UNESCO 2000b: 22).

However, there are important issues that the two reports do not focus on or address which are important for evaluating the state's advance towards sustainable development.

Though the authors of the ASD Report state that it focuses mainly on environmental stresses, they were aware of the centrality of health to development. They mention, as explained above, that the health policy in Qatar copes well with the international proclamations of health issues and that the country is investing heavily in expanding its health services to improve the quality of life of its citizens and that all health-outcome indicators have improved markedly in the past two decades. However, the report does not mention, in detail, the challenges presented by the health-care sector other than that there are lifestyle diseases such as obesity, high blood pressure, diabetes and heart disease that are on the rise and putting increased demand on health services.

The State of Qatar, though it is the leader in the region in providing medical services to its citizens and has the highest density of physicians and hospital beds, indeed ahead of the norm for developed countries, and though the government-run Hamad Medical Corporation meets high standards (Kotilaine 2009: 4), has a healthcare system that is experiencing, and will experience, an unprecedented rise in the demand for healthcare because of population growth and rising life expectancy. Population growth is due, as mentioned, to demand for expatriate workers to support many large-scale development projects (ASD Report: 46). Rising life expectancy is evident with the over-65-year-olds as the fastest-growing age group. As a result, the rate of increase in the demand for medical services has exceeded the general population growth rate (Kotilaine 2009: 2)

Another challenge that the medical sector faces is the heavy reliance on expatriate physicians and nurses. In 2007, foreign physicians comprised 74 per cent of the total (ibid.: 21). This reliance on foreigners is set to continue for some time to come. The reason is that local educational institutions are currently insufficient to produce the numbers of clinical professionals needed to staff the state's healthcare services. In Qatar, Weill Cornell Medical College, established in 2001, is currently the only local medical school. It offers an integrated program of pre-medical and medical studies leading to the MD degree. The first class of fifteen physicians graduated in May 2008. Though enrolment has grown rapidly from 25 first year pre-medical students in the fall of 2002 to over 240 students in the fall of 2009 (Weill Cornell Medical College 2009), the number of new local medical graduates is not expected to keep pace with the population growth. The high dependency on expatriate medical staff has negative impacts on the healthcare sector. Continuity of service, including the personal relationship between doctor and patient, is continuously broken with many expatriate medical staff preferring to return home after a few years to be replaced by new ones, who leave after a certain time and so on. In addition, non-Arab expatriates face the problem of communication with local people. Mutual misunderstanding may result in misdiagnosis and prescribing incorrect medication (Kotilaine 2009: 21–22).

The reliance on the rest of the world is, if anything, even greater in the case of pharmaceuticals, with 85 per cent of all medicines being imported. The GCC pharmaceutical companies, which largely produce generic medicines, also face problems with sourcing skilled labour, with only a few local institutes providing courses in pharmacology (ibid.: 3). Qatar University's College of Pharmacy, established in 2008, is the first and only pharmacy school that offers a degree program. It currently has three approved academic degree programs: the Bachelor of Science in Pharmacy, Doctor of Pharmacy and Master of Sciences in Pharmacy degree programs. The first bachelor's degree class was enrolled in September 2007 and Qatar's first eighteen graduates are expected in 2011. The first Doctor of Pharmacy degree class will be admitted in September 2011 and the first graduates are expected in 2012. The first master's degree class will also be admitted in September 2011 and the first graduates are expected as early as 2013.

The ASD Report does not focus on the social aspects of development. Empowerment of women, for example, is a recent social phenomenon in Qatar. It is seen in families' encouragement of their daughters to learn until they get a university degree (the ASD Report notes that boys have much lower enrolment rates in tertiary education). It is also seen in the encouragement of females to do the same jobs as males, in the increasing occupation of high positions by women, in their enjoying the same health services as men. These practices, as Yousef Obaidan (vice president of the Qatari National Human Rights Committee) says, are officially supported by the state, which is increasingly providing Qatari women with political, social and economical rights (Obaidan 2008: 71). The few distinctions in some homes between brothers and sisters reflect old remaining but diminishing customs. And while the unemployment rate for women (3.8 per cent in 2004) is higher than for men (1 per cent in 2004), this is due to women mostly choosing occupations that are oversubscribed currently, such as teaching and clerical jobs in the government sector (Almaliki and Alrubai: 40).

In 2010, the Social and Economic Survey Research Institute (SESRI) of Qatar University published a summary of an omnibus survey it conducted in which a large and representative sample of Qatari citizens participated. The intention was to gather information about the attitudes and opinions of Qatari people on a number of topics of importance to the Qatari society. In asking participants about gender issues, the results show that attitudes were generally positive towards women working outside the home, with 8 out of 10 agreeing or strongly agreeing that women should be allowed to work outside the home if they wish; the attitudes were similar towards married and unmarried women (SESRI 2010: 4). The results also show that the majority reject wife beating: only 32.8 per cent of male respondents and 24.2 per cent of female ones accept wife beating (ibid.: 5). As for household decisions, 96 per cent said that women participate in household decisions (ibid.). These results reflect attitudes that increasingly empower women. These attitudes have to be reinforced because women constitute potential human resources that have an important role in the country's development.

However, moving towards a knowledge-based and post-carbon economy does not necessitate, as the ASD Report claims (15), that Qatari females will constitute the same ratio of the labour force as in industrialized countries. If women in the labour force are lower in Qatar, it does not imply that it will hinder development. Development is neither gender dependant nor measured by the ratio of females working outside the house. It can be argued that women staying home to nurture the children is better for family society. What is needed for development is a collaborative effort by all, regardless of the ratio of either gender in the waged labour force or the nature of work each does.

The ASD Report mentions urbanization as one of the challenges Qatar is facing, pointing out the need to review and assess it during the preparation of Qatar's first National Development Strategy, 2010–2015. Some of the adverse implications urbanization has on development are mentioned in the ASD Report while discussing other issues. Urbanization is a demographic as well as a cultural process, involving population's movement from rural areas to cities. In Qatar, urbanization has featured a change in people's economic activities resulting in a change in the social lifestyle. In 1950, 30 per cent of people lived in towns with most Qatari living in the semidesert (*badiya*) and leading a nomadic lifestyle (Al-Mohannadi and Al-Hity 2010: 27). The harsh environment characterized by hot weather, sandy storms, poor soil and scarce fresh surface as well as groundwater shaped life in pre-oil Qatar, with people largely relying on fishing, pearl diving, some trade, agriculture and animal herding – life was hard (Alkhayyat 2000: 56). With the discovery of oil and gas, the country has moved to a petroleum-based economy enhancing living standards and turning nearly all Qatar's population into an urban one (Al-Mohannadi and Al-Hity 2010: 28).

One consequence of today's high standard of living is the prevalence of obesity. According to the WHO's most recent study of Qatar, almost 70 per cent of males and 80 per cent of females are obese, which contributes, as noted, to other associated illnesses such as high blood pressure, heart disease and type 2 diabetes (Peninsula 2010). Rapid urbanization has also had adverse environmental impacts. With increasing population, 'more demands are placed on the use of natural resources and more non-biodegradable waste is generated which makes it difficult to improve the quality of the environment' (Darkoh and Rwomire 2003: 11). The report does not mention that the designs of most recent buildings in Doha, as described by the Arab Forum for Environment and Development Report (2009) are unsustainable (as are those in other GCC cities such as Dubai and Abu Dhabi). They are huge buildings with large areas of glass façade that consume much electricity in air conditioning, contributing heavily to GHG emissions (AFED 2009: 21).

While recognizing the critical role of research, the ASD Report focuses exclusively on the need for natural science research. It stresses the need to raise the quality of education in mathematics and sciences, of the need for research that can help meet the challenges of climate change and the transition to a low carbon economy and work that can solve environmental problems focusing on water, energy and emissions. It argues for the promotion of medical sciences. However, social science research is important too because human behaviour impinges on a number of environmental issues and needs to be brought to the attention of policy makers. These include: how human activities alter the environment, how environmental change affects society and individuals and what may prompt society to intervene. These areas relate to political activity, economic structures and social organizations and institutions (Salih 2003: 487).

Raising awareness is a key social factor in advancing sustainability. It cannot be reduced to policies and regulations. All citizens need to participate in all stages, starting with identifying challenges and goals, suggesting plans and policies and monitoring their execution and effectiveness. This requires education of all citizens to the issues and challenges, the necessary behavioural changes to consumption patterns and the importance of participating in all steps to advance sustainability. It is necessary to incorporate 'sustainability' in the curricula, thus guaranteeing awareness among school and university students – the next generation – of the need for advancing sustainable development

Another reason for getting as many people as possible engaged in the drive to sustainability is that persons in the same society may have different views that affect the way they interpret and frame the issues. Failure to engage them or, at least, representatives of these viewpoints in meaningful discussion inhibits governmental agencies to build the necessary societal consensus to implement policies effectively. Research conducted in 1982 in the United States found that senior managers most frequently cited lack of public acceptance as the most significant barrier to successfully implementing policies taken away from stakeholders' participation (Bradbury and Rayner 2002: 21, 22).

The ASD Report does not give much consideration to the integration of national efforts to combat existing problems and to advance development through exchange of resources. It mentions collaboration in education with the establishment of Education City (1995) where the Qatar Foundation supports international educational institutions to provide world-class education, and also the establishment of Qatar Science and Technology Park that helps organizations develop and commercialize their technologies. It refers to the adoption of the 2002 Arab Initiative on Sustainable Development that provides an opportunity for the League of Arab States to coordinate efforts in promoting and monitoring progress towards sustainability. These collaborative initiatives may help in solving problems, but are not enough to guarantee advancing sustainable development. One major problem that can delay development – not only in Qatar, but anywhere – is shortage of human and natural resources. The Arab states, taken individually, lack human resources and/or one or more natural resources. Resource exchange between Arab states could solve this problem. For instance, gas and oil from the Gulf states Algeria and Libya can meet Arab needs of energy; the rich soil along the Nile River in Sudan and Egypt can satisfy Arab agricultural needs. Egypt can provide other Arab countries with skilled manpower in many service sectors and so on. With political will that builds on an understanding that development can proceed through integration and exchange of effort and resources across the Arab world, an ambitious development plan can be put into effect.

Global governmental issues also demand attention. Governments more than individuals can avoid countries harming one another, and need to integrate to solve one another's problems. There are sufficient natural resources and technologies to secure the basic needs of all people on earth.

Shortage of resources and lack of technology to solve problems are often the result of indifference of some governments towards others. If there is a need to educate people about their responsibilities in preserving the environment for the sake of others, governments need also to recognize their roles and responsibilities in helping *one another*. No country working alone can solve the problems that face us such as global warming. Only coordinated national efforts can solve such problems and advance sustainable development for all. Only when governments act with such integrity can it be claimed that sustainable development is truly ethical.

Notes

1. One publication that challenged existing orthodoxies and had an impact on Western thought in the late 1950s and probably heralded the ecological movement of the 1960s was a major symposium volume, entitled *Man's Role in Changing the Face of the Earth* (Thomas 1956). This book identified the human forces that had changed the state of the biosphere. Several components of the biosphere as well as aspects of society responsible for changes in the environment were discussed directly or indirectly with emphasis on technology, urbanization, industry and trade (see Darkoh and Rwomire 2003: 3, 4).

References

Abaza, H., and A. Baranzini (eds.). 2002. *Implementing Sustainable Development*. United Nations Environment Program.

Al-khayyat, H. 2000. *Al-Sokkan Walamala fi Dowal Magles Elta'awon Al-Khaligi* [Population and workforce in the GCC]. Doha: Gameat Qatar, Marka Al-Wathaek Walderasat Al-Ensaneya.

Almaliki, N., and F. Alrubai. N.d. *Summary of the Population Policy: Background Papers in the State of Qatar*. Doha: Permanent Population Committee.

Al-Mohannadi, H., and N. Al-Hity. 2010. *Moshkelat Al-Tanmeya fi Dawlat Qatar fil Al-feya Al-Gadida* [Development problems in the state of Qatar in the new millennium]. Doha: Qatar Wezarat Al-Thakafa Walfonoun Waltoraath.

Barry, J., B. Baxter and R. Dunphy (eds.). 2004. *Europe, Globalization and Sustainable Development*. London and New York: Routledge.

Bradbury, J., and S. Rayner. 2002. 'Reconciling the Irreconcilable.' In *Implementing Sustainable Development*, eds. H. Abaza and A. Baranzini, 15–31. United Nations Environment Program.

Crawford, A. 2003. 'Productivity Growth in Canada and the G7.' In *Sustaining Global Growth and Development*, eds. M. Fratianni, P. Savona and J. Kirton, 35–64. Aldershot: Ashgate.

Darkoh, M., and A. Rwomire. 2003. 'Ideas on Human Impact on Environment and Prospects for a Sustainable Future in Africa.' In *Human Impact on Environment and Sustainable Development in Africa*, eds. M. Darkoh and A. Rwomire, 1–28. Aldershot: Ashgate.

Elliott, J. 1999. *An Introduction to Sustainable Development*. London and New York: Routledge.

General Secretariat for Development Planning. 2008. *Qatar National Vision 2030*. Doha. www.gsdp.gov.qa/portal/page/portal/GSDP_Vision_Root/GSDP_EN/GSDP_News/GSDP%20News%20Files/QNV2030_English_v2.pdf (accessed 1 November 2009).

———. 2009. *Advancing Sustainable Development: Second National Human Development Report*. Doha.

Intergovernmental Panel on Climate Change. 2007. *IPCC 2007 Fourth Assessment Report*. Geneva: Switzerland (accessed 21 October 2010).

Kotilaine, J. 2009 *Healthcare in the GCC*. http://www.ncbc.com/uploads/library/20090630123930aGCC%20Healthcare%20-%20NCBC%20Research.pdf (accessed 2 January 2011).

Obaidan, Y. 2008 *Al-Khetab AlSeyasi Wahokouk Al-Ensan fi Qatar* [The political discourse and the human rights in Qatar]. In *Proceedings of the Conference on the Arab Human Rights in the Contemporary Legal and Political Discourse*, ed. A. Almerri and K. Almonoufi, 67–76. Doha: Al-Lagnalwataneya Lehokouk Al-Ensan.

The Peninsula. 2010. 'The Heavy Weight of Urbanisation,' 3 May. http://www.thepeninsulaqatar.com/q/56-tofol-jassim-al-nasr/1702-the-heavy-weight-of-urbanisation.html (accessed 25 February 2011).

Salih, M. 2003. 'Context, Principles and Practices of Conservation Strategies and Environmental Action Plans.' In *Human Impact on Environment and Sustainable Development in Africa*, eds. M. Darkoh and A. Rwomire, 471–493. Aldershot: Ashgate.

Social and Economic Survey Research Institute. 2010. *First Annual Omnibus Survey: A Survey of Life in Qatar: Summary Report*. Doha: Social & Economic Survey Research Institute, Qatar University.

Thomas, W. L. (ed.). 1956. *Man's Role in Changing the Face of the Earth*. Chicago: University of Chicago Press.

Tolba, M., and N. Saab. 2009. *Arab Environment: Climate Change*. Beirut: Arab Forum for Environment and Development. http://www.afedonline.org/afedreport09/default.asp (accessed 11 May 2010).

United Nations Development Program. 2009. *Arab Human Development Report*. New York: Regional Bureau for Arab States.

United Nations Documents. 1987. *Our Common Future, Ch.2: Towards Sustainable Development*. www.un-documents.net/ocf-02.htm#1 (accessed 18 March 2010).

———. 2000. *Expanded Commentary on the Dakar Framework for Action*, World Education Forum, Paris, 23 May 2000. http://www.un-documents.net/dakar-ec.htm *(accessed 23 March 2010)*.

UNESCO. 2000a. *The Dakar Framework for Action*. http://unesdoc.unesco.org/images/0012/001211/121147e.pdf (accessed 23 March 2010).

———. 2000b. *The Ethics of Freshwater Use: A Survey*. Reykjavik: UNESCO.

―――. 2007. *The United Nations Decade of Education for Sustainable Development (2005–2014)*. http://unesdoc.unesco.org/images/0015/001540/154093e.pdf (accessed 26 December 2010).

―――. 2010a. *Report of the International Bioethics Committee of UNESCO (IBC) on Social Responsibility and Health*. Paris: Social and Human Sciences Sector, UNESCO.

―――. 2010b. *Report of The World Commission On the Ethics of Scientific Knowledge and Technology (COMEST) on the Ethical Implications of Global Climate Change*. Paris: UNESCO.

Walther, G., et al. 2002. 'Ecological Responses to Recent Climate Change.' *Nature* 416: 389–395. http://eebweb.arizona.edu/courses/Ecol206/Walther et al Nature 2002.pdf (accessed 3 February 2010).

Weill Cornell Medical College in Qatar. 2009. http://qatar-weill.cornell.edu/media/reports/2009/graduation2009/documents/WCMC-QoverviewEnglish.pdf *(accessed 12 February 2011)*.

WHO Basic Documents. 2006. Forty-fifth edition, supplement, October. http://www.who.int/governance/eb/who_constitution_en.pdf (accessed 20 April 2010).

World Bank. 2003. *World Development Report 2003: Sustainable Development in a Dynamic World*. New York: A Co-publication of the World Bank and Oxford University Press.

CHAPTER 5

Charting the Emergence of Environmental Legislation in Qatar

A Step in the Right Direction or Too Little Too Late?

Wesam Al Othman and Sarah F. Clarke

Environmental concerns have featured in the legislative process in many parts of the world stretching back as far as the seventeenth century,[1] when fears about public health and sanitation began to emerge, or earlier if practices in Roman times such as the introduction of public baths, sewage systems and fresh-water aqueducts are interpreted as responses to environmental issues. While our impact on the environment started to exceed other animals' impacts many millennia ago when humans first used fire for cooking and heating, it was not until the industrial revolution of the eighteenth and nineteenth centuries that pollution became a widespread and large-scale public and private issue in England, continental Europe and beyond.

Major pollution events in the twentieth century, such as the Exxon Valdez oil spill in 1989 off Prince William Sound in Alaska, and more recently the massive Deepwater Horizon spill in the Gulf of Mexico in 2010, have highlighted the growing significance of maintaining a healthy environment while improving how corporations operate. They have also served to raise public perception about environmental issues and individual, institutional and corporate responsibilities for environmental protection. This has led to calls for stronger and more far-reaching legislative action to minimize future environmental impacts, mitigate existing pollution concerns and resolve the apparent conflict between environmental protection and the rush for development in certain parts of the world. This phenomenon is seen in China where leaders have started to confront the economic, environmental and social costs of unchecked development by putting environmental sustainability on the public agenda, subsequently strengthening existing environmental regulations and issuing a raft of new standards.[2]

Research has shown that stringent legislation is an important factor in reducing environmental impacts, for example toxic chemical usage and emission levels in the United States have been curtailed with strict regulation, while negotiated voluntary initiatives feature prominently in Europe with the mere threat of regulation having a similar level of control (Harrison and Antweiler 2003). In countries of the Middle East, where in many cases environmental legislation is playing 'catch up' to keep up with rates of development, voluntary initiatives play a critical role and companies apply international standards in the absence of locally enforced environmental legislation. It is only belatedly that environmental laws governing, for example, water use, pollution emissions and negative impacts on biodiversity are featuring on the legislative horizon, although several Middle Eastern countries are signatories to various international treaties, such as the Kyoto Protocol or the Convention on Biological Diversity.

The same is true in Qatar and this chapter explores emerging environmental law in the state to determine the effectiveness of the existing legislation, identify obstacles to its implementation and suggest where renewed emphasis and new initiatives are required. It aims to answer the question: Is Qatar doing enough to preserve and enhance its natural environment in the context of large-scale development? Data was collected from legal texts in Qatari law, publicly available documents and research and interviews with specialists of environmental law at the Ministry of Environment, a member of Qatar's Shura Council and residents of the city of Al-Khor, located to the north of Doha.

Environmental Issues in the Gulf Region

Until relatively recently the countries of the Gulf Coordination Council (GCC) had not taken environmental issues seriously. The evidence suggests that the environmental dimension was not incorporated into the development process until the mid-1980s (Hussain 2007: 10). Prior to this, the main economic aim of these countries was to build up an industrial base without concern for the potentially adverse impact that large-scale development might have on the natural environment. However, accelerated development on such a scale has resulted in harmful and negative consequences; on the water through oil spills from container vessels (Al-Mohandi and Al-Hiti 2007: 28), the air through toxic emissions from factories and the soil through the inappropriate disposal of waste. Critically, these countries have depended on environmentally unfriendly technology, much of it designed to exploit non-renewable resources, which in turn has led to further pollution.

Gulf communities depend on oil- and gas-extractive industries to fund economic development and meet their populations' basic needs and advance a prosperous life for all. But meeting people's needs at the expense of the environment, with inadequate regulation of the production process to control resource use and minimize pollution, is potentially unsustainable, such development will not be profitable if it leads in the long term to the destruction of the ecological systems on which the GCC countries depend. The current environmental challenge is to advance environmentally friendly development and reverse some of the unintended consequences of certain aspects of economic activities, notably in oil and gas extraction and processing (Al-Makaawi 1995: 58).

In Qatar, as elsewhere in the region, in order for the exploitation of natural resources to continue to meet the demands of the population for increasing standards of living, a balance must be struck between the needs of people and the needs of the natural environment and other species. This equilibrium has yet to be achieved in many Gulf countries, including Qatar. However, the solution to environmental destruction does not lie in suspending development, but in balanced planning that incorporates environmental considerations and obliges industries to take into account the cost.

In line with the economic growth in the region, Qatar has seen extensive industrial development over the last decade. Reliance on oil and gas and associated industries to 'fuel' development is negatively impacting on the Qatari environment in three respects, i.e. air, water and land (Abdulrahman, Ahmed and Abdulsameer 2002: 28). Critical issues include water scarcity, loss of biodiversity, food security, emissions to air and water and land contamination.

Evidence of Pollution in Qatar

Increases in pollution are evidence that rapid development has impacted negatively on the environment. The accompanying increase in air-pollution rates has become hazardous, for instance reducing quality of life in general and threatening well-being. Rapid urbanization, notably in Doha Qatar's main city and other towns surrounding the capital such as Al Khor and Al Wakra, together with the new industrial cities such as

Mesaieed and Ras Laffan, are adding to the burden. The population of Doha is approximately 1.7 million, with 50 per cent of the residents living in Doha.[3] According to population size, Al Khor, 60 kilometres north of Doha on the east coast, is the next populous city, with 11.5 per cent of the population, followed by Al Wakra, 15 kilometres south of Doha, with 6.6 per cent. The industrial cities of Mesaieed and Ras Laffan are on the east too with the three main cites sandwiched between them, resulting in serious wind-borne factory pollution in all of them.

The Environmental Strategy 2011–2016 points out that air pollution[4] by factories and transport exceeds WHO emissions standards (GSDP 2010: 55–57).[5] Ozone is the most serious preventable air pollution in Qatar which, while a concern in Doha, is a far greater concern outside the capital. This is because of the chemical reaction between nitrous oxide emitted by vehicles and ozone which actually leads to the reduction of ozone in Doha. This means that ozone pollution decreases inside Doha and augments in areas such as Al Khor and Al Wakra (ibid.: 59).[6] Furthermore, the Ministry of Environment's air-quality monitoring stations are inside Doha, meaning that these emissions are underreported.

In areas such as Al Khor and Al Wakra, where the concentration of factory waste are greater and particulate and ozone levels increased, the impact on human health will be greater, having implications for rates of asthma, bronchitis, heart attacks and other cardiopulmonary problems. Residents of Al Khor and Al Wakra regularly express concerns about having factories close by and the adverse impacts on health, notably respiratory diseases.[7] Many industries are struggling to comply with new regulatory limits for NOx emssions issued in 2008–2009 (ibid.: 60–62).

Regarding water pollution, the Environmental Sector Strategy 2011–2016 reports that Qatari water is contaminated (GSDP 2010: 62–63). This is due to leakage from petroleum storage tanks, wastewater from cooling and washing plants, desalination of seawater and sewage waste, in addition to oil spills which percolate with rainwater into groundwater. This pollution appears to have less impact on human health than air pollution, though it has a negative impact on other species of plants and animals and an adverse impact on the marine environment, notably through operational and accidental oil spills (Hussein 2007: 160) combined with large-scale construction and land reclamation along the coast of Qatar, for example around the capital Doha. The large amount of heavy oil-related traffic (e.g. tankers) and oil-related activities (e.g. pipelines and fixed facilities) in the Gulf suggests that the waters around Qatar and the region in general could become some of the most polluted in the world unless strict measures are implemented and enforced.

Emerging Environmental Concerns in Qatar

Until the 1950s, people in Qatar lived a simple economic life with fishing and pearling, animal herding and some cottage industries, together with the importation of basic consumer goods. The economy has since come to depend on the export of oil and gas with the large-scale import of goods. The state's income depended initially on extracting and exporting oil and some oil-related industries (Abdulkareem 1999: 96–97). During this early petro-economy, Qatar, like other GCC countries, did not give much attention to the natural environment. Industrial plants were relatively small compared to today's gas monoliths and had relatively less environmental impacts. Furthermore, global consciousness of the dangers of hydrocarbon exploitation and use was not as pronounced as it is now, as evident in the type of environmental laws that were ratified in other parts of the world at this time. For example, the US Clean Water Act, enacted in 1948 and revised in 1972, set ambitious national standards for water quality that are still being implemented by industries and municipalities (Copeland 2010). An aim was to curb emissions to water sources from all industries, including extractive.[8] In its early formulations, the act focused primarily on point-source pollution, thereby encouraging end-of-pipe technological solutions to factory emissions; it was not a regulatory tool that would lead to major, more systemic changes in how waste and emissions were managed.

In Qatar in the 1980s and 1990s, oil production grew rapidly, increasing GDP from approximately QR 28 billion to 254 billion. It led to the emergence of large-scale oil-related industries (Abdulkareem 1999: 103). As a result, it became necessary for Qatar to enact new pollution laws to regulate the exploitation of resources and to deal with the resulting pollution, with an emerging awareness of the need to preserve marine and terrestrial life.

With the new millennium came the discovery of large reservoirs of gas together with the establishment of new gas-related industries. This coincided with growing concern on the international stage for environmental protection, as demonstrated by the burgeoning number of conferences and symposiums on this issue (Al-Makaawi, Othman and Al-Nasser 1998: 249) and the evolution of an international consensus on issues of sustainable development as enshrined in environmental conventions such as the Montreal Protocol of 1987, the Framework Convention on Climate Change of 1992 and the Bio-Safety Protocol of 2003. A consequence was that key individuals in the legislature of the State of Qatar began to recognize the importance of preserving the natural environment in response to the international community's pressure for enhanced environmental protection

(Al-Hosani 2004: 80). During this period the state issued a raft of laws regulating the production of oil and gas and associated petrochemical industries. These laws focused on the production process and ways of waste disposal, especially of hazardous chemical materials. Laws were enacted to protect marine life in particular.

The sudden and rapid rates of development in Qatar combined with massive increases in population have also put considerable strain on the country's already scarce water resources with pressure on fresh-water supply projected to increase to the year 2030 and beyond if left unchecked (GSDP 2010: 11). Water is fully subsidized for citizens and highly subsidized for foreigners, meaning that there are no incentives to reduce consumption and the environmental consequences will only intensify in the absence of regulatory control.

The rapid increase in the number of gas-production facilities has led to a heightened awareness and acceptance among Qatari government representatives of the importance of environmental management for continued human progress (Abdulkareem 1999: 110). This resulted in the establishment of the Ministry of Environment in 2008, which has a remit to protect the environment. Its vision is to be a leading institution in achieving balance between the protection of the environment and its natural resources, and the requirements of development for a better life for present and future generations. Prior to this, the role of environmental stewardship was held by the Supreme Council for the Environment and Natural Reserves (SCENR),[9] which in turn replaced the Permanent Environmental Protection Committee in 2000.

In view of the need to protect the environment and conserve natural resources while promoting the development of a better life for present and future generations, the State of Qatar has adopted a comprehensive policy (Hussain 2007: 58) covering the following areas:

(1) Initiating assessment processes to determine the impact of development projects on the environment, emphasizing environmental protection.
(2) Making additions and/or modifications to environment related legal framework and accelerating the enactment of these laws.
(3) Establishing environmental information systems for developing resource management.
(4) Protecting the wildlife and biological heritage of Qatar.

Since its establishment in 2008 the Ministry of Environment has been gradually coming to grips with the scale of the task before it. Compared with other countries that have well-established and long-recognized government departments and ministries dealing with environmental matters,[10] its activities are still in their infancy and it has yet fully to develop its capabilities to enable an environmental ethic to be embedded within Qatar's government and economic system such that environmental thinking becomes part of the fabric of Qatari policy making. For example, during the design phase of large-scale industrial, petrochemical and desalination facilities, major infrastructure improvements or large residential developments,[11] the Ministry of Environment require the proposals to undergo either an environmental impact assessment or a less intensive environmental authorization application to determine its impact on the Qatari environment and to regulate pollutants. At present, there are no set criteria and standards for determining which process should be applied. Moreover, a lack of transparency, staffing issues and the absence of clear and cogent guidelines mean that the process is fraught with complexities and uncertainties on both sides leading to delays and costly changes (GSDP 2010: 92–93).

Enactment of Laws in Qatar

Legislative Authority in Qatar is vested in an Advisory Council, known in Arabic as the Shura Council. It is the body responsible for issuance of key laws in the country. Executive Authority is entrusted to His Highness the Emir, assisted by a Council of Ministers (comprising the heads of each ministry). The Emir[12] appoints the prime minister and ministers, accepts their resignations and may relieve them of their posts by Emiri Decree. Judicial Authority is vested in Courts of Law with judgments pronounced in the name of the Emir. No law can be issued unless approved by the Shura Council (the Parliament) (Shura Council 1998: 11). The Shura Council gives the Emir and the Council of Ministers its opinion about the political, economic, cultural, social and other issues facing the country. In addition it gives its view on the laws that the Council of Ministers suggest.

The forty-five members of the Shura Council are appointed by the Emir from among ministers or any other persons thought to have the necessary expertise and abilities. The term of office of the elected members expires when they resign their seats or are relieved of their post. Members of the Shura Council must be from an original Qatari family (i.e. a person holding a Qatari passport does not necessarily qualify), at least twenty-four years old and have no criminal record. The selected members are typically people with social status and with an expertise in different aspects of life (Shura Council 2008: 6–7). The president of the council is chosen through a secret voting system, but the council's first meeting is led by the oldest member. Those holding the positions of president and vice president can be elected more than once.

The Shura Council sits for approximately eight months of the year. Official leave usually runs from July to October although the Emir has the authority to summon an unusual meeting during the official council leave period if necessary (Shura Council 1998: 21–34) or can extend the period if it is in the public interest. The council holds weekly meetings on Mondays. However, the president of the council has the authority to call a meeting anytime if necessary. Usually the council's meetings are open to the public. However, they can be closed-door if necessary (Shura Council 1998: 34). The council's secretariat prepares the agenda for each meeting, which is sent to all members together with full documentation required, allowing members sufficient time to review them.

Any concerned body, whether a ministry, council (such as the Shura Council or Family Council[13]) or indeed the Emir, may prepare a bill and send it to the Legislation Department of the Secretariat for the Council of Ministers that, in turn, reformulates or modifies it to remove any conflicts that may occur with other state laws. Once reformulated, the bill is sent to all ministries for comments or feedback. These must be returned to the Council of Ministers within three weeks, which further revises the bill as needed. A session of the Council of Ministers then discusses the modified bill. If approved, it is sent to the Shura Council which studies the bill through its subcommittees before subsequently discussing it in a public session. Following public discussion, the bill is sent to the Council of Ministers for final formulation. The Council of Ministers sends the bill to His Highness the Emir for signature. The law is then sent to the Ministry of Justice for publication in the Official Gazette. Once published, the law comes into effect, or at a designated date set in the law itself. Some laws state that an executive rule should be issued by the concerned minister to explain the law and necessary executive steps to get, for example, a certain license or initiate a certain procedure referred to in the bill.

There are few avenues for the general public to influence the nature of environmental legislation. A small number of non-governmental organizations such as Friends of the Environment, Qatar Natural History Group and Qatar Green Centre are involved in raising public awareness about environmental concerns. In addition, an increasing number of Qatari businesses are championing environmentally friendly activities through their employees' involvement in socially responsible projects. For example, Doha Bank has organized beach clean-ups and QTel promotes green business practices such as recycling through its highly successful e-recycling initiative (refer to Clarke and Almannai, chapter 15, this volume). However, in general, there is an absence of a culture of engaging the public in comprehensive dialogue with the government on these issues with the exception of relatively low-key day activities, which suffer from a lack of publicity, even though sustainability is one of the pillars of Qatar's National Vision 2030 (refer to Tan, Al-Khalaqi and Al-Khulaifi, chapter 2, and Darwish, chapter 4, this volume).

Key Legislation in Qatar

Qatari law[14] includes considerable legislation regarding protection of the environment dating back to 1970, the state's interest in the environment originating from the time of independence and the establishment of the state. There are seventeen principal environmental laws each with several hundred clauses and articles for their enactment. For example, in 1974, Law (8)[15] regarding public hygiene gives guidelines for the disposal of waste in places designated for that purpose and recommends that people keep trashcans in their homes. Law (4) of 1983 protects the marine life through the identification of specific hunting seasons and the regulation of practices and equipment used. Law (4) of 2002 further regulates animal, bird and reptile hunting. Law (1) was added in 1993 to prevent the destruction of arable land and dredging of beach sand. In 1995, Law (32) protects vegetation through a ban on harmful practices and regulation of animal herding. Law (19) in 2004 relates to the protection of wild fauna and flora and its natural habitats.

The sophistication of environmental law in Qatar has evolved with environmental thinking and international calls for more sustainable behaviours and now reflects a more systemic and holistic view of the problem of environmental degradation. Law (30) of 2002 demonstrates this evolution in thinking, as one of the most important environmental laws in Qatar to date. This law seeks to reduce the immediate and long-term negative side effects of industrial development, maintaining ecosystem balance and limiting pollution by requiring those planning to start up any project, to complete an environmental assessment of their proposal. Law (30) also prohibits the importation, transportation, burial, storage or 'injection' of hazardous waste in the country.

The Qatari legislature enacted Law (3) in 2002 to protect the country from the dangers of radiation. Other laws prohibit the exportation/importation of substances harmful to the ozone and require that these are monitored. In addition to the above, there are further laws that aim specifically to protect and preserve Qatar's wildlife, its natural habitat, and to regulate trade in endangered animals.

The country has also signed twenty-two treaties, both regional and international, to protect the environment. These include the 1969 treaty on marine life protection from oil-based waste and monitoring of ship weight to prevent overloading. Other treaties signed subsequently include those on the transportation and handling of hazardous substances, and in 1983 the Vienna Convention on the Protection of the Ozone Layer.

Difficulties Facing the Execution of Legislation to Protect the Environment

Given that the Ministry of Environment is only in its infancy and Qatar has yet to establish a robust policy and strategic framework for the development of a culture of environmental awareness at all levels of government and society, it is not surprising to discover that there are substantial obstacles to the establishment of environmental legislation to enhance Qatar's environmental record. While it should be acknowledged that the statements in relation to environmental sustainability enshrined in the Qatar National Vision (GSDP 2008) and the subsequent Qatar National Development Strategy (GSDP 2011) are far reaching in their potential impact on all aspects of government policy, their successful implementation lies some distance in the future. What then are the key hindrances to the successful development of environmental legislation in Qatar?

Perhaps the most critical issue restricting the effective transformation of the legal framework in Qatar to one that embraces the concepts of environmental sustainability is the lack of sufficient specialized persons to assess, develop, implement and enforce environmental laws. Not only are there few legal professionals with environmental law experience, but also there is an absence of people with the skills required to monitor and test compliance with the resulting laws. Added to this is the reality that few have the knowledge and expertise to determine and set appropriate environmental standards. As a consequence, while Qatar has moved quickly to ratify international conventions and establish regulatory instruments, progress with implementation of action plans and monitoring of compliance has been slow.

With the absence of locally appropriate specifications for, for example, a particular emission or environmentally hazardous material, it is common for companies operating in Qatar to apply international standards to their operations. This is in part due to these companies' global corporate sustainability policies, but also due to local commitments to social responsibility and employees' personal convictions about environmental stewardship. Corporate ability to move forward on some projects in an environmentally appropriate manner is hampered by the case-by-case approach adopted in the assessment of projects and poor transparency regarding the 'rules of the game' which may change during the process.

Besides this lack of expertise on the various dimensions of sustainable development, which may itself slow the process of implementation of a law once a law has been proclaimed by Emiri Decree, a long and bureaucratic procedure ensues in the execution of a given piece of legislation and some two or three years may elapse before a law is fully in place. This bureaucratic sluggishness is compounded by the absence of cooperation among the country's different governmental institutions which serves to further hinder enactment of legislation. The slowness of the legislative process has resulted in some pieces of legislation remaining incomplete and others being in need of amendment to reflect the current environmental and sustainability agenda of Qatar for years. For example, amendments to Law (4) to protect water sources, including groundwater and seawater, took three years (from 2008 to 2011) to complete.

Effective implementation of environmental laws also relies to some extent on the presence of a robust infrastructure to deal with wastes such as household matter, construction debris, industrial substances, sewage and hazardous waste (see Clarke and Almannai, chapter 15, this volume). The public in general and businesses in particular cannot fully adhere to environmentally sound behaviour in waste disposal and meet legislative and regulatory requirements, for example, without the necessary systems in place to deal with these concerns. Retrospective construction of infrastructure is a common feature of the Qatari landscape due in part to a lack of adequate planning but also the reality that construction cannot keep up with demand. Indeed, the speed of development has resulted in some areas of Qatar not having adequate sewage infrastructure or waste-disposal systems, which results in poor environmental stewardship and on occasions one may see unsightly garbage floating in on the tide or blowing across the desert with the prevailing wind.

Part of the problem stems from a lack of general awareness about, and knowledge of, environmental issues among the population, not helped by the apparent reluctance of the media to report negative or contentious local environmental stories. 'Good-news' stories about the environment are frequently showcased in the media – for example, the Qatar Today Green Awards for Environmental Excellence (*Gulf Times* 2010) – while few column inches are devoted to controversial environmental problems and as a consequence there is little opportunity to raise and debate these issues. Key to the implementation of environmental legislation will be the development of avenues for fostering environmental consciousness among Qatari citizens. While actions have been taken to raise awareness among school children with the advent of various educational programs,[16] much still needs to be done to ensure that all segments of the population are equally environmentally conscious. Steps in the right direction are the regular beach clean-up events organized by the Ministry of Environment (*Gulf Times* 2011a) and environment-themed activities held by various organizations designed to raise environmental awareness. For example, many companies, other organizations and individual families took part in Earth Hour 2011 and environmental topics feature regularly on popular websites such as http://www.iloveqatar.net. However, failure to provide environmental education for the large migrant labour force is likely to hinder the full and effective implementation of environmental legislation, not least due to the multiple languages used by migrant workers, varying levels of education and a variety of ingrained cultural habits of these individuals (see Campbell, chapter 9, this volume). Furthermore, the absence of a clear framework for involving all stakeholders, including the private sector and civil society as well as government entities, in the process of achieving environmental sustainability means that roles, responsibilities, rights and relationships are unclear and participation greatly restricted. The success of the Doha Debates[17] in engaging people in Qatar in discussion and debate on diverse topics illustrates that there is a thirst for this kind of public participation.

The evidence presented by Sillitoe and Alshawi (chapter 10) in this volume regarding the Al Reem Biosphere demonstrates the disconnect between the state's desire to further environmental stewardship through the designation of the reserve area, the implementation and enforcement of environmental legislation to support the reserve's aims and the lack of an educational program or community-driven process to encourage environmental awareness and the development of a common understanding of the purpose of the reserve.

The absence of specialized environmental research centres in Qatar to study particular issues of environmental, social and economic sustainability also contributes to the weak environmental knowledge base among the population in general and policy makers in particular. While research is underway at several universities on specific technological challenges – for example, Qatar University's Material Technology Unit has research programs focused on plastics recycling and the Qatar Sustainability and Water Initiative at Texas A&M University Qatar has a mission to bring together all relevant public and private stakeholders to help make sustainable water and energy utilization a reality – there is no fully functioning, dedicated research facility in Qatar championing issues of sustainable development.[18] The establishment of the Qatar Science and Technology Park and the Qatar National Research Fund and a high-level commitment to develop a strong and robust knowledge-based economy in Qatar will be invaluable to building environmental know-how and providing sets of clear and unambiguous requirements for expertise on sustainability. Critically, sociological research about, for example, the impact of environmental legislation, or the lack thereof, on segments of the population is largely absent. Without a comprehensive program to undertake this type of research, it may be difficult to determine the effectiveness of environmental legislation and how it might need to be modified in the light of public and corporate responses to it. For example, research has shown that ambivalence and negative attitudes towards recycling may stem from an incongruity between beliefs about the importance of environmental stewardship on the one hand and personal attitudes and lifestyle on the other (Ojala 2008).

A Blueprint for the Future of Environmental Legislation in Qatar

Taken together, there are considerable obstacles facing the government of Qatar as it seeks to effectively develop and implement environmental legislation. They suggest an uphill struggle for lawmakers in the years to come. Yet there is a clear political will and public desire to safeguard the environment and maintain quality of life for all in the state as demonstrated by the words enshrined in many documents, not least the Qatar National Vision 2030. This desire is also shown in the gradual emergence of a more sophisticated set of environmental laws in Qatar that take on board issues of global warming, water scarcity, urbanization and demographic change. What appears to be lacking, however, is a high-profile champion tasked with ensuring that the environment is placed front and centre in all policy decisions, a proposal suggested in the 2011 National Development Strategy. Without such a clear 'voice', sustainability may be lost in the maelstrom of economic development where a desire to be the best in the region may win out over environmental conservation, unless, of course, the goal is also to be the best in environmental sustainability.

We have highlighted the need for enhanced skills and education in the area of sustainable development. At its most basic, this relates to teaching members of the public, business leaders and government employees what laws are in place, how to use them and for the laws to be properly enforced. It is not unusual to see flagrant disregard of, for example, littering laws by all levels of society, infringements which appear to go unnoticed and/or unpunished.

There are currently few incentives to act in an environmentally sensitive manner or indeed disincentives not to act with disregard to the environment. This is most clearly demonstrated by fully subsidized water supply for citizens and partially subsidized water for the expatriate community. This ensures wasteful use of an extremely precious resource and places Qatar as one of the world's leaders in per capita water consumption in a desert region where water is scarce by definition. Innovative regulatory support for the protection of this precious resource is undoubtedly needed. In addition, with some of the world's highest per capita waste generation rates, the state could follow Abu Dhabi's lead and introduce innovative laws regulating landfill use, for example to begin to change attitudes and behaviours towards waste materials (see Clarke and Almannai, chapter 15, this volume).

Certainly the state's drive to build a strong and vibrant knowledge-based economy will help to ensure that, over time, local skills are developed to bring about institutional change. A Centre of Sustainable Development charged with undertaking research and education to bring about a sea change in attitudes and behaviours across government departments and in all walks of life would assist the Ministry of Environment in their task. However, a mechanism is required to fast-track environmental education at primary, secondary and tertiary levels and to provide educators with the necessary training and skills set to teach environmental subjects. The presence of a small number of non-governmental organizations such as the Qatar Natural History Group, Qatar Bird Club and Friends of the Environment, which have growing membership, suggests there is a latent desire among the general public to support these kinds of initiatives.

What is clear is that environmental laws properly enforced are only part of the story. Key to environmental sustainability will be winning over hearts and minds and instigating behavioural change to a more sustainable way of life for the people of Qatar. This cannot be left to the final chapter; it must of necessity be woven throughout the story, with environmental laws forming the underlying structure of the narrative.

Acknowledgements

The authors would like to thank Professor Bahaa Dawish, Minya University, Egypt (formerly Department of Humanities, Qatar University), and Ms Hind Al-Sulaiti, Teaching Assistant Department of International Affairs, Qatar University for translating from Arabic sections of this chapter.

Notes

1. For example, in 1671 the Colonial Assembly in South Carolina passed a law that is still in effect: 'should any person cause to flow into or be cast into any of the creeks, streams or inland waters of this State any impurities that are poisonous to fish or destructive to their spawn, such person shall, upon conviction, be punished' (DHEC n.d.).
2. For example, the US EPA-China Environmental Law Initiative is designed to help strengthen the environmental legislative framework in China.
3. Refer to Qatar Statistics Authority, http://www.qsa.gov.qa.
4. Air pollution includes nitrogen oxides (NOx), ozone (O_3) and particulate matter.
5. Dust in the desert environment is primarily responsible for high particulate concentrations in Qatar which also exceed WHO levels. However, the WHO levels are difficult to apply due to the nature of the desert environment and frequent sand storms (GSDP 2010: 57).
6. A study by Qatar Petroleum and Qatar Science and Technology Park modelling ozone exceedances in desert and industrial areas found that measurements for 2008 exceeded standards several hundred times (GSDP 2010: 69).
7. Comments made to the researcher during interviews in October 2009.
8. The production of heavy oil requires massive volumes of water. Produced water can be reused in the production process or treated and used for, for example, irrigation (Veil and Quinn 2008: 49).
9. The SCENR was accountable for all environment-protection responsibilities including protection and enhancement of wildlife and its natural habitats, formulation of policies to protect the environment and realize sustainable development, preparation of environmental legislation and regulations and monitoring the status of existing environment and wildlife protective measures.
10. For example, in the UK the Ministry of Agriculture Food and Fisheries established in 1955 was amalgamated with Department of Environment, Transport and the Regions in 1997 to form DEFRA, the Department of Environment, Food and Rural Affairs. In the United States, the Environmental Protection Agency was established more than forty years ago in 1970.
11. Examples include the Pearl Island development and Lusail Qatar's future city.
12. The Office of the Emir is situated in the Emiri Diwan which houses the Emir's staff and advisors. It is also the place where official business takes place such as meetings with visiting dignitaries.
13. The Family Council deals with matters relating to family, women and children. There are also Municipal Councils comprising men and women elected by direct secret ballot by the public. Those elected hold office for a three-year term. These councils have no legal authority but can make suggestions about the need for, for example, schools, public gardens or sewage system upgrades in a particular municipal area.

14. As indicated by Dr Alaa Badr, legal expert at the Qatari Ministry of Environment (interviewed October 2009).
15. In Qatar, each law is referenced by the year it was enacted and a number.
16. For example, Doha Bank and UNESCO have launched an 'eco-schools' program to encourage schools to take responsibility for their energy consumption (Townson 2011) and the Friends of the Environment Centre in Doha is spearheading a campaign in schools to promote recycling and help establish a recycling industry in Qatar (Gulf Times 2011b).
17. Formed in 2004 by the Qatar Foundation for Education, Science and Community Development, the Doha Debates are a forum to debate contentious local, region and global issues. No government, official body or broadcaster has any control over what is said at the sessions or who is invited. Refer to http://www.thedohadebates.com.
18. Qatar University's Environmental Studies Centre undertakes some environment-related research and monitoring activities.

References

Abdulkareem, N. 1999. *Al-Tanmeya Al-Sena'eya fi Qatar Walkhaleej* [Industrial development in Qatar and the Gulf]. Doha: Dar el-Kotob.

Abdulrahman A., M. Ahmed and S. Abdulsameer. 2002. *Al-Derasat Al-Ejtema'eya fi Mowajahat Alkadaya Al-Bee'eya* [Social studies contra environmental issues]. Cairo: Al-Qahera lelnashr.

Al-Hosani, H. 2004. *Derasat fi Al-Tanmeya Walbee'ah Wadawr Al-Mar'ah* [Studies in development, environment and the role of the woman]. Cairo: Al-Qahera lelnashr.

Al-Makaawi, A. 1995. *Albee'ah Walsehha* [Environment and health]. Alexandria, Egypt: Dar al-Ma'rifa al-Jami'iyah.

Al-Makaawi, A. , W. Al-Othman and F. Al-Nasser. 1999. *Elm Al-Ejtemaa Al-Tebby* [Medical sociology]. Cairo: Al-Ahram Lel-Nashr.

Al-Mohandi, H., and N. Al-Hiti. 2007. 'Masader Al-Meyah fi Dowal Majles Elta'awon Al-Khaligi' [Water resources in the GCC]. *Majallet Al-Joghrafia Al-Khaleejeya* 1: 205–252, special issue on Saudi Arabia.

Copeland, C. 2010. 'Clean Water Act: A Summary of the Law.' Congressional Research Service Report for Congress. www.crs.gov RL30030 (accessed 30 May 2011).

DHEC. N.d. 'A Brief History of Environmental Law.' Columbia, South Carolina: Office of Solid Waste Reduction and Recycling, Department of Health and Environmental Control, Document No. OR-0593 9/09. http://www.scdhec.gov/environment/lwm/recycle/pubs/environmental_law.pdf (accessed 1 June 2011).

General Secretariat for Development Planning (GSDP). 2008. *Qatar National Vision.* Doha, Qatar.

———. 2010. *Environmental Sector Strategy 2011–2016: Phase 1 Situational Analysis.* Draft 4, May. Doha, Qatar.

———. 2011. *Qatar National Development Strategy.* Doha, Qatar.

Gulf Times. 2010. 'Awards Recognition for Green Cause,' 30 November, 8.

———. 2011a. 'Sealine Beach Area Cleaned by Ministry,' 2 March, 14.

———. 2011b. 'Eco-Friends Special Supplement,' May, 8

Harrison, K., W. Antweiler. 2003. 'Incentives for pollution abatement: Regulation, regulatory threats, and non-governmental pressures.' *Journal of Policy Analysis and Management* 22(3): 361–382. http://onlinelibrary.wiley.com (accessed 7 April 2011).

Hussain, A. 2007. *Al-E'elam WalQadaya Al-bee'eya fi Qatar* [Media and environmental issues in Qatar]. Doha: Qatar Books.

Majles Al-Shoura [Shura Council]. 1998. 'Adwaa Al-a Majles Al-Shura' [On the Shura Council], special issue.

———. 2008. 'Daleel Al-la'eha Al-Dakheleya' [Internal draft law], special issue.

Ojala, M. 2008. 'Recycling and Ambivalence: Quantitative and Qualitative Analyses of Household Recycling Among Young Adults.' *Environment and Behaviour* 40 (6): 777–797. http://eab.sagepub.com (accessed 7 April 2011).

Townson, P. 2011. 'Scheme Aims to Make Schools Eco-Friendly,' *Gulf Times,* 3 March, 36.

Veil, J. A., and J. J. Quinn. 2008. 'Water Issues Associated with Heavy Oil Production.' ANL/EVS/R-08/4 Environmental Science Division, Argonne National Laboratory for the US Department of Energy, National Energy Technology Laboratory, November. http//www.evs.anl.gov/pub/dsp_detail.cfm?PubID=2299 (accessed 19 June 2011).

II

Energy and Economic Issues

CHAPTER 6

Sustainable Energy
What Futures for Qatar?

Thomas Henfrey

The transformation of energy is perhaps the distinctive feature of life. Continuous throughputs of energy, the vast majority originally coming from the sun and fixed by photosynthetic plants and microorganisms, allow living systems to maintain themselves in states of dynamic complexity that resist the general trend of matter towards entropy, or disorder. Human societies are no exception: ecological anthropology models them as systems for the management of flows of energy, along with matter and information, mediated by culture (Rappaport 1979; Ellen 1982; Stepp et al. 2003). While to reduce historical trends to changes in patterns of energy relations alone is both an oversimplification and unwarranted generalization (Ellen 1982: 258–259), major shifts in the historical trajectory of the industrialized world can be characterized as reconfigurations in the dominant ways of capturing and transforming natural sources of energy and directing them to human uses (White 1959).

Industrialization was the last such globally significant shift. For most of human history, the dominant primary energy source was sunlight, captured by plants through photosynthesis and passed directly through the food chain (human and animal power, along with untransformed biomass fuels such as wood, dung and fats and oils derived from both animals and plants). Since the industrial revolution, for the majority of the world's population this has been superseded by fossil fuels: first coal, later petroleum and its derivatives, and later still natural gas (e.g. see Barbour et al. 2010). Coal, oil and gas are themselves the remains of living organisms, and their energy content ultimately derives from photosynthesis, but is bound up in matter that has been sequestered in the earth's crust and transformed by geological processes over timescales measured in aeons. In those parts of the world that have experienced industrialization,[1] these products of previous geological eras, along with nuclear fission, power all of the processes necessary for survival and well-being: food production, manufacturing, transportation, construction, the maintenance of basic infrastructure and the habitability of buildings. Abundant reserves of these fuels have brought Qatar and other Gulf states to an important role in the global economy. This role may become more important still as the world prepares for another shift, away from fossil fuel dependency and towards the sustainable use of renewable energy sources.

Energy, Society and Culture

Energy's central role in all human societies means our relationship with it is at the heart of sustainability. This is particularly so in the industrialized world, whose appropriation, transformation and use of energy are afflicted with a chronic lack of sustainability. This is true both directly, in that we rely overwhelmingly on primary energy sources that are in inherently limited supply, and indirectly, in that use of these energy sources has deleterious environmental and social impacts. The combined impact has in recent decades reached such a magnitude that, on a global scale, another revolutionary transformation of our relationship with energy is inevitable (Abramsky 2010). This may occur by choice, through pre-emptive measures that seek to minimize, and eventually eliminate, the social and environmental costs of the ways we currently capture, transform and use energy. Such measures are increasing throughout the world, but their scale and impact are small relative to those of the dominant, 'business as usual' pattern, which evidence suggests is based on economic premises fundamentally incompatible with sustainability (Jackson 2009). Only a dramatic change in this situation can avoid the prospect of the energy revolution occurring by default, as a retrospective response to the potentially disastrous consequences of the persistence of the current model.

The consequences will be momentous for Qatar and other states currently experiencing rapid expansion and industrialization of their domestic economics, fuelled and financed by abundant reserves of fossil fuels. Their social, economic and political aspirations rest on the exploitation of a one-off bonanza of resources on which the rest of the world currently depends (see Gilberthorpe, Clarke and Sillitoe, chapter 7, this volume), but whose use has increasingly evident global impacts. The focus of the present chapter is the contradiction between the need for sustainability and the dependency on non-renewable energy sources – fossil fuels and uranium feedstock for nuclear fission – characteristic of industrial economies worldwide. While emerging states would do well to avoid emulating this pattern, the dominant mode of development on offer is the reproduction of the same technology, economy and institutions, inherently lacking social and environmental sustainability (Unruh and Carrillo-Hermosilla 2006). Qatar has an opportunity – perhaps responsibility – to lead the way in defining and establishing a new relationship with energy consistent with reasonable material aspirations and the reality of life on a planet with finite resources (Meadows et al. 1972; Meadows, Randers and Meadows 2004).

Meeting this challenge will be formidable in the face of the pervasive barriers to sustainable production and consumption of energy outlined below. The argument taken here recognizes that the biosphere's resilience to human disturbance, while considerable, is not infinite. People are capable of modifying their habitat in ways that enhance its capacity to meet their needs (Geertz 1963; Boserup 1965), including in ways that over time enhance biodiversity and other ecological properties (Balée 1994, 1998). History also provides us with numerous examples where failure of human societies to modify worldviews, economic aspirations and/or patterns of social organization incompatible with ecological reality has led to dramatic declines in population and social complexity, and in some cases complete extinction (Santley, Killion and Lycett 1986; McGovern 1994; Schmidt 1994). While I contend that fulfilling the energy needs of growing national and global populations in a sustainable fashion is well within the limits of human ingenuity, to do so will require a radical transformation not only in the ways we provide energy, but of the economic system in which this takes place and the cultural outlook that underpins it (Heinberg 2010). Qatar and the other Gulf states may have a crucial role in providing the alternatives to a global energy system that is inherently unsustainable in many different ways.

Resource Depletion and Peak Supply

The energy supply for most of the industrialized world is fundamentally unsustainable as it relies on primary sources that cannot be replaced by natural processes (at least, not on timescales comparable with those of their use). This creates unavoidable issues of depletion and eventual scarcity, which have in recent years attained a high global profile through increased attention to the phenomenon known as peak oil (Hubbert 1971; Hirsch, Bezdek and Wendling 2005). Peak oil is the point at which supplies can no longer increase in response to increased demand. This may be evident on a variety of scales: for instance, the peak in production from a particular field, from all sources within a single country, and in total worldwide production.

At whatever scale, peak supply is the outcome of complicated inter-actions among several factors. Chief among these are: the size of the re-source; its spatial distribution; its accessibility; the extraction technologies available; the financial costs of extraction relative to market prices; the energetic cost of extraction relative to energy yield; and the environmen-tal and social costs of extraction, transport and use. Difficulties in exact measurement of these variables, some of which are plastic, mean exact prediction of the date of peak oil is impossible. Some have dismissed the prospect of impending oil shortages resulting from either resource depletion or technological constraints, while acknowledging that political factors may in practice restrict supplies (Radetzki 2010). The most recent authoritative study at the time of writing suggests a strong likelihood of a global peak in oil production from conventional sources by 2030, and a significant risk by 2020 (Sorrell et al. 2009).

Peak oil may be the most pressing supply problem, but similar issues apply to other non-renewable fuels. Reported coal reserves are far higher, but sharp rises in demand in growing Asian economies, notably India and China, threaten a short-term global supply crunch (Froggatt and Lahn 2010: 11). Optimistic predictions for future supply may be based on suspect data, and ignore interactions with peak oil that will increase demand for liquid fuels derived from coal (Energy Watch Group 2010a). Supplies of natural gas are more abundant relative to current levels of use, but escalating demand due to the replacement of many current uses of oil with liquefied natural gas is likely to bring about peaks in supply from conventional sources within the next few decades (Bentley 2002). Contrary to reports by the nuclear industry that supplies of uranium feedstocks for nuclear fission are abundant, several independent analyses suggest scarcity within the next few years (Dittmar 2009a; Energy Watch Group 2010b).

Oil, gas, coal and uranium supplied over 90 per cent of the energy traded on world markets in 2008 (IEA 2009). The prospect of their deple-tion raises serious concerns over security of global energy supply (Frogatt and Lahn 2010). In the short term, this will probably benefit Qatar's econ-omy. Although known oil reserves are relatively modest, current exploi-tation rates are also reasonably low, so domestic supply is secure in the immediate future. Meantime, increased global demand for natural gas and its liquid fuel derivates will increase the value of the country's vast gas fields.

There is, in summary, an emerging (but not unchallenged) consensus that global supplies of the most important primary energy sources are on the point of, or very close to, becoming increasingly constrained. Scarcity of supply increases the search for technical improvements in the extraction of oil and other resources, but these inevitably have their costs, financial and otherwise. A key economic consideration for the energy industry, also relevant to energy supply and sustainability more general, is the Energy Return On Investment (EROI). As energy sources become more scarce and difficult to extract, more energy has to be invested for each unit of energy successfully extracted, leading to diminishing returns (Sorrell et al. 2009: 4; Vernon 2010). In addition, it is becoming increasingly clear that diminishing reserves increase the broader social and environmental costs of energy extraction.

Social and Environmental Impacts

In addition to direct depletion there are broader sustainability issues with all of the common non-renewable energy sources. The most pressing and high profile is global warming resulting from the release of carbon dioxide and other greenhouse gases in the combustion of fossil fuels. Although unique in both its scale of impact and political profile, danger-ous anthropogenic climate change is only one form of the social and en-vironmental damage associated with the extraction, transportation and combustion of non-renewable energy sources and disposal of associated waste products.

In the first instance, damage inevitably occurs in accessing uranium fossil fuels and uranium from deposits under the earth's surface and, in many cases, separating them from other materials. The infrastructure associated with extraction, purification, and transportation is often envi-ronmentally and social damaging in its own right. For instance, in the Ec-uadorian Amazon both people and wildlife have been severely impacted by activities associated with the exploitation of large oil and gas reserves that overlap with areas of extremely high biodiversity and territories of indigenous peoples (Finer et al. 2008).

The direct environmental impacts of extraction are unevenly distrib-uted, and for obvious reasons tend to be felt most strongly in the vicin-ity of sites where these resources occur. It might be supposed that these would, to some extent, be compensated by the economic benefits, but in reality this is rarely so. The term *resource curse* characterizes a common, apparently paradoxical situation where for a variety of reasons an abun-dance of valuable natural resources undermines both sustainability and development (Gilberthorpe, Clarke and Sillitoe, chapter 7, this volume). It is a threat that the Gulf states are aware of, and seek to avoid. How-ever, situations where sovereignty over resources and clear political vision combine to ensure that revenues are directed towards genuinely sustainable development, in line with the aspirations of the Qatar National Vision 2030 (see Tan, Al-Khalaqi and Al-Khulaifi, chapter 2, this volume), are the exception rather than the rule.

Both environmental and social impacts of extraction often escalate as resources become more scarce, creating pressure for extraction in places where such activity is more inappropriate due to environmental and/ or cultural constraints, remoteness and/or inaccessibility, difficulty and danger of extraction, or high costs of extraction of sub-optimal resources. Remote and inaccessible sites require more extensive and possibly risky transportation infrastructure, often through areas such as tropical forests ill suited to such development. The Gulf of Mexico oil spill in 2010, which resulted from a failure of inadequately tested technology for deepwater extraction, illustrates the dangers of extracting fossil fuels from technically challenging sites. In addition, exploitation of sub-optimal supplies tips the financial and energetic balance sheets away from non-renewable sources, leading to price increases, declines in profitability and reduced EROI. The extraction of oil from the Canadian tar sands exhibits all of these, consuming vast quantities of natural gas and fresh water while having devastating local social and environmental impacts (Walsh and Stainsby 2010). The tar sands perhaps exemplify how the incidental costs of continued dependence on fossil fuels and nuclear power in the face of declining supplies are becoming ever more dramatic.

Climate Change

Qatar, along with 193 other countries, is among the signatories to the UN Framework Convention on Climate Change, drafted in 1992 as an outcome of the Rio Earth Summit, and at the time of writing is bidding to host the eighteenth UN Conference of the Parties on Climate Change, to be held during 2012. The prominence of climate change in international politics reflects a broad scientific consensus, crystallized through the ongoing work of the Intergovernmental Panel on Climate Change (IPCC 2007), that atmospheric pollution resulting from human activities is already changing the global climate, that these changes will become more dramatic unless urgent measures are taken to mitigate these effects, and the consequences in the absence of such measures could be sufficiently severe to threaten the biosphere's capacity to support the majority of present-day human societies, and perhaps even human life at all.[2] The major cause is the release of the greenhouse gas carbon dioxide[3] through changes in land-use patterns (especially deforestation and other removal of natural vegetation cover), and above all through the burning of fossil fuels.

Carbon naturally circulates in vast quantities through the atmosphere, soils, waters and tissues of living organisms, in what is known as the active carbon cycle. Planetary-scale homeostatic mechanisms balancing the relationship between the removal of carbon dioxide from the atmosphere through photosynthesis in green plants and algae and its production by all living things in respiration and the decay of organic matter, keep atmospheric levels of carbon dioxide within fairly narrow limits. This in turn helps regulate the temperature of the earth's surface, as the concentration of carbon dioxide and other greenhouse gases affects the atmosphere's capacity to retain heat. Fossil fuels represent a vast global store of carbon that is inert and isolated in the inactive carbon cycle, having been sequestered through geological processes that contribute to planetary self-regulation over far-longer timescales than those of the active carbon cycle. Whenever fossil fuels are extracted and burnt, the carbon they contain moves irreversibly from the inactive into the active carbon cycle. Rising concentrations of carbon dioxide in the atmosphere make it more efficient at retaining heat, leading to a rise in average global temperatures.

To the limited extent that international action on global warming has achieved anything at all, it has overwhelmingly focused on the dubious practice of carbon trading. Critics have noted that governments and the business community have been far quicker to establish carbon markets than to establish ways to link these to emissions reductions (Smith 2007; Lohmann 2008). Their ineffectiveness non-withstanding, the allocation of permits to businesses represents the privatization of what was previously a global commons, the capacity of the biosphere to absorb increasing quantities of carbon in the active cycle and so buffer resulting climatic changes (Carbon Trade Watch 2007). This represents a corruption of the logic behind ideas such as 'cap and share' or 'cap and trade', which link implementation and enforcement of a global climate-change mitigation strategy to formal mutualization of the atmospheric commons (Tickell 2008; Matthews 2010; Large 2010: 167–168). While such schemes could, if not appropriated by business interests, both promote fair allocation of responsibilities for decarbonizing global energy supplies fairly and compensate for historical and current inequities in the distributions of the costs and benefits of industrialization, they do not directly address the causes of global warming.

There are two ways to stop moving carbon from the inactive to the active carbon cycle: stop burning fossil fuels, or find some way to return the carbon emitted to the inactive cycle. Options for reducing overall global levels of carbon emissions divide into demand-side measures (reducing total energy demand) and supply-side measures (shifting to less polluting energy sources). Regarding supply-side measures, increased use of natural gas is widely considered an important transitional step (e.g. IEA 2010, 2011), as carbon dioxide emissions per unit of energy released in its combustion are roughly one-third to one-half that associated with other fossil fuels. Qatari reserves contain gas mixed with a high proportion of carbon dioxide. Release of this entrained carbon dioxide during extraction compromises this advantage. It is responsible, together with extremely high levels of individual energy consumption, for Qatar having the highest recorded per capita carbon dioxide emissions of any country in the world, 55.43 tonnes per person during 2007 according to UN data.[4]

Governments and energy companies are giving serious attention to Carbon Capture and Storage (CCS) technology, which by removing carbon dioxide from the mix of exhaust gases at power plants purports to reduce the quantity of carbon released to the active cycle in the combustion of fossil fuels. However, there are doubts over the technical and economic feasibility of all aspects of CCS, especially the prospect of retrofitting existing power stations. The removal and sequestration of entrained carbon dioxide in natural gas reserves, as is currently under development in Qatar, appears one of the more robust applications (Hardisty, Sivapalan and Brooks 2011).

CCS is the most prominent among a range of geo-engineering technologies that have been proposed to address climate change not by direct mitigation of its causes (i.e. reducing levels of greenhouse-gas emissions), but by eliminating its effects. Proposed techniques are generally based on one of two strategies: removing carbon dioxide from the atmosphere, of which CCS is just one of the less ludicrous examples, or by reflecting solar radiation away from the earth. Such technologies are technologically and economically unproven, may raise the prospect of unanticipated environmental side effects and in addition face considerable social and political barriers to their implementation (Shepherd 2009). Critics have also pointed out the folly of relying on non-existent technologies, whose potential consequences cannot be predicted, as the only prospect of avoiding potential environmental catastrophe (Fauset 2008; ETC Group 2010).

Even if it was technologically possible to use the energy in fossil fuels without releasing greenhouse gases into the atmosphere emission, and despite the advantages of natural gas as a less carbon-intensive fuel, continued use of fossil fuels can at best be a stopgap measure. High quality and readily accessible reserves are inherently limited, as already pointed out, and the escalating social and environmental costs of accessing more marginal sources suggest we should cease their exploitation sooner than economic considerations alone might dictate. The only technically proven and long-term prospect for supply-side mitigation is the use of renewable energy technologies.

Renewable Energy Technologies

Renewable energy comes from sources that cannot be depleted, at least on human timescales and/or relative to the intensity of use. The majority of these originally derive from the sun, which can be used directly for heat (solar thermal), converted into electricity (photovoltaic) or used to drive large-scale thermal generation of electricity (concentrating solar power). Solar power can also be harvested indirectly as wind, waves, water flows in rivers (hydro power) or as biomass when converted into the tissues of plants or other organisms. Two other potential sources of renewable energy are heat from the earth's crust (geothermal) and tidal power from the interaction of the earth and moon. The total quantity of energy in each of these is enormous relative to current human consumption, but there are practical and technological limitations to our ability to make use of them on the scale required to match current global demand, let alone accommodate increases.

The main barrier to utilization of solar power is its relatively low intensity (energy per unit area), meaning that it requires large surfaces for energy capture. This is a particular problem with photovoltaic conversion, as the relatively high unit cost of cells and panels typically makes prices several times higher than conventional forms of electricity generation, even under optimum climatic conditions. Existing photovoltaic technology also relies on rare minerals that are in limited global supply (Barras 2009). Concentrated solar power, in which a large reflecting area concentrates sunlight onto a central thermal electricity generator, has greater potential for implementation on large scales in areas with reliably high levels of insolation (Teske 2010: 55). In the Gulf region especially, it may promise a sustainable energy future beyond oil and gas.

Wind energy is also conducive to generation on large scales, particularly offshore. Onshore wind is the only renewable power source that is price competitive with conventional generation technologies under current market conditions. Atmospheric modelling suggests that installing sufficient wind generation to provide for current global energy needs would risk atmospheric disruption comparable in magnitude to some of the worst predictions for global warming (Kleidon 2011). The same conclusions also apply to wave and tidal power: all three are part of natural energy systems that are vital to the earth's capacity to support life, but which are poorly understood. Axel Kleidon's analysis is preliminary, but suggests that there are limits to their sustainable exploitation, meaning that they cannot expand indefinitely to accommodate rising human demand.

Of other renewable energy sources, geothermal and hydro are possible only under specific conditions that occur in a limited number of places.

Furthermore, large-scale hydro can disrupt hydrological cycles and dependent ecological processes and economic activities. The use of biofuels is limited by maximum sustainable harvests of natural sources, and in the case of agrofuels (cultivated plants grown specifically as fuel crops) by the available space for cultivation. Major problems with the first generation of agrofuels included competition with food crops, displacement of small-scale producers and conversion of biodiverse habitats to agricultural monocultures (Levidow and Paul 2010). New generations of biofuels address some of these problems, but the environmental impacts of large-scale implementation remain unclear (Williams et al. 2009). Limitations on biofuel production also limit the use of liquid fuels for transportation. Most projected future energy scenarios foresee widespread electrification of vehicular transport, with vehicles powered by either chemical batteries or hydrogen cells charged from renewable electricity sources.

Nuclear fission merits a mention here only because it is often characterized, spuriously, as a 'low-carbon', 'green' or even 'sustainable' power source. The reason for this is that, unlike fossil fuel combustion, it does not directly produce greenhouse gases. However, full life-cycle analysis – taking into account the mining and refining of uranium, the construction, operation and decommissioning of power plants, and the processing and disposal of wastes including highly dangerous radioactive direct products of the fissioning process and other materials contaminated by exposure to radiation – indicates financial social and environmental costs of sufficient magnitude that the UK government's Sustainable Development Commission argued against nuclear playing a role in the country's energy future (SDC 2006). One of the commission's members publically criticized the government for ignoring this advice (Jackson 2008). The recent incident at Fukushima nuclear power station in Japan has renewed worldwide concerns over the safety of nuclear power, notably in Germany, which in response has discontinued its nuclear programme.[5]

Nuclear fusion is often cited as a long-term solution to problems of energy supply. It could, in theory, provide a long-term source of clean energy, with deuterium, abundant in seawater, as its main fuel, and inert helium as its main product. In practice, claims as to its potential have not translated into progress towards commercial production, and may be based on false premises (Dittmar 2009b).

Existing, proven renewable energy technologies, whether market-ready or not, all have inherent limitations in terms of total supply capacity. Nonetheless, several recent reports show the technical feasibility of meeting proportions as high as 95 per cent of the world's energy needs from renewable sources by 2050, with economic as well as environmental and social benefits (Teske 2010; Singer 2011; UNEP 2011). Plausible technical scenarios for a secure, sustainable energy supply have been devised for Britain (Kemp and Wexler 2010) and a number of other countries, based on maximizing uptake of renewables and eliminating surplus demand, without any reduction in quality of life or economic output.[6] It is possible to imagine similar solutions for the Gulf states. The Qatari government's commitment to exploring such options is demonstrated by such steps as investment in energy research at Qatar Science and Technology Park,[7] collaborations on sustainability research with Chevron[8] and Texas A&M University,[9] along with, surprisingly, the plan to embed solar-thermal generation in stadia built for the 2022 FIFA World Cup.[10] Such commitments are vital if Qatar is successfully to make the transition to a zero-carbon energy economy. In addition to infrastructural development, it will require the embedding of technical knowledge and capacity for research and innovation in domestic institutions. Current investment in 'human capital' and the drive to develop a knowledge-based economy are consistent with these demands (Rahman, chapter 3, this volume).

This chapter does not anticipate the results of these endeavours, nor seek to guide them. It outlines a rough scenario, conscious that the devil is in the details and it is far simpler to propose broad general solutions than to address any of the myriad practical challenges implementation of a national sustainable energy strategy will involve. One obvious step is to take maximum advantage of the potential to exploit indigenous renewable energy sources. Large-scale renewable generation is already possible with concentrating solar power and wind, especially offshore, and tidal and wave power will both become increasingly viable in coming decades. Dispersed small-scale generation using solar thermal, wind, photovoltaic and geothermal (heat pumps) energy can be installed as appropriate to local conditions. It will be necessary to ensure transfer of the technical skills and manufacturing capacity necessary for their continued operation and, where necessary, expansion. Longer term there will be increasing imperatives to minimize dependence on external sources of raw materials by maximizing recycling and efficiency in production methods. Demand-side measures will also be important, minimizing energy consumption throughout the country through appropriate design of building, transportation and manufacturing infrastructure and maximizing reliance on local sources of goods, materials and expertise. While all this is being put in place, Qatar can maximize the use of gas as a transition fuel while minimizing the carbon dioxide emissions and other environmental impacts of its production. Finally, such a programme would be most effective if it integrates further sustainability concerns – especially environmental damage and equity of access to energy supplies – at all stages.

Energy and Sustainability

The technical means exist to produce energy in a way that is more or less sustainable, and appropriate government strategies for investment and research in Qatar mean there is no reason the country cannot make full use of them. A complete switch to renewable sources, closure of production loops through recycling and re-use to minimize input of primary materials in their manufacture, development of the research and production base to maintain this, and minimizing all ancillary environmental damage are all within the country's technical and financial means. However, energy and sustainability have such a complex and intricate relationship that such steps, although imperative, will not be sufficient by themselves.

Throughout the fossil fuel era, expansion of the global economy and incessant rises in humanity's global energy requirements have gone hand in hand. They have also been accompanied by dramatic and worrying declines in the capacity of natural systems to provide vital and irreplaceable ecosystem services (Millennium Ecosystems Assessment 2005; Gilberthorpe, Clarke and Sillitoe, chapter 7, this volume). Troublingly, and despite the translation into national legislation of concerted attention to sustainability in international fora (Al Othman and Clarke, chapter 5, this volume), the link between these phenomena may be intrinsic. The prospect of decoupling economic growth from negative environmental impacts, although an explicit or implicit assumption in much mainstream discourse on sustainability, may in fact be impossible (Jackson 2009). There is no evidence that it is achievable in theory, let alone in practice. While growth is an inescapable precondition for stability in all existing macro-economic models, and no economy has ever grown in size while simultaneously reducing either its carbon or ecological footprint.

Increases of greenhouse gas concentrations to potentially dangerous levels and depletion of readily accessible sources of fossil fuel and uranium feedstocks are the most urgent symptoms of this dilemma, but by no means the only ones. Even in the unlikely event that technical ingenuity allows us to circumvent both the energy and climate crises, future problems resulting from the accumulation of other pollutants, depletion of vital resources such as soil, water or minerals, or the undermining of vital ecological cycles, will eventually prove intractable (Heinberg 2007). The industrialized world's relationship with energy is inherently unsustainable, both in its direct implications, and in its connection with an economic model that is unsustainable in myriad ways.

To date, this situation has persisted through a combination of material, political and cultural factors. Materially, the ability to harness and use large quantities of energy has exaggerated the potential for technological solutions to environmental and social problems to unrealistic levels (Heinberg 2010). Politically, the intertwining of energy-intensive industrial infrastructure with social institutions, including those of governance, creates barriers to escaping fossil fuel dependency (Unruh 2000). In addition, colonial and post-colonial inequalities of political power, and hence control of resources, have allowed this situation to persist: the 'first world' has historically been able to live beyond its means through access to the resources of the 'third world' (Holling, Berkes and Folke 1998). Export of the social and environmental externalities associated with industrialized economies has also contributed to the persistence of the illusion of technical control. Culturally, this is reinforced by the emergence of consumption as a dominant feature of social life (Filk 2009): those living in industrialized economies increasingly seek comfort, status and meaning not in human relationships and social achievement, but in the purchase and accumulation of material goods (Jackson 2006). 'Carbon lock-in' is not only the socio-technical problem identified in its original characterization (Unruh 2000), but has cultural roots that deepen as the material affordances of the industrial world become ever more pervasive features of personal identity and social life.

Dominant trends in international development globalize not only the technical aspects of carbon lock-in (Unruh and Carrillo-Hermosilla 2006), but its institutional and, increasingly, cultural correlates. The energy-intensive infrastructure that supports continual economic growth, and individual aspirations to ever-increasing levels of material consumption that are both driven by and drive it, are becoming not only normalized as the only route to increased well-being, but naturalized as a universal and hence unavoidable human aspiration. Globally, as at other levels, the prospects for escaping carbon lock-in occur at its margins (Unruh 2002). However, the ongoing expansion of capitalism, and the 'techno-institutional complex' that underpins it, is undermining the socio-cultural diversity upon which this depends (Henfrey 2009). In current circumstances the role of countries such as Qatar, whose control over valuable primary energy sources is translating into increasing levels of economic and political power, extends far beyond their borders (also see Darwish, chapter 4, this volume).

We urgently need alternatives to the globally dominant model of relationships among energy, economy and society that has become environmentally and socially dysfunctional (cf. Sillitoe, conclusion this volume). The search for these alternatives depends upon diversity of outlooks, and the Muslim world is still, for now, a part of the globe that retains the potential to deliver, or at least inform them. Just as Western economists have increasingly turned to Islamic finance as an alternative to their own failing economic theory (see Wilson, chapter 8, this volume, and c.f. Gilberthorpe and Sillitoe 2009), and paralleling how attention to the human dimensions of biodiversity conservation has revealed its inextricable links with cultural diversity (Maffi 2001; Sillitoe and Al Shawi, chapter 10; Heckler, chapter 18, both this volume) and a role in this for traditional Arab environmentalisms (El Guindi, chapter 19; Al-Ghanim, chapter 20, both this volume), distinctively Muslim energy sociologies may contribute significantly to the pluralistic global energy culture that will be a necessary foundation of future energy sustainability.

Whether or not the Gulf region can deliver on this potential remains to be seen, and will depend on both international and domestic policy. Internationally, it cannot be achieved by emulating either the infrastructural or economic systems that characterize industrialized society during the fossil fuel era (see Alraouf and Clarke, chapter 13, this volume). Domestically, it is likely to depend on a politics of arrangements that reconcile social responsibility with inclusion and freedom of individual expression (c.f. Porter, chapter 17; Clarke and Almannai, chapter 15, both this volume). There is substantial evidence that sustainability, in any form, is incompatible with hierarchy (Bookchin 2005; Maturana and Valera 1980: xxiv–xxx), and no society that legally discriminates among citizens on any grounds or denies full participation to all (such as long-term resident migrants) can plausibly claim to draw upon its full range of internal diversity. While this chapter does not propose to comment on the morals underlying aspects of domestic policy, with their complex Islamic roots, the practical concerns of establishing a sustainable energy economy in Qatar may compel their reconsideration. The political and social uprisings taking place in many parts of the Arab world at the time of writing – the so-called Arab Spring of 2011, which some commentators have compared to the occupation of global financial centres on Wall Street – show the potential for such radical review.

Notes

1. With a few notable exceptions, such as Danish wind power, Norwegian hydropower, and geothermal energy in El Salvador.
2. Ongoing independent analysis of latest findings and debates on climate change is available at http://publicinterest.org.uk/climate-comms/.
3. Carbon dioxide is neither the only nor the most potent greenhouse gas; it is however the most abundant and the most significant in terms of the links between energy, climate and sustainability. Space constraints limit the discussion here to carbon dioxide emissions associated with energy production.

4. http://unstats.un.org/unsd/environment/air_co2_emissions.htm (accessed 31 May 2011).
5. http://www.bbc.co.uk/news/world-europe-13592208 (accessed 31 May 2011).
6. See http://www.zerocarbonbritain.com/index.php/zcb-world (accessed 31 May 2011).
7. http://www.explore-qatar.com/qatar-today/towards-sustainable-energy (accessed 31 May 2011).
8. http://www.chevron.com/news/currentissues/ccsee/ (accessed 31 May 2011).
9. http://qwe.qatar.tamu.edu/about-qwe/ (accessed 31 May 2011).
10. http://english.aljazeera.net/sport/2010/04/2010428193515919564.html (accessed 31 May 2011).

References

Abramsky, K. 2010. *Sparking a Worldwide Energy Revolution.* Edinburgh: AK Press.

Balée, W. L. 1994. *Footprints of the Forest: Ka'apor Ethnobotany – The Historical Ecology of Plant Utilization by an Amazonian People.* New York: Columbia University Press.

——— (ed.). 1998. *Advances in Historical Ecology.* New York: Columbia University Press.

Barras, C. 2009. 'Why Sustainable Power is Unsustainable,' *New Scientist,* 6 February. http://www.newscientist.com/article/dn16550-why-sustainable-power-is-unsustainable.html (accessed 30 May 2011).

Barbour, I., et al. 2010 (1980). 'Energy and the Rise of American Industrial Society.' In *The Energy Reader,* ed. L. Nader. Chichester: Wiley.

Bentley, R. W. 2002. 'Global Oil and Gas Depletion: An Overview.' *Energy Policy* 30: 189–205.

Bookchin, M. 2005. *The Ecology of Freedom: The Emergence and Dissolution of Hierarchy.* Oakland, CA: AK Press.

Boserup, E. 1965. *The Conditions of Agricultural Growth: The Economics of Agrarian Change Under Population Pressure.* London: Allen and Unwin.

Carbon Trade Watch. 2007. *The Sky is Not the Limit.* Amsterdam: Transnational Institute.

Dittmar, M. 2009a. 'The Future of Nuclear Energy: Facts and Fiction Chapter II: What is known about secondary uranium sources?' arXiv:0908.3075v1 [physics .soc-ph] (accessed 31 May 2011).

———. 2009b. 'The Future of Nuclear Energy: Facts and Fiction Chapter IV: Energy from breeder reactors and from fusion?' arXiv:0911.2628v1 [physics .soc-ph] (accessed 31 May 2011).

Ellen, R. F. 1982. *Environment, Subsistence and System: The Ecology of Small-Scale Social Formations.* Cambridge: Cambridge University Press.

Energy Watch Group. 2010a. 'Peak Coal.' In *Sparking a Worldwide Energy Revolution*, ed. K. Abramsky, 431–438. Edinburgh: AK Press.

———. 2010b. 'Peak Uranium.' In *Sparking a Worldwide Energy Revolution*, ed. K. Abramsky, 398–405. Edinburgh: AK Press.

ETC Group. 2010. *Geopiracy: The Case Against Geoengineering*. Ottawa: ETC Group Communiqué #103.

Fauset, C. 2008. *Techno-Fixes: A Critical Guide to Climate Change Technologies*. London: Corporate Watch.

Filk, R. 2009. 'Consuming Ourselves to Death: The Anthropology of Consumer Culture and Climate Change.' In *Anthropology and Climate Change: From Encounters to Actions*, eds. S. A. Crate and M. Nuttall, 265–276. Walnut Creek: Left Coast Press.

Finer, M., et al. 2008. 'Oil and Gas Projects in the Western Amazon: Threats to Wilderness, Biodiversity, and Indigenous Peoples.' *PLoS ONE* 3 (8): e2932. doi:10.1371/journal.pone.0002932 (accessed 31 May 2011).

Froggatt, A., and G. Lahn. 2010. *Sustainable Energy Security: Strategic Risks and Opportunities for Business*. London: Lloyds.

Geertz, C. 1963. *Agricultural Involution: The Process of Ecological Change in Indonesia*. Berkeley: University of California Press, for Association of Asian Studies.

Gilberthorpe, E., and P. Sillitoe. 2009. 'A Failure of Social Capital: Lessons from Papua New Guinea in the Current Economic Crisis.' *Anthropology News* 50 (7): 15–16.

Hardisty, P., E. M. Sivapalan and P. Brooks. 2011. 'The Environmental and Economic Sustainability of Carbon Capture and Storage.' *International Journal of Environmental Research and Public Health* 8: 1460–1477.

Heinberg, R. 2007. *Peak Everything*. Forest Row: Clairview.

———. 2010. 'Beyond the Limits to Growth.' In *The Post Carbon Reader*, eds. R. Heinberg and D. Lerch, 3–12. Healdsburg: Watershed Media.

Henfrey, T. 2009. *Educating and Engaging Communites: Lessons from Biodiversity Conservation*. Paper presented at RESOLVE conference, London.

Hirsch, R. L., R. Bezdek and R. Wendling. 2005. *Peaking Of World Oil Production: Impacts, Mitigation, and Risk Management*. US Department of Energy, National Energy Technology Laboratory.

Holling, C. S., F. Berkes and C. Folke. 1998. 'Science, Sustainability and Resource Management.' In *Linking Social and Ecological Systems: Management Practices and Social Mechanisms for Building Resilience*, eds. F. Berkes and C. Folke, 342–362. Cambridge: Cambridge University Press.

Hubbert, M. K. 1971. 'The Energy Resources of the Earth.' *Scientific American* 225 (September): 60–70.

International Energy Agency (IEA). 2009. *World Energy Outlook 2009*. Paris.

———. 2010. *World Energy Outlook 2010*. Paris.

———. 2011. *Are We Entering a Golden Age of Gas?* Special Report, World Energy Outlook. Paris.

Intergovernmental Panel on Climate Change (IPCC). 2007. *Climate Change 2007: Synthesis Report. Summary for Policymakers*. http://www.ipcc.ch/pdf/assessment-report/ar4/syr/ar4_syr_spm.pdf (accessed 31 May 2011).

Jackson, T. 2006. 'Consuming Paradise? Towards a Socio-Cultural Psychology of Sustainable Consumption.' In *Earthscan Reader in Sustainable Consumption*, ed. T. Jackson, 367–396. London: Earthscan.

———. 2008. 'A Blatant Failure of Moral Vision,' *The Guardian*, 16 January 2008. http://www.guardian.co.uk/environment/2008/jan/16/nuclearpower.ene rgy (accessed 31 May 2011).

———. 2009. *Prosperity Without Growth.* London: Earthscan.

Kemp, M., and J. Wexler (eds.). 2010. *Zero Carbon Britain 2030.* Machynlleth: Centre for Alternative Technology.

Kleidon, A. 2011. 'How does the earth system generate and maintain thermo-dynamic disequilibrium and what does it imply for the future of the planet?' Submitted contribution to Theme Issue 'Influence of Nonlinearity and Randomness in Climate Prediction' of *Philosophical Transactions of the Royal Society A.* arXiv:1103.2014v1 (accessed 30 May 2011).

Large, M. 2010. *Common Wealth: For a Free, Equal, Mutual and Sustainable Society.* Stroud: Hawthorn Press.

Levidow, L., and H. Paul. 2010. 'Global Agrofuel Crops as Dispossession.' In *Sparking a Worldwide Energy Revolution*, ed. K. Abramsky, 439–452. Edinburgh: AK Press.

Lohmann, L. 2008. 'Carbon Trading, Climate Justice and the Production of Ignorance: Ten Examples.' *Development* 51: 359–365.

Maffi, L. (ed.). 2001. *On Biocultural Diversity: Linking Language, Knowledge and the Environment.* Washington, DC, and London: Smithsonian Institution Press.

Matthews, L. 2010. 'Cap and Share – Simple is Beautiful.' In *Fleeing Vesuvius: Overcoming the Risks of Economic and Environmental Collapse*, eds. R. Douthwaite and G. Fallon, 244–256. Gabriola Island, British Columbia: New Society Publishers.

Maturana, H. R., and F. J. Valera. 1980. *Autopoiesis and Cognition: The Realisation of the Living.* Dordrecht: D. Reidel Publishing Company (Boston Studies in the Philosophy of Science, vol. 42).

Meadows, D. H., et al. 1972. *The Limits to Growth: A Report for the Club of Rome's Project on the Predicament of Mankind.* New York: Universe Books.

Meadows, D. H., J. Randers and D. L. Meadows. 2004. *Limits to Growth: The 30-Year Update.* White River Junction, VT: Chelsea Green Pub. Co.

McGovern, T. H. 1994. 'Management for Extinction in Norse Greenland.' In *Historical Ecology. Cultural Knowledge and Changing Landscapes*, ed. C. Crumley, 127–154. Santa Fe, NM: School of American Research Press.

Millennium Ecosystems Assessment. 2005. *Ecosystems and Human Well-Being: Synthesis.* Washington, DC: Island Press.

Radetzki, M. 2010. 'Peak Oil and Other Threatening Peaks: Chimeras Without Substance.' *Energy Policy*, doi:10.1016/j.enpol.2010.07.049 (accessed 31 May 2011).

Rappaport, R. A. 1979. *Ecology, Meaning and Ritual.* Berkeley, CA: North Atlantic Books.

Santley, R. S., T. Killion and M. Lycett. 1986. 'On the Maya Collapse.' *Journal of Anthropological Research* 42 (2): 123–160.

Schmidt, P. R. 1994. 'Historical Ecology and Landscape Transformation in Eastern Equatorial Africa.' In *Historical Ecology: Cultural Knowledge and Changing Land-*

scapes, ed. C. Crumley, 99–126. Santa Fe, NM: School of American Research Press.

Sustainable Development Commission (SDC). 2006. *The Role of Nuclear Power in a Low Carbon Economy*. London. http://www.sd-commission.org.uk/publications.php?id=344 (accessed 31 May 2011).

Shepherd, J. 2009. *Geoengineering the Climate*. London: The Royal Society.

Singer, S. (ed.). 2011. *The Energy Report*. Gland: World Wide Fund for Nature.

Smith, K. 2007. *The Carbon Neutral Myth*. Amsterdam: Transnational Institute.

Sorrell, S., et al. 2009. *Global Oil Depletion: An Assessment of the Evidence for a Near Term Peak in Oil Production*. London: UK Energy Research Centre.

Stepp, J. R., et al. 2003. 'Remarkable Properties of Human Ecosystems.' *Conservation Ecology* 7 (3): 11. http://www.consecol.org/vol7/iss3/art11.

Teske, S. (ed.). 2010. *Energy Revolution*. Amsterdam: Greenpeace International.

Tickell, O. 2008. *Kyoto 2*. London: Zed Books.

United Nations Environment Program (UNEP). 2011. *Towards a Green Economy: Pathways to Sustainable Development and Poverty Eradication*. www.unep.org/greeneconomy (accessed 31 May 2011).

Unruh, G. 2000. 'Understanding Carbon Lock-In.' *Energy Policy* 28 (12): 817–830.

———. 2002. 'Escaping Carbon Lock-In.' *Energy Policy* 30 (4): 317–325.

Unruh, G., and J. Carrillo-Hermosilla. 2006. 'Globalizing Carbon Lock-In.' *Energy Policy* 34 (10): 1185–1197.

Vernon, C. 2010. 'Future Energy Availability: The Importance of "Net Energy".' In *Fleeing Vesuvius: Overcoming the Risks of Economic and Environmental Collapse*, eds. R. Douthwaite and G. Fallon, 34–42. Gabriola Island, British Columbia: New Society Publishers.

Walsh, S., and M. Stainsby. 2010. 'The Smell of Money: Alberta's Tar Sands.' In *Sparking a Worldwide Energy Revolution*, ed. K. Abramsky, 333–344. Edinburgh: AK Press.

Williams, P. R., et al. 2009. 'Environmental and Sustainability Factors Associated With Next-Generation Biofuels in the U.S.: What Do We Really Know?' *Environmental Science and Technology* 43 (13): 4763–4775.

White, L. 1959. *The Evolution of Culture*. New York: McGraw-Hill.

CHAPTER 7

Money Rain

The Resource Curse in Two Oil and Gas Economies

Emma Gilberthorpe, Sarah F. Clarke and Paul Sillitoe

Concern for the relationship between mineral extraction and economic development has grown since evidence emerged in the 1980s and 1990s to suggest that resource endowment was not as favourable as previously thought (Auty 1993; Sachs and Warner 1999; Gylfason 2001). Evidence of a 'resource curse' challenged existing predictions that mineral[1] wealth would stimulate growth; such predictions were based on the success of the primary industry model[2] applied by conventional economic analysts in the US, Canada and Australia (Rostow 1960; Gelb 1988: 33; Ross 1999: 301). Unfortunately, predictions failed to consider either the 'contained' process of extraction or the consequences of extracting non-renewable resources. As the resource curse literature shows, mineral extraction occurs within enclaves that generate few economic and social linkages; and it is capital – rather than labour – intensive, with the resource becoming less economically viable the more embedded it is.

In this chapter we examine the ways in which the relationship that people develop with royalty income from oil/gas extraction is not necessarily conducive to socio-economic security, particularly when it is not adequately distributed across all segments of the community or linked to other economic activity. We refer to this royalty income as 'money rain' after a Papua New Guinea term that refers to the unearned cash royalties paid to indigenous landowners.[3] It is not dependency on foreign markets (for capital, labour and goods) or the temporary nature of resource income per se – issues identified in the resource curse literature – that concerns us here; what does concern us is the extensive cultural transformation resulting in social and economic insecurity and fundamental changes to the traditional fabric that occur in a 'resource cursed' society.

To illustrate the nature of this change we focus on the type of economy that results from mineral extraction, how it relates to other aspects of the 'resource curse' and the implications of mineral endowment for human relationships. The dynamics of social organization and interaction in diverse global localities are more complex than governments, multinational corporations and donor agencies often realize. A more holistic view of resource exploitation is needed to tackle 'the curse', encompassing the social implications of the 'money rain' phenomenon that occurs in mineral economies where state mechanisms for managing resource rents take the form of indigenous benefits (royalties, services, compensation etc.) that are, crucially, unearned. In this chapter we explore the phenomenon of 'money rain' and the extent to which it applies in two mineral economies – Qatar and Papua New Guinea – with different experiences of the 'resource curse'. The aim is to compare a country often associated with 'the curse' (Papua New Guinea) to a country that is not (Qatar), and assess 'the curse' implications.

There are five characteristics that economists identify as symptomatic of the resource curse. They are: a confined economy, low formal employment, poor fiscal discipline, poor capital investment and low business development. While Papua New Guinea exhibits all of these, Qatar does not. Does this mean that Qatar is avoiding the negative consequences of unrestrained mineral extraction and unprecedented economic growth or will the social impacts, currently not adequately considered, result in the curse being visited on the nation in another form?

Qatar has the highest gross domestic product (GDP) per capita in the Arab world (IMF 2011) and one of the world's fastest growing economies,[4] and, consequently, together with other Gulf States, is rarely mentioned in reference to the resource curse. Yet, the social and cultural changes the country is experiencing are dramatic, having consequences for its long-term prosperity, taking prosperity not merely to be a function of economic wealth, but also encompassing social well-being, environmental sustainability and the degree to which cultural traditions are upheld. Change on the scale experienced by Qatar over the last two decades challenges some deep-rooted social values and conventions and raises the question: To what extent is economic progress synonymous to social progress? The key to avoiding the negative implications of 'money rain' in expanding the country's economic base is achieving a balance between modernity and tradition such that the country may reap the benefits of economic and social development without sacrificing the stabilizing effects of cultural continuity (QNDS 2011:35). The modern Arab, referred to by Saad Ibrahim (1982) as a 'mechanized Bedouin' – a term capturing the resilience and dynamics of traditional Bedouin culture – now jostles for space alongside millions of migrant workers brought in to keep rapid growth going with potentially dramatic social and environmental consequences for the nation.

Papua New Guinea, on the other hand, prior to 2010 had a much slower-growing economy, and unstable development and social indicators (AusAID 2011). It is often associated with the resource curse given the well-documented negative impacts emerging from the country's growing mineral sector (Auty 1993; Auty and Mikesell 1999). Imposed principles of landownership rights and royalty payment mechanisms have altered traditional relationships and caused fragmentation within established socio-political exchange networks, giving rise to resentment and hostility (Gilberthorpe 2007). This enmity is further increased when cash is no longer shared in traditional egalitarian ways but creamed off by a few who have adapted to the new contractual ways of doing business with oil-project operators. An examination of social factors such as kinship, descent and exchange patterns suggest that the 'money rain' phenomenon undermines social cohesion and sustainable relations, which none of the five macro-economic variables listed above address.

Scrutiny of the social consequences of 'the curse' draws attention to social accountability in debates about development in mineral economies and the implications of mineral endowment for socio-economic security. The experiences of Qatar and Papua New Guinea show how two diverse mineral-dependent states with dramatically different socio-political structures are threatened with fragmentation if the sole business model is that associated with primary industry capitalism. This chapter begins with an outline of the key aspects of the resource curse thesis. These are then applied to Qatar and Papua New Guinea to determine the extent to which each country's experience of the hydrocarbons industry conforms to the resource curse thesis. We draw out the similarities and differences between the two cases and highlight how the resource curse theory might be expanded to incorporate more fully the social and cultural implications of mineral extraction.

The Resource Curse Thesis

The term *mineral economies* refers to countries generating 'at least 8% of their GDP and 40% of their export earnings from the mineral sector' (Auty 1993: 3). They comprise approximately one-fifth of developing economies (Auty and Mikesell 1999), including those enjoying economic growth such as Korea, Botswana, Ecuador and Qatar, and those afflicted by corruption and conflict such as Nigeria, Sierra Leone, Bolivia and Papua New Guinea.

According to the standard economic model, increased GDP should lead to higher standards of living, employment, capital investment and growth of small and large businesses in the public and private sectors.

According to Simon Kuznets (1966: 247), this sustained rise builds the 'capacity to supply increasingly diverse economic goods' through the application of 'advancing technology and the institutional and ideological adjustments that it demands'. This view is popular with those who advocate diversification in governments' use of primary industry income to advance economic and social change (Solomon 2000; see also Auty and Mikesell 1999). The key features of such economic development, alongside diversification, are improved employment (building on knowledge and technology), improved fiscal management, capital investment and business development (see Iqbal 2006: 9; Auty 1993). It is the absence of these in many mineral economies that are said to be symptomatic of the resource curse.

The resource curse thesis (or 'paradox of plenty') refers to the observation that some regions and nations with an abundance of non-renewable natural resources such as minerals and fossil fuels, experience less economic growth and development, compared to those with fewer resources (Auty 1993, 2001; Karl 1997; Sachs and Warner 2001; Stevens 2003). According to Gylfason (2001: 848–849), a 10 per cent increase in the contribution of natural capital to a nation's total national wealth (comprising physical, human and natural capital), correlates with an average decrease of 1 per cent in per capita growth per annum compared to other nations. The curse afflicts countries that depend on extractive industry, such as mining. It frequently occurs in emerging capitalist-market economies following major natural resource discoveries, which are often not the blessings that many citizens assume. As politician Juan Alfonzo graphically put it following the discovery of oil in Venezuela: 'oil will bring us ruin … [oil is] the devil's excrement', and, in a similar vein, Sheik Yamani of Saudi Arabia commented: 'All in all, I wish we had discovered water' (cited in Ross 1999: 297).

Corruption is endemic, though not necessarily a given, in many resource-rich countries, and occurs in a wide range of ways. It arises where resource rights and income distribution mechanisms are unclear, often associated with countries without a robust system of governance and weak and unstable institutions that allow the illicit diversion of revenues. It may involve large sums of money. Those in political power may allocate a disproportionate share of the wealth received to a favoured few who, with a vested interest in such arrangements, see that they maintain their authority. Illegal extractive operations may occur through corrupt national politicians colluding with multinational companies that treat corporate responsibility lightly. Where there is weak governance politicians may see no need to promote conditions for economic growth or build up infrastructure beyond that necessary to the natural resource sector.

Corruption may be accompanied by abuses of human rights. The human rights' records of some resource cursed nations are poor with undemocratic, even authoritarian regimes. Political and military leaders control the levers of power and ensure such regimes continue.[5] It is here that serious corruption may feature, as those in government seek to keep those few with sufficient influence happy. In time the desire to control resources can lead to violence (Bannon and Collier 2003). Conflicts over control of resources and allocation of revenues can take many forms. Often they are covert struggles between government factions and ministries, which frequently feed corruption. Sometimes open 'resource wars' occur, as in Angola, with resource rich regions engaging in separatist struggles (Le Billon 2005).

Other commentators point to indirect impacts such as income inequality, contributing to poor economic growth (Papyrakis and Gerlagh 2003). Some resource-rich countries in Latin America and sub-Saharan Africa show signs of rising inequality, prompting some resource curse theorists to predict that depleting reserves will lead to economic decay and social unrest (Karl 1997). They argue that natural windfalls create governments that consume resource rents, triggering inflation, channelling only token dividends into infrastructure and services (Sachs and Warner 2001; Karl 1997; Ross 1999; Gylfason 2001; Auty 2001). But all is not doom and gloom. In resource-rich nations good governance may generate large revenues to foster growth and reduce poverty. A comparison of the political regimes of nations that rely heavily on non-renewable resources between 1800 and 2006 challenges the assumption that they are necessarily authoritarian; indeed the data suggest the reverse, that such countries are more likely to be democratic (Haber and Menaldo 2011). The Extractive Industries Transparency Initiative (EITI) is a coalition of governments, companies and civil society which aims to support improved governance in resource-rich countries through full disclosure of company payments and government revenues from oil, gas and mining.[6]

A related phenomenon is the 'rentier state', a country that derives a substantial part or all of its national revenue from the royalties or rents that it demands from foreign companies exploiting its natural resources (Beblawi and Luciani 1987; Dauderstädt and Schildberg 2006). Citizens may consequently enjoy low or even zero rates of taxation. This divorcing of public revenues from citizens' pockets can arguably promote irresponsible governance and even reinforce the effects of corruption. Subjects may be less watchful of fiscal policies or demanding of efficiencies in government, having a reduced incentive to concern themselves with how the government spends its rent as opposed to tax income, albeit derived from national resources. Moreover, those benefiting disproportionately from mineral resource income may consider an effective civil society a threat to their benefits and take steps to obstruct it.

A consequence of mineral reliance is that countries become heavily dependent on the price of a single commodity and gross domestic revenue becomes volatile through exposure to global market swings in that commodity. Additionally, other economic sectors become less competitive; for instance, as resource revenues cause the exchange rate of the national currency to appreciate, incentives to pursue other economic activities diminish (Van Wijnbergen 1984). This phenomenon became known as the 'Dutch disease' after the Netherlands' experience following the 1959 discovery of North Sea gas, the production of which increased the value of the Dutch Guilder, undermining the ability of exporters to compete internationally. As a result, the economy shrank and a recession occurred. Agriculture and manufacturing sectors are particularly vulnerable to becoming less competitive in world markets, increasing dependence on revenue from natural resource exploitation and vulnerability to price fluctuations. Crude oil prices illustrate the wide fluctuations that can occur, varying between 1999 and 2009 from US$10 to over US$150 a barrel. Recurrent booms and busts further increase exchange rate volatility. Such volatility can seriously upset government planning.

Furthermore, primary extractive industries tend to operate as enclaves with few connections to the rest of the economy, so offering relatively few incentives for economic diversification and growth in other sectors (Hirschman 1958; Gelb 1988). Fossil fuel production creates temporary economic bailiwicks because the crude-petroleum or gas production chain is short (oil or gas are extracted, refined and exported by a single company) which limits wider economic and social linkages (see Humphreys, Sachs and Stiglitz 2007). The only sectors that are likely to enjoy growth with technology transfer are those related to the primary industry, such as local petrochemical refinery operations. The organization of primary industry and the large rent income that it yields inhibit economic diversification, even where governments perceive a need to act. Overall productivity may decline in the longer term, as it is the manufacturing sector that usually grows faster. Attempts to diversify the economy often feature grand public works projects that are equally mismanaged and misguided.

Conversely, many economists and political scientists predicted resource extraction would lead to self-sufficient development, arguing that the wealth earned through mineral export would lead to increased demand that would in turn stimulate production in the agricultural and manufacturing sectors, leading to further foreign investment, competitive activity and development of human capital (Nurske 1958). They argue that the development of infrastructure and economic activity associated with mineral extraction should, if properly managed, lead to sustainable development (e.g. Solomon 2000: 3).

Some left-wing commentators argue that international pressure exerted by powerful states such as the US and other Western nations, via institutions that promote market liberalization such as the World Trade Organization and International Monetary Fund, discourages lesser-developed resource-rich countries from investing in economic diversification, which could act against Western interests and undermine their hegemony. They think that this explains why observers are angered by, for example, Venezuela's nationalization of its oil resources and the public deployment of the wealth they earn to fight poverty rather than business-as-usual private investment in the market economy.

The mineral sector may also pay considerably higher salaries, so distorting employment by attracting the best-qualified persons and depleting other sectors, both private and public, of skilled workers. This can be a problem in lesser-developed nations with a small proportion of the population formally educated and qualified to work in industry and government. However, while the primary industry sector may provide well-paid jobs, they are comparatively few relative to any national economy's labour force and are often occupied by expatriates. The enclaving tendency of such industry can heighten isolation both economically and socially with expatriate employees living as temporary migrants with little commitment to the host country. Some countries that rely heavily on primary industry exports also neglect to invest in human resources, particularly through education (Gylfason 2001: 850–851), as it would reduce the disposable income of those benefiting from revenues. But this is not an invariable effect of the 'resource curse'; a significant fraction of the readily taxable rents that natural resources yield may be invested in the education sector (Stijns 2006).

An abundance of mineral reserves may ironically encourage some nations to increase their debt burden regardless of their high resource rent incomes, the reserves serving as collateral against loans. In the short term this may pay off, if currency exchange rates increase with capital inflows so reducing interest payments on the debt. However, in the long term the risks are considerable with volatile commodity prices, such that in a downturn a nation may struggle to service its debt. For instance, oil-rich Nigeria expanded its national debt during the 1970s oil boom but fell into arrears with the 1980s price falls, triggering penalty interest rates and cessation of bank lending. Such sudden changes in economic fortunes can result in the breaking of contracts, eroding business trust to the further detriment of 'cursed' countries.

It is not only national governments and multinational corporations that are responsible for the decisions that lead to features of 'the curse' in society – notably inhibiting diversity-encouraging, growth-friendly economic management – but the attitude of citizens too. Abundant natural resources may give people a false sense of security and blunt their need to work and dampen entrepreneurial activity. They have sufficient wealth to improve the material quality of their lives immediately with relatively little effort and perceive no need to invest in their nation's productive capacity. They prefer to satisfy their consumer demands straightaway, purchasing imported goods, rather than thinking long term about building up their capacity to supply their own demands. As one commentator put it: 'Rich parents sometimes spoil their kids. Mother nature is no exception' (Gylfason 2001: 850). While not applicable to all resource cursed nations, this relaxed attitude relates to another aspect of 'the curse' that affects all resource-endowed nations: non-renewable resources are, by definition, finite (an effect that has more to do with the cost of extracting embedded resources rather than the resource actually 'running out'). If the wealth these resources generate is not wisely invested by this time to secure the economic capacity necessary to ensure the same national income, the country will experience a dramatic fall in its standard of living.

There has been considerable criticism of the resource curse thesis because of its highly generalized view based on interpretation of macroeconomic trends seen in comparisons of nations' economic statistics. When we look at particular countries in detail we find considerable variation and diversity. Christa Brunnschweiler and Erwin Bulte (2008) illustrate this variety, showing the wide diversity between nations for just one of the factors that economists take as diacritical – per capita income growth. Another recent study confirms the diversity point. A review of World Bank data from 1980 to 2006 covering 53 countries (with 81 per cent of the world's oil reserves), which seeks to accommodate cross-country differences, shows that both short- and long-term growth may correlate positively with oil reserves (Cavalcanti, Mohaddes and Raissi 2011). Resource abundance is not responsible for 'the curse', it is argued, but rather global economic instability, notably volatility in commodity prices is (Ploeg and Poelhekke 2009). The myriad of other dimensions along which societies differ further questions the applicability of 'the curse' theory to all resource-endowed nations. We shall illustrate this diversity in our comparison of Qatar and Papua New Guinea, where we find some similarities but also stark differences.

A further problem, as Brunnschweiler and Bulte point out, is the endogenous (internally referential) nature of the measure used in cross-country analyses – primary exports divided by national income – which does not consequently relate directly to or vary with respect to changes in exogenous factors such as institutional arrangements or conflict. They question the assumed character of causality to challenge the resource curse thesis. The primary exports/national income variable measures the resource *dependence* of economies, not the *abundance* of non-renewable resources, which is supposedly the root cause of 'the curse'. Whilst resource curse theorists argue that a negative correlation between this variable and growth shows that resource extraction leads to slower economic growth, there are other equally valid arguments. It is feasible that poor economic development policies are strangling growth and lead to dependence on non-renewable resource exports. Furthermore, although such resources may occur where there is inefficient government, they do not necessarily undermine institutions; it is equally likely that 'the resource sector is the "default sector" in the absence of decent institutions when nobody is willing to invest in alternative forms of capital' (Brunnschweiler and Bulte 2008: 616). Likewise, while resources may spark conflict, it is just as likely that conflict leads nations to depend on resource extraction in the first place, it is the 'default activity' after other economic activities have collapsed. In this event, 'resources are not a curse to development, but rather a safety net' (ibid. 2008: 617).

The analysis that follows explores the extent to which the experiences of Qatar and Papua New Guinea accord or clash with the curse theory described above. Does the resource curse apply to all resource-endowed countries and does this theory account fully for the realities of the two countries considered here?

Qatar's Experience of Abundant Natural Resources

The Gulf states with booming economies and comprehensive distributive policies seem to avoid 'the curse', albeit they are concerned about managing depleting resources in the future and diversifying their economies to reduce their dependency on oil and gas revenues. The extent of diversification varies greatly and illustrates how caution is required in making generalizations about countries across the region. Bahrain has the most diversified economy with oil and gas accounting for only 11 per cent of GDP (Macropolis n.d.), whereas in Kuwait, Qatar and Saudi Arabia oil and gas approaches 50 per cent or more of GDP (fluctuating with the price of a barrel of oil).[7] This contrasts with the UAE where non-hydrocarbon sectors accounted for more than 71 per cent of GDP in 2009 (Arabian Oil and Gas 2010). However, the International Monetary Fund's most recent Article IV report on Qatar expects the non-hydrocarbon sector to be the main driver of growth, with this sector's revenue forecast to represent

56 per cent of total fiscal income by 2016. The state, however, aims to have a fully financed buffer budget from non-hydrocarbon revenue by 2020 to act as a safety net in the event of hydrocarbon price shocks (John 2012). This suggests that Qatar is positioning itself to side step the 'Dutch disease' encountered by some hydrocarbon resource-endowed nations.

In terms of capital investment (i.e. technology for production and investment in infrastructure such as roads etc.), personnel training and openness to international trade and investment, Qatar is making advances with its commitment to a modernization programme (paid for by oil and gas revenues). But high oil prices from 2003 onwards have reduced pressure to implement economic reform to stimulate the private sector and reduce public services. The Qatar National Development Strategy (QNDS 2011: 5–7), however, shows a commitment to transport, communication, business and financial services, construction, manufacturing and investment in the public and private sectors (see Rahman, chapter 3, this volume).

The population explosion across the Gulf states, linked mainly to a huge influx of migrant workers employed by the construction sector, has left an educated 'oil generation' of nationals with the expectation of a guaranteed income whether or not they show up for work. Due to the nature of 'money rain' for Qatari nationals (see page 165), they are often under-employed and hold a 'relaxed' work ethic. This contrasts dramatically with the experience of migrant labourers, who while benefiting from the jobs created by the development boom, work comparatively hard for few of the benefits enjoyed by the local population, for example, living in substandard accommodation with limited entertainment options (see Gardner, chapter 14, this volume). Furthermore, debt among citizens grows as the oil generation struggle to sustain the standard of living to which they have become accustomed (Marcel 2006: 118–119).[8] This 'spend now, worry about it later' attitude is at odds with the intergenerational equity demanded by principles of sustainability laid out in the national strategies of many governments of the Gulf region (see Tan, Al-Khalaqi and Al-Khulaifi, chapter 2, this volume).

Qatar is not alone. Other Arab nations are experiencing similar changes in their citizen's outlook. As King Faisal of Saudi Arabia observed in an interview: 'In one generation we went from riding camels to riding Cadillacs. The way we are wasting money, I fear the next generation will be riding camels again' (Gylfason 2001: 848). It is an aspect of the resource curse which has serious consequences for the region, not least when the non-renewable resource starts to run out and if insufficient alternative energy sources exist to replace it. To a certain extent the very wealthy members of the ruling elite in these countries will be protected from this eventuality, being able to escape and take up residence elsewhere on the proceeds of their private investments. The wider population will have a harder time adjusting to the inevitable changes. The knock-on implications for the home countries of migrant labourers are of wider concern, dependent as many of these communities are on the remittances of their nationals in the Gulf (see Campbell, chapter 9, this volume).

The need for an intergenerational focus, a central feature of sustainable development, captures a key challenge for economies that depend on exploitation of a non-renewable resource, leaving nothing for future generations at current extraction rates and squandering the wealth. While sustainable development requires a diversified economic base for growth (see Agenda 21 1992), economic reform documents focus less on economic diversification than on the implementation of neo-liberal agendas that are rarely sensitive to the local culture (Gilberthorpe and Banks 2012). The Qatar National Development Strategy (QNDS 2011: 7), for example, identifies three interrelated strategies for sustainable economic development: 'to sustain a high standard of living, to expand innovation and entrepreneurial capabilities and to align economic outcomes with economic and financial stability'. This focus on competitive 'entrepreneurial capabilities' may be at odds with the cooperative values of Bedouin culture, where formerly people favoured modest, collaborative behaviour and few spoke about wealth.

People are rightly concerned about dependence on an oil- and gas-exporting economy with its inherent economic instability brought about by the price volatility of the hydrocarbon market. In the short term, Qatar's economy will continue to be tightly linked to developments in the fossil fuel sector. However, looking forward, policy initiatives are directed at diversification to prepare the country for life beyond oil and gas, as called for at the twentieth World Petroleum Conference in Doha (Jackson 2011). For example, the Qatar Science and Technology Park focuses on high-tech sectors such as life sciences, oil and chemicals, environment, electronics and software development; Qatari Diar continues to forge ahead in real estate development and investment; and Al Jazeera leads in the media and communications sector for the region (QNDS 2011: 49). The successful bid for the 2022 FIFA World Cup will also help to broaden Qatar's economic profile through tourism development and emphasizes the country's pre-eminence as a preferred location for major sporting and cultural events, and international conferences. These initiatives are complemented by considerable national investment in knowledge development among the local population through training and education at, for example, internationally linked university campuses and research centres.

The question remains whether Qatar is able to make the leap from an extractive to a knowledge-based economy without developing a manufacturing base, the traditional path to diversification and economic development. In the space of a few decades, Qatar has been transformed from nomadic pastoralism and coastal pearling villages to sprawling cityscapes (see Alraouf and Clarke, chapter 13; Gardner, chapter 14, both this volume; Melamid 1987: 103). It appears that it is set to go through further reinvention, into a knowledge economy, potentially making it even more unrecognizable from its previous, some might say, tranquil and environmentally harmonious past. The cultural changes required in this phase will surely be as difficult and complex to orchestrate, if not more so, than the changes in physical infrastructure of the previous phase. Money 'raining' down on the country's citizens may fund the material changes but hearts and minds will be harder to transform. Regardless of the major changes in their way of life and increasing outside influences, the Qataris currently remain secure in their culture, with its deep Islamic roots. They are also fiercely patriotic and proud of their heritage. Strong tribal allegiances and lineage-based loyalties, rules of endogamy,[9] tribal distributive customs and the *majlis* system (forum for decision making) have all survived the oil and gas bonanza. While some of the obligations established and maintained between individuals and groups through kin networks are being eroded by intensified politicking and changing expectations among the younger generation, men still spend much time sitting in *majlis* discussing issues. Moreover, a conservative form of Islam dominates all spheres of life, which sets limits on the change possible. For example, many Qatari women still wear the full veil in public by choice. However, high incomes may threaten some fragmentation and inequalities in the future, undermining the social cohesion and security that characterize traditional culture. To date, these relationship issues and their 'curse' potential have been less well addressed in analyses of resource-endowed nations such as Qatar. A secondary consideration is the income inequity between Qatari nationals and the migrant workforce and the tensions this may create in the long term. It is not sufficient to argue that these workers are better off than they would be in their home countries.

The scale and pace of development and economic diversification in Qatar raises other concerns, not least in terms of climate-change issues. Qatar topped the world in per capita rates of carbon dioxide emissions in 2007 with rates approximately three times that of the United States (see Sillitoe's introduction to this volume; Reuters 2010) due to profligate energy use, including natural gas processing, water desalination and electricity production.[10] The fact that Qataris do not have to pay for either their water or electricity supplies, and both are heavily subsidized for other residents, is thought to contribute to high rates of energy use.[11] A large change in attitudes and behaviour is necessary to ensure the conservation of precious resources for future generations. Without this transformation, money rain (in the form of subsidies) could drag the country quickly towards the less documented and accounted for consequences of resource endowment, with over consumption leading to water and energy scarcity and environmental decline.

With construction continuing apace and requiring ever more foreign workers to provide the labour, water and food security have become an additional concern. The Qatar National Food Security Programme launched in 2008 is addressing this issue. The chairman of QNFSP, Fahad Al Attiyah, aims to 'jumpstart an entire industry in Qatar',[12] to tackle the threat of scarce water resources by focusing on renewable energy, desalination and water management and to reduce dependence of food imports by dramatically increasing agricultural production and food processing (Townson 2011).[13]

The political system in Qatar features a hierarchy of the Emir, ruling family, businessmen, sheikhs and kinsmen within tribal patron-client networks of reciprocity, obligation and cooperation, which British colonialism institutionalized formally (Crystal 1989: 432). The arrival of the oil industry in the 1940s strengthened it further when the Emir was, according to Crystal (1989: 433), 'careful to distribute revenues in politically useful ways', engendering further stratification, uneven distribution of wealth and subsequent lack of political participation (see also Ibrahim 1982; Marcel 2006). The social mechanisms may have already been in place to facilitate the distribution of revenues, but these networks and institutions have changed somewhat with petro-resource exploitation (Crystal 1989: 439). We see the recalibrating of Bedouin values of loyalty, equality and obligation in the face of mineral-led modernization, with far reaching socio-political implications.

Qatar has three mechanisms for distributing revenue: through royalties to the national population, through social services and through state employment (Crystal 1989; Marcel 2006). The income from oil and gas reaches all Qataris (who make up less than 14 per cent of the total population according to the 2010 census) so that even the poorest 'are today healthier and better housed, educated, and fed than ever before' (Crystal 1989: 433–434). They receive a family allowance, free education, healthcare, subsidized housing and, as mentioned, free water and electricity. The state's capacity to distribute resource rents across all sectors has ensured domestic tranquillity and created apparent 'political apathy' for, as in other Gulf states (with the exceptions of Bahrain and to a limited extent Oman) no social group has reason to challenge the established political regime (see Crystal 1989: 427–428; Marcel 206: 107; see Gardner, chapter 14, this volume). A recent decree issued by the Crown Prince granting a salary increase to public sector employees and retirees among Qatari civilians and military personnel illustrates this process. It raised the gross salaries of all Qatari employees by 60 per cent with effect from 1 September 2011 and salaries of defence personnel of officer rank by 120 per cent (Toumi 2011). The decision has forced many private sector employers to follow suit with similar pay rises for Qatari employees, while expatriate staff doing similar jobs receive no such increases. While this initiative serves to maintain harmony within the Qatari populous, enabling them to pay off debts and cope with inflationary tendencies, it reinforces the paternalistic relationship between the state and the Qatari public and the 'something for nothing' attitude. 'Money rain' such as this does little to incentivize Qataris to improve productivity. It may however generate disharmony with the non-Qatari workforce and create financial problems for private companies raising the cost of doing business.[14]

Qataris have long benefited from the state's 'national employment' and 'knowledge-based economy' campaigns (GSDP 2011; see also Crystal 1989: 434). These policies ensure government employment with large bureaucracies. In parts of the Gulf, kin commitments influence recruitment processes and many jobs are superfluous and redundancies and firings unknown (Marcel 2006: 108–110). Qatar also has a large expatriate population. The labourers from Arab and non-Arab States (largely Asian) work, as mentioned, on construction projects. Many European expatriates work in construction too and in oil and gas and service industries (Melamid 1987) and increasingly in the education, science and research sectors to supply the necessary know-how for the knowledge-economy projects. Coping with this million plus population of largely single male workers is a major challenge in respect of the support systems required to feed, water, house and medically care for so many people, and manage their environmental impact. Their presence also influences the social fabric of the country; for example, large numbers of men congregate on the weekends in downtown areas, having nowhere else to go for their recreation. Recently, the Central Municipal Council announced a new commercial and entertainment facility for bachelors located in the industrial area west of Doha, recognizing the important role played by the migrant workforce in building the economy and the need to protect and enhance their welfare to meet commitments to international human rights organizations (Adly 2012). The resource curse theory does not adequately account for this changing social fabric within resource-endowed nations such as Qatar, as outlined previously. While a higher standard of living is encouraging entrepreneurship and diversification among the migrant population, in line with standard economic models, managing the complex dynamics remains a challenge.

Some economists argue that tax gathering and redistribution are necessary to a stable and sustainable economy (Hirschman 1958). In mineral economies, the state does not need to tax people and so prudent fiscal arrangements are often lacking (Gelb 1988; Gylfason 2001) and corruption may be rife, as noted earlier. Qataris, for instance, pay no income tax. This gives the State a certain autonomy from citizens (Brynen 1992: 74). In Saudi Arabia the separation between the state and citizens has led, according to Kiren Chaudhry, to political apathy (Marcel 2006: 107). Recognizing transparency as a critical issue to the country, Qatar recently established an Administrative Control and Transparency Authority with the aim to move the country to the top ten in terms of transparency worldwide. Among the Authority's responsibilities is to probe cases of misuse of public office and misuse of public funds.[15] It is argued, as noted previously, that with an effective tax system citizens become more interested in what governments do with their money, ensuring a degree of fiscal efficiency. During the oil-price collapse of 1986, for example, some Gulf states incurred debt through foreign borrowing to maintain the rentier lifestyle rather than imposing taxes on their populations (cited in Marcel 2006: 108). The World Bank, International Monetary Fund and World Trade Organization have all called for the Gulf region to raise taxes to help create sustainable economies (ibid. 2006: 116). The State of Qatar is launching a budget reform programme to address the issue of fiscal arrangements (QNDS 2011: 8), but this will not be easy. Tax reforms are invariably difficult to make and a 'no-tax policy' hard to reverse with an 'oil generation' used to spending large sums on imported consumer items, with scant positive impact on the local economy.

It appears from this analysis that although Qatar does not exhibit the five characteristics of a resource cursed nation presented in the introduction to this chapter, it is encountering other challenges, not least those of managing the social transformations going on within the country and its (un)sustainable development trajectory. These factors are less well explored in the resource curse literature and are crucial to a full understanding of the implications of being a resource-endowed country. Without the necessary holistic interpretation and policy formation, resource endowment in Qatar may indeed become a curse.

Papua New Guinea: Resource Abundance and Social Disintegration

Like Qatar, Papua New Guinea's resource-dependent economy shows the economic anomalies associated with royalties, or 'unearned income'. Unlike Qataris, however, Papua New Guineans who receive royalties live within an environment that is remote from the market, the majority comprising a rural population living off the land with socio-political arrangements that centre locally on kin networks and social exchange transactions that promote cohesion and material security equally for all. Papua New Guineans draw the royalty wealth, the 'money rain', into traditional systems of exchange rather than using it to fund consumption as in the urban metropolises of the Gulf states. But the relationship that people develop with 'money rain' is neither conducive to socio-economic security nor to sustainable development. The way individuals interact with 'money rain' in Papua New Guinea emphasizes the critical part society and culture play in propagating 'the curse'.

Papua New Guinea's environmental and cultural landscape has changed significantly over the last century. The country is rugged and varied spanning a range of ecological systems, from rainforests and grasslands, to wetlands and sandy beaches. It has a history of mineral exploration and extraction, featuring two mining 'crises' on Bougainville and Ok Tedi in which cultural conflict was prominent between the companies and State on the one hand and indigenous populations on the other (Filer 1990; Kirsch 2006). Since Independence in 1975, Papua New Guinea has embarked on a resource-development pathway. It seeks to advance sustainable development through various corporate social responsibility (CSR) activities.

Economic growth is driven largely by the mineral-resources sector. Oil and gas revenues accounted for more than 10 per cent of GDP (and about 40 per cent of government revenues) in 2008 (Ochirkhuu and Takahashi 2010) and mining revenues (minerals and metals) accounted for approximately 18 per cent. Papua New Guinea has a more diversified economy than Qatar, with a growing agricultural sector that includes coffee, cocoa, timber, rubber and palm oil production. The latter, with its increasing importance to the alternative energy market, is potentially important for Papua New Guinea's future sustainable development. Whilst the State aims to increase agricultural production in rural areas, there is an ongoing problem of access and engagement. Access to the country's rural interior is limited with no roads currently linking isolated areas to the capital.

If we consider Papua New Guinea in terms of the five characteristics identified as symptomatic of the resource curse by economists – a confined economy, low employment, poor fiscal discipline, poor capital investment and low business development – we can see that it is an exemplar of each. The 'money rain' is confined by the system of royalty distribution (see below) to areas where mineral extraction occurs, areas that have few linkages to the wider national or international economy. In terms of employment, Papua New Guinea has few in paid work with its high rural population (87 per cent) and self-sufficient agricultural lifestyle. Literacy is ambitiously estimated at 57 per cent (of those over fifteen years of age) but employment opportunities are minimal. Those living near (or migrants to) regions hosting primary industry have poor employment opportunities because of low labour requirements on the one hand and lack of skills on the other.

Papua New Guinea has more fiscal arrangements than Qatar. Employees pay income tax, although beneficiaries of income from petroleum, mining and gas are exempt (TFF 2009: 27). There is a school-fee system and charges are made for medical services. Landowners in mining regions receive free permanent housing with running water and electricity but these facilities are not provided in oil-producing areas where inhabitants live in more 'traditional' settings (Gilberthorpe 2007). New businesses in rural regions are exempt from income tax for a ten-year period, except those in mineral-producing areas (TFF 2009: 38). The country has tax incentives for employers (e.g. 100 per cent accelerated depreciation deduction) and employees (e.g. taxable wages subsidy) in the non-mineral exporting sector (TFF 2009: 30–34), and a tax credit scheme for infrastructural development within the mineral sector (TFF 2009: 36). Business development in the private, non-mineral sector is limited even with the tax exemptions in place, whilst business development in the mineral sector is hampered by high taxation and conflicts caused by envy (Gilberthorpe 2009).

Not only is Papua New Guinea without the scale or pace of development seen in the Gulf states, but it is also without a similar 'modernization programme'. It does, however, have a development partnership with Australia (PNG-Australia Partnership for Development) established in 2008 to address the Millennium Development Goals with a bi-sector commitment to education, health, transport infrastructure and law and justice. It also has a sustainable development programme (Papua New Guinea Sustainable Development Program Ltd.) that is funded by profits from the Ok Tedi copper and gold mine (see PNGSDP 2009). Its mission is: 'Promoting development that meets the needs of the present generation and establishes the foundation for continuing progress for future generations of Papua New Guineans' (PNGSDP 2009) through transport infrastructure, water supplies, education and smallholder investment (aquaculture, rubber etc). This 'development' is restricted to a few urban centres, including the capital Port Moresby, and to regions in the vicinity of mining and oil developments where 'modernization' or 'development' takes the form of various 'benefits', particularly infrastructure (generally in mining rather than oil/gas zones) and cash royalties.

So whilst Papua New Guinea appears to have a more diverse economic base and extensive taxation system than Qatar, it seems to be a victim of the resource curse whilst Qatar and other Gulf states appear to escape it. Why is this? Part of the answer might be located in the vast difference in rural/urban populations and the cultural features influencing the emergence of new economies. The majority of Qatar's population live in urban areas linked by a rapidly developing infrastructure giving them access to the emerging 'knowledge-based economy' and other development opportunities, whereas the opposite is true for Papua New Guinea. The majority of Papua New Guineans live rurally, as noted, and have a subsistence-based lifestyle where kinship and exchange remain dominant social forces. They have limited access to services and markets, and demand for imported goods is low. 'Money rain' thus stimulates a rural, indigenous 'economy' rather than a national one. At state level, development is seen as an effect of industrial activity and 'fair exchange' for the environmental devastation inevitably caused by mineral extraction.

The assumption that 'development' accompanies large-scale resource extraction has its foundations in a number of historical factors including colonization and missionization. The colonial era saw the introduction of manufactured goods such as steel tools and other processed foods, along with Western ideologies of law and order, systems of authority that challenged existing stateless arrangements and all-purpose cash. At Kutubu, the location of the country's main oil-extraction facility, there is no plantation economy or large-scale cash cropping (only smallholdings of vanilla and coffee), nor is there much tourist activity. Missionaries proselytized against local beliefs and institutions, and the colonial authorities prohibited ceremonial activity, warfare and cannibalistic practices, although ceremonial activity was revived in the 1990s (Busse, Araho and Turner 1993). Whilst cash was introduced during the colonial and missionary era and impacted on the distribution of resources and exchange activity, the basic principles of socio-economic networks spanning the wider Kutubu region persisted (Gilberthorpe 2007; Weiner 1988). This indicates the importance of the social principles underpinning relationship networks and the value attached to the kinship connectivity that facilitates individual mobility (Gilberthorpe 2007).

Unlike the national systems of revenue distribution in the Gulf, in Papua New Guinea not all citizens benefit from royalty wealth. The Papua New Guinea government devised a land-title system that legally recognizes indigenous groups as customary landowners, as institutionalized in the Land Groups Incorporation Act of 1974 (see Glaskin and Weiner 2007). The act was based on the assumption that corporate groups have a collective interest in land and resources, an assumption refuted some time ago (Wagner 1974; Sillitoe 1979). The act has led to the implementation of fixed, landownership models in regions affected by mineral extraction. It is the introduction of this ideology of 'development' that links 'landowners' to resources that feeds the 'curse' in Papua New Guinea via the 'money rain' phenomenon. Whilst the system ensures that some of the population receives royalties, it is criticized for foregrounding corporate/State concerns over indigenous well-being. The Papua New Guinea revenue-distribution system (representative of many others) allows the State and corporate sectors to keep royalties to a minimum by confining the scope of benefits. It passes responsibility for redistribution from companies to indigenous groups whilst appearing to ensure that CSR objectives are met (see Sillitoe and Wilson 2003; Filer, Burton and Banks 2008; Gilberthorpe and Banks 2012).

In Papua New Guinea's oil sector, landownership is regulated through the Incorporated Land Groups (ILG) system under which groups living within the vicinity of the central production facility, employee camps, airport, roads, and pipeline can register as an ILG and receive cash royalties as well as other resource-generated benefits (compensation, future generation funds, basic services and infrastructure, and [minimal] labour opportunities). Consequently, only a small number of people receive cash royalties. This is at odds with traditional principles of social interaction and organization and has created several problems (Gilberthorpe 2007). The reduction of a complex traditional system to a legally instituted one has created 'haves' and 'have-nots', and led to social fragmentation that in turn has had a significant impact on the security offered by socio-political exchange networks. In a 'traditional' setting, wealth is not accumulated as capital but exchanged to earn social capital (Sillitoe and Wilson 2003: 251). Royalties are distributed through a system of imposed hierarchy (from a chairman to ILG leaders to kin) that creates new distributive pathways and alliance structures, leading to a build-up of resentment, hostility and conflict because revenues fail to circulate within the traditional socio-political exchange system where obligation, trust and loyalty are central principles.

The individual pursuit of wealth and cash hoarding encouraged by these capitalist arrangements has allowed a small number of 'entrepreneurs' to capture resource rents. These persons arrange contracts with the oil-project operators, particularly in construction, maintenance and security. Yet, these few (male) individuals run the risk of detaching themselves from the security of established social networks because they place themselves outside the sphere of social obligation and support. Failing to share cash in the traditional way based on an egalitarian ethos, such entrepreneurs find themselves at increased risk from resentful individuals and groups with whom they break long-standing networks of reciprocity. The isolated individual in pursuit of wealth finds himself threatened by a hostile majority and dependent not only on an unreliable and unsustainable resource economy, but also on weak ties that carry no obligation of economic and social security (Gilberthorpe and Sillitoe 2009).

The Papua New Guinea case demonstrates how the 'money rain' phenomenon weakens social cohesion by promoting political and economic inequalities where primary industry depends on depleting resources and is volatile. Social and economic security (and thus well-being) is put at serious risk as social networks break down at an ever-increasing rate (Gilberthorpe and Sillitoe 2009).

Transforming 'Money Rain' Impacts

This chapter shows the mistake in assuming that states such as Qatar are immune to the resource curse because their GDP is high, they have 'modernization programmes' in place and they have booming cosmopolitan metropolises. If we focus only on economic factors we see growth in a limited sense (see Papyrakis and Gerlagh 2004); if we consider wider social issues, including kinship, descent and exchange patterns, we begin to see how these are also vulnerable to 'the curse' and play a central role in the consumption of resource rents. While generating tax revenue, diversifying the economy, stimulating employment and exports are important, so are social considerations associated with unemployment, changing family structures and increasing stratification. The key questions emerging from this comparative study are: Does the reduced scale of 'modernization' in Papua New Guinea make it less susceptible to an unsustainable post-extraction scenario? And can 'modernized' Qataris sustain a non-mineral state?

What the 'money rain' phenomenon shows is the impact royalty wealth can have on social organization and interaction that links to 'the curse'. The sociology of the 'money rain' phenomenon requires greater critical attention, moving beyond the role played by economic modernization in achieving and maintaining sustainable development and overcoming or avoiding the resource curse. Nation states, NGOs, international agencies and multinational corporations need to focus more on 'the human factor' to counteract 'the curse' and achieve sustainability.

At the national level, Papua New Guinea faces the challenge of deploying resource rents to benefit a majority rural population and achieve sustainable economic growth. Qatar faces considerable challenges in managing the social implications of its vast development projects and their consequent environmental impacts, not least in relation to the migrant workers required to implement these plans. Shifting from an extractive industrial base to a 'knowledge-driven' economy presents other problems for Qatar given the expertise required within a relatively short space of time (one or two generations) and the fact that buying in knowledge is unsustainable in the long run.

'The curse' is a particularly urgent area of concern because mineral economies are vulnerable to predicted falls in demand for oil and gas, particularly in the face of climate change and alternative energy discourse. Qatar is vulnerable to future shocks and downswings due to the weakness of its non-hydrocarbon sector. Papua New Guinea perhaps less so, as long as its subsistence economy remains intact. In short, States such as Qatar and Papua New Guinea need to be more attuned to *all* the variables when addressing extraction and the dangers of the resource 'curse', as illustrated by the relationship between the 'money rain' phenomenon and local populations.

Notes

1. For ease of understanding, *mineral* is used in reference to both hard rock and petrochemical resources.
2. A model based on the fur and cod industries.
3. The term 'money rain' derives from the Melanesia Pidgin *mani ren* that refers to the unearned cash royalties paid to indigenous landowners.
4. For comparative world growth data by country refer to http://www.index mundi.com/facts/indicators/NY.GDP.MKTP.KD.ZG/compare.
5. The socially driven uprisings that began in 2011 across parts of the Arab world, known colloquially as the Arab Spring, suggest this status quo may be changing in this region.
6. Refer to http://eiti.org for a list of participating countries. At the time of writing, neither Papua New Guinea nor Qatar were signatories. The United States has signaled its intent to implement the EITI.
7. See Shaheen 2010; Redpath 2011.
8. For example, loans, advances and overdrafts in the UAE rose to DH 43.9 billion in the year to March 2008, a 38 per cent increase over the same period in 2007 (*Khaleej Times* 2008).
9. Endogamy (cousin marriage) remains prevalent in several countries (see El Guindi, chapter 19, this volume). While there has been a decline in cousin marriages among people in Jordan, Lebanon, Morocco, Mauritania and the Palestinian population in Israel, the practice is increasing in Qatar, the United Arab Emirates and Yemen.
10. Qatar is disadvantaged by having production-based emissions attributed to it and a small population. The country's emission data would be greatly reduced under a consumption-based accounting system.

11. Qatar is one of the highest consumers of water per capita per day, using around 310 litres per day – more than double the average for West European countries. Studies show that Qataris used 1,200 litres per person per day in 2009, while expatriates consumed 150 litres per person per day during the same year (*The Pennisula* 2009).
12. Agricultural production of dates, dairy, grapes, meat, fruit and vegetables contributes only 0.1 per cent of total GDP (see Melamid 1987).
13. Refer to http://www.qnfs.gov.qa.
14. See for example http://www.qatar-tribune.com/data/20110921/content.asp?section=nation4_1.
15. Qatar ranked twenty-second in Transparency International's rankings in 2011 and first among Middle Eastern countries. Refer to http://www.transparency.org.

References

Adly, A. 2012. 'Plan to Build Leisure Zone for Bachelors Welcomed,' *Gulf Times*, 11 March, 12.

Agenda 21. 1992. http://www.un.org/esa/dsd/agenda21/index.shtml (accessed 28 March 2011).

Arabian Oil and Gas Staff. 2010. 'Non-Oil Sector Grows to 71.6% of GDP for UAE,' 30 May. http://www.arabianoilandgas.com/article-7409-non-oil-sector-grows-to-716-of-gdp-for-uae/1/print/ (accessed 6 December 2011).

AusAID. 2011. 'PNG–Australia Partnership for Development.' http://www.ausaid.gov.au/publications/pubout.cfm?ID=3419_4132_845_3563_3801&Type= (accessed 11 January 2012).

Auty, R. 1993. *Sustaining Development in Mineral Economies: The Resource-Curse Thesis*. London: Routledge.

———. 2001. 'The Political Economy of Resource-Driven Growth.' *European Economic Review* 45 (4–6): 839–846.

Auty, R., and R. F. Mikesell. 1999. *Sustainable Development in Mineral Economies*. London: Clarendon Press.

Bannon, I., and P. Collier (eds.). 2003. *Natural Resources and Violent Conflict: Options and Actions*. Washington: World Bank.

Beblawi, H. 1990. 'The Rentier State in the Arab World.' In *The Arab State,* ed. G. Luciani, 85–98. Berkeley: University of California Press.

Brunnschweiler, C. N., and E. H. Bulte. 2008. 'Linking Natural Resources to Slow Growth and More Conflict.' *Science* 320 (5876): 616–617.

Brynen, R. 1992. 'Economic Crisis and Post-Rentier Democratization in the Arab World: The Case of Jordan.' *Canadian Journal of Political Science* 25 (1): 69–97.

Busse, M., N. Araho and S. Turner. 1993. *The People of Lake Kutubu and Kikori: Changing Meanings of Daily Life*. Port Moresby: PNG National Museum and Art Gallery.

Cavalcanti, T. V. de V., K. Mohaddes and M. Raissi. 2011. 'Does Oil Abundance Harm Growth?' *Applied Economics Letters* 18 (12): 1181–1184.

Crystal, Jill. 1989. 'Coalitions in Oil Monarchies: Kuwait and Qatar.' *Comparative Politics* 21 (4): 427–443.

Dauderstädt, M., and A. Schildberg (eds.). 2006. *Dead Ends of Transition: Rentier Economies and Protectorates.* Frankfurt: Campus Verlag.

Filer, C. 1990. 'The Bougainville Rebellion, the Mining Industry and the Process of Social Disintegration in Papua New Guinea.' *Canberra Anthropology* 13 (1): 1–39.

Filer, C., J. Burton and G. Banks. 2008. 'The Fragmentation of Responsibilities in the Melanesian Mining Sector.' In *Earth Matters: Indigenous Peoples, the Extractive Industry and Corporate Social Responsibility,* eds. C. O'Faircheallaigh and S. Ali, 163–179. London: Greenleaf Publishing.

Gelb, A. (and associates). 1988. *Oil Windfalls: Blessing or Curse?* New York: Oxford University Press.

Gilberthorpe, E. 2007. 'Fasu Solidarity: A Case Study of Kin Networks, Land Tenure and Oil Extraction in Kutubu, Papua New Guinea.' *American Anthropologist* 109 (1): 101–112.

———. 2009. *Development and Industry: A Papua New Guinea Case Study.* Canterbury: CSAC.

Gilberthorpe, E., and G. Banks. 2012. 'Development-Free Zone? CSR Discourse and Social Realities in Papua New Guinea's Mineral Extraction Sector.' *Resources Policy.*

Gilberthorpe, E., and P. Sillitoe. 2009. 'The Construction of Social Capital in the Current Economic Crisis: Lessons from Papua New Guinea.' *Anthropology News* 50 (7): 4–5.

Glaskin, K., and J. Weiner. 2007. *Customary Land Tenure and Registration in Australia and Papua New Guinea: Anthropological Perspectives.* Canberra: ANU E-Press.

General Secretariat for Development Planning (GSDP). 2011. http://www.gsdp .gov.qa/portal/page/portal/GSDP_Vision_Root/GSDP_EN/Organisational_ Structure/Economic_Affairs_Department/KBE (accessed 11 April 2011).

Gylfason, T. 2000. 'Resources Agriculture, and Economic Growth in Economies in Transition.' *Kyklos* 53 (4): 545–580.

Haber, S., and V. Menaldo. 2011. 'Do Natural Resources Fuel Authoritarianism? A Reappraisal of the Resource Curse.' *American Political Science Review* 105 (1): 1–26.

Hirschman, A. O. 1958. *The Strategy of Economic Development.* New Haven, CT: Yale University Press.

Humphreys, M., J. D. Sachs and J. E. Stiglitz. 2007. 'Introduction.' In *Escaping the Resource Curse,* eds. M. Humphreys, J. D. Sachs and J. E. Stiglitz, 1–20. New York: Columbia University Press.

Ibrahim, S. E. 1982. *The New Arab Social Order: A Study of the Social Impact of Oil Wealth.* Boulder, CO, and London: Westview Press and Croom-Helm.

International Monetary Fund (Country Information) (IMF). 2011. http://www.imf .org/external/country/index.htm (accessed 12 April 2011).

Iqbal, F. 2006. *Sustaining Gains in Poverty Reduction and Human Development in the Middle East and North Africa.* Washington, DC: The World Bank (Orientations in Development Series).

Jackson, R. 2011. 'Britain Encourages the Region to 'Diversify' Beyond Hydrocarbon,' *Gulf Times,* 6 December, 13.

John, P. 2012. 'Non-Hydrocarbon Income Poised for Big Leap in Qatar,' *Gulf Times,* 12 February, 1.

Karl, T. 1997. *The Paradox of Plenty: Oil Booms and Petro-States.* Berkeley: University of California Press.

Khaleej Times. 2008. 'UAE Faces Consumer Debt Crisis,' *Khaleej Times,* 31 August. http://www.menafn.com/qn_news_story_s.asp?StoryId=1093210111 (accessed 6 December 2011).

Kirsch, S. 2006. *Reverse Anthropology: Indigenous Analysis of Social and Environmental Relations in New Guinea.* Stanford, CA: Stanford University Press.

Kuznets, S. 1966. 'Modern Economic Growth: Findings and Reflections.' *American Economic Review* 63 (3): 247–258.

Le Billon, P. 2005. *Fuelling War: Natural Resources and Armed Conflicts.* Abingdon: Routledge.

Macropolis. N.d. 'Bahrain's GDP: Bahrain to Diversify its GDP.' http://www.marcopolis.net/bahrains-gdp-bahrain-to-diversify-its-gdp-diversification-of-bahrains-gdp.htm (accessed 6 December 2011).

Marcel, V. 2006. *Oil Titans: National Oil Companies in the Middle East.* London and Washington, DC: Chatham House and Brookings Institution Press.

Melamid, A. 1987. 'Qatar.' *Geographical Review* 77 (1): 103–105.

Nurske, R. 1958. 'Trade Fluctuations and Buffer Policies of Low-Income Countries.' *Kyklos* 11 (2): 141–154.

Ochirkhuu, E., and K. Takahashi. 2010. 'Papua New Guinea: Selected Issues Paper and Statistical Appendix.' International Monetary Fund Country Report No 10/163 June 2010. www.imf.org/external/pubs/ft/scr/2010/cr10163.pdf (accessed 1 December 2011).

Papyrakis, E., and R. Gerlagh. 2003. 'The Resource Curse Hypothesis and its Transmission Channels.' *Journal of Comparative Economics* 32: 181–193.

The Peninsula. 2009. 'Qatar Tops Per Capita Water Use in the World,' *The Peninsula,* 20 March. http://www.thepeninsulaqatar.com/qatar/147343-qatar-tops-per-capita-water-use-in-world.html (accessed 1 December 2011).

Ploeg, F. van der, and S. Poelhekke. 2009. 'Volatility and the Natural Resource Curse.' *Oxford Economic Papers* 61 (4): 727–760.

Papua New Guinea Sustainable Development Program (PNGSDP). 2009. http://www.pngsdp.com/ (accessed 31 May 2011).

Qatar National Development Strategy (QNDS). 2011. 'Qatar: General Secretariat for Development Planning.' http://www.gsdp.gov.qa/portal/page/portal/GSDP_Vision_Root/GSDP_EN/NDS (accessed 11 April 2011).

Redpath, S. 2011. 'Qatar to Soften Oil and Gas Dependency.' *World Finance* (January–February): 1C–2C. www.qinvest.com (accessed 1 December 2011).

Reuters. 2010. 'FACTBOX: Qatar Tops World in Carbon Emissions Per Capita,' *Reuters,* 14 November. http://www.reuters.com/assets/print?aid=USLDE6AB1KT20101114 (accessed 1 December 2012).

Ross, M. 1999. 'The Political Economy of the Resource Curse.' *World Politics* 51 (2): 297–322.

Rostow, W. W. 1960. *The Stages of Economic Growth: A Non-Communist Manifesto.* Cambridge: Cambridge University Press.

Sachs J. D., and A. M. Warner. 1999. 'The Big Push, Natural Resource Booms and Growth.' *Journal of Development Economics* 59 (1): 43–76.

———. 2001. 'The Curse of Natural Resources.' *European Economic Review* 45 (4–6): 827–838.

Shaheen, A. R. 2010. 'Saudi Arabia's Oil Sector GDP Plunges 40%,' *Gulf News,* 6 January. www.gulfnews.com, (accessed 1 December 2011).

Sillitoe, P. 1979. *Give and Take.* New York: St. Martin's Press.

Sillitoe, P., and R. Wilson. 2003. 'Playing in the Pacific Ring of Fire: Negotiation and Knowledge in Mining in Papua New Guinea.' In *Negotiating Local Knowledge: Power and Identity in Development,* eds. J. Pottier, A. Bicker and P. Sillitoe, 241–272. London: Pluto.

Solomon, M. H. 2000. *Growth and Diversification in Mineral Economies Planning and Incentives for Diversification.* South Africa: The Mineral Corporation.

Stevens, P. 2003. 'Resource Impact: Curse or Blessing? A Literature Survey.' *Journal of Energy Literature* 9 (1): 3–42.

Stijns, J.-P. 2006. 'Natural Resource Abundance and Human Capital Accumulation.' *World Development* 34 (6): 1060–1083.

Tax Facts and Figures Papua New Guinea (TFF). 2009. 'Papua New Guinea: PricewaterhouseCoopers.' http://www.pwc.com/en_PG/pg/publications/assets/2009-png-tax-facts-figures.pdf (accessed 27 May 2011).

Toumi, H. 2011. 'Public Sector in Qatar to get 60% Pay Rise,' *Gulf News,* 7 September. http://gulfnews.com/news/gulf/qatar/public-sector-in-qatar-to-get-60-per-cent-pay-rise-1.862595 (accessed 20 December 2011).

Townson, P. 2011. 'Dryland Nations' Group to be Named Within 2 Years,' *Gulf Times,* 6 December.

Wagner, R. 1974. 'Are There Social Groups in the New Guinea Highlands.' In *Frontiers of Anthropology,* ed. M. J. Leaf. New York: Van Nostrand.

Van Wijnbergen, S. 1984. 'The "Dutch Disease": A Disease After All?' *The Economic Journal* 94 (373): 41–55.

CHAPTER 8

Islam and Sustainable Economic Development

Rodney Wilson

There has been more concern with meeting immediate needs in the Islamic World than with longer-term issues of sustainability, as much of the region remains poor. Debate and writing on environmental issues in this region has therefore largely lagged behind elsewhere. It is worth noting that the 1.2 billion Muslims account for only 10 per cent of carbon dioxide emissions, while the United States, with less than a quarter of that population, is responsible for 20 per cent.

Following the Kyoto and Copenhagen conferences on climate change, Muslim academics and activists are nevertheless giving increased attention to environmental issues, not least because many predominately Muslim countries have become victims of greenhouse warming. Literature is starting to appear that draws on Islamic teaching and considers the relevance of faith and belief for policy on climate change. The methods associated with *ijtihad*, the application of Islamic principles to contemporary issues, which have proved so successful with respect to the development of modern Islamic finance, can potentially be drawn on to make a unique contribution to the climate change debate (Ansari 1992).

It is first necessary to consider Islamic teaching and its applicability to sustainable development. This chapter examines Islamic views on the custodianship of resources and asks whether trading in carbon credits is legitimate from a moral standpoint. It evaluates the stance of the governments of predominately Muslim countries to the climate change debate and the involvement of Islamic activists and non-governmental organizations (NGOs) in the run-up to the Copenhagen climate change conference and subsequently.

Secondly, this chapter considers how Islamic financing methods work and whether they can contribute to more sustainable outcomes than conventional finance. The greed that drove the real estate bubble prior to 2007 and the development of assets that were ultimately to prove toxic was clearly unsustainable. Islamic financial principles suggest a more cautious approach to finance based on risk sharing and the avoidance of speculative dealings (Wilson 2008). On the other hand, the involvement of some Islamic financial institutions in Dubai's overexpanded property sector raises questions about how far Islamic financial practice has been consistent with *shari'a* teaching.

This chapter will finally investigate the parallels between the objectives of Islamic finance and those of the ethical or socially responsible investment (SRI) movement. Many of the SRI funds concern ecology and biodiversity and avoid supporting activities that cause environmental damage. The extent to which Islamic funds and investment companies share these objectives is considered, as well as the screening methodologies used to distinguish between acceptable and unacceptable activities and what can be done to persuade businesses to change their practices in order to promote sustainability.

The Applicability of Islamic Teaching to Environmental Issues

In the Qur'an, there are passages that not only deal with spirituality and worship, but also many verses that relate to human activity and the social order. These provide a point of reference for scholars of *fiqh*, Islamic jurisprudence, who have a responsibility to provide answers to questions that arise through history as human society changes. As mentioned, the work of *fiqh* scholars is referred to as *ijtihad*, and includes attempts to address the issues of environmental sustainability and climate change from an Islamic perspective consistent with the basic principles of the Qur'an's teachings.

In particular, in the Qur'an the earth is regarded as the creation of Allah, the source of all life, including plants, animals and humankind (2:164). Human need for nature is not only to supply resources for food and shelter, but also to nurture the human soul (Nasr 2003: 96). Yet the Qur'an refers to mankind's lack of awareness of the holistic nature of the creation: 'The creation of the heavens and the earth is far greater than the creation of mankind. But most of mankind do not know it' (40:56).

Islam views nature as linked to Allah, and the relationship between the two is referred to by the Arabic word *ayat*, meaning the sign (Hussain 2007: 10). This word also refers to verses in the Qur'an which are signs of Allah's presence. The Qur'an reveals the word of Allah, and signs of his work are to be found in nature: 'There are certainly signs in the earth for people with certainty; and in yourselves. Do you not then see?' (52: 20–21).

Those who ignore the signs out of ignorance, and destroy or abuse natural habitats, are defiling the work of the Almighty. Moderation in consumption is urged, as Allah has provided abundant resources for mankind, and shortages reflect human greed and waste: 'It is He who produces gardens, both cultivated and wild, and palm trees and crops of diverse kinds and olives and pomegranates both similar and dissimilar. Eat of their fruits when they bear fruit and pay their dues on the day of their harvest, and do not be profligate. He does not love the profligate' (6: 142).

Researchers concerned with Islam and the environment have also examined the policy implications of the application of the teachings of the Qur'an to Muslim societies. In particular, the rulings of Abu Bakr, who was the first of what are referred to as the four rightly guided caliphs who succeeded the Prophet, are instructive. He not only ordered that his armies should not harm women, children and the infirm, but also they should not harm animals, destroy crops or cut down trees. He was concerned both with the establishment of justice and respect for nature (Khalid 2002: 335).

Islamic Views on Sustainable Development

The Islamic view of the goals of development is much wider than that of mere material advance. It sees development in terms of the realization of socio-economic justice and well-being, with the latter being equated with the Arabic word *falah,* which implies spiritual fulfillment as well as material well-being (Chapra 1998: 2). In other words, Islam advocates a balanced approach to development taking account of spiritual as well as material needs; indeed, it is the former, not the latter, that ultimately matter. In contrast, the capitalist development paradigm that emphasizes material advance as measured by such indicators as gross national product takes no account of environmental costs and negative externalities, where material advancement often only benefits a minority. An obsession to maximize consumption is unlikely to lead to long-term satisfaction from an Islamic perspective, which teaches that material goods can become false gods, and that those who pursue them will be idolaters.

In contemporary Islamic writing, there is concern with both how development occurs and the direction it takes. This chapter considers the former when it examines Islamic finance. The latter involves the important concept of *tazkiyah*, which can be interpreted as purification through development (Ahmed 1976: 2–4). Development outcomes can be moral or immoral, and it is concern with the morality of development that *tazkiyah* applies. Development should not be viewed as a process of attaining material perfection, but rather as a spiritual journey involving the uplifting of the soul. The stress is on personal and social development rather than simply the accumulation of worldly goods. Ultimately, worldly goods, no matter how magnificent and luxurious, though not condemned, are transitory whereas with spiritual development comes an appreciation of eternity. Even for those who are non-believers and sceptics, it is evident that the production and accumulation of goods, which has implications for resource use, has environmental consequences (such as pollution). Spiritual experiences may be enhanced by the construction of fine mosques, which are calm places and involve little carbon emission in contrast to secular leisure developments designated for frantic activity.

The great Muslim historian and philosopher of the fourteenth century Ibn Khaldun had a moral theory of development which he attributed to good governance. A just ruler would inspire trust and confidence, encouraging workers to give of their best and not worry about how they would be remunerated as they specialized and moved beyond subsistence production. Ibn Khaldun, like Adam Smith four centuries later, believed that specialization would result in an increase in wealth and a thriving state. Unfortunately, in Ibn Khaldun's view the progress was unsustainable, as the wealth, rather than satisfying material aspirations, actually increased greed, including that of rulers who would seek to raise taxes to pay for their ever more lavish consumption. It was not the supply of resources that caused the problems, as these represented the bounty of Allah; rather it was the distortions created by excessive unjustified demand. Ultimately this would cause social dissent and even rebellion, resulting in the collapse of the hitherto successful economy. Many of the symptoms of malaise identified by Ibn Khaldun arguably have applicability to the peaks of modern business cycles, as in 2007 before the financial crisis.

A central theme of contemporary Muslim studies of development is whether Islam is helpful or an obstacle to economic development. Proponents of the latter view contrast the rapid spread of Islam in its early years and the great advances of Islamic civilization with the relative stagnation in the nineteenth and early twentieth century when Western civilizations became dominant. Some attribute the Muslim world's economic stagnation and the marginalization of Islamic teaching to the irrelevance of *fiqh*, Islamic jurisprudence, to the real world, especially with the spread of *sufism* or mysticism. Others attribute it to moral decay, and apply Ibn Khaldun's analysis of the causes of decline to Muslim societies from the nineteenth century onwards (Chapra 2000: 173–177). Alternatively, yet others blame Western colonialism and imperialism, a view that became increasingly prevalent as the influence of the European powers increased and the Ottoman Empire weakened (Keddie 1994). In other words, both external and internal factors account for the malaise.

Markets and Sustainable Economic Empowerment

These views do not challenge the desirability of economic development or its sustainability. Some have nevertheless questioned the compatibility of economic development, as conventionally measured in terms of gross domestic product growth, and adherence to Islamic values, especially Malaysian writers (Hasan and Sadeq 1990: 11–12). In particular, they question production priorities and whether what is produced in a market system actually meets social needs, especially if the income distribution is skewed with large disparities between the rich and poor. However, markets are generally viewed from an Islamic perspective as a natural and normal vehicle for business transactions, and few writers argue that the state should take over the role of the market and have a monopoly of resource allocation, not least because states can become corrupt. The concern is more with income distribution, where Islamic inheritance law, the creation of *waqf* or charitable endowments and *zakat* alms giving can help empower the less economically affluent, addressing imbalances in the market. The encouragement of charitable giving, including through the tax system, is seen as a legitimate way of helping the poor.

There are detailed rules for the establishment and administration of *waqf* and the management of *zakat* to ensure that there is no abuse of state power. Similarly, it is recognized that markets need to be regulated to ensure buyers and sellers are not exploited, but state intervention is through the *hisbah*, a body that functions as an arbitrator in commercial transactions taking account of Islamic teaching (Abdullah 2010: 12–14). Although primarily concerned with eradicating corruption in buying and selling and combating monopoly, the remit of the *hisbah* extends beyond fair trading to ensuring that what is produced and sold has not caused social harm as is the case with manufacturing resulting in pollution or damage to natural ecosystems.

Redistributive policies can contribute to the maintenance of a social equilibrium, but whether they contribute to environmental sustainability is debatable and can only be answered by studying empirical data. Unfortunately, Gini coefficient data, which measures income distribution, is unavailable for most Muslim countries.[1]

Private property, which is necessary for markets to function, is recognized as being legitimate in Islam, and property can be inherited, and bought from and sold to others. Property ownership in Islam is not merely concerned with rights, but also obligations. Ultimately, property owners are accountable to the Almighty for how they use their property. Some may own more property than others, but with the benefits from this come additional responsibilities. Concentrated ownership may be justified if those exercising control are more competent and trustworthy than those with little or no property.

An important concept applicable to property management is *khalifah,* which refers to Muslim rulers, who ultimately face judgment on how they perform their duties. This concept not only applies to national political governance by a *caliph,* but also to corporate governance and the management of assets more generally. The implication of *khalifah* is that owners should exercise stewardship over the assets they control, ensuring that these are used responsibly and in appropriate ways. The latter could encompass sustainability.

Shari'a jurisprudence provides for the leasing of property and rent is regarded as a legitimate return to the owners. An Islamic lease, known as *ijara,* is the equivalent of an operating lease rather than a financing lease, as with the latter most of the responsibility for the maintenance of the property gets passed on to the tenant. This is regarded as unfair, as in Islamic teaching the owner must retain most of the obligations pertaining to the property to justify the rent payments. In other words, landlords have a long-term responsibility for the sustainability of the property, and tenants, who may only be leasing for a short period, are viewed as having less responsibility, a realistic approach with tenants in occupation for a limited time.

To be *shari'a* compliant, expenditure must be on goods and services which are permissible (*halal*) rather than prohibited (*haram*) such as alcohol or activities like gambling. This applies not only to current consumption, but also investment, which is why the latter features screening criteria, which will be discussed later. Trading in most goods is permissible – indeed, Islamic teaching regards trading as a legitimate means of making a living, in contrast to the income from usury or *riba,* which is regarded as illegitimate: 'Those who charge usury are in the same position as those controlled by the devil's influence. This is because they claim that usury is the same as commerce. However God permits commerce and prohibits usury' (Qur'an 2:275).

There is no need to enter debate about whether *riba* constitutes all interest payments or simply usury here, but what is clear is the legitimacy of trade.

Trading in Carbon Credits

A carbon credit is purchased by governments, corporations or even individuals who have a moral duty to decrease their carbon footprint. The
proceeds can be used for investment in carbon emission–reduction technologies. Carbon credits can be regarded as a tax on pollution, with less
pollution resulting in a lower liability. They are designed to provide an incentive to limit emissions that cause greenhouse gases and climate change.
Companies that succeed in this can sell their carbon credits to others, who
may not be able to reduce their emissions in the short term, but will in turn
have an incentive to tackle pollution in the longer term.

In Islamic teaching, a distinction is drawn between trading in 'goods'
and trading in 'bads'. This is of relevance to the use of carbon credits as
they enable the purchaser to pollute. Although the aim of carbon credit
trading may be laudable, the creation of monetary incentives to reduce
emissions by forcing polluters to pay, creating a market in rights to pollute, could be regarded as dubious from an Islamic perspective. Trading
in 'goods' has merits, but trading in 'bads' such as rights to pollute could
be regarded as *haram.*

There are five arguments in support of this view. Firstly, pollution has
environmental consequences for others. Regardless of whether the pol-
luter pays or not, these will remain. Cash from carbon credit levies will not
compensate for the environmental degradation caused by the pollution.

Secondly, rich polluters, whether countries or large profitable companies,
can afford to pay for carbon credits, whereas the poor cannot. Hence there
are clearly inequities in the entitlements resulting from such arrangements.

Thirdly, much of the trading in carbon credits is by buyers and sellers who do not actually intend to use the carbon credits, but are solely
motivated by short term financial gain. Carbon-credit trading is a form of
derivatives transactions, which are not permissible under *shari'a.*[2] Islamic
teaching condemns speculative dealings and trade that serves only a financial rather than a material purpose.

Fourthly, what is being traded with carbon credits is a right which
relates to the future rather than the present. Trading in future contracts is
also forbidden under *shari'a*, as only spot contracts for immediate delivery
are acceptable.

Finally, trade in carbon credits is *haram* because of the uncertainty and
potential ambiguity regarding what is being bought and sold. In addition
to prohibiting *riba*, Islamic teaching abhors *gharar*, which is usually translated as contractual or legal uncertainty. In so far as carbon credits represent assets, they are intangibles, whereas Islamic contract law requires
what is being traded to be precisely defined. Furthermore, it is not clear

that the actual pollution covered by carbon credits can be effectively monitored and how transparent the process will be. Carbon trading credits relies on trust, but there will inevitably be questions about how trustworthy polluters actually are.

The Responses of Muslim Country Governments to Kyoto

Government responses in the Muslim world to the international debates and initiatives prior to and after the signing of the Kyoto Protocol largely reflected perceptions of national interests rather than Islamic teaching. Those Muslim countries that would be the most severely affected by climate change were eager to sign up to the protocol, the first being the Maldives which signed on 16 March 1998 (this Indian Ocean archipelago could be the first country in the world to disappear if sea levels rise due to global warming). Muslim states surrounding the Sahara were also quick to sign and ratify the Kyoto Protocol as they have already experienced the effects of climate change as grazing land reverts to desert and water supplies dry up. These Muslim states include Niger, which signed in 1998, and Mali, which signed in 1999. Bangladesh, a Muslim state that experiences monsoon flooding annually and severe typhoons that may worsen with climate change, ratified the Kyoto Protocol in 2001.

The oil-exporting Muslim countries were more cautious about how to respond to Kyoto, as they recognized that energy-saving policies and switching to alternative non-carbon supplies could potentially damage their economies in the long run. They felt little pressure to sign, as the United States had not yet ratified the Kyoto Protocol, although eventually in 2005 most finally did ratify, including Saudi Arabia, Kuwait, Qatar and the UAE together with Iran. Egypt, which exports only limited amounts of oil and gas, also signed in 2005, and this was followed by Turkey, Kazakhstan, Iraq and Brunei in 2009. Indonesia, the most populous Muslim country, had previously ratified in 2004, and Pakistan, an oil-importing state, ratified in 2005.

As part of the ratification process, countries were asked to review their methodologies for the compilation of greenhouse gas emissions. Saudi Arabia was cautious in its response, stressing that it had the status of a developing country and that the principle of common but differentiated responsibilities must be considered in developing any future methodologies related to greenhouse gas inventories (Saudi Arabia 2004). In practice this can be used to justify less stringent requirements. The response stated that bodies such as the Organization of Petroleum Exporting Countries (OPEC) should be involved in future discussions. The implication was that this could strengthen the negotiating position of oil-exporting countries. Furthermore, Saudi Arabia indicated that it would not include fuel sold to shipping companies or airlines when compiling its national totals.

The most ambitious scheme for sustainable development among the Gulf Cooperation Council (GCC) countries is the Masdar initiative of Abu Dhabi, which involves the creation of a new carbon-neutral city. This is discussed elsewhere in this book, but a key question is why Abu Dhabi has taken this initiative given that most of its economy depends on hydrocarbon exports and that global carbon neutrality would undermine it. The promoters of the project see it giving Abu Dhabi a leadership role in sustainable development, as the first energy exporter to take such an initiative, and it can also be seen as part of a move to long-term diversification. The aim is to diversify Abu Dhabi's economy by making it a pioneer in alternative energy. The Masdar project could however be undertaken anywhere, and the promotional material for the initiative appears to be entirely secular, with no reference to local cultural values or norms. The city will have homes, schools, restaurants, theatres and shops for 40,000 residents and 50,000 commuters from elsewhere. There is however no mention of it having a mosque. The architecture is supposed to be inspired by traditional souks and wind towers, but so are many of the themed and highly unsuitable developments in Dubai and elsewhere. It is unclear how many local citizens will actually live in Masdar.

International Islamic Organizations with a Possible Sustainable Development Mandate

At a global level, it is the Organization for Islamic Cooperation (OIC), comprising fifty-six predominately Muslim countries, which is the relevant forum for discussions and resolutions on sustainable development issues. It encompasses both Sunni and Shia states, and provides an opportunity for dialogue between Iran, Iraq and the GCC states, as well as bringing together the many Muslim countries in Africa and Central Asia, and, importantly, Malaysia, Indonesia, Bangladesh and Pakistan. The charter of the OIC has three clauses dealing with sustainable development which are worth quoting in full (OIC 1972: 1–2):

(1) To endeavour to work for revitalizing Islam's pioneering role in the world while ensuring sustainable development, progress and prosperity for the peoples of Member States;

(2) To promote cooperation among Member States to achieve sustained socioeconomic development for effective integration in the global

economy, in conformity with the principles of partnership and equality;

(3) To preserve and promote all aspects related to environment for present and future generations.

The OIC's remit is to encourage cooperation between Islamic countries and defend the interests of Muslims. Although developmental issues have been addressed at its summits, there has been no debate so far on climate change issues. As with the Arab League,[3] much of the focus has been on Palestine at the political level, although more recently there has been debate on terrorism and extremism, which the OIC seeks to counter by portraying a moderate image to combat Islamophobia.

The two subsidiaries of the OIC relevant to sustainable development are the OIC Fiqh Academy and the Islamic Development Bank (IDB), both based in Jeddah. The OIC Fiqh Academy comprises well-respected Islamic scholars with the authority to deliver *fatwa* (rulings) on how Islamic teaching should be applied to the modern world. Most of their work has concerned medical ethics, where many moral dilemmas arise, and Islamic finance. There has been no research conducted by the OIC on the issuance of possible *fatwa* on sustainable development issues.

The IDB has functioned as a type of World Bank for Islamic nations since its establishment in 1974, mainly through the provision of developmental assistance, largely by concessional loans. Its funding is *shari'a* compliant rather than being interest based, with costs being covered through fees and equipment rentals. The costs are comparable to those of other conventional providers of development assistance such as the Asian and African Development Banks. As it tends to follow development fashion, its publicity and media releases make many references to sustainable development, but it does not have a specific sustainable development programme. Together with the Federal Government of the UAE it supports the work of the International Centre for Biosaline Agriculture (ICBA) that was established in Dubai in 1999. One of the goals of the ICBA is to support the sustainable development of agriculture in arid desert regions, many of which occur in Muslim countries.

The IDB subsidiary, the Islamic Research and Training Institute (IRTI), also based in Jeddah, has sponsored research on sustainable development issues which it has published (Khaf 2003). The work has largely focused on the sustainability of Islamic financial systems rather than ecosystems.

The changing global economic order during the last decade has given significantly greater power to Muslim countries to influence the international economic agenda, especially with the shift from the Group of Seven (G7) to the Group of Twenty (G20). Saudi Arabia, Turkey and Indonesia are represented on the G20 as three of the world's largest economies. Recently, G20 meetings have largely focused on the international financial crisis and how banking regulation can be strengthened in its aftermath. However, there is the possibility of sustainable development featuring on its agenda as an alternative to the United Nations framework for dealing with climate change, especially given the failure of the Copenhagen conference. At the G20, the three predominately Muslim countries have yet to assert themselves or agree to any collective position, but the forum could be used to provide an Islamic input on matters of concern, including sustainable development.

Muslim Environmental Activism
Prior to the Copenhagen Conference

Following the Kyoto conference, there was increasing awareness in many parts of the Muslim world, especially in Bangladesh, of the connection between climate change and the deteriorating environment. Those voicing concern included academics, journalists, religious leaders and NGOs. Conferences and seminars were held addressing environmental issues, with participants looking to Islamic teaching for guidance in relation to the moral and ethical questions.

There are two academic studies and two academic initiatives that have influenced the thinking of Muslim climate change activists. The first post-Kyoto study by Khalid Fazlul provided a broad perspective on the issues (1999). It is essentially a literature review covering the teaching of the Qur'an and *fiqh* scholars on environmental issues. The second study by Mawil Izzi Dien also reviewed Islamic teaching and the views of *fiqh* scholars, but was more forward looking and written in language that will be familiar to all those researching climate change, both Muslim and non-Muslim (Dien 2000). Mawil Dien's study sees the development of Islamic environmental ethics as an ongoing process, and he relates concepts of Islamic economic justice to the environment.

One of the initiatives was an academic conference in the United States on Islam and ecology, which resulted in an edited book (Foltz, Denny and Baharuddin 2003). The issues covered were wide ranging, from the challenges of reinterpretation of Islamic teaching to specific topics such as ecological justice and human rights for women in Islam, to the environment and family planning. The final section, containing three interesting contributions, inspirationally entitled 'the Islamic garden as a metaphor for paradise', highlights the spiritual rewards from careful management of the environment.

The other initiative was a series of seminars held at the Oxford Centre of Islamic Studies in association with the Centre for Environmental Policy and Understanding of Green Templeton College, now re-launched as the Policy Foresight Programme. The last seminar, in 2006, addressing the impact of climate change on the Islamic World, stressed the unsustainable nature of consumerism and how technological change to maintain it would only create further problems (Oxford 2006). It was agreed that if climate change could be seen as a security issue there would be a greater probability of serious action to reduce greenhouse gas emissions.

There are relatively few Islamic NGOs focused on environmental issues, but one of the most high profile is the Islamic Foundation for Ecology and Environmental Sciences. It launched a project in Zanzibar in 2000 to provide for more sustainable fisheries. Hitherto local Muslim fisherman had adopted the practice of using dynamite for fishing, seriously damaging coral reefs and fish habitats. The Muslim fisherman changed their practices following an educational programme on alternative methods of fishing that pointed out that such practices were in conflict with Islamic values (Van Der Meulen 2009).

In July 2009, ahead of the Copenhagen Conference, the Muslim Association for Climate Change Action (MACCA) was founded, with its headquarters in London. Although an NGO, it has financial support from the Ministry of Awqaf and Islamic Affairs in Kuwait, where an initial workshop was held in 2008 to discuss how to take matters forward. An inaugural conference was held in Istanbul the following year, which endorsed a seven-year action plan to deal with global warming issues in a manner consistent with Islamic values. A conference held in Jakarta in November 2009, immediately prior to the Copenhagen conference, concluded that help should be sought from the West to support existing environmental projects in Muslim countries, with Western Muslims playing a mediating role.

MACCA has set several specific objectives. One is working towards a Green Hajj, which the Saudi Arabian Ministry of Hajj has endorsed. The aim is to encourage more environmentally friendly travel and make pilgrims aware that 'the care of creation is an act of faithfulness' (Earth Mates Development Centre 2009). The construction of green mosques is planned to showcase best practice in heating, lighting and environmentally friendly design. Two or three cities in the Muslim world are to be designated as targets for green initiatives with measures taken to ensure their development becomes more sustainable. Lessons learnt will subsequently be applied to ten other cities in the Muslim world. MACCA also envisages the production of educational materials on environmental issues for use in schools and *madrassas* that train Islamic clergy. There is even provision for the printing of the Qur'an on paper that comes from sustainably managed forests.

Islamic Finance for Sustainable Development

Islamic banks and other *shari'a*-compliant financial institutions have proliferated during the last four decades, with the largest concentration in the energy-based economies of the Gulf. This has occurred with rising oil and gas revenues, the utilization of which should be, at least partially, in compliance with the religious values of the region's Muslim population. On the Arab side of the Gulf, Islamic finance has widespread popular support and up to one-third of bank accounts are designated as being *shari'a* compliant. In the Islamic Republic of Iran, all banking has been *shari'a* compliant since the Law on Interest-Free Banking was enacted in 1983.

The question arises as to whether Islamic finance is more likely to promote sustainable development than conventional financing – not just in the Gulf, but worldwide. From the perspective of sustainability, running a financial system from revenue from a depleting resource is questionable unless Islamic finance can contribute to economic diversification into other production with a long-term future. Islamic banks proved to be financially sustainable during the global financial crisis of 2008 as there were no institutions that collapsed or had to go to the regulatory authorities or governments for financial assistance. This was partly explained by Islamic banks largely managing their financing from deposits rather than from inter-bank borrowing, the cost of which soared after banks lost faith in each other following the collapse of Lehman Brothers and Bear Sterns. Furthermore, much of the financing of Islamic banks is for the acquisition of real assets rather than financial securities, which to some extent protected Islamic banks from the downturn in financial markets.

Nevertheless, Islamic banks have not been immune from the economic recession of 2009 following the financial crisis, and many institutions were involved in real estate finance. When the property market crashed in countries such as Dubai, Islamic banks, like their conventional counterparts, inevitably found that many of their clients could no longer meet their financial obligations. Provision has therefore had to be made for impaired assets, and some debts have been written off. Two Dubai providers of Islamic mortgages, Amlak and Tamweel, are being restructured so that they will be able to become viable once again (Wilson 2009: 32).

The dilemma facing Islamic bankers is that the economies where business is generated are very open, increasing their vulnerability to global financial cycles. Yet if they choose isolation, it is doubtful if this would be financially sustainable. The early experience with Islamic credit unions serving rural communities in Pakistan and Egypt in the 1960s was not encouraging as they needed government subsidies to continue, and in Egypt's case the Mit Ghamr savings bank was nationalized and became part of the Nasser Social Bank. There have been several experiments with *shari'a*-compliant microfinance, but none has taken off and achieved financial viability, although organizations such as the Islamic Financial Services Board (IFSB), a body that provides regulatory standards, would like to see more initiatives of this kind (IFSB 2010: 24–25).

Islamic Ethical Investment

Although Islamic financing methods will not guarantee financial sustainability, the need for *shari'a* compliance has implications for how finance is allocated. In particular, funds can only be advanced for activities that are viewed as *halal* or permissible. This is referred to as 'sector screening', which involves a similar methodology to that used by ethical and socially responsible mutual funds, although the latter largely focus on preventing the financing of activities which damage the environment or involve exploitation, such as the employment of child labour in sweatshops. Islamic investment also involves financial screening, which means eliminating institutions that are heavily leveraged, as this involves *riba* financing.[4] In practice this means Islamic funds cannot be used to finance conventional banks (Wilson 2004).

The Dow Jones Islamic Market Sustainability Index represents the first attempt to combine the Islamic sector and its financial screens with the criteria for selection of listed companies based on an assessment of their environmental sustainability (Dow Jones Indexes 2009). Each of the 2,500 largest companies in the Dow Jones World Index is invited to participate in a corporate sustainability assessment. The companies are then assigned a score based on their corporate sustainability performance assessed from the information provided. The average error margin is determined by reviewing a random sample of the companies. Companies selected for inclusion are periodically reviewed to check that they still meet the sustainability criteria.

Conclusion

It is necessary to be realistic rather than idealistic about how far Islamic finance as presently practiced can contribute to sustainable development.

Ecologically friendly investment is inherently *shari'a* compliant, but permissibility is not the same as being enthusiastic or proactive towards investment in projects such as solar- or wind-energy generation. *Shari'a*-compliant investment is primarily concerned with adherence to rules, which are ultimately divinely inspired, and less about socially inspired values. Nevertheless, *shari'a*-compliant investment can be combined with SRI, not least as both use screening criteria to determine what investments are appropriate, rather than solely looking at projected rates of return. SRI is not concerned with how funds are dispersed, but this is of concern to Islamic financial institutions which cannot provide interest-based loans. Rather, in Islamic finance the returns are justified on the basis of risk sharing, which may fit well with the venture-capital requirements of ecologically sustainable projects that can so easily be damaged by excessive short-term debt.

It is apparent from this chapter that Islam has a distinctive approach to issues of climate change and sustainable development. Muslim activists and researchers in this field are interested in dialogue with other faith groups to explore how far joint efforts can go in the achievement of common goals for the long-term benefit of all. In October 2007, a group of 138 Muslim scholars representing all Islamic denominations addressed an open letter to Christian Church leaders calling for dialogue on issues of mutual concern (Christian Muslim Youth Forum 2008). As part of the response, on 19 June 2008 the World Bank hosted delegates from the National Association of Evangelicals, an American Christian organization and representatives from Morocco's Ministry of Islamic Affairs and religious television. The theme was 'creation care', with the discussion centred on how both Muslims and Christians could promote awareness of climate change issues amongst the faithful.

Because tackling climate change is as much about changing social attitudes as it is about winning the support of governments, the role of faith-based initiatives can be crucial. Action on climate change is much more likely to be successful within the Muslim world if it can be seen as entirely consistent with Islamic values, indeed as helping to both defend and promote those values. On the wider global front, Islamic researchers and activists are already cooperating with those of other faiths, in recognition of their mutual vulnerability and in order to ensure that a better environment is passed on to future generations.

Notes

1. The Gini coefficient is the most widely used measure of inequality which varies between zero, indicating complete equality, with, for example, 50 per cent

of a population having 50 per cent of the income, and one, which indicates complete inequality with one person having the entire income.

2. A derivative is an agreement or contract that is not based on an exchange of tangible goods.

3. An international organization representing twenty-two Arab states founded in 1945.

4. Leveraging is the proportion of debt or borrowing which a company has in relation to the value of its share capital. High leveraging can indicate excessive risk taking, often involving speculation. In *fiqh*, Islamic jurisprudence, a ratio of debt to equity which exceeds one-third is regarded as excessive, and therefore *haram*.

References

Abdullah, A. 2010. 'Harking Back to Hisbah: Kuala Lumpur,' *Accountants Today*, 12–14.

Ahmed, K. 1976. *Studies in Islamic Economics*. Leicester: Islamic Foundation.

Ansari, .M. I. 1992. 'Islamic Perspectives on Sustainable Development.' *American Journal of Islamic Social Sciences* 8 (4): 394-402.

Chapra, M. U. 1998. 'Islam and Economic Development: A Discussion within the Framework of Ibn Khaldun's Philosophy of History.' In *Proceedings of the Second Harvard University Forum on Islamic Finance*, 1–10. Cambridge, MA: Harvard University.

Chapra, M. U. 2000. *The Future of Economics: An Islamic Perspective*. Leicester: Islamic Foundation.

Christian Muslim Youth Forum. 2008. 'Christian-Muslim Dialogue on Climate Change.' Washington. http://www.cmyf/uploads/2/9/0/6/2906152/muslim_-_christian_dialogue_on_climate_change.pdf.

Dien, M. I. 2000. *The Environmental Dimensions of Islam*. Cambridge: Lutterworth Press.

Dow Jones Indexes. 2009. 'Methodology: Dow Jones Islamic Market Sustainability Index.' New York.

Earth Mates Development Centre (EMDC), United Nations Development Programme and Alliance of Religions and Conservation. 2009. 'Draft of the Muslim Seven-Year Plan to Deal With Global Climate Change.' London: EMDC.

Fazlul, K. 1999. *Islam and the Environment*. London: Ta Ha Publishers.

Foltz, R., F. M. Denny and A. Baharuddin. 2003. *Islam and Ecology: A Bestowed Trust*. Cambridge, MA: Harvard University Press.

Hasan, A. and M. Sadeq. 1990. *Economic Development in Islam*. Selangor: Pelanduk Publications.

Hussain, M. 2007. 'Islam and Climate Change: Perspectives and Engagement.' http://www.lineonweb.org.uk/Resources/reading.htm.

Keddie, N. R. 1994. 'The Revolt of Islam, 1700 to 1993: Comparative Considerations and Relations to Imperialism.' *Contemporary Studies in Society and History* 36 (3): 463–487.

Islamic Financial Services Board, Islamic Development Bank and Islamic Research and Training Institute. 2010. 'Islamic Finance and Global Financial Stability.' Kuala Lumpur and Jeddah.

Khalid, F. M. 2002. 'Islam and the Environment.' In *Encyclopedia of Global Environment Change, Volume 5: Social and Economic Dimensions of Global Environmental Change,* ed. Peter Timmerman, 332–339. Chichester: John Wiley.

Nasr, S. 2003. 'Islam, the Contemporary Islamic World and the Environmental Crisis.' In *Islam and Ecology: A Bestowed Trust,* eds. R. Foltz, F. Denny and A. Baharuddin, 85–105. Cambridge, MA: Harvard University Press.

Organization of the Islamic Conference (OIC). 1972. 'Charter,' 1–15. Jeddah.

Oxford Centre for Islamic Studies and Policy Foresight Programme. 2006. 'Synopsis of the Seminar on The Impact of Climate Change on the Islamic World.'

Saudi Arabia. 2004. 'Review of Methodological Work under the Convention and the Kyoto Protocol: (Information on National Systems under Article 5, Paragraph 1, Of the Kyoto Protocol for the Preparation of National GHG Inventories).'

Van Der Meulen, E. F. 2009. *Islam Inspired Green Initiatives Deserve Western Support.* Amsterdam: NRC Handelsblad.

Wilson, R. 2009. 'The Development of Islamic Finance in the GCC.' London School of Economics: Kuwait Programme on Development, Governance and Globalization in the Gulf States.

———. 2008. 'Islamic Economics and Finance.' *World Economics* 9 (1): 177–195.

———. 2004. 'Screening Criteria for Islamic Equity Funds.' In *Islamic Asset Management: Forming the Future for Shari'a Compliant Investment Strategies,* ed. Sohail Jaffer, 35–45. London: Euromoney Books.

III

Environmental Issues

CHAPTER 9

Linking Local and Global in the Sustainable Development of Biodiversity Conservation

Ben Campbell

When sustainable development became a principal policy paradigm at the end of the 1980s, it thrust together human development needs and environmental protection in a marriage of interests that were previously imagined to be mutually incompatible. The 1992 Rio Earth Summit's vision of Agenda 21 forefronted the planet's diverse set of biomes as needing care, both to prevent climate change and species loss, and to achieve improved livelihoods and social justice. Anthropologists' and other social scientists' contributions to the formation and subsequent life-career of sustainable development have been especially significant in bringing field experiences and case studies to bear on general understandings of the concept, its permutations and transformative potential.

This chapter asks how we would recognize sustainable development if we saw it. I attempt to answer this question by thinking with the place-based resources of an anthropologist's parochial knowledge, and stretching them in new directions to track the evolution and visibility of sustainable development. Knowledge gained about a certain place, with its specific cultural-ecological dynamics of sustainability, has suddenly found a new horizon of enquiry, and context of relevance by having set foot in Qatar – as have others from that certain place. Viewing the connections that make parochial sustainable development possible involves materializing a network that will unlikely be visible to those in whose hands its fate lies. There are vital sustainable development consequences upstream, in communities where Qatar has become a destination for labour in search of employment.

People are coming for many reasons (Gardner 2011), but many come from communities in South Asia, where traditional sources of production and consumption have disappeared, in search of livelihood substitution strategies. If it were not for employment in Qatar, many households would find it extremely difficult to make a living. Recent data mentioned by Gardner from the UN Economic and Social Commission for Western Asia suggest that the Gulf states are the source of remittances of more than US $26 billion in value, which is a higher figure than that for the United States in the global scheme of things (ibid.: 15). Despite this being the case, 'scholarship and baseline data about the fundamental aspects of these migration flows remain in their infancy' (ibid.: 22). Poverty, population pressure and conflict are common causes for South Asians to look for work in the Gulf. There is, however, another outcome of the remittance economy, which is to give the biodiversity conservation projects operating in many of the rural migrants' homelands a greater chance of being sustainable. Remittances from overseas labourers now provide families with a buffer against hunger. In previous generations, domestic shortfalls pushed households to take valuable plant and animal materials from South Asian forests to barter and exchange for food.

As someone who in the late 1970s first heard about sustainable development as a novel and radical possibility, the twists and turns through which the concept has travelled are a source of constant surprise. The message of this chapter is to follow connections of sustainable development that are on the move, and to be aware of beneficial and risky aspects of sustainable development that have mobility as an intrinsic feature. An argument raised in the chapter questions methods for approaching sustainable development, the units and scales standardly brought to bear and how to make visible the multiple linkages between migration and development processes.

Post-Agrarian Movements

To provide some theoretical context to the general discussion of migration and development, it is worth looking at assumptions concerning what sustainable processes might look like, and at what scale they might be expected to be visible. This has implications for the empirical case study on the dynamics of sustainability in Nepal that is to follow. One important perspective that challenges deeply held assumptions is expressed by Jonathan Rigg. He asks if investment to support small-scale agricultural production in developing countries makes sense in the context of migrant labour trends, and

> whether the present state of affairs in the Rural South will have any historical resilience. In other words, do the present and the past offer a reasonable

guide to the future? … [N]ot only are non-farm activities becoming central to rural livelihoods but also … an increasing number of rural households have no commitment to farming whatsoever. It is not, therefore, just a question of weighting and balance, but of a more profound transition from one way of making a living to another. (2006: 181)

Rigg goes on to quote Piers Blaikie, John Cameron and David Seddon's (2002) study of poverty and development in west central Nepal, based on a longitudinal view of more than seven hundred households over twenty-five years: 'The original model underestimated the capacity of the global labor market to provide work and remittances to sustain rural life and to stave off a more generalized crisis' (2002: 1268–1269, cited in Rigg 2006: 182).

The argument in Rigg's article builds by discussing evidence from a number of studies, such as that by Afsar (2003), which indicate that in Bangladesh the flow of remittances into rural areas has had positive effects in terms of actual productivity of farming, increased use of machinery, levels of agricultural wages and availability of land for farm tenants. On the back of such evidence, Rigg proposes that the population of areas of Asia and Africa where agricultural development has been promoted to reduce poverty may do better by upping sticks and joining the mobile labour force. He argues: 'The best means of promoting pro-poor growth in the countryside may have less to do with supporting small-holder farming, whether through land redistribution or policies of agricultural development, and more to do with endowing poor people with the skills so that they can escape from farming and, perhaps, escape from the countryside' (2006: 196).

Rigg identifies a powerful normative value among sectors of the development community who give preferential treatment to models of change that keep farming families on the land. In the light of persistently favouring land-based livelihood options, migration is seen as dislocation or deviation from deep-rooted channels of improvement: 'It is when villages are fragmented by modernity, when village production is undermined by industrialization, and when villagers are extracted from their natal homes that things are perceived to go wrong' (ibid.: 187). This has been termed the 'yeoman farmer fallacy' (Farrington et al. 2002: 15).

Glick Schiller and Faist , in their reflections on linkages between migration and development, similarly point out that 'migration has mutated from being a problem for economic development to being a solution. … Hopes [for development] are pinned on labour migrants, especially temporary ones, sending financial remittances to their countries and locales of origin' (2010: 7)

Faist notices that commentators who look approvingly on the new positive view of migration for development are at risk of seeing development in aggregate terms of raised income levels, rather than attending to what precise consequences for development are occurring in the sending countries (Faist 2010: 86). This is the key issue that the rest of this chapter explores. In the core community focused on here, there are very significant changes underway in the relationship of the migrant households and their possibilities for sustainable livelihoods. This involves their ability to switch to patterns of consumption that depend on cash exchange for large areas of their domestic needs. This in turn has made possible a viable relationship to 'participatory' forms of biodiversity conservation promoted by national parks and protected areas. Cash-acquired food, clothing and shelter have replaced the previous generation's dependence on supplies for growing their own food, and relying on forest products to barter or sell in exchange for items of need.

Where this chapter takes issue with Rigg is in the singular alignment of remittance-oriented livelihoods with solutions for sustainability in the global south. It concurs with Faist and Glick Schiller in calling for more rigorous examination of migration and development in ethnographic terms that explicitly challenge the drawbacks of 'methodological nationalism' and 'sedentarist bias', so as not to lose sight of the specific differences that are being made on the ground. This has impacts for how projects and processes can be assessed as sustainable or not, in terms of their consequences for the ability of poor households to adjust their livelihood strategies to engage in unprecedented ways with new labour markets, and at the same time continue to struggle for rights, respect and resilience in their own development as communities in their national societies, with much to offer the future prospects for biodiversity conservation that could better incorporate local knowledge and livelihood skills.

The New Remittance Ecology

Nepal has been predominantly imagined as a peasant society stuck in a pre-modern, culture-bound relationship to land and livelihood. Factors of historical mobility were commonly ignored (except migration to join mercenary Gurkha forces or tea plantations) prior to the last decade. Today the scale and impacts of recent migration trends are recognized to be immense. Well over 10 per cent of the population is abroad, and there is no greater contributor to national income than migrant remittances, which now exceed all other combined sources of income (Graner 2010). The question is whether Nepal is a 'rural' or 'agricultural' society. As Andrew Graner notes, village communities where the overall dependence is on remittance income means it is 'largely inappropriate to refer to these households as agricultural ones' (ibid.: 25). She identifies the mid-1990s collapse of Nepal's carpet industry as a key factor in analyzing the circumstances in which overseas migration took hold. She argues for an institutional analysis of migration that moves beyond methodological individualism for understanding what are mistakenly referred to as 'flows' of labour and capital (as if similar to some natural process), rather than a distinct conjuncture of dynamic institutional arrangements both within Nepal and globally. After the downfall of the carpet industry and loss of income, Nepalese government and manpower agencies looked for new markets to employ workers (ibid.: 38).

Looking at the communities of migrant workers from Nepal to Qatar (approximately 300,000 in 2009), Tristan Bruslé attempts to enquire into their experiences beyond the headlines in the Nepali press about the workers' 'horrendous conditions', ' indecent treatment' and being considered as 'slaves' (*gulam*; 2010b: 155). In the labour camp he studied, most of the people were employed in office and cleaning jobs, rather than in the construction industry, and there was a larger proportion of higher castes among them than in Nepal's population as a whole. He noted 'there is a correlation between caste, wealth and migration to Gulf countries' (ibid.: 160). At the time of Bruslé's research in 2008, an amount of US $550–$1,100 was required in order to embark on migration to the Gulf, depending on the commission taken by various handlers. This put Gulf migration beyond many potential Nepali migrants, for whom Malaysia is a cheaper alternative. In 2008 the basic net salary was US $55 a month, though the average wage in the labour camp was US $98. There is no minimum wage as such in Qatar, but the Nepalese embassy rules that it should be US $77. Bruslé comments there is 'little or no power to bargain' once the Nepali workers discover the salary they are actually paid does not correspond to what was written on their contracts (ibid.: 166). The film by Nepali filmmaker Kesang Tseten, *In Search of the Riyal*, includes several interviews with Nepalis who have regularly not been paid on time, and not been given leave to attend funerals. Yet the film confirms that Nepalese labour has a comparative reputation for not complaining about employment conditions. If this were to change, the numbers of Nepalis recruited would probably fall off.

The case study in this chapter considers the relationships between local and global elements of economy and environment as they have evolved through implementation phases of sustainable development programmes in the context of the Himalayas. These relationships have changed in ways that could not at all have been foreseen at the outset of the sustainable journey. The key themes that emerge concern interconnectedness and movement. Surprising relationships have emerged from historical trends and events that have helped bring about certain sustainable development objectives. These emphasize that field-based knowledge is required to reinvigorate how sustainability is conceived, communicated and assessed for points of least resilience.

Anthropologists working on projects for sustainable development have tried to see what is happening 'on the ground'. There tend to be a number of ways in which their understandings of development differ from economists, who normally assume human motivations and perceptions to be universal. The ethnographic concern for local distinctiveness and unpredictability provide methodological entry points for scrutinizing 'off-the-shelf' policy prescriptions. Beyond the rhetoric of sustainable development as a generic panacea for all ills, field-based observations of policy implementation, and the effects of local communities' engagement with the implications of given policies, allow understandings of sustainable solutions to emerge, located in real-world conditions and historical processes.

A key perspective argued in this chapter is that sustainable development projects to improve the relationships between villagers and protected area authorities in the Himalayas have demonstrated a 'sedentarist' bias. They have made assumptions about the social and economic characteristics of poor village communities. These imagine a finite number of community members and a finite set of environmental resources of which those community members can be deemed legitimate 'users'. Sustainable development's conceptual underpinnings were formed in the debates over poverty and environmental degradation in the late 1980s. At this time, the notion of common property resources management offered a notable alternative to the bleakness of individual self-interest assumed in to the 'tragedy of the commons' thesis. The common property resources approach used rational choice theory combined with calculations of carrying capacity to argue the case for local governance of the commons, backed up by numerous ethnographic case studies. However, this did not adequately recognize the fluidity of the social fabric interweaving mountain communities' mutual dependence with regards to forests and pastures. Ironically, it is migration to foreign labour markets, such as the Gulf countries, that has provided the conditions in which the sedentarist model has managed to have some viability. With this new global context, the realities of rural society in the developing world, and especially in South Asia, were to transform dramatically over two decades, as communities once thought of as 'peasantries' tied to the soil became participants in global migrant networks.

What Difference Did Sustainable Development Make in Policies for Biodiversity Conservation?

Many national parks and protected areas were originally based on the principle of 'minimal human interference'. In the 1870s, the US national parks and the colonial Indian Forest Department were formed to provide a defence against the uncontrolled use of timber and forest lands for development (Grove 1993; Tucker 1991; Saberwal 1999; Campbell 2005).

The model of protecting authentic, pure nature devoid of human presence may have been viable for Yellowstone Park, but not for developing world countries with numerous rural poor, resentful that local forests became inaccessible (Stevens 1997). In the post–World War II era of development, national economies increased growth by exploiting environmental resources (rivers and forest soils) to boost agricultural production, but concerns expressed by wildlife organizations regarding disappearing species like rhinos and tigers led to the creation of pockets of nature protection. With the perceived threats of population explosion uppermost in the 1970s (Ives and Messerli 1989), a band of national parks were created in the Himalayas to hold back the pressure of demographic growth on natural environments. The consequences for local communities of parks policed by the military were severe. Nature protection did not prove popular, and became associated with coercive, unjust and poverty-exacerbating policies. In this era, the brute alternatives of either promoting economic growth or protecting nature were too inflexible for the many thousands of households that happened to find their villages within national parks. The unsustainability of coercive conservation, and the need to find alternatives that would reconcile environmental protection with legitimate subsistence needs of the poor led to a significant policy rethink. Similar processes were at work internationally after the 1982 Venezuela meeting of the International Union for Conservation of Nature and Natural Resources (IUCN).

In Nepal, the wisdom of taking use rights away from local communities and imposing central bureaucratic control over forests had been significantly questioned in a number of interventions by anthropologists, among whom the work of Christoph Fürer-Haimendorf was prominent. He had observed that the arrival of the forest department in district capitals had displaced local management structures. Among the Sherpas of the Everest region, he argued the indigenous institution of *shing ki nawa* had provided a local figure with responsibility for monitoring timber use, overseeing arbitration of disputes and administering fines for misdemeanours (Fürer-Haimendorf 1975). According to Stanley Stevens (1993), Fürer-Haimendorf in fact lumped together a number of distinct institutions, roles and responsibilities into the category of *shing ki nawa,* and what needs to be taken into account is the remarkable diversity of categories of forest and local arrangements for their management, even if the modern-style idea of conservation (with an indigenous equivalent of a forest-protection officer) was not exactly the principle behind them. Be that as it may, the reality of a relatively weak state, and the hard-to-access remote mountain regions made it propitious to favour indigenous institutions of community forestry (Springate-Baginski and Blaikie 2007). By 1978, Nepal had some of the most progressive legislation in the world for initiating community-based natural-resource management. However, when the suggestion was being mooted in the early 1980s to create yet another national park in the Annapurna region, where a huge number of tourists come each year (approximately 60,000), the local community feared the consequences of state administration backed by a military presence, and made a case for a novel approach to protected areas in the form of the Annapurna Conservation Area Project (ACAP), that would rely on community grassroots development in conjunction with environmental protection.

The example of ACAP fed into policy thinking around the Rio Earth Summit. Sustainable development approaches to biodiversity conservation implied recognition that local communities should receive tangible benefits from environmental protection, and that conservation had to be with local *consent* (Brandon and Wells 1992). Turning around the coercive approach previously characteristic of national parks would involve modifying villagers' rights regarding access to resources in buffer zones in national parks such as Sagarmatha (Everest), Chitwan and Langtang. The UNDP's People and Parks program set about creating buffer zones in which villagers would have legitimate use rights, and monitor their resource use within a user-group committee structure, according to a constitution approved by the national park. In return for compliance with the buffer-zone committee system, villagers could then apply for funds for small development projects (such as enterprise training for the micro cheese factory in figure 9.1), claiming a share of between 30–50 per cent of the park's income (from tourist entry permits, harvesting licenses, fines etc). The buffer zone concept, implemented in Nepal's national parks from 1996 onwards, mediated the classic conflict of interests between development and biodiversity concerns. It gave recognition to local governance and decision making, and provided a collaborative platform for village user-group leadership to enter productive dialogue with state officials. The civility and mutual benefit between people and park was markedly different from the intimidating, militaristic and largely prohibitive face presented by the national parks prior to the buffer zone era.

When I started fieldwork in Nepal at the end of the 1980s, the villagers' relationship to the park authorities was characterized by considerable suspicion, concealment and fear of reprisal from the national park for routine provisioning for livelihood needs from their forest environment. The area for the Langtang National Park was selected with the aim of conserving a representative section of Nepal's central Himalayan chain, including an

Figure 9.1. Beneficiaries of buffer zone development funds that funded equipment and training for making a local cheese known as *durga.*

altitudinal range from subtropical to alpine, containing rare stands of forest with Himalayan larch, and populations of musk deer and red panda. The park was also justified in the 1970s to protect the upstream watershed of a hydroelectric plant, and as a support to a tourist trekking route up to Langtang village (Borradaile et al. 1977; IUCN 1993). When villagers told me of how, prior to the advent of the park, they used to move their yaks (see figure 9.4), cattle and water buffaloes collectively in coordination with those of the village headman, they spoke of a system which saw to the common interests of all households. This system of public regulation of local livestock movements applied a pasture-fee levy for the transit of animals from other villages, that was channelled through tribute offered to a place-deity, and protected pastures and field crops according to seasonal access cycles. Perhaps this was somewhat nostalgically idealized, but a key principle of this local management system was that in return for tribute and respect shown to the headman (several days of labour every year, and the head of any animal killed), the villagers in turn were entitled to meet their subsistence needs from the forest (clearing swiddens to grow potatoes, taking timber and bamboo to sell or barter for grain, (see figure 9.2). In this sense there was a 'moral ecology' at work that provided a safety net for livelihoods, which the arrival of the national park undermined.

Market Alternatives to Forest Wealth

As mentioned above, the Annapurna Conservation Area Project provided a model for thinking about more politically and economically sustainable relationships to protected areas in Nepal. Direct income from tourism, and development funds distributed by ACAP for village communities to broaden their small income-generation enterprises would help to ease villagers off their traditional dependence on forest resources. In retrospect, it appears that the Annapurna area was an exception rather than a norm to hold up for other protected areas to emulate. Tourism numbers in Nepal have not recovered to the levels of the mid-1990s (one of the reasons for so many rural Nepalis to go to the Gulf for work). The expectation of ACAP that tourism would provide for communities a cash alternative to forest depletion has not been a generalizable strategy to follow for communities in other protected areas.

ACAP's much-vaunted international reputation as an example of successful grassroots environmental protection depended significantly on cash income from its convenient location near popular trekking routes, and also on overseas remittance wages, for effective substitution of non-forest resources in villagers' livelihood and consumption patterns. Isabelle Sacareau (2003) has argued that ACAP has for the most part succeeded in delivering development outcomes in return for forest-protection management, where numbers of tourists are significantly higher. It is therefore vulnerable to any changes in the characteristics of the trekking tourism industry. Indeed, in the east of Nepal, in Makalu Barun, the community conservation area was so desperate for tourists to come to its newly built hotels, that the Village Development Committee chairman I met was threatening to interrupt helicopter flights heading for the base camp by ambushing them at landing pads (Campbell 2005b).

The tie-up of sustainable biodiversity conservation with resource substitution and alternative livelihoods marks a particular direction for strategies to achieve sustainable development. It helps to see these historically, as products of events located in distinct political and economic times. For consideration of future choices of strategies, and in order to apprehend the range of possible outcomes that chosen strategies can lead towards, it is worth contemplating alternative scenarios. These could support communities in ways that are not founded to the same extent on looking for external income sources. They could include proactive management of the park, such as productive vegetational succession, or investing in training the local villagers in skills and knowledge about biodiversity, or medicinal herb processing. Villagers could be included as co-managers of conservation areas, assisting in environmental restoration, landslide prevention, education programmes and contributing to people's pride in their locality as a world biodiversity hotspot. Local community members are often present and aware of forest conditions in more locations within protected areas than staff from outside who are unfamiliar with the environment. Villagers could be involved in participatory ecological monitoring and apply their skilled labour in holding back invasive species or offering community support for scientific research as field guides and assistants.

An unforeseeable set of political and market circumstances occurred from the mid-1990s that makes the ongoing chances for successful participatory biodiversity conservation heavily dependent on non-local economic circumstances. The progress of biodiversity conservation is most unlikely to be visible in the far-off places where the people who once took what they needed from the Himalayan forests are now earning wages on top of construction cranes in Doha, or in furniture factories in Kuala Lumpur. What we see in those places is cheap labour. The complex domestic rationales for migration are not apparent, nor are the institutional hierarchies that enable people to arrive in distant lands for work. Even less visible will be the fact that the fate of the forests back home now lies in the search for foreign earnings. The heavy dependence on cash income to provide alternative resources for domestic consumption, rather than finding help to reinvigorate local subsistence and renewable-energy technologies led to livelihood solutions being sought externally to the village economy in market exchange (the main exception in this respect has been the spread of trout farms, but these do rely on imported feeds and materials). Residents of the Langtang National Park became increasingly reliant on migrant employment in India for seasonal work outside the village economy. Subsequently, from the early 2000s the Gulf and Malaysia offered better prospects as destinations for non-agricultural earnings. The civil war in Nepal intensified this out-migration as the conflict deepened after 2001 (Graner [2010] writes that it is very hard to gauge how many people migrated from villages as a consequence of the conflict. She mentions estimates from 10,000 to 600,000). The civil unrest put on hold the national park's buffer zone initiatives for several years. This militated against progressive scenarios for biodiversity conservation. Effective cooperation on local ecological and community relationships, promoting resilience in agro-pastoral practices for village food security, could have provided a tangible defence against economic fluctuations, promoting both local income generation and conservation values.

The focus from the early 1990s on looking to the international labour market to provide alternative resources for the support of household livelihoods, diminishing the pressure of harvesting on forests and thereby protecting biodiversity, has forced much of the male workforce in particular to join the flow of migrant labour. The stories that Gardner (2011) reports of migrants regularly being underpaid or having pay deferred are confirmed by the level of uncertainty expressed by villagers back home struggling to make ends meet. It is not only irregularity of cash flow that is to the detriment of the quality of lives of the women, children and elderly. They are left to cope with feeding themselves with less available labour. Table 9.1 demonstrates the extent of involvement in labour migration to various destinations in 2009 among households in the village of Tengu in the Langtang National Park. Graner's (2010: 37) figure for districts of origin of migrants to the Gulf and Malaysia indicate that far heavier rates of out-migration are recorded from East Nepal. For the year 2008, Graner discusses the variable reliability of different sources of statistics, but puts the probable figure of remittances from Qatar and Saudi Arabia combined at between 60–90 billion rupees (in the region of US $1 billion). World Bank data gave remittances as 12 per cent of Nepal's GDP in 2005 (2007: 11). The same report showed 19 per cent of households in Nepal to have received remittances in the previous twelve months and there was a higher proportion in rural areas and among the poor (ibid.: 75).

The shift from occasional short-distance seasonal migration to long-term, long-distance migration has resulted in many returning migrants considering themselves outside the subsistence labour economy. They do not join in with domestic production in the fields when they are back home, and plan for further migratory moves. This impacts severely on the remaining domestic workforce, particularly on the ability to participate in the rounds of reciprocal exchange labour by which the most inten-

Table 9.1. Village labour migrants by destination country (households = 52)

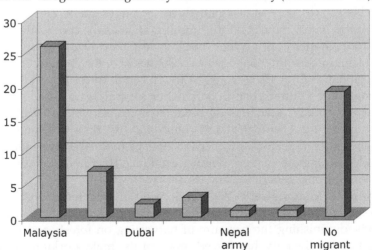

sive phases of the agricultural cycle have been conventionally managed (Campbell 1994). By 2011 it was clear that the same emphasis was not put on growing finger millet as during the twentieth-century decades of subsistence cropping intensification. Finger millet had been the crop which yielded more harvest by input of transplanting labour in the early monsoon rains. It can be either intercropped with maize up to an altitude of roughly 1,500 metres, or grown as a single crop up to 2,000 metres. Calculations of the cash value of labour increasingly affect subsistence decision making, such that today the return for every 3,000 rupees spent on labour groups in cultivating finger millet is hardly 1,000 rupees worth of harvested crop.

Rethinking Sustainability in a Migrant Universe

The way that sustainability entered mainstream development paradigms from the late 1980s followed the predominant neo-liberal approach (Woodhouse 2002). It was assumed that the environment would only be given value in the world of the globalizing economy by appealing to the logics of marginal utility maximizers. The route to halting environmental degradation was to find sources of cash to replace the income and barter value previously derived from forest products and territories that were now either prohibited or accessed by payments for licenses. Twenty years on we can see the consequences of this particular channelling of livelihood options. The market has not simply behaved as a mechanism for allocating prices for environmental services based on scarcity, or for transacting one kind of valued service or good for the value and functional equivalence of another. The park takes a thousand rupees from each tourist coming to experience the trekking holiday of a lifetime, and tells the villagers that if they cannot pay the licence fees for harvesting fir tree roofing shingles, bamboo and plants such as *Daphne nepaulensis* (for local paper making, see figures 9.2, 9.3, & 9.5), they will have to buy alternatives in the bazaar. The effects have been far reaching in putting village labour into the global orbit of West and East Asia's growing economies. Villagers are propelled into taking leave of the village economy for periods of two years or more to seek in temporary foreign migration an answer to the mismatch between ends and means back home. One Tamang woman coined a phrase to sound like a real (Tamang) place name to summon up the sense of 'a place as far away as anyone could imagine' (*Kana tang-tang*). Villagers have to go wherever they can, as the forest, which was previously their safety net against poverty in the pre-park dispensation of people's deep-rooted environmental entitlements, is increasingly hard to use legitimately. They now have to

Figure 9.2. Temperate bamboo (fodder, baskets).

Figure 9.3. *Abies spectabilis* (building timber, roofing shingles).

Figure 9.4. Yak-cow hybrids (dairy herds).

Figure 9.5. *Daphne nepaulensis* (paper making).

budget monetarily for consumption needs, such as paying for building materials by sending sons abroad, rather than take timber from the forest, or by acquiring food through bartering bamboo products during the annual hungry gap in subsistence consumption, as villagers used to do.

This is not how recent history inevitably had to turn out. There could have been other means for protecting biodiversity that need not have relied to such an extent on economizing the non-human environment, through a pricing regime that put routine and potentially sustainable use practices beyond the budget of local communities (O'Neill 2007; Martinez-Alier 2002). Alternative scenarios might have focused on the power relations of forest-dependent communities, and the areas where lack of power translated into ecologically destructive activities (by villagers, by forest security personnel and by the acts of a variety of persons excluded from legitimate use rights). More focused engagement of local community interests to protect biodiversity, with investment in the skills and training of youth to bring them into participatory alignment with the purpose and running of the park, and attract their commitment for the greater future value of a participatory protected area of which local communities could see their children as beneficiaries, could have promoted a project of shared dialogues on the local science and practice of ecologically sound livelihoods.

Subsistence Value in the Forest

The global effect of labour migration has been to alter significantly the conditions for sustainable development as regards biodiversity conservation. Considerable responsibility for the successful continuity of forest protection regimes now lies with the economies of countries such as Qatar. It is unlikely that employers of Nepalese village labour in other countries have any awareness or interest in the unintended consequences of their hiring practices. Whatever the long-term durability of employment relations between Nepal's villages and Qatar's construction industry and Malaysia's furniture factories, the linking of participatory programmes to market logics of alternative livelihoods has made the forest biodiversity of the Himalayas hostage to the fortunes of far-off decisions about manpower levels, and perceptions of risks and advantages in hiring labour from one country rather than another. A check and balance of ecological value should be considered for future rethinking of sustainable development, as a counter to the periodic up- and downturns of market exchange value. Economics as if people and environment mattered might be too utopian to expect soon, in which case ecological value needs to be recognized methodically through alternative criteria of value. Some examples would include participatory mapping of environmental well-being, to implement active monitoring and remedial measures against landslides, invasive species and climate change effects, with direct benefit demonstrable for both biodiversity and villagers.

A New Mobility Paradigm for Sustainable Environmental Protection

The effects of migration and mobility need to be brought into thinking about sustainable development not only in terms of Rigg's arguments over the positive impacts on rural poverty in South Asia in the opening section of this chapter and the linkage drawn through the analysis presented here between conservation management in Nepal and global labour markets. The integration of mobility also needs to happen at a more fundamental level at multiple scales for ecological processes and human activity over time and space to be realistically aligned. This includes the local scale, where sustainable use of natural resources is often attempted by first restricting mobility. Sustainability of people and resources has tended to be thought of in terms of fixity. There is a 'sedentarist' bias in the conception of fixed territories with environments of certain carrying capacities to protect, and communities of beneficiaries to include in devolved governance regimes observing sustainable harvesting levels. As yet, there have been surprisingly few studies that explore the connections between sustainable biodiversity conservation and migrant labour. This is despite several authors having worked on both themes within Nepal (Graner 1997; Graner and Seddon 2004; Kollmair, Müller-Böker and Soliva 2003). Susan Thieme and Ulrike Müller-Böker refer to the major reasons for (male) migration out of northwest Nepal as: 'poverty, unemployment, a scarcity of natural resources, and the only recently ended Maoist insurgency' (2010: 107). This out-migration leaves women behind to keep households going by livelihood strategies that include 'illegal gathering of products from the nearby Khaptad National Park' (ibid.: 112).

The pervasive 'sedentarist visions' (Bruslé 2010a, citing Sheller and Urry 2006) concerning rural societies in the developing world need to be questioned. Michael Kearney (1996) reflected on the effects of labour globalization on the societies of rural Mexico. He addressed the 'polybian' (adapted to multiple locations and subject positions) migrant-behaviour patterns of people often known as 'peasants'. Given the labour destinations of Mexican migrants in the US agricultural sector, he characterized the notion of sustainable development (projects of persuading poor com-

munities into ever deeper dependence on sedentarized, land-based subsistence economy) as running counter to rural Mexicans' adventurous
quest for improved livelihoods by moving between diverse locations. Sustainable development programmes, as characterized by Kearney, would
consign rural communities to live in poverty, compliantly stuck in place,
with their livelihoods homeostatically dependent on the natural yield potential of particular local ecologies. Such a negative view of sustainability
is not necessary if mobility becomes a flexible dimension of the paradigm
for sustainable thinking, and the final section of this chapter will attempt
to sketch out certain ways this can come about.

Vertically Sustainable Livelihoods

A livelihood perspective is required in looking at the complexity of a variety of kinds of movement in operation. It means not simply privileging
techno-managerial visions of utility with respect to natural carrying capacity as determining sustainable outcomes. Evoking 'livelihood' should
not put out of view elements of social life that link up communities of
different scales in ritual or symbolic networks as well as in more directly
material exchanges. These are often not attributed use value in their lived
practice, as forms of social relations, but occasions do occur when being able to call on someone as belonging to a network of trust can prove
useful. Connections through ritual kinship are one such example of locally sanctioned social capital. Idioms of 'classificatory' connection to a
common hearth, an ancestral clan or personal histories spent working
in different communities can further contribute to livelihood opportunities enabled by social networks that actively include people and kinds of
exchange across territorial or ethnic boundary edges. Mountain communities survive by being able to call on other communities' locational advantage. Village communities are not self-sufficient or harmonious units,
and are disposed through internal conflicts and interests to make alliance
with external others. Mobility as a feature and solution to many livelihood problems opens up not only international and 'internal' migrations
(from hills to lowlands), but also the responses of households, neighbourhoods and regional societies to adapt, channel and keep available a range
of livelihood pathways. Such ridge-top perspectives for livelihoods in
upland Asia has recently been presented as characteristic of 'Zomia' by
James Scott (2009), referring to the historical scatter-zone societies on the
margins of the valley-based power centres of India and China, reliant on
strategically diverse small-scale trade, swiddening, pastoralism and forest
environments rather than surplus grain production.

The Tamang-speaking people, for example, talk about seeking their livelihood between the ecological extent of the juniper at the tree line, and the palm in the valley bottom. This necessarily entails mobile agro-pastoral subsistence practices, as resources are not found in one location (as with consolidated irrigated rice farming). Livelihood opportunities are distributed in times and places that require relocating every two weeks to a month, moving animals to new pastures, or planting, weeding or harvesting crops scattered in different locations and varied crop rotations. Livelihoods are taken care of by keeping on the move, being conscious of what priorities most need seeing to. And today they include calculating whether it is more worthwhile to keep a household member in the village subsistence orbit or encourage him or her to leave to join siblings, cousins or friends working elsewhere in migrant labour for a couple of months or a couple of years.

Verticality has its own specialist literature in anthropology and geography. The Andes and Himalayas frequently inspire comparative reflection, and John Murra's (1972) typology for the economic and social interdependence of vertically distributed ecological niches has prompted a number of Himalayan counterparts (Molnar 1982; Orlove and Guillet 1985; Stevens 1993). Fürer-Haimendorf (1975) famously argued that the propensity to trade among higher-altitude dwellers was necessary to supplement their inadequate subsistence base, and that the produce from different zones was managed on the basis of an ecological complementarity of needs and affordances. The northern 'adventurous traders' had skills, networks and beasts of burden to join up supply and demand between communities in different locations. Many of them descended to the lower hills every winter. Richard English (1985) more specifically linked long-distance trans-Himalayan trading patterns and political systems, emphasizing the connections with profits and the locations of fortress kingdoms on given routes. Wim Van Spengen (1999) likens the Tibetan margins to Fernand Braudel's characterization of the Mediterranean 'économie monde' that brought diverse shores and their mountain hinterlands into communication. Van Spengen tracked the movements of the Manangba after World War II, and subsequently the fall-off of the salt trade to Tibet, who followed opportunities in India and Southeast Asia. Robert Rhoades, combining experience from both the Andes and Himalayas, proposes the powerful notion of mountain peoples' interdependent 'politics of location' (1997: 27), arguing that sustainable development in mountains has to address the specificities of locatedness and the connections to other people in other places. Locatedness brings certain advantages and disadvantages, and problems of integration. Himalayan anthropology has recorded a host of responses to altitude factors in subsistence strategies, ranging from transhumant livestock patterns, diverse agricultural cropping systems and social institutions of ritual kinship linking people in differently located communities. Movement between places over seasons, and transporting what is high-value, low-volume from top to bottom, has been a vital way of keeping livelihood connections open. When community forest regulations in west Nepal prevented sheep and goats from passing through (in the name of sustainable development!) in the 1980s, and the flocks were given up, famine followed in subsequent years due to lack of transport. The World Food Organization still pays helicopter flights to keep the uplanders, who once had a low carbon transport system, fed (*Kathmandu Post*, 24 September 2011).

While the move from overpopulated hills to areas of available cultivable land in Nepal's lowlands has been a theme of the last fifty years, it has remained the case that mobility has tended to be seen by the development community and social scientists as something to remedy, as almost pathological (Bruslé 2010a). The presumption of sedentary peasant fixity to land was scripted perhaps unconsciously into the notion of legitimate resource users in participatory conservation projects. If mobility is to be discussed now, it is important not to overgeneralize but note variation, the ingenuity and inventiveness in the last two decades with which people have responded to livelihood challenges by different strategies of accumulation and shifting residence. Ian Fitzpatrick (2010) recounts how in east Nepal the discovery of profitable cardamom growing in the hills led to subsequent reinvestment of capital in external migration, via new lowland settlements that acted as a springboard to employment opportunities elsewhere.

Conclusion: The Sustainable Challenge

If commentators of the developing world in the twentieth century were fired up over 'the peasant question', how might this change with the environmentally reconfigured horizon of sustainable development? And to repeat the question raised in the opening of this chapter, how would we recognize sustainability if we saw it? Steven Sanderson (2005) provides some reflections on the first of these questions. He bemoans the fate of 'development economics' that once attended to the specific characteristics of the global south, but was bulldozed out of any distinct identity by the force of neo-classical orthodoxy. He makes a number of observations about the invisibility to what he calls 'mono-economics' of human experiences of poverty in places where biodiversity issues are critical. He argues that once the problems of developing countries were given no special consideration by economic orthodoxy for their particular historical, cultural and geographical circumstances, and the claim for universal economic validity pushed aside state-led interventions, 'the set of implementation tools that went along with that claim never showed itself to be compatible or even very interested in the special problems of development, much less sustainability' (2005: 327). He advocates by contrast a strong focus on local conditions rather than allowing perceptions of value by markets to dominate. However, he concludes in his advocacy of the value of local knowledge of empirical conditions that 'alleviating poverty and conserving biodiversity will take place in the most difficult settings, places of extreme ecological vulnerability, very low population densities and no state presence' (ibid.: 331). Nowhere in his article is the word *migration* mentioned, except in reference to songbirds, antelopes and Monarch butterflies. It is a case of the missing migrants. The peasant question has shifted, with peasants themselves relocating their terms of engagement with livelihood issues. Some may have been helped on their way by excessively protectionist biodiversity conservation, or at least, less than proactive agro-ecological management options within protected areas.

The result for protected areas is in many ways unfortunate, as the ecologically skilled and relatively cheap resident workforce available till a decade ago to assist with ecological restoration, soil erosion measures, biodiversity monitoring, invasive weed control and re-afforestation is now adjusting to a different set of livelihood parameters. The message given out by 'fortress conservation' was inadequately tempered by more moderate and less misanthropic versions of how environmental protection could be a pro-poor strategy for communities often neglected by development. There might be nostalgia for days when 'development economics' referenced local contextualization and case-specific non-sectorial analysis, but the expanding phenomenon of remittance economies has put the conventional distinctions aside. There needs to be some stock taking of the full impact of the market in places where the proposal to remedy poverty and ecological decline by turning the attention of the poor away from local environments towards enterprise and cost-benefit accounting in foreign labour markets, has gambled the future of local environments by placing a massive stake on the fortunes of distant centres of commercial activity. Rigg's sound arguments about benefits accruing to areas of poverty in rural Asia from migration as a general phenomenon are accepted, but there is an invisibility within this aggregate picture of the impact that migration has on the possibilities for progressive change in the negotiations between indigenous communities and biodiversity authorities over rights of forest use and the inclusiveness of perspectives that are needed for long-term forest care. This scenario calls for research, especially to further understanding of the implications of different approaches to agro-ecological livelihood development. On the migration end of the spectrum, as Bruslé admits, the information is thin: 'Although the Gulf countries have emerged as a major destination since 2000, scientific studies about Nepalese migrants in the Middle East are non-existent' (2010b: 1154). It is necessary to connect up the increasingly distant interdependent points that have emerged regarding the sustainability of human-environmental relationships, and reveal to decision makers the points of vulnerability with livelihoods and life diversity that global economic changes are likely to bring about.

Jobs provided in Qatar and other Gulf countries help environments in distant places, where the success of projects protecting biodiversity with sustainable development benefits now rely on incomes to villagers from remittances. This should be more widely appreciated. Experience since Rio '92 indicates that uncertainty in reliable forecasting behaviour is common, and underlines the need to think of people in local and global interactions as mobile citizens whose behaviour needs to be geared to a sustainable planet. Sustainability implies reflecting on the environmental consequences of livelihood choices, and making visible emerging patterns stemming from interventions to promote development, sustainable and otherwise. There have been lost opportunities of community participation in active management of protected areas using local skills and knowledge – contributions that bureaucratic forms of environmental governance cannot make. It is time that projects made a difference by using local common sense, in this case adopting migrant-aware practices of environmental governance.

References

Afsar, R. 2003. Dynamics of poverty, development and population mobility: The Bangladesh case. Ad Hoc Expert Group Meeting on Migration and Development, Economic and Social Commission for Asia and the Pacific (ESCAP), Bangkok, August 27–29. Available from http://www.sdnpbd.org/sdi/interna tionaldays/wed/2005/bangladesh/migration/document/Bangladesh_rita.pdf.

Blaikie, P., J. Cameron and D. Seddon. 2002. Understanding 20 years of change in West-Central Nepal: Continuity and change in lives and ideas. *World Development* 30(7), 1255–1270.

Borradaile, L., et al. 1977. *Langtang National Park Management Plan*. Durham University Himalayan Expedition. HMG/UNDP/FAO Project NEP/72/002 Field document no. 7.

Brandon, K., and S. Wells. 1992. 'Planning for People and Parks.' *World Development* 20 (4): 557–570.

Bruslé, T. 2010a. 'Nepalese Migrations: Introduction.' *European Bulletin of Himalayan Research* 35–36: 16–23.

———. 2010b. 'Who's in a Labour Camp? A Socio-Economic analysis of Nepalese Migrants in Qatar.' *European Bulletin of Himalayan Research* 35–36: 154–170.

Campbell, B. 1994. 'Forms of Cooperation in a Tamang Community of Nepal.' In *Anthropology of Nepal: Peoples, Problems and Processes,* ed. M. Allen, 3–20. Kathmandu: Mandala.

———. 2005a. 'Introduction to Re-Placing Nature: Changing Trajectories in Protection Policies and Ethnographies of Environmental Engagement.' *Conservation and Society* 3 (2): 280–322.

———. 2005b. 'Nature's Discontents in Nepal.' *Conservation and Society* 3 (2): 323–353.

English, R. 1985. 'Himalayan State Formation and the Impact of British Rule in the Nineteenth Century.' *Mountain Research and Development* 5: 61–78.

Fitzpatrick, I. 2010. 'Cardamom, Class, and Change in a Limbu Village in East Nepal.' DPhil Thesis, Oxford University.

Fürer-Haimendorf, C. 1975. *Himalayan Traders: Life in Highland Nepal.* Delhi: Oxford University Press.

Gardner, A. M. 2011. 'Why Do They Keep Coming? Labor Migrants in the Gulf States.' In *Migrant Labor in the Gulf: Summary Report,* 5–6. Doha: Georgetown University Centre for International and Regional Studies, Summary Report no. 2.

Glick Schiller, N. & Thomas Faist. 2011. *Migration, Development and Transnationalism* Critical Interventions: A Forum for Social Analysis. Berghahn.

Graner, E. 1997. *The Political Ecology of Community Forestry in Nepal.* Saarbrücken: Verlag für Entwicklungspolitik.

———. 2010. 'Leaving Hills and Plains: Migration and remittances in Nepal.' *European Bulletin of Himalayan Research* 35–36: 24–42.

Grove, R. 1993. *Green Imperialism: Colonial Expansion, Tropical Island Edens and the Origins of Environmentalism, 1600–1860.* Cambridge: Cambridge University Press.

International Union for Conservation of Nature and Natural Resources (IUCN). 1993. *Nature Reserves of the Himalaya and the Mountains of Central Asia.* Oxford: Oxford University Press.

Ives, J. & B. Messerli. 1989. *The Himalaya Dilemma: reconciling development and conservation.* London: Routledge.

Kearney, M. 1996. *Reconceptualizing the Peasantry.* Boulder, CO: Westview Press.

Kollmair, M., U. Müller-Böker and R. Soliva. 2003. 'The Social Context of Nature Conservation in Nepal.' *European Bulletin of Himalayan Research* 24: 25–62.

Martinez-Alier, J. 2002. *Environmentalism of the Poor: A Study of Ecological Conflicts and Valuation.* Cheltenham: Edward Elgar.

Murra, J. 1972. 'El Control Vertical de un Maximo de Pisos Ecologicos en la Economia de la Sociedades Andinas.' In J. Murra (ed) *Inigo Ortiz de Zuniga, Visita de la Provincia de Leon de Huanuco en 1562,* Huanuco, Peru: Universidad Nacional Hermilio Valzida, pp. 429–476.

Nelson, F. 2008. 'Conservation and Aid: Designing More Effective Investments in Natural Resource Governance Reform.' *Conservation Biology* 23 (5): 1102–1108.

O'Neill, J. 2007. *Markets, Deliberation and Environment*. London: Routledge.

Orlove, B., and D. Guillet. 1985. 'Theoretical and Methodological Considerations on the Study of Mountain Peoples: Reflections on the Idea of Subsistence Type and the Role of History in Human Ecology.' *Mountain Research and Development* 5 (1): 3–18.

Rhoades, R. 1997. *Pathways towards a Sustainable Mountain Agriculture for the 21st Century: The Hindu Kush-Himalayan Experience*. ICIMOD, Kathmandu.

Rigg, J. 2006. Land, Farming, Livelihoods, and Poverty: Rethinking the Links in the Rural South. *World Development* 34: 180–202.

Saberwal, V. 1999. *Pastoral Politics: Shepherds, Bureaucrats, and Conservation in the Western Himalaya*. Delhi: Oxford Univeristy Press.

Sacareau, I. 2003. Gestion des Resources et Evolution des Paysages au Sein de l'Annapurna Conservation Area Project. L'example du Modi Khola. In: *Histoire et Devenir des Paysages en Himalaya* (ed. J. Smadja), pp. 417–445. CNRS Editions, Paris.

Sanderson, S. 2005. 'Poverty and Conservation: The New Century's "Peasant Question".' *World Development* 33 (2): 323–332.

Scott, J. 2009. *The Art of Not Being Governed*. New Haven, CT: Yale University Press.

Sheller, M., and J. Urry. 2006. 'The New Mobilities Paradigm.' *Environment and Planning A* 38 (2): 207–226.

Springate-Baginski, O., and P. Blaikie. 2007. *Forests, People and Power: The Political Ecology of Reform in South Asia*. London: Earthscan.

Stevens, S. 1993. *Claiming the High Ground: Sherpas, Subsistence, and Environmental Change in the Highest Himalaya*. Berkeley: University of California Press.

——— (ed.). 1997. *Conservation through Cultural Survival: Indigenous Peoples and Protected Areas*. Washington, DC: Island Press.

Thieme, S., and U. Müller-Böker. 2010. 'Social Networks and Migration: Women's Livelihoods Between Far West Nepal and Delhi.' *European Bulletin of Himalayan Research* 35–36: 107–121.

Tucker, R. 1991. 'Resident Peoples and Wildlife Reserves in India: The Prehistory of an Idea.' In *Resident Peoples and National Parks: Social Dilemmas and Strategies in International Conservation*, eds. P. West and S. Brechin, 40–50. Tucson. University of Arizona Press.

Van Spengen, W. 1999. *Tibetan Border Worlds*. London: Kegan Paul.

Woodhouse, P. 2002. 'Development Policies and Environmental Agendas.' In *Development Theory and Practice: critical perspectives*, eds. U. Kothari and M. Minogue. Palgrave: Basingstoke. pp. 136–156.

World Bank. 2007. *Access to Financial Services In Nepal*. Aurora Ferrari with Guillemette Jaffrin and Sabin Raj Shrestha. Finance and Private Sector Development Unit South Asia Region. Conference Edition (PDF accessed 18 October 2010).

CHAPTER 10

Conservation and Sustainable Development
The Qatari and Gulf Region Experience

Paul Sillitoe with Ali Alshawi

One response to humanity's unsustainable use of natural resources and consequent degradation, even destruction of the environment, is to establish conservation areas, to protect nature and preserve biodiversity at least in limited selected regions. The consequences of human activities are particularly graphic in marginal and harsh environments such as the deserts of the Middle East, where some regions, which appear denuded of plant and animal life, can look to the outsider like barren moonscapes. It is widely agreed that such conservation measures are necessary for a range of reasons: to ensure on-going healthy functioning environments; to protect unique habitats and possibly unique species (as extinction is forever); to conserve the global genetic bank (not knowing what aspects of the world's natural heritage may be of future value); and to meet our emotional needs and aesthetic esteem of nature (IUCN; World Conservation Monitoring Centre 1994).

Confronted by the environmental consequences of oil and gas extraction and rapid urban development, the government of Qatar has shown a strong commitment to conservation in its 2030 National Vision (GSDP 2008), where under the fourth development pillar, concerning the environment, it says that the state seeks 'to preserve and protect its unique environment and nurture the abundance of nature granted by God'. The government has signalled the seriousness of its intent in declaring the Al Reem region, approximately one-tenth of the country's land area, a conservation reserve under the UNESCO Man and Biosphere (MAB) programme.[1] The total area of the core and buffer zones is approximately 1,190 square kilometres, with a transition zone (which falls outside the Al Reem Reserve area as protected by Emiri Decree) taking the area to 2,024 square kilometres or nearly 18 per cent of the country (UNESCO 2007: 4). The reserve is situated in the northwest of the Qatar peninsula (see figure 10.1), within parts of the Jemailiya and Madinat Al Shamal municipalities. The two towns of Jemailiya and Al Ghuwairiya are located on the highway that marks the reserve's eastern boundary.

Experiences within the Al Reem Biosphere raise some intriguing questions about assumptions that inform conservation currently. A range of approaches has featured in conservation over the past century or so. Currently popular is co-management that includes the participation of the local population. This follows problems with conservation reserves that

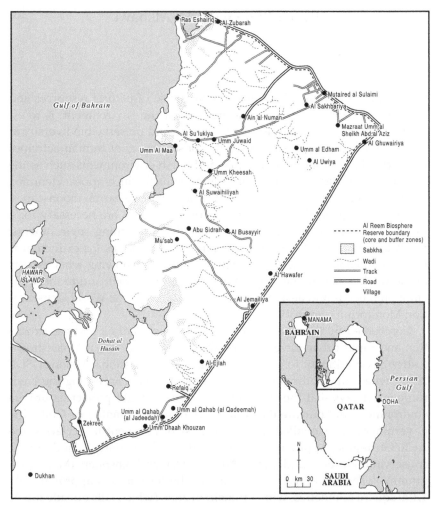

Figure 10.1. Al Reem region (see table 10.2 for population).

sought to protect nature by excluding previous resource users. It is argued that local people are more likely to abide by restrictions on access and resource use if they are party to devising these and understand what they aim to achieve. Furthermore, local communities also have much knowledge of the local region, their activities often contributing to the environment seen today. This has led recently to the promotion of the idea of bio-cultural diversity and the need to promote its continuance. However, the assumptions underpinning this view may not hold where rapid social and cultural change occurs, such as is happening in Qatar. This chapter explores the implications of such change for participatory co-management and the consequences for the oversight of conservation areas, drawing on the Al Reem experience.

From Exclusion to Inclusion

A growing recognition of ecological damage following industrialization prompted the establishment of national parks, and most recently biosphere reserves, to protect the environment and promote conservation. These parks aimed initially to minimize human interference in the natural environment (Grove 1994; Spence 1999; Wilshusen et al. 2002), after Yellowstone, the first such park. But it has become increasingly apparent that the exclusion of humans from such areas leads to considerable problems, even conflicts (Neumann 1998; Zerner 2000). In an attempt to reduce local resentment with parks that interfere with previous land use, various schemes have been devised (Tuxill and Nabhan 2001). One such scheme involves the designation of zones that differ in access and human activities permitted, as planned for Al Reem; these comprise core zones where classic conservation measures apply and humans are largely excluded through to buffer and transition zones where varying human activities are permitted that interfere in nature.

It was also realized that the activities of local people contribute to the current environment; often they manage aspects of it. As pristine, untouched nature is rare, humans have to be considered along with other animals that inhabit any region in thinking about conservation (MacNeely 1997; Posey 1999). Human land use is often an integral aspect of the shape and nature of today's landscape – for example, if the park authorities stopped sheep grazing in the South Downs National Park in England (designed a park in 2011; National Parks Commission 2008), the current rolling chalk grassland that they seek to conserve would become scrub woodland. It is arguable that appreciation of local practices will improve conservation interventions in both the ecological and sociological senses,

as these often represent understanding rooted in highly sustainable adaptations past from generation to generation (Baines 1985); for example,
Arabs have managed to live for centuries in delicate desert environments
without apparently irreparably degrading their resources (Chatty 2003a
and b). As Joseph Hobbs (2006: 785–786) notes: 'Over thousands of years
of experience, pastoral nomads have devised effective means of predict-
ing and reacting to changing environmental opportunities. Many of these
people have created what social and ecological scientists would call "sustainable use" practices or "ethnoconservation" systems, making them
ideal partners for modern conservation and development efforts.' This
has led to the emergence of the idea of bio-cultural diversity to indicate
that human activities may support, not threaten biodiversity.

The co-management approach, which aims to involve local people in
park management, resulted, utilizing participatory methodologies that
have emerged in development in the last two decades or so. It is necessary
to involve people not only because they have knowledge relevant to making any reserve a success but also to ensure that the management regime
is socio-culturally appropriate and complies with their expectations, such
that they will consent to it (Campbell 2004). While socio-cultural and environmental particulars vary from one region to another, it is now widely
acknowledged that success of such initiatives depends on the informed
approval and co-operation of local populations; excluding people does
not work (Grove 1994; Neumann 1998; Knight 2000). But it is a challenge
to incorporate local aspirations, activities and knowledge in a way that
does not lead to disputes that thwart the objectives of conservation and
matches government development goals (Saberwal, Rangharajan and Kothari 2001; Swiderska et al. 2008). A key aspect of winning local consent
and co-operation is the ability to identify points of potential conflict and
devise strategies to resolve them in the interests of all stakeholders.

The central assumption of bio-cultural diversity, namely that local
knowledge and practices are sustainable, having a long history of being adapted to exploit a region's resources while maintaining ecosystem
integrity (Smith and Meredith 1999; Laird 2002), breaks down with rapid
social change and economic development (Ghimire and Pimbert 1997; Al-
Rowaily 1999; Chatty 2003b), such as has occurred in the Gulf for instance
(Chatty 1996; Cole and Altorki 1998: 111–1134; Mundy and Musallam
2000; Gardner 2003), which can result in confusion and discord, as actors
differ in their understanding and interpretation of events. The cultural
dimension of bio-cultural diversity changes to such an extent that human
management and/or interference in the environment becomes potentially
destructive from a nature-conservation perspective. The formulation of a
reserve's management strategy becomes considerably more complex, as

all parties have to learn what may be an ecologically sustainable adaptation under the changed conditions (Chatty n.d.). This is the position currently in the Al Reem region, where understandings of what conservation comprises under conditions of extensive social change vary considerably.

Although designated a biosphere, current management does not meet UNESCO's expectations. We seek to gauge the extent to which this may be a response to local views about the reserve, subtly communicated to the government via tribal networks. In addressing these issues, this chapter draws on a survey conducted to ascertain local knowledge of conservation in the Al Reem region and attitudes towards proposed measures to protect the environment,[2] using the results to explore some of the contradictions and contested ideas that characterize conservation; prompting the question: what next? The overall results are mixed: while 67 per cent of respondents knew that Al Reem was designated a reserve, only 34 per cent were aware of planned management proposals, and positive support ranged from 51 per cent to 58 per cent for the four proposed interventions. These are: (1) the erection of exclosures (fenced areas to exclude stock and act as seed banks), (2) reinstatement of the traditional *hima* grazing system, (3) controls on vehicular access and (4) restrictions on hunting activities. While nearly three-quarters of respondents claimed to know what conservation is, only a small number could provide a definition, such as 'It is preserving the environment'.[3] The chapter reviews these data for any patterning to responses according to various criteria – such as respondents' age, gender, nationality – to further understanding of issues.

Al Reem Environment and Land Use

The Al Reem Reserve comprises a fragile desert environment that experiences a harsh climate, where unsound land use can lead to serious degradation of natural resources. It comprises subtropical desert with hot humid summers and short semi-dry winters. Average temperatures range from 26°C to 30°C, regularly exceeding 45°C in summer, and rainfall is infrequent and low, averaging 34 millimetres (figures 10.13 and 10.14). The geology is Tertiary limestone. The landscape is largely flat, much of it barren and arid. It comprises undulating *hamadas*, gravel plains, which are strewn with rocks of varying sizes, fine particles blown away to leave a rocky desert floor. Features include shallow *rowdah*, depressions resulting from subterranean karst erosion and collapse, which contain young fine colluvial sediments, often supporting denser vegetation. They are crisscrossed by *wadi* channels, shallow short-lived stream runnels, often filled with windblown and waterborne deposits, which are also often comparatively well vegetated. Near the coast are *sabkha*, saltflats comprising salty crusts over silt-sand formed by intense evaporation of saline water (Barth and Böer 2002). Beaches consist of marine sand and gravel mixed with numerous small cone shells, sometimes cemented into friable conglomerate. In the south of the reserve are *hofuf*, limestone mesas, wind eroded into striking mushroom-shaped formations. The soils are rocky shallow lithosols and calcareous sandy loams. Vegetation comprises dwarf shrubs, succulents and some small trees (*Lycium shawi*, *Zygophyllum qatarense*, *Limonium axillare* and *Acacia ehrenbergiana* predominating; Abdul-Majid 2008: 41), plus desert annuals after rainfall. The saltflats support dispersed halophytes – such as *Limonium* and *Halopeplis* (see Batanouny 1981, and Abulfatih, Abdelbari and Ibrahim. 2001).

The changes that have occurred in land use and settlement in the region as a whole during the second half of the twentieth century intimate the extent of the shift in people's relationship with their environment. Contemporary land-access arrangements are a mix of the old and new – that is, tribal customary practice combined with state bureaucratic regulation (Wilkinson 1983; Hiatt 1984). It reflects the tension between tribe and nation that has a long history throughout Arabia.

Tribal organization has long structured socio-political arrangements in the Gulf region including Qatar, and continues to inform it (see Cole

Figure 10.2. The arid Al Reem landscape.

1975, 1982; Lancaster 1981; Ingham 1986; Ferdinand 1993). The system basically comprises an arrangement of agnatically defined nesting groups of increasing size from the family up to the clan and tribe (Peters 1990). Descent groups are identified with certain *dirah* 'territories' (see Wilkinson 1983), albeit they conceive of this identification flexibly. Such groups did not think of their territories as bounded areas to which they have exclusive rights of access (Montigny-Kozlowska 1983). According to Donald Cole (1975: 33), 'access to pastures blessed by rainfall … [is an] open matter in which the rights of first come, first-served prevail', and William Lancaster (1981: 123) says that people 'never felt that they owned the grass or water … grass and rain come from God and is free to all'. Livestock owners were consequently free to herd their stock in any region there was adequate pasture regardless of tribal affiliation (Webster 1996: 482–483). So if one region received good rainfall and had plentiful pasture, Bedouin came from far away to graze animals there, although not their territory – albeit members of different clans of the same tribe may have traced, or possibly even maintained, distant kin links. It was rights to water wells (*biyr*) that anchored tribes and clans to geographical locales (Cole 1975: 33–36; Ferdinand 1993). According to people they are centuries old; in the past, they sometimes fought over access. They were the location of summer tent encampments, called *ed*, 'place adjacent to well', or *bidiy*, 'water trough'. Those with rights to the water congregated there with their herds, leading a nomadic existence the rest of the year, sometimes moving large distances.

Regarding tribal affiliation, the survey data reveal no evident trend with respect to knowledge of conservation and support of planned management interventions according to affiliation (table 10.1). The data however suggest that members of tribes that have well/land rights within the reserve, although informed about conservation, are less supportive of biosphere status and future management plans than those who have no tribal affiliation. This suggests that those more closely associated with the region are more suspicious of biosphere status and future conservation plans.

A consequence of the traditional rangeland access system was not only that people spread the risk of poor pasture in any season and shared the benefits of abundant pasture, but also that they moved over large areas. There are reports of pastoralists moving not only across large parts of Saudi Arabia but also as far as Kuwait, Jordan and Iraq. While there is no call for people to move stock such large distances today with tanker water and imported fodder, some continue to move stock between Qatar and Saudi Arabia. The manner in which they transport animals, often in flat-bed trucks, signifies their different place in life today, whereas previ-

Table 10.1. Responses by tribal affiliation (% - note 100% balance includes non-responses).

Tribe	Number of responses	Know that Al Reem is a reserve?		Know what conversation is?		Defined conservation	Good that Al Reem is a reserve?		Know of planned management interventions?		Exclosures		Hima grazing system		Vehicular access		Restrictions on hunting	
	.	Y	N	Y	N		Y	N	Y	N	G	B	G	B	G	B	G	B
Al Hajiri*	13	85	15	92	8	8	69	31	31	46	23	54	39	39	31	46	54	23
Al Mansuri*	16	56	25	75	6	6	63	0	19	31	13	25	31	6	25	13	25	6
Al Nuaimi*	6	83	0	83	0	0	83	0	33	67	100	0	83	17	100	0	100	0
Al Shawani*	11	82	18	82	18	36	82	18	27	55	46	27	55	9	55	9	55	18
Al Mura	7	29	29	43	14	0	57	0	43	43	86	0	71	0	57	14	57	43
Al Subai'i	3	67	33	33	33	0	100	0	0	100	67	0	33	0	33	0	67	0
Other	4	50	25	50	25	25	75	0	50	25	75	0	75	0	75	0	75	0
None	32	84	9	78	16	25	72	13	44	41	59	31	66	16	72	13	41	41

*= well/land owners within the Reem reserve

Y = yes, N = no, G = good, B = bad

ously animals carried humans and their possessions. The reason given for this movement is differences in government fodder subsidies. While those who register their animals with the Qatari authorities[4] are eligible for a 50 per cent subsidy, fodder is cheaper in Saudi Arabia. While some Qatari nationals may have stock in Saudi and have camps there, the Saudis do not apparently come in the opposite direction and use kin/clan connections to herd stock in Qatar. The differences in fodder prices are probably a factor, and there are also legal obstacles regarding registration of livestock and campsites. Nonetheless, if Saudi tribal relatives turned up with stock, people said that they would welcome them, while being somewhat surprised at such an unusual occurrence.

Figure 10.3. Camels in truck at Al Ghuwairiya.

Sedentarianism has increased in recent decades and nomadism has ceased, albeit those with well rights on the Qatar peninsula may have a history of more sedentary ways, their movements less extensive than those living in other parts of Arabia because the region enjoyed higher rainfall previously, families not necessarily having to move large distances to find pasture. Also, many of them were not solely dependant on nomadic pastoralism for their livelihoods but participated in other aspects of the local economy; some of those living near to the Gulf coast worked in the pearling industry in the summer months, for instance, moving on with their herds for the rest of the year. Whatever the case, control of wells has transformed into the right to build permanent dwellings with the establishment of villages (*kariya*) adjacent to wells (Katakura 1977). The significance of these locales for water is reflected in their names. The village name Khouzan, for instance, derives from *kazenah*, 'to hold, keep, reserve', after a small depression in the local terrain where water collects, and Umm Al Qahab likewise comes from the slightly undulating surface, supplying hollows where water collects after rainfall. The name Abu Sidrah, 'father Sidrah', comes from the Sidrah tree (*Ziziphus* spp.), which grows prolifically adjacent to water sources, and Refaiq may be a corruption of *refeeq*, 'friend', signifying a place where one found a welcome adjacent to a well.

There are several small settlements dotted around the reserve, many located off the highway that bounds it (see figure 10.1). According to Ministry of the Environment staff,[5] the numbers of households in the villages of the Al Reem region are shown in table 10.2.

Today's villages were all established in similar ways with those who claimed rights to the wells at these places building houses adjacent to them. The tribal and clan affiliations of these persons and their descendants currently living there include the Beniyhaeza (Al Shahwani, Al Ay-

Table 10.2. Number of households (permanent settlements).

Settlement name	households	Settlement name	households
Zekreet	19	Al Busayyir	8
Khouzan	6	Abu Sidrahh	5
Umm Al Qahab	14	Al Suwaihliya	8
Al Refaiq	15	Umm Kheesah	5
Al Ejlah	1	Al Ghuwairiya	~65
Jemailiya	~75	Ain Al Numaan	6
Al Hawafer	1	Umm Al Edham	3
At other places, migrant workers only			

adiy and Al Ajaep clans), Al-Manasiya (Al Masif) and Al-Nayemi (Al Mansor). Those living in villages currently talk about their fathers/grand-fathers settling down and building houses with the development of the Dukhan oilfield, which is located just to the south of the Al Reem Reserve (figure 10.1), probably in the early 1950s, many of them finding work there as labourers. Other clan relatives working for the oil companies joined the village founders. The village populations have grown, until today they largely comprise *bideda*, 'extended families' of kin. Sometimes people refer to villages as *al hezara*, 'immigrant (locales)', changed places where fami-lies now live 'newly' (like immigrants) all the time.

Initially the founders built houses using mud-faced local stone and wood with corrugated iron roofs, some of which still stand in a ruinous state today, abandoned following the construction of more substantial dwellings from imported building materials. These comprise modest fam-ily houses compared to the modern mansions of Doha, often gathered around a small *masjid*, 'mosque', and *majlis*, 'men's day room', the latter ranging from traditional carpeted tents with open fire and scattered floor cushions to air-conditioned buildings with tinted double-glazing, electric hob and plasma TV (figures 10.4 and 10.5). Both within the village and on the outskirts are various enclosures and buildings for animals built from a range of materials including wire mesh, corrugated iron, bricks etc. There are small areas under cultivation, including some *tamar*, 'date palm', groves.

Figure 10.4. A tent at Zekreet.

Figure 10.5. Houses and mosque at Umm al Qahab village.

According to the survey data, there is some correlation between respondents' place of residence and knowledge of conservation and attitudes to interventions (table 10.3). Those living in the small settlements within the Reem reserve are slightly better informed about conservation but are less supportive of planned management interventions. This parallels the previous tribal pattern, indicating that those more closely associated with the region are more suspicious of biosphere status and future conservation plans.

While the majority of residents lived permanently in these settlements until the 1980s, many have since moved to Doha for employment and schools, becoming weekend visitors. Those who continue to live permanently are largely farmers with livestock, although some have other occupations in the region, such as schoolteachers (who may engage in some farming too). Several are elderly couples whose adult children and grandchildren work and live elsewhere (largely in Doha) and come as visitors. The survey data show that most persons associated with the Reem region are not employed on the land; many have white-collar jobs in Doha city. Nonetheless they often keep animals there, continuing their forebears' pastoral activities, albeit no longer nomadic. When cross-tabulated, these occupation data show no pattern with respect to knowledge of conservation and opinions about planned interventions (table 10.4).

Those residing in the Al Reem region also fall into two groups according to nationality, either Qatari or other. Households employ many migrants, largely Asians, as labourers and domestic servants, many of whom

Table 10.3. Responses by place of residence (% - note 100% balance includes non-responses).

Place	Number of responses	Know that Al Reem is a reserve?		Know what conversation is?		Defined conservation	Good that Al Reem is a reserve?		Know of planned management interventions?		Exclosures		Hima grazing system		Vehicular access		Restrictions on hunting	
		Y	N	Y	N		Y	N	Y	N	G	B	G	B	G	B	G	B
Al Rufaiq*	11	64	36	64	36	46	91	0	36	55	64	36	73	9	73	18	64	27
Khouzan*	8	38	25	50	13	13	50	0	13	38	13	25	38	0	25	13	25	0
Zukreet*	13	100	0	100	0	23	46	54	23	46	31	46	46	31	31	39	62	8
Um Al-Zabd§	3	0	100	0	100	0	67	0	0	100	33	67	67	33	100	0	67	33
Al-Ghuwairia†	21	95	5	91	10	24	91	5	52	43	52	48	71	19	81	19	38	57
Al-Ituriya†	6	50	0	33	17	0	50	0	17	83	100	0	100	0	83	17	83	17
Al-Jemailiya†	31	68	23	71	16	3	71	10	39	39	52	13	48	13	52	10	48	19
Dukhan†	6	33	67	83	17	17	100	0	17	17	33	0	17	0	33	0	33	0
Other	4	75	25	75	25	0	75	0	50	25	50	25	75	0	75	0	75	0
None given	12	33	58	67	25	0	83	0	33	50	67	0	50	8	58	0	58	17

*= small settlements within the Reem reserve; § = camel camp; † = large settlements outside reserve

Table 10.4. Responses by occupation (% - note 100% balance includes non-responses).

Occupation	Number of responses	Know that Al Reem is a reserve?		Know what conversation is?		Defined conservation	Good that Al Reem is a reserve?		Know of planned management interventions?		Exclosures		Hima grazing system		Vehicular access		Restrictions on hunting	
		Y	N	Y	N		Y	N	Y	N	G	B	G	B	G	B	G	B
Administration	8	38	38	75	0	0	63	0	25	38	63	0	63	0	63	0	50	13
Govt Ministry	5	60	0	60	0	20	40	20	0	40	20	40	0	40	40	20	0	40
Engineering	6	67	33	67	17	0	100	0	33	33	50	17	50	0	33	17	50	17
Security	8	88	13	88	13	25	88	13	38	25	25	75	63	25	75	13	38	38
Education	25	56	32	76	12	12	72	8	20	44	48	12	48	8	48	12	44	16
Student	10	70	10	80	0	10	60	0	50	40	60	10	40	20	50	10	40	40
Domestic	6	67	33	33	67	33	83	0	33	67	100	0	83	0	83	0	50	33
Camel herder	4	0	100	0	100	0	50	0	0	100	25	75	75	25	100	0	75	25
Employee	31	87	10	87	10	19	81	16	48	42	58	29	68	16	65	23	65	23
Other	6	83	17	67	33	0	83	17	33	67	67	17	83	0	67	17	83	0
None given	6	67	33	67	33	17	67	17	50	50	17	33	33	17	33	17	50	17

[Other = imam, retired, post office, social work, self-employed; Security = police, army, security guard; Education = teacher, school sponsor; vice principal; Engineering = oil industry, telecommunications, systems engineer; Employee = unspecified] reside permanently in the region (figure 10.6) – or at least for much of the time that they work in Qatar (others may travel to and fro with their Qatari employers). The large numbers of migrant labourers, comprising something like 80 per cent of the country's population, are another aspect of the dramatic social changes that have occurred with exploitation of petroleum reserves (Kapiszewski 2001; Campbell this volume). The trend noted previously for those with close associations to the Reem region being more suspicious of biosphere status and future conservation plans is again evident when respondents are compared by nationality (table 10.5). While knowledgeable of conservation issues, Qataris are less likely than migrants to support any proposed management measures. This is significant given that current inactivity with respect to implementing conservation measures in the Reem region is largely a political issue and the Qataris are those with political influence, exerted in some measure on the Emir-headed government via tribal networks.

Temporary herding camps (*mukaiyem*) also occur in the region (figure 10.7). While only Qataris can apply for a licence to establish such camps, those living at them are overwhelmingly (if not exclusively) non-Qataris such as Sudanese, Bengalis and Nepalis, who herd the stock. There are on average between four and eight migrant workers residing at such camps. Similarly, elsewhere in Arabia: 'The everyday herding of almost all the livestock on the Saudi Arabian range is left to hired shepherds, usually

Figure 10.6. The house of a migrant worker in Umm Al Qahab village.

Table 10.5. Responses by nationality (% - note 100% balance includes non-responses).

Nationality	Number of responses	Know that Al Reem is a reserve?		Know what conversation is?		Defined conservation	Good that Al Reem is a reserve?		Know of planned management interventions?		Exclosures		Hima grazing system		Vehicular access		Restrictions on hunting	
		Y	N	Y	N		Y	N	Y	N	G	B	G	B	G	B	G	B
Qatar	92	73	16	75	13	16	72	11	34	45	50	26	55	14	55	15	49	24
All non-Qatar	23	39	61	61	39	4	83	4	35	48	57	17	57	13	70	9	61	17
Other Gulf	7	57	43	71	29	0	86	14	71	29	57	14	43	29	57	29	43	43
Other Arab	3	0	100	67	33	0	100	0	0	33	33	0	33	0	33	0	33	0
N. Africa	10	40	60	60	40	10	90	0	20	60	60	20	60	10	80	0	70	10
Asia	3	33	67	33	67	0	33	0	33	67	67	33	100	0	100	0	100	0

[Other Gulf = Oman, Iran; Other Arab = Jordan, Syria; N. Africa = Sudan, Egypt, Mauritania; Asia = India, Pakistan, B'desh]

expatriates' (Cole and Altorki 1998: 121). They again are permanent residents in that they stay in these places for the life of the camps (or so long as in the employ of the Qatari licence holder). According to data supplied by the Ministry of Municipal and Agriculture Affairs,[6] there are thirty-nine camps in the Al Reem Reserve (see table 10.6 and figure 10.2 for locations).

When selecting a camp place, people look for somewhere there are no others, either encampments nearby or homesteads. They avoid stony locales, looking for level *ramel*, 'sandy', sites. Camps where livestock are herded are usually situated inland because of the danger of animals wandering onto the *sabka*, 'salt flats', that are common adjacent to the sea in the Al Reem region, falling through the saline crust and becoming stuck. Some stock-camps are established by villagers in the desert away from their settlements; others belong to persons from outside the region. The people at Refaiq, for example, have a camp at Al Khashina, which is about a 10 to 15-minute drive away. Other villages – such as Khouzan and Umm Al Qahab – have no stock-camps, keeping all animals (camels, sheep and goats) in pens around the settlement. The majority of Qatari men with residence rights in the Al Reem region keep some animals. According to staff in the Jemailiya office of the Ministry of Environment, there are sixty-four village-dwelling permit holders who herd stock in the region, who may or may not maintain stock-camps elsewhere from the village.

Figure 10.7. A camel camp at Al'jla.

Table 10.6. Temporary camps. Five have no licensed stock and are recreational camps only (marked *). Table 10.2 lists Qura Abu Raghed camp in Jemailiya Municipality, as in the Ministry records, although this is incorrect.

Location name & map no.	*Location name & map no.*	*Location name & map no.*
Jemailiya Municipality:		
1. Abu Suf	12. Qatna	23. Sini' Alghadriyat
2. Al-Humailat	13. Qura Abu Raghed	24. Sulaimiyat Bu'ina
3. Al'jla	14. Qura Alqaraf	25. Um Alkhuraq
4. Al-Khashina	15. Rowdat Azza*	26. Um Al-Zabd*
5 Alnafayed	16. Rowdat Khalifa	27. Um Juwaid*
6. Al-Qamirya*	17. Shamal Al-Gazlaniya	28. Um Khayeesa
7. Barbiyat	18. Shamal Al-Jamailiya	29. Um Qarn
8. Baseeteenat	19. Shamal Alsuwaihla	30. Wady Al-Ja'da
9. Fushakh	20. Sharq Al Ghuwairiya	31. Wasee'
10. Janoub Bu Ghamara	21. Sharq Wady Al-Ji'da	32. Widyan Alsahm
11. Juda	22. Shukeek	
Madinat Al-Shamal Municipality:		
33. Alfahadat	36. Janoob Lushai'	39. Shamal Al-Nu'man
34. Idgheesheeyat	37. Maroob	
35. Janoob Abwab	38. Nu'man*	

The state bureaucracy features a system of permits that controls the establishment of stock-herding camps and hunting activity (Al Othman and this volume). It is necessary to obtain a permit issued by the Ministry of the Environment to establish a camp and also to register animals kept there; rules that apply not only to the Al Reem region but all rural Qatar. There are two broad classes of stock-camp permit holder: *mazarah*, persons who 'own earth', that is have permanent houses in the region, and *azba*, non-residents who have a permit to establish a temporary camp. In this way the state seeks to regulate pastoral activity and directly influences contemporary land use. The system of regulation, which is subject to local political manipulation, is now allowing persons without a pastoralist heritage to herd animals by legitimating access to territory that previously would not have been possible without necessary tribal connections. A Qatari can establish a stock-camp anywhere he chooses in rural areas (figure 10.8); he does not need to have had ancestors camping and herding there previously. The blurring of customary practice by state intervention parallels the changes that are occurring in herding arrangements, and reflects

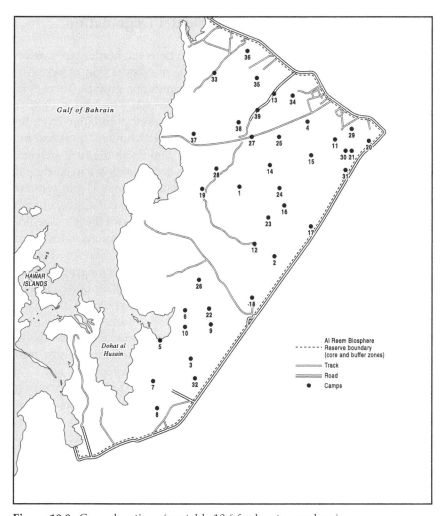

Figure 10.8. Camp locations (see table 10.6 for key to numbers).

the major shifts and the multiple layered nature of the cultural change that is happening with government interventions.

The tendency noted previously with respect to opposition to the biosphere is evident again when we compare the reason that persons are in the Reem region with their knowledge of conservation and attitudes to interventions (table 10.7). While those who have ancestral rights to water and land are more knowledgeable about conservation, they are generally more negative about proposed conservation measures, which several see as restricting their activities.

Population and Environmental Degradation

The traditional strategy of open competition between herders for pasture is not only compromised today by bureaucratic restriction of access to rangeland and sedentary lifestyle but also population growth. There is no census of those living in the Al Reem Reserve region. The UNESCO MAB Nomination File (2007: 14) estimates the permanent population from the 2004 National Census (according to Zones within Municipalities and human settlement distributions) to be 400–500 persons in the core area and approximately 8,000 in the buffer zone (three-quarters male). According to Ministry of Environment briefing notes, the population is 11,160 persons, which is still tiny compared to Qatar's total population of approximately 1.6 million persons. While these demographic statistics for the Reem region are on the high side, and presumably include the populations of Jemailiya and Al Ghuwairiya towns, they give a density of population way beyond what the region supported previously. Whatever the demographic position, the survey data suggest a nonchalant attitude. Respondents were asked about the size of their households, to test the hypothesis that those with larger households, who probably had more children, might be more conscious of future environmental problems and conservation needs (table 10.8). The data do not support this hypothesis; if anything, those from larger households are more opposed to proposed interventions.

It is the large numbers of animals being herded that are thought responsible for environmental degradation, as way beyond the region's natural carrying capacity (similarly in Saudi Arabia; Webster 1996: 483–485), which proposed conservation measures seek to control. While calculation of carrying capacity presents difficulties, available stock figures and contemporary herding practices suggest that it is exceeded by a large margin (tables 10.9 and 10.10).

These data are indicative only. We might assume that one snapshot in time gives a representative indication of stocking levels, but monitoring animal numbers is difficult. For example, while there is the 50 per cent fodder subsidy incentive for owners to register their animals, they do not necessarily do so, but may transfer plastic registration ear tags between animals.[7] Also, stock numbers can fluctuate, possibly widely according to comparative data from briefing notes supplied by the Ministry of the Environment[8]; according to these, animal totals in the Al Reem region two years previously (April 2007) to those in tables 10.9 and 10.10 were: 947 camels, 181 cattle, 9,073 sheep, 8 horses and 17 donkeys. The variation in these animal statistics probably reflects to some extent the fact that stock currently herded in the Al Reem region is not confined there but may be moved considerable distances elsewhere, which further confounds attempts to calculate herd levels commensurate with conservation.

Table 10.7. Responses by reason for being in region (% - note 100% balance includes non-responses).

Reason	Number of responses	Know that Al Reem is a reserve?		Know what conversation is?		Defined conservation	Good that Al Reem is a reserve?		Know of planned management interventions?		Exclosures		Hima grazing system		Vehicular access		Restrictions on hunting	
		Y	N	Y	N		Y	N	Y	N	G	B	G	B	G	B	G	B
Well/land rights	69	81	15	86	9	17	78	13	36	45	46	33	58	17	55	20	52	26
Labour	19	32	68	53	47	5	90	0	26	53	53	21	63	5	68	5	63	11
Other	6	100	0	50	50	50	67	17	50	33	83	17	67	0	83	0	33	33
None given	21	38	29	52	14	0	52	5	29	43	57	0	43	10	52	5	48	19

[Other = married, visitor]

Table 10.8. Responses by household size (% - note 100% balance includes non-responses).

Household Size	Number of responses	Know that Al Reem is a reserve?		Know what conversation is?		Defined conservation	Good that Al Reem is a reserve?		Know of planned management interventions?		Exclosures		Hima grazing system		Vehicular access		Restrictions on hunting	
		Y	N	Y	N		Y	N	Y	N	G	B	G	B	G	B	G	B
2–6 persons	26	62	23	73	8	12	73	8	19	42	50	8	46	4	50	4	50	8
7–10 persons	25	68	24	80	12	8	64	20	36	44	52	20	56	12	56	16	68	8
11–19 persons	22	68	23	64	27	5	86	5	50	41	59	32	82	5	59	23	55	32
20–40 persons	9	67	22	78	11	11	78	0	22	56	44	22	33	33	44	22	44	22
No response	33	67	30	70	27	15	73	9	36	49	49	36	61	15	70	12	39	39

Table 10.9. Village animal numbers (*mazarah* rights) in Al Reem region. Data in this and the table 10.10 (of March 2009) kindly supplied by the Department of Animal Resources (Ministry of Municipal and Agriculture Affairs).

	Camels	Cattle	Sheep	Goats
No. villages with	12	12	16	16
No. homesteads with	32	29	52	41
Total animals	728	272	4,806	2,653
Mean per homestead	22.8	9.4	92.4	64.7
Range by homesteads	1–99	1–90	2–402	3–220
Standard deviation	22.9	16.6	90.3	47.3

Table 10.10. Stock-camp animal numbers (*azba* rights) in Jemailiya and Madinat Al Shamal Municipality regions of the Al Reem Reserve (total number of camps owning stock is 39). Five locations had two separate stock licenses in different names and treated as separate camps.

	Camels	Cattle	Sheep	Goats
No. camps with	22	7	25	21
Total animals	803	57	2,528	1,059
Mean per camp	36.5	8.1	101.1	50.4
Range between camps	1–102	3–15	2–285	2–129
Standard deviation	27.8	4.2	75.4	36.7

Nonetheless, as pointed out, such stock movements are minimal compared to previously when herders moved with their animals over large areas, whereas today they are constrained not only by national borders and a system of government-imposed permits but also by internal borders and highways. The Al Reem region is tiny compared to the area the Bedouin previously roamed over (Cole 1975; Wilkinson 1983; Ferdinand 1993); land degradation seems unavoidable with so many animals kept in such a relatively confined space. While sustainable herding seems a forlorn hope at current stocking levels with available land resources, there is evidence that resources may previously have sometimes been inadequate too. Periodic fighting and raiding of stock – celebrated today in poetry at large social events such as weddings – is possibly evidence that resources were insufficient on occasions with variation in annual rainfall and so on, leading to violent confrontations over rangeland and water sources (Sweet 1965). Dawn Chatty (2006: 11) for instance refers to 'frequent skirmishes ... as tribes struggled to lay claim to the most fertile parts of the semi-arid and arid lands'. In respect of raiding, Lancaster (1981: 123) proposes an intriguing interpretation of the *khuwa* system of protection payments (where people paid others not to raid them, so opting out of the raiding 'game'). He argues that it ensured ecological balance: 'for the return from grazing must exceed the amount of *khuwa* to be of economic benefit to the payer, so *khuwa* regulated the numbers grazing … [it] became a regulatory mechanism for an ecological balance' (ibid.: 123). It shows the limits of traditional practices in the modern world. Various anecdotes further indicate that people may not always have been as free in allowing others access to their water-well region's resources as the customary 'rules' of open grazing access suggest. This is the case in the Zekreet region of Al Reem where they used to say that the deer were blind, intimating that it was particularly poor in resources to deter others from visiting the area.

When stock exceeded rangeland resources previously, the ecological safety valve was animal deaths, bringing numbers down to levels supportable on available resources; there are historical reports of people losing many animals during drought periods. Today's coping mechanism, when carrying-capacity limits are exceeded beyond anything imaginable previously, is less brutal. It rests on the import of fodder and water. Animals depend on a ration of imported feed, the sheep and goats largely on *alef,* 'alfalfa'[9] (*Medicago* spp.), and the camels on *shuwar,* 'oatmeal', mixed with water; other fodder includes barley, *rodus, jibt,* dry bread and dates. In some settlements, farmers cultivate areas of alfalfa on irrigated plots of land, particularly in the northern Al Reem region,[10] but nowhere near enough to feed current numbers of animals. Although traditional wells are currently dry (figure 10.9), some of the water used for irrigation comes

Figure 10.9. A dry well at Khouzan village.

from local sources, diesel pumps tapping into groundwater via tube wells. Drinking water, together with further water used for irrigation, is brought to villages in water tankers from municipal deep wells.[11] This threatens longer-term, even irreversible degradation, by both depleting aquifers faster than rains can replenish them (water supplies eventually diminishing), and increasing soil salinity (until the land can no longer support crops).[12]

Animal Herding Arrangements Today

The environmental costs of herding are partly exported elsewhere through the import of fodder, much of it from overseas, and trucking of water. This compromises assessment of these costs, as the local region is not a closed ecological system regarding herding activities (Yamaguchi this volume). The locally unsustainable character of contemporary herding arrangements – way beyond available local resources – is not apparently an issue currently, with potentially significant conservation implications. With imported animal feed and tanker-supplied water, there is no competition over available grazing, as there was previously, to trigger any ecological readjustment. The current arrangement is only possible by having other places share some of the environmental burden, and would be unsustainable without oil and gas revenues to fund it. Participation in the global marketplace has changed people's relationship with their environment. They no longer have to follow the nomadic lifestyle of their forefathers to ensure adequate grazing and water for their herds but can remain in the same place year round. The contemporary pastoral regime is not sustainable in the context of the local ecosystem, being dependent on petroleum income that generously funds Qatari employment and subsidizes people's herding activities – such that they can afford to purchase the large volumes of imported fodder necessary to keeping so many animals and truck water to otherwise barren places. A question from a conservation viewpoint is the extent to which we are today witnessing a state-sponsored so-called tragedy of the commons (Al-Rowaily 1999), with government-subsidized fodder and water supplies and permit controls effecting environmentally damaging changes in traditional communal land management strategies.

The large numbers of animals relative to local water supplies and pasture resources reflect the dramatic changes that have occurred in animal husbandry in recent decades (Cole and Altorki 1998: 111–134; Gardner 2003). The supply of imported fodder and availability of water tankers have not only led to radical changes in pasturing arrangements and way of life, but are also party to the changing place of animals in Qatari life, the very reasons for keeping stock. Some families continue to herd a few goats, sheep and camels to supply themselves, as previously, with meat and milk, albeit augmenting what they consume with food purchased using cash incomes from other employment, enjoying a dramatically enlarged, and possibly improved diet compared to previously (obesity and associated health problems are now an issue; Hediger et al. 2006; Riva et al. this volume). Others keep more animals, notably goats and sheep, and to a lesser extent cattle, to supply the local Qatari market with meat, in addition to their families (e.g. via the large wholesale animal market off Salwa Road in Doha).

While some continue to earn a proportion of their living through raising sheep and goats, few depend on camel herding to any extent. Nonetheless some people continue to keep large numbers of camels. Although some camel owners and their families in Al Reem villages, together with migrant workers at stock-camps, consume some camel milk and meat,[13] many now keep camels not primarily for food but as status symbols; they are important regarding their sense of cultural identity, for demonstrating social standing and wealth. While camels traditionally featured as wealth in Bedouin communities, they were previously linked directly to subsistence requirements – a successful man could support a large family from his herd, a mark of social standing and renown. Today, camel ownership is still the mark of success for some, animals serving as stores of surplus wealth, like gold jewellery (but which unlike gold, can reproduce more wealth). It is an intriguing transformation of custom with globalization (Cole 1981; Chatty 1996), camels serving today as investments of income deriving from the country's vast hydrocarbon reserves that permit the foregoing unsustainable arrangements. In a review of the changes that have occurred during the three decades that he has known the Al Murrah tribe, Cole (2006: 380) talks about pure-bred camels in Saudi Arabia taking 'on a new value in a prestige economy'. In Qatar, camels sell for tens, even hundreds of thousands of riyals (some even change hands for over a million riyals). There are camel shows at which animals judged best (by size, body shape, coat colour etc.) can win their owners large sums of prize money (a million or more riyals). Other highly valued animals are juveniles that can run fast, which are trained as racing camels (Khalef 1999); again winners earn their owners large sums (figure 10.10).[14] The parallel with racehorses is apposite, in which the rich also invest large sums.

The keeping of camels has become an aspect of Gulf Arab cultural identity in a globalizing world (Lancaster 1981: 103; Montigny-Kozlowska 1989; Cole 2006: 380); for former desert dwellers it is something that marks them out, while ensuring some continuity with their past.[15] We should not expect economic logic necessarily to apply when something achieves such

Figure 10.10. A racing camel at Al Shahaniyah track.

iconic status. While overstocking and the poor condition of the range-land mean that keeping animals is costly, when discussing fluctuations in the price of fodder, for instance, Al Reem informants said that it does not influence the number of animals they keep. Consequently, price manipulation may not prove particularly effective in seeking ways to protect the environment from overgrazing – even if politically acceptable. The changed place of animals in contemporary Qatari society has profound environmental repercussions, pushing any ecological accounting askew. There are significant implications regarding reserve management where animal owners invest disproportionately in their herds for social status reasons rather than to earn their economic livelihoods.

A review of the survey data according to animal ownership supports these conclusions (table 10.11), with those who herd animals in the Reem region more resistant to proposed management measures, albeit they are well informed about conservation issues. This trend further underlines the pattern noted previously, where those more closely associated with the region, in this case herding animals there, are more suspicious of talk about conservation.

The trend is even more pronounced when the animal ownership data are disaggregated according to numbers of animals owned (table 10.12). The more animals herded, the more marked the tendency.

Table 10.11. Responses by animal ownership (% - note 100% balance includes non-responses).

Animal Ownership	Number of responses N	Know that Al Reem is a reserve? Y	N	Know what conversation is? Y	N	Defined conservation	Good that Al Reem is a reserve? Y	N	Know of planned management interventions? Y	N	Exclosures G	B	Hima grazing system G	B	Vehicular access G	B	Restrictions on hunting G	B
Own animals:	58	65	27	72	16	11	66	16	31	41	47	23	49	17	47	17	51	16
Camels, goats and sheep	30	90	7	93	3	13	67	20	33	43	40	30	50	17	50	17	43	20
Camels only	9	56	44	67	22	22	78	11	44	33	67	22	67	11	67	11	67	22
Goats and sheep only	13	62	23	62	23	8	85	0	31	54	62	23	62	23	54	23	62	23
Unspecified	6	50	33	67	17	0	33	33	17	33	17	17	17	17	17	17	33	0
No animals	29	45	38	59	21	3	76	3	28	41	55	3	52	0	52	7	59	7
No response	28	75	25	79	21	25	82	4	43	54	57	43	71	18	82	14	46	46

Table 10.12. Responses by number of animals owned (% - note 100% balance includes non-responses).

No. animal Owned	Number of responses N	Know that Al Reem is a reserve? Y	N	Know what conversation is? Y	N	Defined conservation	Good that Al Reem is a reserve? Y	N	Know of planned management interventions? Y	N	Exclosures G	B	Hima grazing system G	B	Vehicular access G	B	Restrictions on hunting G	B
<50 animals	15	47	33	60	20	7	80	0	47	27	67	13	53	20	60	13	47	33
50–100 animals	9	67	33	100	0	11	78	22	44	33	44	22	56	11	56	11	56	11
>100 animals	16	100	0	94	6	25	88	13	38	38	31	38	50	19	38	25	44	13

While it is thought that participatory approaches to development, which allow expression of local knowledge and practices, are the best way to ensure their incorporation into projects, we should not romanticize these; not all local understanding and aims lead to activities that necessarily respect biodiversity, particularly in times of rapid change. We have to ask if ownership of camels, goats and sheep is too important an indicator of social status for Qataris to contemplate modifying current practices and restricting the size of their herds. So long as owners can import fodder and truck in water, is the state of the rangeland immaterial? In other words, current economic arrangements allow expression of the cultural estimation of stock ownership – owning many animals – without regard to environmental costs. Not so long ago such attitudes would have cost nomadic herders their livelihoods by degrading the pastures on which they and their animals depended. As Cole comments ominously, 'the new pastoralism is fragile, a luxury' (2006: 391).

Return to Exclusion Zones?

The change in perceptions about stock ownership in Qatar and Arabia more generally imply a breakdown of the idea of bio-cultural diversity as a way to promote and manage conservation. The cultural dimension has shifted to such an extent with rapid social change that human activities become environmentally destructive. The restricted movement of people and stock today questions the applicability of local knowledge to environmental management when this knowledge and associated practices depended on more extensive movement of people and stock over much larger regions (Chatty 2003a); it is rather like expecting local knowledge of elephant ecology in Indochina, which depends on animals moving over vast areas of jungle, to apply to animals penned up in a zoological park. Not only has rangeland access changed considerably but also animal herding arrangements as described, from nomadic camel-borne pastoralism dependant on tribally controlled access to pasture over wide areas and rights to water wells in certain locales, to sedentary herding featuring four-wheel drive vehicles, water tankers and imported alfalfa hay and oatmeal fodder (Cole 1981, 2003; Cole and Altorki 1998; Chatty 1996; Gardner and Finan 2004).

The assumptions of co-management are compromised, namely that local people's knowledge and practices will jive with conservation of the environment and sustainable use of resources, and we have the re-emergence of the 'Yellowstone model' of national parks that prohibit or heavily control human activities to protect the environment. This is evident in UNESCO's proposals for the Al Reem Biosphere Reserve, which feature as mentioned core conservation zones (where people will be excluded and nature strictly protected from human activities) and a buffer zone (where protection measures will be less stringent).[16] But this prospect leads to a number of contradictions.

What sort of environment do we seek to conserve? The 'Yellowstone model' aims for pristine nature untouched by humans, whereas today's environment is partly due, as noted, to generations of human activity in most regions. For example, the uplands in Britain would be forested – as they were before humans deforested them – if people ceased managing them as grouse moors and grazing for sheep with periodic burning of heather etc. So excluding people will presumably result in a changed, albeit eventually 'natural' environment, so far as possible on a planet where hydrological and atmospheric systems are global. But if current human activities continue in the Al Reem region, we have the prospect of a changed – and in ecological terms degraded – environment. Viewed from the perspective of the local ecology, these activities have apparently gone haywire recently, no longer being sustainable but damaging the ecosystem. Whatever way we contemplate the future, the environment is likely to differ from previously, as it is improbable that people will revert to their previous nomadic livelihood strategy.

A Yellowstone-type park seems an improbable prospect politically, even though the Qatar government owns 90 per cent of the region (UNESCO 2007: 32) previously held under the tribal common property regime. It would require a large extension of government authority beyond current arrangements. These involve the Ministry of Environment overseeing, as noted, the licensing of campsites and the registration of animals. Only Qatari citizens can apply for such permits to establish stock-camps and herd animals.[17] The government distinguishes three types of camp that need Ministry clearance:

(1) Camps established by residents of villages, who may apply to have a year-round camp with animals; they have to renew the licence annually. This represents bureaucratic rubberstamping of customary practice, as it has evolved contemporarily.

(2) Camps established by non-residents who own stock; these are issued for up to six months, after which permit holders have to reapply; they may move on anywhere in rural Qatar (i.e. out of Al Reem region).

(3) Camps established by non-residents without animals; these are issued for up to four months in winter only; they are for recreational purposes.

Permit holders can only have one camp at any time in all Qatar but can move from one location to another, having secured a permit for the new place. The Ministry staff checks that the animals are appropriately registered with the Department of Animal Resources at the General Department for Agriculture Research and Development. This is undertaken for health reasons – to monitor stock movements and know the whereabouts and numbers of animals in the event of disease outbreak – another aspect of the considerable changes in herding practices.

In theory, the current system of animal registration and camp licensing gives the government the authority to regulate animal numbers, but there is scant evidence of any attempt to do so in the Al Reem region. To go further than these current arrangements seems politically unlikely, as it would require intruding into people's lives more than probably acceptable. Current reserve management and the attitude of rangers reflect political reality, albeit to the frustration of international agencies, which see the declaration of a reserve without any apparent action to make it a reality. The frustration felt at UNESCO is evident in a recent *Gulf Times* article (James 2010), which refers to overgrazing and threatened biodiversity loss, a UNESCO spokesman commenting that 'the present state of Al Reem Biosphere Reserve is the same as that of outside the reserve. It has been selected, identified, a little bit of work has gone into it, but I find it highly disappointing that nothing has been done over the last three years'.

While the current Al Reem situation suggests the prioritizing of environmental and biodiversity protection, extending to the imposition of rules to regulate access to and use of the region's resources, this may not be politically feasible. The biosphere core and buffer zones have yet to be fully implemented. While Qatar is an absolute monarchy, where the Emir is both head of state and government and directly accountable to no one, there is a tradition of consultation and rule by consensus, symbolized in every citizen having the right to appeal to the Emir personally. He and the government he appoints are obliged, in the interests of political stability, to consider the opinions of leading civil and religious notables, such as tribal Sheiks who represent the views of their fellow tribesmen. It is unlikely that popular opinion would support measures to make Al Reem a protected area where access and use of resources are strictly controlled or that the government could enforce such without serious social unrest, as it would amount to excluding the population from a large part of the country.

Participation in the Reserve

We return to the 'participation model' as the only viable option. But local Qataris are already participating in reserve activities, and daily management is under their control via the Ministry of Environment in Doha; many rangers are Al Reem residents who herd animals and hunt there. The question is how to facilitate participation that supports conservation. The local population needs to understand the issues and agree that conservation of the environment is necessary before it will sign up to or enforce any rules regulating access to and use of its region's resources, that is agree to a certain level of protection – as current indifference of Al Reem rangers and management indicates. As the UNESCO person cited above observes, 'A biosphere reserve management committee was established initially and UNESCO invited me to be a part of it, but that committee never met.'

While the results of the survey assessing people's awareness of and attitudes towards the reserve and conservation issues give grounds for optimism, several persons spoke out against the declaration of the region as a biosphere. Why have it, they asked, when there was so little rain and so scarcely any vegetation to protect and little pasture for animals anyway, however managed? They also see the government as duplicitous, pointing out for example that the army conducts exercises in the region, damaging plants and greatly disturbing the wildlife; how can this square with having declared a reserve there? And conservation schemes of the Ministry of Environment have furthered scepticism. Attempts to reintroduce *reem* gazelle into the region, for example, have been mismanaged, resulting in the death of many animals. According to Ministry of Environment briefing notes, in April 2007 there were 120 gazelle (released?) in the Al Reem region. An elderly man at Zekreet described how the Ministry had employed him, as he knows the region intimately, on a small stipend to look out for the gazelle (to provide water and fodder as necessary) but suddenly stopped doing so. 'Who', he asked angrily, 'is looking after the gazelle now'? 'No one', he replied, 'so in hard times like now they are dying.' Such experiences understandably make residents somewhat cynical of talk about a reserve and conservation.

During discussions, some persons became further animated at the suggestion that their activities, notably grazing of animals, were responsible for the apparent environmental degradation seen in the Al Reem region. For example, the first page of the UNESCO MAB Nomination File (2007: 2) refers to 'desert gravel plain ecosystems … partially degraded through overgrazing', and elaborates further 'the greater-than-carrying capacity density of grazing animals … has reduced natural grazing material to extremely sparse densities.… This trend needs to be reduced through zonation and limitations on grazing animals' (ibid.: 30). There is the possibility of stereotyping here (Chatty 2003b), such as imposing a tragedy of the commons view (see Al Rowaily 1999) on a land-use system, which as indicated, is intricate and needs to be understood in all its complexity. For instance, Chatty (2006: 12) points to an 'academic critique … [of] international and national land use paradigms which have sought to blame the Bedouin for what was widely regarded as man-made land degradation and desertification…. questioning government claims of widespread desertification and range degradation due to Bedouin overgrazing and other pastoral activities'.

Local people maintain that they and their forbearers have always been good custodians of the environment, pointing out, like Bedouin elsewhere, that they have herded stock in the region for generations without undue destruction of the vegetation (Lancaster and Lancaster 1999). And a recent survey of vegetation in the Al Reem region supports their claims, concluding that 'human activities do not have a significant impact on either species richness or vegetation cover' (Abdul-Majid 2008: 49). The owners of stock, whether kept in villages or camps, manage their animals closely. They keep many camels, sheep and goats in pens during the daytime (figures 10.11 and 10.12), probably because of the poor grazing available locally. Camels, sometimes hobbled with a rope tied between their front legs, may be allowed to roam unattended during the day, as they return to village or camp water source by evening. Goats and sheep, on the other hand, need shepherds in attendance if allowed to browse in surrounding country in the daytime (similarly in neighbouring Saudi regions; Webster 1996: 485). They are herded near village or camp, whereas

Figure 10.11. Penned camels at Al Busayyir village.

Figure 10.12. Sheep in pen at Refaiq village.

camels may wander further off. While some camels roam free and graze what they find in the desert, and some goats wander free in villages, they are few compared to total numbers of animals, which suggests that it may be inappropriate to blame the poor condition of vegetation in the region on overgrazing. This is certainly the view of local people. They point out that having a shepherd control flocks means that the animals do not roam freely and graze destructively of vegetation, particularly goats that are notorious for heavily browsing plants. Camels, on the other hand, they point out are more fastidious feeders and after nibbling some foliage from a plant move on to the next one.

Hunting is also cited by some as impacting heavily on wildlife and contributing to ecological degradation. It is an important activity for some men in the Al Reem region, not for what it brings to the cooking pot, as previously, but again as an aspect of their Arab identity, particularly the use of falcons; twenty out of the twenty-three survey respondents said that they hunt with falcons, some also use dogs and guns. It is a unique aspect of their desert cultural heritage – whereas people around the world hunt with guns and dogs, only in southwest Asia do they regularly use falcons. These birds, like camels, can change hands for large sums (e.g. prices quoted by falcon sellers at Souq Waqif market run to hundreds of thousands of riyals). In some Al Reem villages, men keep falcons in specially built aviaries of wire netting. While these are not always obvious, the pigeon lofts that supply food for these birds of prey are, comprising wire mesh structures on stilts with empty five-gallon tins stacked sideways up a wall as nesting boxes. It affords owners some sport and their falcons some exercise to release them to catch a pigeon to feed on. They only hunt during the winter months, between the dates that the government advertises (e.g. on the TV) as open season; days spent hunting varies widely according to respondents. The houbara bustard (*Chlamydotis undulata macqueenii*) and cape hares (*Lepus capensis*) are favourite prey species.

When hunting activity is cross-tabulated with persons' responses to plans to restrict hunting in the biosphere region (table 10.13), there is a correlation, perhaps expectably. Those who hunt regularly oppose the putting in place of conservation measures that restrict their activities; the survey data indicating that the more they hunt, the less they view restrictions favourably.

Hunting is a male activity but no trend for or against restrictions is evident when the survey responses are compared according to respondents' gender (table 10.14). Nor is there any correlation with respect to other conservation measures, albeit men profess to know more about conservation issues (although proportionally more females gave a definition).

When asked what they thought was responsible for the current poor condition of vegetation and wildlife in the region, if it is not, as is asserted, due to overgrazing and poor animal management or excessive hunting, local persons said that it was due to lack of sufficient rainfall for several years past. Some persons went on to attribute the poor rainfall and the region's consequent desiccation to the will of Allah, punishing people for their sins. One of the sins mentioned is the greed of some families today, not sharing the country's newfound wealth. The fencing off of areas for the larger farms of the better off, so stopping others from grazing stock freely across the country, was also mentioned as a grievance, restricting their freedom of movement (this is a long-standing source of tension between pastoralists and farmers throughout the Middle East). According to others, the region's current desiccation may be partly attributable to climate change (Gardner and Finan 2004). While current climate change model predications suggest decreased and erratic rainfall for the Gulf region, climate data from Dukhan (the nearest meteorological station to the Al Reem region) do not support the view that the region is experiencing either declining rainfall or increasing temperatures (figures 10.13 and 10.14).[18] The extent to which environmental change and degradation is due to climate change is debatable and demands further research, which is to be expected with the issue currently subject to dispute globally. Either way, local ideas about environmental degradation will inform opinions about the role and relevance of the MAB Reserve and acceptance of pro-

Table 10.13. Response to hunting restrictions by hunting activity (% - note 100% balance includes non-responses).

Hunting activity	Number of responses	Restrictions on hunting	
		G	B
1–30 days	9	67	33
31–100 days	13	8	69
Sometimes	14	57	29
Don't hunt	57	75	18
No response	22	5	0

Table 10.14. Responses by gender (% - note 100% balance includes non-responses).

Gender	Number of responses	Know that Al Reem is a reserve?		Know what conversation is?		Defined conservation	Good that Al Reem is a reserve?		Know about planned management interventions?		Exclosures		Hima grazing system		Vehicular access		Restrictions on hunting	
		Y	N	Y	N		Y	N	Y	N	G	B	G	B	G	B	G	B
F %	31	55	29	61	23	16	71	7	32	48	68	10	71	3	68	3	52	23
M %	84	71	24	77	17	13	76	11	35	44	45	30	51	17	55	18	51	23

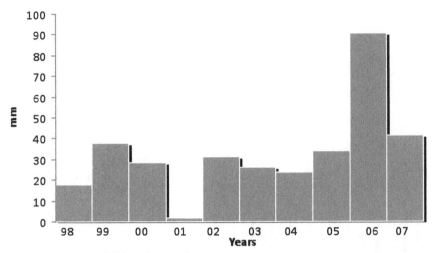

Figure 10.13. Rainfall (total annual).

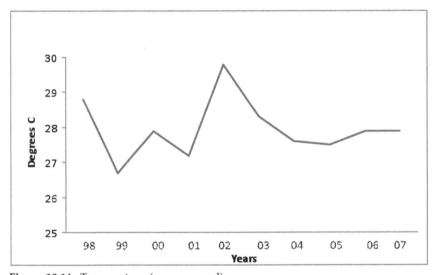

Figure 10.14. Temperature (mean annual).

posed management measures to promote conservation, and so need to be taken seriously.

Education in Conservation

Local opinion thinks that the government is not fully aware of the problems those living in the Al Reem region face. Many of the issues encountered in the course of the survey are similar to those reported elsewhere in the Gulf region where there are similar plans to promote biodiversity conservation (cf. Chatty n.d.). There is understandably widespread concern about the extent to which the declaration of the region a reserve will affect local lives, such as imposing new restrictions on the herding of animals or right to hunt. On the other hand, there is considerable support detectable for investment that might protect or even improve the natural environment – which it is widely agreed is showing signs of stress. But it seems that many Qatari may be unaware of the consequences of their actions in a world greatly changed from that of their grandparents, not that they are indifferent to their peninsula becoming a virtual moonscape dotted with urban sprawls.

In order that the local population can participate meaningfully in planning and implementing of conservation management measures it needs the necessary knowledge. Understanding of what the designation of the Al Reem region as a MAB Biosphere Reserve implies, appears limited from the survey returns. For example, it might be expected that a large majority of people in the region know that they are living in a biosphere reserve and the implications, whereas only 33 per cent claim to know anything about planned management interventions to improve the state of natural resources in the region. In this regard, more awareness of conservation is an educational matter, to inform people about the issues (UNESCO 2007: 27–28), so that they appreciate the urgency of taking action to protect the environment, and the majority will support it and make a participatory park a reality. This is to reiterate UNESCO's point about the need to promote 'public awareness activities aimed at varying sectors of society' (ibid.: 8). Any education policy could profitably draw on the extended family group structure of local communities, to facilitate the efficient dissemination of information widely via kin networks.

But it is not straightforward. Education takes time, even generations, to have an effect, while the environmental problems are urgent and demand conservation measures today (Makrakis 2006). But imposing an immediate Yellowstone-like solution is not an option politically, even if ethically justifiable – by, for example, appealing to universal needs and values, namely that all humans, regardless of culture and history, do not presumably wish to see planet Earth so despoiled that it is no longer a place fit for us to live. Furthermore, there is a danger that promoting education might be seen as advocating ethnocentric brainwashing to the Western conservation view (suspected by some as cover for continued Western economic hegemony, as evident at the Copenhagen and Cancun climate world summits). In this event the promotion of biodiversity conservation becomes a Western imposition to be resisted, or at least the reasons given for it being necessary, which in the Reem region focus on the actions of the local population that are held responsible for degradation.

When the survey data are reviewed according to respondents' education level, the pattern agrees somewhat with expectations, with those who have no schooling being least knowledgeable (table 10.15). But other than that the data evidence no clear pattern, with those who have only primary schooling equally or more knowledgeable about conservation and supportive of interventions.[19] The foregoing occupation data support the counter-intuitive trend regarding education, with neither those employed in education nor currently students markedly better informed about conservation issues or supportive of measures. The absence of correlation with education is encouraging in one aspect, namely it questions disquiet about formal education amounting to brainwashing over conservation.

Furthermore, whereas we might expect younger persons to be more aware of conservation issues, as these feature increasingly in education, this is not so. The survey data indicate that knowledge of conservation and attitudes to interventions do not vary with age (table 10.16). Younger respondents are no more informed about conservation in general or Al Reem in particular. There is even a trend for them to disagree that it is a good thing that the Reem region is a reserve and to judge the implementation of proposed management interventions negatively.

Any education programme should respect what people think and know, and exercise cultural sensitivity in promoting awareness of, and discussion of environmental issues, so that they may conclude for themselves what conservation action is necessary and the participatory park model become a reality. Such promotion of locally informed discussion and avoidance of ethnocentric impositions opens the prospect of building on cultural practices, beliefs and knowledge to further conservation efforts (Stevens 1997; Laird 2002; Sillitoe 2006). It means co-opting Arab concepts and experience to the reserve's conservation ends (El Guindi this volume), so involving the local population more meaningfully in its management, such that they may better appreciate its aims as clearly related to what they already know and believe (Baines 1985; Colchester 2003). This reiterates another point made in the UNESCO MAB Nomination File about the importance of local knowledge featuring in any future plans for the reserve; for example, its reference to 'the use of traditional ecological knowledge in research studies' (UNESCO 2007: 9). It relates to the possibility of reinstating bio-cultural diversity assumptions. Another way to support building awareness of the importance of environmental protection and reaffirm the traditional conservation ethic is to establish robust networks of research and policy experts, both locally and internationally, to support local initiatives and promote sustainable development that proceeds in harmony with environmental conservation.

Table 10.15. Responses by education level (% - note 100% balance includes non-responses).

Education Level	Number of responses	Know that Al Reem is a reserve?		Know what conversation is?		Defined conservation	Good that Al Reem is a reserve?		Know of planned management interventions?		Exclosures		Hima grazing system		Vehicular access		Restrictions on hunting	
		Y	N	Y	N		Y	N	Y	N	G	B	G	B	G	B	G	B
No school	6	17	83	0	100	0	33	33	0	100	33	67	67	33	83	0	83	17
Primary/Middle School	16	81	19	88	13	25	88	6	56	31	44	38	63	19	63	19	44	31
High School	31	74	16	74	13	16	77	10	32	48	65	16	58	13	65	10	48	32
University	50	68	26	94	8	12	74	12	30	44	48	22	54	12	52	16	58	10
No response	12	46	23	39	31	8	54	8	46	31	62	15	62	0	54	15	54	15

Table 10.16. Responses by age (% - note 100% balance includes non-responses).

Age [yrs.]	Number of responses	Know that Al Reem is a reserve?		Know what conversation is?		Defined conservation	Good that Al Reem is a reserve?		Know of planned management interventions?		Exclosures		Hima grazing system		Vehicular access		Restrictions on hunting	
		Y	N	Y	N		Y	N	Y	N	G	B	G	B	G	B	G	B
15–24	16	69	13	69	13	13	63	0	44	44	44	38	50	25	63	13	31	56
25–44	71	66	24	73	16	13	72	14	30	44	49	25	56	13	56	16	54	18
45–59	22	59	41	73	27	18	86	5	41	46	73	5	64	0	68	5	64	9
>60	4	75	25	50	50	25	100	0	50	50	50	50	75	25	50	25	75	25

[Y = yes, N = no, G = good, B = bad]

Local Environmental Knowledge and Conservation

A key question is the extent to which local environmental knowledge and practices are still extant, and then to ask how the Al Reem Reserve authorities might profitably employ them. For instance, is there a working memory of the traditional *hima* community-based grazing arrangements of Bedouin pastoralism that left areas fallow for vegetation to regenerate (Draz 1979; Batanouny 2001: 32–34; Chatty 2003b; Hobbs 2006: 787–788), sufficient to further the objectives of biodiversity conservation? When we raised the issue of the practice of *hima* rotation of grazing areas, some maintained that they continue to practice it. They also said that they try to restrict the access of strangers to parts of their region, although the manner in which they do so is unclear. Again, this is to mobilize people's sense of identity as herders of animals, through practices such as *hima* fallow arrangements, to further the objectives of biodiversity conservation, which is to turn round one of the perceived causes of environmental degradation to serve its protection.

While Bedouin pastoralists may have followed practices that protect natural resources from overexploitation, current behaviour suggests that these may not equate with a Western-like awareness of the need for biodiversity conservation. Otherwise, why do people, including reserve rangers mandated to promote conservation, evidence such apparent indifference to contemporary damage to the environment in their behaviour? It is necessary, as noted, to beware of idealizing local knowledge, as shown by the survey of people's opinions of various proposed conservation measures. Regarding the four interventions under consideration in the Al Reem Biosphere Reserve: (1) 49 per cent of respondents thought that the establishment of exclosures would be good as 'it will protect local shrubs and trees', while others thought it 'bad because it will limit freedom of movement'[20]; (2) 56 per cent thought the re-establishment of the community-based *hima* grazing system was a good idea as 'it will preserve the animal resources', while others thought it no benefit 'as Qatar only has a small amount of land'; (3) 53 per cent thought control of vehicular access a good thing 'because it will protect the environment', while others thought it bad 'because it will limit our freedom'; and (4) 56 per cent thought a prohibition on hunting locally a good idea 'because it will preserve wild animal numbers', while others opposed it 'because it is the tradition of our ancestors'. The overall level of agreement for all four proposed conservation interventions combined was 54 per cent.

The idea of bio-cultural diversity and possibility of co-opting local knowledge and practices to conservation goals may imply the need to conserve culture, as well as nature (UNESCO 2006–2009). But this is a contentious idea with a controversial history featuring salvage ethnography and attempts to save traditions. The picture is mixed across Arabia, including Qatar; while rapid economic development is leading to changes in identity with little evident concern to preserve some aspects of Arab culture, there is a fierce desire to protect other aspects, notably those with a religious association (Al-Ghanin this volume). The restoration of previous practices that promoted sustainable resource use will not be successful unless culture bearers can see the point and want to do so. If the prospects of turning the clock back to previous ecologically balanced ways of life or excluding people and imposing Yellowstone park–style conservation are inadequate-cum-inappropriate to tackle problems of human activity currently degrading the environment in contemporary Qatar, a viable way to proceed may be to promote a new sustainable accommodation between human population and environment. This relates to attempts by well-meaning authorities, which perceive a need to conserve nature, to introduce outside-brokered conservation-framed interventions, such as proposals to promote environmentally friendly tourism, particularly eco- and cultural tourism (Richtzenhain et al. 2008), and camel dairy farms (UNESCO 2008).[21] But similar to the reinstatement of previous sustainable land-use practices, the development of such new practices that accord with conservation are only likely to prove successful if they resonate with local people and their expectations too (Chatelard 2006). In other words, they need to be developed collaboratively to meet with local approval and to take root. Any imposition will probably prove unsustainable, which returns us to the centrality of participation for successful interventions.

Regarding tourism, the omens from the survey are mixed. Residents seem fairly tolerant of tourists, considering the numbers that pass through some villages, especially at weekends. Many pass through Zekreet on their way to visit the popular Abrouq area with its interesting wind-eroded mesa formations. According to the Sudanese caretaker at the Abrouq 'fort' film set, he sees about forty-five vehicles a day over a weekend (Friday and Saturday), but only five vehicles a day during the rest of the week. This possibly represents the highest rate of tourist visits to the Al Reem region; the Ras Abrouq peninsula being popular with expatriate tourists, few of whom venture deep into the desert elsewhere. Residents said that they do not mind them passing through Zekreet village on the whole, although someone has constructed a speed hump to slow vehicles down and some mentioned that they are fed up with having to help persons ignorant of desert-driving conditions who get into trouble. They are happy to see visitors enjoying the beaches and sea, so long as they behave reasonably, not speeding through villages or leaving litter. But some expressed anger at seeing visitors, particularly joy-seeking youngsters, damaging the land, driving recklessly off tracks, damaging vegetation,[22] or leaving rubbish after camping for a night or two (a permit is not necessary for such short stays), which they have to clear up so that it does not harm grazing stock; animals have been known to die because they ingest refuse.[23]

Where to Next?

Biodiversity conservation raises complex issues and we should not anticipate straightforward solutions to the problems posed by the establishment of bioreserves such as Al Reem (Nelson 2008). It can be difficult for deskbound policy makers, researchers and planners to understand the local viewpoint and allow it expression. For instance, concerns for freedom of movement, mentioned several times, are a common issue among nomadic pastoralist populations and have long featured in their relations with sedentary farming neighbours and nation states that throughout history have sought to curtail their liberty. In other words, it is a deep-rooted cultural issue. It can be challenging to appreciate the significance of such values and accommodate for them. Some local ideas and wishes may likely conflict with those of outside authorities with respect to measures deemed necessary to biodiversity conservation. The survey findings suggest this is so. They broadly accord with the 'NIMBY' acronym. Qataris appear no different to people elsewhere when faced with proposals to establish conservation reserves. They are willing to support these in principle as worthwhile initiatives, so long as 'not in my back yard' or too disruptive of their lives and inconvenient.

Striking a balance between economic development and environmental conservation is a challenge facing many communities around the world; often short-term development proceeds at the expense of long-term conservation, particularly where there is no tradition of conservation. Until the petroleum bonanza, many communities in the Gulf and wider Middle East region subscribed to an unwritten philosophy of conservation. It featured a mindset that enabled people to survive in a harsh and unforgiving desert environment; they were 'living' conservation long before it became a sustainable development buzzword. But the coming of a rapidly growing fossil fuel–funded economy with extensive infrastructure development and escalating materialistic consumption threatens not only to overwhelm this approach to life but also the natural environment. The local population is experiencing rapid economic and social change, moving from a nomadic to a settled lifestyle in less than half a century, with profound implications. It is likely to experience confused and contradictory aspirations as it seeks to adapt to the new situation, as evident for example in the struggle to accommodate tribal ways and values to an urban existence. A cost of so-called economic globalization—where Qatar's market participation is largely dependent on the unsustainable exploitation of abundant non-renewable gas and oil reserves demanded by an energy-hungry world—appears to be that sustainable use of renewable natural resources and the environment take second place.

What are the implications of such attitudes, combined with recent lifestyle changes that distance people from the land, for the participatory co-management of conservation areas? In light of the evidence, is it possible to argue for such management of protected areas? The answer is 'yes and no, it depends'. It depends on whether we take an ecological or a social view. Where rapid change occurs, as in Qatar, and people's activities are environmentally out of whack, the ecological implication is that we need to turn the clock back to the imposition of conservation areas and to centrally managed approaches that seek to control access and local activities, even the prohibition of some to protect wildlife. But experience tells us that such an approach is unlikely to meet with success socially; the survey returns indicate the extent to which the local population will probably resent such restrictions on use of resources, making them politically unfeasible. As to where they go next, that is for the various stakeholders involved in the Al Reem Biosphere Reserve to work out. Wherever they go, they are likely to encounter issues that will keep researchers and policymakers occupied for the foreseeable future, given that Al Reem is a largely unknown region to outsiders. We need to substantiate the extent to which people's activities are contributing to degradation and how any conservation interventions may ameliorate it. And local involvement will be critical to the policy framing of such enquiries into human-environmental relations (UNESCO 2007: 23).

Notes

We are grateful to Mariam Abdel-Hafiz, one-time research assistant for the Sustainable Development Initiative at Qatar University, for assistance coordinating the surveys that feature in this chapter and data analysis (conducted during work undertaken for Qatar-Shell GTL Ltd; Sillitoe et al. 2009), and our colleague Abdul Karim Al-Amir Hassan for his valuable help. Thanks also for helpful comments from participants in the Sustainable Land Development and Wildlife Conservation (2B-2) session at the 2011 International Conference on Sustainable Systems and the Environment (ISSE 11) held at the American University of Sharjah, at which a version of this chapter was given. We also thank Sarah Clarke for her careful reading and comments on the chapter.

 1. Established by the Supreme Council for the Environment and Natural Reserves in 2005, following declaration of its protected status by Emiri Decree 7

(2005), the region became a biosphere in UNESCO's MAB programme in 2007 (UNESCO 2007: 5; SCENR 2007).

2. The survey comprised a brief questionnaire administered to a sample of individuals/households to gauge knowledge and opinions of Al Reem MAB Reserve. We administered some questionnaires directly during visits to the Al Reem region with the assistance of a team of Qatar University student interviewers (we thank the following students from the Departments of Social Sciences and Biological and Environmental Sciences for assistance with the conduct of the two surveys: Saoud Ali Al Adba, Rashed Ali Al Merri, Mohd Saad Al-Dosari, Mohd Saeed Masoud, Saeed Rashid Sebaih, and Mohammed Ahmed Sorour; and Momina Adel Zakzok, Hayat Khalaf Al-Japiry, Hana Khalaf Almohammed, Afra Mubarak Al-Hajri, Shamsa Abdullah Salim Al-Khanjari and Mona Haider Al-Lawati). Although this is the ideal way to conduct such a survey using trained interviewers, the time constraints and problems encountered finding and interviewing certain members of the population, due to sensitivities of doing research in this region, prompted us to resort to the distribution of questionnaires through schools (we thank the teachers and students at Jemalieeya and Zekreet boys' and girls' elementary and high schools for their ready cooperation with the surveys, which helped us achieve a statistically adequate sample). Seventy-five respondents completed the questionnaires.

3. Obscure wording of the question in Arabic may partly explain why so few respondents provided definitions.

4. The Ministry of Municipal and Agriculture Affairs, Department of Animal Resources.

5. Information kindly supplied by Mr Khalid al-Enzi and Mr Hameed.

6. We thank Dr Kassem Nasser Al-Qahtani and Hussain Aseri and the staff in the Department of Animal Resources at the General Department for Agriculture Research and Development for kindly making these data available to us.

7. Staff at the Ministry talked about people messing around with registration numbers on tags, albeit such practices are illegal. (It is not possible to tamper with camel registration as this involves a microchip inserted into the animal's neck.)

8. Ministry of the Environment briefing notes entitled 'Al-Reem Reserve: Man and Biosphere Reserve' kindly supplied by Khalid Helal Al-Enzi.

9. The English term *alfalfa* derives from the Arabic term *al-fasfasa* for green fodder.

10. According to the Ministry of the Environment briefing notes on the reserve, there are seventy-four farms in the region covering 1,839 hectares.

11. People own water bowsers and receive payment from the government for transporting water to their villages.

12. The UNESCO Nomination File (2007: 30) makes the same point. In Oman, the use of increasingly salty groundwater has resulted in large areas of land becoming sterile.

13. They do so seasonally, milking largely during the winter months, for although a camel will lactate for one year, herders milk animals for only some of this time, ceasing when the cow is pregnant again.

14. Racing camels are rarely kept in remote places such as Al Reem camps and more usually in stables adjacent to the Al Shahaniya racing track, which is situated in the centre of the Qatar peninsula about half way between Al Reem and Doha.

15. The identity issue is a complex one, for as Cole (2006: 380) points out, prized camels 'had genealogies and histories that were intertwined with those of their owners'.

16. Webster (1996: 492) makes similar recommendations for the Jubail Reserve on the Saudi Arabian Gulf.

17. Either married Qatari men who own registered animals or unmarried men over thirty years in age; those married to Qatari women can also apply, claiming the right in their wife's name (their children may subsequently claim permits in their own names if Qatar residents).

18. Meteorological data supplied by Department of Meteorology, Qatar Civil Aviation Authority.

19. The large proportion of respondents with university-level education is probably an artefact of the survey method; those with higher education possibly more likely to complete the questionnaire.

20. Note that some of the responses suggest that respondents did not understand what an exclosure is, confusing it with enclosure. See Chatty 1998 for discussion of enclosures to protect wildlife such as oryz.

21. An increasingly popular market-informed approach to conservation is to advocate that people are remunerated for the ecosystem services of protected natural environments. But there is little mileage in this approach in desert contexts where – unlike forest watersheds – there is little vegetation to fix CO_2 and release O_2, and scant water catchment function etc. And national income from hydrocarbon revenues far exceeds any ecosystem service remuneration yet contemplated – so this market solution is unlikely to fly.

22. According to one botanical study however, the passage of a single vehicle may benefit plant growth by creating a shallow indentation where rainwater collects (Brown and Schoknecht 2001) – although this is at odds with orthodox opinion (Vollmer et al. 1977).

23. When long-term camp permit-holders move camp, they should clear up the previous site as a condition for securing a new permit, and Ministry staff are supposed to go and check that they have done so properly when they reapply.

References

Abdul-Majid, S. 2008. 'Vegetation Mapping and Anthropogenic Effects in Al-Reem.' MSc dissertation, University College London.

Abulfatih, H., E. M. Abdelbari and Y. M. Ibrahim. 2001. *Vegetation of Qatar.* Doha: University of Qatar.

Al-Rowaily, Saud L. R. 1999. 'Rangeland of Saudi Arabia and the "Tragedy of Commons".' *Rangelands* 21: 27–29.

Baines, G. 1985. 'Draft Programme on Traditional Knowledge for Conservation.' *Tradition, Conservation and Development* 3: 5–13.

Barth, H.-J., and B. Böer (eds.). 2002. *Sabkha Ecosystems: Volume I: The Arabian Peninsula and Adjacent Countries.* Dordrecht: Kluwer Academic Publishers (Tasks for Vegetation Science 36).

Batanouny, K. H. 2001. *Plants in the Deserts of the Middle East.* Berlin: Springer.

———. 1981. *Ecology and Flora of Qatar.* Doha: University of Qatar.

Brown, G., and N. Schoknecht. 2001. 'Off-Road Vehicles and Vegetation Patterning in a Degraded Desert Ecosystem in Kuwait.' *Journal of Arid Environments* 49: 413–427.

Campbell, B. 2004. 'Indigenous Views on the Terms of Participation in the Development of Biodiversity Conservation in Nepal.' In *Investigating Local Knowledge: New Directions, New Approaches,* eds. A. Bicker, P. Sillitoe and J. Pottier, 149–187. Aldershot: Ashgate.

Chatelard, G. 2006. 'Desert Tourism as a Substitute for Pastoralism?' In *Nomadic Societies in the Middle East and North Africa: Entering the 21st Century,* ed. D. Chatty, 710–736. Leiden: Brill Publishers.

Chatty, D. 1996. *Mobile Pastoralists: Development Planning and Social Change in Oman.* New York: Columbia University Press.

———. 1998. 'Enclosures and Exclusions: Conserving Wildlife in Pastoral Areas of the Middle East.' *Anthropology Today* 14 (4): 2–7.

———. 2003a. 'Mobile Peoples and Conservation: An Introduction." *Nomadic Peoples* 7 (1): 5–16.

———. 2003b. 'Environmentalism in the Syrian Badia: The Assumptions of Degradation, Protection and Bedouin Misuse.' In *Ethnographies of Conservation: Environmentalism and the Distribution of Privilege,* eds. D. Anderson and E. Berglund, 87–99. New York and Oxford: Berghahn Books.

———. 2006. 'Introduction: Nomads of the Middle East and North Africa Facing the 21st Century.' In *Nomadic Societies in the Middle East and North Africa: Entering the 21st Century,* ed. D. Chatty, 1–29. Leiden: Brill Publishers.

———. n.d. 'Adapting to Biodiversity Conservation: The Mobile Pastoral Harasiis Tribe of Oman.' Unpublished manuscript.

Colchester, M. 2003. 'Indigenous Peoples and Protected Areas: Rights, Principles and Practice.' *Nomadic Peoples* 7 (1): 33–51.

Cole, D. P. 1975. *Nomads of the Nomads: The Al Murrah Bedouin of the Empty Quarter.* Chicago: Aldine Publishing Company.

———. 1981. 'Bedouin and Social Change in Saudi Arabia.' In *Change and Development in Nomadic Pastoral Societies,* eds. J. G. Galaty and P. C. Salzman, 128–149. Leiden: Brill (International Studies in Sociology and Social Anthropology vol. 33).

———. 1982. 'Tribal and Non-Tribal Structures among the Bedouin of Saudi Arabia.' *Al-Abhath* 30: 77–93.

———. 2003. 'Where Have the Bedouin Gone?' *Anthropological Quarterly* 76 (2): 235–267.

———. 2006. 'New Homes, New Occupations, New Pastoralism: Al Murrah Bedouin, 1968–2003.' In *Nomadic Societies in the Middle East and North Africa: Entering the 21st Century,* ed. D. Chatty, 370–392. Leiden: Brill Publishers.

Cole, D. P., and S. Altorki. 1998. *Bedouin, Settlers, and Holiday-Makers: Egypt's Changing Northwest Coast.* Cairo: American University in Cairo Press.

Draz, O. 1979. 'Revival of the *Hema* System of Range Reserves as a Basis for the Syrian Range Management Program.' In *Proceedings of 1st International Rangeland Congress,* ed. D. N. Hyder, 100–103. Denver: Society for Rangeland Management.

Ferdinand, K. 1993. *The Bedouins of Qatar.* London: Thames and Hudson.

Gardner, A., and T. J. Finan. 2004. 'Navigating Modernization: Bedouin Pastoralism and Climate Information in the Kingdom of Saudi Arabia.' *The MIT Electronic Journal of Middle East Studies* 4: 59–72. http://web.mit.edu/cis/www/mitejmes/.

Gardner, A. 2003. 'The New Calculus of Bedouin Pastoralism in the Kingdom of Saudi Arabia.' *Human Organization* 26: 267–276.

General Secretariat for Development Planning (GSDP). 2008. 'Qatar National Vision 2030.' Doha.

Ghimire, K. B., and M. P. Pimbert (eds.). 1997. *Social Change and Conservation: Environmental Politics and Protected Areas.* London: Earthscan.

Grove, R. 1994. *Green Imperialism.* Delhi: Oxford University Press.

Hediger, V., et al. 2006. *Gulf Cooperation Council Health Care 2025.* New York: McKinsey and Company.

Hiatt, J. M. 1984. 'State Formation and the Encapsulation of Nomads: Local Change and Continuity Among the Jordanian Bedouin.' *Nomadic Peoples* 15: 1–11.

Hobbs, J. J. 2006. 'Guidelines for the Involvement of Nomadic Pastoralists in Conservation and Development.' In *Nomadic Societies in the Middle East and North Africa: Entering the 21st Century,* ed. D. Chatty, 785–799. Leiden: Brill Publishers.

Ingham, B. 1986. *Bedouin of Northern Arabia: Traditions of the Al-Dhaf'ir.* London and New York: KPI (distributed by Routledge and Kegan Paul).

International Union for the Conservation of Nature and Natural Resources (IUCN). Homepage, http://www.iucn.org/.

James, B. 2010. 'UNESCO Team Calls for Al Reem's Conservation,' *Gulf Times,* 4 December.

Kapiszewski, A. 2001. *Nationals and Expatriates: Population and Labour Dilemmas of the Gulf Cooperation Council States.* Reading: Ithaca Press.

Katakura, M. 1977. *Bedouin Village: A Study of a Saudi Arabian People in Transition.* Tokyo: University of Tokyo Press.

Khalef, S. 1999. 'Camel Racing in the Gulf: Notes on the Evolution of a Traditional Cultural Sport.' *Anthropos* 94: 85–106.

Knight, J. (ed.). 2000. *Natural Enemies: People Wildlife Conflicts in Anthropological Perspective.* London: Routledge.

Laird, S. (ed.). 2002. *Biodiversity and Traditional Knowledge: Equitably Partnerships in Practice.* London: Earthscan (People and Plants Conservation Series).

Lancaster, W., and F. Lancaster. 1999. *People, Land and Water in the Arab Middle East: Environments and Landscapes in the Bilâd as-Shâm.* London: Routledge.

Lancaster, W. 1981. *The Rwala Bedouin Today.* Cambridge: Cambridge University Press.

MacNeely, J. 1997. 'Interaction Between Biological Diversity and Cultural Diversity.' In *Indigenous Peoples, Environment and Development.* Copenhagen: International Working Group for Indigenous Affairs, document 85.

Makrakis, V. 2006. *Preparing United Arab Emirates Teachers for Building a Sustainable Society.* Crete: University of Crete E-media Publications.

Montigny-Kozlowska, A. 1983. 'Les Determinates d'un fait de la notion de territorie et son evolution chez les Al-Naim de Qatar.' *Production Pastorale et Societe* 13: 111–113.

———. 1989. 'Les lieux de l'identite des Al-Na'im de Qatar.' *Maghreb-Machrek* 123: 132–143.

Mundy, M., and B. Musallam (eds.). 2000. *The Transformation of Nomadic Society in the Arab East.* Cambridge: Cambridge University Press.

National Parks Commission. 2008. *Report of the National Parks Commission.* London: HMSO.

Nelson, F. 2008. 'Conservation and Aid: Designing More Effective Investments in Natural Resource Governance Reform.' *Conservation Biology* 23 (5): 1102–1108.

Neumann, R. P. 1998. *Imposing Wilderness: Struggles Over Livelihood and Nature Preservation in Africa.* Berkeley: University of California Press.

Peters, E. L. 1990. *The Bedouin of Cyrenaica: Studies in Personal and Corporate Power* (ed. by J. Goody and E. Marx). Cambridge: Cambridge University Press.

Posey, D. A. (ed.). 1999. *Cultural and Spiritual Values of Biodiversity: A Complementary Contribution to the Global Biodiversity Assessment.* London: Intermediate Technology Publications (for the UN Environment Programme).

Richtzenhain, M., et al. 2008. *Towards Environmentally Friendly Tourism in Arabian Biosphere Reserves: Case Study: Al Reem, Qatar.* Doha: UNESCO.

Saberwal, V., M. Rangharajan and A. Kothari. 2001. *People, Parks and Wildlife: Towards Coexistence.* New Delhi: Orient Longman.

Supreme Council for Environment and Natural Reserves (SCENR). 2007. Protected Area Action Plan 2008–2013. Department of Wildlife Conservation, SCENR (see http://www.cbd.int/doc/world/qa/qa-nbsap-oth-en.doc).

Sillitoe, P. 2006. 'Ethnobiology and Applied Anthropology: Rapprochement of the Academic with the Practical.' *Journal of the Royal Anthropological Institute* Special Issue (ed. R. Ellen) 1: 119–142.

Sillitoe, P., et al. 2009. Socio-Economic Survey Report for Qatar Shell Proposed Biodiversity Offset Investment at Al Reem Biosphere Reserve. Submitted to Qatar-Shell GTL, Al Mirqab Tower, Doha, 52 pp.

Smith, W., and T. C. Meredith. 1999. 'Identifying Biodiversity Conservation Priorities Based on Local Values and Abundance Data.' In *Cultural and Spiritual Values of Biodiversity,* ed. D. A. Posey, 372–375. London: Intermediate Technology Publications.

Spence, M. D. 1999. *Dispossessing the Wilderness: Indian Removal and the Making of the National Parks.* Oxford: Oxford University Press.

Stevens, S. (ed.). 1997. *Conservation Through Cultural Survival: Indigenous Peoples and Protected Areas.* Washington, DC: Island Press.

Sweet. L. 1965. 'Camel Raiding of North Arabian Bedouin: A Mechanism of Ecological Adaption.' *American Anthropologist* 67: 1132–1150.

Swiderska, K., et al. 2008. *The Governance of Nature and the Nature of Governance: Policy that Works for Biodiversity and Livelihoods.* London: International Institute for Environment and Development.

Tuxill, J., and G. P. Nabhan. 2001. *People, Plants and Protected Areas*. London: Earthscan.

UNESCO. 2007. Al-Reem Reserve: UNESCO MAB Biosphere Reserve Nomination File, submitted to the Supreme Council for the Environment and Natural Reserves, State of Qatar.

———. 2008. *The Camel Farm Project: From Tradition to Modern Times*. Doha: UNESCO Office.

Vollmer, A. T., et al. 1977. 'The Impact of Off-Road Vehicles on a Desert Ecosystem.' *Environmental Management* 1 (2): 115–129.

Webster, R. M. 1996. 'People, Resources and Conflicts of Interest in the Jubail Marine Wildlife Sanctuary' In *A Marine Wildlife Sanctuary for the Arabian Gulf: Environmental Research and Conservation Following the 1991 Gulf War Oil Spill*, eds. F. Krupp, A. H. Abuzinada and I. A. Nader, 480–495. Frankfurt: Senckenberg Institute.

Wilkinson, J. C. 1983. 'Traditional Concepts of Territory in South East Arabia.' *The Geographical Journal* 149: 301–315.

Wilshusen, P., et al. 2002. 'Reinventing a Square Wheel: Critique of a Resurgent "Protection Paradigm" in International Biodiversity Conservation.' *Society and Natural Resources* 15 (1): 17–40.

World Conservation Monitoring Centre. 1994. *United Nations List of National Parks and Protected Areas*. Gland: IUCN.

Zerner, C. (ed.). 2000. *People, Plants and Justice: The Politics of Nature Conservation*. New York: Columbia University Press.

CHAPTER 11

Promoting Sustainable Development in Marine Regions

James Howard

Coastal nations are often, economically, highly dependent on the rich diversity of marine life found in their waters. Their economic development is reliant on continued or expanding income from such marine resources. Such important economic assets need safeguarding from the threats of overexploitation. To a large extent, most countries seek to protect their national waters for their own use; however, these are complex systems and simple protection for economic gain does not equate to sustainable resource use. The concern with marine ecosystems is their 'invisible' nature; it was popularly believed until recently that they are inexhaustible and the threat of extinction a minor one (Roberts and Hawkins 1999). If future generations are to benefit from these assets, we need changes in how these resources are managed, protected and harvested. Many 'developed' countries' marine resources until recently have suffered from ignoring sustainable practices resulting in irrecoverable loss of diversity and ecosystem function. Developing countries can avoid a similar deterioration of their marine resources by implementing sustainable forms of management in conjunction with other development goals.

One of the main arguments for marine conservation is to protect the functioning of ecosystem services. These tend to be taken for granted until they are suddenly absent or change. Losses to biodiversity ultimately affect ecosystem services provision (Dietz and Adger 2003). The ocean provides many services from influencing landmass temperatures to protection from storms and natural disasters, to cycling material globally, and detoxifying and sequestering wastes, and providing societal and scientific values. While these services are difficult to put a value on, several studies have attempted to measure the value of ecosystem services to highlight their importance and how expensive it is to try and restore them if possible. A much-cited valuation of the world's natural capital and ecosystem services showed that marine ecosystems provide 63 per cent of all global ecosystem services (Costanza et al. 1997: 12). In a further economic valuation, using similar methods, Qatar's aquatic ecosystem services are estimated at US $5.5 billion annually, which is almost a hundred times the country's terrestrial services (Martínez et al. 2007: 259). This shows the value of managing marine resources effectively, which despite providing far more services have received less priority than terrestrial ecosystems because they are 'out of sight, out of mind'.

Over 80 per cent of the population of more than 50 per cent of countries worldwide lives on the coasts, and with coastal populations predicted to increase by 42 per cent between 2007 and 2015 (Martínez et al. 2007) there will be growing pressure on coastal and marine resources, further reducing ecosystem services and functions. Since the start of the new millennium the coastline of Qatar has been drastically altered in places with continuing natural gas and oil exploration and drilling, yet the coastline is less degraded in comparison to the coastlines of some developed and developing countries, which should be a further impetus to preserve these areas carefully and ensure planned and managed use.

Most economically viable marine resources are now exploited at maximal and often unsustainable levels, few marine ecosystems in the world remain underexploited and none remain at historical natural levels of diversity (Jackson et al. 2001). Even before 1950 and the introduction of modern commercial fishing, the megafauna of our oceans, large species such as whales, turtles and sharks had been overharvested (ibid.). The importance of recognizing what was abundant in the past helps in planning for sustaining resources for the future and safeguarding remaining populations. Finding the balance between preventing extinctions and maintaining healthy ecosystem services, and ensuring livelihoods and income for current and future generations is challenging as they are often seen in opposition (Cheung and Sumaila 2008).

Biodiversity conservation is often implemented independent of human needs with exclusion of people often seen as the solution, yet many studies highlight that where conservation ignores social priorities it tends to fail (Christie 2004). As threats to the natural biota are largely attributed to human activities, calls to conserve and develop sustainably must involve and include humans within the management model (Cheung and Sumaila 2008). Recently there has been a move towards an ecosystems-based management strategy (EBM) which combines preservation of the entire ecological system with consideration of the social situation and local stakeholders' needs, as previous single-stock management methods have largely failed to halt species decline and ecosystem deterioration

(Leslie and McLeod 2007). The many threats to marine ecosystems need to be understood and identified in order to find solutions and alter our behaviour.

Major Threats to Marine Ecosystems

It has been shown that there are multiple stressors to marine environments, including both environmental shocks such as hurricanes, tsunamis, El Niño events and human-induced stressors such as pollution and fishing. When these stressors act synergistically, they consequently reduce the resilience of previously healthy ecosystems. The lower the resilience of the overall ecosystem, the lower its ability to withstand occasional environmental shocks, such as warming events or tsunamis and large storms, which are predicted to occur more frequently in the future due to climate change (Hughes and Connell 1999). It is crucial to reduce human pressures on these stressed systems, including minor threats, to allow them to regain their intrinsic resilience. Since the 1970s, the trade in aquarium reef fish in tropical reef areas has been practised on a large commercial scale and it was thought to have an insignificant effect on reefs and fish communities (Bruckner 2000). But it is potentially a serious threat given our knowledge of synergistic factors and the decrease in resilience of reefs around the world (Wabnitz et al. 2003). Our knowledge of the oceans and the complex ecological interactions and processes is minimal in comparison to terrestrial systems and yet there are important discoveries to be made, which may provide solutions to combat the threats facing our oceans. Further study to understand the complex interactions of these threats is needed alongside continued remediation.

Climate Change

Climate change is a threat to biota and ecosystems across the globe, and is seen as a priority area for research and intervention. Governments worldwide are finally acting on predictions, though the indirect effects and knock-on effects that a rise in global temperature could cause remain unclear. It is beyond the scope of this chapter to examine in detail the effects of climate change on marine resources, however a few examples highlight the seriousness of this threat. For the tropical marine environment the predictions are bleak (Hughes et al. 2003). John Veron et al. (2009) predict that with increasing atmospheric carbon and greater acidification of the ocean, major coral bleaching events may occur almost every year within twenty years. If no drastic reduction in carbon emissions occur soon, it is likely that coral reefs, which are some of the most productive ecosystems on earth (Connell 1978), will become extinct within the next thirty to fifty years (Veron et al. 2009). Sea temperatures are already rising, forcing mobile marine life to move pole-wards to cooler waters, where previously they did not exist. Sessile marine organisms, including those contributing to many habitat forms, such as coral reefs or sponges, will have little chance to escape the increasing temperatures and will have to adapt or die out. The Gulf around Qatar supports some healthy coral reefs in coastal areas although the reefs of the Arabian Gulf are some of the most highly stressed in the world, with factors as diverse as light and oil pollution to harmful algal blooms and overfishing being to blame.

In the time frame climate change is occurring, there is little chance of adaptation. Ice caps and glaciers are melting at unprecedented rates, altering the salinity and sea level of the oceans; this could alter sea-current direction and intensity, altering organism distribution and productivity (Overpeck et al. 2006). To highlight the seriousness of this issue, I give two examples. An alteration in sea currents would change where and when phytoplankton blooms occur, as these move on ocean currents. As the primary producers of the ocean, a change in their distribution would be disastrous for entire food webs in tropical, temperate and polar waters, causing shortages at every step of the food chain. Only the most mobile or adaptive species will survive. It is still not possible to predict such shifts accurately. The second example relates to the lag time between when carbon levels are reduced enough to stop further increases in temperature. For air, that lag time is small, one or two years perhaps, but for seawater the lag is in the order of decades if not centuries. Even if carbon emissions were reduced today to pre-industrial levels, sea temperatures would continue to rise for the next thirty to fifty years. Currently, carbon concentrations in the atmosphere exceed 380 parts per million. Reductions are needed soon as a tipping point is believed to exist, after which reductions in carbon emissions will not prevent severe effects on our marine and terrestrial environments (Hoegh-Guldberg et al. 2007). Our high consumption of fossil fuel–based energy now are negatively affecting those of the next generation.

Habitat Loss and Fragmentation

The loss of habitat is directly related to an exponential loss in species diversity and for marine ecosystems, as in terrestrial ecosystems, this remains a serious and long-term threat both in terms of current loss but also future recovery and restoration. Many current fishing practices use methods which impact heavily on habitats. Examples include bottom trawling of the seabed, which damages many benthic structures in the net's path, such as rocks and deep sea reefs and amid growing concern of the long-term effects of this, efforts are being made to ban such fishing practices (Roberts 2002). Dynamiting to catch fish is practised throughout tropical waters. It is an easy way to kill fish, but all habitat within the immediate explosion zone is pulverized in the process. Similar levels of regrowth and diversity of habitats such as coral reefs after dynamiting are unlikely due to the loss of hard substrate for new corals to grow on and other stressors inhibiting regeneration. Fishermen then move to intact areas and the destruction expands with increasing conflict over decreasing resources. Another example of drastic habitat loss in tropical areas concerns mangroves, with estimates of over a third of cover removed globally (Alongi 2002). Mangroves are valuable in providing storm defence, nurseries for juvenile fish and invertebrates and bio-filtration of terrestrial runoff. Their benefits were noted after the 2004 Asian tsunami where greater damage occurred in areas where natural coastal defences, such as mangroves and coral reefs, had been removed during coastal development. Both these habitats occur in Qatar and the Arabian Gulf and need managing carefully. Mapping is necessary to quantify distribution and avoid destruction of rare habitats, which has recently received attention in Qatar through funding from Dolphin Energy in mapping and quantifying the health of coral reef areas (Alkendi and Chandler 2008; Richer 2008).

Pollution

The world's oceans have been seen, and still are seen, as the world's dustbin, with everything from plastics to chemicals to human waste dumped in the seas. Again, the vast size of the oceans led people to think there could be little effect of waste dumping. The effects are increasingly evident. The Pacific subtropical gyre, a slow-moving clockwise sea current, accumulates plastic and other waste in the ocean and is said to cover an area twice the size of Texas, large amounts of waste from this mass are deposited daily on Hawaiian beaches and have to be cleared at high expense to prevent damage to beaches. Molecular tests have shown the components of plastic occur in the lowest levels and smallest members of the oceans' food chains, showing just how far this synthetic material has contaminated marine ecosystems (Derraik 2002). As fisheries become overexploited and collapse, people have turned to alternatives such as aquaculture. Its exponential growth worldwide has been hailed a development success in many developing countries yet the pollution cost can be extremely high. For example, tiger prawn farming in sheltered tropical waters has resulted in widespread mangrove clearance and anoxic conditions near to the shore due to the fouling of the water by the high concentrations of prawns as well as the addition of antibiotics and high levels of nutrients and additives to encourage rapid prawn growth. These often have disadvantageous knock-on effects on other species in the vicinity of these in situ farms, such as disease and parasites spreading to neighbouring marine populations. The Chile salmon farms were ravaged by disease recently and the business has collapsed, destroying livelihoods and reducing the health of wild populations (Barrett, Caniggia and Read 2002).

Domestic and industrial waste is directly pumped into the sea and also arrives in the sea indirectly through runoff. Agricultural runoff also adversely affects the marine environment, as high concentrations of fertilizers accumulate in the sea especially in inshore areas and regions with low tidal current. This causes extensive algal blooms and seaweed growth which results in anoxic conditions and smothers other organisms. Large anoxic zones have occurred near the seabed from the shores of Florida and the southeastern United States far out to sea. They are 'dead zones', as low oxygen levels prevent most life forms existing (Dybas 2005). Coastal zones are the most productive areas of our oceans and most at risk from pollution. The risks to human health as well as marine life from pollution cannot be ignored in any sustainable development plan. Some improvements have been made through strict legislation and waste-treatment programs and developing countries need to do likewise as their contribution to waste and pollutants increases.

Invasive Species

As in terrestrial ecosystems, the arrival of invasive species is a seriously negative consequence of human migration and travel. Ballast water in ships is changed in different localities and may transport eggs, larvae and adult organisms from one area of the world to another, where they may out-compete the native fauna or flora, altering the ecosystem in the process. This has occurred off the west and south coasts of South Africa where the faster-growing, hardier Mediterranean mussel species has out-competed the local species and reduced local diversity (Robinson et al. 2005). Attempts are being made now to stop ships changing ballast in coastal waters where it is more likely for invasives to obtain a foothold and dominate. With the high volumes of shipping in the Gulf, the threat of invasives from other parts of the world is very apparent. Escapes of non-native species from aquaculture facilities are also causing problems to local food chains and wildlife. The temptation to use non-native species is driven by short-term profits and not a long-term sustainable perspective. Further legislation is needed to protect native marine flora and fauna and prevent unnecessary introductions of invasives.

Overharvesting from Fisheries

It was believed that wild-capture fisheries could provide for the escalating demand for seafood by an ever-increasing and more affluent human population. But world fish catches peaked in the 1980s and 1990s, and the catch of most commercially important species has since declined, prompting shifts to new forms of management such as EBM (Leslie and McLeod 2007). The complex dynamics between fishing and management objectives often leads to conflict, which demands restructuring of current management techniques with more co-management initiatives or ecosystem rebuilding models (Pomeroy et al. 2010). However, many fisheries practices remain unsustainable due to overcapacity of fishing fleets, poverty, lack of alternative livelihoods, poor incentives not to fish, large demand, a lack of law enforcement and political will compounded by a lack of data (Pauly et al. 2002). Often government inaction, scientists' refusal to address practices that have proved disastrous for fisheries in the past, and heavy pressure from fishing lobbies has resulted in unsustainable harvests, often leading to stock collapse. One of the most infamous examples concerns North Atlantic cod (*Gadus morhua*) stocks, which were depleted during the 1980s and 1990s and have not recovered since (Myers et al. 1997). It is the profitability of harvesting marine resources that leads to overfishing. The cod stocks in the North Sea are similarly threatened and fishery scientists urge major reductions in catch or closure of the fishery (Cook, Sinclair and Stefansson 1997). But stakeholders are unable to agree if the stock is resilient enough to be sustainably harvested and fishing continues at unsustainable levels with stock collapse widely predicted (see Yamaguchi this volume). Over 90% of global fish stocks are either fully exploited or overexploited or have collapsed (Roberts and Hawkins 1999) with predictions of all major worldwide stocks collapsing by 2050. This would be disastrous, not only for the economies of coastal nations that depend on productive fisheries but also for the loss of ecosystem services.

Coral reefs, for example, make up only 0.1 per cent of the marine environment but supply protein and ecosystem services to tens of millions of people, especially in developing countries (Pauly et al. 2002). However, many coral reef fisheries cause wide-scale damage to the reefs, as coral is broken while catching fish in nets, such as the trade in aquarium reef fish in Sri Lanka (Wood 1985). The volume of fish removed from the relatively small reefs is high and, according to historical records and fishers' observations, targeted fish populations have diminished drastically (Wilhelmsson et al. 2002). Negative environmental impacts, such as the Asian tsunami, have also severely damaged the reef structure and ecology (Rajasuriya 2005). Future regeneration of the reefs and fish populations and local community incomes depends on a holistic and well-structured approach to management. A potential solution in any overfished system is to set up extensive marine protected areas for overharvested species, such as North Atlantic cod, to allow for stock replenishment (Christie 2004).

A growing number of fisheries have become 'sustainable' through certification schemes such as that of the Marine Stewardship Council (MSC), which assess fisheries' sustainability based on a multitude of criteria (Agnew et al. 2006). This is necessary to supply future demand for seafood (at present, 85 per cent of seafood originates from wild catch, with aquaculture making up the rest). Paradoxically, we cannot provide enough seafood at present to satisfy worldwide demand, let alone from sustainable sources, yet a start is being made by projects and work done by the MSC. Aquaculture looks set to increase its provision to meet increasing worldwide demand (Naylor et al. 2000). The protection of wild stocks and their future viability however, is paramount. Many current fisheries are wasteful; the catch is often processed into fish oils and animal feed. The harvesting of krill from the Southern Ocean to provide animal feed is an example. Krill forms the basis of one of the most productive food chains in the marine world, and removing large volumes of krill will affect all species in Antarctic waters from fish to penguins to whales. Another challenge is bycatch waste, those non-target fish and other organisms caught, which are not used. There are estimates of 18–35 million tonnes of bycatch for every 50 million tonnes of targeted catch in the world fisheries (Hall, Alverson and Metuzals 2000). Many other examples of wasteful fishing practices exist. Shark finning is an example, the fins are so valuable that only these are taken and the dying shark is thrown back to the sea (Lewison et al. 2004), severely depleting populations in many areas.

Overfishing in reef areas can result in further imbalances. Both ornamental and seafood fisheries are selective regarding the size and species of fish they harvest, and they often reduce the population of large predators and herbivorous fish (Hughes and Connell 1999). This disrupts the food chain, an example is the increase in jellyfish in many commercial fishing grounds around the world from North America to Africa, where predators have been removed by overfishing. Plagues of harmful species occur in the Great Barrier Reef in Australia, such as crown of thorn starfish, which eat coral polyps, and are linked to increased nutrient inputs and overfishing of predators (Brodie et al. 2005).

278 | James Howard

Compounding many of these threats and resulting from many of them is the increase of emergent and resurgent diseases[1] in marine environments. These have been documented in marine mammals and coral reefs, as these are well-studied marine groups, but disease may be increasing at all taxonomic levels. New pathogens have been recorded in species such as North Atlantic bottlenose dolphin, sea lions and dugongs, which threaten the fecundity and stability of these populations (Bossart 2007). Reasons for new epidemics and diseases occurring include climatic shifts and anthropogenic activities. High stress through unusual climatic conditions allow pathogens to infect hosts opportunistically and human movement allows unknown pathogens to interact with previous isolated host populations (Harvell et al. 1999). A striking example is the die off of *Diadema antillarum* sea urchins in the Caribbean reefs due to an unknown pathogen, resulting in an explosion of large, long-lived algae species that are smothering corals (Hughes and Connell 1999).

Confronting the Challenges with a Multidisciplinary Approach

Due to our reliance on the marine environment for a variety of needs from food and recreation to ecosystem services, it is common for conflicts to arise between conservation groups, fishers and other stakeholders. To take all these aspects into account and to make the required changes toward sustainable marine resource utilization and practices an interdisciplinary approach is needed. Interdisciplinarity cannot be limited to individual threats and concerns, as this has proved ineffective in the past. It needs to encompass the many threats and include all stakeholders who use the marine resources in a particular region. My own study of the ornamental reef fish trade in Sri Lanka sought to further understanding of the ecological and conservation problems, and stakeholders' concerns and attitudes to government management and/or foreign conservation interventions. To do this, inclusive, interdisciplinary research was carried out to identify the priorities and challenges that need addressing to improve the ornamental fish trade and the marine resources upon which it relies and make suggestions for alternative livelihoods.

Such an integrated approach at a larger management scale is EBM, which is gradually being applied around the world. In coastal zones there is integrated coastal zone management (ICZM) which features the same multidisciplinary approach. All Gulf countries need to adopt these management frameworks, as they share the same common resource and regional cooperation will benefit all in the long term. The costs of implementing ICZM will be saved in the mid to long term against the cost of mitigating mistakes made by unplanned development. ICZM has proved the best solution in highly degraded areas, despite the many challenges of such integrated work. Some Gulf countries such as Iran are implementing it, beginning sustainable coastal preservation (Pak and Farajzadeh 2007).

Other examples, which have relevance to the Gulf marine ecosystems, where such integrated management is needed include seagrass ecosystem conservation (Kenworthy et al. 2006) and the inclusion of socio-cultural issues in fisheries regulation and management (de la Torre-Castro and Lindström 2010). Challenges remain in developing these strategies, but with more proactive thinking to predict issues that will affect marine resources in the midterm, with international will and research the prospects are hopeful.

Marine Resources in Qatar

The Arabian Gulf surrounding Qatar's peninsula provides resources and ecosystem services to the country. The Gulf is a unique marine environment globally. It is highly stressed due to strong salinity and temperature fluctuations due to limited connectivity to the Indian Ocean through the Strait of Hormuz, which is narrow, and allows little mixing of waters from the Gulf with the open ocean (Pilcher et al. 2000). The Gulf has higher salinity levels than the open ocean, between 40 and 70 parts per thousand, but can reach levels of 200 parts per thousand in some areas,[2] due to the intense solar radiation and high evaporation rates of the seawater (Carpenter et al. 1997). Large seasonal temperature fluctuations occur, more synchronous with air temperature, given the Gulf's semi-enclosed nature. Specialist adaptations are common in marine flora and fauna resulting from these unusual environmental conditions, as well as from the high levels of petroleum hydrocarbons in the earth's crust which leach into the marine environment.

These unique conditions give the area importance for the study of changing climate; if plant and animal species have higher tolerances and special adaptations, these may, perhaps aid our understanding and ability to conserve species more at risk from climate change. An example is the zooxanthellae in corals in the Gulf that do not die with higher-than-average water temperatures; these could be paired with less hardy corals in areas where higher sea temperatures are resulting in bleaching events with no coral regrowth. Such adaptations have the potential to aid habitat restoration and rehabilitation in this region and elsewhere.

Qatar's territorial waters are a diverse environment with 955 marine species described. There are still species being discovered and yet this region trails other regions of the world in marine taxonomic work and Qatar has the poorest record for Gulf countries (Richer 2008). Research is needed to protect and use such an intricate and diverse resource, to document species present, to map their distribution and to increase understanding to devise effective management plans. Qatari waters support large populations of marine mammals and large fish predators; species such as dugongs, whale sharks, rays and other sharks are present, which are the signs of healthy food webs in the ocean. The Arabian Gulf is an extremely important area for dugongs, as it harbours the second largest population globally, estimated at approximately 7,000 individuals (Richer 2008). Surveys of dugongs in 1986 and in 1999 recorded the largest group sighting ever of over 600 individuals off the west coast of Qatar and dugong abundance had changed little over that time period. Despite this, dugongs still face a number of anthropogenic threats in the Gulf, dugongs have been impacted in the past by oil spills, entanglement in disused fishing nets and illegal poaching (Preen 2004). To sustain the balances in the food chain, these populations need to be protected by establishing marine protected areas, which additionally may generate further revenue through marine tourism. Zones between Qatar and Bahrain and between Qatar and UAE have been suggested as potential protected-area sites as the largest concentrations of dugongs observed from surveys were found there (Preen 2004). Dugongs rely on seagrass beds for their continued survival and seagrass areas are some of the most productive marine ecosystems supporting over 600 species, yet worldwide they are a sensitive and threatened habitat (Richer 2008). The seagrass meadows around Qatar need protection as they not only sustain the dugong populations but also are a significantly important habitat for shrimp and prawn populations (Al-Maslamani et al. 2007). The shrimp fishery was closed in Qatar in 1993 due to overfishing and habitat reduction; however, with sufficient protection of seagrass beds and intertidal mudflats, this may yet resume and be a profitable and sustainable fishery.

The entire marine environment in this region is anthropogenically stressed due to the unprecedented rapid human development with the discovery of oil and natural gas, from which the region has become wealthy and geo-politically important. The threats described are not unusual in this region and are likely to be acting in synergy on certain ecosystems and organisms accelerating their decline and reducing local diversity. Major threats include the oil and gas leaks from refineries, rigs and wells, brine wastewater returned from desalination plants, overfishing and coastal development resulting in habitat loss (Abuzinada et al. 2008).

There are many desalination plants in the region delivering fresh water to the population, with groundwater resources already overexploited. The desalination process involves returning hot, high salt and chlorine concentrated water back to the sea. Both demersal[3] and pelagic[4] species can be negatively affected by the changes in seawater chemistry caused by the desalination procedure (Latteman and Höpner 2008; Nour El-Din 2004). Legislation exists in Qatar to regulate chlorine levels, the main biocide in water discharged from desalination plants but there is a need to set these limits according to scientifically formulated cooling-water discharge allowances. The industries involved can also be developing cleaner and more environmentally benign technologies (Macdonald et al. 2009). One such step taken by QatarGas is the use of pulse chlorination to prevent marine fouling in the plants, which reduces the amount of chlorine used (ibid.; Richer 2008). Enforcement of the new and upcoming legislation to treat water before returning it to the sea is a priority.

Asia's fishing fleet is growing each year as the human population increases and ever more people become dependent on marine resources for their livelihoods. Fisheries are often deeply rooted in cultural tradition as skills and expertise are passed down through generations with certain communities dominating the fishing sector in many countries. The artisanal fishery in Qatar is one with large social and cultural significance, preserving local heritage and customs. This fishery is sustainable in Qatar with its more varied catch and profitable as it outperformed a major trawling company between 1980 and 1992 (Al-Ansi and Priede 1996). Demersal fishing is a common commercial form of fishing in the Arabian Gulf and provides substantial income to Gulf countries (Feidi 2005). In Qatar, 71 per cent of marine landings comprised demersal species between 1988 and 1993; however, it is thought that many demersal fish and prawn species have been overexploited and nursery areas have been degraded in the southern Arabian Gulf (Siddeek, Fouda and Hermosa 1999). Recommendations made over ten years ago to ensure sustainable demersal fisheries have been adopted but management efficacy is often questioned. The recommendations include reducing fishing effort, enforcing closed seasons and areas and preserving a viable marine environment (ibid.).

Grouper and bream species are highly targeted in the waters off Qatar, with over 40 per cent of fish catch comprising emperors (*Lethrinus* sp.) and groupers (*Epinephelus* sp.) in 2001 (FAO 2003). There is concern that there is no upper catch limit in Qatar; fish catch is regulated by restricting the number of boats, which has remained fairly constant over time; however, larger boats with better fishing gear are replacing smaller boats and the landed catch has increased by 14 per cent annually between 2000 and 2005 (Richer 2008). Other fisheries' modellers have shown that a decrease in fishing effort on species such as groupers in Qatar waters would be the best strategy to avoid stock collapse and is needed alongside other mechanisms to control catch such as closed seasons and protected areas (Barr et al. 2010).

The accumulation of various pollutants in caught fish for consumption needs to be monitored regularly in such a human-affected system. One study investigated whether heavy metal levels had increased in fish caught in Qatari waters after the 1991 oil spill in the Gulf; however, no significant increase was found (Kureishy 1993). Other studies have assessed the levels of heavy metals and pathogens in various fish species consumed in Qatar and the findings showed levels were well within safe limits for human consumption (Al-Jedah and Robinson 2001).

According to an FAO study, the potential for fisheries' expansion in the Gulf region is high and could provide Arab countries' second largest source of revenue after oil (Feidi 2005). The sector provides valuable protein for a population, ensures food security and reduces reliance on food imports, to which some Arab countries are subject, it may alleviate poverty too by providing employment. To expand fisheries responsibly is a long-term process, involves multidisciplinary teams and requires good governance, sound resource management, conservation and investment in fishery infrastructure (Feidi 2005).

A major indirect threat to the marine environment is the burning of fossil fuels, and due to this Qatar has one of the highest national carbon dioxide outputs in the world at 69 tonnes CO_2 per person per year. Most of this CO_2 output derives from obtaining oil and gas from the earth's crust and not from burning the processed fossil fuels within Qatar. Most of the gas and oil is exported around the world and burnt in other countries. With high oil consuming countries showing little concerted effort to curb their emissions and few feasible clean energy alternatives at present to meet soaring world energy needs, it appears that Qatar's petroleum resources will continue to remain in high demand. An increase in CO_2 concentrations in the atmosphere is already causing both an increase in temperature and acidity of the oceans, with lethal effects to marine organisms. Qatar should seek a more sustainable manner of growth, alongside greater efforts to reduce carbon emissions and source cleaner energy sources as the growing pressure to reduce world emissions may result in penalties and restrictions placed on countries with high carbon outputs in the future (see Henfrey, this volume). A long-term view is needed to address this issue as in all sustainable development initiatives.

Other indirect threats include harmful algal blooms that may occur due to activities elsewhere altering the environment, impinging on Qatar's coastline and destroying valuable resources. Late 2008 saw the first ever recorded observation of a large *Cochlodinium polykroides* harmful algal bloom in the Arabian Gulf which, from studies in other parts of the world, is renowned for returning regularly, causing regular widespread mortality to fish, invertebrates and living habitat (Richlen et al. 2010).

A concern regarding the rapid rate of coastal and marine industry development is the lacklustre implementation of environmental protection or enforcement of existing marine protection legislation in many Gulf countries, including Qatar (Richer 2008). Enforcement of legislation is a cornerstone of a robust ICZM and/or EBM schemes, which ensure that building and altering the coastal and/or marine zone is carried out in a sustainable manner. In Qatar, procedures such as environmental impact assessments are carried out on certain projects to determine the extent of environmental damage. Where some destruction or alteration is unavoidable, the appropriate remediation and restoration should be implemented (Richer 2008).

Dredging and infilling of the seabed causes major changes, potentially destroying important benthic marine habitats, and changing sea currents and water mixing, which can affect planktonic food supply. When currents are altered, erosion and deposition occur in different places, damaging areas previously unthreatened and altering others with sand deposition (Peterson, Hickerson and Johnson 2000). The many artificial islands, harbour walls and protective bunds constructed in and around Doha and other coastal areas of Qatar may have these negative impacts if they are not carefully planned with appropriate environmental impact assessments to assess likely implications for currents.

Construction of the Ras Laffan port expansion and Dolphin Energy pipeline damaged highly sensitive seagrass areas, but the area was not remediated. Rather, funding was provided by the energy company for scientific surveys elsewhere. This had its benefits; however, remediation of destructive activities cannot be diverted to other areas, as this leaves loopholes for future development projects. Corals were also damaged but translocation of over 4,000 hard coral colonies was carried out by QatarGas, rather than creating an artificial reef; the company states there are high survival rates (Kilbane et al. 2008). Artificial reefs were created in Qatari waters by 2008 through a collaborative pilot project involving Continental Shelf Associates, a US corporation, Dolphin Energy of Qatar, the Ministry of Environment, the Ras Laffan Environmental Association and Qatar University to assess the potential of artificial reefs as a remediation measure to coral sites damaged by coastal oil and gas exploration and development. Monitoring of these recently constructed artificial reefs is on-going (Continental Shelf Associates 2007).

There are five species of turtles that occur in the Gulf, however only one, the hawksbill turtle, *Eretmochelys imbricate,* a critically endangered and protected species in Qatar and worldwide, nests along the northeastern beaches of Qatar and some offshore islands. Important nesting sites are the beaches bordering the Ras Laffan Industrial City, where the threat of destruction of suitable nesting habitat is high. However, funded by the Ras Laffan Industrial City and coordinated with Qatar University, identification of nesting areas and the determination of their ranges using satellite tracking of turtles was carried out and an on-going regular monitoring and protection program of their nesting sites is in operation (Al-Ansi 2010).

The Way Forwards

There are many problems facing Qatar and the Arabian Gulf and potential solutions. The most productive habitat existing in the Gulf is coral reefs. They are possibly the most sensitive of all marine environments to change. Some areas have already been destroyed while others are at risk of a similar fate. The need for marine protected areas containing coral reefs is a priority (Keller et al. 2009). Further to this, reclamation of damaged coral areas should be attempted, which could involve coral transplantation from healthy reefs. Coral farming is expanding in tropical areas and could be developed to provide livelihoods selling farmed coral to the aquarium trade. Restoration of mangrove ecosystems can be combined with integrated aquaculture systems, restoring services and productivity and providing higher economic returns than mangroves alone. In addition, artificial reefs have seen some success in the tropics and those in Qatari waters may prove beneficial; currently, the financial and environmental costs of decommissioning ships are high, and they can be treated and sunk to form artificial reefs where marine organisms including coral can settle and flourish; these may serve as dive tourism businesses, enhancing local economies.

Many people living and working in coastal and marine regions need to adapt to changing circumstances. Ability to adapt and diversify income-generating opportunities will be necessary to withstand global change and unpredictable climatic events (Berkes and Jolly 2001). Interdisciplinary projects and community-inclusive programmes will raise awareness of conservation efforts and increase preparedness for future change. All stakeholders can contribute, combining local knowledge and scientific knowledge to develop appropriate alternative livelihoods for those dependent on threatened or degraded marine resources. Compliance with new ideas and commitment to preservation and altered lifestyles will be greater with inclusive approaches. In the case of the Sri Lankan ornamental trade in aquarium reef fish, the government is now developing a co-management framework for this fishery; fishers admit there is a problem and a need for change, seeing their diminishing incomes and worries for their children's future. There is enthusiasm to participate in the decision-making process, tenure systems are in place controlling coastal access and reef rehabilitation work is on the agenda. Due to a lack of funding in Sri Lanka and minimal cooperation between various stakeholders, progress is slow in changing ideas and policies; despite this, the outlook looks promising. In a wealthy country such as Qatar, similar ideas can be adopted and the process move far quicker to halt diversity and ecosystem services losses.

The laissez-faire attitude of open access fisheries has seen its failure in driving high exploitation rates and should be phased out (Pauly et al. 2002). The 'Tragedy of the Commons' (Hardin 1968) is often cited as the reason for the decline in fish stocks and overall oceanic health. With the advent of Economic Exclusive Zones,[5] there has been a shift towards demarcating ownership of marine resources at a national level. The principles of sea tenure need to be further developed, with increases in demand and pressure on resources, allowing for dedicated access fisheries at community or nationwide levels. Sea tenure systems devised at village level are managed by the community and locally policed (Pomeroy et al. 2010). A change to this form of access usually results in lower exploitation rates and higher biomass (Hilborn 2007). Consensus is possible within reliant communities with ownership rights defined and incentives to conserve resources, allowing people to continue harvesting and deriving an income from marine resources. Further incentives are needed to reduce bycatch and encourage habitat preservation, as dedicated access tends to restore target species stocks only (Hilborn 2007). These general ideas need to be adjusted to specific fisheries, to reduce conflict between stakeholders and enhance sustainability.

Research is a top priority and needs added investment in Qatar, which falls behind every other surrounding Gulf nation with respect to papers published on marine issues and ongoing projects (Richer 2008). We need data and regular monitoring particularly in areas subject to development. For successful community management, stakeholders need to be aware of the issues and potential actions through education and outreach programs. Coastal development should be undertaken through integrated coastal zone-management plans with the compulsory use of environmental impact assessments, which ultimately ensure restoration and rehabilitation occurs after construction projects. Environmentally sensitive design is a burgeoning area of research and industry, and is a must for future sustainable coastal development.

It is a challenge working in an interdisciplinary framework involving government, industry and the public. With often-diverse interests and goals, finding consensus is often complex. The reason for failure in some well-intentioned sustainability projects is lack of political motivation and disagreement between different powerful sectors. The benefits of sustainable development projects and management need to be clear to all stakeholders and procedures put in place to allow changes and reward those who comply. It is time to put increasingly urgent global debates about sustainable development into action at national and local levels, instilling such development as a way of life for future generations.

Notes

1. New diseases to science or ones that have been absent for at least twenty years and are now appearing again.
2. Typically, seawater salinity is in the range of 31–38 parts per thousand in the world's oceans, with an average salinity of 35 parts per thousand.
3. Demersal fish are species that feed and live on, in or near the seabed.
4. Pelagic species live and feed in the water column and often cover large distances and can be both predators and prey.
5. Economic Exclusive Zones (EEZs) are waters bordering coastal countries over which they have sovereign rights to explore, exploit, conserve and manage the resources found there. EEZs can extend up to two hundred nautical miles from the shore and were introduced to reduce conflict and a strategy to avoid the 'Tragedy of the Commons'. EEZs became recognized under the United Nations Convention on the Law of the Sea in 1982.

References

Abuzinada, A. H., et al. 2008. *Protecting the Gulf's Marine Ecosystems from Pollution.* Switzerland: Birkhäuser Verlag.

Agnew, D., C. et al. 2006. *Environmental Benefits Resulting from Certification Against MSC's Principles and Criteria for Sustainable Fishing.* London: MRAG UK Ltd and Marine Stewardship Council.

Al-Ansi, M., and I. G. Priede. 1996. 'Expansion of Fisheries in Qatar (1980–1992): Growth of an Artisanal Fleet and Closure of a Trawling Company.' *Fisheries Research* 26: 101–111.

Al-Ansi, M. A. 2010. 'Efforts in the State of Qatar to Conserve and Monitor Endangered Marine Turtles.' *Qatar Foundation Annual Research Forum Proceedings*: EEO10.

Al-Jedah, J. H., and R. K. Robinson. 2001. 'Aspects of the Safety of Fish Caught Off the Coast of Qatar.' *Food Control* 12: 549–552.

Al-Maslamani, I., et al. 2007. 'Feeding Ecology of the Grooved Tiger Shrimp *Penaeus semisulcatus* De Haan (Decapoda: Penaeidae) in Inshore Waters of Qatar, Arabian Gulf.' *Marine Biology* 150: 627–637.

Alkendi, M. Y., and M. Chandler. 2008. 'A Successful Stakeholder Partnership-The Dolphin Energy Experience Coral Reef Habitats of the Arabian Gulf.' In *SPE International Conference on Health, Safety, and Environment in Oil and Gas Exploration and Production.* Nice, France: Society of Petroleum Engineers.

Alongi, D. M. 2002. 'Present State and Future of the World's Mangrove Forests.' *Environmental Conservation* 29: 331–349.

Barr, M., A. El-Sayed and A. Osman. 2010. 'The Use of Per Recruit Models for Stock Assessment and Management of Greasy Grouper *Epinephelus tauvina* in The Arabian Gulf Waters off Qatar.' *Tropical Life Sciences Research* 21: 83–90.

Barrett, G., M. I. Caniggia and L. Read. 2002. '"There are More Vets than Doctors in Chiloé": Social and Community Impact of the Globalization of Aquaculture in Chile.' *World Development* 30: 1951–1965.

Berkes, F., and D. Jolly. 2001. 'Adapting to Climate Change: Social-Ecological Resilience in a Canadian Western Arctic Community.' *Conservation Ecology* 5: 18.

Bossart, G. 2007. 'Emerging Diseases in Marine Mammals: From Dolphins to Manatees.' *Microbe* 2: 544–549.

Brodie, J., et al. 2005. 'Are Increased Nutrient Inputs Responsible for More Outbreaks of Crown-of-Thorns Starfish? An Appraisal of the Evidence.' *Marine Pollution Bulletin* 51: 266–278.

Bruckner, A. W. 2000. 'New Threat to Coral Reefs: Trade in Coral Organisms.' *Issues in Science and Technology* 17: 63–68.

Carpenter, K. E., et al. 1997. *Living Marine Resources of Kuwait, Eastern Saudi Arabia, Bahrain, Qatar, and the United Arab Emirates: FAO Species Identification Field Guide for Fishery Purposes.* Rome: FAO.

Cheung, W. W. L., and U. R. Sumaila. 2008. 'Trade-Offs Between Conservation and Socio-Economic Objectives in Managing a Tropical Marine Ecosystem.' *Ecological Economics* 66: 193–210.

Christie, P. 2004. 'MPAs as Biological Successes and Social Failures in Southeast Asia.' In *Aquatic Protected Areas as Fisheries Management Tools: Design, Use, and Evaluation of these Fully Protected Areas,* ed. J. B. Shipley, 155–164. Bethesda, MD: American Fisheries Society.

Connell, J. H. 1978. 'Diversity in Tropical Rain Forests and Coral Reefs: High Diversity of Trees and Corals Is Maintained Only in a Non-Equilibrium State.' *Science* 199: 1302–1310.

Continental Shelf Associates. 2007. 'Artificial Reefs in Qatar.' http://www.csaintl .com/energy-industry-projects-summaries/item/399-artificial-reefs-in-qatar.

Cook, R. M., A. Sinclair and G. Stefansson. 1997. 'Potential Collapse of North Sea Cod Stocks.' *Nature* 385: 521–522.

Costanza, R., et al. 1997. 'The Value of the World's Ecosystem Services and Natural Capital.' *Nature* 387: 253–260.

de la Torre-Castro, M., and L. Lindström. 2010. 'Fishing Institutions: Addressing Regulative, Normative and Cultural-Cognitive Elements to Enhance Fisheries Management.' *Marine Policy* 34: 77–84.

Derraik, J. G. B. 2002. 'The Pollution of the Marine Environment by Plastic Debris: A Review.' *Marine Pollution Bulletin* 44: 842–852.

Dietz, S., and W. N. Adger. 2003. 'Economic Growth, Biodiversity Loss and Conservation Effort.' *Journal of Environmental Management* 68: 23–35.

Dybas, C. L. 2005. 'Dead Zones Spreading in World Oceans.' *BioScience* 55: 552–557.

Food and Agriculture Organization of the United Nations (FAO). 2003. 'Information on Fisheries Management in the State of Qatar.' http://www.fao.org/fi/fcp/en/QAT/body.htm.

Feidi, I. 2005. 'Fish Supply and Demand in the Near East Region.' In *FAO GLOBEFISH Research Programme*. Rome: FAO.

Hall, M. A., D. L. Alverson and K. I. Metuzals. 2000. 'By-Catch: Problems and Solutions.' *Marine Pollution Bulletin* 41: 204–219.

Hardin, G. 1968. 'The Tragedy of the Commons.' *Science* 162: 1243–1248.

Harvell, C. D., et al. 1999. 'Emerging Marine Diseases: Climate Links and Anthropogenic Factors.' *Science* 285: 1505–1510.

Hilborn, R. 2007. 'Defining Success in Fisheries and Conflicts in Objectives.' *Marine Policy* 31: 153–158.

Hoegh-Guldberg, O., et al. 2007. 'Coral Reefs Under Rapid Climate Change and Ocean Acidification.' *Science* 318: 1737–1742.

Hughes, T. P., et al. 2003. 'Climate Change, Human Impacts, and the Resilience of Coral Reefs.' *Science* 301: 929–933.

Hughes, T. P., and J. H. Connell. 1999. 'Multiple Stressors on Coral Reefs: A Long-Term Perspective.' *Limnology and Oceanography* 44: 932–940.

Jackson, J. B. C., et al. 2001. 'Historical Overfishing and the Recent Collapse of Coastal Ecosystems.' *Science* 293: 629–637.

Keller, B., et al. 2009. 'Climate Change, Coral Reef Ecosystems, and Management Options for Marine Protected Areas.' *Environmental Management* 44: 1069–1088.

Kenworthy, W., et al. 2006. 'Seagrass Conservation Biology: An Interdisciplinary Science for Protection of the Seagrass Biome.' In *Seagrasses: Biology, Ecology and Conservation*. eds. A. W. D. Larkum, R. J. Orth and C. M. Duarte, 595–623. Netherlands: Springer.

Kilbane, D., et al. 2008. 'Coral Relocation for Impact Mitigation in Northern Qatar.' In *Proceedings of the 11th International Coral Reef Symposium*. Ft. Lauderdale, FL.

Kureishy, T. W. 1993. 'Concentration of Heavy Metals in Marine Organisms Around Qatar Before and After the Gulf War Oil Spill.' *Marine Pollution Bulletin* 27: 183–186.

Latteman, S., and T. Höpner. 2008. 'Impacts of Seawater Desalination Plants on the Marine Environment of the Gulf.' In *Protecting the Gulf's Marine Ecosystems from Pollution*, eds. A. H. Abuzinada, et al., 191–236. Switzerland: Birkhäuser Verlag.

Leslie, H. M., and K. L. McLeod. 2007. 'Confronting the Challenges of Implementing Marine Ecosystem-Based Management.' *Frontiers in Ecology and the Environment* 5: 540–548.

Lewison, R. L., et al. 2004. 'Understanding Impacts of Fisheries Bycatch on Marine Megafauna.' *Trends in Ecology and Evolution* 19: 598–604.

Macdonald, I. A., et al. 2009. 'Industrial Cooling Seawater Antifouling Optimisation Through the Adoption of Pulse-Chlorination.' http://www.nt.ntnu.no/users/skoge/prost/proceedings/gas-processing-doha-2009/fscommand/o09.pdf.

Martínez, M. L., et al. 2007. 'The Coasts of Our World: Ecological, Economic and Social Importance.' *Ecological Economics* 63: 252–272.

Myers, R. A., J. A. Hutchings and N. J. Barrowman. 1997. 'Why Do Fish Stocks Collapse? The Example of Cod in Atlantic Canada.' *Ecological Applications* 7: 91–106.

Naylor, R. L., et al. 2000. 'Effect of Aquaculture on World Fish Supplies.' *Nature* 405: 1017–1024.

Nour El-Din, N. M. 2004. 'Impact of Cooling Water Discharge on the Benthic and Planktonic Pelagic Fauna Along the Coastal Waters of Qatar (Arabian Gulf).' *Egyptian Journal of Aquatic Research* 30: 150–159.

Overpeck, J. T., et al. 2006. 'Paleoclimatic Evidence for Future Ice-Sheet Instability and Rapid Sea-Level Rise.' *Science* 311: 1747–1750.

Pak, A., and M. Farajzadeh. 2007. 'Iran's Integrated Coastal Management Plan: Persian Gulf, Oman Sea, and Southern Caspian Sea Coastlines.' *Ocean and Coastal Management* 50: 754–773.

Pauly, D., et al. 2002. 'Towards Sustainability in World Fisheries.' *Nature* 418: 689–695.

Peterson, C. H., D. H. M. Hickerson and G. G. Johnson. 2000. 'Short-Term Consequences of Nourishment and Bulldozing on the Dominant Large Invertebrates of a Sandy Beach.' *Journal of Coastal Research* 16: 368–378.

Pilcher, N. J., et al. 2000. 'Status of Coral reefs in Arabian/Persian Gulf and Arabian Sea region (Middle East).' In *Status of Coral Reefs of the World*, ed. C. Wilkinson, 55–64. Australia: Australian Institute of Marine Science.

Pomeroy, R., et al. 2010. 'Ecosystem-Based Fisheries Management in Small-Scale Tropical Marine Fisheries: Emerging Models of Governance Arrangements in the Philippines.' *Marine Policy* 34: 298–308.

Preen, A. 2004. 'Distribution, Abundance and Conservation Status of Dugongs and Dolphins in the Southern and Western Arabian Gulf.' *Biological Conservation* 118: 205–218.

Rajasuriya, A. 2005. 'The Status of Coral Reefs in Sri Lanka in the Aftermath of the 1998 Coral Bleaching Event and the 2004 Tsunami.' In *Coral Reef Degradation in the Indian Ocean (CORDIO): Status report 2005*, eds. D. Souter and O. Linden, 83–96. Kalmar: CORDIO.

Richer, R. 2008. *Conservation in Qatar: Impacts of Increasing Industrialization.* Center for International and Regional Studies (CIRS), Georgetown University, School of Foreign Service in Qatar.

Richlen, M. L., et al. 2010. 'The Catastrophic 2008–2009 Red Tide in the Arabian Gulf Region, with Observations on the Identification and Phylogeny of the Fish-Killing Dinoflagellate *Cochlodinium polykrikoides.' Harmful Algae* 9: 163–172.

Roberts, C. M. 2002. 'Deep Impact: The Rising Toll of Fishing in the Deep Sea.' *Trends in Ecology and Evolution* 17: 242–245.

Roberts, C. M., and J. P. Hawkins. 1999. 'Extinction Risk in the Sea.' *Trends in Ecology and Evolution* 14: 241–246.

Robinson, T. B., et al. 2005. 'Marine Alien Species of South Africa: Status and Impacts.' *African Journal of Marine Science* 27: 297–306.

Siddeek, M. S. M., M. M. Fouda and G. V. Hermosa Jr. 1999. 'Demersal Fisheries of the Arabian Sea, the Gulf of Oman and the Arabian Gulf.' *Estuarine Coastal Shelf Science* 49: 87–97.

Veron, J. E. N., et al. 2009. 'The Coral Reef Crisis: The Critical Importance of <350 ppm CO_2.' *Marine Pollution Bulletin* 58: 1428–1436.

Wabnitz, C., et al. 2003. *From Ocean to Aquarium.* Cambridge: UNEP-WCMC.

Wilhelmsson, D., et al. 2002. 'Monitoring the Trends of Marine Ornamental Fish Collection in Sri Lanka.' In *Coral Reef Degradation in the Indian Ocean (CORDIO): Status Report 2002*, eds. O. Linden et al., 158–166. Kalmar: CORDIO.

Wood, E. 1985. 'Exploitation of Coral Reef Fishes for the Aquarium Trade.' A *Report to the Marine Conservation Society.* Ross-on-Wye: Marine Conservation Society, U.K.

CHAPTER 12

Biodiversity Conservation and Sustainability

Friends or Enemies?

Nobuyuki Yamaguchi

During the twentieth century, environmental concerns have become politically, economically and socially important across the world, and this trend continues, or is even accelerating, during the first decades of the twenty-first century (Macdonald and Service 2006; Sodhi and Ehrlich 2010). Two key concepts appear regularly in discussions about environmental issues, namely biodiversity conservation and sustainability. The United Nations declaration of 2010 as the International Year of Biodiversity highlighted the importance of these two concepts, as did the United Nations Conference on Sustainable Development (RIO+20) in 2012 (to mark the twentieth anniversary of the 1992 United Nations Conference on Environment and Development [the first Earth Summit] held in Rio de Janeiro, Brazil, in 1992). These two concepts are associated with positive images regarding environmental issues, and hence they are vaguely assumed to be mutually consistent if not completely synonymous. On the contrary, when we look closely at biodiversity conservation and sustainability, the relationship is more complex and surprisingly sour. It is arguable that the two concepts are not mutually compatible regarding their definitions and associated values (Callicott and Mumford 1997; Newton and Freyfogle 2005). Furthermore, lack of sufficient data often prevents conservation scientists from empirically teasing out the complex relationship between biodiversity conservation and sustainability (Mulder and Coppolillo 2005). This data deficiency raises a suspicion, from a natural science viewpoint, that sustainability may be 'mere hopes about the future' (ibid.), or 'merely a comfortable illusion created under the lack of information' (Hambler 2004).

Biodiversity Conservation

This chapter discusses why sustainability causes such confusion and can even be antagonistic to biodiversity conservation. It argues firstly that the definition of biodiversity is not compatible with widely accepted ideas about sustainable use of renewable natural resources, which are based solely on biomass and overlook variety. Secondly, units that we use for assessing biodiversity and sustainability tend to be arbitrarily chosen, and may not be bioenvironmentally meaningful. Thirdly, in practice, we do not have enough data to assess biodiversity or sustainability. Fourthly, sustainability may be more achievable where we reduce biodiversity, eliminating organisms that are not readily compatible with anthropogenic activities such as 'destructive' wildlife.

What is Biodiversity?

Although the main focus of this chapter is to confound our understanding of sustainability, it is firstly necessary to understand what we mean by the problematic concept of biodiversity. At the first Earth Summit in Rio de Janeiro, biodiversity was defined as 'the variety among living organisms from all sources, including, amongst others, terrestrial, marine and other aquatic ecosystems and the ecological complexes of which they are a part; this includes diversity within species, between species and ecosystems' (Hambler 2004). This definition highlights the comprehensiveness of the biodiversity concept, including variety amongst all living organisms and ecological complexes. In other words, biodiversity is an umbrella term for all nature's variety. But this definition is not easy for conservation scientists to handle objectively because such a comprehensive view is not practically compatible with quantitative science which focuses on a limited number of key parameters to measure or assess biodiversity either empirically or theoretically.

Conservation scientists have been working on identifying parameters (including proxies) that can meaningfully represent biodiversity and be analyzed quantitatively and objectively (Ricotta 2005; Caro 2010; Gaston 2010). It is amongst the urgent challenges that face conservation scientists today. They largely agree that important parameters include taxonomic diversity (e.g. species richness), genetic diversity and ecological diversity (Campbell 2003; Gaston 2010), which are not mutually exclusive. Some may add other parameters such as molecular diversity, although this overlaps considerably with genetic diversity. Anthony Campbell (2003) suggests molecular biodiversity occurs within the individual, between individuals of the same species, between related species, within and between phyla and ecosystems and throughout evolution (including a crucial evolutionary role for 'hidden' molecular biodiversity in 'bad' genes).

Some measures of biodiversity, such as vertebrate species richness on a small island, are easier to handle than are others, such as diversity of ecological functions on a continent (Hambler 2004; Ricotta 2005). Therefore scientists tend in practice to express biodiversity in terms of limited measures of organismal diversity, often numbers at a given taxonomic level, particularly species (Gaston 2010). Needless to say, measuring species richness alone omits certain important aspects of variation, such as localized behaviours. Also, some argue that an area-based approach, such as an ecosystem-based approach, needs more attention in biodiversity conservation contexts. This chapter focuses on species, genetic and molecular diversities.

Naturalness: Another Controversial Concept

Anthropogenic activities may increase, as well as decrease biodiversity (Macdonald and Service 2006). For example, genetically modified organisms, if they do not exterminate other organisms, increase biodiversity of the planet. Also, introducing invasive species, a serious conservation problem today (Yamaguchi et al. 2004b, 2004c; Macdonald et al. 2010; Rands et al. 2010), may increase biodiversity in some places. These examples question the assumption in conservation discussions that increasing biodiversity is a 'good' thing.

Some conservation scientists argue for the importance of biodiversity being 'natural', although another vague concept difficult to assess quantitatively. What is natural (Angermeier 2000; Yamaguchi et al. 2004b; Willis and Birks 2006)? This question cannot be solved easily due to the existence of two major schools of (philosophical) thoughts – one believes humans should be considered part of nature, and the other believes the opposite.

Whether one considers humans as part of nature or not, all largely agree that genetically modified organisms that depend on so-called modern technologies are not natural. However, when we consider the activities of human hunter-gatherers not dependent on 'modern' technologies, much disagreement occurs between those two schools of thoughts (Angermeier 2000; Mulder and Coppolillo 2005). To avoid conservation arguments becoming too arbitrary and even logically inconsistent, some scientists have been seeking to define *naturalness* (Angermeier 2000; Czech 2004) to serve as a basic standard for assessing 'natural' biodiversity.

In contrast to other disciplines where naturalness is not an issue (e.g. physics, chemistry or evolutionary biology), 'human' influence on Earth is responsible for the existence of conservation biology, as 'human' health

prompts the existence of medicine. It therefore seems logically legitimate to treat anthropogenic factors as distinct, and to contrast them with
naturalness – otherwise, as I discuss later, some conservation arguments
disintegrate including the idea of sustainability. Although we can argue
philosophically about what is natural and what is anthropogenic according to our value-based opinions, the scientific challenge is to distinguish
between them such as to allow quantitative analysis (Angermeier 2000;
Czech 2004). For example, the date of European colonization of North
America is sometimes used to separate natural and non-natural states of
the continent partially because it is a convenient clear cut-off point and
appeals to many people's perceptions. It also has very considerable environmental impacts (left alone, it is unlikely the Sioux would have built
freeways and New York!). However, it is increasingly clear that 'unsustainable' impacts of anthropogenic activities on large terrestrial mammals
during the Upper Palaeolithic (end of the Pleistocene and early Holocene)
were more widespread than thought previously (Mulder and Coppolillo
2005), becoming detectable by 50,000–10,000 years ago (Alroy 2001; Brook
and Bowman 2002, 2004; Yamaguchi et al. 2004a; Bar-Oz, Zeder and Hole
2011). European colonization of North America was merely one episode of
human input on the environment, long after such anthropogenic influences
are first detectable, although it dramatically influenced local biodiversity.
Conservation scientists should use the date that anthropogenic impacts become detectable for the first time, which is less arbitrary than dating these
to subsequent events, however dramatic. The foregoing argument suggests
that to understand the 'natural' biodiversity, conservation scientists need
to go back in time substantially further than some do currently.

Biodiversity Changes Naturally

Biodiversity changes all the time. For example, the number of species of
mammals today is estimated to be c. 4,600 whilst it was '0' (nil) until c.
200 million years ago (although mammal-like reptiles were there for the
previous c. 100 million years) of the c. 4.5 billion years of the history of this
planet (Kemp 2005). Conserving the 'natural' biodiversity of the earth is
not synonymous with preserving the current status quo, such as freezing
one scene of a movie, but paying attention to the 'natural' processes (e.g.
evolutionary processes) behind the changes of biodiversity, viewing the
entire movie.

Although it may be relatively easy to identify natural conditions in
some cases, in others cases it is difficult to distinguish these from anthropogenic effects (figures 12.1a, b). The challenge facing conservation scientists is to find combinations of parameters (e.g. species richness) and
scales (e.g. temporal, spatial, taxonomic) that effectively distinguish natu-

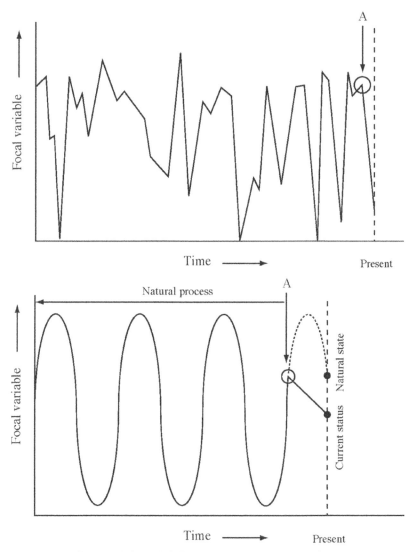

Figure 12.1a, b. Possibility of deducing what is 'natural' today.

(a) Human activities start to increase along the time axis at A, and are associated with the subsequent decrease of the focal variable (e.g. population size). However, the decrease is not distinct from decreases previous to A, and also the changing pattern of the focal variable appearing stochastic, at the time scale shown. Therefore, it is not possible to deduce what is 'natural' today.

(b) Human activities again start to increase at A, and are associated with the subsequent decrease of the focal variable. Although the decrease is not unique at the time scale shown (the variable has reached similar low levels previously), it is uniquely distinguished against the background cycle. If human impacts had not occurred, 'natural' changes of the focal variable would be expected to follow the dashed line.

ral from anthropogenic. Then, it may be possible to hypothesize the state of current natural biodiversity without human influence (figure 12.1b).

For example, the maned modern lion (*Panthera leo*) is currently found only in sub-Saharan Africa and India. However, on the basis of its deduced colonization history during the late Pleistocene – early Holocene – it is possible that the modern lion could have expanded its distribution to the Palaearctic region (e.g. Europe and central to northern Asia) if there had been no humans (Yamaguchi et al. 2004a). Conservation scientists can deduce, based on available evidence, the possible natural state of the lion not only concerning geographical distribution, but also population size and genetic diversity (Barnett et al. 2006, 2009).

Such a deduced/hypothesized measure helps conservation scientists to assess the current status of biodiversity in the context of the organisms' (evolutionary) history, although it is clearly unrealistic to restore the natural biodiversity today.

Sustainability

Linguistically, *sustainability* is an adjective dressed up as a noun, just like *reality* – in other words it is a philosophical nightmare. In a similar way that *reality* means 'state(s) of things as they actually exist', *sustainability* is defined as the 'capacity to endure for a long(er) term'. Consequently, unlike biodiversity, sustainability depends on viewpoints in the first place (useful examples and discussions are seen throughout this volume). There is a large number of ways to view sustainability in different fields, including politics (e.g. sustainable policy), economics (e.g. sustainable economic development) and social (e.g. sustainable urban community planning), as well as bioenvironmental (e.g. ecological sustainability; see Sillitoe introduction this volume). A phenomenon may be classified as sustainable from one point of view but unsustainable from another. For example, depending on time scale: from an ecological longer-term view the harvest of slow-growing species such as mahogany trees may be considered unsustainable, but from a shorter-term economic view be judged sustainable (Mulder and Coppolillo 2005; see Sillitoe conclusion this volume). For the sake of simplicity, this chapter focuses on the sustainability as assessed on bioenvironmental grounds, notably the sustainable use of natural resources (see also Al Othman and Clarke, chapter 5; Sillitoe and Alshawi, chapter 10; Howard, chapter 11, all this volume).

All organisms on the planet are connected to each other through very complex interlinkages. According to the laws of thermodynamics, no organism can exploit the environment for nothing (Hambler 2004). Earth is practically a finite system – i.e. there is only a limited total number of atoms on this planet that does not appear to change substantially enough on short(er) timescales to influence many organisms' lives. It is inevitable that when some organism exploits resources also used by other organisms, the first group impacts on the second. For example, if we harvest grasses to feed sheep to produce food, our activity influences their alternative possible fates such as wild gazelles grazing on the grasses. However, quantitatively analyzing the complex interlinkages between organisms is currently in its infancy (ibid.).

The foregoing arguments suggest that (bioenvironmental) sustainability does not seem to be consistent with the laws of natural sciences. Also, it is only possible to conceive of quantitatively analyzing sustainability if the following three conditions are met. Firstly, and probably most importantly, we need to take a clear anthropocentric view. Without this condition, relevant bioenvironmental arguments become too complicated. Secondly, we need to focus on simple relationships between humans and only as few arbitrarily chosen units/resources as possible, such as one species, the biomass of one local population or water quality of one stretch of a river. Thirdly, we need to discuss phenomena within arbitrarily chosen spatial and temporal scales, which are usually (much) smaller in comparison to planet-wide processes and geological time frames. When we find a stable equilibrium between human activities and the monitored parameter(s), the focal anthropogenic activities are considered sustainable.

Single Parameter Approach

In many cases, sustainability of natural resources is assessed on only one quantitative parameter, notably the biomass (e.g. population size, combined weight/volume harvested etc.). It is widely accepted that when a harvesting activity (e.g. fishing) does not decrease the resource level (e.g. fish stock), the activity is sustainable. The focus on biomass suggests that current assessments of sustainability pay little attention to biodiversity, which concerns variety (e.g. species, genetic and molecular diversities) and not biomass alone. The recent exploitation and recovery of the northern elephant seal (*Mirounga angustirostris*) illustrate the point. The northern elephant seal was nearly hunted to extinction towards the end of the nineteenth century with the estimated total population less than 100 before protected and the population increased to present levels at more than 100,000 animals (Stewart et al. 1994). Nevertheless, it is suggested that the species lost a substantial proportion of its genetic diversity due to the population bottleneck, and is unlikely to recover it as quickly (Hoelzel et al. 2002). The 'successful recovery' story is not as successful as thought based on increase in population size (i.e. biomass) when we consider genetic biodiversity. Quantifiable bioenvironmental parameters other than population size are often not available currently for species other than charismatic vertebrates such as lions, brown bears and elephants (Hortal, Lobo and A. Jiménez-Valverde 2007; Régnier 2009), and so inevitably, conservation scientists tend to assess sustainability using biomass parameters.

Even where we simply consider the relationship between humans and one other organism, conservation scientists face basic (theoretical and empirical) problems incorporating biodiversity into sustainability assessment. Nonetheless, some may argue that if sustainable practices conserve an 'appropriate' population size of focal organisms, they contribute to conserving biodiversity. But this view is flawed too.

Maximum Sustainable Yields

Resource managers such as foresters and fisheries officers have considered sustainability for many years in attempting to harvest in ways that maintain long(er)-term yields. The ideal target to aim for was set by the concept of 'Maximum Sustainable Yield' (MSY; Hambler 2004; Mulder and Coppolillo 2005). The MSY gives the greatest harvest while maintaining the stock of organisms over the long(er) term: birth and growth replace individuals harvested (or died by other causes). It is possible to assess sustainability using this approach that focuses on a single quantitative parameter (biomass). The MSY theoretically depends on the ideas of both logistic growth and density-dependent competition, visualized in figure 12.2 as a sigmoid (or logistic) population growth curve, although whether these ideas are directly and unconditionally applicable to the real world is debatable (Mulder and Coppolillo 2005; Van Vliet et al. 2010). In brief, sexually reproductive organisms at low population densities may not efficiently find members of the opposite sex, so compromising their reproduction rates (the left one-third of the graph in figure 12.2). When the population increases and its population density reaches a certain level, organisms reproduce at their maximum intrinsic rates resulting in rapid population growth (the middle one-third of the graph in figure 12.2). Then, as density rises further, competition (e.g. for food, space and over reproduction) starts to reduce survival and reproduction rates, and eventually, the population stabilizes at level K, which is the carrying capacity of the environment (the right one-third of the graph in figure 12.2).

The following equation incorporates harvest into this simple model (Milner-Gulland and Mace 1998): $dN/dt = rN((K-N)/K) - H$ (where N is the population size, t is time, r is intrinsic rate of increase, K is the (average) carrying capacity and H is harvesting rate). In theory, where population growth follows the sigmoid curve (figure 12.2), the greatest growth rate occurs where population density is neither low nor high (figure 12.3).

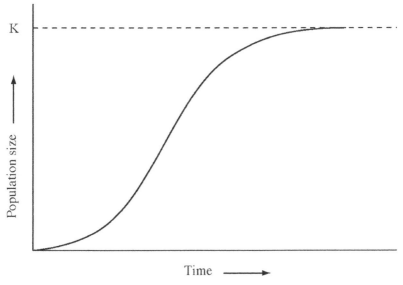

Figure 12.2. A sigmoid (or logistic) population growth curve. Population growth slows down as the population size approaches the carrying capacity (K), and eventually stops.

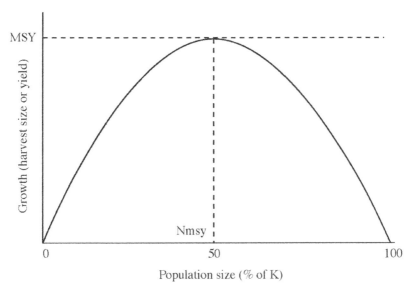

Figure 12.3. Population size, population growth and maximum sustainable yield. The population size is shown as a percentage (%) of the carrying capacity (K). The maximum sustainable yield (MSY) occurs at the highest population growth rate (at population size N_{msy}; the graph shows N_{msy} at 50 per cent of K, whereas N_{msy} depends on the biology of each species).

A sustainable harvest should not decrease the population size (N): if the harvesting rate is equal or lower than MSY (H ≤ MSY), it is judged sustainable.

Independent of Population Size

The above defines sustainability as depending on harvest rate (H) being lower than MSY under given carrying capacity. It is worth noting that it does not include the biomass (e.g. population size). In other words, sustainability can be achieved regardless of the population size. Figure 12.4 shows sustainable harvest for three different-sized populations. It shows that sustainability and resource level (e.g. population size) are effectively independent. Humans may deplete natural resources, even destroy habitats (i.e. decrease the carrying capacity for the focal species), and maintain an illusion of sustainability until the moment the resources become extinct. Needless to say, in practice, a few key factors including demand and accessibility strongly influence harvest rate (H). For example, even if the demand for a fish species is high, if accessibility is low, fisheries may not be able to harvest it economically, which implies sustainability of sorts

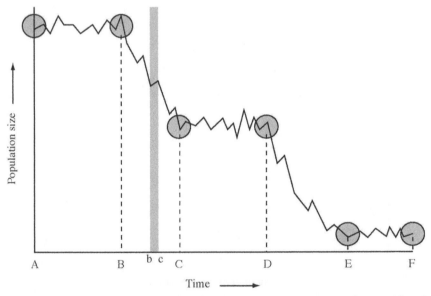

Figure 12.4. Resource level and sustainability. Harvest activity may be considered sustainable between A and B, C and D and E and F, whilst unsustainable between B and C and D and F. Although there is an unmistakable trend of population decline between A and F, viewed over a shorter time frame (b–c), the population is increasing.

under the commercial extinction (not biological extinction) of the species. This situation occurs between E and F in figure 12.4 where the population is much lower than the unsustainable stage between B and C. Even in this simple model based on a single resource, the widely accepted notion of sustainability is not necessarily positively associated with population size, let alone biodiversity.

Post-Depletion Sustainability

The phenomenon of post-depletion sustainability contradicts biodiversity conservation (Cowlishaw, Mendelson and Rowcliffe 2005). For a long time, humans have observed the disappearance of some organisms from areas which we dominate. For example, Georges-Louis Leclerc, Compte de Buffon (1785) described 'Man's industry augments in proportion to his numbers; but that of the other animals remains always the same. All the destructive species, as that of the lion, seem to be banished to distant regions, or reduced to a small number, not only because mankind have increased, but because they have also become more powerful, and have invented formidable arms which nothing can resist.' More than two hundred years later, it is suggested that significant disparities exist between the needs of (local) peoples and species with large territorial requirements exist, and preservation of biodiversity demands a different strategy than sustaining landscape qualities for continued human exploitation (Kellert et al. 2000; Antrop 2006; Rands et al. 2010). Yet, in the so-called developed world, such as Europe, in spite of the extinction (or near extinction) of some species, there are many species of plants and animals that do not appear to be endangered. This phenomenon is 'post-depletion sustainability' where following the overexploitation of vulnerable species, those remaining are 'robust' enough to survive in the human-dominated landscape, and may be harvested in a sustainable way to meet the demands of communities, at least at current harvest levels (Cowlishaw, Mendelson and Rowcliffe 2005).

Similarly, where an area of land is exploited with low(er) anthropogenic impacts, for a certain amount of time, it may become so-called semi-natural, where nominal, although misleading, sustainability occurs that is substantially different from the 'natural' (Hambler 2004). Many such nominally more sustainable 'semi-natural' areas, such as secondary forests, are distributed around the world and offer potential for biodiversity conservation (Chazdon et al. 2009) albeit many are in a 'post-depletion sustainability' state. The value of such 'semi-natural' or occasionally exploited areas for 'natural' biodiversity conservation is generally lower than that of more primitive natural areas (Hambler 2004; Barlow et al. 2007).

Many endangered species are vulnerable to anthropogenic activities, and hence sustainability may not be achieved as long as vulnerable species are included into the equation because they are likely in decline in most cases. When the endangered species are extinct (so no need of including them into equation any longer), sustainability may be achieved between anthropogenic activities and the remaining more 'robust' species. But one of the top priorities of biodiversity conservation is to protect as many endangered species as possible; the extinction of each is a loss of diversity (Nee and May 1997; Mace, Gittleman and Purvis 2003). The relationship between biodiversity conservation and sustainability appears antagonistic.

Arbitrary Unit Syndrome

The spatial and temporal units (or scales) used are important when measuring quantitative parameters, yet there are few general rules guiding choice of unit to evaluate biodiversity conservation or sustainability (Willis and Whittaker 2002; Caro 2010). Figure 12.5 shows a hypothetical situation concerning the occurrence of a fish species around Qatar. In 1990, the fish population is distributed around the coastline of Qatar, with a strong hold on the western coast. By 2010, the distribution range has shrunk substantially. However, if the monitoring area (i.e. spatial unit) is the southeast part of the country, the range has increased, whereas if one investigated the changes beyond the waters around the country (i.e. increasing the spatial scale), the picture may differ again. It is possible that conservation scientists may draw contradictory conclusions if they choose spatial units arbitrarily. This is similar with temporal scale, as figure 12.4 illustrates. If we analyze the trend between Time-A and Time-F, we will detect a clear trend of population decrease. However, if we take the trend between Time-b and Time-c, we detect a population increase. The further issue regarding temporal scale is the constant erosion of people's memories over time, resulting in the Shifting Baseline Syndrome (Pauly 1995), where each generation resets its perception of the benchmark (e.g. the biomass of fish stocks considered 'sufficient') in the face of declining natural resources. This phenomenon has a corrosive influence on concepts within resource management including biodiversity conservation and sustainability assessment (Baker and Clapham 2004; Jennings and Blanchard 2004; Mulder and Coppolillo 2005; Manning, Lindenmayer and J. Fischer 2006).

A further problem, due to funding arrangements, is that the duration of a typical conservation project is only a few years. Also, limited resources restrict projects to small geographical areas. Consequently, they tend to

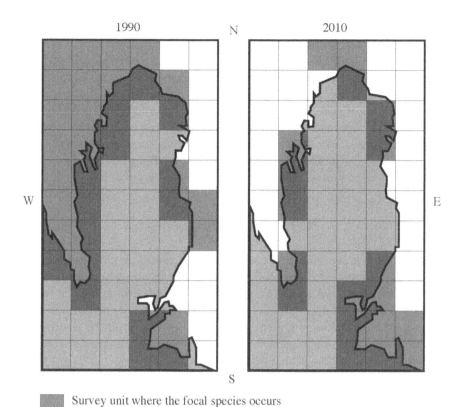

Survey unit where the focal species occurs

Figure 12.5. A hypothetical example: a change of the distribution of a fish species around Qatar between 1990 and 2010 (N in the figure indicates north, S is south, E is east and W is west).

focus on issues relevant to small(er) spatial scales and short(er) temporal scale. The typical project may not even cover a single generation (the period between birth and first reproduction), or a single individual's home range, of many endangered medium- to large-sized vertebrates, whose survival is a conservation priority. It is clear that conservation scientists face considerable practical difficulties obtaining meaningful bioenvironmental data to assess biodiversity conservation and sustainability.

It is also important to pay attention to units other than the spatial and temporal. Conservation scientists may focus on taxonomic units such as species or genus, or ecological units such as community or ecosystem. In spite of advances in ecosystem delineation and classification, natural ecosystem boundaries are often harder to define than those between internally coherent taxa, such as species (Mace, Possingham and Leader-Williams 2007) with the possible exception of landwater interfaces (Karr 1999; Czech 2004). Although the boundaries of some areas are clearly defined (e.g. Kruger National Park, Iran or European Union), such areas are often delimited without consideration of bioenvironmental issues. At the same time, and frustratingly, it is likely that a scientifically justified unit will not correspond to a practical management unit in the real world (Caro 2010).

There is a scale- and unit-related dilemma. Firstly, current practical limitations may not allow conservation scientists to assess biodiversity sustainability according to appropriate scientifically meaningful bioenvironmental units. Secondly, if they could work on such scientifically justified units, the results may not be directly applicable to ongoing practical conservation, or worse, the projects may not be funded at all.

Value-Based Judgments

We should not overlook that conservation decision making has been, is and will be based on 'consumer choice', wherein the question 'how many of this species do we want' may be answered with little reference to scientific evidence (Stankey and Shindler 2006). Disagreements due to different value judgements (e.g. personal preferences) may hinder us making appropriate decisions to conserve biodiversity and manage our activities more sustainably (if possible) for the benefit of future generations. Conservation scientists are striving to find some quantifiable standards, less value dependent, to assess biodiversity conservation and sustainability.

Balanced View or a State of Chaos?

Although human activities invariably seem to decrease biodiversity in the longer term (May, Lawton and Stork 1995), in the shorter term (and on a local scale) they may increase it by providing extra resources or creating certain levels of environmental disturbances (e.g. Intermediate Disturbance Hypothesis: local biodiversity is maximized when ecological disturbance is neither too rare nor too frequent; Connell 1978; Whittaker, Willis and Field 2001). For example, creating artificial water holes in arid areas probably increases some wildlife populations, and may reduce short-term extinction risk. However, based on 'naturalness' as discussed above, if an area naturally supports a low level of biodiversity, increasing it through human activities is just as unnatural as decreasing naturally rich biodiversity.

If one taxon consists of ten closely related extant species, and another only one, then losing one of the former might be considered less important than losing the latter because this would mean the loss of the evolutionary history of an entire taxon (e.g. biodiversity; Nee and May 1997; Purvis,

Mace and Gittleman 2000; Mace, Gittleman and Purvis 2003). It may be possible, however, that the former has been increasing naturally in diversity whilst the latter has been decreasing naturally. In such a case, where a taxon is 'naturally' more diverse than another, there might be an argument for retaining that intra-taxon biodiversity, or maintaining the process that increases its intra-taxon biodiversity further. Furthermore, common taxa, due to their commonness, may play important roles concerning ecosystem function in comparison to rare taxa (Ganson and Fuller 2008). In this context, a dominant species in decline because of anthropogenic influence may be given as much attention (if not more) as a species that is naturally rare, even if the total population size of the former is larger.

What are we to make of the 'semi-natural' habitats discussed above created by human woodland and agricultural management, and the plant and animal species adapted to them, where these owe their success to obsolete (yet clearly anthropogenic) management systems. Some argue that efforts to conserve those habitats and associated organisms are 'gardening' (Hambler and Speight 1995), and should not attract limited resources allocated for biodiversity conservation, while others argue that as such 'semi-natural' habitats are widespread around the world, they should be incorporated into biodiversity conservation programmes (Hambler 2004; Chazdon et al. 2009).

Diverse arguments from different viewpoints may help us form a balanced view. But, there is a risk that such differences may create a state of chaos, stymieing effective decision making. A way to avoid chaos is to use scientific evidence to guide our decisions. But, do we have enough data to assess the deficit that humanity owes nature?

Lack of Data

Conservation scientists may theoretically assess 'natural' biodiversity quantitatively, if we accept the concept of naturalness, free from the perils of a shifting baseline, and they should be able to improve the assessment of sustainability with increased bioenvironmental relevance by carefully choosing appropriate units (or scales). Relevant theoretical work and modelling, let alone practice, require more information than we have currently about species' genetic and molecular diversities and various ecological functions beyond biomass issues. Nonetheless, lack of information and practical problems should not prevent theoretical work on both biodiversity and sustainability to help us understand our impact on the planet, and to plan biodiversity conservation and more sustainable use of natural resources. We can deduce past conditions, important to understanding long-term trends from the literature, museum collections, hunting records, archaeological and palaeo-ecological findings (Hortal, Lobo and Jiménez-Valverde 2007; Régnier et al. 2009). For example, advances in ancient biomolecular techniques increasingly allow scientists to trace changes in species' genetic diversity and demography from the end of the Pleistocene onwards (Driscoll et al. 2007; Barnett et al. 2009; Bar-Oz, Zeder and Hole 2011). Some obstacles may take longer to overcome, depending heavily on the development of appropriate methodologies. The methodology-dependent approach to understanding biodiversity and assessing sustainability bioenvironmentally will allow us to better to evaluate humanity's impacts, and help us to save the planet from humans for humans.

Illusions Resulting from Data Deficiency?

The aims of conserving biodiversity are not theoretically compatible with widely accepted notions of sustainability based on biomass and ignoring variety. Furthermore, in practice, we do not have enough data to assess biodiversity or sustainability. For example, in one of rare cases where some data are available, it is estimated that fishing has reduced by c. 97 per cent the 'natural' biomass of large fish weighing 4–16 kilograms in the North Sea (Jennings and Blanchard 2004). It is inconceivable that such a loss has not impacted the ecosystem including variety of other organisms (e.g. species, genetic and molecular diversities), as well as various ecological functions. Ironically, as illustrated, it is possible to present the changed situation as sustainable so long as harvesting does not reduce the remaining biomass – i.e. the remaining c. 3 per cent of the North Sea fish stock can be harvested in a sustainable way. Politicians, economists and others may present such sustainability at a 'low' level of resource as a positive message to mask the magnitude of the devastation that humans are visiting on ecosystems and maintain current arrangements. Nevertheless, it is not easy to prove it wrong when somebody would insist 'there is no hard evidence to prove humans cannot achieve sustainable use of natural resources' thanks to the current data deficiency. Sadly, such data deficiency may continue in the future for a long time (or even indefinitely).

Acknowledgements

I thank Paul Sillitoe and Sarah Clarke for their editorial work, encouragement and patience. I also thank Paul Sillitoe, David W. Macdonald and Clive Hambler for their comments and discussions.

References

Alroy, J. 2001. 'A Multispecies Overkill Simulation of the End-Pleistocene Maga-faunal Mass Extinction. *Science* 292: 1893–1896.

Angermeier, P. L. 2000. 'The Natural Imperative for Biological Conservation.' *Conservation Biology* 14: 373–381.

Antrop, M. 2006. 'Sustainable Landscapes: Contradiction, Fiction or Utopia?' *Landscape and Urban Planning* 75: 187–197.

Baker, C. S., and P. J. Clapham. 2004. 'Modelling the Past and Future of Whales and Whaling.' *Trends in Ecology and Evolution* 19: 365–371.

Barlow, J., et al. 2007. 'The Value of Primary, Secondary and Plantation Forests for Amazonian Birds.' *Biological Conservation* 136: 212–231.

Barnett, R., et al. 2009. 'Phylogeography of Lions (*Panthera leo*) Reveals Three Distinct Taxa and a Late Pleistocene Reduction in Genetic Diversity.' *Molecular Ecology* 18: 1668–1677.

———. 2006. 'The Origin, Current Diversity, and Future Conservation of the Modern Lion (*Panthera leo*).' *Proceedings of the Royal Society B: Biological Sciences* 273: 2119–2125.

Bar-Oz, G., M. Zeder and F. Hole. 2011. 'Role of Mass-Killing Strategies in the Extirpation of Persian Gazelle (*Gazella subgutturosa*) in the Northern Levant.' *Proceedings of the National Academy of Sciences of the United States of America* 108: 7345–7350.

Brook, B. W., and D. M. S. J. Bowman. 2002. 'Explaining the Pleistocene Megafaunal Extinctions: Models, Chronologies, and Assumptions.' *Proceedings of the National Academy of Sciences of the United States of America* 99: 14624–14627.

———. 2004. 'The Uncertain Blitzkrieg of Pleistocene Magafauna.' *Journal of Biogeography* 31: 517–523.

Buffon, G. L. L. C. 1785. *Natural History, General and Particular, Second English Edition Volume 5* (translated into English by W. Smellie). London: W. Strahan and T. Cadell.

Callicott, J. R., and K. Mumford. 1997. 'Ecological Sustainability as Conservation Concept.' *Conservation Biology* 11: 32–40.

Campbell, A. K. 2003. 'Save Those Molecules! Molecular Biodiversity and Life.' *Journal of Applied Ecology* 40: 193–203.

Caro, T. 2010. *Conservation by Proxy*. Washington: Island Press.

Chazdon, R. L., et al. 2009. 'The Potential for Species Conservation in Tropical Secondary Forests.' *Conservation Biology* 23: 1406–1417.

Connell, J. H. 1978. 'Diversity in Tropical Rain Forests and Coral Reefs.' *Science* 199: 1302–1310.

Cowlishaw, G., S. Mendelson and J. R. Rowcliffe. 2005. 'Evidence for Post-Depletion Sustainability in a Mature Bushmeat Market.' *Journal of Applied Ecology* 42: 460–468.

Czech, B. 2004. 'A Chronological Frame of Reference for Ecological Integrity and Natural Conditions.' *Natural Resources Journal* 44: 1113–1136.

Driscoll, C. A., et al. 2007. 'The Near Eastern Origin of Cat Domestication.' *Science* 317: 519–523.

Gaston, K. J. 2010. 'Biodiversity.' In *Conservation Biology for All*, eds. N. S. Sodhi and P. R. Ehrlich, 27–44. Oxford: Oxford University Press.

Gaston, K. J., and R. A. Fuller. 2008. 'Commonness, Population Depletion and Conservation Biology.' *Trends in Ecology and Evolution* 23: 14–19.

Hambler, C. 2004. *Conservation*. Cambridge: Cambridge University Press.

Hambler, C., and M. R. Speight. 1995. 'Biodiversity Conservation in Britain: Science Replacing Tradition.' *British Wildlife* 6: 137–147.

Hoelzel, A. R., et al. 2002. 'Impact of a Population Bottleneck on Symmetry and Genetic Diversity in the Northern Elephant Seal.' *Journal of Evolutionary Biology* 15: 567–575.

Hortal, J., J. L. Lobo and A. Jiménez-Valverde. 2007. 'Limitations of Biodiversity Database: Case Study on Seed-Plant Diversity in Tenerife, Canary Islands.' *Conservation Biology* 21: 853–863.

Jennings, S., and J. L. Blanchard. 2004. 'Fish Abundance with No Fishing: Predictions Based on Macroecological Theory.' *Journal of Animal Ecology* 73: 632–642.

Kellert, S. R., et al. 2000. 'Community Natural Resource Management: Promise, Rhetoric, and Reality.' *Society and Natural Resources* 13: 705–715.

Kemp, T. S. 2005. *The Origin and Evolution of Mammals*. Oxford: Oxford University Press.

Macdonald, D. W., and K. Service (eds.). 2006. *Key Topics in Conservation Biology*. Oxford: Blackwell Publications.

Macdonald, D. W., et al. 2010. 'The Scottish Wildcat: On the Way to Cryptic Extinction Through Hybridisation: Past History, Present Problem, and Future Conservation.' In *Biology and Conservation of Wild Felids*, eds. D. W. Macdonald and A. J. Loveridge, 471–491. Oxford: Oxford University Press.

Mace, G. M., J. L. Gittleman and A. Purvis. 2003. 'Preserving the Tree of Life.' *Science* 300: 1707–1709.

Mace, G. M., H. P. Possingham and N. Leader-Williams. 2007. 'Prioritising Choices in Conservation.' In *Key Topics in Conservation Biology*, eds. D. W. Macdonald and K. Service, 17–34. Oxford: Blackwell Publications.

Manning, A. D., D. B. Lindenmayer and J. Fischer. 2006. 'Stretch Goals and Backcasting: Approaches for Overcoming Barriers to Large-Scale Ecological Restoration.' *Restoration Ecology* 14: 489–492.

May, R. M., J. H. Lawton and N. E. Stork. 1995. 'Assessing Extinction Rates.' In *Extinction Rates*, eds. J. H. Lawton and R. M. May, 1–24. Oxford: Oxford University Press.

Milner-Gulland, E. J., and R. Mace. 1998. *Conservation of Biological Resources*. Oxford: Blackwell Science.

Mulder, M. B., and P. Coppolillo. 2005. *Conservation Linking Ecology, Economics, and Culture*. Princeton, NJ: Princeton University Press.

Nee, S., and R. M. May. 1997. 'Extinction and Loss of Evolutionary History.' *Science* 278: 692–694.

Newton, J. L., and E. T. Freyfogle. 2005. 'Sustainability: A Dissent.' *Conservation Biology* 19: 23–32.

Pauly, D. 1995. 'Anecdotes and the Shifting Baseline Syndrome of Fisheries.' *Trends in Ecology and Evolution* 10: 430.

Purvis, A., G. M. Mace and J. L. Gittleman. 2001. 'Past and Future Carnivore Extinctions: A Phylogenetic Perspective.' In *Carnivore Conservation*, eds. J. L. Gittleman et al., 11–34. Cambridge: Cambridge University Press.

Rands, M. R. W., et al. 2010. 'Biodiversity Conservation: Challenges Beyond 2010.' *Science* 329: 1298–1303.

Régnier, C., B. Fontaine and P. Bouchet. 2009. 'Not Knowing, Not Recording, Not Listing: Numerous Unnoticed Mollusk Extinctions.' *Conservation Biology* 23: 1214–1221.

Ricotta, C. 2005. 'Through the Jungle of Biological Diversity.' *Acta Biotheoretica* 53: 29–38.

Sarker, S. 2006. 'Ecological Diversity and Biodiversity as Concepts for Conservation Planning: Comments on Ricotta.' *Acta Biotheoretica* 54: 133–140.

Sodhi, N. S., and P. R. Ehrlich (eds.). 2010. *Conservation Biology for All.* Oxford: Oxford University Press.

Stankey, G. H., and B. Shindler. 2006. 'Formation of Social Acceptability Judgments and their Implications for Management of Rare and Little-Known Species.' *Conservation Biology* 20: 28–37.

Stewart, B. S., et al. 1994. 'History and Present Status of the Northern Elephant Seal Population.' In *Elephant Seals Population Ecology, Behaviour, and Physiology*, eds. B. J. Le Boeuf and R. M. Laws, 29–48. Berkeley: University of California Press.

Van Vliet, N., et al. 2010. 'Effects of Small-Scale Heterogeneity of Prey and Hunter Distributions on the Sustainability of Bushmeat Hunting.' *Conservation Biology* 24: 1327–1337.

Whittaker, R. J., K. J. Willis and R. Field. 2001. 'Scale and Species Richness: Towards a General, Hierarchical Theory of Species Diversity.' *Journal of Biogeography* 28: 453–470.

Willis, K. J., and H. J. B. Birks. 2006. 'What is Natural? The Need for a Long-Term Perspective in Biodiversity Conservation.' *Science* 314: 1261–1265.

Willis, K. J., and R. J. Whittaker. 2002. 'Species Diversity Scale Matters.' *Science* 295: 1245–1248.

Yamaguchi, N., et al. 2004a. 'Evolution of the Mane and Group-Living in the Lion (*Panthera leo*): A Review.' *Journal of Zoology* 263: 329–342.

———. 2004b. 'Craniological Differentiation amongst the European Wildcat (*Felis silvestris silvestris*), the African Wildcat (*F. s. lybica*) and the Asian Wildcat (*F. s. ornata*): Implications for their Evolution and Conservation.' *Biological Journal of the Linnean Society* 83: 47–64.

———. 2004c. 'Craniological Differentiation amongst Wild-Living Cats in Britain and Southern Africa: Natural Variation or the Effects of Hybridisation?' *Animal Conservation* 7: 339–351.

IV

Urban and Health Issues

CHAPTER 13

From Pearling to Skyscrapers

The Predicament of Sustainable Architecture and Urbanism in Contemporary Gulf Cities

Ali A. Alraouf and Sarah F. Clarke

In the last decade, and at a remarkable pace, Gulf cities have witnessed unprecedented growth, setting new standards for rates of urbanization and attracting large numbers of immigrants from all over the globe. Lucrative oil revenues have motivated Gulf cities to aim for 'world class status' and, in aspiring to this goal, they have competed to have the highest, the biggest and the longest developments, seemingly the more glitzy and extravagant the better. What are the consequences for the future of Gulf cities? Will the relative absence of sustainable concepts in their strategic development result in negative outcomes? Is the sustainability label applied to some Gulf developments credible? Are Gulf cities planned with people in mind and do they welcome and include social sustainability, urban diversity and promote preservation of traditions and local cultures?

This chapter argues that the transformation from relatively low-tech, desert dwelling, pearling-based settlements to multifaceted, complex oil- and gas-financed economies with dynamic urban landscapes, Gulf communities are failing to heed fully the demands of the sustainability agenda and that there is an urgent need for the implementation of sustainable strategies in the design and development of cities in the region. Moreover, we suggest that much can be learned from traditional Gulf and Middle Eastern architecture, community planning and cultural sensibilities; through a marrying of the lessons of the past with the technological solutions of the future, a context-based urban landscape may emerge with a socially driven character of its own that champions sustainability over and above that which is purely modern and new.

While it has been argued that in developed countries, cities are inherently more sustainable than many other forms of human habitation, in the rapidly developing nations of the Middle East where cities are being 'master planned', with a series of super-modern standalone developments in a sea of sand and empty space, the same argument may not hold true (see Gardner, chapter 14, this volume). It is the responsibility of designers, developers and decision makers in the Gulf to adopt new policies in planning, urban design and architecture; policies that acknowledge that carbon-based energy resources have a limited future, which shift the dominant thinking towards the green design of buildings, neighbourhoods and cities, using new and renewable sources of energy, without compromising the aesthetics of the built environment. Traditional Gulf architecture and urbanism can provide a set of principles and concepts suited to desert contexts, revitalized in contemporary architecture and urbanism. But more than this, the urban landscape and associated technology does not come into being spontaneously. Rather, it emerges out of a social process that shapes its nature, form and function. If truly liveable cities are to be created, that process must include sustainability at all stages. There is no one solution that will emerge from a single discipline. What is required is a cross-disciplinary discourse, one that considers social, political, environmental and cultural aspects and thinks beyond the present and considers the future consequences of our actions. In a region where the political process is driven by tribal loyalties and networks of filial relations, we may need to reframe Western architectural discourse and debate.

Sustainability is more than a buzzword: it is a concept and movement that defines what is needed for civilizations to survive, especially today when facing unprecedented environmental threats. While a new global paradigm is emerging where sustainability is recognized as the future for cities and communities, contemporary Gulf cities are designed and constructed with almost a total disregard for local and global environmental issues. Calls for holistic sustainability in the design of these cities go largely unheeded with the luxury of cheap oil and the illusion of timeless energy resources. While many GCC countries have National Visions that espouse an environmental and sustainability ethic, endorsed at high level; the words are there, but the action is not widespread (see, for example, Tan, Al-Khalaqi and Al-Khulaifi, chapter 2, and Darwish, chapter 4, both this volume). Gulf cities such as Dubai, Doha, Kuwait or Manama continue to fail to adopt sustainable strategies to minimize environmental impacts and preserve the earth's resources for coming generations.

There is no universally accepted definition of sustainability or sustainable development (Beatley 1995). Coined in the 1970s, the term and the ideas behind it have enjoyed varying popularity, as argued by George Okechukwu (2010). At a basic level, the various definitions embody the notion that we require a radical rethink of our relationships with one another (in the present and future) and with the natural environment on which we depend for our survival. Societies must adjust to new realities in order to be sustainable, which includes changes to ecosystems as an inevitable consequence of past development and urbanization and natural limits to population growth. Chris Laszlo (2008) outlines the new competitive environment in which social challenges are becoming lucrative business opportunities. He gives examples of businesses successfully integrating sustainability into their core activities, not only from a sense of moral correctness, but because it makes good business sense. Issues such as climate change and global poverty introduce complexity into strategic decision making and have far-reaching implications for companies. When we apply sustainability principles to the form and function of cities and the public arena, the complexities multiply.

Sustainability and cities is a fundamental issue long overlooked due to limited understanding of development. As Antonia Layard's, Simin Davoudi's and Susan Batty's (2001) volume shows, sustainable development thinking has substantial implications for housing, urban design, planning and property development as well as transport and waste (see Clarke and Almannai, chapter 15, this volume). The need in the Gulf, with its unique culture and demographic profile, is for these principles to be applied to architecture and urbanization in an inclusive manner such that all stakeholders have a place in the emerging cities and quality of life is assured for all. In this chapter, we argue that while traditional architectural patterns and approaches have lessons for today, it is not sufficient to simply bolt these ideas on to new designs or use them for superficial aesthetic effect. What is required is a re-envisioning of the old with the benefit of new technologies, materials, know-how and social capabilities to produce more sustainable ways of living, working, learning and playing.

This chapter begins by framing architecture and urbanization in the context of the global view of sustainable development. It charts the emergence of three trends in architectural design and urbanization in the Gulf region, paying particular attention to the case of Masdar, a futuristic sustainable city in the desert adjacent to Abu Dhabi, capital of the UAE. Examples of traditional architectural techniques and patterns of design and urbanization are used to illustrate how the knowledge of the past may be used to inform the designs of the future. We suggest that the sustainable future of Gulf cities lies in the adoption of a low-carbon compact city model that includes a reinterpretation of these traditional elements through the use of new technologies and techniques and in so doing takes a more holistic and integrated approach to the design of cities. Such a model will be constructed through an understanding, analysis and contemporary reinterpretation of traditional built environment patterns and principles. The chapter concludes with some observations about the future of architecture and urbanism in the Gulf region.

The Global View of Sustainable Development and Cities

Research aims to address the many interrelated aspects of the urban environment from transport and mobility to social exclusion and economic development and crime prevention. But we need to allow for a local focus. According to Charles Handy (1995), we live in an age of paradox: the more high tech and global our world, and the heavier our footprints, the more intensely we need to focus on the local and the critical need for cooperation in the development of sustainable strategies.

John Eger (2000) dates the decline of American cities to 1939 at the World's Fair in Flushing Meadows, New York, where the most popular exhibition was 'The World of Tomorrow' in the General Motors Pavilion. It featured an enormous model of a City of the Future, complete with elevated freeways, on-ramps and off-ramps and shiny skyscrapers separated by miles and miles of asphalt. For General Motors and for the rest of America, the vision became reality, as roads were increasingly built across the country, with more and more families able to purchase their own cars. This urban vision and its realization underline the need for a new and different one for the future and the role of cities.

While a city's configuration may appear static, any planning analysis must consider the relationships between different elements and movement within it. The dynamics of networks (flows of energy, people, goods and information) are fundamental to understanding contemporary cities. The challenge of planning sustainable cities concerns these urban system dynamics. Furthermore, by treating theory as a practical discourse, Adrian Parr and Michael Zaretsky (2010) stress the importance of politics and cultural symbolizations to a sustainable future and argue that no advances can be made in sustainable urban planning, housing or architecture without imagining and nurturing spatial, political, cultural and economic structures that promote the necessary conditions. Steven Moore (2010) also proposes a pragmatic and pluralistic approach to understanding and implementing sustainability. This is necessary, he argues, to achieve the changes required for creating a sustainable future. For him, climate change, widely seen as an environmental crisis, should also be confronted as a cultural crisis. Indeed, John Foster (2008) suggests that we need to progress to a new way of understanding sustainability in the built environment by no longer focusing simply on functionality. Rather, cities should nurture our deep needs, such as those for belonging and well-being. Moreover, winning the 'war' on climate change requires a shift of emphasis from a fear of the coming future to one which embraces the challenges ahead as an opportunity for rebirth and renewal. This will necessitate a holistic perception of sustainability which requires us to accommodate the immeasurable (Bell and Morse 2008), that is, shift from a wholly quantitative assessment of the built environment to one that includes qualitative methods.

The phenomenon of increasing world urbanization intensifies the need for a more sustainable approach to development. In 1960 there were only about 5 megacities with a population of over 10 million inhabitants; by 2000, this number had risen to 19, and will increase to 22 in 2015, most in developing countries. The number of cities with 5 million inhabitants or more is projected to rise from 46 in 2003 to 61 by 2015. In 2003, 33 of the 46 cities with 5 million or more inhabitants were in less developed countries, and by 2015, 45 out of the 61 are expected to be in less developed regions (UN-Habitat 2009). In the twentieth century, human numbers increased four-fold globally – from 1.5 to 6 billion – and the consumption of resources by urban populations went up sixteen-fold (World Bank 2010) with the trend set to continue.

Data from recent United Nations Development Programme (UNDP) reports, including 'The path to achieving Millennium Development Goals' (UNDP 2010a), the Human Development Report (UNDP 2010b) and the Arab Human Development Report (UNDP 2009b), highlight the critical situation of urban growth and resource use. Cities occupying 3–4 per cent of the world's land surface use 80 per cent of its resources, and discharge most solid, liquid and gaseous waste. They are responsible for two-thirds of global energy use and are major contributor of greenhouse gas (GHG) emissions that cause climate change. Every year we burn at least one million years' worth of fossil fuels. Buildings alone consume one-third of the total energy. In 2030, according to Energy Efficient Cities Initiative report (World Bank 2010), cities will consume over 73 per cent of the world's energy, with 4.9 billion people (60 per cent of the world's population) inhabiting cities. Urban built-up areas in developing countries will triple. If business as usual continues, cities will then emit 75 per cent of the world's greenhouse gases (GHG). Developing countries will be responsible for 81 per cent of urban energy use. Thus, by any analysis, the sustainable design of cities is critical to achieving global sustainability. It is a reality acknowledged by the Sustainable Cities and Agenda 21 programmes of the UN. Moreover, counter to common expectations, industry consumes less energy annually than buildings and transportation. For example, in the UK, energy consumption in buildings and transportation comprises more than 78 per cent of the total energy consumed, with the remainder used by industry (DTI 2005). This suggests that attention to how we build our cities and move around/between them will substantially reduce energy consumption and put us on a path to sustainability.

Contemporary Gulf Cities: The Dilemma of Growth

Gulf cities are experiencing unprecedented economic growth with governments and business investing heavily in infrastructure, real estate and industrial developments. These cities attract people from all over the world, mainly migrant workers and skilled expatriates vital to the completion of numerous construction and industrial projects and education initiatives. All countries in the region have followed the same approach to development with the oil/gas boom; new housing projects, modern institutional buildings and substantial upgrading of infrastructure. It is possible to delineate three paradigms of development in the emerging cities of the Gulf.

The first is a desire to take twentieth-century modernization to new highs and secure a place on the global stage. A well-known example is Dubai, one of the UAE's seven emirates, which has established a Gulf and Arab 'urban brand'. This paradigm is termed the *Dubaization* phenomenon (Alraouf 2006). It is characterized by iconic developments in Dubai such as 'Palm 1, 2 and 3' and 'The World' which are constructed on elaborate artificial islands.

There is competition between Gulf cities to imitate Dubai's 'success story' with similar developments across the region. Many cities have undergone a process of construction, deconstruction and reconstruction of their identities resulting in a sameness across the Gulf region with iconic structures and real estate fantasies dominating cities. For example, Manama's waterfront in Bahrain bears a striking resemblance to Dubai, with its World Trade Centre and Financial District developments (figure 13.1), as does the downtown area of Doha (figure 13.2). As a model of urban development, Dubai and similar cities in the Gulf are based primarily on images and icons rather than sustainable concepts and strategies, resulting in degradation of locality and a lack of social cohesion or uniqueness; should every downtown area in the region look the same?

The second paradigm, *Knowledgefication*, represents a move towards a knowledge-based economy with a view to the post-oil era. It comprises a shift from a focus on real estate creation to urban development that fosters the growth of a knowledge economy. Knowledgefication includes urban features such as contemporary university campuses, hi-tech centres of innovation, research institutes and state-of-the-art IT facilities. Such a shift is

Figure 13.1. The fast-changing Manama waterfront. Photograph by Sarah F. Clarke.

Figure 13.2. Skyline of the financial downtown area of Doha overlooking the Gulf. Photograph by Haider Raifey.

evident in Dubai, Doha, Manama, Abu Dhabi and Riyadh (Alraouf 2005a, 2008b). Knowledge economies depend on educated and skilled people and the challenge is to create an environment that encourages creativity and knowledge transfer (Landry 2000; Florida 2004; Carrillo 2005; Chen and Dahlman 2005). A prime example of this approach is the Qatar Foundation (QF), located in Doha and founded in 1995; the stated aim of which is to develop people's abilities through investments in human capital, with the aim of raising competencies and quality of life.[1]

The third paradigm, *Sustainablization*, signifies a concern for developing sustainable cities, with sustainability at the centre of development strategies and aspirations. A prime example in the Gulf region is Masdar City, billed as the world's first zero-carbon, zero-waste, car-free city, designed by Norman Foster and Partners in Abu Dhabi, UAE. It is a model that has the potential to be replicated regionally and internationally. Yet, there is a danger here that sustainability is being used as a marketing tool for real estate projects, which are a main component of Masdar, and not as a comprehensive approach to urban life. It also raises questions about what happens in the spaces between sustainable cities and where the boundaries of sustainability are since these cities will require an army of workers transported in from less sustainable locations (see Gardner, chapter 14, this volume). A comprehensive analysis is needed to evaluate the credibility of Masdar as a model to be followed. The Bahrain World Trade Centre (BWTC), with its large wind turbines spanning twin towers, is another example of Sustainablization, albeit on a smaller scale than Masdar. Billed as a testament to 'an underlying commitment to environment and sustainability' (BWTC 2008), the BWTC is the world's first commercial development to incorporate a wind turbine into its structure, which, it is estimated, will save 55,000 cubic kilograms of carbon emissions annually (figure 13.3). However, the presence of an exclusive shopping mall in the lower levels of the development, replete with prestigious brand names, implies a schism between the sustainability espoused by the building's designers and the culture of consumption it serves; the wind-energy technology simply gives the BWTC superficial 'green' credentials.

How ready are Gulf states to move towards the sustainable urban paradigm? Referring to the SWOT analysis in table 13.1, GCC countries have significant financial resources from oil and gas revenues to fund preparations for a post-oil world. In addition, a unique strength is their deliberate attempts to diversify economies in the region, making them well placed to support a more sustainable paradigm through investment in knowledge-based urban development, tourism, 'green' industry, financial services and education. Moreover, many have made a commitment to preserve cultural heritage. These factors, combined with a clear political will to

Figure 13.3. The wind turbine of the World Trade Centre, Bahrain. Photograph by Sarah F. Clarke.

champion sustainability and an open-door policy for assistance from out-side, suggest that the Gulf may achieve a sustainable future.

On the other hand, there are a number of weaknesses and threats to achieving sustainable urban development in the region. The population in general has limited awareness and understanding of sustainability and its significance for future well-being. In addition, the rate of population increase in Gulf cities is phenomenal. For instance, the population of Qatar rose to almost 1.7 million in 2010 from 0.74 million in 2004. This equates to 128 per cent over the six-year period. Around 95 per cent live in urban locations, according to Qatar Statistics Authority data.[2] Furthermore, the Gulf states' demographic structure is characterized by a large percentage of expatriates, in some cases exceeding 70 per cent of the total population. This segment of the population has temporary-resident status. Expatriates are likely to have limited loyalty to their country of residence and as such less stake in its sustainability; many live in substandard housing, have little job security and do not benefit from the region's wealth in the same way as the local population.

There is a developing legal and institutional framework for dealing with environmental concerns in the GCC countries (see Al Othman and Clarke, chapter 5, this volume). However, in contrast to elsewhere, there are few civil society institutions and non-governmental organizations that are engaged in public discourse about issues of environmental protection and sustainability. Other threats to progress on sustainability in the region include vulnerability to uncontrollable global market forces and unstable regional political conditions which may negatively impact investment

Table 13.1. SWOT analysis of Gulf states' readiness for sustainable development.

Strength	Weakness
• Political commitment • Existence of legal and institutional frameworks for the urbanization process and environmental protection • Availability of financial resources • Commitment to preserve cultural heritage • Plans for diversified economies	• Lack of understanding of sustainable development requirements • Impact of civil society • Weakness of communication between stakeholders • Demographic structures
Opportunities	**Threats**
• International recognition of the strategic importance of the Gulf region • Strong will of foreign investors • Open-door policy for outside assistance about sustainability	• Loss of cultural heritage • Uncontrollable global market conditions • Deliberate changes in natural environment • Climate change impacts • Unstable regional conditions • Natural/human-made disasters

opportunities. Unanticipated impacts from deliberate changes to the environment, particularly in coastal regions where land reclamation continues on an unprecedented scale (as in Bahrain, figure 13.4), could also be a major threat to sustainability along with climate change impacts.

Taken as a whole, this analysis suggests that while there are some drivers that support sustainability in the region, there are substantial constraints on the ability of Gulf states to embrace and act on the sustainability agenda. However, one dimension they have yet to exploit fully is their traditional Middle Eastern and Gulf architectural heritage which, used in conjunction with modern technologies, could provide a route to a more sustainable urban future.

Roots of Gulf Sustainable Architecture and Urbanism

Buildings designed with a view to environmental sustainability represent the renewal of an ancient approach to architecture. As we look to reduce our reliance on the world's non-renewable energy resources, there is much we can learn from previous civilizations that lived in sustainable settlements (Pearson 1989). Traditional architecture and urbanism can contribute to the future of Gulf cities, being sustainable, smart, and providing

Figure 13.4. Land reclamation on the Manama northern coast, Bahrain. Photograph by Sarah F. Clarke.

numerous lessons on how to achieve harmony between people and their surrounding environment. In years gone by, traditional Arab and Gulf communities had a harmonious, even sacred relation with nature. Indeed, there are references in the Qur'an to this relationship. For example, a governing principle clearly stated in the Qur'an is for followers not to abuse nature or destroy the environment. Muslims are commanded: 'And do not cause disruption/corruption/mischief/chaos on earth after it has been so well ordered/organized' (Qur'an 7:56). In the Gulf, lives depended on this respect, understanding and sensitive interaction with natural surroundings.

Green and sustainable design today has its roots in traditional architecture. The world's vernacular building traditions show great variety and ingenuity (Oliver, Vellinga and Bridge 2008). The traditional Gulf cities of Jeddah, Doha, Dubai and Manama were people- and environment-friendly settlements. As Norman Foster commented on his first step in designing the Masdar Project (Ouroussoff 2010), asserting that the crucial point was to go back and understand the basics, how Gulf communities could create liveable environments where the air can feel as hot as 150°F.

The architectural and urban heritage of many Middle Eastern communities is smarter than that encountered in today's Gulf cities and urban settlements (Hakim 1986; Mortada 2003; Al Hathloul 2004). For example, formerly buildings were designed with wind towers and natural ventilation systems, windows were small and positioned carefully, walls were thick for natural insulation and the buildings were orientated to make best use of shade. External wooden panels (*mashrabih* in Arabic) with intricate geometric carving aided airflow without compromising the need for privacy. These wooden external curtains were cleverly used, especially in upper floors where women gather, to maintain their freedom while affording privacy. *Mashrabih* also reduced glare resulting from a very sunny desert environment by fragmenting light through its small geometrical parts, creating an interesting tapestry of light and shade. Today buildings are the reverse; villas typically have large windows, poor insulation (thin walls), exposed roofs, lack of shade and electric air conditioning units. Traditional architecture can be drawn on as a counter balance to current architectural practices in Gulf cities. As Besim Hakim (1986) suggests, the architecture of Muslim communities has creatively come up with many appropriate solutions throughout the ages. Indeed, Christopher Alexander (1979) notes that traditional architecture in different locations around the world is a direct expression of human needs, the availability of materials and local climate. It is an expression of a way of life and a culture and as such, for him, there is one timeless way of building, it is thousands of years old, and the same today as it always has been; it marries human needs with environmental appropriateness.

However, we do not argue that learning from history implies ignoring advances in science, communication and technology. On the contrary, historical solutions combined with technological advances can help Gulf cities became sustainable using a mix of appropriate solutions. Ed van Hinte and colleagues (2003) argues that contemporary sustainable architecture is smart in its design and implementation. It utilizes technology and science to create buildings that, for example, require a minimum amount of material and energy. While technology certainly has a role to play in improving the sustainability of Gulf states, care must be taken not to lock cities or areas within cities into a technology that may limit the ability to become more sustainable in the future as external circumstances change. Reinterpreting traditional built environments to advance sustainable architecture may present intellectual and creative challenges for architects and designers trying to match personal and corporate needs with demands for sustainability. By successfully marrying the aspirations of the Gulf people for all that is modern and new with a more sustainable way of life, hi-tech solutions and state of the art products can be seamlessly integrated into locally appropriate designs that respect the cultural heritage of the region, the social norms of the community and the harshness of the climate. This mirrors the approach of traditional communities the world over who have sustained themselves for centuries by matching social and cultural needs with environmental realities. Modern materials and techniques are used increasingly in buildings in the Middle East, although the results are often poor in quality and expensive and do not meld with cultural traditions. Traditional building techniques and processes have depended, by their nature, upon locally available materials that may be cheaper and more suited to the local climate and culture. The key is to balance old techniques and traditions with the smart technological solutions of today. In design terms, these are expressed in planning, urban design and architectural patterns as follows.

Traditional Architecture: Process and Patterns

Traditional architecture is based on a collective vision, often resulting in a harmonious and appropriate built environment (Rapoport 1969; Steele 1997). Architecture acquires a certain quality when construction features hand-crafted processes using traditional techniques. Architectural masterpieces across the globe have been built this way. The architect-builder-inhabitant was the 'Master Builder', on the site designing and building, deeply involved intellectually and emotionally. These masterpieces involving craftsmanship are more emotionally satisfying as the result of a unique process of design and building (Alexander 1977, 1979). They transcend time representing a smart relation between man, space and surrounding environment (Jacobson 2002).

The vernacular buildings that stand the test of time reflect an ability to design and build harmoniously with the environment. Wind towers, *badgir* or *malqaf* in Arabic, for instance, were used across the Arab world to provide ventilation to homes as well as passive cooling for food storage and water. Some wind towers were built in conjunction with underground water channels, *faggora* in Arabic, so increasing humidity and the cooling effect. A response to the local climate, wind towers spread from Iran to many cities in the Middle East. Yet, it is disappointing to see that this unique locally appropriate 'air-conditioning' solution is used today as an artificial adornment on buildings to somehow flavour them with traditional heritage sentimentalities. There are many examples of this superficial embellishment in Gulf cities, including Aldar villas in Bahrain (figure 13.5), Souq Waqif in Doha or Madienat Al Jumeriah in Dubai where wind towers feature as add-on decorative elements without any use value. In contrast, wind towers were reinvented in the research institute building at Masdar city to provide a state-of-the-art contemporary version of an old yet inspiring traditional solution. This is a crucial distinction since it calls for a shift from using traditional elements as decoration to revitalizing their use. Additionally, it invites architects, designers and engineers to see the value in smart and sustainable traditional solutions and use them as a springboard for contemporary solutions related to our time, technology and way of life.

In Gulf cities today it is not unusual to see large Bedouin-style tents (*khaima* in Arabic), constructed out of camel-hair panels adjacent or added on to modern villas. Used as a community room (*majalis* in Arabic) for meetings and celebrations, typically with the modern luxury of electric air-conditioning units, it is hard to imagine this traditional form of meeting place completely replaced by the white modern marques and more permanent fixtures used by some. Indeed, strong respect of long-held local traditions and values suggest that there will always be a need for meeting spaces of this type. Domes and vaulted roofs also feature heavily in traditional architecture, most obviously in mosques. These types of roofs increase shade and shadow on and around the built environment, creating different pressure zones to allow for increased air movement and providing another mechanism for improved air circulation in buildings. Today, with the advent of electric air conditioning, domes and vaulted

Figure 13.5. The use of wind towers as a decorative element in contemporary architecture in Bahrain. Photograph by Sarah F. Clarke.

roofs are incorporated into designs for decorative and aesthetic reasons, though they will help to keep the ambient temperature down.

We distinguish three main categories of design patterns in discussing the smartness and appropriateness of Middle Eastern and Gulf traditional architecture and urbanism. The influential work of Christopher Alexander inspires these patterns (Alexander 1977). Their recognition results from a comprehensive analysis of traditional buildings and settlements within the Gulf and Middle East (Alraouf 2005b, 2008b). The three categories are planning patterns, urban design patterns and architectural patterns. Planning patterns focus mainly on the morphology and overall structure of the conurbation. Urban design patterns concern how buildings and surrounding spaces relate to one another. Architectural patterns are responsible for creating liveable, harmonious and sustainable buildings. Table 13.2 gives examples of traditional Gulf architecture and urbanism that can be used to guide the advancement of a more appropriate and sustainable relationships-built environment, grouped as architecture, urban design and planning patterns.

Two recent projects in Gulf cities demonstrate the value of such patterns in creating more sustainable built environments. The first is the re-

Table 13.2. Sustainable patterns of traditional Gulf architecture and urbanism.

Planning Patterns	Architectural Patterns
1. *Settlement volume and location*: Compacted, organic form and close to water sources and green vegetation.	1. *Smart geometry*: Geometrical and organic buildings that reject rigidity and modularity of modern designs.
2. *Appropriate network of roads*: Emphasize walkability via shaded narrow pedestrian streets.	2. *Local customs* (urf) *in design and building construction*: Respecting local traditions and values.
3. *Pedestrian networks*: Fully integrated with settlement activities and main functions.	3. *Courtyard as a positive space*: The inner garden and heart of the building.
4. *Natural windbreak*: Native trees and bushes surrounding the settlement.	4. *Intimate/private spaces and places*.
5. *Settlement borders and barriers*: Use of sand as natural shield. Gated walls for privacy and defence.	5. *Accumulated architecture*: Organic growth as community changes. Complex building composition for better climate protection.
6. *Productive green fields* (bustan): A source of beauty and to produce fruits and vegetables for households.	6. *Green boundaries*: Green walls of local trees for building protection against harsh weather and sand storms.
7. *Water well location and accessibility*: Protection and wise use of natural resources.	7. *Domes and vaults*: Roofs that give maximum shade.

Urban Design Patterns	
1. *The Mosque*: Sacred order and geometry.	8. *Tents*: Light structures to cover walkways and open spaces.
2. *Oasis Centre*: Creating places for people typically around water source.	9. *Local materials*: Palm, stone, clay, sand.
3. *The market* (souq) *as a social and public space*: Enhancing people interaction.	8. *Wind towers* (badgir): Utilizing wind for natural ventilation.
4. *Community school* (madrasa): A knowledge centre for all community members.	10. *Limited external windows and openings*.
5. *The value of waterfront*: The unique relation between Gulf settlements and water.	11. *Breathing thick walls*: Externally and internally to protect inner spaces and allow natural ventilation.
6. *Integration of mosque, souq and public spaces*.	12. *Layers of building*: Green layer, walls and gates, external walls and wooden screens (*mashrabih*).
7. *Organic growth of architectural masses*: Building growth is based on needs and is organic and dynamic, rejecting rigid plans.	

habilitation of the traditional core of Muharraq city in Bahrain, which had suffered severe deterioration and decay due to years of neglect. The redevelopment of the area acknowledges the value of traditional patterns exhibited in the urban fabric and architecture. Yet, in the ongoing rehabilitation and transformation of old neglected houses into cultural centres, libraries, a traditional craft centre and other buildings meeting community needs, the project uses contemporary technologies, materials and design. A balance has been achieved between the value of the past and the significance of contemporary technologies in the development. By preserving the narrow winding alleyways and high walls that were a feature of the neighbourhood, developers were able to maintain the natural cooling effect of the passageways. Indeed, there is a significant fall in ambient air temperature as one strolls around the streets of this revitalized area compared to adjacent modern spaces, demonstrating the effectiveness of traditional urban design patterns. Moreover, visitors are surprised by the cooling effect of the natural ventilation systems still used in some of the restored buildings, an example of the architectural patterns highlighted in table 13.2.

The second example is Msheireb, the 'Heart of Doha', in downtown Doha, under construction at the time of writing. The main objective of this project is to bring people back to the heart of Doha, Qatar's largest city. In doing so, the consultant and developers have incorporated traditional patterns of Gulf architecture and urbanism and are creating a contemporary Qatari architectural and urban language in a scheme that innovatively balances modernity with traditionalism. Thus, the Msheireb project is finding and using the same principles suggested in table 13.2 to achieve continuity between the past, the present and the future. The developers emphasize their commitment to using timeless techniques inherited from the traditional built environment. For example, in relation to climate issues, an ultimate goal is to use old and new technologies to achieve maximum comfort with minimum energy use.[3]

The contemporary challenge for architects and urban planners is to design modern developments that advance on the patterns outlined in table 13.2 incorporating new materials and technologies, with a mind to features that enable social interaction and meet cultural needs. For instance, some projects in the Gulf have introduced wind towers, such as Masdar Institute of Technology, Princess Nora University and King Abdullah University of Science and Technology. The latter campus will incorporate a distinctive blend of traditional regional architecture with modern styles and amenities. Understanding how to manage the microclimate is the foundation of this integrated campus design to create comfortable spaces despite a harsh natural environment. According to the environmental consultants, wind towers are integrated in courtyards to ensure the walkability and liveability of the main spaces.[4] The vision of the design team is to have buildings that work better within their environment, by creating opportunities for natural ventilation, so reducing overall campus energy consumption and enhancing visual, acoustical and thermal comfort.

These examples demonstrate the shift towards green architecture and urbanism in the Gulf and the potential for traditional architecture to enhance the sustainability of design. Yet two issues remain open to scrutiny. First, is this design effort enough in Gulf cities that are experiencing some of the fastest rates of urbanization and development in the history of mankind? Second, how can we evaluate the integrity and credibility of such green and sustainable initiatives? We distinguish between a 'green rush' model that uses traditional elements as a marketing tool and an integrated approach that takes a holistic view blending traditional with modern to achieve more sustainable urban development.

Current Gulf Sustainable Initiatives: A Green Rush?

The oil-rich Gulf region has attracted inward investment from energy-intensive industries such as aluminium smelting and cement production. Another intensive use of energy is the desalination of seawater that Gulf states rely on for their water supplies in a desert region where water is scarce and the fast-growing populations are using up groundwater quickly.[5] Moreover, electricity demand has been growing at 8–9 per cent a year, faster than the growth recorded in any other region of the world, underlying the need for swift action to build cities that minimize electricity use.

This unsustainable use of energy has prompted the somewhat belated application of green design principles to developments, principles that are both fashionable and marketable. In the Gulf states, in the absence of tax breaks or legislation (see Al Othman and Clarke, chapter 5, this volume), few have considered the long-term performance of their buildings other than some internationally recognized developers and investors. However, there are some moves towards a sustainability policy. For example, in May 2008, the Abu Dhabi government launched an initiative called *Estidama* (meaning 'sustainability' in Arabic) which includes a green-building rating system. In addition, both Qatar and the UAE have established chapters of the Green Building Council to raise awareness and promote sustainability in the built environment. Opening in late 2011, the Qatar National Convention Centre (QNCC)[6] is the first convention and exhibition centre of its kind being built to the Gold Standard of LEED, the internationally recognized green-building rating system. And, in 2010, Qatar launched its Qatar Sustainability Assessment System requiring all major projects to undergo an environmental assessment process.[7]

While these initiatives are promising, development in Gulf states has a unique dimension that may constrain progress towards sustainability; governments and their investment arms in the region are responsible for, and engaged in, most of the development. In Qatar, as in other emerging GCC countries, the state partially finances and manages major development companies. As a result, the ability of international developers to embrace more sustainable practice will be constrained without the full commitment of the government at all levels to sustainability performance measures. For example, the mega–real estate companies Barwa, Qatari Diar and Msheireb Properties, all with large government stakes, are shaping Qatar's urban development. The immense size of these companies' projects means that they will have a dramatic impact on the future sustainability of the Qatari built environment – witness, for example, The Heart of Doha in downtown Doha as previously noted and Lusail City to the north of Doha's financial district, a new city for 80,000 residents and capacity for more than 120,000 employees and visitors. Some of these real estate companies use slogans to emphasize the sustainable nature of their new projects. For example, Msheireb bills itself as the world's first sustainable downtown regeneration project, which uses traditional Qatari architectural language and aims to achieve one of the highest concentrations of LEED certified buildings in the world.[8] It remains to be seen whether they achieve this aspiration.

In assessing the credibility of these efforts we need to consider their economic, ecological and equity dimensions in accordance with the sustainability vision, as defined at the Sustainable City Conference in Rio 2000. This definition declares that a sustainable conurbation functions to ensure a quality of life desired by the community, without restricting the options of future generations or causing adverse impacts within and beyond the urban area (Batte and McCarthy 2001). The full adoption of this as a vision for Qatar, for example, implies that the large migrant labour force currently residing in substandard living conditions must be part of the regeneration and renewal process with proper consideration in city designs.

Landownership norms in Qatar and other Gulf states may also constrain the move towards sustainability. The state, represented by the ruling families, is the sole authority that grants land either to citizens or foreign investors. With generous loans to help citizens build their own homes, they secure the loyalty of their people, maintaining political stability. Such stability, rare in the Middle East with its conflicts and struggles, is necessary to ensure continued investment in development projects. Sustainability is strongly related to stability, peace and democracy. However, societies living on generous governmental grants, which promote dependence and favour consumption, such as is the case of most Gulf states, may find it difficult to promote the radical changes in behaviour and attitudes demanded by the move to more sustainable cities. The reality is, of course, that the current sources of wealth are not endless and therefore, change is inevitable. Masdar city is one uniquely Gulf solution looking to the future but is it indeed sustainable?

Masdar: Sustainable City or Sustainable Bubble?

Masdar City, twenty miles from the centre of Abu Dhabi, is being promoted as a sustainable model of urbanism, one which, its supporters suggest, could be the model of Gulf cities for a post-carbon age. The virtual cornerstone of Masdar City – the world's first carbon-neutral, zero-waste, car-free city – was laid by Sheikh Mohammed bin Zayed Al Nahyan, Crown Prince of Abu Dhabi on 9 February 2008. It was a visually stunning production depicting life in the city, a 1,483-acre project that will include commercial and manufacturing space dedicated to developing eco-friendly products, a university, housing and the headquarters for the Future Energy Company that is spearheading the initiative: 'We are creating a city where residents and commuters will live the highest quality of life with the lowest environmental footprint.... Masdar City will become the world's hub for future energy. By taking sustainable development and living to a new level, it will lead the world in understanding how all future cities should be built' (Dr. Sultan Al Jaber, CEO Masdar, quoted in Masdar Institute 2008).

Although the desert might seem an unlikely location for such a sustainable undertaking, it affords Masdar year-round solar power. The city will feature construction that resists high temperatures with attention to shading and use of slab cooling. Its design is rooted, the design firm Foster and Partners claim, in the Arabic tradition of walled cities, with photovoltaic panels capable of generating 130 megawatts covering Masdar's external, mainly stone walls. Along the site's northern edge the walls will be more permeable to let in the breeze. Electricity will also come from photovoltaic cells integrated into rooftops and a 20-megawatt wind farm. The city's water will come from a solar-powered desalination plant. Shaded paths will make walking more bearable in the region's extreme heat. The wind and photovoltaic farms, as well as plantations to supply the city's biofuel factories, will be situated on surrounding land. The biofields will also help reduce waste by acting as carbon sinks to offset gases produced in the factories and they will be irrigated with grey water drawn from the city's water-treatment plant.

Masdar will be developed in phases centred on two plazas. The first phase includes construction of a 60-megawatt photovoltaic power plant that will supply electricity for constructing the rest of the city. This phase was partially completed in 2010. It includes Masdar Institute of Technology buildings which incorporate a modern interpretation of a wind tower. Masdar Institute was established on 25 February 2007 and in spring 2011 had 170 students from 32 countries. It is affiliated with the Massachusetts Institute of Technology (MIT) with 30 per cent of the student population housed on site. Its students will be encouraged to participate in the development of the city while working on graduate degrees in sustainability. The Masdar Institute is the world's first graduate-level institution dedicated to the study and research of advanced energy and sustainable technologies. The partnership with MIT includes assistance in the development of graduate degree programs and recruitment of faculty and senior-level administration, joint collaborative research and outreach that encourages industrial participation in research and development activities.[9]

Designers and project managers estimate that it will take ten years to build the entire city, with structures ultimately occupying nearly half of the site. When complete, Masdar will be home to 45,000 people and attract an additional 60,500 daily commuters, some of whom will arrive via a new rail line.

Foster and Partners have blended high-tech design and traditional regional architecture into an interesting model for a sustainable community, in a country where oil revenues allow it to build almost anything (witness the world's tallest tower in Dubai). The aim is to realize a vision, in which local tradition and the drive towards modernization are not in conflict: 'The environmental ambitions of the Masdar Initiative – zero carbon and waste free – are a world first. They have provided us with a challenging design brief that promises to question conventional urban wisdom at a fundamental level. Masdar promises to set new benchmarks for the sustainable city of the future' (Sir Norman Foster, quoted in Ouroussoff 2010).

More critically, Foster's design reflects the gated-community mentality that has been spreading around the globe and is becoming a feature of contemporary Gulf urbanism. What Masdar represents is this global phenomenon: the growing division of the world into refined, high-end enclaves and vast formless ghettos where issues like sustainability have little immediate relevance. It is the culmination of the trend towards suburban gated communities: a self-reliant society, lifted on a platform and outside the reach of most of the world's citizens, including those who live in nearby Emirates' cities. The futuristic city's utopian purity, and its isolation from the life of the older city next door, seems grounded in the belief that the only way to create a truly harmonious community, is to cut it off from the world at large (Ouroussoff 2010). If it maintains this sense of isolation how will it ever attain the richness and texture of a proper city? While Masdar is an attempt to create an alternative to the ugliness and inefficiency of the development responsible for demolishing the fabric of Middle Eastern cities for decades – the suburban villas slathered in superficial Islamic-style décor and gargantuan air-conditioned shopping malls – the result, Mr. Foster acknowledges, has a Disneyland feel: 'Disneyland is attractive because all the service is below ground, we do the same here – it is literally a walled city. Traditional cars are stopped at the edges' (ibid.: 2).

The credibility of this utopian vision of a Gulf city of the future is being evaluated by independent monitoring to monitor if the project lives up to its billing. Andrew Revkin (2008) points out that it is surprising that this sustainable urban initiative occurs not in some green hub such as Oregon, but in the Gulf, fuelled as much by the need to find a post-petroleum business model as environmental concern. He questions if Masdar as a car-free, solar city could set a new standard for green design because attempts at such green communities have had mixed results. For instance, Arcosanti, the ecotopian town in the Arizona desert started three decades ago, remains a work in progress, now being encroached on by Phoenix's suburban expansion. Similarly, China has embarked on building rural communities and cities designed to limit environmental impacts, with help from American partners, but recent reports disclose many problems (ibid.). Will Masdar end up a white elephant (or camel) in the desert?

Challenges for Sustainable Gulf Cities

As noted previously, there is limited environmental awareness in the Gulf where few citizens have yet confronted the challenges or consequences of the global environmental crisis. It is consequently difficult for Gulf governments to persuade people to integrate sustainable principles in their lives. Yet, these Gulf states share many challenges in common including scarce supplies of fresh water, land vegetation and few natural resources except oil and gas. Poverty is unknown except amongst the migrant work force and relatively small segments of the local population, with countries such as Qatar, Kuwait and the United Arab Emirates having some of the highest income per capita worldwide.

The Masdar city project and similar smaller-scale urban initiatives in the Gulf promulgate a rosy picture in promoting a sustainable future. However, some predict excess urban capacity such that in five- to ten-years' time planners and developers will not be able to utilize all provided spaces. Moreover, sustainability is not presented as a new way of life to be adopted by local Gulf communities. While Masdar's promoters emphasize a car-free environment, they fail to explain how they will achieve the required social and cultural changes. The UAE is currently home to some 2 million vehicles of which 1.3 million are passenger cars. Abu Dhabi has recorded the largest change with a 700 per cent increase in the number of vehicles over the last five years according to the UAE's roads and transportation authority.[10] In this region, citizens travel exclusively by car and its cities suffer considerable traffic chaos. Luxury sports cars, gas-guzzling sports utility vehicles and even tank-like Hummers all jostle for space on Gulf highways, their owners buoyed by record oil prices that are forcing some motorists in the West to ditch cars for bicycles.

Recent investments in public transportation in Dubai are another illustration of the cultural barrier to be overcome against public transportation. At the time of writing, Dubai has a two-line monorail system covering a great portion of the city's main destinations. Yet, passenger usage figures suggest that it is only used by some expatriates. In interviews conducted by the author (Alraouf 2008b), local people emphasized that the system was for expatriates and not for their use. Local people in Dubai, Bahrain and Qatar are united in their attachment to car usage. Qatar also is in the process of planning a combined underground, on-ground and above-ground rail network to support new developments and to cope with the 2022 World Cup traffic. Who will use it? The uptake of this system by the population will substantially affect the sustainable performance of Doha in the future.

An Alternative View of Gulf Urbanism: The Concept of Compacted Cities

Many problems characterize Gulf urbanism: sprawling and fragmented urban fabric, fragile public transportation, a car culture and centralized services. More critically, it promotes an unsustainable style of living, one which is energy intensive and where its citizens reside in large houses with high rates of water and electricity consumption. Contemporary Gulf cities are low-density car-dependent places. The more they grow horizontally at low density, the more citizens will rely on cars for transportation. Reducing carbon emissions is necessary to achieve sustainable urbanism and is a major sustainability challenge in the region. Qatar is the latest Middle Eastern country to begin to aggressively push towards reducing per capita CO_2 emissions and embrace a low-carbon economy. The country's need for new initiatives to reduce greenhouse gases gained global attention after a 2008 UNDP Human Development Report revealed Qatar's per capita CO_2 emissions to be the highest in the world at 79.3 tonnes per capita, well above the ninth-ranked United States (UNDP 2008).

In an attempt to explore new paths towards better, sustainable ways of urban living, Darko Radovic (2009) proposes a radical change in the way we conceive cities. His theory of eco-urbanity advocates the compact-city concept. A compact city is simply a high-density urban development. Its development strategy is to control the spread of urban suburbs into open lands. The scale of compact cities enhances the sustainability of urban living by allowing walking, cycling and efficient public transportation; it reduces journeys and improves quality of life (Jenks, Burton and Williams 1996: 297). Urban compactness also enhances and encourages social interactions. New developments should have a mix of uses. The concept of the compact city challenges the modern planning paradigm that promotes zoning and separate land uses. Zoning may be straightforward and economic under current conditions, but it isolates residents and enslaves them to the use of cars. As Richard Rogers (1998) argues, mixed-use centres of development are more appropriate to an environmentally conscious planning process and he points out the importance of public space within sustainable city centres. Public spaces should include gardens and allocated spaces for children and families to respect Gulf traditions of privacy.

Historic examples of compact European and Middle Eastern cities have attracted the attention of planners and architects. They represent a model of high-density settlement where sustainable principles are evident. Cities such as Florence, Bath and Fez are examples of successful compact cities. We argue that the compact-city model offers an effective route to a more sustainable future for Gulf cities, particularly if it also incorporates elements of traditional Gulf architecture, community planning and cultural sensibilities, together with contemporary urban technology to improve living in harsh desert environments.

From Sprawl to Compact to Low-Carbon Gulf City: Towards an Implementation

Our re-envisioned compact city model also offers a route to a low-carbon Gulf city. The main intention of suggesting the compact model as a more relevant planning concept for contemporary Gulf cities stems from a commitment towards reducing negative environmental impacts and to promote a more liveable and enjoyable human-friendly environment. A holistic approach to a low-carbon Gulf city considers three levels of design and planning. First, the building level, which should incorporate all principles of sustainable architecture, green design and environmental planning. Second, at the urban district level investment should be geared towards low-carbon infrastructure; walkable districts are a prime concern at this level. Third, the city- and urban-planning level needs to move from a sprawling to a multipolar city model that features several local self-sufficient centres linked together by an efficient public transportation system.

Qatar's new master plan (Elshabani and Reiter 2007) is based on the concept of multicentres and hubs of development linked by rail and road networks, and seeks to restrain the sprawling horizontal expansion of the country's cities. The issue of transportation, noted above, presents a fundamental challenge. Qatari citizens would consider using public transport as a socially degrading and unwanted equality. Still, a comprehensive public transport network in Qatar and between Gulf cities, fully utilized by the large expatriate and migrant work force, would at least alleviate some of the problems on the roads and reduce carbon emissions. Car sharing, car clubs and company or school travel plans may help if they can be made to be attractive in the region. Add to this the people-friendly infrastructure that this approach requires and the path to a sustainable city is clearer. It would include, for example, comfortable pedestrian-priority zones, pavements and public spaces with walking and cycling routes, which are currently rare or non-existent in Gulf cities. The quality and performance of infrastructure is as important as the individual buildings that it serves.

A well-designed, sustainable Gulf city will provide a better quality of life for all, being a healthier, less-polluted and quieter place to live and work in. Streets should be designed as vents to help counteract the 'urban heat-island' effect. This requires large tree canopies to provide shade and cool streets and buildings in summer. In the Gulf where water is scarce, this necessitates using recycled grey water, including runoff from window and vehicle washing. Rooftop gardens will also be a feature of a sustainable city, situated on both public and private buildings; the former may be an extension of public spaces.

These are the conditions that will help contemporary cities transform themselves into knowledge and creative cities (Florida 2002; Florida, Franke and Verhagen 2006; Landry 2006). They will attract a greater range of creative people to live and work. Such an environment makes a city an attractive place for businesses to relocate and invest in. Creating markets and opportunities for low-carbon businesses and new green technologies will make cities more future competitive.

In their pursuit of a sustainable future, Gulf cities need to make better use of existing resources. This includes waste, water and energy. A city should also aim to be inclusive, its identity reflected in its buildings and spaces and their uses – a place accessible to all regardless of ability and which embraces different cultures. Gulf cities need to be designed and developed with respect for religious, ethnic, national, gender and wealth differences built to accommodate this human mosaic, celebrating and fostering diversity.

Sustainability is also about the rejection of the consumption culture and a move towards a balanced attitude towards every aspect of life (Jayne 2006). In Gulf cities, shopping malls are the new *souqs* – traditional Arab markets – where people enjoy endless opportunities for consumption in air-conditioned environments. A low-carbon Gulf city promotes more local, independent shopping outlets negating the need to drive to such malls as currently. Without a socio-cultural revolution bringing such radical changes, achieving true sustainability will be a mere fantasy in Gulf states. The current sustainability models adopted in Gulf cities give too little attention to social dynamics. The increasing gap between the over-represented and dominant corporate sector and the under-represented and subordinate working classes that make up a large part of today's Gulf megalopolises make these particularly complex. It is necessary to consider the unique demographic structure of the Gulf, where expatriates comprise an average of more than 50 per cent of the population and 80 per cent of the work force consists of single men. The population of the Middle East and North Africa region exceeded 432 million people in 2007, half of them less than twenty-four years of age, which is the youngest population of any region in the world (UNDP 2009a). The region also has the second highest urbanization rate and an annual urban growth rate – second only to Sub-Saharan Africa – at 4 per cent in the past two decades (ibid.). It is vital to include youth in urban plans and tap its potential. There is a need to identify mechanisms to engage these under-represented segments of society at the earliest stage in urban development and renewal projects if cities are to achieve a holistic interpretation of sustainability.

Conclusion

Gulf cities have witnessed an unprecedented pace of development during the last decade. It features sprawling urbanism, wasteful use of natural resources including fresh water, loss of vegetation and lack of awareness of sustainability issues. The concept of the compact low-carbon city was introduced in this chapter as an appropriate approach to counter this reality. Contemporary Gulf cities need to attain sustainability to cope with the eventual depletion of their carbon resources or replacement by clean sources. Undoubtedly, a post-carbon paradigm has to inform the future of Gulf cities. But more than this, architects, planners and users need to be educated about the value of traditional architecture in contributing to appropriate solutions to the problems facing contemporary Middle Eastern cities. Architecture in the Gulf, as elsewhere, should creatively reflect and maintain local culture as a way of counteracting the 'look-alike' mentality that permeates the region. Smart architecture does not reject technology. On the contrary, it is an invitation for architects and designers to draw on different technologies, not only high-tech ones. As we have shown in this chapter, the vernacular and traditional architecture and urbanism of Arab and Gulf communities has an important role to play in contemporary design and may provide a route to more sustainable Gulf cities, allowing iconic development and real estate fantasies to be replaced by a more sustainable vision. For sure, architecture and urbanism should do more with less. We need to teach ourselves and the next generation to look to the long term, remembering that sustainability and environmental justice are intergenerational as well as international issues. There is a danger that developments such as Masdar City will become isolated oases of sustainability linked to highly unsustainable locales of architectural and consumer excess. The success of sustainable architecture lies in its ability to bridge the gaps between these havens, marrying local necessity with global needs.

Notes

1. For more information refer to http://www.qf.org.qa.
2. Refer to Qatar Statistics Authority, http://www.qsa.gov.qa.
3. Interviews and private correspondence between Alraouf and Tim Makower, Partner, Allies and Morrison Architects, Lead Architect for Msheireb during 2010 and 2011.
4. http://www.rwdi.com.
5. It is estimated that 75 per cent of global desalination took place in the Middle East in 2010 (http://www.worldenergyoutlook.org).
6. http://qatarnationalconventioncentre.com.
7. Refer to http://www.qsas.org.
8. http://projects.msheireb.com/.
9. Refer to http://web.mit.edu/newsoffice/2009/mitei-masdar-0119.html.
10. http://www.rta.ae.

References

Alexander, C. 1977. *A Pattern Language*. New York: Oxford University Press.
———. 1979. *The Timeless Way of Building*. New York: Oxford University Press.
Al Hathloul, S. 2004. 'Planning in the Middle East, Moving Toward the Future.' *Habitat International* 18 (5): 641–643.
Alraouf, A. 2005a. 'Knowledge Cities: Examining the Discourse: Smart Villages, Internet Cities or Creativity Engines.' Proceedings of the International Symposium on Knowledge Cities, The World Bank and Arab Urban Development Institute. Medina, Saudi Arabia, 28–30 November.
———. 2005b. 'The Origins of Smart Architecture: Reinterpreting Traditional Intelligent Buildings and Spaces.' Intelligent Building – Middle East 2005. International Conference for Buildings Concepts, Materials and Technologies, Manama, Kingdom of Bahrain, 5–7 December.
———. 2006. 'Dubaization vs. Glocalization: Territorial Outlook of Arab/Gulf Cities Transformed.' The 9th Sharjah Urban Planning Symposium, Sharjah, United Arab Emirates, 2–4 April.
———. 2008a. 'The Dilemma of Sustainable architecture in Gulf Cities.Unsustainable Developments and Energy Conservation.' International Conference on Energy Conservation, Kingdom of Bahrain, 16–18 June.
———. 2008b. 'Middle Eastern Knowledge Cities: The Unfolding Story.' In *Knowledge Based Urban Development: Planning and Application in the Information Era*, eds. T. Yigitcaular and V. Koray, 240–259. Hershey, PA: IGI Global Publishing, USA.
Batte, G., and C. McCarthy. 2001. *Sustainable Ecosystem and Built Environment*. London: Wiley Academy.
Beatley, T. 1995. 'The Many Meanings of Sustainability.' *Journal of Planning Literature* 9 (4): 339–342.
Bell, S., and S. Morse. 2008. *Sustainability Indicators*. London: Earthscan.
Bahrain World Trade Center (BWTC). 2008. 'Bahrain World Trade Center Implements Large Scale Recycling Initiative.' Press Release Manama, 28 August. www.bahrainwtc.com (accessed 20 March 2011).
Carrillo, F. J. 2005. *Knowledge Cities: Approaches, Experiences, and Perspectives*. Oxford: Butterworth-Heinemann.
Chen, D., and C. Dahlman. 2005. *The Knowledge Economy, the KAM Methodology and World Bank Operations*. Washington, DC: The World Bank Press.
Department of Trade and Industry (DTI). 2005. *UK Energy in Brief*. London: Department of Trade and Industry, Energy Publications.
Eger, J. 2000. 'Cities: Smart Growth and the Urban Future.' *The San Diego Union Tribune*, 13 February. http://www.smartcommunities.org/pdf/smart/SmartGrowth.pdf.
Elshabani, A., and U. Reiter. 2007. 'The Transport Master Plan for Qatar.' http://cgi.ptv.de (accesed 20 September 2011).
Florida, R. 2002. *The Rise of Creative Class*. New York: Basic Books.
———. 2004. *Cities and the Creative Class*. London: Routledge.
Florida, R., S. Franke and E. Verhagen. 2006. *Creativity and the City: How the Creative Economy is Changing the City*. Rotterdam, NL: NAI Publishers.

Foster, J. 2008. *The Sustainability Mirage.* London: Earthscan.

Hakim, B. S. 1986. *Arabic-Islamic Cities: Building and Planning Principles.* London and New York: Kegan Paul International.

Handy, C. 1995. *The Age of Paradox.* Boston: Harvard Business School Press.

Hinte, van E. et al. 2003. *Smart Architecture.* Rotterdam: 010 Publishers.

Jacobson, M. 2002. *Patterns of Home.* Newtown, CT: The Taunton Press, Inc.

Jayne, M. 2006. *Cities and Consumption.* London: Routledge.

Jenks, M., E. Burton and K. Williams (eds.). 1996. *Compact City Series: The Compact City: A Sustainable Urban Form?* London: Routledge.

Landry, C. 2000. *The Creative City: A Toolkit for Urban Innovators.* London: Earthscan Publications Ltd.

———. 2006. *The Art of City Making.* London: Earthscan Publications Ltd.

Laszlo, C. 2008. *Sustainable Value.* California: Stanford University Press.

Layard, A., Davoudi, S. and S. Batty (eds.). 2001. *Planning for a Sustainable Future.* London: Routledge.

Masdar Institute. 2008. 'Ground Breaking Marks Start of Masdar City.' Press release, 10 February. www.masdar.ac.ae (accessed 17 October 2010).

Moore, S. A. (ed.). 2010. *Pragmatic Sustainability: Theoretical and Practical Tools.* London: Routledge.

Mortada, H. 2003. *Traditional Islamic Principles of Built Environment.* London: Routledge Curzon.

Okechukwu, U. (ed.). 2010. *Sustainable Development.* New York: CRC Press.

Oliver, P., M. Vellinga and A. Bridge. 2008. *Atlas of Vernacular Architecture of the World.* London: Routledge.

Ouroussoff, N. 2010. 'Arabian Desert, a Sustainable City Rises.' http://www.nytimes.com/2010/09/26/arts/design/26masdar.html (accessed 23 November 2010).

Parr, A. and M. Zaretsky. 2010. *New Directions in Sustainable Design.* London: Routledge.

Pearson, D. 1989. *The Natural House Book.* New York: Simon & Schuster.

Radovic, D. (ed.). 2009. *Eco-Urbanity: Towards Well-Mannered Built Environments.* London: Routledge.

Rapoport, A. 1969. *House Form and Culture.* London: Prentice-Hall.

Revkin, A. C. 2008. 'Car-Free, Solar City in Gulf Could Set a New Standard for Green Design,' *New York Times,* 5 February. http://www.nytimes.com/2008/02/05/science/earth/05city.html (accesseded 4 May 2010).

Rogers, R. 1998. *Cities for a Small Planet.* Boulder, CO: Westview Press.

Steele, J. 1997. *Sustainable Architecture: Principles, Paradigms, and Case Studies.* New York: McGraw-Hill.

United Nations Development Programme (UNDP). 2008. *Human Development Report 2007/8: Fighting Climate Change: Human Solidarity in a Divided World.* New York.

———. 2009a. *Human Development Report: Overcoming Barriers: Human Mobility and Development.* New York.

———. 2009b. *Arab Human Development Report: Challenges to Human Security in the Arab Countries.* New York.

————. 2010a. *The Path to Achieving the Millennium Development Goals: A Synthesis of Evidence from Around the World.* New York.

————. 2010b. *Human Development Report, 20th Anniversary Edition: The Real Wealth of Nations: Pathways to Human Development.* New York.

UN-Habitat. 2009. *Planning Sustainable Cities: Global Report on Human Settlements.* New York: United Nations.

World Bank. 2010. *Energy Efficient Cities Initiative Report.* New York: World Bank Energy Sector Management Assistance Program. http://www.esmap.org/esmap/sites/esmap.org/files/FINAL_EECI_broREV3b.pdf (accessed 13 August 2011).

CHAPTER 14

How the City Grows

Urban Growth and Challenges to Sustainable Development in Doha, Qatar

Andrew M. Gardner

In the short historical trajectory of sustainable development, attention to the idea of urban sustainability has been a particularly late addition. Cities, as industrial nodes and as spaces of dense human habitation, have long been portrayed as antithetical to sustainability. This longstanding rural bias has a sensible legacy, for among their many qualities, cities are locations where the detritus of our human existence congeals and, perhaps more to the point, where the scale of that detritus becomes most visible. And although sustainable development is a relatively new paradigmatic force, the notion that cities are somehow inappropriate or problematic venues for human habitation has a much longer and storied history in both European and Middle Eastern traditions. In the latter tradition, Ibn Khaldun portrayed the city as a culturally refined but morally corruptive space.[1] Centuries later, these same conceptions of the city percolated through European and American thought, and eventually came to serve as the backdrop to substantial portions of classic Western social theory, perhaps most clearly distilled in the Jeffersonian fetishization of the agricultural livelihood (and a corresponding mistrust of the city and its denizens). These conceptions of the city persevere, and today it is more common than ever to find the romanticized portrait of pre-civilized and decidedly non-urban human functioning as a conceptual antidote to the excesses of our contemporary, capitalist and highly urban world. In North America, these perceptions cling to the Native Americans and First Nations of that continent; in Arabia, the same notions adhere to the Bedouin pastoral nomads who traditionally populated the interior of the Peninsula.

The new focus on urban sustainability rejects this history. Certainly the notion that pre-capitalist and non-urban humans lived lives 'in balance' with nature has been challenged by a constellation of scholars who together purvey a more supportable contention that in the history of humankind, *some* people seem to have found *some* sort of balance with their natural environment in *some* places for *some* period of time (e.g. Lansing 1991; Diamond 2005; Smith and Wishnie 2000; Hames 2007). Presently, however, other factors are also driving the increased attention to urban sustainability. First, there is the stark reality of the previous decade – one in which we passed from a primarily rural species to a primarily urban one. More than half of the human population now dwells in cities, and we face a future that looks ever more urban. The task of collectively creating a more sustainable future must necessarily contend with the primary location of our species' habitation. Second, a coterie of scholars have pointed to the inherent efficiencies of urban life (Owen 2009; Light 2001, 2003; see also Keil 2005). In cities, human habitation is dense. People live in close quarters, often stacked upon one another in apartment buildings and other densely efficient dwellings. They live close to commercial centres and to the services they require, and can often access those centres and services by mass transit or on foot. Urban populations in developed nations generally require less per capita infrastructure, and specifically less of the expensive infrastructure that must (ideally) bring water, electricity, gas and asphalt to the domicile, as well as the infrastructure that must (again, ideally) carry away waste. As these scholars argue, proximity and density make the city inherently efficient, and their calculations suggest that the urbanite's ecological footprint is typically smaller by several degrees of magnitude than her suburban or rural counterpart. In other words, within the domain of developed countries, persuasive arguments have been made that cities are, by design, inherently *more* sustainable than many other forms of human habitation.

Sustainable Development and the City

Another facet of urban sustainability, and one perhaps less clearly articulated in the literature, is that cities are increasingly prominent actors in the vanguard of the sustainability movement. When it comes to developing, declaring, and deploying sustainable goals, cities themselves serve as important units of collective action. Perth, Australia; Portland, Oregon; Vancouver, British Columbia, and countless other cities today function as key stakeholders in the collective enacting of sustainable goals (Newman and Jennings 2008). One can envision a variety of different reasons at work here. Even the largest cities are able to develop cohesive identities capable of articulating sustainability initiatives. Cities also provide an integrated political unit in which citizen groups – that is, neighbourhood groups and other voluntary organizations that operate on a local level – can feasibly assert their interests, in contrast to federal systems in which the voices of these groups are lost in the scale and scope of national-level politics. Cities are a principal apex for those energies that gather strength at the grass-roots level, and they comprise a much more manageable target for change than national or global systems. Perhaps cities also replicate the context described by Raymond Firth in his ethnographic work with the Tikopians. By his analysis, the small island presented a cohesive and limited resource domain to the island's denizens. Every adult was aware of the limitations presented by his or her environment, and with no accessible frontier past which more resources might be discovered or, perhaps more to the point, past which more resources might be imagined, the Tikopians eventually established a notably sustainable pattern of human/environmental inter-action. Contemporary cities, of course, are quite different from isolated Pacific islands; indeed, cities are central nodes in the global production, circulation and consumption of commodities and the resources those commodities draw upon. But cities do provide their inhabitants with a bounded unit with which to think – a demarcated social and geographi-cal space to which collective and potentially sustainable aspirations can be affixed. Cities' successes in articulating and implementing sustainable goals have further distanced urban space from its traditional position as the antithesis of sustainability movements.

The increasing prominence of the city in the sustainable development discourse, however, does not correlate with the distillation or progres-sive coherence in that concept's meaning. To the contrary, the concept of sustainable development is broadly used in the contemporary world, and over the course of its expanding currency it has come to mean many different things to many different people. A review of sustainable devel-opment's many meanings and the tectonic frictions underlying its ongo-ing florescence is beyond the scope of this chapter, and has been well described by others (e.g. Adams 2001; Baker 2006).[2] This chapter, however, asserts a classic and critical definition of sustainable development that, in the contemporary era, might also be posited as a radical perspective: sustainability and sustainable development are far-reaching concepts that require fundamental changes in our relationship to the environment, in the structure of our social relations, and in the ideas and values we hold dear. I suggest this definition of sustainable development as radical be-cause of the scope of change it requires. Like other scholars, I see many of the capitalist imperatives of the contemporary world forging societies that aspire to constant and competitive growth, a feature that is by defi-nition antithetical to sustainability (e.g. Broswimmer 2002). At the same time, I contend that this take on sustainable development is also a classic one, in the sense that our ability to ensure future generations can meet their needs – a feature fundamental to many enduring definitions of the concept – remains a fine metric by which we can measure our progress (if any) towards this goal (see Baker 2006 for a similar argument). This also suggests that the appropriate goal for our collective aspirations should be sustainability, rather than sustainable development, particularly for those wealthy countries and populations that already fit the description of 'developed'.

This brief sketch of a radical (yet classical!) take on sustainable development merits more attention and analytic support, but as noted, those arguments have been made elsewhere at great length (e.g. Adams 2001; Baker 2006). With the above definition of sustainability and its relation to the urban form in place, this chapter considers the potential challenges of implementing a meaningful and substantive version of sustainability in the wealthy and highly urban state of Qatar and, by proxy, the neighbouring GCC states. Qatar has explicitly expressed a commitment to sustainable development, and has integrated sustainability-oriented frameworks into both its national vision and the urban master plan for Doha, the single urban agglomeration on the small peninsula.[3] While this public and state-driven adoption of sustainable development can be read as a sign of sustainable development's growing significance, many would agree that Doha and the other astonishing cities of the Arabian Peninsula would probably look no different today if the goal of sustainable development had been rejected or altogether ignored rather than adopted.[4]

The purpose of this chapter, then, will be to consider the potential challenges of implementing a meaningful, substantive and radically transformative version of sustainability in Doha and, by association, in the other wealthy and highly urban states of the Arabian Peninsula. After a brief overview of city and society in Qatar, I will frame the remainder of the article around three dilemmas I see as central obstacles to the successful deployment of a meaningful sustainability in this city.

Khaleeji Society and the Cities of the Arabian Peninsula

With some justification, the six Gulf states of the Arabian Peninsula are often treated as a single socio-political and cultural unit. This affiliation is perhaps best represented by the term *al khaleej*, an Arabic term used to refer to the six Gulf states (Kuwait, Saudi Arabia, Bahrain, Qatar, the United Arab Emirates and Oman) in their entirety, with connotations of the social and cultural homogeneity resulting from the strong commonalities in the history of these states' development. The roots of this affiliation stretch deep into history. In environmental terms, all of the Arabian Peninsula is an arid desert with extraordinarily sparse resources. Two principal and symbiotically intertwined livelihoods historically predominated in the region. A town-based society comprised of settled and largely urban peoples (in Arabic, *hadhari*) was built upon the foundation of trade. This trade included both maritime commerce and caravan-based trade to the peninsula's interior. In some parts of Arabia, limited agricultural production also occurred (particularly in Oman, parts of Saudi Arabia and Bahrain). Along the coastal regions of the Persian Gulf, these town-based peoples also took to the sea, and prospered from pearl production, fishing, piracy and trade, thereby forging a significant merchant class.[5] The livelihoods of the urban peoples enmeshed in these activities were historically intertwined with the second predominant livelihood, practiced by Bedouin pastoral nomads (in Arabic, *badawi*) who made use of the vast spaces between these villages and towns. While the division between *badawi* and *hadhari* was wrought long ago, and while these categories have historically demonstrated more flexibility than this superficial description would suggest, the bifurcation between settled peoples and nomadic pastoral peoples has been held in place for centuries by the genealogical logic of tribalism. This tribalism has been reaffirmed through the political organization of the contemporary Gulf state (and particularly so in Qatar).

To some degree, all six of the Gulf states historically shared a position on the margins of the British Empire. British relations with the region were administered via British India, although Arabia played an insubstantial role in the Empire for much of the eighteenth and nineteenth centuries. Perhaps the most important commonality in these six states' histories is the discovery of oil. All six of the Gulf states possess (or once possessed) significant petroleum resources; states and economies were constructed around the wealth generated by this resource. Today, Qatar and its neighbours are often described as rentier states. In practice, significant portions of oil profits are diverted to a vast social welfare apparatus. Paramount to these transfers and to the organization of these states is the public sector: immense portions of the contemporary GCC economies are operated through the public or quasi-public sector. Citizens in Qatar and the other Gulf states today expect public sector jobs, and the state is constructed around the twin role of disbursing state-held wealth (its traditional twentieth-century role) and guiding the states' diversification plans away from petroleum dependency. While citizens of Qatar and the other Gulf States enjoy limited political participation via municipal elections and consultative bodies, all the Gulf states are controlled by hereditary extended families (or tribes) – the Al Thani clan in Qatar, the Al Khalifa clan in Bahrain and so forth. In analytic terms, the welfare state and limited political participation common to all the Gulf states have been conceptually linked: scholars suggest that citizens have begrudgingly yielded their political rights in exchange for the astonishing benefits of welfare systems that convey wealth from state to citizen (Luciani 1987; Beblawi 1987; Kamrava 2009; see also Dresch 2006: 201). In public discourse, the leading families of Qatar and the other Gulf states conceptualize their role as cosmopolitan stewards of states whose principal task is to guide the more traditional and conservative components of the respective citizenries to modernity.

Qatar and the neighbouring Gulf states are, per capita, among the wealthiest states in the world. Citizens typically receive (and expect) subsidized or free utilities, land, education, medical care, no-interest loans and, often, public sector jobs. Most Qataris, for example, dwell in extremely large freestanding 'villas', employ a small to large staff of domestic servants, and drive new or relatively new cars. Oftentimes that car is a Toyota Landcruiser, a model that seems to function as a marker of citizenship in contemporary Qatar. It is not unusual to encounter families with six, eight or ten cars. While the wealth of Qatar and the other Gulf States can be perceived at the level of the individual citizen, much of the state-controlled wealth has been ploughed into development plans, and much of that development is urban in nature. Museums, heritage centres, sports arenas, skyscrapers, offshore islands, amusement parks, conference centres, national mosques, residential developments and many other components of urban development are directly or indirectly funded with the wealth generated by oil rents. Indeed, the pace of this urban development long ago surpassed the domestic labour supply. Today in Qatar, well over 1 million of the 1.6 million inhabitants of the small country are foreign residents, and the largest portion of that foreign population is made up of construction workers (typically from South Asia). Despite some of the highest natural growth rates in the developed world, in Qatar and several of the other wealthy GCC states citizens comprise an increasingly small portion of the overall population: the scale of transnational labour migration, driven largely by urban development, continues to outpace natural growth.

Thus, urban development is a central feature of the contemporary Gulf. Indeed, as Sharon Nagy (2000: 128) has noted, 'The public has come to accept, and expect, government action in the realm of development and maintenance of the built environment.' In most of the Gulf states, rural populations have migrated to the city, producing one of the most urbanized collection of states in the world. In Kuwait, Qatar, Bahrain, Oman and the Emirates, the large primate cities are also defined by their function as political capitals. As I have argued elsewhere, the astonishing urban projects that rise in the Gulf also serve a symbolic function: Gulf cities are the trophy cases of a people and its leadership, and are directly intended to convey a particular message about the arrival of modernity in the region to a global audience (Gardner 2008, 2009). Sustainable development has emerged as an important discursive element in this urban development. Although the mission of constructing a more sustainable urban future is often tied to plans for the respective states' diversification away from oil dependency, the Gulf states also recognize sustainable development as an emergent and symbolically important attribute of the cosmopolitan modernity purveyed by other wealthy, urban and developed nations in the world.

With that brief background in mind, I now turn to three fundamental and intertwined challenges to the implementation of a meaningful form of sustainable development in the region.

Sustainable Development as a Threat to Political Stability in the Gulf States

In the petroleum-rich state of Qatar, the unparalleled pace of urban development has become more than a fact of life for the inhabitants of the city. Indeed, the pace itself has become emblematic of the city-state's global identity; urban development has taken on a fetishistic quality that pits Qatar against the neighbouring Gulf states in a competition for superlative standing. In this competition, Formula One racetracks, large human-made islands, stadiums capable of hosting global sports tournaments, extraordinary skyscrapers, satellite campuses of American universities and a variety of other mega-features of the urban landscape function as the symbolic capital by which these states assert their position in the vanguard of a cosmopolitan rendition of modernity (see Nagy 2000 for an insightful analysis). This conversation with the rest of the world has a second purpose, for in asserting their modernity through urban construction, the Gulf states simultaneously forge unified nationalisms over the complex allegiances and heterogeneous traditions of their citizenries. Like the Statue of Liberty or the Eiffel Tower, the supermodern components of the Gulf city seek to symbolically construct a homogenous idea of nation, and thereby elide the differences characteristic of Gulf populations – the differences between *hadhari* and *badawi*, between Shi'a and Sunni or between citizens of Arab descent and those of Persian descent (see Nagy 2006; Longva 2006). As this line of reasoning suggests, these cities and their dramatic expansion can be best understood in symbolic terms.

More practically, however, the supermodern components of these urban landscapes are also portrayed as the infrastructure for an economically diverse future. Tourism and the ongoing development of 'knowledge-based economies' to which many of these urban development projects are tied are central features of Qatar and its neighbouring states' plans to wean their economies from petroleum dependency. Around the Gulf, similar diversification plans are largely intended to recapture capital that, for the time being, flows away from the Gulf states. A representative example of this sort of urban development project is 'The Pearl', a massive residential and commercial development constructed on a human-made island off the coast of Qatar. As a freeholder zone in a state that allows only Qatari citizens to own property, the residential development seeks to capture rent and investment monies that, in the past, have been channelled by foreign residents working in Qatar to other locations around the globe. In this sense, the astonishing urban commercial/residential developments characteristic of the region are, as a whole, portrayed as a form of sustainable development, in that they seek to shift economies from their obviously unsustainable dependence on petroleum resources to a potentially more sustainable and diversified economic foundation for the post-petroleum era.[6]

Yet while urban development, and particularly the trophy architecture of contemporary Doha, Dubai and the neighbouring cities occupies the spotlight, the political economy that drives this urban development is decidedly offstage. Moreover, the product of urban development includes much more than those architectural constructions whose symbolic resonance achieves global currency. Surrounding the tall buildings, museums and new universities is a sprawling sea of more mundane construction perhaps best typified by the housing compound and the apartment building. In all the Gulf states, the skilled foreign class needed to build, staff and maintain these supermodern cities is most typically housed in one of these two residential forms, as opposed to the free-standing homes (or 'villas') preferred by many *khaleeji* citizens, and the labour camps that house many of the unskilled transnational migrant workers.[7] Apartment buildings, I will assume, are familiar to readers. Compounds, while certainly not unique to the Gulf, are perhaps unique in their ubiquity in the region. Compounds in the Gulf states are characterized by the tall walls that surround them and a single entrance with a staffed security gate. Compounds may include villas (large single-family homes), apartments and often a combination of the two. Many compounds contain central recreation facilities, a small store and other services. Combined with the proliferating apartment buildings springing up in many of the Gulf cities, these compounds serve the burgeoning transnational middle class at work in the region, and while they pale in the shadows of the symbolically laden super-constructions that garner global attention, understanding the political economy of their proliferation will lay bare the essence of my argument: a confluence of forces at work in the Gulf states has produced a spatially hungry system that directly challenges initiatives for sustainable development.

As this contention suggests, I wish to add a third facet to our understanding of the astonishing urban development characteristic of the region. In addition to its purported economic function of capturing global flows of capital, and in addition to building the idea of nation over the heterogeneous social reality of the Gulf states, the process of urban development has become a central conduit for the transfer of wealth from state to citizen, and hence key to the political legitimacy of the extended families that politically (and economically) control each of the Gulf states. A parallel argument has already been established in academic literature concerning the public sector in the Gulf states. In Qatar and all the Gulf states, public sector employment functions as a primary conduit for the transfer of state-controlled petroleum wealth to its citizen-constituents. In all of the Gulf states, foreign workers and entrepreneurs are the foundation and majority of the private sector. Citizens, meanwhile, are almost entirely employed directly by the state in public sector jobs. In Qatar, over 95 per cent of the citizen-workforce is employed in the public sector: they work directly for the ministries comprising the state, for the public utilities that serve both migrants and citizens, in the police force and national guard and in many other capacities.[8] A variety of reasons have been cited for the citizenry's preference for work in the public sector. These reasons include high pay and benefits of these state-provided jobs; the often gender-segregated offices that fit the cultural norms of the region (and thereby foster women's entry into the job market); the predominance of Arabic in these workplaces (as opposed to English in much of the private sector); and the timings of work in the public sector (typically, 7:00 AM to 1:00 PM). In my own previous work, I have focused on the underlying logic of the public sector, and argued that over the previous decades this sector of the labour market provided a differentiable system where qualities uniquely possessed by citizens – familial and tribal networks, and *wasta* (an Arabic term that is roughly equivalent to social capital) – could be used to secure employment in the public sector, thereby insulating citizens from the competitive meritocratic logic of a private sector in which many are poorly positioned to compete (Gardner 2010). Perhaps more to the point, however, social scientists have suggested that these public sector jobs function as the primary channel for the transfer of wealth from state to citizen, and thereby comprise the keystone in the legitimacy of the Gulf states' leadership (e.g. Willoughby 2008). Indeed, employment is conceived as an integral part of the constellation of entitlements citizens expect from the state.

In the context of a state dependent on extraordinarily large flows of foreign labour (in Qatar, for example, there are more than eight foreigners for every citizen), real estate functions as a second vital conduit for the transfer of petroleum wealth from state to citizen (see Dresch 2006: 202; also Gardner 2009). With the exception of a few special economic zones and freeholder developments scattered around the region, only citizens can own property in the Gulf states.[9] In Doha, property ownership functions as the foundation of a scenario typical throughout the Gulf: the Qatari state, in conjunction with a constellation of transnational energy corporations, directly controls the wealth resulting from the sale of the state's petroleum reserves. In addition to controlling this wealth, the state assumes the responsibility of guiding the nation's infrastructural, economic and social development. In one of its various capacities – through ministries, universities, hospitals or quasi-statal industries – the state hires foreigners to come and design, construct, manage and operate the components of its developing city. The vast majority of the professional class arriving on the peninsula work directly or indirectly for the public sector, and the ministries, institutions, and companies for which they work place them in housing compounds or buildings owned by other citizens. The citizens who own these compounds and buildings then accumulate the profits generated by the astronomical rents characteristic of the region – in Doha, for example, villas in compounds can easily rent for US $4,000 or more per month. The suburban horizon of Doha is now filled with these compounds, and with citizens now outnumbered almost ten to one by foreign residents, the scale of this transfer can hardly be overstated: rental properties, in the guise of a workforce dedicated to urban development, comprise one of the principal mechanisms for transferring wealth from the state to its citizenry.

Yet transfers through rental properties are only the frontline of this political economy of urban development. The construction of an imagined compound, for example, includes the efforts and energies of a constellation of other businesses – the company that makes cement, the company that owns the trucks to move material and equipment to the site, the manpower agency that brings construction workers from South Asia to the Gulf and the firm that designs the villas and apartments in the compound. And once the foreign workforce is placed in the compound, villas must be furnished, automobiles much be purchased and children's tuition must be paid. Indeed, vast portions of the contemporary Gulf economies are oriented towards the project of urban growth, and countless citizens, as the owner/sponsors of these various enterprises, depend directly on these transfers (and, more obliquely, upon the state's ongoing promotion of urban development as a national priority).

What I suggest, then, is that urban development has become an integral component of the implicit contract between state and citizen in the Gulf states. In its current configuration, this system is dependent upon an ever-present and ever-increasing flow of foreigners to the Gulf states.[10] Put another way, the expanding contingent of foreigners employed to assist and guide the Gulf states' development collectively function as the currency by which wealth is transferred from state to citizen. The highest rewards go to those citizens who, in terms of urban development, operate at the largest scale. The crux of the argument, then, reverses the apparent logic of this arrangement: it is not this urban development that forges new social relations in the Gulf, but rather the ongoing articulation of indigenous social relations that drives urban development.[11] Expanding families, and particularly expanding powerful families, require urban development. Guiding that development is what young, well-placed citizens do, and it is the basis of their and their family's economic power.

A meaningful and substantial commitment to sustainability must include some provisions for controlling urban sprawl and, eventually, shifting away from a growth-based economy. By briefly examining the political economy of urban growth in the Gulf states, however, I suggest that the model of urban growth in Qatar presents a strikingly unsustainable socio-political and economic template for the near future. This model, while publicly conceptualized as merely the pathway towards a rapidly approaching endpoint (the depletion of petroleum resources and a diversified socio-economic future to cope with that reality), and now promoted in the discourse of sustainable development, has become deeply interlocked with the social and cultural fabric of the contemporary Gulf state. Citizens' notions of entitlement, their expectations of the state and the high natural growth rate in the region only fuel the situation. Reining in urban growth will undermine one of the two principle conduits by which wealth is transferred from state to citizen, and political stability in the region is partially contingent upon the legitimacy produced by these transfers. Hence a more sustainable model of urban growth represents a significant potential threat to political stability in the region.

Sustainable Development in a Top-Down Society

The role urban development plays in maintaining tribal and interfamilial relations in the respective Gulf states is a testament to the intricacies by which modernity, development and the state itself have been integrated into the complex and often divisive social relations that previously predominated in the region. While urban development functions as a mechanism for maintaining traditional forms of stratification in these Arabian societies, the top-down character of political and social power in the region also poses significant challenges to the implementation of meaningful sustainability in the region. In this section, I consider how the precepts developed by several decades of thought concerning sustainability and sustainable development might founder in the contemporary Gulf.

Over four decades of its articulation, sustainable development has come to encompass a variety of grassroots approaches, community-based initiatives, activisms and proposals for re-engineering contemporary forms of democracy. In development theory, these 'bottom-up' approaches emerged in the aftermath of the collapse of the centralized, monolithic and universalizing approach to development. The new paradigm sought to put people first, and to build participatory models for a successful and sustainable form of development (e.g. Chambers 1983, 1994; Cernea 1991). Bill Adams (2001) suggests that the incorporation of indigenous knowledge and community-based approaches was central to contemporary sustainable development, and more recent attention to the nexus between sustainable development and environmental justice clearly portrays the ongoing legacy of the American civil rights movement in sustainable development (Agyeman, Bullard and Evans 2003: 7). For many post-Marxist environmental scholars, participatory models and grassroots approaches are more than just an efficient means to a more sustainable end – they are the end goal in and of themselves. Franz Broswimmer's call for an 'ecological democracy', for example, is based on the contention that the protection of other species and their habitat will require that 'ordinary citizens be able to take part at the grassroots level in decision-making that effects their environment' (2002: 98). These participatory, community-based and inherently democratic frameworks are particularly prominent in the ongoing conceptualization of urban-focused sustainable development (Newman and Jennings 2008: 156).

Many popular books concerned with the implementation of sustainability in developed nations conclude with a chapter concerning what a person can do in order to make a difference with these issues (e.g Brown 2008; Orr 2009). The basic premise of these concluding chapters seems to be two-fold: first, we can and should make significant changes in our own lives and households; and second, we can and should vote and politically mobilize to help those ideas percolate into law and governing structures. What I suggest, then, is that a close reading of the sustainable development literature confirms the centrality of a democratic foundation to the ongoing articulation of sustainable development's goals, as well as the methods and practices by which those goals can be achieved. Furthermore, while a significant portion of 'mainstream' sustainable development assumes this essentially democratic foundation, a significantly larger portion of what I have described as radical/classical sustainable development does the same, particularly in those radical renditions of sustainable development that challenge state-based deployment of a sustainability friendly to the interests of a corporate-dominated economy. Similarly, much of urban sustainability theory and practice suggests that individuals must have more power and control over the environment they live in and depend upon. In much sustainability theory, this power and control is portrayed either explicitly or implicitly in democratic terms.

Considering the assuredly non-democratic political structure of Qatar and the other Gulf states, how transferable is the package of ideas and methods operating under the banner of sustainable development? Qatar and its neighbouring states lack many of the political and social components that play a central role in the practice of sustainable development. Civil society in the region is generally perceived as absent, anemic or imported (Kamrava 2009; Reiche 2010). Claims of indigeneity are muted or absent: those Bedouin groups with claims of indigeneity are not participants in the growing congress of global indigenous peoples. Citizens rarely form neighbourhood groups or action committees to assert sustainability initiatives. In the larger lexicon of sustainability practice, this suggests that 'increasing awareness', which seems to perennially serve as the most palatable aspect of a typical sustainability campaign, would not have the same sort of traction here as one might expect elsewhere in the world. Because citizens in Qatar and the other Gulf states rarely have the power to elect the officials who might configure social and environmental policy, the impact of grassroots organization – or, simply changing citizens' perspectives on the importance of the environment – is structurally de-linked from its conceptual fruition in policy and law. Instead, political power in the region is strongly top-down: leaders assume the role of configuring appropriate policy for state and citizenry, and citizens generally yield individual or personal responsibility for social, economic or environmental change to that leadership. This top-down approach is evident in the broad penchant for master planning, the strikingly opaque and primary driving force behind sustainable development in the region (which I will consider in more depth in the next section).

While my basic contention, then, is that the social, cultural and political context of the contemporary Gulf state meshes poorly with many of the central assumptions of sustainable development theory and practice, one might also consider the potential advantages of the top-down political structure of Qatar and the other Gulf states in building a more sustainable future. Significant policy steps towards sustainability are, in many ways, simply one decree away from reality in the contemporary Gulf. Combined with the possibilities produced by the astonishing wealth of these states, the top-down structure of policy decision making yields a nimbleness that might potentially benefit sustainability, for policy decisions avoid the mire of congressional or parliamentary politics typical of Western and democratic forms of governance. Furthermore, I would also add that even foreigners with a few months of experience in the Gulf states can quickly perceive that simply classifying these societies as 'non-democratic' does little justice to societies in which citizens are, in many senses, quite capable of voicing their concerns through indigenous familial and tribal networks. While citizens may lack the capacity to elect representative leaders, other networks, including tribal and familial associations, social networks and professional connections provide ample opportunity for many citizens to assert their opinions to policy makers and power holders. These very same networks challenge the rigid definitions of civil society developed in the west and purveyed broadly in the critiques levied against the region. So perhaps the better question is this: how can these indigenous forms of social relation and consultation come to play an instrumental role in building a sustainability drive at the grassroots or community level?

With those important caveats aside, the centralized and top-down nature of political power in the Gulf states has resulted in a highly filtered rendition of sustainable development. In practice, the models of sustainability promoted and adopted by the state focus heavily on technological innovation and infrastructural development. These particular aspects of sustainable development mesh seamlessly with the imperative of urban development described in the previous section, while simultaneously marginalizing the more threatening socio-cultural and political facets of the sustainability paradigm.

Master Planning and the Perils of Supermodernism

In practice, the imperative of urban development and the top-down political structure of the Gulf state coalesce in urban master planning. As the primary avenue by which sustainable development is articulated in the contemporary Gulf states, master planning drives urban development – an urban development, as I have argued above, that is a socio-political necessity in the typical Gulf state. Master planning also confirms the central role of the state and its hereditary leaders in that urban development and, therefore, in the extrapolation of urban sustainable development. In addition to reinforcing the top-down structure of political power, and in addition to fuelling the transfer of wealth via urban development, the discourse of master planning in the Gulf produces an urban form that diverges significantly from the models and best practices that have accumulated in decades of conversation about urban sustainability and sustainable development. More specifically, I will argue that the super-modernism that results from urban master planning in the Gulf city con-signs sustainability to a spatial discourse antithetical to its meaningful implementation.

The modern Gulf home is behind a tall wall. The wall itself delineates the property and yields a culturally normative degree of privacy to the family that resides behind that wall. The private spaces inside these walls are often highly manicured, carefully tended and surprisingly green. This managed and manicured private space contrasts sharply with the inter-stitial land between and beyond these walls. From a vista anywhere in the suburbs of Doha, one can observe a strange combination of elements: high walls that shield private space from view, towering mansions that peer over the walls that surround them and chaotic interstitial space that fills the space between and beyond these ubiquitous walls. This interstitial space is of particular note – piles of construction debris lay abandoned, ad hoc dirt lanes become shortcuts between boulevards, sidewalks peter out in the hardscrabble desert and garbage blown by the wind accrues against the exteriors of these walls (see figure 14.1). In passing from these chaotic and abandoned interstitial spaces into the private spaces of the family property, one crosses the distinct threshold between disorder and order.

This sharp contrast is not consigned to the residential level. Aspire Park, for example, is the agglomeration of stadiums, parkland and athletic facilities built to host the 2006 Asian Games (see figure 14.2). This highly managed and modernistic space abuts two large shopping malls. It now functions as a public park, and is cared for by a small army of South Asian custodians, gardeners and guards. The interior of the park echoes James Holston's description (1989) of Brasilia and James Scott's (1998) critical description of the urban results of high-modern design. Humans struggle to make use of the intricately planned spaces and pedestrian boulevards that carefully connect the various facilities of the park. They are dwarfed by the surroundings, and even when people are about the park feels al-most empty. In contrast to the centre of this planned space, the periphery of the park is chaotic: rickety chain-link fences demarcate the transition to unplanned interstitial space. Walking paths simply end in a rocky dirt lot; grass fields suddenly give way to gravel or sand. Indeed, the threshold one encounters upon entering walled private property is replicated at this supermodern scale: at the interstices of the massive planned develop-

Figure 14.1. Debris outside the wall of a housing compound. Photograph by Kristin Giordano.

ments and trophy projects typical of the Gulf city, the managed and mani-cured gives way to empty lots, debris, gravel and sand.

The lived experience of dwelling in the modern Gulf city, then, in-volves movement back and forth across the threshold between modern-istic planned spaces and the chaos of the interstitial space that surrounds them. I suggest this experience is indicative of one of the principle pat-terns of the Gulf city: the energy, planning and management of the Gulf city is directed inwardly at the discrete units of urban space. Surrounding these planned and modern spaces is the field they punctuate – an inter-stitial urban domain seemingly beyond the gaze of urban planners. This pattern can be traced across scales in the Gulf city: the threshold observed at the level of the individual residence is replicated at the level of the su-permodern structures that now proliferate in the urban environment of the region.

Figure 14.2. Aspire Park grounds on the weekend. Photograph by Kristin Giordano.

The term *supermodernism* has a long and vibrant pedigree (Ibelings 1995; Auge 1995). Here, I am interested the portion of that discussion which concerns the expanding scope of these planned modern spaces. In the Gulf states, rapid urban development and the extraordinary wealth flowing through the region have continually expanded the scale of the typical component of urban development. The planning and construction of hotels, particular buildings, parks or mosques continues, but increasingly larger spaces are being incorporated into this supermodernist and highly planned spatial discourse.[12] In part, *supermodernism* refers to the expansive scale of these constructions, a spatial discourse in which whole planned communities, discrete 'cities', offshore islands and other vast planned spaces sprout in and around the city. In Doha, for example, The Pearl development, which was briefly described earlier in this chapter, is a resort-like residential and commercial development constructed on a large human-made island just north of the city. It is intended to be home to some 40,000 residents in a combination of private villas and tall apartment buildings. The Pearl includes dozens of restaurants, high-end hotels, a marina, commercial space and, perhaps most problematically, only four lanes of road connecting it with the mainland peninsula. Similarly, 'Education City' is a vast complex of American Universities and other institutions located in what is for the time being the periphery of urban Doha. In Dubai, these supermodern spaces have proliferated for years: 'Internet City' is a free economic zone and information technology park; Media City is a tax-free zone intended to attract the media industry active in the region; Knowledge Village is a tax-free and foreign-ownership zone intended as a community for human resources management professionals; International Humanitarian City is an independent free zone authority that houses institutions devoted to internationally-focused humanitarian aid and international development; the Masdar Project in Abu Dhabi is a sustainable city (intended to have a zero-carbon footprint) capable of housing approximately 50,000 people upon completion. These are only a handful of the numerous examples that, as I have already suggested, are emblematic of the spatial discourse central to urban development in the region – a spatial discourse that, following others, I refer to as supermodernism (e.g. Ackley 2007).

In other published work, I have envisioned this spatialization of the urban form as a strategic plan to compartmentalize foreign matter, to segregate that foreign matter, and to thereby assert the predominance of indigenous culture and its sovereignty over the vast flows of people and culture hosted by the Gulf states.[13] This explanation echoes the conceptualization of graduated sovereignty as one of the principle tools by which Asian states strategically grapple with neoliberal flows (Ong 2006). Here, however, my focus is on the implications of this pattern of urban development for the expressed goal of sustainability in the urban centres of the region. The supermodern compartmentalization of urban development in Doha, Dubai and the other Gulf cities functions as the principal frame for urban sustainability: in Masdar City, the region's first and largest attempt to construct a 'sustainable' city, we see the significant capital at hand devoted to the sorts of sustainable goals that other cities only dream of, particularly through the utilization of a constellation of technologies targeting net-zero carbon emissions (Reiche 2009, 2010; Sgouridis and Kennedy 2009). Qatar now has its own plans for an 'Energy City' that will use the latest green technology, rely heavily on solar energy and work carefully to improve air and water quality while reducing the waste stream (Reiche 2010). These projects interlock with the political economy of urban development, for their construction and ongoing maintenance relies upon the foreign labour that transfers wealth from state to citizenry. Supermodern urban development also confirms the top-down structure of political power in the Gulf states – even if the projects are not directly implemented by the state, the land grants and permits for developments of this scale require intricate connections with the top echelons of the Gulf state. But my concern here is with the product of this system and, more specifically, with the friction between urban supermodernism and sustainability.

I suggest two essential and interrelated flaws inherent to the spatial discourse evinced by these projects and plans. First, descriptions of Masdar City footnote the fact that some 40,000 to 60,000 workers will commute to the planned city on a daily basis. Throughout the Gulf, these supermodern projects and monumental spaces are the visible stage presented to the cosmopolitan global audience. Behind the stage curtain, however, lie the support industries, service facilities and labour camps that house these immense labour forces. In Qatar, the South Asian labour force that builds, cleans, maintains and serves the various supermodern projects and urban spaces in Doha typically resides in the Industrial Area, a gritty and expansive grid of industry and labour camps at the periphery of the city. Similar areas exist in most of the Gulf cities, and plans for extensive 'Bachelor Cities' abound in planning circles throughout the Gulf. This offstage activity is central to the day-to-day operation of the Gulf city. It belies the discrete and compartmentalized presentation of these supermodern spaces, and in this case, challenges the logic of Masdar's calculation of its sustainability – how can a discrete and bounded 'sustainable city' account for the impact of the vast labour force that traverses the backstage/frontstage divide every workday?

Second, the compartmentalization of sustainability to a master-planned development essentially consigns sustainability initiatives to the status shared by the constellation of other principles, ideas and whims guiding the spatial articulation of the Gulf city. In other words, a 'sustainable city' located on the periphery of Abu Dhabi frames sustainability as a thematic attraction – a symbolic commodity scavenged from environmental and urban discourses to exemplify the modernity of the nation (see Hubbert 2009). In this spatial discourse, sustainability is therefore on par with the industry of 'Industry City' in Dubai, with education in Doha's 'Education City' or with the opulent Venetian conception of The Pearl offshore residential community in Qatar. Moreover, the spatial compartmentalization of sustainability to one of many master-planned supermodern Gulf spaces corresponds with the ideological compartmentalization of sustainability as both distinct and equivalent to the constellation of other objectives of the contemporary nation-state.[14] While the master-planning frame preserves the political economy of urban development and the centralization of power in the state and its leadership, it contrasts with the central contentions of the meaningful rendition of sustainability sketched at the outset of this chapter: forging a sustainable future requires comprehensive action in all facets of urban existence. There can be no compartmentalized solutions.

The contemporary Gulf city suggests that, as humans, we are capable of working together to construct and perhaps maintain these discrete and highly managed places – a skyscraper, a shopping mall, a home, a park, even a vast master-planned residential community. But a short trip around Doha or any of the other Gulf cities also suggests the difficulty of linking these discrete, managed spaces together into a functional and potentially sustainable whole. This observation leaves me with questions. Can a sustainable urban environment really be master planned? Can we connect all the complex pieces and parts that comprise a planned city? Or is the managed and manicured perfection of modernism and its master plans an elusive goal? Will these chaotic interstitial spaces always exist? And will the cities of the Gulf always need a dirty backstage, like the bachelor cities now being constructed around the Gulf, or Doha's industrial area, where I spend my weekends interviewing migrant labourers who live in a Doha that most middle class residents never see?

Conclusion

In her introductory comments to a recent conference, Qatar University's president, Dr. Sheikha Abdulla Al-Misnad, expressed an interest in how sustainability might serve as a counterbalance to the sense of entitlement and, more broadly, the rampant consumerism that has taken hold amongst the citizens of the *khaleeji* states.[15] Two decades ago, Sulayman Khalaf described something quite similar to the problem identified by the university's president – a broad set of cultural conditions that manifest themselves in the individual as what he describes as 'the notion of unlimited good' (1992). In my own conversations with Qatari citizens, the extraordinary level of consumption typical of the Gulf citizen is often juxtaposed with the impoverished past from which many citizens' parents and grandparents emerged. Petroleum wealth, often conceived as a blessing from Allah in reward for the penurious past, has provided them with an era of plentitude. At the current juncture, that consumer culture is the focus of much conversation but very little scholarship in the Gulf states. In a sense, these broader cultural issues lurk behind the more focused analysis I have provided here, and certainly merit more sustained attention.

In my analysis I have attempted to delineate three arenas of potential difficulty for the implementation of a substantial and meaningful sustainability. To recapitulate, I first suggest that urban development has become an integral conduit for the transfer of state-controlled wealth to its citizenry, and that interrupting urban development in the interests of long-term sustainability will potentially disturb the legitimacy constructed by the political leaders in the GCC states. Second, I contend that the socio-political organization of the GCC states poorly matches the fundamentally democratic assumptions under-girding both theory and praxis in sustainability. Finally, I question whether a meaningful and transformative form of sustainable development can truly be master planned for the urban environment. As I suggest, the predominant spatial discourse of urban development in the region produces highly organized and managed spaces, but also seems to produce interstitial and backstage spaces of a strikingly different character. None of the conditions described here are consigned to the Gulf alone, and it's certainly true that the implementation of the meaningful, substantial and transformative sustainability I chart at the outset of this chapter would face significant, if not insurmountable, challenges in a variety of socio-cultural settings. With significant reservoirs of capital at hand, however, the Gulf States seek to move rapidly towards these expressed goals. This chapter seeks to chart several significant problems that have yet to enter the public discourse about sustainability in the region.

Notes

This chapter was originally presented as 'Doha and Sustainability: An Overview of Urban Sustainability and Four Questions' for the second International Social Sciences Symposium: Sustainable Development: Issues and Challenges, Qatar University, 4 November 2009.

1. See von Sivers (1980) for a longer discussion of Ibn Khaldun's conception of the city.
2. Adams (2001) constructs his analysis of the florescence of sustainable development thinking around what he calls the mainstream and the counter-current definitions. Baker provides a more complex categorization, including idealists, proponents of a strong version of sustainable development, proponents of a weak version of sustainable development, and proponents of an approach consigned to controlling pollution (Baker 2006: 30–31).
3. Two of many published examples include (Qatar 2006a, 2006b).
4. This is not to suggest the same critique does not apply to most cities of the world.
5. These coastal towns were important nodes of social and cultural heterogeneity in the region. The entirety of the region also shares a history in the ambit of

British imperialism, largely administered via British India. All of the states are deeply Islamic and, with the exception of Oman, Sunni, although a significant Shi'a population resides in western Saudi Arabia and in Bahrain.

6. Reiche (2009: 379) briefly makes this point in his discussion of the impetus behind Abu Dhabi's construction of Masdar City.

7. Nagy (2006) details the proliferation of the villa in Qatar as a force of social change.

8. While the line between the public and private sector is difficult to clearly delineate in the Gulf states, a variety of sources point to the ongoing centrality of the government in supporting industries and apportioning jobs to citizens (Qatar 2007: 26; Berrebi, Martorell and Tanner 2009; Willoughby 2008; Niblock 2007).

9. Although the proliferation of these spaces led Basar (2007: 103) to note a 'freehold revolution' in the extrapolation of Dubai's urban model.

10. Indeed, one suspects that the plans for a tourist-based economy have misapprehended the flow of skilled foreign labour employed in the region as evidence of an economically substantial population interested in recreational travel to the Gulf states.

11. It is also of note that as a result of this arrangement both state and citizen have configured and idealized roles as stewards of the development process.

12. See Nagy (2000) for a portrait of master planning in Doha a decade ago.

13. See Ong 2006 and Gardner 2010, 2009, 2008.

14. It should be noted that Masdar was conceived as an innovative supermodern space from which sustainable ideas and practices would eventually flow to Emirati society at large, a process Reiche (2010: 2) refers to as 'policy transfer'.

15. Dr. Sheikha al-Misnad, keynote address, the Second International Social Sciences Symposium, Qatar University, 5 November 2009.

References

Ackley, B. 2007. 'Permanent Vacation: Dubai, Circa 2005.' In *With/Without: Spatial Products, Practices and Politics in the Middle East*, eds. Shumon Basar, Antonia Carver and Markus Miessen, 33–50. Dubai: Bidoun Inc and Moutamarat.

Adams, W. M. 2001. *Green Development: Environment and Sustainability in the Third World. Second Edition*. London: Routledge.

Agyeman, J., R. D. Bullard and B. Evans. 2003. 'Joined-up Thinking: Bringing Together Sustainability, Environmental Justice and Equity.' In *Just Sustainabilities: Development in an Unequal World*, eds. J. Agyeman, R. D. Bullard and B. Evans, 1–16. Cambridge, MA: MIT Press.

Auge, M. 1995. *Non Places: Introduction to the Anthropology of Supermodernism*. London: Verso.

Baker, S. 2006. *Sustainable Development*. London: Routledge.

Basar, S. 2007. 'The Freedom to Create: How Dubai Makes Room for Exception.' In *With/Without: Spatial Products, Practices & Politics in the Middle East*, eds. Shumon Basar, Antonia Carver and Markus Miessen, 102–107. Dubai: Bidoun Press.

Beblawi, H. 1987. 'The Rentier State in the Arab World.' In *The Rentier State*, eds. H. Beblawi and G. Luciani, 85–98. London: Croon Helm.

Berrebi, C., F. Martorell and J. C. Tanner. 2009. 'Qatar's Labor Markets at a Crucial Crossroad.' *Middle East Journal* 63 (3): 421–442.

Brown, L. 2008. *Plan B 4.0: Mobilizing to Save Civilization.* New York: W. W. Norton & Company.

Browsimmer, F. J. 2002. *Ecocide: A Short History of the Mass Extinction of Species.* London: Pluto Press.

Cernea, M. M. 1991. *Putting People First: Sociological Variables in Rural Development.* Second Edition. New York: Oxford University Press.

Chambers, R. 1983. *Rural Development: Putting the Last First.* New York: John Wiley.

———. 1994. 'The Origins and Practice of Participatory Rural Appraisal.' *World Development* 22 (7): 953–969.

Diamond, J. 2005. *Collapse: How Societies Choose to Fail or Succeed.* New York: Viking/Penguin.

Dresch, P. 2006. 'The Place of Strangers in Gulf Society.' In *Globalization and the Gulf*, eds. John Fox, Nada Mourtada-Sabbah and Mohammed al-Mutawa, 200–222. London: Routledge.

Gardner, A. 2008. 'Consumer Culture in Al Khaleej.' Paper presented at the annual meeting of the American Anthropological Association, San Francisco, CA, 21 November.

———. 2009. 'The Amalgamated City: The Alternatives of Wealth in the Neoliberal Landscape of Doha, Qatar.' Paper presented at the annual meeting of the American Anthropological Association, Philadelphia, PA, 5 December.

———. 2010. *City of Strangers: Gulf Migration and the Indian Community in Bahrain.* Ithaca, NY: ILR/Cornell University Press.

Hames, R. 2007. 'The Ecologically Noble Savage Debate.' *Annual Review of Anthropology* 36: 177–190.

Holston, J. 1989. *The Modernist City: An Anthropological Critique of Brasilia.* Chicago: University of Chicago Press.

Hubbert, J. 2009. 'Green and Global: Sustainability in the 2008 Beijing Olymics and the 2010 Shanghai World Expo.' Paper presented at the annual meeting of the American Anthropological Association, Philadelphia, PA, 3 December.

Ibelings, H. 1995. *Supermodernism: Architecture in the Age of Globalization.* London: Nai Publishers.

Kamrava, M. 2009. 'Royal Factionalism and Political Liberalization in Qatar.' *The Middle East Journal* 63 (3): 401–420.

Khalaf, S. 1992. 'Gulf Societies and the Image of Unlimited Good.' *Dialectical Anthropology* 17: 53–84.

Keil, R. 2005. 'Progress Report: Urban Political Ecology.' *Urban Geography* 26 (7): 640–651.

Lansing, S. J. 1991. *Priests and Programmers: Technologies of Power in the Engineered Landscape of Bali.* Princeton, NJ: Princeton University Press.

Light, A. 2001. 'The Urban Blind Spot In Environmental Ethics.' *Environmental Politics* 10: 7–35.

Light, A. 2003. 'Urban Ecological Citizenship.' *Journal of Social Philosophy* 34: 44–63.

Longva, A. 2006. 'Nationalism in Pre-modern Guise: the Discourse on Hadhar and Badu in Kuwait.' *International Journal of Middle East Studies* 38: 171–187.

Luciani, G. 1987. 'Allocation vs. Production States: A Theoretical Framework.' In *The Rentier State*, eds. H. Beblawi and G. Luciani, 63–82. London: Croon Helm.

Nagy, S. 2000. 'Dressing Up Downtown: Urban Development and Government Public Image in Qatar.' *City and Society* XII (1): 125–147.

———. 2006. 'Making Room for Migrants, Making Sense of Difference: Spatial and Ideological Expressions of Social Diversity in Urban Qatar.' *Urban Studies* 43 (1): 119–137.

Newman, P., and I. Jennings. 2008. *Cities as Sustainable Ecosystems: Principles and Practices.* Washington, DC: Island Press.

Newman, P., and J. R. Kenworthy. 1999. *Sustainability and Cities: Overcoming Automobile Dependence.* Washington, DC: Island Press.

Niblock, T. 2007. *The Political Economy of Saudi Arabia.* London: Routledge.

Ong, Aihwa. 2006. *Neoliberalism as Exception: Mutations in Citizenship and Sovereignty.* Durham, NC: Duke University Press.

Orr, D. 2009. *Down to the Wire.* New York: Oxford University Press.

Owen, D. 2009. *Green Metropolis: Why Living Smaller, Living Closer, and Driving Less are the Keys to Sustainability.* New York: Riverhead/Penguin.

Qatar. 2006a. *Sustainable Development Indicators in Qatar.* The Planning Council, December.

———. 2006b. *Human Development Report.* The Planning Council.

———. 2007. *Turning Qatar into a Competitive Knowledge-Based Economy: Qatar Knowledge Economy Project.* Government of Qatar Planning Council, 21 May 21.

Reiche, D. 2009. 'Renewable Energy Policies in the Gulf Countries: A Case Study of the Carbon-Neutral "Masdar City" in Abu Dhabi.' *Energy Policy* 38: 378–382.

———. 2010. 'Energy Policies of Gulf Cooperation Council (GCC) Countries: Possibilities and Limitations of Ecological Modernization in Rentier States.' *Energy Policy* (2010), doi:10.1016/j.enpol.2009.12.031

Scott, J. 1998. *Seeing Like a State: How Certain Schemes to Improve the Human Condition have Failed.* New Haven, CT: Yale University Press.

Sgouridis, S., and S. Kennedy. 2009. 'Tangible and Fungible Energy: Hybrid Energy Market and Currency System for Total Energy Management. A Masdar City Case Study.' *Energy Policy* 38: 1749–1758.

Smith, E. A., and M. Wishnie. 2000. 'Conservation and Subsistence in Small-Scale Societies.' *Annual Review of Anthropology:* 493–524.

von Sivers, P. 1980. 'The Agrarian Foundations of Society according to Ibn Khaldun.' *Arabica* 27 (1): 68–91.

Willoughby, J. 2008. 'Segmented Feminization and the Decline of Neopatriarchy in the GCC Countries of the Persian Gulf.' *Comparative Studies of South Asia, Africa and the Middle East* 28 (1): 184–199.

CHAPTER 15

Sustainable Waste Management in Qatar

Charting the Emergence of an Integrated Approach to Solid Waste Management

Sarah F. Clarke and Salah Almannai

Looking towards downtown Doha your gaze alights immediately on the gleaming tower blocks of the business district soaring beside the sea, shimmering brightly in the desert heat. Bringing your gaze closer to your immediate surroundings, the contrast is stark, for the dominant feature is typically rubble, heaps of it, intermingled with all manner of the detritus of daily life – plastic bags, empty food cartons, disused paper and shards of metal. You name an item of rubbish and it's there, everywhere in fact, an inevitable consequence of rapid development. And, for development, read construction. Villas appear seemingly within weeks, with carefully tendered gardens and yards behind high walls, creating a private oasis that enables families, particularly local women, to go about their daily lives unseen in their personal space. Outside, there may be rubbish strewn across the street or an unsightly garbage bin brimming with waste, yet inside all is in order. And few there seem to be bothered by this incongruity that may jar Western sensibilities, brought up on a diet of endless slogans: Reduce, Reuse, Recycle! Keep it Tidy!

How can this be? Only a generation or so ago, desert-dwelling families took great care of their immediate environment, recognizing its fragility and importance to their community's ongoing well-being (see for example Lancaster 1997; Cole 1975). Not so long ago – let's say fifty years before – the only waste the people of the Gulf would have generated would have been date stones, palm fronds and camel bones, all of which could be safely thrown away in the environment for nature to take its course. What changed attitudes in such a short space of time?

Developed and developing nations alike face the unrelenting challenge of how to deal with the waste generated by everyday human activity. Academics, policy makers and environmental campaigners have devoted much attention to the most economically effective and environmentally sustainable methods of dealing with the mountain of waste, trash, garbage, rubbish, call it what you will, that is generated on a daily basis worldwide (for example Uiterkamp, Azadi and Ho 2011; Alhumoud, Ghusain and Al Hasawi 2004; and Phillips et al. 2010). As countries move along the 'development path' and become more sophisticated in their manufacturing techniques, construction needs and technology uptake, ad hoc methods for dealing with waste are no longer able to cope with the amount of waste and associated negative environmental and health concerns. Add to the mix high rates of population growth, rapidly changing consumption patterns and the continual expansion of mega-cities and the resulting waste mountain becomes an issue that we cannot ignore.

Waste and Sustainability

Chapter 21 of Agenda 21 – the blueprint for the protection of the planet and its sustainable development drawn up at the Rio 'Earth Summit in 1992 – states that 'environmentally sound management of wastes was among the environmental issues of major concern in maintaining the quality of the Earth's environment' (UNESCO 1992: para21.1). Subsequently, at the World Summit on Sustainable Development in 2002, governments reaffirmed the importance of solid waste management, calling for attention to be given to waste prevention and minimization, reuse and recycling. This concern arose from the realization that poor solid waste management not only impacts the well-being of the environment but also the quality of life of those living in locations where there are ineffective waste systems, including negative health implications and adverse socio-economic effects. Developed and developing countries face the same challenge, albeit with different characteristics – that is, how should municipalities deal with the ever-growing mountain of waste?

This chapter focuses on municipal solid waste, which includes all forms of household waste, garden and landscaping 'green' waste and waste from small commercial and retail outlets. It excludes hazardous waste, construction and demolition waste, industrial waste and all types of wastewater including sludge. In other words, municipal solid waste is everything collected and treated by municipalities; only part of which comes from households. However, reference is made to other waste streams, where appropriate, since responses to the issue of waste within a country or region necessitates attention to the entire system of waste generation – i.e. the multiple inputs and outputs of interconnected waste streams. This reflects the reality that integrated solutions to the problem of waste are a necessity.

Research shows that countries with high annual income (more than US $10,000 per capita per year) generate proportionally greater volumes of municipal waste per capita per year than lower-income countries (Bogner et al. 2007: 592; Al Yousfi n.d.: 4). In response, governments of many developed nations have introduced a range of integrated waste management options that reflect the solid waste management hierarchy espoused by the United Nations Environment Programme (UNEP). This hierarchy favours prevention or reduction of the production of waste at source, reuse of materials in the waste stream in their current forms, recycling, composting or recovery of materials for use as direct or indirect inputs into new products, energy recovery by incineration, anaerobic digestion etc., reduction of the volume of waste prior to disposal and, as a last resort, disposal of the residue in an environmentally sound manner, for example, to landfill (UNEP 2005: 9).

In contrast, until recently, the rapidly developing nations of the Middle East[1] have opted for landfill as the sole and preferred waste management option.[2] This is despite the fact that failure to pay adequate attention to solid waste management incurs a penalty later, not least in terms of resources lost and a dramatic negative impact on the environment. It reflects not only an absence of adequate waste management infrastructure capable of coping with the volume of waste but also a lack of awareness about the importance of dealing with waste in an environmentally sound manner, reflecting limited education and public knowledge about environmental issues in general. A dearth of information or inaccurate data also contributes to poor coordination and planning of waste management.

Cultural traditions in the region also affect waste generation rates, consumption patterns and the degree of participation in public programmes. For example, in recent years people tend to provide large amounts of food at celebrations (weddings, 'Id al-Fitr and 'Id al-Adha, Ramadan etc.), much of it ending up uneaten and disposed of in landfill (Alhumoud, Ghusain and Al Hasawi 2004: 553). The excesses seen today differ from, for example, Donald Cole's (1975: 133–135) experience of breaking fast during Ramadan with the Al Murrah Bedouin of Saudi Arabia when there 'was a minimum of ritual and we only had the barest of necessities'. Today, there are also large month-to-month fluctuations in household waste generation, particularly during the hot summer months in the Gulf when many expatriate and local households travel outside the region. This reality contrasts with the behaviour and know-how of the former Bedouin communities of the region who, as a semi-nomadic people, were compelled to live in harmony with the natural cycles of the harsh desert environment and respect and protect it. The apparent disconnect is also at odds with Islamic traditions which call for the faithful to safe guard the beauty of the earth (Anon 2011a).

This chapter describes the approach to municipal solid waste management (SWM) in Qatar, and charts the emergence of a more integrated approach to SWM against a backdrop of developments in waste management across the Gulf region and in the context of the overall character of the waste problem in the country. It presents some conclusions about the factors which hinder or promote best practice in waste management in Qatar along with recommendations aimed at securing more sustainable waste management. Finding satisfactory solutions to the management of solid waste is an important part of the country's move towards a more sustainable way of life; a goal espoused by H. H. the Emir of Qatar and set out in the Qatar National Vision 2030 (see Tan, Al-Khalaqi and Al-Khulaifi, chapter 2; and Darwish, chapter 4, both this volume).

Information was collected through a series of informal conversations with various stakeholders involved in dealing with different aspects of waste management in Qatar including policy makers, planners, corporate executives and members of the public, particularly in Abu Hamour, negatively impacted by waste issues (e.g. emissions from factories), together with data obtained from publically available documents relating to waste management in Qatar and the region. In addition, a short survey was conducted of a small sample of Qatar University students' attitudes to recycling and data was used from an undergraduate class on sustainable development relating to household waste. Further details about the characteristics of the waste management problem in Qatar were obtained from a waste management workshop attended by more than thirty interested parties including Ministry of Environment employees, waste management experts, business leaders and researchers in the field of waste.[3] Lack of accurate and inconsistent data and an unwillingness of some parties to divulge the true nature and scale of the waste problem in Qatar mean that there is some disagreement over the figures for different waste streams, a lack of clarity about how waste is currently handled in Qatar and the exact nature of proposed waste management strategies. Where necessary we highlight these inconsistencies and research limitations. Despite these shortcomings, we demonstrate that Qatar, as other countries in the region, faces a challenging waste problem that requires at the very least a multipronged strategy to minimize its environmental, social and economic impact.

The Gulf Region's Waste Problem

Countries of the Gulf region hold the unenviable status of being among the most affluent, resource-using, and consequently waste generating, nations of the world, with the UAE and Qatar ranking first and second in their ecological foot prints (WWF 2010: 37). Estimates of the volume of solid waste generated in 2009 in the Gulf Cooperation Council (GCC) region range from 80 million to 120 million tonnes per annum rising to 130 million tonnes by 2014,[4] with the greater part (50 per cent or more) originating from construction and demolition activities[5] and municipal waste accounting for more than 30 per cent (Anon 2011b; Gautam 2009; Bruyer 2011).[6] More than 60 per cent of the waste originates from Saudi Arabia, 20 per cent from the UAE, with Kuwait, Bahrain, Oman and Qatar accounting for the rest (approximately 5 per cent each; Anon 2011b). This equates to daily per capita waste generation rates in excess of 1.5 kilograms, with Abu Dhabi having some of the highest solid waste rates in the world at 1.8 kilograms (including all forms of solid wastes; Ahmad 2011). Furthermore, taking the Arab region as a whole, some predict municipal solid wastes alone (i.e. excluding construction and demolition, hazardous and industrial waste) could by 2020 exceed 200 million tonnes per year (Al Yousfi n.d.: 3).

Weaknesses in waste management in the Arab region have not gone unnoticed. This is particularly so in countries such as Egypt where a significant proportion of waste goes uncollected and hazardous waste is improperly handled. It is leading to a gradual move towards an integrated approach to waste management starting with reduction and reuse and aiming to reach high percentages of recycling while moving away from the use of landfill as the defacto repository for refuse (Tolba and Saab 2008: XV). For example, Abu Dhabi has recently introduced a Waste Generation Tariff system[7] with the ambitious goal of reducing waste production from commercial, industrial, construction and demolition activities by 80 per cent of its current volume by 2018 (Ahmad 2011). In addition, the country's Estidama (meaning sustainability) initiative launched in 2008 includes a building-design methodology that mandates a minimum of 30 per cent construction-waste recycling (Platt 2011).

The need for a more cohesive approach to waste management has also resulted in the formation of various high-profile national organizations in countries of the Middle East. Typically, these organizations are tasked with developing a coordinated and sustainable response to the problem of waste, for example the Centre for Waste Management in Abu Dhabi, and Bee'ah (meaning environment), a public-private partnership in Sharjah that aims to be one of the best integrated waste management and environmental companies in the region. A result of these initiatives is that waste is no longer viewed exclusively as an inevitable consequence of development, but rather it is seen increasingly as a resource that when properly managed can produce benefits, for example waste to energy conversion or greenhouse gas mitigation (Bogner et al. 2007: 611). This is demonstrated in Abu Dhabi where new legislation permits the use of recycled aggregates in construction projects enabling a fledgling market to develop for this type of material (Theil 2011).

Characteristics of the Solid Waste Problem in Qatar

The Peninsula of Qatar has a total land area of approximately 11,521 square kilometres, with flat and rocky terrain and sand the main features of its desert landscape. Over the last three decades Qatar has undergone a period of extensive development and industrialization, rapidly transforming this barren landscape into a vibrant multifaceted metropolitan setting unrecognizable from its desert past, when a predominantly Bedouin population lived a semi-nomadic life and with some settlements in coastal areas (see for example Sillitoe and Alshawi, chapter 10, this volume). At the same time, the economy has moved from one that was largely rural, dependent on fishing, pearling and animal husbandry, to a booming oil- and gas-based economy centred on the large conurbation of Doha, neighbouring cities of Wakra and Al Khor and the new industrial cities of Mesaieed and Ras Laffan in the south and north respectively. Today there are major highways cutting west to east and north to south allowing industrial, commercial products and waste to be transported the length and breadth of the country with ease. These developments are set to continue in, for example, the infrastructure to host the Qatar 2022 World Cup, and the furious pace and scale of development is likely to be maintained as Qatar's Vision 2030 is brought to fruition (refer to Tan, Al-Khalaqi and Al-Khulaifi, chapter 2, this volume); some estimates put the forecasted growth in GDP for 2011 at 20 per cent compared to 6.5 per cent for other developing economies (John 2011). It is difficult to imagine the Arabia of not-so-long-ago when tent-dwelling Bedouin tribes lived in the region and 'there were no paved roads, no telegraphs, no telephones, no electricity, no booming cities filled with people from outside Arabia, no gigantic gas flares to light the night skies' (Cole 1975: 138, describing Saudi Arabia). This image contrasts vividly with the vision of, for example, the Lusail City development on the east coast of Qatar, 15 kilometres north of Doha's city centre, which aims to be a distinctive twenty-first-century iconic city with a full array of community facilities that meet sustainability criteria at all stages from design, through construction and use, thereby minimizing environmental impacts and waste generation.[8]

A knock-on effect of this dramatic and rapid growth is an increased demand for services to facilitate the needs of an ever-expanding population which at the last census stood at 1.7 million, representing an increase of 128 per cent between 2004 and 2010 (QSA 2010a: 2). More than 70 per cent of the population lives in Doha and the neighbouring suburb Al Rayyan (QSA 2010b). A unique characteristic of this population, common to the majority of GCC countries, is that it comprises a large percentage of migrant workers whose numbers and nationalities fluctuate annually primarily dependent upon construction demands[9] (see Campbell, chapter 9, this volume). This means that the nature and characteristics of municipal solid waste (MSW) can change year after year and that figures valid one year may be out of date the next (Alhumoud, Ghusain and Al Hasawi 2004). What is sure is that population growth on this scale will be accompanied by a commensurate growth in solid waste from municipal, industrial and commercial sources. In fact, 2,175 tonnes of MSW were generated per day in Qatar in 2010, representing approximately 30 per cent of total waste generated, equivalent to 7,000 tonnes per day when industrial waste, construction and demolition waste and hazardous waste are included (GSDP 2011: 225). Left unchecked, for 2011 it is estimated that MSW will increase to 2,500 tonnes per day with an anticipated annual growth rate of approximately 10–15 per cent per annum (Piggott 2011). The picture is broadly the same across the GCC, although caution should be exercised when making comparisons between countries as definitions of municipal waste may vary (see table 15.1). What is clear, however, is that there is a huge and growing amount of waste to be processed, a pattern also reflected across OECD (Organization for Economic Cooperation and Development) countries (UNEP/GRID-Arendal 2004).

The scale of the waste problem in Qatar is confirmed by a waste audit of households conducted by a group of Qatar University students in spring 2011. Weekly glass, paper, aluminium cans, plastic and food waste ranged from a low of 0.83 kilograms per family member per week to, in one case, 30 kilograms and averaged 1.14 kilogram per person per day for a group of twenty-six students.[10] Only one student reported that their household regularly recycled glass, paper, aluminium cans and plastic, with one other student stating that her family distributed surplus food to their neighbours. A similar picture was found in survey of eleven social-work students: while all eleven students supported the idea of recycling as a way to improve the environment and Qatar society, six indicated that they had never considered recycling themselves and most had no knowledge of recycling or were too lazy to bother, as this respondent observed: 'Yes,

[I've thought about recycling] but I'm too lazy most of the time. I wish if [*sic*] there was a place where people do that for you.' Two respondents stated that recycling should not take place in residential areas as it would become a burden and one felt that as Qatar was a small country, recycling would not have a big impact in the wider scheme of things.[11]

Composition of MSW in Qatar and the region in general has many of the characteristics of that elsewhere in the world, comprising a mix of organic, paper, glass, metals and plastic. However, there is one notable exception; in contrast to the USA and UK for example, where organic waste is estimated as less than 20 per cent of the total, in countries of the Middle East it constitutes more than 40 per cent with assessments for Qatar being in the region of 60 per cent (Al Maaded et al. n.d.). The large percentage of organic waste is generally explained by local people as due to 'cultural differences' referring to the tendency to provide more food than is necessary at functions to show true Arab hospitality. As noted by William Lancaster in his study of the Rwala Bedouin (1997: 43–44), reputations were traditionally built on a person's ability to demonstrate Bedouin virtues of honour, bravery, generosity, political acumen and mediatory skills. The only way of distinguishing one man from another was by his reputation, monetary wealth having little meaning, as the only wealth at that time was camels. The aim was to demonstrate one was 'a "rajul tayyib" – a good man: a man who demonstrates bravery without rashness, generosity without ostentation, political sensibility without double dealing' (ibid.: 45). At public feasts, when food had to be abundant, there was a fine line between providing sufficient food to demonstrate generosity while not overegging it; too much would effect a man's reputation just as badly as too little (ibid.: 64). Today, with abundant food at buffets held for family celebrations, religious holidays and national festivities, the meaning of Arabic (Bedouin) generosity seems to have changed.

Jasem Alhumoud (2005: 144) notes that across the GCC about 1.4 million tonnes per year of organic material could be made available as feedstocks for composting facilities. This potential resource, he argues, is lost due to inefficiencies, high operating and maintenance costs, lack of technical support and inefficient management. No reference is made to attempts to reduce the volume of organic waste. However, there is evidence of improvements in organic-waste recycling. For example, in the Emirate of Sharjah, the capacity of the country's organic waste–management facility has been increased from 100 tonnes per day in 1978 to 400 tonnes per day in 2009 with the plant producing 28,087 tonnes of high-quality compost in 2010 (Hantoush 2011). Qatar's Domestic Solid Waste Management Facility,[12] the first of its kind in the region, is designed to accept approximately 1,180 tonnes of organic and green waste a day of which around 857 tonnes will be suitable for composting (see below).

Table 15.1. Best estimate of current and projected municipal waste in selected GCC countries.

Country	Population (million)	Waste Generation (tonnes/day)	Annual Waste Generated (millions, tonnes/year)	Projected Rate of Increase	Per Capita Waste Generation (kg/day)[a]
Qatar[b]	1.7 (2010)	2,500 (projected 2011)	>0.8 (estimate for 2010)	10–15%	1.65 (2008)
Kuwait	2.74 (2010)[c]		~1.6 (2007)[d]	21%	n/a
Saudi Arabia	27.4 (2010)[e]		12[f]	n/a	1.4 (2008)
Bahrain	1.23 (2010)[g]		1.5 (2010)[h]	n/a	
Sharjah[i]		2,000 (yr 2010)			>2 (2010)
Abu Dhabi	0.93 (2007)[j]		5.9 (2007/8) (including 4.745 construction waste)[k]	13 million tonnes by 2030[l]	4.2 (2008)

a MEED 2011
b GSDP Qatar 2011
c World Bank 2011
d Al Mudh'hi 2011
e World Bank 2011
f Warnock 2009
g Bahrain Census 2010
h FACT Bahrain 2011:32
i Bee'ah 2011
j www.uaeinteract.com
k CWM A–D 2011
l CWM A–D 2011

Awareness among the local population that waste is at best a nuisance and at worst a health hazard is shown by the experience of residents in Abu Hamour[13] on the southern edge of the capital. This suburb is near to a light-enterprise industrial area and is close to a large open-air wholesale market supplying fruit, vegetables, fish and live animals for slaughter (e.g. sheep). These, together with a camel market, generate unpleasant smells. A nearby fertilizer plant and a plastics factory's emissions add to the general noxious mix. Garbage is a common sight in the neighbourhood's streets; bad odours and airborne pollutants a daily occurrence. As one resident noted, referring to the accumulation of solid waste outside the factory: 'I don't know whether these residues [wastes] are thrown from utility vehicles after being collected [elsewhere] from the streets ... or if companies have taken advantage of the lack of control in this place. Whatever the case, it's not pleasant'. Another resident suggested: '[There] is now an urgent need to transfer the current factory to another place, especially if population growth continues close to it. Also, safety controls are lacking [as demonstrated] by the factory fire which broke out last year [2008] and resulted in foul odours and toxic fumes across the neighbourhood. In fact [we] often notice that the wind smells ... in and around the factory and as far away as the airport [approximately 5 kilometres].' All interviewees called for the ministry responsible to act on this issue otherwise the entire area would be contaminated and health negatively impacted. Their concerns raise the question: What has been the government's response to the types of problems faced by residents in Abu Hamour and elsewhere?

Towards Integrated Waste Management in Qatar

The Qatar National Vision 2030 sets out a clear mandate for environmental responsibility and sustainable behaviour across all aspects of Qatari life by calling for a balance between development needs and protection of the environment (see Tan, Al-Khalaqi and Al-Khulaifi, chapter 2; and Darwish, chapter 4, both this volume). The Vision underscores the need for a comprehensive response to the mountain of waste being generated in the State; it requires not only infrastructure development but also changes in attitudes and behaviour towards waste, not least to engender an ethic of waste minimization in the country. Implementation of the National Vision is realized via the National Development Strategy (NDS; GSDP 2011) which calls for a multifaceted strategy to contain levels of waste generation by households, commercial sites and industry and for much more of what is generated to be recycled. The strategy endorses the UNEP waste management hierarchy referred to earlier and aims to move Qatar up that hierarchy to promote increased waste avoidance and to provide a more integrated sustainable response that considers waste before it is generated rather than on the way to landfill (ibid.: 224).

The NDS calls for 'supporting recycling, incentivizing waste reduction, promoting source separation and developing a robust recycling sector' with targets of 38 per cent recycling by 2016 compared to a current level of 8 per cent (ibid.: 225–226). This will be achieved by encouraging waste minimization and waste segregation at source, processing municipal waste at the Domestic Solid Waste Management Facility (described below), and industrial waste at proposed material recovery facilities. Within the NDS framework, fourteen sector strategies are under development including an Environmental Sector Strategy which covers four key areas: Water Management, Energy Intensity and Climate Change, Pollution and Biodiversity.[14] In addition, the Qatar National Master Plan, which will guide the development of Qatar for the next twenty-five years, contains two policies on solid waste management: ENV8[15] National Waste Management Strategy that includes a requirement for recycling and the use of recycled materials before development projects are approved, and ENV9 Sites for Waste Management Facilities that states that premises should be built to meet international standards of best practice.[16] In addition, the policy framework developed in 2009 notes the need for a Solid Waste Management Plan to coordinate waste management responsibilities and planning activities.

Previously, general responsibility for environmental issues and corresponding legislation and regulation came under the remit of the Permanent Environment Protection Committee formed in 1981. This committee was superseded by the Supreme Council for Environment and Natural Reserves in 2000 which in turn was replaced by the Ministry of Environment in 2008. While the Ministry of Environment has primary responsibility for developing and implementing plans to protect the natural environment including that of appropriate waste management, day-to-day responsibility for collection and disposal of all domestic waste falls to the Ministry of Municipality and Urban Planning's (MMUP) General Cleaning Project, 'Q Kleen'. While each municipality[17] has its own schedule, infrastructure and some private-sector contracts for collecting and disposing of waste, their activities all come under the authority and direction of MMUP. Q Kleen has approximately 3,000 employees and 1,000 vehicles including refuse collection trucks, skip loaders, mini refuse trucks, open trucks, street sweepers and compactor trailers.

Currently the majority of municipal waste in Qatar is collected from large kerb-side dumpsters, skips or wheelie bins at more than 50,000 locations. There is no source separation and households typically dispose of their garbage in plastic bags of all shapes and sizes or simply throw it away loose such that it is easily dispersed by the wind or disturbed by feral cats, presenting an unsightly nuisance and health hazard to local communities. Dumping and thoughtless discarding of waste is an issue as evidenced by miscellaneous piles of rubbish here and there around residential, commercial and industrial areas, in the desert and by the sea-shore. This indicates the absence of a 'keep-it-clean' culture and individual responsibility for waste. Yet Islam, as with many other faiths, speaks of the need for people to act as trustees and keepers of the earth, to cherish and preserve its beauty and goodness and to avoid excess and waste: 'Do not be extravagant for Allah does not love the wasteful' (Qur'an 96:141, cited in Anon 2011a).

Collected MSW is loaded on to trucks and transferred by road to trans-fer stations a short distance from Doha.[18] Prior to 2011, all domestic waste was subsequently moved from the stations by trailer and disposed of in an open landfill area at Umm Alafai which accepts domestic (non-hazard-ous)[19] waste, construction and demolition wastes,[20] bulky wastes and used car tyres,[21] of which there are several million that present a fire hazard during the hot summer months. The intention is to phase out the use of this landfill and transfer domestic waste to the waste management facility. In 2005–2006 scrap recovered from the landfill totalled 0.09 per cent of the daily flow of waste into the landfill.[22] Before April 2008 any company was allowed to recover materials from the landfill as long as they were regis-tered under the General Cleaning Project of the MMUP. Since then, only seven companies have permission to recover materials: one scrap collec-tor, four plastic collectors and two paper collectors, meaning that a small amount of recycling continues at the landfill. In addition, a compost plant at Mesaieed produces 300 tonnes per day of compost from biodegradable domestic waste (GSDP 2011: 225). These initiatives, together with some private, corporate driven recycling initiatives (described below) enable some 8 per cent of MSW to be recycled.

Umm Alafai, with a total area of 2 kilometres, was constructed in the 1980s. It was not originally designed as a sanitary landfill. Waste is covered daily and greenhouse gas emissions are released above the landfill. This situation is common in developing countries where properly designed and maintained landfills are uncommon. It is a problem being tackled in Kuwait where dumping of solid waste in landfills over a twenty-five-year period has resulted in serious environmental and health impacts and prompted a major rehabilitation and remediation programme of landfill sites by the Kuwait Environment Public Agency (Al Mudh'hi 2011).

In addition to municipality-run domestic-waste collection, there are also a small number of private waste collection schemes operating in Qatar, as well as corporate recycling initiatives. For example, The Pearl, a flagship, upmarket Riviera-style island development off the east coast of Qatar close to downtown Doha, incorporates an innovative waste management system which transports waste through underground pipes at speeds of up to 70 kilometres per hour, removing the need for unsightly refuse-collection bins, a particular concern in a development that projects an exclusive image. Known as Envac, the underground system dealt with 42.5 tonnes of waste in March 2011 and is capable of handling 3,720 tonnes per month once The Pearl development is fully occupied (UDC 2011).[23] Waste collected via chutes is compacted, transported off the island on a daily basis and presently taken to landfill until it can be accepted by the facility at Mesaieed. In the Pearl's configuration of Envac, there is no source separation of waste, with the exception of 'not allowed' waste.[24] However, in keeping with the developer's environmental ethos, regular environmental awareness events are held to educate residents about environmental issues such as waste minimization and recycling (which may be introduced at The Pearl at a later date). Adopting a more traditional approach, Dulsco Qatar (established in 2007) collects and disposes of non-hazardous solid and liquid waste from residential and commercial locations by private contract but under the regulation of the MMUP, using trucks, skips and compactors similar to Q Kleen. In addition, there are a number of private recycling schemes which serve commercial enterprises[25] and corporate-sponsored waste minimization initiatives.

In 2000, in recognition of the limitations of the existing MSW management system in Qatar, the government launched a project to develop an integrated domestic solid waste management (DSWM) facility capable of accepting all of Qatar's domestic solid waste. The contract was awarded to Keppel Seghers. The company designed the facility with four key concepts in mind, namely, integration (i.e. taking a systems view of waste), sustainability (balancing development needs with environmental concerns), environmental improvement and protection and flexibility (to allow for future changes in technology and demographics). The integrated DSWM facility is located on a 300-hectare site south of Doha in Al Wakra municipality. It is designed to process 2,300 tonnes of MSW per day, up to 627 tonnes of which can be separated out for recycling, 857 tonnes can be composted and 922 tonnes used as input for a waste to energy plant (table 15.2).

Integrated waste management systems treat waste streams, collection, treatment and disposal methods as one system in order to produce environmental benefits along with economic efficiency and social acceptability (McDougal et al. 2001: 15). Using this approach, the DSWM's waste-to-energy plant will be a source of renewable energy, with a maximum en-

Table 15.2. Breakdown of daily domestic solid waste to be accepted at DSWM facility (in tonnes). *Source*: Piggott 2011

	Waste from transfer stations/ public	Recyclables for separation	Compostable for composting	Combustibles for WTE plant
Organic MSW	1,076		753	323
Paper	120			120
Plastics	368	184		184
Metals	92	83		9
Glass	81			81
Others	138			138
Green waste	104		104	
Slaughterhouse waste	25			
Pre-separated glass	81	81		25
Pre-separated paper	179	179		
Waste from plant process				43
TOTAL	**2,300**	**627**	**857**	**922**

ergy export potential of 33 megawatts at 66 kilovolts. In addition, the compost plant will produce more than 150,000 tonnes of compost per year and over 90,000 tonnes of liquid fertilizer. An above-ground landfill area will receive treated incineration bottom ash (non-combustible residue of the incineration process), cement-stabilized fly ash and street sweeping wastes (mostly sand).

By moving forward with this type of integrated approach, the National Development Strategy suggests that a 38 per cent recycling rate is achievable without any reduction in waste generation rates, but with some degree of source separation and implementation of material-recovery facilities (GSDP 2011: 226). However, the lack of opportunities for in-home source separation means that waste is currently contaminated before collection, incineration and conversion to energy or composting without recovery of all the recycled material. Given the NDS proposals for increased recycling, in the short term this is likely to involve mixed municipal solid waste taken to recovery facilities rather than separation by households unless new infrastructure is created. The NDS notes that improvements in public education and awareness about environmental issues in general and recycling in particular are critical to the achievement of the recycling targets (GSDP 2011: 225). A sea change in public attitudes may also be required if waste reduction and recycling is to be seen as everyone's responsibility, adopted out of respect for future generations (Ng, Al Khalaqu and Al Abdullah 2011). The survey of social work students undertaken for this chapter suggests that there is a latent desire among these young adults for recycling with all respondents stating that they would support recycling if it was available. Whether they would use it in practice remains to be seen; research has shown that a positive attitude towards recycling may not necessarily manifest itself in changed behaviour (Ojala 2008). A detailed study of a multifaceted waste-awareness and -education campaign in the Western Riverside Waste Authority area of central London found that simply creating awareness and generating a supportive attitude to recycling did not change recycling behaviours, particularly if there were real and perceived barriers to recycling, for example inadequate storage in homes (Thomas et al. 2004).

Critics argue that the DSWM facility is already too small given anticipated levels of MSW generation and that it locks Qatar into a system that uses non-source separated waste that fails to encourage people to recycle and reduce waste. Indeed, anecdotal evidence suggests that there is a de-facto assumption that source separation in Qatar will not work in the short term because of the significant cultural hurdles that are to be overcome. Simply put, recycling in Qatar is a challenge and only the most environmentally committed currently attempt it. Recycling bins are few and far between and those that exist tend to be hidden or placed in inconvenient locations. Moreover, contamination of different waste receptacles is common. For example, at the Katara Cultural Village seafront development opened in 2010 there are cleverly disguised recycling bins, shrouded in white ornately carved covers in keeping with the style of the development, but not conducive to encouraging the general public to recycle. This contrasts with the approach in many countries of the West where recycling containers are large and highly visible (e.g. brightly coloured) and in Bahrain where the Recycle for Charity organization has stationed large, red, white, blue and green recycling bins in pedestrian areas such as cinemas, schools and supermarkets.[26] However, there are coloured recycling bins in some 'family only' parks in Qatar where single men are not allowed access.

While recycling by individuals on a large scale is not generally an option in Qatar,[27] a number of private companies run schemes serving educational, retail, commercial and industrial locations. These are prompted by individual concerns for environmental protection, corporate social responsibility and sustainable development policies, and industry best practice rather than a regulatory requirement or municipal driver. Indeed, there are currently no regulatory mechanisms mandating recycling or the use of recyclable materials in projects[28] and there are no incentives in place to encourage recycling or indeed disincentives to not recycle such as a landfill tax or tariff system. Without these there is little to support a recycled products and services industry, except perhaps altruistic reasons such as a personal belief it is the right thing to do. Private recycling typically comprises companies arranging individual contracts with organizations for the collection of their recyclable materials. These projects are relatively small. For example, Al Haya Waste Management has collected 55 tonnes of paper and 8.5 tonnes of plastic bottles for recycling in one year from one office tower in the West Bay area of Doha.[29] The success of Qatar Telecom's (Qtel[30]) E-Waste Recycling Programme demonstrates that given the right circumstances (i.e. making things easy for users) recycling could be successful in Qatar; 27 tonnes of e-waste were collected in the first seventy-two days of the programme (Anon 2010). Mobile phones can be disposed at Qtel outlets and larger items such as TVs and kitchen appliances on 'Big Drop' days. Not only have the public readily engaged with this initiative but also large corporations have taken part. E-waste collected in this manner is shipped to Singapore for reprocessing. This programme was developed in conjunction with the Ministry of Environment to enable people safely to dispose of potentially environmentally hazardous e-waste and is in advance of a proposed e-waste law which is in the drafting stage. A similar programme in the UAE collected 600 tonnes of e-waste and 300,000 old mobile phones in three years (Kanady 2010).

Where Next for Household Waste in Qatar?

Qatar will not solve its domestic solid waste problem in the near future. It may take years to convince households to buy into a campaign to reduce, reuse and recycle waste, not least because there is simply no infrastructure to support such an initiative. The necessary changes in attitudes and behaviour are further hindered by the unique characteristics of the population, which comprises multiple nationalities with widely differing cultural and educational backgrounds and experiences. A consequence is that any programme to raise awareness about the importance of effective and efficient solid waste management, as espoused in the National Development Strategy, must be multipronged and operate at all levels, with clear and decisive enforcement. The current disregard of existing littering laws by individuals from all walks of life is discouraging. However, the growing and active membership of the Qatar Bird Club and Qatar National History Group suggest developing interest in protection of Qatar's natural environment.

Key to implementation of a comprehensive recycling and waste minimization programme will be the empowerment of unskilled migrant workers and household staff (i.e. maids, drivers, gardeners) to act in an environmentally responsible manner. At a most basic level, if employers do not recognize the need for recycling, then household staff will not be allowed to separate the household rubbish. In addition, those who are already socially disadvantaged, such as the large migrant labour force, may see little point to participation in a recycling scheme unless it directly benefits them. Their waste generation will also be substantially different to those of more affluent groups of expatriates and locals, both in volume and character, meaning that different collection systems may be required for each group. While many bachelors live in controlled living quarters on the outskirts of Doha they descend on the capital in considerable numbers on Fridays. In addition, large numbers of people congregate on public beaches, at the Inland sea area, in parks and on the Corniche at weekends. These times and locations represent important opportunities to educate people about the importance of the thoughtful disposal and recycling of litter, opportunities that to date have been missed, with the exception of volunteer initiatives to clean up some areas. Shopping malls are also places were large numbers of people congregate and yet there are no obvious recycling facilities and few waste bins. The network of mosques and other religious premises across the country represents another important avenue that could be used in any campaign to instil an environmental ethic in the population.

In some countries, notably in Europe, systems for charging for household waste have been implemented or are under consideration as a response to European directives that require, for example, significant reductions in biodegradable waste going to landfill (Dresner and Ekins 2010). It is hard to imagine such an approach being implemented in Qatar, a country where nationals get their water and electricity free and these resources are heavily subsidized for non-nationals. Tax-based systems also require the support of programmes to educate users of the system and regulation to overcome market barriers to promoting reuse and recycling (for example permitting recycled materials to be used in construction, such as rubber from tyres in asphalt). According to Simon Dresner and Paul Ekins (2010), low participation in kerb-side recycling is due primarily to problems of information, awareness, motivation and culture. But the choices individual consumers make about decisions to recycle are highly influenced by the nature of waste management and recycling infrastructure where they live.

Put simply, if recycling is not convenient and easy, people who wish to recycle will be constrained in their ability to participate. And, those who do not wish to recycle will not be penalized in the absence of a tariff or penalty system. The extent to which a tariff system would work in Qatar has yet to be fully tested by the research community. It may be that a uniquely Arabic system for household recycling and waste minimization needs to be developed that recognizes and responds to the distinctive cultural landscape in the Gulf not least the country's Bedouin heritage. The Arab Recycling Initiative supported by UNESCO and designed to provide a platform for this type of locally focused initiative comprises a programme for the development of an ethic of environmental stewardship and waste minimization in the Gulf region.

One way to begin to instil strong environmental values is through the education of young people. The story of Rashid the Recycler, his sister Dana and cousins from across the Arab region, developed by UNESCO and Qatar's Ministry of Environment, is helping to spread the recycling message to school children.[31] However, what is striking in Qatar is the number of seemingly independent schools' initiatives that have been launched recently, among them UNESCO's and Doha Bank's 'Eco Schools' programme, Msheireb Properties' 'Green Programme for Schools' (GPS), the Indian Schools' project supported by the Institution of Engineers of India and the Friends of the Environment Centre 'Award for Schools' (established in 1996). All these programmes are designed to raise awareness about environmental issues and recycling and have locally specific elements. What is missing is a way for them all to work together towards their common goal; a collaborative network of environmental knowledge and learning would support their aims and help to minimize duplication. In addition, teacher training, not mentioned in reports about the above programmes, should not be overlooked. Moreover, there is no campaign to educate university students or transform universities into centres of sustainable learning and practical action. If and when Qatar introduces a separation-at-source waste system, an army of trained volunteers, drawn potentially from universities, will be needed not only to explain the need but also how to use the system. In addition, it will take time to convince a sceptical public that separated materials are not intermingled and contaminated in a truck down the road on their way to the materials recycling facilities proposed in the National Development Strategy.

Household waste is not the most pleasant of topics, concerning the detritus of everyday life. When its collection and removal goes wrong the impacts are far reaching, witness the waste crisis in southern Italy or breakdown in waste management in areas of conflict and regions hit by disasters. Instilling in people the idea that the environment beyond the four walls of their compound or yard is as important as the private space within will be an important element of the environmental steward-ship called for in Qatar's National Development Strategy and any waste management programmes that follow. While the need for a well-known and respected figurehead to champion environmental concerns has been highlighted in the Environmental Sector Strategy, what are also needed are Champions of Waste tasked with making (the lack of) waste important to the country's future while acting as catalysts for the spread of best prac-tice across the country.

The sustainable management of waste has been identified by the UN as a critical issue in securing sustainable development. This chapter has illustrated the complexities of dealing with municipal solid waste in a country where the rate and scale of development is unprecedented and where there are distinct cultural and social dimensions that shape the re-sponse to the issue of waste. There are deeply held Arab (Bedouin) beliefs and values that may provide a route to a uniquely Arab response to ef-ficient waste management, one which favours moderation and respect for the environment over unrestrained excess. These have yet to be fully ex-ploited. Through its National Vision and Development Strategy, Qatar has emphasized the importance of establishing a knowledge-based economy that promotes education as a key element of development. Assuming that the sustainable management of waste is championed at all levels in this knowledge-development process then Qatar has a major contribution to make in demonstrating how waste minimization can become a driver of environmental sustainability in rapidly developing nations. The steps that have been taken by the government to date demonstrate a clear commit-ment to tackling and indeed solving the issue of the effective management of municipal solid waste.

Notes

1. Though considered developing nations, many of the countries of the Middle East have high GDP per capita. For example, in 2009 Qatar had a GDP per capita of US $65,495, Kuwait $38,876, UAE $38,284 and Bahrain $35,561 (GSDP 2011: 45).
2. It should be noted that countries of the Middle East are not alone in this ap-proach; the United Kingdom also has a poor record on developing alternatives to landfilling and on recycling (Dresner and Ekins 2010) and other developing countries, such as India and Tanzania, are also faced with the need to improve recycling capabilities (Uiterkamp, Azadi and Ho 2011).
3. The authors would like to thank Paul Sillitoe, Shell Chair of Sustainable Devel-opment at Qatar University, and Hind Al Sulaiti and Tara Thompson, teaching

assistants at Qatar University, for their assistance in the organization of the workshop What a Load of Rubbish! Reducing Waste for a More Sustainable future in Qatar, 6 March 2011, Sustainable Development Initiative, Department of International Affairs, College of Arts and Sciences, Qatar University.

4. By comparison, in 2009 Americans produced about 243 million tonnes of MSW, or about 4.3 pounds (1.95 kilograms) waste per person per day. Currently, in the United States, 33.8 percent is recovered and recycled or composted, 11.9 percent is burned at combustion facilities and the remaining 54.3 percent is disposed of in landfills (http://www.epa.gov/osw/nonhaz/municipal/, accessed 18 July 2011).

5. Construction and demolition waste accounts for up to 80 per cent of the solid waste stream in some countries of the Middle East, e.g. Abu Dhabi, reflecting high rates of development (Ahmad 2011).

6. The disparity in the estimates of the volume of waste reflects a general lack of accurate data, non-uniform definitions of categories of waste and ill-defined annual variations in many countries (Bogner et al. 2007: 591).

7. Companies will be charged fees based on the rate of waste produced annually, according to the type of activity and the size of the facility. Fees will range from Dh 225 to Dh 50,000 per tonne annually. Dh 225 is 45 per cent of the cost incurred by the government to dispose of 1 tonne of waste. Companies will be able to reduce their tariff through a commitment to recycling and waste reduction (Ahmad 2011).

8. It is mandatory for all public and civic buildings to be designed to meet 4-star Qatar Sustainability Assessment Standard (QSAS), while all other buildings must reach a minimum 2-star rating. For more information refer to www .lusail.com.

9. For example, the total population of the UAE is estimated at 8.26 million in 2010, of which 7.32 million are non-UAE nationals (UAE-NBS 2011).

10. This data forms part of a study by students to calculate their households' ecological footprint. The all-female students were on the Sustainable Development course in the Department of Social Sciences at Qatar University. The total sample size was thirty-eight with twelve students providing incomplete data.

11. Data from a short, opened questionnaire-based survey on recycling conducted by Dr Salah Almannai during a social work course, Spring 2010, Department of Social Sciences, Qatar University.

12. At the time of writing, the Domestic Solid Waste Management Facility was offline pending the issuance of the final 'Taking Over' certificate by the Ministry of Municipality and Urban Planning, signifying that the contractor Keppel Seghers has met all the project requirements. However, the DSWM facility began accepting waste in December 2010 and has processed over 100,000 tonnes to date (private e-mail correspondence with Geoff Piggott, regional manager Middle East and North Africa, Keppel Seghers Engineering Singapore). It currently receives 1,000 to 1,400 tonnes of waste per day (Jackson 2011).

13. Interviewed Autumn 2009 by Salah Almannai.

14. The final report (February 2011) has not been released for public dissemination at the time of writing. It identifies key outcomes and goals within each area.

15. The nomenclature ENV8 refers to the policy number within the National Master Plan.

16. These policies are in the process of being finalized and have yet to be released for full public scrutiny. The information cited here was obtained from the Qatar University workshop on waste, endnote 3.

17. At the time of writing, there were seven municipalities: Doha, Al Rayyan, Al Wakra, Al Khor, Al Daayen, Al Shamal and Umm Salal.

18. There are currently four transfer stations: Doha South with a capacity of 900 tonnes/day, Doha West (900 t/d), Doha Industrial (300 t/d) and Dukhan (150 t/d), with a fifth planned at Al Khor (150 t/d). These have all been built or upgraded under the DSWM project described below. Prior to the project the transfer stations were open dumps.

19. There is a separate site for dealing with hazardous waste near Umm Said.

20. Landfills at Rawdat Rasheed and Al Owaina primarily accept construction and demolition waste.

21. For example, the Seashore Group (www.seashoregroup.com.qa) has a tyre recycling plant capable of processing 30 tonnes per day. However, they are restricted in their ability to make use of the recycled rubber as at the time of writing Qatari law does not permit the use of recycled materials in asphalt, for example, as is common practice in other parts of the world.

22. Data obtained from GSDP unpublished Environmental Sector Strategy 2011–2016, Final, February 2011.

23. Similar high-tech waste collection systems have been launched in Abu Dhabi to reduce the number of daily trips by refuse trucks and an underground vacuum system is part of the Abu Dhabi island development (Ahmad 2011).

24. The Envac system used at The Pearl cannot deal with all forms of waste: for example, bulky waste (furniture, cardboard), spongy waste (cushions, pillows) or waste emitting offensive odours (animal feces). These are collected and disposed of separately.

25. Many of these initiatives focus on industrial waste. For example, the Seashore Group deals with waste from Ras Laffan Industrial City, Mesaieed industrial area and Al Khor city. The company does not directly manage any recycling, rather it sends recyclable materials to government-approved recycling facilities in Qatar.

26. Recycling for Charity collects and processes the waste and finally sells it to the local and world market. For every tonne collected the company donates to local charities (http://www.recycling-for-charity.com).

27. Employees from RasGas and QatarGas living at the Al Khor Housing Community can make use of Qatar's first source waste separation initiative enabling them to recycle paper, aluminium cans and plastic water bottles.

28. In some cases Qatar will need to amend legislation to permit the use of recycled materials where research has proven their efficacy. This has been demon-

strated in Abu Dhabi where the viability of a Construction Waste Processing Facility depended on changes in specifications and ministerial approval to permit the use of recycled aggregates, in road construction for example, thereby creating a market for the product (Theil 2011).

29. Private correspondence with the general manager of Al Haya Waste Management, Qatar.

30. Qatar Telecom (Qtel) is the telecommunications service provider licensed by the Supreme Council of Information and Communication Technology (ictQATAR) to provide both fixed and mobile telecommunications services in the state of Qatar (http://www.qtel.qa). Qtel was rebranded as Ooredoo in February 2013.

31. http://portal.unesco.org/science/en/ev.php-URL_ID=4835&URL_DO=DO_TOPIC&URL_SECTION=201.html (accessed 24 July 2011).

References

Ahmad, A. 2011. 'Abu Dhabi to Bill Waste Generation,' *Khaleej Times Online*, 6 March.

Alhumoud, J. M. 2005. Municipal solid waste recycling in the Gulf Cooperation Council States. *Resources, Conservation and Recycling* 45: 142–158.

Alhumoud, J. M., I. Al Ghusain and H. Al Hasawi. 2004. 'Management of Recycling in the Gulf Co-operation Council States.' *Waste Management* 24 (2004): 551–562.

Al Maaded, M., et al. n.d. 'An Overview of Solid Waste Management in Qatar.' Unpublished working paper.

Al Mudh'hi, S. F. 2011. 'Waste Management in Kuwait, an Overview.' Paper presented at MEED Waste Management, 21–22 February.

Al Yousfi, A. B. n.d. *Sound Environmental Management of Solid Waste: The Landfill Bioreactor.* Bahrain: UNEP Regional Office for West Asia (ROWA).

Anon. 2010 'Huge Response to Qtel E-Waste Recycle Project,' *Gulf Times*, 23 September, 6.

———. 2011a. 'Living in Harmony with Our Surroundings,' *Gulf Times*, 4 March, 13.

———. 2011b. 'GCC Produces 80m Tonne [*sic*] Waste Yearly,' *Khaleej Times Online*, 7 April.

Bahrain Census. 2010. General Results. http://www.census2010.gov.bh/results_en.php (accessed 31 March 2011).

Bee'ah. 2011. 'Public-Private Partnerships Working Effectively in Tandem.' Paper presented at MEED Waste Management, 21–22 February.

Bogner, J., et al. 2007. 'Waste Management.' In *Climate Change 2007: Mitigation, Contribution of Working Group III to the Fourth Assessment Report of the Intergovernmental Panel on Climate Change*, eds B. Metz et al., 587–618. Cambridge: Cambridge University Press.

Bruyer, C. 2011. 'Financing Waste Projects in MENA.' Paper presented at MEED Waste Management, 21–22 February.

Cole, D. P. 1975. *Nomads of the Nomads: The Al Murrah Bedouin of the Empty Qatar.* Arlington Heights, IL: Harlan Davidson.

Centre of Waste Management Abu Dhabi (CWM A-D). 2011. 'Waste in the Emirate of Abu Dhabi.' http://www.cwm.ae//index.php?page=waste-in-auh (accessed 31 March 2011).

Dresner, S., and P. Ekins. 2010. 'Charging for Domestic Waste in England: Combining Environmental and Equity Considerations.' *Resources, Conservation and Recycling* 54: 1100–1108.

FACT Bahrain. 2011. The BIG Green Issue, February, 29–39.

Gautam, V. 2009. 'Solid Waste Management in the Gulf Region: Challenges & Opportunities.' http://www.globe-net.com/articles/2009/december/17/solid-waste-management-in-the-gulf-region-challenges-opportunities-.aspx?sub=11 (accessed 4 July 2011).

General Secretariat for Development Planning (GSDP). 2011. *National Development Strategy 2011–2016: Towards Qatar National Vision 2030.* Doha.

Hantoush, S. 2011. 'Organic Waste Recycling in Sharjah.' Paper presented at MEED Waste Management, 21–22 February.

Jackson, R. 2011. 'Qatar's residents urged to reduce waste generation,' *Gulf Times,* 22 December, 10.

John, P. 2011. '20% GDP Growth Forecast,' *Gulf Times,* 1 May, 1.

Kanady, S. 2010. 'E-waste Law soon; draft in the works,' *The Peninsula,* 15 June (accessed 28 June 2010).

Lancaster, W. 1997. *The Rwala Bedouin Today.* Second edition. Long Grove, IL: Waveland.

McDougal, F. R., et al. 2001. *Integrated Solid Waste Management: A Life Cycle Inventory.* Second edition. Oxford: Wiley- Blackwell Publishing.

MEED. 2011. Proceedings of MEED Middle East Business Intelligence Conference on Waste Management, 21–22 February.

Ng S., A. Al Khalaqu and N. E. Al . 2011. 'Qatar National Development Strategy (2011–2016) Waste Management and Recycling.' Paper presented at the workshop What a Load of Rubbish! Reducing Waste for a More Sustainable Future in Qatar, Qatar University, 8 March.

Ojala, M. 2008. 'Recycling and ambivalence: Quantitative and qualitative analyses of household recycling among young adults.' *Environment and Behaviour* 40(6): 777–797.

Phillips, P. S., et al. 2010. 'A Critical Review of a Key Waste Strategy Initiative in England: Zero Waste Places Projects 2008–2009.' *Resources, Conservation and Recycling* 55 (2011): 335–343.

Pigott, G.A. 2011. 'The Middle East's First Integrated Domestic Wastes Management Facility in Qatar: A progress update.' Paper presented at the workshop What a Load of Rubbish! Reducing Waste for a More Sustainable Future in Qatar, Qatar University, 8 March.

Platt, G. 2011. 'Sustainable Infrastructure Development: Planning for Management of C&D Waste.' Paper presented at MEED Waste Management, 21–22 February.

Qatar Statistics Authority (QSA). 2010a. *Results of the 2010 Census of Population, Housing and Establishments.* Doha.

————. 2010b. 'Population by Sex and Municipality Table 1.1.' http://www.qsa .gov.qa/QatarCensus/Pdf/Population_by_sex_and_municipality.pdf (accessed 29 April 2011).

Theil, C. 2011. 'Implementing a Construction Waste Processing Facility in Abu Dhabi, UAE.' Paper presented at MEED Waste Management, 21–22 February.

Thomas, C., et al. 2004. 'Changing Recycling Behavior: An Evaluation of Attitudes and Behavior to Recycling in the Western Riverside Area of London.' Paper presented at the Waste 2004 Integrated Waste Management and Pollution Control Conference, September, Stratford-upon-Avon, UK. www.oro.open.ac.uk (accessed 20 July 2011).

Tolba, M. K., and N. W. Saab (eds.). 2008. *Arab Environment Future Challenges: Report of the Arab Forum for Environment and Development.* Beirut, Lebanon: AFED.

UAE National Bureau of Statistics (UAE-NBS). 2011. 'Table: National Population of Emirate and Sex (2010 mid-year estimates).' http://wwwuaestatistics.gov.ae (accessed 31 March 2011).

United Development Corporation (UDC). 2011. E-mail correspondence with Environment Department, United Development Corporation, Qatar, April.

United Nations Educational, Scientific and Cultural Organization (UNESCO). 1992. *Agenda 21: UN Economic and Social Development Division for Sustainable Development.* http://www.un.org/esa/dsd/agenda21/res_agenda21_21.shtml (accessed 11 December 2011).

United Nations Environment Programme (UNEP). 2005. *Solid Waste Management.* Osaka, Japan: UNEP IETC.

United Nations Environment Programme / GRID-Arendal (UNEP/GRID-Arendal). 2004. 'Projected Trends in Regional Municipal Waste Generation.' UNEP/GRID-Arendal Maps and Graphics Library. http://maps.grida.no/go/graphic/pro jected_trends_in_regional_municipal_waste_generation (accessed 25 April 2011).

Uiterkamp, B. J. S., H. Azadi and P. Ho. 2011. 'Sustainable Recycling Model: A Comparative Analysis Between India and Tanzania.' *Resources, Conservation and Recycling* 22: 344–355.

World Bank. 2011. World Development Indicators. http://data.worldbank.org/ data-catalog/world-development-indicators (accessed 21 December 2011).

World Wide Fund (WWF). 2010. *Living Planet Report.* Gland, Switzerland.

Warnock, M. 2009. 'Severe Need for Saudi Waste Solution,' *ConstructionWeekOnline,* 16 September, article 6382.

CHAPTER 16

Sustainable Development and Health

From Global to Local Agenda

Mylène Riva, Catherine Panter-Brick and Mark Eggerman

Sustainable development of a region and the health of its people are intrinsically linked. This is emphasized in the first principle of the 1992 Rio Declaration: 'Human beings are at the centre of concerns for sustainable development. They are entitled to a healthy and productive life in harmony with nature' (United Nations 1992). It is argued that sustainable development cannot be achieved without a healthy population, and that the health of a population cannot be maintained without healthy environments (von Schirnding 2002a), such that 'health' is both an indicator of and a resource for sustainable development. In this chapter, we take up these arguments to illustrate the interrelationships between the socio-cultural, economic and environmental 'pillars' of sustainable development, and how these are underpinned by good health (von Schirnding and Tobin 2002). Concerns for sustainable development and global health pose significant challenges, are at the top of the international agenda and demand specific frameworks for action.

Health is defined as 'a state of complete physical, mental and social well-being and not merely the absence of disease or infirmity' (WHO 1946). Two hallmarks of this definition are that it is holistic, linking physical states with both emotional and social experiences, and that it strives towards positive outcomes related to well-being, rather than the absence of disease. As such, the definition of health comes close to that of happiness, but with the fundamental difference that health is a human right, while happiness is not (Panter-Brick and Fuentes 2010). Sustainable development, in turn, is economic and social development that 'meets the needs of the present without compromising the ability of future generations to meet their own needs' by irreparably damaging the environment (WCED 1987). The economic, socio-cultural and natural environment 'pillars' of sustainable development also correspond to the 'social determinants of health', i.e. the socio-environmental conditions in which people are born and live. These two dimensions of human experience are thus closely interlinked. Indeed, one recent editorial in *The Lancet* (2009) highlighted a definition of health that went far beyond medical considerations, as the 'ability to adapt' that is in terms of our human capability to respond to changing environmental conditions.

We begin by reviewing the international agenda, detailing some of the key standpoints taken at international conferences on sustainable development, health and health care. We trace parallels in the 'calls for action' to achieve sustainable development and to achieve rights to health, in relation to the need for actions across different sectors of society and at multiple levels of governance: namely, calls for integrated local, national and global action to achieve goals for good health and sustainable development. We examine health indicators within the GCC states and priorities and strategies for action to tackle the social and environmental determinants of health. Throughout this chapter, we highlight issues critical for inter- and intragenerational equity, issues that call for a political and scientific agenda than addresses the many tensions currently engendered from rapid population growth, shortfalls in economic development, and worrying health profiles.

The International Agenda on Sustainable Development: Linkages with Health

Sustainable development is concerned with balancing environmental, social and economic objectives in order to maximize societal well-being, both in the present and the future (von Schirnding 2002a), within the carrying capacity of supporting ecosystems. This demands good governance at local, national and global levels, and also well-orchestrated intersectoral efforts. Within a remit focused on sustainable development, health issues have received increasing attention, due to the premise that health and development are 'intimately interconnected' (United Nations 1992). Three summits, led by the United Nations, made such linkages explicit.

'Our Common Future'

In 1987, the United Nations World Commission on Environment and Development (WCED) published a groundbreaking report entitled *Our Common Future*, in which good health was recognized as the foundation of human welfare and productivity. The argument was made that sound health policies are essential for sustainable development. In this early report on sustainable development, health was discussed largely in relation to the poverty and environmental conditions of developing countries. The issues highlighted included communicable diseases such as malaria and HIV/AIDS, malnutrition and diseases linked to water and sanitation. Health was also discussed in relation to fertility rates and rapid population growth, and issues of family planning and reproduction. It was argued that existing action with respect to health policy and health care provision was not sufficient and that social and economic policies were needed to complement provision of primary health care and health education programs.

Agenda 21

In 1992, the United Nations Conference on Environment and Development (UNCED), also known as the Earth Summit held at Rio de Janeiro, produced a blueprint for programmatic action related to sustainable development. This was known as Agenda 21, namely, an agenda for the twenty-first century, voted in by no less than 178 heads of government, to take action at global, national and local levels to intervene in areas where humans directly affect the environment with respect to climate change. This agenda contributed to raising health issues as key dimensions of sustainable development (United Nations 1992), and to establishing key partnerships between governments and other forms of global or local governance.

The first principle of the 1992 Rio Declaration on Environment and Development stated, as quoted in the introduction, that humans are at the centre of concerns over sustainable development and are entitled to a healthy and productive life in harmony with nature. Chapter 6 of Agenda 21 emphasized the fundamental commitment, within sustainable development, to protect and promote health: 'Health ultimately depends on the ability to manage successfully the interaction between the physical, spiritual, biological and economic/social environment. Sound development is not possible without a healthy population. ... Conversely, it is the very lack of development that adversely affects the health condition of many people, which can be alleviated only through development' (United Nations 1992: 42).

Key steps to protect and promote health, specified in Agenda 21, included: meeting the primary health needs of rural, peri-urban, and urban populations; controlling communicable diseases such as HIV/AIDS, malaria and sanitation/water-related infections; meeting challenging health conditions associated with poor living conditions; and reducing health risks from environmental hazards and pollution. In addition, it highlighted the protection and promotion of health of vulnerable groups, e.g. children, women, indigenous people, the elderly and the disabled, as a prerequisite for sustainable development. In addition, Agenda 21 saw prevention and health promotion programmes as particularly relevant to achieving goals of health equity, namely the right to health across all population groups within society.

A More Central Place for Health

A decade later, in 2002, the United Nations World Summit on Sustainable Development (WSSD), held in Johannesburg, reaffirmed its commitment to the Rio Declaration and the full implementation of Agenda 21 (United Nations 2002). The WSSD declaration asked each and every one of us to take notice of the serious problems that affect our children's future. It reaffirmed the Rio agenda on: poverty eradication as an indispensable requirement for sustainable development; linkages between population health and sustainable development; and vulnerable groups. In comparison to Rio, however, it placed a greater emphasis on social and economic issues, and on local, as opposed to global, agendas (von Schirnding 2005).

One contribution to WSSD was an initiative, led by UN Secretary General Kofi Annan, identifying five thematic areas to provide impetus for international action on sustainable development: Water, Energy, Health, Agriculture, and Biodiversity and Ecosystem Management (WEHAB; von Schirnding and Tobin 2002). As a result, health issues featured more centrally, bringing to the fore issues in relation to communicable diseases, water, sanitation and air pollution. For the first time, WSSD also called for programmes to tackle chronic diseases, such as cardiovascular diseases (CVD), diabetes, obesity, cancer and respiratory diseases, and their associated risk factors, namely tobacco, alcohol, poor diets, physical inactivity, mental health problems, injuries and violence (article 54.O). Further priorities for health-related action included strengthening the capacity of health care systems to deliver basic health services to all population groups, to implement global commitments to combat HIV/AIDS, to reduce respiratory diseases and problems resulting from air pollution and to phase out human exposure to lead (e.g. in lead-based paint) and other sources of contaminants. A key message, in this wide-ranging health agenda, was that sustainable development cannot be achieved where there is a high prevalence of incapacitating illnesses, while population health cannot be maintained without healthy environments (von Schirnding 2005).

In recent years, health issues in relation to sustainable development have been increasingly linked to global actions to tackle climate change (Costello et al. 2009) and to eliminate poverty; this is represented in the two themes of the next United Nations Conference on Sustainable Development in 2012 (referred to as 'Rio+20') which are green economy and poverty eradication (www.uncsd2012.org). In brief, the prominence of health issues within the international discourse on sustainable development has grown rapidly over the last two decades. This has been paralleled by an increased recognition that the social, economic and environmental conditions in which people live are pre-conditions for good health.

The International Agenda on Health: Linkages with Sustainable Development

In 1978 the International Conference on Primary Health Care in Alma-Ata (in present-day Kazakhstan) called for a holistic definition of health and launched the rallying call of 'health for all' as a fundamental human right (WHO 1978). It also recognized the importance of economic and social development to realize this goal, namely equity in access to health care, thus enlarging the scope of health-related action to include sectors other than health services per se. The conference raised concerns regarding health inequalities between developed and developing countries, as well as inequalities within countries. Thus, three decades ago, in a time of Cold War, economic crisis, reduction in public spending and emerging diseases, economic and social development was already posited as intrinsically linked to population health.

Primary health care (PHC) was the key to deliver 'health for all by the year 2000', the strategic means to attain a level of health that would enable each and every individual to lead a socially and economically productive life (ibid.). Primary health care is 'essential health care based on practical, scientifically sound and socially acceptable methods and technology made universally accessible to individuals and families in the community through their full participation and at a cost that the community and country can afford to maintain at every stage of their development in the spirit of self-reliance and self-determination' (article VI). The fundamentals of PHC are thus based on values relating to: active community participation, social relevance, involvement of sectors other than solely the health care sector, health services provision, health protection and promotion and use of appropriate and effective technologies. PHC was to be an integral part of a country's health system and of the social and economic development of local communities. It constitutes the first tier of care by which individuals, families and communities engage with a national health system.

In market-based economies, countries varied in the extent to which they embraced the social and political goals of Alma-Ata, undermined as they were by the proponents of selective PHC, more focused on the medical strategies (vs. comprehensive strategies as originally intended by

PHC) that accelerated the tempo but reduced the scope of health care programmatic interventions. In today's developing-countries context, PHC is set against a context characterized by the coexistence of communicable diseases, malnutrition and reproductive health issues, on the one hand, and non-communicable diseases on the other, a 'double burden of disease' that poses considerable challenges to health systems (Gillam 2008).

Since the declaration of Alma-Ata, rapid health gains were noted in the GCC and EMR countries, facilitated by improvements in literacy, economic development and access to clean water and sanitation (Sabri 2008). Political commitments to the goals and principles of PHC clearly have had positive impact within the region, despite variation in levels of implementation and health care financing and provision (ibid.). Recently EMR countries met at the 'Qatar Primary Health Care 2008: The Foundation of Health and Wellbeing' conference, where they reaffirmed that 'the primary health care approach is the main strategy to achieve better health and well-being for the people of the Region'. They reiterated their 'commitment to primary health care and its values and principles of universal access and coverage, based on equity and social justice, community involvement and health as a basic human right' (Qatar Declaration 2008). Through this declaration, member states recognized that they need to respond quickly to a changing global geo-political, socio-economic, informational, technological and climatic landscape, given the challenge posed to health systems. Actions towards sustainable development are needed to address the wider determinants of health.

Millennium Development Goals for Equity in Health

One of the most remarkable international agreements on health, poverty reduction and development were the Millennium Development Goals (MDG): a call for action at the local, national and international levels by the United Nations in 2000 to eradicate poverty and its many dimensions by 2015. The eight MDG address targets to eradicate poverty and hunger (MDG1); achieve universal primary education (MDG2); eliminate gender inequality (MDG3); reduce child (MDG4) and maternal mortality (MDG5); reverse the spread of HIV/AIDS, tuberculosis and malaria (MDG6); reverse the loss of natural resources and biodiversity and improve access to water, sanitation and good housing (MDG7); and establish effective global partnerships (MDG8) (United Nations, http://www.un.org/millennium goals). These goals (table 16.1) are broken down into twenty-one quantifiable targets, with measurable success specified across more than sixty indicators. Goals and targets are to be implemented through partnerships between developed and developing countries, to foster a national and

Table 16.1. The Millennium Development Goals and specific targets to achieve by 2015. *Source*: http://mdgs.un.org/unsd/mdg/Resources/Attach/Indicators/OfficialList2008.pdf

Goals	Targets
Goal 1: Eradicate extreme poverty and hunger	Target 1.A: Halve, between 1990 and 2015, the proportion of people whose income is less than one dollar a day
	Target 1.B: Achieve full and productive employment and decent work for all, including women and young people
	Target 1.C: Halve, between 1990 and 2015, the proportion of people who suffer from hunger
Goal 2: Achieve universal primary education	Target 2.A: Ensure that, by 2015, children everywhere, boys and girls alike, will be able to complete a full course of primary schooling
Goal 3: Promote gender equality and empower women	Target 3.A: Eliminate gender disparity in primary and secondary education, preferably by 2005, and in all levels of education no later than 2015
Goal 4: Reduce child mortality	Target 4.A: Reduce by two-thirds, between 1990 and 2015, the under-five mortality rate
Goal 5: Improve maternal health	Target 5.A: Reduce by three quarters, between 1990 and 2015, the maternal mortality ratio
	Target 5.B: Achieve, by 2015, universal access to reproductive health
Goal 6: Combat HIV/ AIDS, malaria and other diseases	Target 6.A: Have halted by 2015 and begun to reverse the spread of HIV/AIDS
	Target 6.B: Achieve, by 2010, universal access to treatment for HIV/AIDS for all those who need it
	Target 6.C: Have halted by 2015 and begun to reverse the incidence of malaria and other major diseases
Goal 7: Ensure environmental sustainability	Target 7.A: Integrate the principles of sustainable development into country policies and programmes and reverse the loss of environmental resources
	Target 7.B: Reduce biodiversity loss, achieving, by 2010, a significant reduction in the rate of loss
	Target 7.C: Halve, by 2015, the proportion of people without sustainable access to safe drinking water and basic sanitation
	Target 7.D: By 2020, to have achieved a significant improvement in the lives of at least 100 million slum dwellers

(continued on next page)

Table 16.1. continued

Goals	Targets
Goal 8: Develop a global partnership for development	Target 8.A: Develop further an open, rule-based, predictable, non-discriminatory trading and financial system
	Target 8.B: Address the special needs of the least developed countries
	Target 8.C: Address the special needs of landlocked developing countries and small island developing states
	Target 8.D: Deal comprehensively with the debt problems of developing countries through national and international measures in order to make debt sustainable in the long term
	Target 8.E: In cooperation with pharmaceutical companies, provide access to affordable essential drugs in developing countries
	Target 8.F: In cooperation with the private sector, make available the benefits of new technologies, especially information and communications

international environment conducive to development, the elimination of poverty and health equity. While the eight goals are set on an international scale, targets and indicators are country specific, representing guides to measure performance against the specified goals. The choice of targets and indicators are tailored to fit with a country's specific situation and development needs.

Globally, progress towards the MDGs is encouraging, yet considerable efforts are required if goals are to be met by 2015. Not all countries are on track to meet these goals, with the least progress in Africa and South Asia, regions where there is urgent need of meeting the MDGs. Recent reviews report that: eradication of extreme poverty and hunger is on course to be attained and remarkable progress has been made towards reversing trends in HIV/AIDS, tuberculosis and malaria; there is insufficient or slow progress towards achieving provision of universal primary education, reduction of maternal and child mortality and promotion of gender equality and empowerment of women; environmental sustainability is compromised in many parts of the world, notably due to extreme climate and natural events, and the global economic crisis has put unexpected strain on local economies and global aid to developing countries (Hogan et al. 2010; United Nations 2010; Waage et al. 2010).

EMR countries are relatively on track to meet the MDGs, with goals already or very likely to be achieved in relation to the eradication of poverty and hunger and universal primary education; for example, in GCC countries enrolment rates in primary education are already above 85 per cent (United Nations 2005). GCC countries have also seen a significant reduction in childhood mortality rates between 1990 and the mid-2000s, with rates being equal or less than 10 per thousand live births. Although still high in Saudi Arabia, childhood mortality rates were reduced from 34 to 18.6 per thousand between 1990 and 2005, while infant mortality rates decreased from 44 to 21.7 per thousand over the same period. In Saudi Arabia, a further challenge to health equity is to narrow the disparities in child and infant mortality rates that exist across urban and rural areas. Finally, with regards to maternal mortality, all countries are expected to achieve a 75 per cent reduction of death rates and increase the proportion of births that are attended by skilled health personnel. With respect to communicable diseases (MDG6), malaria no longer poses a real threat, while HIV/AIDS prevalence is increasing, albeit from a very low level.

A contentious MDG relates to the promotion of gender equality, given that countries have set themselves different targets and are using different indicators to measure 'success'. In the GCC countries, the educational achievements of women are noteworthy: there are more women than men enrolled in higher education, although this might reflect cultural practices that favour sending men abroad for post-secondary education; it is also possible that women engage in higher education because of a lack of job opportunities or attitudes towards women working outside the home (United Nations 2005). This 'success' for women on the education front is not necessarily translated into economic and political participation, or participation in the labour force which is mainly composed of men (there is also a large influx of male migrant workers, in response to GCC policies regulating the construction sector, and of women in the housekeeping and nursing sectors; United Nations 2005). With respect to MDG7, progress has been made in GCC states to address the challenges of sustainable development in relation to environmental degradation and pollution, but this is harder to quantify given sparse data. The energy sector, dominated by the oil and gas industry, is the most significant economic sector in the region and is associated with increases in CO_2 emission, air pollution and negative impacts on water and marine resources and ecosystems (see Howard, chapter 11, this volume). Attaining sustainable oil and gas development in the region (see Henfrey, chapter 6; Gilberthorpe, Clarke and Sillitoe chapter 7, both this volume) is thus a prerequisite for sustaining long-term population health. Another noteworthy target (MDG8) relates to international cooperation and collective responsibility at the global level, to foster an environment conducive to pro-poor development. In this respect, the GCC has made significant contributions to development assistance, with investments of US $13.7 billion between 2000 and 2003 (United Nations 2005). This progress has to be set within the context of the current economic crisis, the impacts of which have been particularly severe in some of the GCC states.

Health Promotion: Healthy Public Policies, Supportive Environments and Community Action

We now turn to health promotion, the values and principles of which align closely with those of primary health care. Almost thirty years ago, the Ottawa Charter for Health Promotion defined health promotion as 'the process of enabling people to increase control over and to improve their health' (WHO 1986). It focused on five key strategic actions. The first was building healthy public policy, by putting health on the agenda in all sectors of society and at all levels of government, so decision makers would be aware of, and responsible for, the likely health consequences of their policies aiming to modify the social determinants of health. The second was creating supportive environments for health, by recognizing the inextricable links between people's health and social, economic and natural contexts. The third was strengthening community action in setting priorities, making decisions, planning strategies and implementing them to achieve better health. The fourth was developing personal abilities by providing information, education for health and enhancing life skills, in order to increase the options available to people to exercise control over their own health and their environments, and to make choices conducive to health. The final strategy was to reorient health services towards health promotion and disease prevention, beyond responsibilities for providing clinical and curatives services and in line with the values of primary health care.

In 2005, the Bangkok Charter for Health Promotion in a Globalized World sought to address critical factors such as the rising inequalities within and between countries, new patterns of consumption and communication, commercialization, global environmental change and urbanization. In addition, it highlighted the rapid and often adverse social, economic and demographic changes affecting working conditions, learning environments, family patterns and the cultural and social fabric of communities (WHO 2005). These factors influence health and demographic transitions in countries of the Eastern Mediterranean Region (EMR) and are certainly at play in GCC states. To manage the challenges of globalization, the Bangkok Charter posited that coherent policy must be developed across all levels of governments, United Nations' bodies and other organizations, including the private sector – stressing that health issues need to be 'everybody's business'. The Bangkok Charter recognized that globalization, as well as posing new challenges to health, provides new opportunities for co-operation to improve well-being and reduce transnational health risks, including enhanced information and communications technology, and improved mechanisms for global governance.

In the EMR, actions for health promotion are informed by the Ottawa Charter, by regional resolutions such as the 1989 Amman Declaration on Health Promotion through Islamic Lifestyle (WHO Regional Office for the Eastern Mediterranean [EMRO] 1996), and by health education programs such as the publication series 'The Right Path to Health' (www.emro.who .int/publications/HealthEdReligion/Index.htm). In addition, the Strategy for Health Promotion 2006–2013 aims to assist EMR countries in creating and maintaining environments leading to better health and quality of life, focusing on the unique strengths and opportunities of the Region (WHO EMRO 2008: 17). This strategy encompasses a life-course perspective that recognizes that physical and social exposures during gestation, child-hood, adolescence, adulthood and old age all influence health trajectories; targeting interventions to the social determinants of health and to settings where people live, work and play; and the use of evidence to inform deci-sions, and best practice to select effective interventions. Importantly, these approaches have to be tailored to the national context, and based on health needs and priorities defined through participatory processes that involve a wide range of stakeholders. The strategy embraced the view that local communities are at the centre of health promotion activities, such that community participation needs enhancement at all levels of development and policy implementation. Thus governance for health promotion oper-ates across different levels.

This last point is illustrated, for example, through community-based initiatives (CBI) which complement primary health care efforts by target-ing the social determinants of health through bottom-up community en-gagement and intersectoral collaboration (Assai, Siddiqi and Watts 2006). The aim of CBI is to create development policies that are supportive to health while fostering community empowerment, local governance and equitable access to health care. CBI include programmes such as Health Promoting Schools (http://www.who.int/topics/school_health_pro motion/en/) and Healthy Cities and Healthy Villages (Khosh-Chashm 1995). Because health needs vary across communities, local leadership and community engagement are crucial factors in identifying and achiev-ing health-related goals. CBI have been implemented in the EMR since 1988 (WHO EMRO 2009); among GCC states, examples of successful CBI implementation are found in Oman and in Saudi Arabia (box 16.1).

Box 16.1. Community-Based Initiatives Implemented in Oman, 2004–2005, and Saudi Arabia, 2007

Oman: The Nizwa healthy lifestyle project aims to reduce morbidity and mortality related to non-communicable diseases among teachers at the Nizwa School for girls. Following programmes of public awareness and healthy school promotion initiatives, a group of teachers decided to take action to tackle their sedentary lifestyles. They identified a high level of obesity among staff and attributed part of this as due to lack of public or private venues for women to exercise. During the academic year, female teachers raised sufficient money to purchase fitness machines to equip a room provided by the school in support of this healthy lifestyle project, with the hope to extend the use of the gym to girl students and to other women in the community (WHO EMRO 2009).

Saudi Arabia: In the community of Bukariyah, an organic vegetable market was built as a result of collaboration between the municipality, the Ministry of Agriculture Al-Qaseem University, private companies and the community with the aim to increase access to healthy food. The market was also used to raise community awareness about the nutritional benefit of fruits and vegetable consumption with the aim of changing unhealthy diets (WHO EMRO 2009).

Source: http://www.emro.who.int/cbi/publications/success-stories.html

---

Another potential 'tool' for health promotion in the region is Health Impact Assessment (HIA). HIA has been defined as a 'combination of procedures, methods and tools by which a policy, program or project may be judged as to its potential effects on the health of a population, and the distribution of those effects within the population' (WHO European Centre for Health Policy 1999). HIA is thus a framework for evaluating, comprehensively, the positive and negative health impacts of development programmes with a view to insure sustainable development and the creation of environments supportive of good health. It is underpinned by a holistic model of health, recognizing multiple sectors of influence on health and by values such as equity, participation and sustainable development. The intent of HIA is to inform and influence the decision-making processes (not delay or constrain decision), through community involvement and partnership, such that development programmes or projects lead to improved population health.

Within the EMR, HIA is mainly conducted within the Environmental Health Impact Assessment (EHIA) framework which is gaining impetus in the region (see, for example, Al Othman and Clarke, chapter 5, this volume) given that it is now requested by most international development banks before agreement is reached to support development projects (Hassan et al. 2005; IPIECA/OGP 2005). The main difference between HIA and EHIA is that the former can be conducted on development projects not *directly* impacting on the natural environment (e.g. building of a supermarket, new economic policy) and therefore relates more directly to the social determinants of health. HIA and EHIA have the potential to influence decision making by raising awareness about the links between health and the social, economic and physical environment; by helping decision makers identify, assess, mitigate and optimize potential health impacts of the decision; and by helping those affected by the policy to participate in its formulation and decision making (Kemm and Parry 2004). Whereas the potential for governance and health promotion of CBI is situated at more the local level, HIA also has the potential to address the more upstream social determinants of health, if applied to assess the impacts of health and well-being of development policies and projects at a strategic level.

The 'Pillars of Sustainable Development' and the 'Social Determinants of Health'

The pillars of sustainable development are defined as the economic, socio-cultural and environmental conditions in which people are born, live, learn, work, reproduce and get older. They operate across international, national and local levels and influence population health and well-being though the provision of opportunities, or constraints, for people to lead healthy and happy lives. Together, these three 'pillars' are known as the 'social determinants of health' (SDH), i.e. the specific features and pathways by which social and environmental conditions impact on health. The SDH receive specific attention since they are modifiable by informed action (Krieger 2001), such as public policies and development programmes and projects. They are the 'causes of the causes' of poor health, the 'upstream' determinants of health as opposed to 'downstream' determinants pertaining to biological processes. And consequently, in terms of governance, the recent WHO Commission on the Social Determinants of Health has forcefully argued that what matters most for health is concerted action to tackle the linkages between social and health inequalities. The evidence is incontrovertible that social inequalities are the root of poor health, and that 'social inequalities are killing people on a large scale' (Commission of Social Determinants of Health 2008). This has been a rallying call for improving the health of nations and achieving international, regional and local health equity.

Thus health is, to a large extent, about the environment and its sustainable development, not just a matter of biological processes and access to care. This is best illustrated when considering health care expenditure in relation to life expectancy (see the WHO Global Health Observatory, http://apps.who.int/ghodata/). The United States spends more on health care per capita than any other country (US $7,245 in 2007), yet the average life expectancy (seventy-eight years) is similar to the life expectancy of other countries spending considerably less on health care, such as Cuba ($585) and Costa Rica ($488). One reason for the discrepancy between spending and life expectancy is that these averages are masking considerable inequalities between different geographic areas and groups of the population within countries (Wilkinson and Pickett 2009) and by differences in the social policy context (Avendano and Kawachi 2011). In the United States, for example, one study estimated that 886,202 deaths could have been prevented between 1991 and 2000 if mortality rates between whites and African Americans were equalized, in contrast to 176, 633 lives saved by medical advances over the same period (Woolf et al. 2004). The conclusion has been drawn that 'achieving equity may do more for health than perfecting the technology of care' (ibid.).

Figure 16.1 illustrates the social determinants of health in relation to the pillars of sustainable development, with a focus on the SDH at play in the GCC countries (the figure is adapted from the Social Model of Health presented by Göran Dahlgren and Margaret Whitehead [1991] and from the DPSSEEA [driving forces, pressures, state, exposures, health effects and actions] model of the WHO [von Schirnding 2002b; WHO 1997]). It represents ways in which various driving forces, at the global level, generate pressures at the national level, which in turn impact the state of the community's environment and human health. The figure needs to be read in a non-linear fashion: interactions take place across rows, representing the international, national and local level, and across columns, representing the different conditions of living environments.

Figure 16.1 shows that global driving forces at the international level include processes related to media, tourism, and population growth, trade and economic agreements, new technologies, climate change, food production and water and energy policies. These forces impact on health directly, as when climate change leads to increase in temperature and rises of communicable diseases such as malaria (Husain and Chaudhary 2008), and indirectly, as possibly unforeseen health consequences of existing social and economic policies. At the national level, it is well established that economic and social policies create structural barriers and/or opportunities for communities to maintain supportive environments for health. And at the community level, several systematic reviews of the

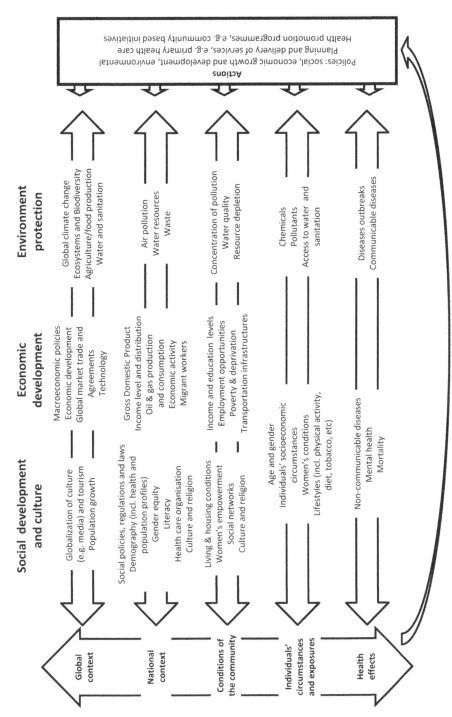

Figure 16.1. Overview of the social determinants of health in relation to the pillars of sustainable development in the GCC states.

scientific literature have conclusively shown that health status depends on living and housing conditions, employment opportunities, education levels, access to water quality and sanitation and community social networks. Most available data on these issues are from countries within the Organization of Economic Cooperation and Development (OECD); in the GCC states, the evidence base regarding links between community-level environments and variation in health outcomes is still very limited. Indeed, urgent research is needed to document how these linkages interplay in the Gulf region.

The 'upstream' SDH have consequences on population and individual health through a variety of pathways that include: social and economic status (usually measured by household income or expenditures), employment status, education attainment, gender roles, health-related risk behaviours (such as smoking, physical inactivity, unbalanced diet) and exposure to chemicals and pollutants in the natural, home and work environment. For example, an earlier study in the city of Aleppo, Syria, reported that people with less education were statistically more likely to report a clustering of CVD-relevant risk factors (hypertension, obesity and smoking) in comparison to people with more education (Maziak et al. 2007).

Links between the upstream determinants of health, health promotion, disease prevention and provision of health care services are represented in figure 16.2. 'Upstream' from the waterfall, we find the societal

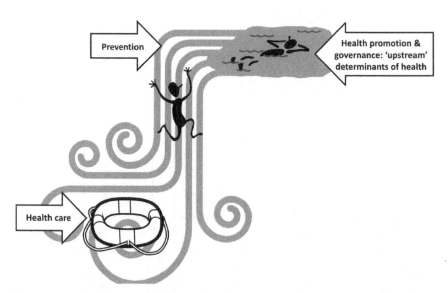

Figure 16.2. Health systems: from health promotion to health care.

and environmental conditions that support healthy and happy lives, including those listed in the MDG. This is the area of health promotion, i.e. interventions aiming to create supportive environment for health, healthy public policy and community engagement, and to enable people to take control over and improve their health. Prevention is situated downstream from health promotion and corresponds to interventions aiming to influence individuals to adopt healthier lifestyles, e.g. smoking-cessation programs, and to prevent ill health, e.g. cancer screening. Once individuals become ill, i.e. fall down the waterfall, health care systems become important in reducing the individual burden of disease by providing means (treatments) to stay afloat. Investing in more upstream interventions aimed at improving societal and environmental conditions of daily living for everyone in the population will clearly alleviate pressure on health care systems.

Health and Social Development in the Eastern Mediterranean Region (EMR) and Gulf Cooperation Council (GCC) States

In GCC countries, health indicators and their determinants (table 16.2) have significantly improved since the 1970s. Nonetheless, these states face new health challenges and new pressure on their health systems: chronic diseases and associated risk factors are on the rise both globally and locally, and some of the highest rates of diabetes and obesity are found amongst GCC nationals.

An emerging health concern for the Gulf region is in the area of non-communicable (chronic) diseases. These pose a considerable disease burden and result in a loss of economic output (Lim et al. 2007). Non-communicable diseases include malignant cancers, diabetes, cardiovascular diseases, neuropsychiatric disorders, as well as chronic diseases of the digestive, respiratory, genitourinary and musculoskeletal systems (e.g. ulcers, asthma, nephritis, arthritis, rheumatism). Collectively they are a major cause of death and disability worldwide, accounting for an estimated 51 per cent of the global burden of disease in 2008 (Mathers and Loncar 2005).

In the EMR, non-communicable diseases account for 47 per cent of the region's burden of disease; this is expected to rise to 60 per cent by the year 2020 (Khatib 2004). As summarized in Ruth Mabry et al. 2010a, higher prevalence of obesity, type 2 diabetes and other chronic diseases in the GCC countries is similar to developed countries; at least 25 per cent of the adult population have hypertension; four out of six countries of the GCC (Kuwait, Oman, Saudi Arabia and United Arab Emirates) are in the

Table 16.2. The social determinants of health[a] and health indicators in the Gulf Cooperation Council.[b] *Source*: 2008 Country profiles available from the Eastern Mediterranean Regional Office of the World Health Organization, available at http://rho.emro.who.int/rhodata/?theme=country [When this chapter was first written, 2008 data for Bahrain was not available].

	Qatar	Kuwait	UAE	Oman	Saudi Arabia
Area in thousands square kilometres	11.58	17.82	83.60	309.50	2000.00
Total population in thousands	1,449	3,640	4,765	2,743	24,807
% Urban population	100	100	80	71	85
Indicators of social determinants of health					
% Population growth rate	5.2	9.3	6.2	2.2	2.3
% Population below 15 years	14.5	19.6	19.1	36.2	32.2
% Population 65 years and over	1.1	1.6	0.9	2.2	2.8
% Dependency ratio	31.1	27	24.9	62	64.9
Total fertility rate (R) per woman	2.4	2	2	3.1	3.2
% Adult literacy rate 15+ years	91	94	70	81	88
% Adult literacy rate 15+ years, men	94	95	71	87	90
% Adult literacy rate 15+ years, women	88	91	68	74	85
% Gross primary school enrolment ratio	103	100	86	99	99
% Gross primary school enrolment ratio, boys	105	100	85	99	100
% Gross primary school enrolment ratio, girls	102	100	88	99	97
% Gross secondary school enrolment ratio	105	100	76	90	94
% Gross secondary school enrolment ratio, boys	102	100	80	92	99
% Gross secondary school enrolment ratio, girls	109	100	82	87	90
% Population with sustainable access to improved water source	100	100	100	75	100
% Population with access to improved sanitation	100	100	100	89	99

Indicators of health					
Crude birth rate per 1,000 population	11.9	15	15	25	24.1
Crude death rate per 1,000 population	1.3	1.6	1.7	3.1	3.9
Total life expectancy at birth (years)	77.8	77.4	76.9	72	73.4
Male life expectancy at birth (years)	77.8	76.9	75.6	70.4	72.4
Female life expectancy at birth (years)	77.9	77.8	78.6	73.6	74.5
Newborns with low birth weight (%)	8.1	8.0	3.2	9.2	5.0
Infant mortality rate (per 1,000 live births)	7.7	9	7.8	10.1	17.4
Under five mortality rate (per 1,000 live births)	9.5	10.5	9.6	13	21.1
Maternal mortality ratio (per 1,0000 live births)	12	2	0	23	15
% Smoking among adults, total	14	18	-	-	22
% Smoking among adults, men	24	35	-	-	37
% Smoking among adults, women	3.1	2.9	-	-	6
Coverage with primary health care services indicators					
% Population with access to local health services	100	100	100	98	-
Antenatal care coverage (%)	100	100	100	99	96
Births attended by skilled health personnel	100	100	100	99	96
% One year olds immunized[c] for (2008): BCG	98	94	98	100	98
DPT3	97	99	92	99	98
OPV3	97	99	94	100	98
Measles	95	99	92	100	97
HBV3	97	99	92	99	98

[a] Value can exceed 100% as a result of grade repetition and school entry at ages younger or older than the typical age at that grade level

[b] No information is available for Bahrain

[c] BCG: Bacille Calmette-Guerin; OPV3: Three doses of oral poliovaccine, not including supplemental immunization doses; DPT3: Three doses of combined diphtheria–pertussis–tetanus vaccine; HBV3: Three doses of hepatitis 3 vaccine

top ten countries globally in the prevalence for diabetes; and cardiovascular diseases are the leading cause of death (Mabry et al. 2010a). The high prevalence of overweight and obesity in some GCC countries is exceeding that of some developed countries (e.g. with prevalence ranging from 46.2 per cent to 74.5 per cent among men and between 49.5 per cent and 79.2 per cent among women, in Oman and Saudi Arabia respectively [as summarized in Mabry et al. 2010b]). Higher prevalence of overweight and obesity is observed among women compared to men whereas in Western countries, the prevalence is usually higher among men.

A GCC-wide review found that the prevalence of metabolic syndrome (a group of risk factors that occur together and increase the risk for coronary artery disease, stroke and type 2 diabetes) was 10 to 15 per cent higher than in most developed countries, with generally higher prevalence rates for women (Mabry et al. 2010a); the authors highlighted the need to address modifiable risk behaviours, including lack of physical activity, prolonged sitting time and diet.

A recent study documenting cancer incidence in the GCC countries observed that, despite a similar overall pattern in cancer across these countries, the magnitude of the cancers and cancer sites varied between the countries (Al-Hamdan et al. 2009). For example, higher proportions of paediatric cancers are observed in Saudi Arabia, higher incidences of cancer of the stomach are observed among Omani and Emirati men and lung cancer among women was among the top five cancers in Bahrain only, ranking second in this country. Important inequalities were also observed in lung cancer among men, with incidence being seven times greater in Bahrain than in Saudi Arabia.

Non-communicable diseases reflect significant global change in diet habits, physical activity levels and tobacco use (Berger and Peerson 2009; Shara 2010) as a result of industrialization, urbanization, economic development and increasing food market globalization. Globally, these 'modifiable behavioural risk factors' explain about 75 per cent of these chronic conditions. In the EMR, rapid social, economic and environmental changes have occurred in the past few decades, presenting a continual challenge to health in the region. In the GCC states, the impacts of globalization are being felt not only through the opening of economic markets, but also through a change in general 'lifestyles' associated with specific health-related risks that concern efforts for public health promotion and prevention. One of the most significant changes has been associated with the oil industry boom. Since the 1970s, previously nomadic populations have settled into large cities or peri-urban areas, changing regional profiles. The rapid construction of highway networks coupled with low fuel prices has underpinned growth in the use of private cars, leading to reduced physical activity. Diets have undergone considerable change too, with increased consumption of salt and high saturated fat. The value put on hospitality by people in the region often takes the form of lavish meals. Such cultural practice, in conjunction with the availability of 'junk food', has the potential to influence weight-related problems in the region. Furthermore, most of the food in the GCC is imported from African countries, creating unsustainable growing pressures on global food supplies. Tobacco consumption, in the form of chewing tobacco, smoking cigarettes and/or use of waterpipes (*shisha* or *hookah*) is on the increase, especially among women (Maziak et al. 2004a) and young adults (Maziak et al. 2004b).

Other factors contribute to the increase non-communicable disease burden in the GCC countries. Cousin marriage is a common practice (estimated to range from 20 per cent in Bahrain to 58 per cent of marriages in Saudi Arabia) seen to increase family cohesion and cultural and social compatibility (Aljasir et al. 2009; Panter-Brick, 1991). Close consanguinity increases the risks of genetic diseases in cases where a child carries a double dose of deleterious recessive alleles, risks that are especially visible where family sizes are large (Aljasir et al. 2009; Panter-Brick, 1992). It is also linked with an increased incidence of adult-onset diseases such as cancer, hypertension and mental health disorders (Bener, Hussain and Teebi 2007). Premarital counselling is obligatory in Bahrain and in Saudi Arabia, and is encouraged in the rest of the GCC countries; the organization and nature of newborn screening programs vary between countries (Aljasir et al. 2009).

This evidence points to the need for a concerted public health effort to reduce risk factors for non-communicable diseases and to establish a national system for the monitoring and the surveillance of risk factors (Khatib 2004). Unless GCC state-driven health care systems develop policy responses to such challenges, non-communicable diseases will produce an unsustainable drain on human and financial resources, and potentially negate the improvements in health and longevity realized over recent decades (Al-Lawati, Mabry and Mohammed 2008). A widely publicized assessment of GCC health care forecasted unprecedented rises in demand and cost by 2025, driven by a doubling of the population, a large growth in the proportion of elderly citizens, a higher prevalence of diabetes and cardiovascular diseases, a more than doubling of requirements for hospital beds and a continued dependence on expatriate medical and technical staff to provide health care (Hediger, Mourshed and Lambert 2006). Furthermore, in some countries of the Gulf, migrant workers outnumber national citizens, creating new pressures on urban planning, socio-cultural identity and provision of services likely to influence health-related behaviours and outcomes.

Conclusions

Sustainable development in the GCC states and the health of its people are intrinsically linked. Throughout this chapter, we have highlighted the interrelationships between health and overall social and economic development, as well as the need for effective political governance and community participation, to reach stated goals of health equity and sustainable development.

GCC states face a set of health-related issues which have been identified by the WHO as global concerns, particularly the increase in non-communicable diseases and related rise in health care demands. However, there are distinct structural and social factors that distinguish GCC countries from the WHO Eastern Mediterranean region as a whole – a region which includes countries as diverse (in terms of wealth and political stability) as Afghanistan and Qatar. Oil and gas wealth has underpinned vast improvements in health care provision and longevity in the GCC, but also led to a shift in the burden of disease, and consequently the nature of the demand for health services. There is a need to address particular public health concerns, such as the increases in inactive lifestyles, smoking and obesity, the need to provide specialized care for the growing number of older GCC citizens and gendered health issues arising from cultural and religious restrictions on female activity. Growing numbers of people with non-communicable diseases such as diabetes, cardiovascular disease and cancer will require more specialized and expensive health care services, including a greater demand for palliative care. Such demands require medical and technical expertise, the majority of which is currently provided by expatriate health care workers.

Concerns for sustainable development and global health pose significant challenges, and are steadily rising to the top of the international agenda. Keeping them at the top of the agenda demands specific frameworks for action at both global and local levels of decision making. Compelling, effective and sustainable action is required to produce health systems that are better integrated into pressing social and economic agenda.

References

Al-Hamdan, N., et al. 2009. 'Incidence of Cancer in Gulf Cooperation Council Countries, 1998–2001.' *Eastern Mediterranean Health Journal* 15 (3): 600–611.
Al-Lawati, J., R. Mabry and A. Mohammed. 2008. 'Addressing the Threat of Chronic Diseases in Oman.' *Preventing Chronic Diseases* 5 (3): A99.

Aljasir, B., et al. 2009. 'Population Health Genomics in Member Countries of the Cooperation Council for the Arab States of the Gulf.' *Kuwait Medical Journal* 41 (3): 187–204.

Assai, M., S. Siddiqi and S. Watts. 2006. 'Tackling Social Determinants of Health Through Community Based Initiatives.' *British Medical Journal* 333: 854–856.

Avendano, M., and I. Kawachi. 2011. 'The Search for Explanations of the American Health Disadvantage Relative to the English.' *American Journal of Epidemiology* 173 (8): 866–869.

Bener, A., R. Hussain and A. S. Teebi. 2007. 'Consanguineous Marriages and their Effects on Common Adult Diseases: Studies from an Endogamous Population.' *Medical Principles and Practice* 16: 262–267.

Berger, G., and A. Peerson. 2009. 'Giving Young Emirati Women a Voice: Participatory Action Research on Physical Activity.' *Health & Place* 15 (1): 117–124.

Commission of Social Determinants of Health. 2008. 'Closing the Gap in One Generation: Health Equity Through Action on the Social Determinants of Health.' Geneva: World Health Organization (WHO).

Costello, A., et al. 2009. 'Managing the Health Effects of Climate Change.' *The Lancet* 373: 1693–1733.

Dahlgren, G., and M. Whitehead. 1991. 'Policies and Strategies to Promote Social Equity in Health.' Institute for Future Studies, Stockholm.

Gillam, S. 2008. 'Is the Declaration of Alma Ata Still Relevant to Primary Health Care?' *British Medical Journal* 336 (7643): 536–538.

Hassan, A., et al. 2005. 'Environmental Health Impact Assessment of Development Projects: A Practical Guide for the WHO Eastern Mediterranean Region.' Amman: Regional Centre for Environmental Health Activities, WHO Regional Office for the Eastern Mediterranean.

Hediger, V., M. Mourshed and T. Lambert. 2006. *Gulf Cooperation Council Health Care 2025.* New York: McKinsey & Company.

Hogan, M. C., et al. 2010. 'Maternal Mortality for 181 Countries, 1980–2008: A Systematic Analysis of Progress Towards Millennium Development Goal 5.' *The Lancet* 375: 1609–1623.

Husain, T., and J. R. Chaudhary. 2008. 'Human Health Risk Assessment Due to Global Warming: A Case Study of the Gulf Countries.' *International Journal of Environmental Research in Public Health* 5 (4): 204–212.

International Petroleum Industry Environmental Conservation Association and International Association of Oil & Gas Producers (IPIECA/OGP). 2005. 'A Guide to Health Impact Assessments in the Oil and Gas Industry.'

Kemm, J., and J. Parry. 2004. 'What is HIA? Introduction and Overview.' In *Health Impact Assessment,* eds. J. Kemm, J. Parry and S. Palmer, 1–14. Oxford: Oxford University Press.

Khatib, O. 2004. 'Noncommunicable Diseases: Risk Factors and Regional Strategies for Prevention and Care.' *Eastern Mediterranean Health Journal* 10 (6): 778–788.

Khosh-Chashm, K. 1995. 'Healthy Cities and Healthy Villages.' *Eastern Mediterranean Health Journal* 1 (2): 103–111.

Krieger, N. 2001. 'A Glossary for Social Epidemiology.' *Journal of Epidemiology and Community Health* 55 (10): 693–700.

The Lancet. 2009. 'What is Health? The Ability to Adapt.' *The Lancet* 373 (9666): 781–781.

Lim, S. S., et al. 2007. 'Prevention of Cardiovascular Disease in High-Risk Individuals in Low-Income and Middle-Income Countries: Health Effects and Costs.' *The Lancet* 370: 2054–2062.

Mabry, R., et al. 2010a. 'Gender Differences in Prevalence of the Metabolic Syndrome in Gulf Cooperation Council Countries: A Systematic Review.' *Diabetic Medicine* 27: 593–597.

———. 2010b. 'Evidence of Physical Activity Participation Among Men and Women in the Countries of the Gulf Cooperation Council: A Review.' *Obesity Reviews* 11: 457–464.

Mathers, C., and D. Loncar. 2005. 'Updated Projections of Global Mortality and Burden of Disease, 2002–2030: Data Sources, Methods and Results.' Geneva: WHO.

Maziak, W., et al. 2004a. 'Gender and Smoking Status-Based Analysis of Views Regarding Waterpipe and Cigarette Smoking in Aleppo, Syria.' *Preventive Medicine* 38 (4): 479–484.

———. 2004b. 'Tobacco Smoking Using a Waterpipe: A Re-emerging Strain in a Global Epidemic.' *Tobacco Control* 13 (4): 327–333.

———. 2007. 'Cardiovascular Health Among Adults in Syria: A Model from Developing Countries.' *Annals of Epidemiology* 17: 713–720.

Panter-Brick, C. 1991. 'Parental Responses to Consanguinity and Genetic Disease in Saudi Arabia.' *Social Science & Medicine* 33 (11): 1295–1302.

———. 1992. 'Coping with an Affected Birth: Genetic Counseling in Saudi Arabia.' *Journal of Child Neurology* 7: 69–72.

Panter-Brick, C., and A. Fuentes. 2010. 'Health, Risk, and Adversity: A Contextual View from Anthropology.' In *Health, Risk, and Adversity,* eds. C. Panter-Brick and A. Fuentes, 1–10. Berghahn Books. New York.

Qatar Declaration. 2008. 'Health and Well-Being Through Health Systems Based on Primary Health Care.'

Sabri, B. 2008. 'Thirty Years of Primary Health Care in the Eastern Mediterranean Region.' *Eastern Mediterranean Health Journal* 14 Suppl: S12–14.

Shara, N. M. 2010. 'Cardiovascular Disease in Middle Eastern Women.' *Nutrition, Metabolism and Cardiovascular Diseases* 20 (6): 412–418.

United Nations. 1992. Conference on Environment and Development, Rio de Janeiro.

———. 2002. World Summit on Sustainable Development, Johannesburg.

———. 2005. *The Millennium Development Goals in the Arab Region.* New York.

———. 2010. *The Millennium Development Goals Report 2010.* New York. http://www.un.org/millenniumgoals/pdf/MDG%20Report%202010%20En%20r15%20-low%20res%2020100615%20-.pdf.

von Schirnding, Y. 2002a. 'Health and Sustainable Development: Can We Rise to the Challenge?' *The Lancet* 360 (9333): 632–637.

———. 2002b. *Health in Sustainable Development Planning: The Role of Indicators.* Geneva: WHO.

———. 2005. 'The World Summit on Sustainable Development: Reaffirming the Centrality of Health.' *Globalization and Health* 1: 8.

von Schirnding, Y., and V. Tobin. 2002. 'A Framework for Action on Health and the Environment.' WEHAB Working Group.

Waage, J., et al. 2010. 'The Millennium Development Goals: A Cross-Sectoral Analysis and Principles for Goal Setting after 2015.' *The Lancet* 376: 991–1023.

World Health Organization (WHO). 1946. 'Preamble to the Constitution of the World Health Organization.' New York.

———. 1978. 'Declaration of Alma Ata.' International Conference on Primary Health Care, Alma-Ata, USSR, 6–12 September, Geneva.

———. 1986. 'Ottawa Charter for Health Promotion.'

———. 1997. 'Health and Environment in Sustainable Development.' Geneva.

———. 2005. 'The Bangkok Charter for Health Promotion in a Globalized World.' Geneva.

WHO Eastern Mediterranean Region (WHO EMRO). 1996. 'Health Promotion Through Islamic Lifestyles: The Ammam Declaration.' Cairo, Egypt.

———. 2008. 'A Strategy for Health Promotion in the Eastern Mediterranean Region.' Cairo, Egypt.

———. 2009. 'Community-Based Initiatives Success Stories - 2.' Cairo, Egypt.

WHO European Centre for Health Policy. 1999. 'Health Impact Assessment: Main Concepts and Suggested Approach.' Gothenburg Consensus Paper, December, Copenhagen, WHO Regional Office for Europe.

Wilkinson, R., and K. Pickett. 2009. *The Spirit Level: Why More Equal Societies Almost Always Do Better.* London: Allen Lane.

Woolf, S., et al. 2004. 'The Health Impact of Resolving Racial Disparities: An Analysis of US Mortality Data.' *American Journal of Public Health* 94: 2078–2081.

World Commission on Environment and Development (WCED). 1987. *Our Common Future.* Oxford: Oxford University Press.

V

Cultural and Social Issues

Exploring Collaborative Research Methodologies in the Pursuit of Sustainable Futures

Gina Porter

This chapter focuses on the role of collaboration in the pursuit of more sustainable futures. It builds on and reinforces the argument presented by James Howard in chapter 11 on marine resources, where it is concluded that a broader, interdisciplinary understanding is required of the complex interactions between the many players and sectors involved in sustainable development. It starts by reflecting on the value of collaborative endeavour for researching sustainability and emphasizes the particular value of interdisciplinary approaches. This type of research requires partnerships and collaboration between many stakeholders, including alliances beyond research institutions (with formal and informal institutions found in government, NGOs, the private sector and communities), as this chapter considers. Collaborative research is then examined within the specific context of community participation, which is widely viewed as fundamental to research focused on sustainable futures: the value and the potential limitations of participatory field methods are explored. Personal experience from studies conducted at an irrigation project on the Keta Lagoon in Ghana and elsewhere in Africa is used to illustrate the discussion. Links are also made to reports of similar research conducted in the Middle East. Development interventions can be notoriously unsustainable, being prone to failure and waste of resources. The examples presented show how participatory approaches can promote the sustainability of development interventions themselves.

Building Interdisciplinary Approaches to Research in Sustainable Development

It is important to distinguish what is meant by *interdisciplinarity*, as opposed to *multidisciplinarity*. The two terms are often used interchangeably, but they are not the same: whereas multidisciplinarity involves different experts working in parallel, interdisciplinarity requires dialogue, interactions and integration across areas of expertise (Strathern 2005: 82). This is a harder task and one less commonly achieved in practice. Ravi Kanbur (2002; see also Hume and Toye 2006) argues that interdisciplinarity requires deep integration of concepts and methodologies – it is a demanding approach to research because it is necessary to learn the logic of other disciplines and integrate with those logics, without compromising the standard of rigour in one's own discipline. Multidisciplinarity, by contrast, implies separate disciplinary research followed by efforts to achieve overall analytical synthesis. This avoids the risk of diluting the conceptual and methodological standards of one's own discipline. It is consequently a less hazardous enterprise, but arguably lacks the full potential that interdisciplinary work offers for the creation of new understandings.

David Hulme and John Toye (2006, in the context of a discussion about crossdisciplinary[1] work in development research on poverty, inequality and well-being) note that there are strong incentives to stay within disciplinary boundaries, not least the single-subject peer review which characterizes university research assessment exercises in the United Kingdom and elsewhere. They also observe that the inclination to interdisciplinarity varies across the social sciences, with economists generally less interested than others. This they link, in part, to the professional status accorded to economists in most countries and the presence of a professional economist cadre in government with whom academic economists can easily interact through their shared understandings. Further, they observe that while economists 'mix well with more powerful people' (ibid.: 1095), anthropologists and sociologists are less ready to mix and empathize with those in power – and that such values and attitudes 'may be both reinforced and reproduced by the notable gender disparities between the disciplines'. Hulme and Toye propose that while such barriers continue, multidisciplinary work built over time through seminars, meetings etc. could subsequently aid evolution of systematic interdisciplinary research. I would argue further that one of the most effective means of achieving preliminary interdisciplinary exchange among academic researchers is for disciplinary specialists to come together in the field. An interdisciplinary research project at Keta Lagoon, Ghana, is used below to illustrate this point, but also to emphasize the importance of extending interdisciplinarity beyond the academic community to include a wide range of stakeholders.

Interdisciplinary Collaboration at Keta Lagoon, Ghana

This Keta Lagoon project in Ghana, which took place over a decade ago, was something of a personal revelation in terms of recognizing the potential for interactions and engagement with other disciplines and a wide range of stakeholders. It offers a useful starting point for a discussion about collaboration. The project, which could be described as interdisciplinary in essence (though the researchers did not call it such until late in the project), led each of the participant academics to an understanding of a fairly complex local development issue that, on reflection, they recognized was considerably deeper than they might have individually achieved separately. It also enabled an engagement with other stakeholders beyond the academy in a more effective manner than might otherwise have been achieved.

The three academic researchers – a man from the nearby Ghanaian university department of Crop Science and two women from UK universities (a plant scientist working in a development research centre and a development geographer) – had come together in a small Land-Water Interface Programme project, funded by the UK Department for International Development (DFID). Our task was to characterize environmental conditions and associated management issues in the Keta area of Ghana. For each of us, the experience of working in a multidisciplinary team was relatively new and, until then, had mostly consisted of group meetings and field studies with colleagues from our own disciplines. However, fortuitously we found ourselves together in the field and, with limited access to transport and a deadline to produce a review of key environment-related issues, elected to work closely together at selected sites.

The research site in the Anloga area of Ghana consisted of a narrow, intensively cultivated area located on a sandbar separating Keta lagoon from the sea. Here, traditional irrigation from wells (drawing water from a shallow freshwater perched aquifer) and stringent regulation of planting dates for the main cash crop (shallots) had enabled an intensive permanent irrigated vegetable production system to be built up at the lagoon side of the sandbar over a period of more than a century. Population pressure had led to intensification of agriculture on this narrow littoral, including additional wells and recent expansion of irrigation into higher areas of the sandbar away from the lagoon side using electric pumps, encouraged by a World Bank–sponsored programme. The unit responsible for implementing the project in the Ministry of Agriculture had apparently agreed to monitor the environmental impact of the electric pumps but, at the time we undertook our fieldwork, it was clear that a number of environmental problems were emerging. In brief, our combined studies of the physical and political economy/ecology contexts and our discussions with a wide range of community members in the field, as we observed, interviewed and measured, brought to the fore the significant dangers of saltwater intrusion, a lack of crop regulation in newly cultivated areas (increasing the danger of pest infestation) and women farmers being potentially marginalized through reduced access to land and water (Porter, Young and Dzietror 1997).

Drawing on our interdisciplinary research findings (which built on and were supported by earlier individual studies by social scientists, hydrologists, sociologists and geographers at the University of Ghana, Legon), we arranged a community meeting and together presented a strong argument about the interconnectedness of current environmental and social trends and their potentially negative implications for future livelihoods in the community. However, it was clear that there was little local political will to enforce new regulations among the community's leading farmers, who were accruing high profits. We also raised our concerns with the relevant ministries in Accra, but pressure from the powerful local farmers union for irrigation expansion was paramount in shaping ministry attitudes to development at Anloga. Moreover, the irrigation engineer/hydrologist on the World Bank–funded project was merely expected to determine any environmental impact of proposed water extraction and distribution and devise operation and management plans to minimize negative impacts.

We circulated a preliminary report expressing concern about water extraction, lack of monitoring and associated issues to the Environmental Protection Agency in Accra and, via DFID, to the World Bank in Washington. Shortly afterwards, the World Bank sent a consultant engineer to investigate conditions at Anloga and, on the basis of his report (which confirmed our concerns), the scheme was halted until a study of extraction rates along the Keta strip had been made. The World Bank intervention to halt the scheme caused substantial local trouble and political manoeuvring: questions were reportedly raised in the Ghanaian parliament. Our report had requested urgent monitoring, not stoppage of the scheme, but there was little we could do once the World Bank intervened directly, apart from helping to establish a monitoring scheme (a UK hydrology Masters student worked with staff from Ghana's Water Resources Institute to establish the extent of the freshwater aquifer and its susceptibility to change).

Building Alliances Beyond the Academy

The Keta research project was highly instructive for the team, not only because we found that working multidisciplinarily in the field acted as a catalyst to interdisciplinarity, but also because it raised wider issues around interdisciplinary working beyond the academy. The project highlighted the importance of building partnerships and collaborations between the researchers and local community, governmental representatives and others to shape and inform our study. With hindsight, we might have avoided some of the difficulties we encountered during the project had we had stronger collaborative relationships with all stakeholders from the start and organized stakeholder meetings involving all parties at an early stage, rather than interacting with individual groups separately for most of the fieldwork. Regular multi-stakeholder dialogue with the diverse interests involved – from poor women farmers through to the World Bank – would have increased costs (beyond the tight budget we had available for the study) but could have been highly beneficial, especially in avoiding the World Bank's peremptory action.

The Consultative Group

The experience has encouraged me to establish a Country Consultative Group (CCG), or sometimes a more local Consultative Group (CG), at the commencement of every research project that I have led since the Keta project, and to see this group as key in shaping, developing and disseminating ensuing research. I would define the CCG/CG as the coming together of a range of stakeholders (both local and external to the project) in regular meetings from the start of the project, aimed at garnering advice and support, ensuring dissemination of project information and influencing policy. Membership of the Consultative Group will vary, depending on the nature of the project, but may include local community, local government, central government, local and international NGOs, the private sector, academics and the research team.

Choosing potential CCG members requires careful consultation with in-country research collaborators, given the power issues surrounding who is on the group, how representative they are of their constituency, how they will interact together and so on. In a child mobility study, where we worked in Ghana, Malawi and South Africa (see www.dur.ac.uk/child .mobility/), we had Country Consultative Groups in Ghana and Malawi and more local Consultative Groups in two provinces of South Africa. The Ghana CCG, for instance, included teachers, academics and staff from the transport unions and a police woman- and child-protection unit, in addition to representatives from government ministries, local government and NGOs. Our aim here and elsewhere has been to engage key practitioners and policy makers with influence who will not simply delegate at random. We have found that a maximum of about twenty members seems to work best in terms of achieving wide coverage of interests while ensuring a manageable group (and containing costs).

While there may be difficulties in terms of power relations and consequent voice where the status of Consultative Group members is diverse, such that careful management will be needed, there can also be substantial potential benefits. Such encounters can bring rare interactions and insights. In a project where the CCG included staff from two government departments, for instance, the comments of a local community member of the CCG precipitated a heated discussion between the government staff. This was highly enlightening to other CCG members since it revealed how interdepartmental competition was delaying development projects in our research location.

Building stakeholder partnership and ownership from the *beginning* of research has much to recommend it. Regular meetings – usually at six-month intervals (depending on the project timescale) – allow stakeholders to give advice, support and to contribute to ongoing analysis and dissemination. They help avoid duplication of research which has already been done, since local stakeholders tend to have more information regarding earlier research and key contacts than is readily available in official records and are usually keen to ensure time and money is not spent on replication of earlier work. Joint stakeholder meetings have the potential to encourage debate and reflection about past work that may not emerge in one-to-one discussions with individuals. The CCG can also help counter misinformation and political manoeuvring which may otherwise delay or devalue the work: a CCG would have been helpful, for instance, in getting a monitoring scheme in place at an earlier date or at least avoiding some of the political problems ensuing from the World Bank's halting of the Keta lagoon irrigation project. The CCG also offers a potential route to policy influence and change, especially if policy makers operating at national level are included. Key ministry staff may not have the time or inclination to travel out to research sites to talk to individual stakeholders but can often be persuaded to join a CCG organized by others. The CCG can then open a relatively neutral space in which less powerful stakeholders are able to interact with policy makers: despite power differentials, sensitive facilitation can ensure that a range of voices is heard and informs policy.

The venue of the CCG is important. If possible we have found it advisable to find a neutral space, ideally near the project site, but often the meeting place has to be in a national or regional capital to ensure certain stakeholders attend (though this raises costs). In terms of meeting arrangements, the following usually works well: a first CG meeting early in the project; then six-monthly (half-day) meetings; and a final project meeting at/after the end of project workshop. Dissemination of project information and outputs is usually ongoing throughout and after the project end.

From experience of using the Consultative Group approach over a number of projects, it is easier to bring influential national stakeholders into positive membership in countries with small populations and a strongly networked middle class. In such contexts an influential academic researcher can often bring a minister to the table, simply because he is a former classmate! In terms of project type, it is easier to develop stronger stakeholder engagement in: (a) action research where there are interventions ongoing, (b) situations where specific groups perceive they are misunderstood and see the Consultative Group as a route to improved understanding, and (c) smaller projects where the focus is relatively narrow and stakeholders have strong reasons to address the project focus. The funding context can also be significant. Some CG members may perceive meetings funded by external sources (bilateral/multilateral donors) as principally a potential source of largesse, including daily allowances and a free lunch. (It is also possible that such funded CG meetings may impact negatively on stakeholder involvement in locally funded projects that are perceived to offer fewer potential perks.) The CCG is about building ownership, albeit there are potential problems of hijack by individual interest groups, issues of cost control etc. When encountered, such problems have to be resolved during the project life course, but they are unlikely entirely to take away the value of the group interaction.

Working with NGOs and CBOs

Non-government organizations (NGOs) are now ubiquitous in many parts of the world, but a comprehensive definition is impossible, given the 'competing arguments and the practical slippages that are often made in academic, policy and practitioner usage' (Alikhan et al. 2007: 8). The discussion below focuses on 'development' NGOs, i.e. organizations constituting one small part of civil society which have as their purpose improvement in people's lives and operate on a not-for-profit basis (ibid.). Many academics now recognize the benefits that can be gained from working with community-based organizations (CBOs) and NGOs (although the initial impetus for such partnerships has often emerged from funding agency and donor requirements rather than any commitment to collaboration). There has been a very rapid growth in development NGOs in the Arab world in recent years (Abdo 2010) and, despite some potential challenges (discussed below), it is likely that interest in collaborative work with NGOs will increase among academics researching in the Middle East region.

Staff representing international NGOs (INGOs), local NGOs and CBOs can be valuable members of Consultative Groups, but they may also be involved in a more hands-on way in a project as research collaborators. International NGOs often have impressive networks that link to key development actors including donors. NGO collaboration also offers the potential for joint work towards interventions, especially since NGOs often employ large numbers of trained field staff who possess substantial local knowledge regarding development issues and intervention potential and may have extensive networks which can be called upon to support interventions. For their part, NGOs may gain the benefit of academic perspectives and analytical capacities unavailable 'in-house' (Roper 2002).

Barbara Cottrell and Jane Parpart (2006) observe that the rewards of successful collaboration between academics and NGOs are many, but the challenges are considerable, particularly around different notions of change, processes and dissemination of findings. Clashes of expectation are likely to occur (as reported in a Sri Lanka case study by Cathrine Brun and Ragnhild Lund [2010]). NGO-academic collaborations can be problematic, because of different organizational structures, funding patterns and objectives. Funding pressures are significant in both the NGO and university sectors but take different forms. In practice, NGOs are commonly highly dependent on donor funds to maintain the trained field staff they need to support their interventions, whereas academics face hurdles such as research assessment exercises imposed by the funding councils which bring to bear strong pressures to publish. Among NGOs, a focus on success and associated under-reportage of failures is relatively widespread, especially in smaller organizations, due to their dependence on donors: there is a perception that only positive results will be rewarded with further financial support. Deborah Eade (2007) observes that despite a focus on capacity building, many conventional NGO practices contribute to short-termism, tunnel vision and upwards accountability, 'based on the assumption that the transfer of resources is a one-way process' (ibid.: 630). Academics, for their part, commonly face pressures from their home institutions to produce rigorous (time-consuming) research for publication in specialist scholarly journals (ideally single-authored) in order to attract further funding to the universities. To NGOs this can seem excessive, even exploitative, both in terms of their own objectives and the needs of the communities with which they are working.

NGOs commonly emphasize partnership as part of their ethos which academic researchers may find more difficult to put into practice, given their usual experience of individually defined research strategies and single-authored papers. In term of objectives, academic focus is often on observation, analysis and interpretation and around obtaining the 'big picture' (Cottrell and Parpart 2006: 18), whereas NGOs, especially at the field-staff level, more commonly focus on practical grass-roots change. Interactions with government can further complicate matters in NGO-academic collaborations. On the one hand, NGO activism may lead to strained NGO-state relations which can impact negatively on research. On the other hand, too cosy a relationship between NGO and state (possibly at its most pernicious in the case of the so-called GONGOs – government NGOs) can also create difficulties for academic researchers, especially when the state requires access to sensitive and confidential information (Paluck 2008).

Clearly, much depends on the individual NGOs and academics concerned in the research collaboration. Initial agreement is vital regarding the nature of the collaboration – its goals, respective partners' needs, capacities and interests in the collaborative enterprise, timescales etc. – *before* the research commences (Roper 2002). An understanding of the nuances of the different organizational cultures, ways of working and the interplay of individual personalities will inevitably emerge as the project proceeds. Jonathan Fox's suggestion (2006: 31) that for activist-scholar partnerships to work, there must be 'an understanding of the other, respect for difference, shared tractable goals, and a willingness to *agree to disagree*'[2] is relevant to many other collaborative contexts. However, serious disagreement also has the potential to derail research and harm participating individuals and communities.

Working With Communities: Participatory Approaches to Field Research

While academic collaborations with NGOs are commonly crucial to achieving broader policy impact for research, grass-roots community perspectives and collaboration are a necessary foundation for research and associated interventions focused on sustainable development. Without grass-roots commitment, sustainable futures are unlikely to be achieved.

In the Middle East, interest in participatory approaches to field research for sustainable development is growing (though detailed observations of participatory approaches in action are rare). Mathew M. Abang et al. (2007), for instance, strongly advocate a community participatory farming systems approach to the management of an aggressive parasitic weed, broomrape (*Orobanche* spp.), which is severely affecting the livelihoods of farmers in the region. They found that farmers continue to use ineffective management practices that exacerbate the problem, rather than adopting new technologies which have been developed to control the weed and link the development of more sustainable management practices directly to the need for better understanding the specific socio-economic characteristics of individual farming systems and a community-based integrated management approach. Another example, which resonates directly with the Keta strip case study discussed earlier, concerns sustainable water management in Iran (Balali, Keulartz and Korthals 2009). In Iran, mechanically pumped wells have been promoted since the 1962 Land Reform Act. Many landowners and farmers now prefer to use pumped wells and have abandoned their traditional underground irrigation systems (Qanats) and associated community water organization in preference for individual profit: 'an "every man for himself" mentality' (ibid.: 102). Mohammad Balali observes that recent interest in reviving the Qanat system across the Middle East and integrating this with modern water supply systems would help reconnect people with nature and promote greater ecological awareness but that this will require participatory community action (and advocates multi-stakeholder platforms, which could draw on the Consultative Group concept discussed earlier in this chapter).

One way of building community participation widely employed by NGOs, is through the employment of 'PRA', Participatory Rural Appraisal, or 'PLA', Participatory Learning and Action'.[3] The origin of these participatory approaches can be traced back to earlier Rapid Rural Appraisal (RRA) which, in turn, has its roots in applied anthropology and farming systems research, where the focus is on complex interlinked relationships (Sillitoe, Dixon and Barr 2005: 7-12). The philosophy behind the approach is that outsiders need to learn from insiders and that insiders can analyze their own problems. Whereas early RRA focused on rapid assessment by outsiders, who then left the field with the data and often made their final decisions with little or no community involvement, PRA emphasizes the importance of community ownership of information, analysis and conclusions. Its widespread adoption owes much to the persuasive writing of Robert Chambers (for example, 1983, 1997, 2001).

Triangulation is one of the key elements of PRA: i.e. collecting information from diverse sources to increase reliability and reduce bias. Data is commonly collected in PRAs by a multidisciplinary team of insiders and outsiders, men and women, using a range of tools and techniques. The aim is to reduce bias by actively seeking out diverse groups, including those potentially least likely to be considered: the poorest, the disabled, the illiterate and least educated, those living in remote locations etc. Another key feature of PRA is flexibility – the research focus and methods will be regularly reviewed and possibly revised during fieldwork to respond to changing circumstances, understandings and ongoing analysis. In terms of procedure, PRA often starts with a team workshop including community participants, to identify the approach, methods, objectives and topics for investigation. Field research may take place in phases, with each phase followed by an interim review of data which sets the agenda for the next phase. The final analysis takes place immediately at the end of fieldwork and findings are discussed with the whole community.

A full PRA normally starts with a review of baseline data, to identify issues and avoid duplication. The range of methods includes semi-structured interviews with checklists (with individuals and key informants) and gathering other information through focus group discussions, accompanied by careful direct observation to cross-check responses. Other tools commonly employed in PRA include oral histories and timelines, ranking and scoring exercises to explore local preferences and perceptions (including wealth or well-being ranking to aid understanding of community dynamics), construction of maps and diagrams (to show local resources, social mapping of where various groups live etc.), accompanied transect walks to view and discuss community resources, mobility maps (to show where different groups travel and key interconnections with other places), seasonal calendars (to indicate crop sequences, rainfall and temperature patterns, income-generating activities, health and disease, income patterns etc.), time trends (to show changes over time of migration patterns, population size, rainfall, resource extraction, area under cultivation etc.), historical profiles (identifying major historical events in the community) and organizational (Venn) diagrams to show how key institutions and individuals link together in decision making etc. Individual PRAs may employ a very limited range of tools from this list and could form just one component of a larger study. In research on rural poverty in Iran, for instance, Dariush Hayati, Ezatollah Karami and Bill Slee (2006) started with an etic (outsider) perspective from extension experts and a review of conventional development indicators before moving to a PRA exercise with villagers limited to ranking households by wealth and identifying key poverty indicators. They concluded that the combination of emic (insider) with etic approaches was particularly powerful in assessing poverty and designing poverty alleviation measures.

The analysis of the data collected in the PRA may simply consist of a detailed description or 'characterization' of the community and its resources, or a more systematic analysis using a framework of key themes with data organization to address each (as in the work by Hayati, Karami and Slee 2006). It may incorporate group discussion of themes as a route to analysis and possibly some statistical analysis, if quantitative data has been collected. On the basis of this analysis, possible options for specific interventions towards sustainable development may be explored, with reference to benefit to community members, equity, feasibility etc. and possibly subsequently written up as an NGO or CBO proposal to be pursued with potential funders.

This PRA approach is attractive as a way to facilitate community development support in the NGO sector, including participatory monitoring of environmental change (for which see Abbott and Guijt 1998 for an early review). It may start in a multidisciplinary way but the approach is geared towards building interdisciplinarity of the kind described at the start of this chapter: dialogue, interactions and integration across areas of expertise are central. It also emphasizes qualitative research, though it may include quantitative studies.

Potential strengths and weaknesses of PRA have been discussed for many years. Strengths include: promotes understanding of community capacities and problems among participants; includes a wide range of stakeholders (including NGOs and local government staff), gives the community more influence over local development interventions; ensures the community has an understanding of any ensuing development projects and thus promotes commitment to such projects; ensures local priorities; brings rapid results which are accessible to the community; is cheaper to undertake than large formal development surveys; can produce unanticipated information; is less intrusive than a formal questionnaire survey. Weaknesses include: the results are likely to only apply to the communities where the work takes place and do not have generic application; biases can still creep in where the team misses an issue; it is difficult to verify the results because of the qualitative nature of the research; the results can be impressionistic if the research is not conducted systematically; decision makers often favour quantitative data and may give little weight to information they perceive as largely anecdotal (Gosling with Edwards 1995).

Over the past fifteen years, participatory research and, in particular, the power relations involved in participation, have been subject to intense scrutiny by academics. The critique goes beyond PRA to include a wide range of participatory approaches. An edited collection of papers entitled *Participation: The New Tyranny?* (Cooke and Kothari 2001) has been particularly influential in bringing concerns to a wide audience. Those identified include perceived inadequacies in the conceptualization of power that leads to failure to recognize how participation can be skewed to the powerful (and with careful behind-the-scenes facilitation may reflect the personal agendas of one or two powerful staff; see Kapoor 2005); how the poor may be romanticized and essentialized; the way rigid structures may be imposed on existing, informal truly participatory structures; the time inputs required of local participants which may impact negatively on their earning capacity; in some cases it is less efficient than a top-down decision equally acceptable to most stakeholders; the reality that group work is not always a positive experience for many individuals and that PRA can encourage a consensual view of community which is potentially dangerous, as bringing a diversity of voices to the fore inevitably raises the possibility of conflict (Guijt and Shah 1998).

Many commentators have observed the need for more careful analysis of the political context in which participatory research takes place (e.g. Williams 2004; Hodgson and Schroeder 2002). In particular, Giles Mohan and Kristian Stokke (2000) observe that PRA downgrades the significance of the state by putting emphasis on the local and suggest there is need to examine the political use of the 'local' by actors, while Marjo Bartelink and Brenda Buitelaar (2006), in the context of a Dutch-funded action research project in Yemen, argue that political and public discourses and agendas of both donor and recipient countries need careful consideration. David Mosse (2003) provides a detailed case study of participatory development in India which highlights issues around the rhetoric of partnership and rituals of collaboration, linking directly to many of the points raised above.

In the context of sustainability issues in Ghana's coastal zone, raised earlier, the practicalities of popular participation are similarly doubtful. Government efforts towards the promotion of decentralized environmental management through district committees have been substantially hampered not only by the complexities of coping with competing local interests but also by funding shortages. For example, participatory community development requires funding for transport fares for community members from remoter areas. The proliferation of local NGOs established as a response to donor demand and purportedly focused on environmental issues but with little technical knowledge has not led to ecologically sustainable development in this coastal region. Perhaps more disturbingly, among district authorities, NGOs and even the general populace, there seems to be a widespread view that tree planting is a universal panacea for environmental problems (Porter and Young 1998). As Paul Sillitoe observes in his introduction to this book, not all local communities necessarily subscribe to worldviews that may promote sustainable interventions: there is a real possibility of environmentally unsustainable participation. Promoting local knowledge per se may have wider negative impacts.

Participatory methodologies are constantly evolving, partly in response to ongoing critiques. For instance, community researchers may themselves be trained to undertake peer research and become the lead researchers in a project (Porter and Abane 2008). The challenges of participatory communication are also attracting attention and will have particular significance in the promotion of sustainable futures (Dagron 2009). Nonetheless, the need for a continued critical approach to participation and the promotion of local knowledge in sustainable development remains: avoidance of tokenistic participation; more careful group formation when research teams are established; more sophisticated, reflexive understandings of power; a longer-term deeper approach to empowerment which emphasizes participation as an ongoing, iterative process, not a single event; and avoiding reification of any particular form of knowledge (Parfitt 2004; Hampshire, Hills and Iqbal 2005; Sillitoe and Marzano 2008). As such, it is necessary to ask some key questions: What is the political and cultural context for the participatory work envisaged? Who wants to introduce participation and why? Do local people want to participate and are they able to? How will findings about negative ecological impacts be treated?

Conclusion

The sustainability debate needs to extend beyond environmental issues per se. This chapter has emphasized the importance of participatory approaches based on collaboration and partnership for promoting the sustainability of development interventions. In the absence of grass-roots participation, many development interventions end in failure and the waste of environmental resources: however, grass-roots participation is not enough, in itself, to ensure success of development projects (however that 'success' is assessed). As we have observed, political environments need to be conducive both to grass-roots participation and to the wider organizational and policy environments on which sustainable development also depends. In addition, we have to recognize the potential for successful grass-roots participation of current community members to lead to environmentally *unsustainable* futures in years or decades to come. This takes us squarely back to the issues raised by Paul Sillitoe in the book's conclusion regarding the politics of sustainable development and the potential conflicts between community perspectives and the wider world, where environmentally unsustainable participation is not simply a vague possibility but a feasible outcome. It raises some very uncomfortable questions, not least about the rights of any group to interfere in another society, even if the intervention is for a perceived greater good.

Notes

1. Scholars disagree on terminology and distinctions between *interdisciplinarity*, *crossdisciplinarity* and *transdisciplinarity*. Hulme and Toye (2006: 1086) define

cross-disciplinary work as 'any analysis or policy recommendation based on questions, concepts or methods of more than one academic discipline'. Crossdisciplinarity is sometimes referred to as transdisciplinarity, which has been defined as involving transcendence of disciplinary boundaries within academia, using new strategies for the construction of knowledge, but elsewhere considered as transcending academia to enter society (Wesselink 2009).

2. Italics in the original. Many scholars identify themselves as activists, though this sometimes creates resentment among sceptical community partners (Cottrell and Parpart 2006). It also raises major ethical issues associated with activism outside one's own community (likely to be particularly contentious when researching in another country).

3. In this section on PRA I have drawn on the excellent basic toolkit devised by Gosling with Edwards (1995). PLA Notes, published from 1988 onwards, offers clear, short case studies and 'how-to-do' articles on a wide range of participatory approaches/methods, including no. 60 (December 2009) on community-based adaptation to climate change, which is available in Arabic. See Sillitoe, Dixon and Barr 2005 for an illustrated guide with substantial detail regarding specific methods.

References

Abang, M. M., et al. 2007. 'A Participatory Farming System Approach for Sustainable Broomrape (*Orobanche* spp.) Management in the Near East and North Africa.' *Crop Protection* 26 (12): 1723–1732.

Abbot, J., and I. Guijt. 1998. 'Changing Views on Change: Participatory Approaches to Monitoring the Environment.' SARL discussion paper no. 2, July.

Abdo, N. 2010. 'Imperialism, the State, and NGOs: Middle Eastern Contexts and Contestations.' *Comparative Studies of South Asia, Africa and the Middle East* 30: 238–249

Alikhan, F., et al. 2007. 'NGOs and the State in the Twenty-First Century: Ghana and India.' INTRAC, Oxford.

Balali, M. R., J. Keulartz and M. Korthals. 2009. 'Reflexive Water Management in Arid Regions: The Case of Iran.' *Environmental Values* 18 (1): 91–112.

Bartelink, B., and M. Buitelaar. 2006. 'The Challenges of Incorporating Muslim Women's Views into Development Policy: Analysis of a Dutch Action Research Project in Yemen.' *Gender and Development* 14 (3): 351–362.

Blackburn, J., and J. Holland (eds.). 1998. *Who Changes? Institutionalising Participation in Development.* London: IT Publications.

Brun, C., and R. Lund. 2010. 'Real-Time Research: Decolonizing Research Practices – or Just Another Spectacle of Researcher-Practitioner Collaboration?' *Development in Practice* 20 (7): 812–826.

Chambers, R.1983. *Rural Development: Putting the Last First.* London: Longman.

———. 1997. *Whose Reality Counts? Putting the First Last.* London: IT Publications.

———. 2001. *Participatory Workshops: A Sourcebook of 21 Sets of Ideas and Activities.* London: Earthscan.

Cooke, B., and U. Kothari (eds.). 2001. *Participation: The New Tyranny?* London: Zed Books.

Cornwall, A., and K. Brock. 2005. 'What do Buzzwords do for Development Policy? A Critical Look at "Participation", "Empowerment" and "Poverty Reduction".' *Third World Quarterly* 26 (7): 1043–1060.

Cottrell, B., and J. Parpart. 2006. 'Academic Community Collaboration, Gender Research and Development.' *Development in Practice* 16 (1): 15–26.

Dagron, A. G. 2009. 'Playing With Fire: Power, Participation and Communication for Development.' *Development in Practice* 19 (4–5): 453–465.

Eade, D. 2007. 'Capacity Building: Who Builds Whose Capacity?' *Development in Practice* 17 (4–5): 630–639.

Fox, J. 2006. 'Lessons From Action-Research Partnerships: LASA/Oxfam America 2004 Martin Disking Memorial Lecture.' *Development in Practice* 16 (1): 27–38.

Gosling, L., with M. Edwards. 1995. 'Toolkits: A Practical Guide to Assessment, Monitoring, Review and Evaluation.' Save the Children Development Manual 5. London: Save the Children.

Guijt, I., and M. Shah (eds.). 1998. *The Myth of Community: Gender Issues in Participatory Development.* London: IT Publications.

Hampshire, K., E. Hills and N. Iqbal. 2005. 'Power Relations in Participatory Research and Community Development: A Case Study from Northern England.' *Human Organization* 64 (4): 340–349.

Hayati, D., E. Karami and B. Slee. 2006. 'Combining Qualitative and Quantitative Methods in the Measurement of Rural Poverty: The Case of Iran.' *Social Indicators Research* 75 (3): 361–394.

Hickey, S., and G. Mohan (eds.). 2004. *Participation – From Tyranny to Transformation? Exploring New Approaches to Participation in Development.* London: Zed.

Hodgson, D. L., and R. Schroeder. 2002. 'Dilemmas of Counter-Mapping Community Resources in Tanzania.' *Development and Change* 33 (1): 79–100.

Holland, J., and J. Blackburn (eds.). 1998. *Whose Voice? Participatory Research and Policy Change.* London: IT Publications.

Hulme, D., and J. Toye. 2006. 'The Case for Cross-Disciplinary Social Science Research on Poverty, Inequality and Well-Being.' *Journal of Development Studies* 42 (7): 1085–1107.

Kapoor, I. 2002. 'The Devil's in the Theory: A Critical assessment of Robert Chambers' work on participatory development.' *Third World Quarterly* 23 (1): 101–117.

———. 2005. 'Participatory Development, Complicity and Desire.' *Third World Quarterly* 26 (8): 1203–1220.

Kesby, M. 2000. 'Participatory Diagramming: Deploying Qualitative Methods Through an Action Research Epistemology.' *Area* 32 (4): 423–435.

Kanbur, R. 2002. 'Economics, Social Science and Development.' *World Development* 30 (3): 477–486.

Mohan, G., and K. Stokke. 2000. 'Participatory Development and Empowerment: The Dangers of Localism.' *Third World Quarterly* 21 (2): 247–268.

Morgan, D. L. 1997. *Focus Groups as Qualitative Research*. Thousand Oaks, CA: Sage.

Mosse, D. 2003. 'The Making and Marketing of Participatory Development.' In *A moral critique of Development: In Search of Global Responsibilities,* eds. P. Quarles van Ufford and A. K. Giri, 43–75. London: Routledge.

Paluck, E. L. 2008. 'Methods and Ethics with Research Teams and NGOs: Comparing Experiences Across the Border of Rwanda and Democratic Republic of Congo.' Revised version of a paper presented at the Annual Meeting of the American Political Science Association, Chicago, 29 Aug–2 Sept 2007.

Parfitt, T. 2004. 'The Ambiguity of Participation: A Qualified Defence of Participatory Development.' *Third World Quarterly* 25 (3): 537–556.

Porter, G., and A. Abane. 2008. 'Increasing Children's Participation in Transport Planning: Reflections on Methodology in a Child-Centred Research Project.' *Children's Geographies* 6 (2): 151–167.

Porter, G., et al. 2010. 'Where Dogs, Ghosts and Lions Roam: Learning from Mobile Ethnographies on the Journey from School.' *Children's Geographies* 8 (2): 91–105.

Porter, G., and E. Young. 1998. 'Decentralised Environmental Management and Popular Participation in Coastal Ghana.' *Journal of International Development* 10: 515–526.

Porter, G., E. Young and A. Dzietror. 1998. 'Pressures on an Intensive Irrigated Cash-Crop System in Coastal Ghana.' *Geoforum* 28 (3–4): 329–340.

Pretty, J., et al. 1995. *A Trainer's Guide for Participatory Learning and Action*. London: IIED.

Roper, L. 2002. 'Achieving Successful Academic-Practitioner Research Collaborations.' *Development in Practice* 12 (3–4): 338–345.

Strathern, M. 2005. 'Experiments in Interdisciplinarity.' *Social Anthropology* 13 (1): 75–90.

Sillitoe, P., P. Dixon and J. Barr. 2005. *Indigenous Knowledge Inquiries: A Methodologies Manual for Development*. London: ITDG.

Sillitoe, P., and M. Marzano. 2009. 'Future of Indigenous Knowledge Research in Development.' *Futures* 41 (1): 13–23.

Wesselink, A. 2009. 'The Emergence of Interdisciplinary Knowledge in Problem-Focused Research.' *Area* 41 (4): 404–413.

Williams, G. 2004. 'Evaluating Participatory Development: Tyranny, Power and (Re)Politicisation.' *Third World Quarterly* 25 (3): 557–578.

CHAPTER 18

On the Importance of Culture in Sustainable Development

Serena Heckler

A criticism levelled at development is that it may be detrimental to non-Western cultures, with some arguing that it represents an imposition of Western values on people who may have radically different views and perspectives. When combined with the failure of many development interventions, the issue of how development may address cultural, as well as economic and technical, sustainability has come to the forefront of international development policy and practice.

This chapter considers different ways that culture has been incorporated into development including: the importance of culture for well-being; the need to sustain socio-cultural identity and diversity; the participation of all stakeholders in decision making in order to ensure that cultural values shape policy and practice; the significance of a human rights–based approach to sustainability; the use of indicators of socio-culturally sustainable development; and a few ways in which actors are seeking to make their own cultures more sustainable. It gives examples of sustainable development projects which make culture their central focus, including the work of the international COMPAS (Comparing and Supporting Endogenous Development) Network, the Peruvian group PRATEC (the Andean Project for Peasant Technologies[1]) and development initiatives by the Shuar people of Ecuador. I argue that to avoid the pitfalls of previous development paradigms, organizations adopting the cultural turn must use their greater understanding of other socio-cultural perspectives to cast a critical eye on their own structures and practices with a view to giving local people more autonomy to find their own pathways to development.

Background

What we now think of as international development was originally conceived as a modernizing concept, where social and cultural elements of certain societies would have to become more like so-called developed societies to enable economic advancement. A famous quote by the United Nations illustrates the philosophy underpinning this development paradigm as it first emerged in the post–World War II period: 'There is a sense in which rapid economic progress is impossible without painful adjustments. Ancient philosophies have to be scrapped; old social institutions have to disintegrate; bonds of caste, creed and race have to burst; and large numbers of people who cannot keep up with progress have to have their expectations of a comfortable life frustrated' (United Nations, Department of Social and Economic Affairs, *Measures for the Economic Development of Underdeveloped Countries*, 1951, quoted in Escobar 1995: 3).

However, by the 1980s, it had become clear that this approach to development had failed to produce the economic prosperity that it had promised in many parts of the world. This realization, combined with a growing concern for the environmental destruction to which the modernizing development paradigm had contributed, gave rise to the paradigm of sustainable development.

One of the key innovations of sustainable development was to combine environmental, economic and socio-cultural concerns. It was no longer accepted that a single-minded focus on improving economic indicators would resolve the dire situation of the world's poor or the natural environment. Indeed, the concept of sustainable development is often modelled as a Venn diagram with three interlocking circles representing economy, environment and society and/or culture (figure 18.1).

However, use of the term *culture* in sustainable development contexts has varied considerably. Part of the difficulty is in the way it has been defined in different contexts and different academic disciplines. Early on,

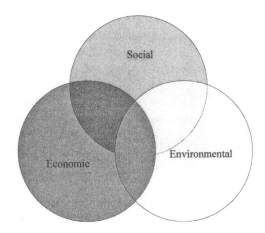

Figure 18.1. A Venn diagram of sustainable development.

anthropologists saw it as a '"bundle" of [coherent] beliefs and practices' (Radcliffe 2006: 9) that inform and inflect all sorts of social and economic activities. This idea of culture has become prominent in the media and non-anthropological circles (ibid.), where 'culture' is often equated with ethnic or racial groups. Anthropologists have refuted this idea of culture, seeing it as something much more fluid and strategic. They no longer consider culture to comprise bounded and discrete units, but rather see it as constantly interacting with 'other cultures', changing with those interactions. Sarah Radcliffe identifies key dimensions to the culture concept as it is currently held by (many) anthropologists (ibid.): its flexibility, its strategic deployment by different actors to make interventions, its contested content and its interplay between material and symbolic components.

In this sense, the concept of 'culture' is better conceptualized as suggested by the World Commission on Culture and Development as 'ways of living together' (WCCD 1996: 14). I will return to this definition below, but it is important to note that defining culture in this way makes it difficult to distinguish between social and cultural issues. Rather than attempt to do so, I wish to emphasize their interrelatedness and the importance of incorporating both into development. Hence, although I often use the term *culture,* I also refer to issues that some might consider to be social.

This chapter reviews four ways in which the culture concept has been used in sustainable development: (1) culture as a useful tool for sustainable development; (2) the post-development critique that sustainable development is grounded in and comes from a particular socio-cultural perspective; (3) the 'cultural turn' that holds that culture and cultural diversity are inherent and innate goods which are vital to well-being; and (4) the most recent push to create sustainable cultures. I present each approach as it is presented by its proponents in more or less chronological order. As each successive approach was often developed from an acknowledgement of weaknesses or failures of the previous ones, I touch upon key critiques and weaknesses of each of the approaches throughout the chapter. However, space prevents a full consideration of all of the arguments that these different approaches have generated over the decades.

Culture as a Tool for Sustainable Development

The first and arguably most common way in which culture has been integrated into sustainable development is as a tool to assist the implementation of development projects. It was acknowledged that many projects failed for socio-cultural reasons, but whereas in the conventional development paradigm the socio-cultural context was seen to be the problem (i.e. the failure of the project was fault of the beneficiaries), in sustainable development the problem was often seen to be the failure of development practitioners to understand and work within the socio-cultural context of the beneficiaries (i.e. the failure was the fault of poor planning or execution). This represented a major shift in thinking and was greeted with enthusiasm by some practitioners: development would be more sustainable if only we could make it locally relevant. A quote from a USAID worker in Egypt illustrates this approach: 'In every culture there is something that works, and the thing is to find out what that is. Is it the headman, the religious leader, community pressure, or the police? Find out what it is and use it' (1995, quoted in Elyachar 2002: 509).

Vijayendra Rao and Michael Walton (2004) suggest that international development agencies expect that by taking local cultures into account and 'using them', development projects will: (a) increase the participation of civil society actors; (b) guarantee social cohesion; and (c) regularize decision making. Radcliffe argues that this has been operationalized through the concepts of governance, social capital and participation (2006: 22). Given that these concepts are central to sustainable development today, it is useful to look at them in more detail.

It is often argued that development has failed because of bad governance – i.e. corruption and lack of participation. This has led to an emphasis on so-called good governance (figure 18.2).

Figure 18.2. The primary elements of good governance as envisioned by the UN Economic and Social Commission for Asia and the Pacific (UNESCAP, http://www.unescap.org/pdd/prs/ProjectActivities/Ongoing/gg/governance.asp).

Within this context, social capital is broadly defined as the social glue or 'norms and social relations embedded in the social structures of society that enable people to coordinate action and achieve desired goals' (Narayan 1999, in Laurie, Andolina and Radcliffe 2005: 474). The idea has been to place social capital alongside economic capital as a means of measuring and evaluating development. From this perspective, it is a resource to be used, but it also must be maintained or increased by a development project (Gilberthorpe and Sillitoe 2009).

The concepts of governance and social capital are related to the idea of participation, which is a fundamental principle of sustainable development. Intertwined with the idea of an environmentally, economically and socially sustainable development, is the belief that the impetus for development, its goals and foci, should be decided by those at the grass-roots level – the beneficiaries of development. It was thought that if development practitioners listened carefully to the concerns, priorities and problems of the intended beneficiaries, development would not only be more successful, but also more relevant to the lives of the people it sought to help, i.e. more sustainable. This bottom-up style of development contrasts sharply with the top-down style where the governments and technical experts of developed countries consider it to be their moral duty to share their knowledge and expertise with developing countries.

It soon became apparent that incorporating the viewpoints of recipients into development projects in any meaningful way was not simply a matter of holding a few meetings, but rather involved a major restructuring of the whole process of development. It was with a view to carrying out this restructuring that the participatory approach was developed in the 1980s (Chambers 1984; Chambers, Pacey and Thrupp 1989). In the subsequent two decades, much has been written about participation in development, and I only highlight a couple of key issues here.[2]

The fundamental idea of participatory development is that it is 'a process through which stakeholders influence and share control over development initiatives, and the decisions and resources which affect them' (World Bank, in Dalal-Clayton and Bass 2002: 178). This involves a radical reconfiguration of the entire decision-making structure including (from Dalal-Clayton and Bass 2002):

- More flexible priority setting;
- Not establishing aims and objectives until after the project start-up (must be set with input from all possible stakeholder groups);
- Committing time and energy to reach underrepresented or marginalized groups *on their own terms* – if you don't reach them, the failure is not theirs, but yours;

- 'Experts' relinquish control;
- Different research methodologies;
- An ability to understand and deal with economic, technical, *and* social issues and an open-minded approach to what the problems are. This means multidisciplinary teams and mutual respect within those teams (see Porter, chapter 17, this volume);
- New ways of measuring development success – local perspectives on success may differ from those of development practitioners.

In practice, this ideal has rarely been realized and the literature is full of examples where *participation* has been used as little more than a buzzword to lend credibility to a project. Barry Dalal-Clayton and Stephen Bass (2002: 179) give a good example of this (table 18.1).

Table 18.1. Some perceptions of participation in the Bangladesh Flood Action Plan and in rural planning in Tanzania. *Source:* Adapted from Adnan et al. 1992; and Kikula and Pfliegner 2001.

Villagers
• 'Participation is about doing something for everyone's benefit' (villager).
• 'Oh yes, the foreigners were here one day, last month. But they only went to school and spoke in English. We are not educated. We could not understand' (a poor peasant).
Government Officials
• 'Yes, we're doing people's participation. We have had people working in Food for Works programmes since the seventies' (top official in Bangladesh Water Development Board).
• 'Your idea regarding women's participation is not correct for the overall national interest.'
• 'But what will be our role if we are to have complete participation?'
• 'True participation is too expensive.'
• 'Participation takes too long and is wasting time.'
• 'There are limits to participation because somebody ultimately has to decide.'
• 'I did the work plan myself on behalf of the district staff' (district planning officer, Tanzania).
Foreign Consultants
• 'Another idea from the social scientists. Only slogans! First "poverty alleviation". Then "women" and "environment". Now "people's participation"! It's just a new fad!' (engineer).
• 'You have to consult my socio-economist, not me. I have no time for this participation. I'm working 12 hours every day on the project' (FAP team leader).

In fact, despite the use of the buzzword *participation* in many projects, many different types of so-called participation have been identified (table 18.2).

Table 18.2. Types of participation in local-level development. *Source:* Dalal-Clayton and Bass 2002, from Pretty 1997.

	Type	Characteristics
1	Manipulative participation	Participation is simply a pretence.
2	Passive participation	People participate by being told what has been decided or has already happened. Information shared belongs only to external professionals.
3	Participation by consultation	People participate by being consulted or by answering questions. No share in decision making is conceded and professionals are under no obligation to take on board people's views.
4	Participation for material incentives	People participate in return for food, cash or other material incentives. Local people have no stake in prolonging practices when the incentives end.
5	Functional participation	Participation is seen by external agencies as a means to achieve project goals, especially reduced costs. People may participate by forming groups to meet predetermined project objectives.
6	Interactive participation	People participate in joint analysis, which leads to action plans and the formation or strengthening of local groups or institutions that determine how available resources are used. Learning methods are used to seek multiple viewpoints.
7	Self mobilization	People participate by taking initiatives independently of external institutions. They develop contacts with external institutions for resources and technical advice, but retain control over how resources are used.

Obviously the goal is to work towards the bottom end of this table (rows 6 and 7), but all too often the word *participation* is used in the sense of rows 1–3.

Truly participatory development usually requires more time, energy, flexibility and resources to get off the ground. Most contentiously, it often involves the relinquishing of control by those who are accustomed to making the decisions. However, the payoffs, at least in theory, are worth it: participation is the only way to make the development sustainable.

Advancements in Participatory Development

The concepts of social capital, governance and participation have been thoroughly critiqued by various commentators. If we take participation, for instance, people who were encouraged to 'participate', often in the sense of rows 1–3 in table 18.2, have no real influence over the process. Some development practitioners have acknowledged this and have moved beyond the idea of participation to look at issues such as 'enfranchisement' (Green and Chambers 2006). Another term that is regularly used instead of or alongside *participation* is *empowerment* (Cornwall and Brock 2005). These terms focus not only on a person or group's presence at a particular event or signature on a particular document, but what actual power they have to effect change and influence the process. Empowerment is seen as a means of overcoming what is often perceived as passivity or dependency on the part of recipients.

Another key advancement in thinking that has occurred in participatory development is recognition that 'local' recipients are themselves a diverse and complex group. Some projects found that when they engaged with local decision making and governance structures, they ended up exacerbating internal conflicts or inequalities. For instance, men might benefit from development at the expense of women, or one ethnic group, tribe or clan at the expense of another depending on who captured the ear of the project staff. This could cause conflict in the community, not only threatening the project, but also the well-being of the people. There was therefore an emphasis on 'widening participation' in which a number of tools and tactics were incorporated to ensure that marginalized groups participated. Some key methods include (from Dalal-Clayton and Bass 2002: 206–224):

- Social mapping: to identify wealth distribution and diverse socio-economic groups;
- Joint management strategies;
- Participatory learning and action: all participants learn to carry out all the methods while doing them. The emphasis is on facilitating local processes of learning and analysis, sharing knowledge and building partnerships, rather than on the outcomes;
- Participatory rural appraisal: local people undertake their own appraisals.

In summary, then, the new perspectives and approaches inherent in the sustainable development approach stimulated the advance of participatory or bottom-up approaches. According to some, this has led to significant advancements in the way that development projects are designed and implemented. In particular, it has promoted a toolbox of methods that seek to ensure that the development process incorporates local concerns and perspectives. Nevertheless, post-development thinkers argue that the very concept of sustainable development is fundamentally flawed.

Sustainable Development Derives From a Particular Culture

In recent decades, a serious critique of both development and sustainable development has emerged. This critique, known as post-development (Rahnema and Bowtree 1997; Ziai 2007), draws in part from Edward Said's concept of Orientalism (1978) and has been largely developed by thinkers from the Arab and Islamic world. A seminal work, *Encountering Development* (Arturo Escobar 1995), along with a range of other works (Hobart 1993; Apffel-Marglin with PRATEC 1998; Crush 1995; Rahnema and Bawtree 1997) argued that despite good intentions, the discourse and practice of sustainable development is justified by the assumptions of a particular worldview, i.e. Western or Euro-American cultural perspectives, responsible for the very problems that sustainable development seeks to address.

To illustrate this argument, I return to the quote by the USAID development worker in Egypt, in which he calls for the development worker to 'find what works' in every culture and use it. The subtext of this quote is that the development worker is qualified to judge traditional knowledge and to arbitrate 'what works', for what purpose and for whose interests. What is not useful by his or her own criteria doesn't 'work' and therefore is … what? To be discarded? To be ignored? To be changed?

A number of recent case studies have shown that development projects often misinterpret 'what works' in particular cultures. They also show how introducing sustainable development into a particular society can lead to wide-ranging unintentional changes, and that the way 'development' is perceived in that society can be quite different from how it is intended by project staff (Mosse 2005; West 2007; Wright 2009; Gilberthorpe 2009).

It is increasingly argued that Western science is only one of many types of knowing, rather than a widely assumed universal truth (Sillitoe 2002, 2007). When we begin to understand that many societies have their own ways of understanding and interacting with the world, we also begin to understand that many of the core concepts and methodologies of development – from the desirability of a certain kind of relationship between the individual and the state to 'management plans' and 'cost benefit analysis' – come from a particular vision of the world and our relationship with it that may be completely inimical to local and traditional ways of seeing things.

Arturo Escobar (1995) argues that the Brundtland Commission and other early proponents of sustainable development used a particular worldview 'shared by those who rule [the world]' (1995: 195) of what economies, ecosystems and societies could and should be. In *Our Common Future*, 'the environment' emerges as something separate from people and the economy, something that should be 'managed' by 'planners' and 'experts'. Escobar writes, 'The concepts of planning and management embody the belief that social change can be engineered and directed, produced at will' (ibid.: 194). He goes on to assert that 'no longer does nature denote an entity with its own agency, a source of life and discourse' as it is often perceived in local and indigenous cultures, but rather a 'resource' to be managed by experts. Thus, argues Escobar, the very idea of sustainable development is an imposition of outside values, an inherent contradiction that dooms the concept to failure from the outset.

Most importantly, post-development thinkers argue, the power differentials that created the problems we see today are perpetuated by the sustainable development paradigm. For instance, the representation of the developing world as 'poor, problematic, needy, passive recipients' (Maiava and King 2007: 84) continues under sustainable development, as does the structural blindness to the myriad of solutions that have been developed locally to the problems normally addressed by international development. Instead, the people qualified to solve these problems are 'experts' trained in universities. With its introduction of yet another technical aspect that must be examined and described by 'experts' – i.e. the environmental aspect, as it is defined by the West – sustainable development continues down the route of denying the possibility that the world's poor have the knowledge for successful development, thereby rendering them 'ignorant' (Hobart 1993). Thus, the primary issue, argue post-development thinkers, is the inequality inherent in the global economy, an inequality that is maintained and perhaps increased under the paradigm of sustainable development (Sachs 1997: 293).

A few go on to suggest that we have wrongly identified the underlying problem. They argue that to solve the problems conventionally seen to be the purview of sustainable development, we should not be concerned with changing the behaviour of the poor, but rather with changing the behaviour of the rich, notably their out-of-control consumption (Sachs 1997: 298–299; Wilkinson and Pickett 2009).

These are important issues and deserve our consideration, but in the meantime, marginalized people around the world continue to die from preventable causes, species are going extinct at an unprecedented rate and the gap between rich and poor continues to widen. Thus, I do not agree that intentional development should be abandoned. Instead, I agree with those who have taken on board these critiques and work to establish new ways of doing development. One of these new ways has been the so-called cultural turn in development.

Culture and Cultural Diversity Are Vital to Well-Being

Proponents of the 'cultural turn' argue that it is about acknowledging that the major issues that development needs to address, including the economic and environmental, are socio-cultural issues (Nederveen Pieterse 2001; Watts 2006). Moreover, culture itself is seen as a resource essential to well-being. A milestone in this process was the publication of *Our Creative Diversity*, also known as the Pérez de Cuéllar Commission, by the World Commission on Culture and Development in 1995.

Our Creative Diversity was significant in redefining the role of culture in development. It states that 'development divorced from its human or social context is growth without a soul' and argued that 'poverty of a life, in this view, is not caused only by the lack of essential goods and services, but also a lack of opportunities to choose a fuller, more satisfying, more valuable and valued existence' (WCCD 1996: 14). The report defines culture as 'ways of living together' and the authors argue that the 'cultural dimensions of human life are more essential than [economic] growth' (WCCD 1996: 14). Culture is seen to contribute to well-being in several key ways, including giving meaning to existence; sustaining the physical environment; preserving family values; and protecting civil institutions. Hence a thriving cultural and spiritual life free from suppression or acculturation is no longer seen as a hindrance or help to development, as per the United Nations and USAID quotes above, but rather a desirable outcome in and of itself.

Our Creative Diversity also argues that development must not be assessed by economic growth alone, but also to the values of 'fostering of respect for all cultures and for the principle of cultural freedom' (WCCD 1996: 15). In focusing on culture as being inextricably related to values, the report argued for recognition of two fundamental principles: the principle of equality and the principle of respect for human diversity (van der Staay 1996). From these principles it advocated the idea of global ethics, which it claims are shared by all world cultures and religions:

- Human rights (including environmental rights)
- Democracy and civil society
- Recognition of the rights of minorities
- The peaceful solution of and a rational approach to conflicts;
- Intergenerational responsibility

Following on from *Our Creative Diversity*, in 2005, UNESCO finalized the Convention on the Protection and Promotion of the Diversity of Cultural Expressions.[3] As of January 2012, 118 countries were party to this legally binding, international agreement in which several articles highlight the importance of culture in sustainable development (UNESCO 2007):

- Article 2 para 6: **Principle of Sustainable Development:** Culture is a rich asset for individuals and societies. The protection, promotion and maintenance of cultural diversity are an essential requirement for sustainable development for the benefit of present and future generations.
- Article 13: **Integration of culture in Sustainable Development:** Parties shall endeavour to integrate culture in their development policies at all levels for the creation of conditions conducive to sustainable development and, within this framework, foster aspects relating to the protection and promotion of the diversity of cultural expressions.

Taken as a whole, these policy documents have been part of a wider change in the focus and intention of international development over the past ten to fifteen years. One result in this change in focus is the development and increasing popularity of the Human Rights–Based Approach (HRBA).

The Human Rights–Based Approach to Development

A clear and concise definition of the HRBA is to be found on 'Partner Portal', a website for participatory video:

> The human rights-based approach provides a framework for looking at development based on international human rights standards. The aim is that this approach will protect and promote people's rights rather than just their needs. It is about recognising poverty as a question of powerlessness and aiming to address this. Above all it is about expanding people's lives and choices to live the lives they value and the empowerment of people to decide what this process of expansion should look like.[4]

To reiterate, the HRBA is *rights* based, rather than *needs* based. And the emphasis is on empowerment, which means to give local people the tools, confidence and ability to meaningfully participate. This may include providing education, building confidence, forming groups and networks that can influence decision-making processes, or simply helping to overcome practical barriers to their participation.

To properly understand how HRBA moves beyond the participatory approach detailed above, consider the following. There is a common saying that has often been cited by sustainable development advocates: 'Give a man a fish and he'll eat for a day, teach him how to fish and he'll eat forever.' This saying has been seen as a metaphor for the sustainable development approach, where 'giving a man a fish' was seen to represent the conventional development approach, but 'teaching him how to fish' was a much more sustainable way to improve his lot. Nevertheless, through the post-development critiques, it became clear that there was something wrong with this attitude to development. Namely, it is condescending to assume that local people do not eat fish because they do not know how to fish; it imagines poor people as helpless, needy and ignorant. In fact, the HRBA assumes that the reasons the man is not eating fish are any of a multitude of structural and social barriers. He may no longer have access to fishing territory, that territory may have been rendered unproductive through pollution by actors outside his control, and, furthermore, he may not want to be a fisherman – he may have aspirations to do other things with his life. This metaphor may be applied to many sustainable development projects, where the practitioners assume that they know what the beneficiary's goals are and what the source of their problems may be.

A problem remains from a post-development perspective, namely the unspoken assumption that 'empowering' people means to teach them to see development, identify the problem, act and evaluate the outcomes like Western project staff. As Rosemary McGee has noted, the very concept of participation only makes sense 'when the impetus or framework for a development activity is located outside people's lifeworlds' (2002: 92). People do not 'participate' in their own initiatives. A farmer does not 'participate' in her farming, or a student in his learning. Instead, development practitioners should perhaps think of themselves as participating in local initiatives.

However, it must also be recognized that, at the local level, people still have to contend with a broader power structure, including international economic and political interests, not of their own making. They have urgent needs that many believe the international community is morally obligated to meet even if the thorough overhaul of the current world system advocated by post-development thinkers does not immediately come to pass. We should not ignore or dismiss the critiques of the post-development movement, but there is still a role for development practitioners to facilitate meaningful negotiations between local people and the power and resource structures that currently exist. In other words, the role of professionals should not be to train locals to be 'experts', but rather to help local people and organizations to find their own pathways to development.

To break away from the underlying assumptions that have rendered previous versions problematic, sweeping changes will have to occur in development structures, including practitioners rethinking what it means to be an 'expert', who has control over decision making, who decides what the problems are that need to be solved and who comes up with the solutions. As can be seen from table 18.1, this will be a giant task and space only allows a brief consideration of some of these issues. However, a key aspect of development practice that is worth highlighting because of what it illustrates about the centrality of socio-cultural issues in development is how we measure outcomes of development projects.

Socio-Cultural Indicators of Sustainable Development

When given the opportunity, local people will define the goal of development in their own way. As the World Bank's publication *Voices of the Poor* (2002) emphasized, they do not focus entirely on increasing per capita income or GDP, but also on more intangible elements of well-being. To again quote 'Partner Portal':

> [It was] based on a study of 80,000 poor and marginalised people world wide who spoke about poverty as they experience it. Their responses highlight that poverty is not just a question of a lack in services and commodities such as health and education they also brought up less well addressed issues. They talked about issues of emotional integrity, respect and dignity, social belonging, cultural identity, organisational capacity, political representation and accountability; issues of powerlessness.[5]

To reflect these priorities, development must be measured and evaluated differently. How can 'emotional integrity' and 'respect and dignity' be measured? Recently, considerable work has been done on this at the international level. The International Indigenous Forum on Biodiversity (IIFB) has undergone a round of international consultations to come up with indicators to measure progress towards the Millennium Development Goals and the targets of the Convention on Biological Diversity. It is argued that indigenous concerns are missing from the indicators originally proposed to evaluate progress towards these goals (Tebtebba 2008: ix). Hence, the IIFB has worked to have these concerns recognized and included in international agreements. It is notable that the resulting indicators focus largely on socio-cultural issues, with only one of twelve strands focusing explicitly on economic – or in their words, material – well-being (table 18.3).

Table 18.3. Global summary of the core thematic issues recommended by the IIFB. *Source:* Tebtebba Foundation 2008: 44.

1. Security of rights to territories, lands and natural resources
2. Integrity of cultural heritage
3. Respect for identity and non-discrimination
4. Culturally appropriate education
5. Fate control
6. Full, informed and effective participation
7. Health
8. Access to infrastructure and basic services
9. Extent of external threats
10. Material well-being
11. Gender
12. Demographic patterns of peoples

It can be seen from the categories in table 18.3 that these indicators echo many of the concerns expressed in the *Voices of the Poor* report. Many challenge the normal way of doing sustainable development and are elusive: how does one measure 'fate control'? How can it be established that participation is full, informed and effective? At the root of all of this is a demand for a shift in power, which is one of the most difficult changes to effect. Given the entrenched belief of many policy-makers, donors, politicians and scientists that they know the best way to 'develop' a society, how can it be made evident that other concerns, priorities and needs, not only exist, but must be taken into account if development is to be successful? Certainly, a first step towards doing this is to make these concerns, priorities and needs visible through appropriate indicators.

Examples of Sustainable Development That Sees Culture as Vital to Well-being

As a means of illustrating what culture-based development looks like, I now consider several examples of ways of working that put cultural issues in the centre of development projects. They demonstrate how culture and sustainable development may interact and how the ideas of participation and empowerment are fundamental in this process.

The Comparing and Supporting Endogenous Development Network (COMPAS) is an international network of research and development institutions that implement 'field programmes to develop, test and improve endogenous development (ED) methodologies'. According to the COMPAS website: 'Endogenous development is based on local peoples' own criteria of development, and takes into account the material, social and spiritual well-being of peoples.'[6] COMPAS has developed a logo that echoes the sustainable development Venn diagram, but it has some crucial differences (figure 18.3): instead of making the economic a key aspect of develop-

ment, as is seen in the sustainable development Venn diagram, the economic is embedded within the human world and the material is embedded within the natural world. Notably, this approach to development elevates the spiritual to a central position. The Venn diagram implicitly suggests that the three domains of the sustainable development model – the socio-cultural, the environmental and the economic – are not seen as being appropriate by all development beneficiaries. Commenting on the

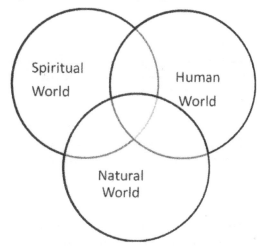

Figure 18.3. The logo for COMPAS, which echoes the Venn diagram for sustainable development, but the central principles are different. *Source:* Haverkort, van 't Hooft and Hiemstra 2002: 31.

Venn diagram, Bertus Haverkort, Katrien van 't Hooft and Wim Hiemstra (2002: 31) observe: 'Together these notions form the worldview or cosmovision that describes the role of [the supernatural], the perceived relationship between humans and nature, and the way natural processes are explained. On the basis of these perceptions, people organize themselves and determine their interventions in nature as well as their religious activities.'

A consequence of emphasizing the spiritual is the identification of different goals for development. In an echo of the World Bank's *Voices of the Poor* study, COMPAS suggests that for many people aspects of well-being besides income level are of equal or greater importance, for instance social cohesion, having and caring for children and maintaining spiritual life, not only privately but in society and in relation to the natural world (ibid.: 32). This emphasis on the family and spiritual life is, of course, extremely important in the Arab world. Islamic traditions of charity and community provide the basis of models for endogenous development in the Gulf region.

The Peruvian NGO, PRATEC shares this emphasis on the spiritual. PRATEC (Andean Project of Peasant Technologies by its Spanish initials)

is a non-profit organization that aims to reinforce Amazonian and Andean culture and agriculture. It was formed in the 1990s as a result of the founders' disillusionment with the participatory approach to development (Appfel-Marglin and PRATEC 1998) and works with a network of indigenous Andean and Amazonian communities in the execution of actions aiming to strengthen their cultural identity and therefore, their well-being. The founders of PRATEC note that 'there is a recognition among traditional authorities … that their present lack of well-being is due to a generalised loss of respect for each other, for their deities and nature' (Ishizawa and Rengifo 2009: 60). This is seen to be partially the fault of a school system that has taught children to value only exogenous culture. As a result, PRATEC has worked with local communities to incorporate traditional values, rituals and social relations into teaching methods and curricula.[7] The aim is not only to instil respect for elders, but also greater proficiency in the students' native language and a more centred and mature perspective from which to learn those elements of the exogenous culture that will help them succeed in their chosen careers. For instance, teachers say that children learn reading, writing and arithmetic with more enthusiasm and have a better work ethic when taught solely in their native language and largely about and with the community and their families until they are eight or nine years old.

Across the border in Ecuador, I have worked with people whose priorities show many affinities with this approach. The Shuar are an indigenous group living in the Amazon region of southeast Ecuador. They are interested in development, but are unsatisfied by the various types of development projects that have been imposed upon them. As a result, they have begun to plan and execute their own projects and to establish and act upon their own priorities for development.

In 2010, Shuar NGO, Corporation UNSA, planned a project to establish ecotourism industries in several remote Shuar regions. However, rather than focus exclusively on the infrastructure necessary to run these businesses, the projects begin with local studies to document and 'revitalize' Shuar traditions and practices. In justifying this emphasis on cultural revitalization, the author of the project proposal cites both social and environmental consequences of the loss of tradition and cultural identity: '[The] effects [of loss of traditions and culture] are especially worrying for younger generations, many of whom have become acculturated and thus have low self-esteem…. We Shuar, who were once a culture well adapted to its environment, who once cared for and protected our home and our habitat, we have now been converted into devourers and impulsive predators' (document written February 2010, translated from Spanish by the author).

This example suggests that the immediate goal of development for the Shuar is not to increase income but rather to strengthen Shuar society and ethnic identity. Just like with the Andean communities with whom PRATEC works, the Shuar see the loss of respect for their elders and their ways of living as a key factor in their general decline in well-being. From this perspective, then, economic, legal and rights-based development can only occur if the properly moral enactment of social relationships – embedded within a particular cultural context – is healthy and functional.

Whether these projects represent real solutions to development's most stubborn problems remains to be seen. Do they adequately respond to the concerns of post-development thinkers? I know that the projects run by PRATEC, COMPAS and Shuar NGOs make a significant impact on people's lives. Importantly, they do not unilaterally identify the needs of a community, decide what is to be done and how, and enter that community with a detailed action plan, but rather they forfeit such power and work with local people to help them identify their own problems, come up with solutions and act on them in their own manner.

The role of international development professionals, then, should not be to lead and implement development projects, but rather to create conditions and support local communities to lead and implement their own. Appropriate roles for development professionals might include collecting and disseminating best practice, sharing ideas and expertise, facilitating networks and providing the institutional contexts and structures in which local people can overcome limitations and build capacity to address their own problems. This includes providing platforms upon which local people can have their own perspectives, concerns and expertise heard by decision makers and funders.

Gulf countries, with their strong cultural institutions, notably Islamic banks, development agencies and faith-based NGOs, are well placed to be leaders in culture-based development. A number of Islamic thinkers and intellectuals have made important and lasting contributions to the cultural turn in development. Nevertheless, to continue to set the standard of culture-based development, Gulf countries must continue to emphasize human rights, faith-based values and the importance of culture and not solely focus on economic indicators and outcomes.

Creating Sustainable Cultures

The fundamental point made by the post-development theorists was that sustainable development should not address the resource use by the poor, but rather the resource use by the wealthy. The natural resource consumption of most countries with high GDP, including many of those in the Gulf, is far beyond levels that the planet can sustain. Hence a vital task for sustainable development is, or should be, to decrease the resource use of wealthy nations and people. Many members of wealthy societies have accepted this argument at least partially and have come up with grassroots, institutional and government projects which seek to make their own communities more sustainable. Many readers of this volume will be members of university communities, so it is fitting to end this chapter by briefly touching upon some university projects that seek to encourage sustainable cultures (e.g. Bartlett and Chase 2004).

In *Creating a Culture of Sustainability: How Campuses are Taking a Lead*, the US office furniture company Herman Miller describes part of its Corporate Social Responsibility programme which supports initiatives to encourage more sustainable lifestyles (Herman Miller Inc. 2005). The report reviews a range of campus initiatives that seek to teach and instil sustainability as a value in their communities. These comprise four elements:

- Involve the campus community: get students, academic and non-academic staff involved in collecting data, developing policies and action plans
  - E.g. Pennsylvania State: Ecology students carried out a study of a building as an ecosystem – what was used, what was thrown away – then devised a plan for cutting the ecological impact in half. This plan was negotiated with senior administrators and estates and buildings staff (see Uhl 2004)
  - Non-academic staff are often sidelined in these programmes, but they are key in implementing policies and action plans, so must be involved in negotiating and planning them
- Integrate sustainability into the taught curriculum:
  - Environmental studies programme
  - Broad incorporation of sustainability into other subjects (hidden curriculum), such as teaching environmental literacy, green chemistry experiments, sustainable business programme, environmental law and green architectural and design accreditation (for example the US Green Building Council's Leadership in Energy and Environmental Design [LEED] certification)
  - Teaching critical thinking skills by enabling discussion, a skill which is essential for weighing opinions and ideas and finding a voice in a sustainable community
- Visible symbols of a commitment to sustainability:
  - Do new builds meeting LEED standards? Are they zero emissions? Are they architecturally striking?

- ○ Green landscaping, for example xeriscaped or traditional grounds and gardens
- • Reaching out beyond campus:
  - ○ Offering accreditation courses for professionals (green business or LEED)
  - ○ Consulting on and/or initiating sustainable projects

A key underlying principle is that sustainability is a process. Since students take their experiences from university with them as they disseminate throughout society, such projects will eventually have much wider impacts than the measurable reduction in resource use of any individual campus. This report thus offers guiding principles, examples and references to help encourage sustainability in the broader community and a commitment to the ideal of sustainability amongst the lenders and policy makers of the future.

Conclusion

Culture, once seen as a barrier to development, is increasingly viewed as central to successful sustainable development. Given that it determines 'ways of living together', it is central to well-being. In recent decades, attempts have been made to render culture measurable in the same way that environmental services or income are, for example through the concepts of social capital, good governance or participation. However, these attempts to systematize or quantify the socio-cultural have not led to as many successful development initiatives as was originally hoped.

Post-development theorists argue that this is because many of the assumptions that render classical development problematic also underpin the sustainable development model. Namely, that the idea and shape of development was based on a particular cultural perspective in which a particular cultural model represents 'successful development' – the goal being to make other cultures more like the 'successful' one. While the conventional development model measured development success economically – whereas sustainable development added some other indicators, such as natural and social 'resources' – it still assesses these in ways that are intelligible only to certain types of experts.

Partly in response to these critiques, development has undergone a so-called cultural turn, where culture is seen as key to successful development. The best examples of the cultural turn seek to move away from viewing recipients as ignorant and helpless and focus instead on structural barriers that prevent them from helping themselves. However, in this chapter, I argue that this approach will only improve upon previous endeavours if changes are made to development structures, embedding more flexibility to support truly local development initiatives and ceding control to allow development to be planned, guided and evaluated from distinct socio-cultural perspectives. Rather than focusing our attention, yet again, on how local communities need to improve, we need to focus our attention on improving the development concepts and structures that seek to support them.

Acknowledgements

This research was made possible by a Nuffield Early Career Development Fellowship (NCF/32406). I also thank Paul Sillitoe for his comments on earlier drafts of this chapter.

Notes

1. Literally 'Proyecto Andino de Tecnologías Campesinas'.
2. I base much of the following discussion on a chapter in the *Sustainable Development Strategies Resource Book* (Dalal-Clayton and Bass 2002).
3. http://www.unesco.org/new/en/culture/themes/cultural-diversity/cultural-expressions/the-convention/convention-text/.
4. http://partnerportal.gn.apc.org/HRBA (last accessed 6 April 2010).
5. http://partnerportal.gn.apc.org/HRBA (last accessed 6 April 2010).
6. http://www.compasnet.org (last accessed 6 April 2010)
7. PRATEC (2003). The Ritual Nurturance of the Chacras in the Andes, video. http://partnerportal.gn.apc.org/PRATEC.

References

Adnan, S. et al. 1992. *People's participation, NGOs and the flood action plan: an independent review.* Dhaka: Oxfam-Bangladesh.

Apffel-Marglin, F., with PRATEC. 1998. *The Spirit of Regeneration: Andean Culture Confronting Western Notions of Development.* London: Zed Books.

Bartlett, P. and G. Chase (eds.). 2004. *Sustainability on Campus: Stories and Strategies for Change.* Cambridge, MA: MIT Press.

Chambers, R.. 1984. *Rural Development: Putting the Last First.* London: Longman Group.

Chambers, R., A. Pacey and L. A. Thrupp. 1989. *Farmer First: Farmer Innovation and Agricultural Research.* ITDG Publishing.

Crush, J. 1995. *Power of Development.* London: Routledge.

Dalal-Clayton, B., and S. Bass. 2002. 'Participation in Strategies for Sustainable Development.' In *Sustainable Development Strategies: A Resource Book,* chapter 6, 177–225 (available online). London: Earthscan, with UNDP, OECD.

Elyachar, J. 2002. 'Empowerment Money: The World Bank, Non-Governmental Organizations, and the Value of Culture in Egypt.' *Public Culture* 14 (3): 493–513.

Escobar, A. 1995. *Encountering Development.* Princeton, NJ: Princeton University Press.

Gilberthorpe, E. 2009. 'Pathways to Development: Identity, landscape and industry in Papua New Guinea.' In *Landscape, Process and Power: Re-evaluating Traditional Environmental Knowledge,* ed. S. Heckler, 122–139. New York: Berghahn Books.

Gilberthorpe, E., and P. Sillitoe. 2009. 'A Failure of Social Capital: Lessons from Papua New Guinea in the Current Economic Crisis.' *Anthropology News* 50 (7): 15–16.

Green, J., and W. Bradlee Chambers. 2006. *The Politics of Participation in Sustainable Development Governance.* Tokyo: UN University Press (available online).

Haverkort, B., K. van 't Hooft and W. Hiemstra. 2002. *Ancient Roots, New Shoots: Endogenous Development in Practice.* London: Zed Books.

Heckler, S. 2004. 'Tedium and Creativity: The Valorisation of Manioc Cultivation by Piaroa Women.' *Journal of the Royal Anthropological Institute* 10: 241–259.

Herman Miller Inc. 2005. *Creating a Culture of Sustainability: How Campuses are Taking a Lead.* http://www.hermanmiller.com/hm/content/research_summaries/wp_Campus_Sustain.pdf.

Hobart, M. 1993. *An Anthropological Critique of Development: The Growth of Ignorance.* London: Routledge.

Ishizawa, J., and G. Rengifo. 2009. 'Biodiversity Regeneration and Intercultural Knowledge Transmission in the Peruvian Andes.' In *Learning and Knowing in Indigenous Societies Today,* eds. P. Bates et al., 59–72. Paris: UNESCO.

Laurie, N., R. Andolina and S. Radcliffe. 2005. 'Ethnodevelopment: Social Movements, Creating Experts and Professionalising Indigenous Knowledge in Ecuador.' *Antipode* 37 (3): 470–496.

Maiava, S., and T. King. 2007. 'Pacific Indigenous Development and Post-Intentional Realities.' In *Exploring Post-Development: Theory and Practice, Problems and Perspectives,* ed. A. Ziai, 83–98. London: Routledge.

McCallum, C. 2001. *Gender and Sociality in Amazonia: How Real People are Made.* Oxford: Berg.

McGee, R. 2002. 'Participating in Development.' In *Development Theory and Practice: Critical Perspectives,* eds U. Kothari and M. Minogue, 92–116. Basingstoke: Palgrave.

Mosse, D. 2005. *Cultivating Development: An Ethnography of Aid Policy and Practice.* New York: Pluto Press.

Nederveen, P. 2001. 'The Cultural Turn in Development: Questions of Power.' In *Development Theory: Deconstructions/Reconstructions,* ed. P. Nederveen, 60–72. London: Sage.

Perruchon, M. 2003. *I am Tsunki: Gender and Shamanism among the Shuar of Western Amazonia.* Uppsala Studies in Cultural Anthropology 33. Uppsala: Acta Universitatis Upsaliensis.

Radcliffe, S. 2006. *Culture and Development in a Globalizing World.* London: Routledge.

Rahnema, M., and V. Bawtree. 1997. *The Post-Development Reader.* London: Zed Books.

Rao, V., and M. Walton. 2004. *Culture and Public Action.* Stanford, CA: Stanford University Press.

Sachs, W. 1997. 'The Need for the Home Perspective.' In *The Post-Development Reader,* eds. M. Rahnema and V. Bawtree, 290–300. London: Zed Books.

Said, E. 1978. *Orientalism.* London: Penguin.

Schech, S., and J. Haggis. 2000. *Culture and Development: A Critical Introduction.* Oxford: Blackwell.

Sillitoe, P. 2002. 'Globalizing Indigenous Knowledge.' In *Participating in Development: Approaches to Indigenous Knowledge,* eds. P. Sillitoe, A. Bicker and J. Pottier, 108–138. London: Routledge.

———. 2007. 'Local Science vs. Global Science: An Overview.' In *Local Science vs. Global Science: Approaches to Indigenous Knowledge in International Development,* ed. P. Sillitoe, 1–22. New York: Berghahn Books.

Skelton, T., and T. Allen. 1999. *Culture and Global Change.* London: Routledge.

van der Staay, A. 1996. 'Book Review: *Our Creative Diversity.*' *International Journal of Cultural Policy* 3 (1): 169–175. http://www.powerofculture.nl/uk/archive/report/review.html.

Tebtebba Foundation. 2008. *Indicators Relevant for Indigenous Peoples: A Resource Book.* Baguio City, Philippines: Tebtebba Foundation.

Uhl, C. 2004. 'Process and Practice: Creating the Sustainable University.' In *Sustainability on Campus: Stories and Strategies for Change,* eds. Peggy Bartlett and Geoffrey Chase, 29–48. Cambridge, MA: MIT Press.

UNESCO. 2007. Convention on the Protection and Promotion of the Diversity of Cultural Expressions. http://unesdoc.unesco.org/images/0014/001495/149502E.pdf.

Watts, M. 2006. 'Culture, Development and Global Neo-Liberalism.' In *Culture and Development in a Globalizing World,* ed. S. Radcliffe, 30–57. London: Routledge.

West, P. 2007. *Conservation is Our Government Now: The Politics of Ecology in Papua New Guinea.* Chapel Hill, NC: Duke University Press.

Wilkinson, R., and K. Pickett. 2009. *The Spirit Level: Why More Equal Societies Almost Always do Better.* London: Allen Lane.

World Commission on Culture and Development (WCCD). 1996. *Our Creative Diversity.* UNESCO. http://unesdoc.unesco.org/images/0010/001055/105586e.pdf

Wright, R. 2009. 'The Art of Being Crente: The Baniwa Protestant Ethic and the Spirit of Sustainable Development.' *Identities—Global Studies in Culture and Power* 16 (2): 202–226.

Ziai, A. 2007. *Exploring Post-Development: Theory and Practice, Problems and Perspectives.* London: Routledge.

CHAPTER 19

People, Social Groups, Cultural Practices

From Venn Diagrams to Alternative Paradigms for Sustainable Development

Fadwa El Guindi

I leave sustainability workshops (government or industry-sponsored) held in Qatar[1] with a feeling of déjà vu, wondering about accomplishments since previous workshops, and sceptical about measurable implementation for the future. Usually these workshops consist of colourful, attractive PowerPoint presentations of flow charts and Venn diagrams,[2] in addition to printed reports and declarations, using broad abstract constructs, familiar from other international publications on sustainability. To me these abstract notions of economy, environment, development and even sustainability obscure and marginalize real lives and interacting social groups. Frozen abstract vocabulary and broad international categories fail to reveal the realities of life and the concerns of the people. Stated strategies seem irrelevant to real-life concerns.

There is also a problem with interpreting culture. Heritage constitutes the attempts of states to revive past traditions for identity-construction purposes, which may or may not be accurately representative. Art represents a manifestation of traditions which may be individual, not necessarily cultural, creations. The notion of culture is broader, deeper and wider than heritage and arts. But there is a tendency to reduce it to these two aspects, thus diminishing its wholeness by leaving out non-material depth and intangible complexity meaningful in people's lives, such as the way they view and cognitively interpret their natural, social and cultural worlds.

The Qatar National Development Strategy 2011–2016 (GSDP 2011), builds its proposals on the basis of internationally recognized pillars of development, namely economic development, human development, social development and environmental development (see Tan, Al-Khalaqi and Al-Khulaifi, chapter 2; and Darwish, chapter 4, both this volume). Missing are critical cornerstones of life, considered in this analysis necessary for any success in sustainability, namely social groups and their cultural practices. Real units in human culture and society give meaning and substance to spheres such as environment and economics, but subsumed, as seems to be the case, within the above-mentioned pillars of development, then they are secondary and become marginal in discourse and to policy. Therefore, an alternative paradigm to the Four Pillars is proposed here focusing first on people, social groups and cultural practices, thus shifting emphasis and orientation from abstractions distant from people's lives and concerns to the local level of human life. This paradigm is not simply about a new vocabulary; it re-conceptualizes the notion of sustainability by examining the uniqueness of local life, thus adding cross-cultural applicability, and thus more relevance to Gulf issues.

Informed by anthropological knowledge and building on cross-cultural ethnography, comparative studies and empirical research carried out in Qatar, this paradigm looking at aspects of society and culture is used to critique the Qatar National Development Strategy 2011–2016 (hereafter NDS).

What is Sustainability?

'If people decide that they want to make their salads out of our plants, then we're not going to have any chipmunks.'—*María Hernández, director of US horticulture for the Central Park Conservancy*

I think what María Hernández is referring to concerns the recent trend among American activists eager to eat 'natural' and seek new foods not part of the ordinary 'Anglo' American diet. As they get closer to nature they encroach on nature. As a metaphor, however, Hernández is referring to how one act interactively affects another. Well-intentioned people seeking sustainability may diminish the sustainability of other people, species or natural domains. So, what does sustainability mean?

As 'word du jour', it is employed to cover things ranging from coffee cans to conference titles. Market, industry, government and commercial publishers appropriate the label to promote and justify their products. Thus an already amorphous concept gets bent into many different shapes. It has turned into much hyperbole and little substance, not only overused, but oversimplified. The idea of sustainability practices and goals clashing, as implied in the above quote, is not taken in consideration by policy makers, nor is the idea of local participation.

Vladimir Dimitrov (2003) writes that as a concept sustainable development 'dates back to the early 1970s, and the Club of Rome report "Limits
of Growth" was probably the cornerstone piece of literature that got the
whole freight train rolling'. He then points out that 'in 1987 the authors
of the United Nation's Brundtland report "Our Common Feature" (prepared to examine how human activity impacted the world's natural resources) gave a definition of sustainable development as "meeting the
needs of the present generation without compromising the ability of future generation to meet their own needs"'. Dimitrov reiterates what is
becoming a widespread feeling among academics that sustainability is
becoming a slogan employed variably by 'universities, local communities, nonprofit organizations, states, even some industrial companies',
who call for 'social equity, environmental responsibility and economic
viability' in order to achieve sustainability. 'Sustainable programs', he
writes on his website, 'should be democratic, equitable, environmentally
benign and holistic – while allowing for a healthy economy.' He further
points out how many advocates of true sustainability insist on a systemic
shift in how society addresses issues ranging from resource allocation
to urban planning, adding that 'radical fighters for sustainability appeal
for immediate changes in thinking, in societal values and beliefs, even in
human nature'.

What does *sustainable* development entail that development alone does
not? In conceptualizing development, Susan Baker states upfront that for
it to be sustainable debates must centre on 'our relationship with the natural world, about what constitutes social progress and about the character
of development, both in the North and in the South, in the present and
into the future' (2006: 1). A distinction is made between the dominant,
conventional model of development (Modernization Theory) and the Sustainable Development model which challenges it.

Modernization Theory holds that the more structurally specialized and
differentiated a society is the more modern and progressive it is. It is
more technically sophisticated and urbanized with increased use of markets for the distribution of economic goods and services. Modernization
also brings social changes, including the development of representative
democracy, increased mobility and the weakening of traditional elites,
kinship groups and communities. It promotes individual growth and self-
advancement. Progress is central to understanding the conventional Western modernization model – increased domination over nature and the use
of its resources solely for the benefits of humankind. Dominating nature,
turning it into a resource base, has become a key indicator of human progress. Welfare is measured by consumption and 'standard of living' – it
prioritizes individual interest at the expense of the common good. The

market model of food production in the United States (and elsewhere) epitomizes this orientation.

Market Model of Food Production

In a gripping account summed up in the subtitle of his book, 'A Natural History of Four Meals', Michael Pollan (2006: 68) describes the industrial approach through the story of 'the short, unhappy life of a corn-fed feedlot steer'. Cattle, Pollan tells us, are 'made to eat forage and we're *making them* eat grain' (2006: 77, italics added). Herbivores are fed corn, instead of grass, and, to the shock of many, they were also fed animal by-products until scientists figured out that the practice was spreading bovine spongiform encephalopathy (BSE), more commonly known as mad cow disease. Rendered bovine meat and bonemeal represented the cheapest, most convenient way of satisfying a cow's protein requirement (never mind that these animals are herbivorous by evolution) and so appeared on the daily menus of most feedlots until the Food and Drug Administration (FDA) banned the practice in 1997 (75).[3] Corn is a compact source of caloric energy used to rapidly fatten livestock for slaughter. Eating such meat, however, has been shown to be less healthy, if not unhealthy, for consumers of beef, since it contains more saturated fat and less omega-3 fatty acids than the meat of grass-fed animals.[4] Feeding corn and animal by-products to cattle in the United States goes against nature, sanitation and humaneness, but is compatible with a particularly dominant view that puts market and profit (industry) over people and nature.

Market forces are driving the feeding of corn, instead of grass, to cows, but this is possible because it finds support in a particular prevalent view of nature and animals having mostly 'instrumental value', ignoring any 'intrinsic value' of the natural world. This orientation, as Baker points out (2006), obviously neglects the needs of other non-human species, and as the above description of cow-feeding illustrates, it even subordinates human welfare to profit. The drive for profit simply ignores nature and the balance between life and ecology. But it goes against culture as well, since such practices violate feelings of harmony with nature and undermine quality of life. They cannot therefore be considered good for development, nor, I argue, sustainable.

Such practices accord with the fact that the slaughtering of animals is carefully hidden from ordinary people. In much of the world, animals butchered for food are displayed in full view, whereas in the Anglo United States they are sold sanitized, attractively wrapped, neither seen nor smelled. Most white urban children in the United States are sheltered from such images and grow up unaware of a connection between live animals they see and meat they eat. In their minds the two are separate.

The case of MACOS, the Netsilik film series that was considered a violation of such separateness, illustrates the point, being played out in a political-academic drama that involved anthropologists Asen Balikci[5] and Margaret Mead. The reaction to these films is worth repeating (see El Guindi 2004: 129–138). At first, these films were well received in US schools. But by 1973, 'criticism of MACOS grew loud and began to be heard … voiced by politicians and church folk alike' (ibid.: 135). Congressman John Conlan charged that the Netsilik films undermined morality, patriotism, American values, Judeo-Christian ethics and beliefs and family. The concern was that sheltered American children, otherwise insulated from death in general (human and animal), and the killing of animals to eat in particular, would be traumatized by the 'killing of caribou' for food, particularly given attitudes internalized from romanticized Walt Disney imagery of Bambi, in combination with exoticizing caricatures of indigenous people as 'noble savages' and children of nature. In 1976, Congress became involved in the issue with Margaret Mead defending the anthropological portrayal in a hearing by the Congressional Science and Technology Commission. At that time, according to politicians, school was considered the avenue not to educate American children about different worldviews and realistic relations with animals and nature, but rather to insulate them from other ways of life and from the American market approach to nature, cultivating instead a romanticized view that any killing of animals is brutal. This representation of noble savages 'eating' cute Bambi was not acceptable.

This idealized sheltering of American children from reality contrasts with the existing market reality which brutalizes animals and subordinates nature to profit. As Baker points out, taming wilderness into natural parks, harnessing wild rivers to produce energy and clearing forests for agricultural production is a hallmark of modernization (2006: 1–3). Globalization carries this model forward to the world, across cultural traditions. Nations of the South (through their cooperating governments) are turned into consumers of products and technologies from the North, but more importantly they are expected to adopt the models of change and, subliminally perhaps, views about nature and life. This is part of a progress-centric model of development which stresses the individual and material 'standard of living'. In contrast, Baker sees modern environmentalism as focusing on the wider public and on 'quality of life'. It has emerged as a critique of the modernization and progress model.

This, however, does not go far enough. My proposed paradigm focuses directly on concrete aspects of society and culture: the people, their social groups and cultural practices, to advance understanding of people's relation with nature and their lives. On balance, philosophically at least, the individualistic market perspective is countered in the NDS, although this is obscured by its overall globalized conceptualization of sustainability, essentially Western framed but presumed applicable universally. It expresses concern particularly through the Supreme Council for Family Affairs[6] for traditional social relations and religious values in the face of rapid change. Words like *holism, cohesion* and *integration* are used in different parts of the 'Action Plan' section. In particular, the part devoted to Social Development states that its 'cohesive approach … will cut across all elements of society while enabling related economic, environmental and human development goals'. It goes on to say that policy 'requires coordinated and comprehensive integration of five interrelated social sectors' (GSDP 2011: 163). However, it ends with a paragraph that diminishes the significance of the integrated approach: 'Taken together the objectives form a blueprint to realizing the *QNV 2030*. … Taken individually, these goals offer separate but related frameworks' (ibid.: 164). Using the principle of interrelatedness means that elements taken separately are not meaningful in any theory of society.

Wholeness of culture and holism of approach are part of a particular framework of sustainability necessary, I argue, for sustainability to work. In addition, people, social groups and cultural practices must be centralized in both discourse and action as primary (not secondary or subsumed) foci of concern with direct relevance to development concerns. The new paradigm proposed here includes people's own cultural models of nature – as suggested by Egypt's cats, Turkey's birds and Qatar's falcons and camels discussed next, as examples of Muslim models built on harmony with nature.

Living With Cats, Birds and Falcons

Curiously, walking around Cairo's main streets, into alleys, looking below butchers' chopping stands, on top of restaurant dining tables, on bridges, on freeways or laying leisurely on top of the copying machine in the public library,[7] one will encounter friendly cats. People do not seem bothered by them. Something similar occurs in Turkey regarding birds. Thinking sustainably, on a recent visit to Istanbul I was at first impressed by the proliferation of solar panels on the roofs of private homes and public works. Though less visibly sustainable, I began to notice traditional architecture (see Alraouf and Clarke, chapter 13, this volume) that by design integrates beautiful small structures specifically for use as homes (not cages) for birds.[8] Birds in Turkey are often helped to find food or shelter in the city, and perhaps out of a general altruistic feeling towards animals grew the extraordinary architectural form of stone birdhouses, dovecotes and 'bird castles' of elaborateness and beauty in Istanbul and other old cities.

For millennia, cats have permissively shared Egypt with Egyptians and for longer than 2,500 years birds have shared Istanbul with Turks. Egyptians invoke ancient Egyptian cosmology[9] and Turks find direct support in religious sources. The Qur'an, Sura 67 (Dominion), Ayah 19, states: 'Do they not observe the birds above them, soaring and beating their wings? None can uphold them except God most gracious: Truly it is He who watches over all things.'

According to Saffet Dagdeviren (1989):

'The birds above' are everywhere in Istanbul. Swallows hawk across the parks along the Golden Horn at sunset, and jackdaws tumble in the updrafts against the Byzantine city walls. Every fall there is the spectacular, towering gyre of thousands of white storks that forms over the Bosporus as the birds slowly spiral upward to begin their migration to the south. And there are the pigeons strutting and cooing in front of the Yeni Cami – the New Mosque – waiting for handouts of grain from pious passers-by. Feeding birds, or freeing caged ones, is a meritorious act, the Turks believe. According to the Qur'an, the righteous 'feed, for the love of God, the indigent, the orphan and the captive', and some interpret that verse as calling for charity to animals as well as to humans'.

Birdhouses are beautiful aspects of any building. They are encountered everywhere – on mosques, madrasas, libraries, houses, inns, baths, tombs, bridges, churches, synagogues and even palaces. Some are built specially into the facade of the building in the form of either a single aperture or several side by side. According to the Turkish Cultural Foundation: 'Bird houses are man's humble offering to his winged, feathered friends, and one of the oldest and most important expressions of the love of and compassion for animals.' These provide refuge and protection to birds that range freely through the skies, guarding them from storms, rain, mud, cats and the burning sun.[10] The birdhouses are built on walls that sheltered them from the worst of the sun and from winter winds. High up under cornices or eaves, well out of reach of meddling hands – or claws – they are often built in the architectural style of the building, or the period, they are part of. The quality of the workmanship varies from one birdhouse to another. Irrespective of architectural style established standards set officially must be followed ensuring that birds feel safe (even from cats) and that their homes are constructed on the sunny side of buildings, in a place that is not exposed to strong winds.

Some structures do not extend beyond the façade, as on the Suley-maniye mosque, the New mosque (Yeni Cami) and Buyukcekmece Bridge in Istanbul. Dagdevirn describes (ibid.: 30–33) the tiered birdhouses on the walls of the Selimiye mosque 'with their pronounced eaves, corbelled bay windows and what appear to be the remains of grand staircases, [which] deserve to be called "bird castles"'.[11] On the Yeni Valide mosque or on the Turkology Institute building, Dagdevirn observes how birdhouses indis-putably resemble 'miniature mosques, complete with arabesque carving, minarets and domes'.

While the relation with birds may have early roots, it is conjectured that constructing public birdhouses probably came into vogue in the sixteenth century with the flowering of classical Ottoman architecture. The practice continued into the latter part of the nineteenth century, styles shifting with changes in architectural forms. Bricks, tiles, stone and mortar are the building materials of birdhouses.[12] Beyond being shelters, these are highly ornamental, elegant structures reminiscent of miniature palaces or pavil-ions. Indeed, some of them have feeding and water troughs for finches and sparrows, runways for landing and take-off and even balconies where the birds can venture out and survey their surroundings. Among the loveliest examples of these houses, which are the product of delicate workmanship, are the Yeni Valide, the Ayazma and Selimiye mosques at Uskudar and the building in the inner courtyard of the Darphane at Topkapi Palace[13].

Evidently, birdhouses represent a particular relationship, a symbol of the value and importance Turks place on animals, especially birds. Dur-ing the Ottoman period, certain foundations were established to care and protect animals. Some of these specialized in feeding birds on cold winter days, caring for and treating sick storks and providing food and water to animals in general.

In the Gulf region, Arabians[14] (and particularly Bedouins) are known to have a close relationship with their camels, horses and falcons (see Khalaf 1999; Lancaster 1997; Young 1994, 1996 and 2007), which continues despite urbanization and sedentarization (Abou-Zeid 1959, 1979). Spe-cial relations extend to livestock. According to Donald Cole (2003: 238), Bedouins were strongly linked to the livestock they raised and took care of. There was complete interdependence between Bedouin and livestock. The Bedouin depended on their animals for much of their livelihood and sustenance. This interspecies 'codependency' or symbiosis was a central feature of the old Bedouin economy (Swidler 1973), wherein the livestock constituted a person's and a family-household's capital. These animals were owned individually as private property often by the senior male head of the household as part of an inheritance and/or by purchase. Some were owned by women in the household who acquired them in lieu of a right to inheritance or through purchase. That livestock are owned or used for livelihood does not accurately portray the picture. Considering them 'capital' or describing the relation as 'codependence' overstresses the economic aspect and does not do the relation justice. Animals are not merely considered human food, beasts of burden or capital for individual profit, but they are partners in the human quest for food and companions in raid and trade, and even good to think with and inspire poetry. Without descending into romanticism, the actual relation speaks to a special quality of life. The economic interdependence is more of a partnership, a mutuality as it were, in life, not simply for life.

Before Qatar became a state, many Arabian Qataris were leading mobile, nomadic lives, pursuing livelihoods in close partnership with camels, sheep and goats. Today, settled Qataris may remain close to their animals, having access to areas of land away from and in addition to the residential lot assigned to them, on which they keep animals. 'Land is given by State subsidy but is regulated by stipulations regarding building and regarding the number of animals to be sheltered in it. Expenses of building, buying animals, feed, water, tools are all on the owner of the *'izba* (Arabic for private estate that invokes qualities of farm and ranch). The government concern is to regulate use concerning land and animals. Ten years ago the matter was random. Anybody takes a land and raises animals. The government now is regulating place and manner of land use' (Al-Kuwari 2011b; see Sillitoe and Alshawi, chapter 10, this volume).

Recently[15] a Qatari man, recipient of state granted *'izba* (farm/ranch) where he cares for sheep, goats and chickens, went to visit his sister to inform her how saddened he was because of the death of his *'anza* (goat). He spent more than half an hour fondly talking about the goat that had just died – he talked of her looks, her colour. He then sadly told his sister: 'You know Sarah, this goat is the daughter of Rabbush.'[16] Rabbush was the name of the goat's mother, another goat he mourned when it died. (Al-Kuwari 2011a). Few Qataris today raise animals for subsistence. This man voluntarily keeps animals with no desire to turn them into economic capital. He uses goat milk and chicken eggs for family consumption and kinship gift-giving exchanges. Slaughtering livestock is done by the family only for Islamic 'sacrifice' at the 'Eid festival; the meat is apportioned between family and the needy according to Islamic prescription, and these sacrificial sheep are especially purchased for the purpose (Al-Kuwari 2011b). The relationship with animals, previously partners in life and livelihood, continues to be humanized. In order for the Qatari goat owner to express the depth of his emotions at the death of his goat, he reminded his sister of the goat's position in the genealogy, naming her mother. To this

Qatari man, as to other Qataris, livestock are treated as having kin, whose genealogies are remembered, and are mourned in death.[17] They become extensions of the human kin unit. While animals as economic capital are maintained by hired foreign labour in Qatar, kin animals are directly cared for by their owners.

Falcons also have a special place in Arabian life and ethos. They are housed with people inside their homes. Many houses in Qatar today have a room especially designed and equipped to keep falcons. The birds can be seen (without attracting much local attention) on the shoulders of their owners in public places, even in airports, in queues for official passenger travel procedures. Horses and camels, like falcons, are considered partners with humans in racing and hunting. Both activities are ceremonialized and have a strong presence in the lives of the Gulf people.

What is it that Egyptians and cats, Turks and birds and Arabians and falcons have to tell us about the quality of relations between people and animals? Firstly, there is more to the sphere of culture than arts and heritage. There are non-material aspects to culture not given attention in Qatar's strategy,[18] but which is found in a growing body of scholarship which approaches culture as a cognitive domain. Matthew Lauer and Shankar Aswani (2009: 317) discuss different approaches to knowledge that distinguish between cognitive aspects and other modalities of knowing. In what way do cognitive considerations contribute to sustainability? The element of 'quality of life' includes but goes beyond the material world to cosmologies woven to give coherence to our existence and cognitive models that embed the material in the immaterial, for people care not only for better material-living standards, but for a life of harmony and contentment. Importantly, such local models of harmony existed long before theories of environmentalism were advanced in academe, international organizations or by many governments. The role of culture-derived harmony with life and integration with nature and the importance of Qatar-specific societal issues are discussed next through a critique of some aspects of culture and society mentioned in Qatar's national strategy and action plan.

Critique of the Qatar National Development Strategy 2011–2016

Is Qatar, the internationally rising star of the Arabian Gulf,[19] marching on the right or wrong path in policy and practice towards a sustainable life? A rapidly developing country, it officially expresses concern with sustainability of development. It prides itself in centring sustainability in its action plan. According to an official publication (Planning Council 2006) an interest in environmental issues emerged as early as the 1960s, leading to the formation of the Permanent Committee for the Protection of the Environment in 1981, followed by several decrees and laws, including Law No. 11 of 2000 (see Alraouf and Clarke, chapter 13, this volume), which in turn led to the formation of the Supreme Council for the Environment and Natural Reserves, followed by other committees, programs and initiatives as well as conferences, including 'participation in international conferences, such as in Johannesburg, South Africa, in 2002' (Planning Council 2006: 11). Several international and local conferences have been organized in Qatar in the past few years, some sponsored by government, others by industry.[20]

The Qatar National Development Strategy (GSDP 2011) overlooks certain aspects of society and culture which are the focus of my analysis next. In its foreword, Tamim Bin Hamad Al-Thani, the new Emir of the State of Qatar and head of the Supreme Oversight Committee for Implementing the Qatar National Vision 2030, stated that the strategy is 'a product of consultations with all segments of Qatari society, including the private sector and civil society' taking into account 'cultural and religious values' and the needs of future generations in terms of social, economic and environmental aspects (ibid.: iii). A number of issues suggest themselves in this brief statement. I shall address and problematize three: cultural and religious values, family, kinship and marriage, and finally people's participation in sustainability projects.

Cultural and Religious Values

How are cultural and religious values identified? Are they shared, declared, imposed, assumed or empirically discovered? Cultural understanding of nature and the universe are close to the pulse of people and provide meaning and order in their lives. The rhythm of Islam structures life for Muslims who move into and out of sacred space and time, throughout the day, around the year, forever. Islam interweaves a particular orientation to daily life (El Guindi 2008). Similarly, *renqi*, a folk Chinese concept rooted in the Daoist idea of harmony with nature and physical surroundings, denotes a kind of energy, vitality and dynamism that derives from human presence and from practices consistent with the harmony. Urbanization and development in the town of Kumming threatened *renqi*, whereas traditional cityscapes in Kumming produced vigorous *renqi* human interaction.

In projects of development and for planning change in a sustainable way, this kind of local energy generated from the culture must be ensured. The 'rhythm' and energy characteristic of Muslim life is shown to be of increasing significance in the psychological and cognitive sciences. The concept of 'mindfulness' is relevant – a metacognitive skill, a mode, a heightened state of involvement and wakefulness, with essence for change while situated in the present. It is proposed (ibid.: 157–165) that this mindfulness works on the borderless community of Muslims everywhere. Muslims pray and fast anywhere according to the same rhythm.

Family, Kinship and Marriage

In Qatar, kinship is prevalent and pervasive as an organizing principle of social life. Often it blurs the boundary with civil society. Kinship considerations cannot be ignored in many crucial decisions. State and religious authority in Qatar, as in most of the Islamic world, consider family to be central to society. Much of its regulation is rooted in religion and is subject to *shar'ia* law. Official statements on strategy stress the importance of the family. In a section titled 'Reinforcing Family Cohesion' it is stated that 'most Qatari households remain relatively large … more than 80% of households comprise 5 or more people, and 20% comprise 10 or more. Two-person households are rare, and one-person … even rarer.' This is followed by a statement that supports such a trend: 'having large households is consistent with the national vision and that the government supports cohesive families and large households, since the family is considered the core of Qatari society having a moral and religious obligation to care for its members' (Planning Council 2011: 166–168). Clearly, family is considered central to sustainability.

In a short segment titled 'Reduce Consanguinity Risks', two points are mentioned towards the goal of decreasing 'consanguineous marriages among first cousins from 34% to 27%'. But observations suggesting risk to health in cousin marriages are based on inconclusive studies. Also, a report published in the Qatari media links stability of marriages with cousin marriage. To counter presumed health dangers, two points are made regarding cousin marriage: 'implement educational campaigns on consanguinity … [and] provide counseling to support mandatory premarital screening' (ibid.: 114). In other words the report reduces cousin marriage to inbreeding and places it alongside health matters such as smoking, drugs and tuberculosis, pre-biasing the issue when it is hardly determined by systematic research. It would be more appropriate, I think, if cousin marriage is centred in the context of family and society and is subject to a long-term systematic research.

Policy action should be based on analysis that takes into account the complexity revealed in the process of making development sustainable. The report does not cite scholarly studies as a source for its observations. Cousin marriage cannot be determined by studies relying primarily on survey techniques. My own ongoing study of kinship in Qatar (El Guindi 2010a, 2010b, 2011b, 2012b, 2012c, 2012d, 2013; El Guindi and al-Othman 2013) shows that questions about marrying cousins must use in-depth interviewing utilizing genealogical charting of kin relations since terminology alone and survey responses can be deceptive. There are societal mechanisms, such as suckling practices, which produce incest prohibitions that often prevent first cousin marriages. Understanding these requires systematic analysis of multiple overlapping relations.

People's Participation

Policy in Qatar is described as proceeding on the basis of 'consulting all segments of society'. This implies use of participatory processes in development planning. At least theoretically, participation is taken into consideration in strategy: 'effective consultation and participation of stakeholders or target groups in project design and implementation can raise awareness, create trust, foster ownership, improve project design and increase the chances of beneficial results' (Planning Council 2011: 269). But the gap between strategy reports and reality can be large. The same document points out that participation may not be sufficient and that government must rely on communication and advocacy in the course of implementation. Advocacy campaigns originating from the state constitute public relations projects intended to persuade people to accept, live with and adapt to top-down decisions of change. This is different from allowing free participation by people affected by development and making choices on the basis of their own needs to improve the quality of their lives. Ultimately, asking people to accept top-down change does not work except in the short term, gradually growing into discontent. At issue here is: Who determines the needs of future generations?

The notion of participatory development itself is being problematized in academic circles. At issue is knowledge and expertise. How can we determine what is knowledge and who are the experts, and how do we bring this to bear on sustainability? Ethnographic accounts describe encounters between local populations 'who know' and intruding outsiders 'who don't' but have the power to impose interventions. The mountain Zapotec farmer of Oaxaca represents, according to the study by Roberto Gónzales (2001), local expert knowledge which must be considered seriously in the discourse on sustainability for its relevance to development. Here local knowledge is considered ontologically equal to science.

But science-based government expertise can collide with local knowledge. According to González, the Zapotec 'have continuously cultivated maize, beans, squash, and other crops for more than 5,000 years'. He describes the sophisticated intervention by 'ancient Mesoamerican ancestors [who] domesticated maize from a wild grass', an accomplishment considered by Walton Galinat (1992: 47) as the 'most remarkable plant breeding' of all time (cited in González 2001: 1). Techniques for producing, processing, preserving and preparing the so-called American Trinity – maize, beans and squash – evolved and increased in sophistication to the point where agricultural surpluses supported the civilizations of the Olmec, Maya, Toltec, Aztec, Zapotec and Mixtec, and provided, along with animal proteins, the nutritional needs as societies developed into societies of higher complexity, such as those of Monte Albán, Mitla, Tenochtitlán, among others. Throughout this regional history, sophisticated knowledge about farming and food, subsistence and agriculture, has been passing down through the generations of farmers.

The farmers' mastery of such knowledge struck González, who found it to be far from the stereotypical impression of farmers in Mexico being 'underdeveloped'. Instead he found their production and productivity to be immensely successful. He writes: 'Shortly after arriving in Talea,[21] I witnessed government consultants, mainly agronomists, struggling vainly to understand the complexities of local farming methods. … The visitors *seemed to have a different way of talking about plants, soils, and the weather …* than campesino farmers did' (2001: 2, emphasis added). Regarding the regular visits by government experts to their communities, the Zapotec campesinos told the anthropologist: 'such *experts* have good intentions; they periodically visit but they are *handicapped* because they did not *understand local soils*' (emphasis added). These consultants, the campesinos go on to say, have '*mucha teoríia, poca práctica*' (much theory, little practice). The farmers considered the government experts to be limited by purely theoretical information which lacks local knowledge and direct experience in tilling the soil. Farmers meet with them only to pick up the government-provided fertilizer. The farmers' skill was noted early. For instance, Hernán Cortés (González 2001: 1) observed: 'The ability of these natives in cultivating the soil and making plantations would very shortly produce such abundance that great profit would accrue to the Imperial Crown' (15 October 1524). Ironic perhaps, but the colonial conquistadores of the Americas recognized, albeit with exploitation in mind, the effectiveness of local knowledge.

Interest in indigenous knowledge has grown rapidly in recent years (de la Cadena and Stam 2007; González 2001; Lauer and Aswani 2009; Sillitoe 1998). Researchers and practitioners across many disciplines recognize that local people's knowledge, perceptions and cosmologies can be relevant for planning social and economic change and in the management and monitoring of ecosystem processes and functions. Yet, research shows that not all local knowledge can be considered 'science'. How do scholars of sustainability determine the efficacy, adequacy and sufficiency of local knowledge? Is all local knowledge good simply because it is local? It is not clear who determines sufficiency or insufficiency of people's participation? How are 'consultations' done? Is local knowledge tapped? Are people's traditional skills considered integral to sustainable development?

Paul Sillitoe (1998) is among those who 'heralded this new enthusiasm for indigenous knowledge as a revolution in anthropological method because informants become collaborators in applied projects, rather than just subjects of anthropological inquiry'.[22] He has since modified his position (see Sillitoe, conclusion this volume). Christopher Shepherd writes how over the last few decades 'we have witnessed the meteoric rise of a category of local or indigenous knowledge that has entered the lexicon … for conservation and development' (2010: 629) leading to 'local knowledge packages' (Pottier, Bicker and Sillitoe 2003; Shepherd 2010). But the category and contents of local knowledge has come under scrutiny as it is not self-evidently 'just there' to be discovered, but rather emerges during human encounters. Shepherd uses a case study of conservation of agricultural biodiversity in the Peruvian Andes to explore the 'ways in which local knowledge is mobilized, negotiated, and contested in relation to established and shifting understandings of … "development"' (2010: 629–630). Despite the live debate concerning local knowledge and about participatory methods, the relations between local knowledge, academic research and government instituted plans and policy for development remain in the realm of ideal possibilities, and interaction is marked by unease. Government (including its industry) is often sceptical about local knowledge and scholarly academic research. Sillitoe expresses this point well: 'The scope for disagreement between local populations and development authorities over what comprises development results in agencies behaving as if they do not trust local people's knowledge or the soundness of decisions they reach. Consequently participation, where tried, has proved limited and constrained and has even been manipulated, as agency staff seek to ensure that they remain in control and that their view of development, and necessary action to promote it, remains dominant' (2010).

Local knowledge must be evaluated empirically. Some such knowledge is interesting but cannot be considered expert knowledge. Some folk models serve to justify people's attitudes rather than support sustainable practices. Nor is all development good. In Gambia, for instance, tourism is critical to the economy. But while some Gambians gain economically, it seems that watching the growing tourism in their country, children dream of careers as tourists. They are saying 'when I grow up, I want to be a tourist'. Consumer-based tourist industries influence dreams of Gambians for their future. Can participation in such 'development' improve the lives of ordinary people (El Guindi 2011a)?

In Qatar, a process of Qatarization is being deployed to build a native Qatari workforce. It rightly privileges Qatari nationals over foreigners in job and financial security and opportunity, and should infuse development with local knowledge. But unless this privileging is explicitly linked with building capacity, training in skills and measurable productivity and quality of work, it will not result in helping Qataris develop the necessary skills and work-ethic discipline needed to effectively run their country. Privileging to attain an easy and comfortable life, possible during a nation's temporary affluence, can undermine sustainable development later. De-privileging today may create better Qataris tomorrow, and build a better Qatar for the future.

Conclusion

The social and cultural realms of life are critical to the success of sustainability projects and must be considered in policy plans and discourse. People, social groups and cultural practices must complement broad abstract constructs such as the Four Pillars. Cultural models interweave nature and culture into the various worlds constructed by humans to impose order and harmony on the seemingly disorderly universe. (El Guindi 2012a). There is 'great increase in functional variability among individuals that results from environmental influences on development of the brain … [and] human beings [in turn] alter the environment that shapes their brains' (Wexler 2006). This interwoven knowledge is pertinent to issues of sustainability and respects tradition, local skills, uniqueness of human cultural traditions and the diversity of humanness. It can reveal aspects of integrity and harmony in life. We have seen how cats, birds, falcons and camels, along with cosmic elements of nature such as moon and sun, penetrate the world of humans bringing qualities of balance and harmony – integrity to architecture, rhythm to time and space, mutuality to social worlds.[23]

There is organic wholeness to people with their social and cultural worlds. In order to reveal such wholeness there is a need for serious systematic, empirical research to inform policy. The gap between strategy and action reports and reality can be large. Conclusions are only as good as the studies that produced them. But such research takes time. Government is usually 'impatient' regarding the time taken for rigorous and detailed academic studies. It considers scholarly projects as slow, ambiguous and distant from the real world, and prefers to hire its own 'experts'.[24]

Scientific studies should be the task of free (not commissioned) academic research. Academics consider government or industry action to be quick fixes and expedient solutions, misguided and short lived. They are concerned about how such expediency compromises science and dilutes rigorous systematic research. The proposal here is for sustainability to be informed by systematic ongoing research which focuses on: people, social groups and cultural practices contextualized in local models of the world and carried out as scientific academic studies, un-commissioned and free of constraints. It will lead to knowledge-based sustainability. This is where doing good research can benefit not only building knowledge in the Gulf, but future lives and effective sustainability.

Notes

1. My reaction to such meetings is not unique. The issue is that in such conferences one sees more clearly a disconnect between 'vision' and 'reality', plans and implementation, action and inaction. My own involvement with sustainability issues is related to my being in Qatar from 2006, originally by invitation from Qatar University. In fall 2006 I was entrusted by the administration head to search for an international candidate of distinction to occupy the Shell Qatar Chair in Sustainable Development. Subsequently, I was appointed head of the Department of Sociology. After an extensive search, Paul Sillitoe, editor of this volume, was appointed to the Shell Chair in the Sociology Program and I worked closely with him on building a university-wide initiative of teaching and research in sustainability. Towards this goal, we co-organized the second International Social Sciences Symposium on Sustainable Development. The conference was both international and crossdisciplinary. Participants ranged from sociology, biology, archeology, anthropology, geography, history, philosophy, health sciences and more. Discussion bridged academics, industry and government, Qatar University, Durham University and Doha's Education City. Subsequent to the conference, Paul Sillitoe began to compile essays for this volume on sustainable development. While I did not present a paper at the symposium, this chapter is my intellectual contribution to the project.
2. Often the same PowerPoints are presented by the same people in consecutive conferences. Others are similar in content.
3. Despite the ban, there is an exception for blood products and fat, as rules permit feedlots to feed non-ruminant animal protein to ruminants (bedding, faeces, discarded bits of feed etc.)
4. Pollan (2006: 75) mentions that '[a] growing body of research suggests that many of the health problems associated with beef are really problems with eating corn-fed beef'.
5. Asen Balikci and his team spent thirteen months in the arctic and shot 250,000 feet of 16-millimetre colour film (about 600 rolls) between the summer of 1963

and the spring of 1965. After editing there were nine films in total, divided into parts suited in length for classroom use.

6. These are distributed as booklets and pamphlets published by the Supreme Council for Family Affairs.

7. I once had to coax a library clerk to put a little pressure on the two cats occupying the warmth of the copier as I had to copy documents for a subsequent urgent meeting. The clerk was very reluctant to disturb them.

8. But Istanbul is not Turkey's only landlord catering to birds. From Thrace to Eastern Anatolia, birdhouses are to be found in every place touched by human hands. Kirklareli, Tekirdag, Edirne, Bolu, Bursa, Milas, Antalya, Amasya, Kayseri, Ankara, Nevsehir, Sivas, Erzurum, Sanliurfa, Dogubeyazit are just a few of the Turkish cities with birdhouses.

9. For a detailed analysis of Egyptian cosmology as an aspect of the cognitive model of space and time see El Guindi 2008: 55–69.

10. Bird houses are of such significance in Turkish ethos and architecture that is reflected in local poetry. These are a few lines from Mehmet Zaman Sacliolu's poem 'Bird Houses': 'The outer walls of houses should be bird houses / That take wing when children laugh. / Even if it's winter outside, / The summer sun should rise inside the walls / And happiness will also warm the birds.'

11. The article goes into some detail: 'At the Selimiye mosque the holes in the exterior walls where the scaffolding once was anchored were covered with perforated brick or stone to provide a shelter for the birds. At the Seyit Hasan Paşa madrasa, or religious school, on the other hand, the stone of the wall has been carefully plastered to make a smooth, distinct setting far a palatial, mosque-like dovecote.' It goes on to describe: 'A pair of birdhouses flanks the entrance of the Ayazma mosque in Üsküdar, in the Asian part of Istanbul. One resembles a little köşk, or garden pavilion, of the kind found in many a park and palace courtyard in the city; the other has similar dimensions but a more mosque-like shape, and both are delicately carved and adorned at each roofpeak with the crescent finials visible all over the city.'

12. Those that were made of wood have not survived.

13. Other important buildings with birdhouses in Istanbul include: the Feyzullah Efendi and Seyyid Hasan Pasha Madrasas, the tomb of Mustafa III, Cukurcesme Han and the Ahrida Synagogue in Balat.

14. The term *Arabians* refers to Arabic-speaking people living in Arabia and the Gulf. They may or not be nomadic. Bedouins are all of Arabian origin but today live in many parts of the Arab world.

15. This was note recorded in Arabic by my student research assistant, Shaikha al-Kuwari, during field observations in June 2011.

16. Interview held on 25 August 2011 via Skype. In Qatari, Arabic *rabbush* is derivative from *r-b-sh,* and denotes 'imbalance of behaviour and always in a rush'.

17. It is not that this sentiment is unique to Qataris, but that it is present among Qataris.

18. Note the name of the Qatari 'Ministry of Culture, Arts and Heritage'. It emphasizes the materiality of cultural expressions.

19. Qatar is one of the Arabian Gulf's wealthiest states due to its enormous oil and natural gas revenues. In 2010, the economy grew by 19.40 per cent, the fastest in the world. Due to shortage of skills and training and attitudes stemming from a cultural devaluation of physical work and manual labour, the process of development relies heavily on foreign labour. Population Census figures show Qataris becoming an increasingly smaller population minority in their country. Two issues are live in public debate: the diminishing ratio of Qataris in the population leading to foreign intrusions on the culture and undesirability of cultural interventions, and the perceived threat to Arabic as a national language. Neither is addressed in the National Strategy.

20. Beyond conferences and workshops, Qatar University, the national university, with the support of Qatar Shell, has an initiative focusing on the Department of Social Sciences to integrate the subject of sustainability in teaching and research, emphasizing social and cultural issues. One cannot praise such a move enough, since there is no sustainability without understanding and including the societal and cultural dimensions.

21. Talea del Castro is a Zapotec village in a region called the Rincón (corner) of the Northern Sierra of Oaxaca. For general and more information on the mountain Zapotec, see Nader 1969; and on the Valley Zapotec, see El Guindi 1986, 2006.

22. There is, of course, a long respectable tradition of methodological collaboration with local populations in anthropological inquiry. For a detailed summary, see El Guindi 2004.

23. It is interesting that recent Turkish protests in Istanbul were triggered over a tree and a park.

24. Some of these experts have never published in competitive internationally indexed venues in the subjects of focus. They produce additional government reports that cannot be reviewed for accuracy, transparency and scientific accountability.

References

Abou-Zeid, A. M. 1959. 'The Sedentarization of Nomads in the Western Desert of Egypt.' *UNESCO International Social Science Journal* 11: 550–558.

———. 1979. 'New Towns and Rural Development in Egypt.' *Africa* 49: 283–290.

Al-Kuwari, S. 2011a. Unpublished field observation notes, March–June. Doha, Qatar.

———. 2011b. Interview via Skype, 25 August, New York, Los Angeles.

Baker, S. 2006. *Sustainable Development*. London and New York: Routledge.

Cole, D. P. 2003. 'Where Have the Bedouin Gone?' *Anthropological Quarterly* 76 (2): 235–267.

Dagdeviren, S. 1989. 'Castles in the Air.' *Saudi Aramco World* 40: 30–33.

de la Cadena, M., and O. Starn (eds.). 2007. *Indigenous Experience Today*. Oxford: Berg.

Dimitrov, V. 2003. 'Paradox of Sustainability: A Complexity-Based View.' www .pluriversu.org.

El Guindi, F. 1986. *The Myth of Ritual: A Native's Ethnography of Zapotec Life-Crisis Rituals.* Tucson: The University of Arizona Press.

———. 2004. *Visual Anthropology: Essential Method and Theory.* Walnut Creek, CA: Altamira.

———. 2006. 'Shared Knowledge, Embodied Structure, Mediated Process: The Case of the Zapotec of Oaxaca.' Proceedings, 28th Annual Conference of Cognitive Science Society. http://www.cogsci.rpi.edu/CSJarchive/Proceedings/2006/docs/p2646.pdf.

———. 2008. *By Noon Prayer: The Rhythm of Islam.* Oxford: Berg.

———. 2010a. Final Report, UREP Project 06-012-5-003, The Undergraduate Research Experience Program. Doha, Qatar: Qatar National Research Fund, Qatar Foundation.

———. 2010b. 'The Cognitive Path Through Kinship.' *Journal of Behavior and Brain Sciences* 33 (5): 384–385.

———. 2011a. 'Review of Visual Interventions: Applied Visual Anthropology,' edited by Sarah Pink, 2007. *The Journal of the Royal Anthropological Institute (Man)* 17: 678–679.

———. 2011b. 'Kinship by Suckling: Extending Limits on Alliance.' *Anthropologicheskii Forum (Forum for Anthropology and Culture) Peter the Great Museum of Anthropology and Ethnography (Kunstkamera), Russian Academy of Sciences, Special Forum on Kinship* No 15 (7): 381–384.

———. 2012a. 'Moon, Sun, Desert, Sea: Knowledge of Space, Time and Natural Environment – The Case of Qatar.' In *Proceedings of Workshop Cultural Models of Nature and the Environment: Self, Space, and Causality,* 1–4 September 2011, ed. G. Bennardo, 22–28. DeKalb, IL: The Institute for Environment, Sustainability, and Energy, Northern Illinois University.

———. 2012b. 'Suckling as Kinship.' *Anthropology Newsletter (American Anthropological Association)* 53 (1).

———. 2012c. 'Milk and Blood: Kinship among Muslim Arabs in Qatar.' *Anthropos* 107 (2): 545–555.

———. 2012d. 'Suckling, Adoption and the Incest Taboo: Significance of Studying Kinship for Social Science and for Qatar.' *Annual Research Forum Proceedings (Bloomsbury Qatar Foundation Journals), 2012*42P.

———. 2013. 'Inceste, Adoption Et Allaitment: Logiques et Dynamiques De L'Évitement. Revue Incidence.' *Incidence Revue* 19: 121–137.

El Guindi, F., and W. al-Othman. 2013. 'Transformationality and Dynamicality of Kinship Structure.' *Structure and Dynamics: e-Journal of Anthropological and Related Sciences,* 6 (1).

Galinat, W. C. 1992. 'Maize: Gift from America's First Peoples.' In *Chilies to Chocolate: Food the Americas Gave the World,* eds. N. Foster and L. S. Cordell, 47–60. Tucson: University of Arizona Press.

General Secretariat for Development Planning (GSDP). 2011. Qatar National Development Strategy 2011–2016: Towards Qatar National Vision 2030. Doha, Qatar.

González, R. J. 2001. *Zapotec Science: Farming and Food in the Northern Sierra of Oaxaca*. Austin: University of Texas Press.

Khalaf, S. 1999. 'Camel Racing in the Gulf: Notes on the Evolution of a Traditional Cultural Sport.' *Anthropolos* 94 (1–3): 85–106.

Lancaster, W. 1997. *The Rwala Bedouin Today*. Prospect Heights, IL: Waveland Press, Inc.

Lauer, M., and A. Shankar. 2009. 'Indigenous Ecological Knowledge as Situated Practices: Understanding Fishers' Knowledge in the Western Solomon Islands.' *American Anthropologist* 111 (3): 317–329.

Nader, L. 1969. 'The Zapotec of Oaxaca.' In *Handbook of Middle American Indians*, ed. R. Wauchope, 329–359. Austin: University of Texas Press.

Planning Council. 2006. Sustainable Development in State of Qatar: Report on the Implementation of The Sustainable Development Initiative in the Arab Region. Doha: The Planning Council, State of Qatar.

Pollan, M. 2006. *The Omnivore's Dilemma: A Natural History of Four Meals*. New York: Penguin.

Pottier, J., A. Bicker and P. Sillitoe (eds.). 2003. *Negotiating Local Knowledge: Power and Identity in Development*. London: Pluto.

Shepherd, C. J. 2010. 'Mobilizing Local Knowledge and Asserting Culture: The Cultural Politics of in situ Conservation of Agricultural Biodiversity.' *Current Anthropology* 51 (5): 629–654.

Sillitoe, P. 1998. 'The Development of Indigenous Knowledge: A New Applied Anthropology.' *Current Anthropology* 39 (2): 223–252.

———. 2010. 'Trust in Development: Some Implications of Knowing Indigenous Knowledge.' *Journal of the Royal Anthropological Institute (Incorporating Man)*: 1612–1630.

Swidler, W. W. 1973. 'Adaptive Processes Regulating Nomad-Sedentary Interaction in the Middle East.' In *The Desert and the Sown: Nomads in the Wider Society*, vol. 21, ed. C. Nelson, 23–41. Berkeley: University of California, Institute of International Studies Research Series.

Wexler, B. E. 2006. *Brain and Culture: Neurobiology, Ideology, and Social Change*. London: MIT Press.

Young, W. C. 1994. 'The Body Tamed: Tying and Tattooing Among the Rashaayda Bedouin.' In *Many Mirrors: Body Image and Social Relations*, ed. N. L. Sault, 58–75. New Jersey: Rutgers University Press.

———. 1996. *The Rashaayda Bedouin: Arab Pastoralists of Eastern Sudan*. Fort Worth, TX: Harcourt Brace College Publishers.

———. 2007. 'Arab Hospitality as a Rite of Incorporation: The Case of the Rashaayda Bedouin of Eastern Sudan.' *Anthropos* 102: 47–69.

CHAPTER 20

Contradictory Forces in the Gulf Environment

Old and New Cultural Values and Knowledge

Kaltham Al-Ghanim

Environmental change and resource conservation have become national and international concerns with attention increasingly focused on habitat degradation and destruction threatening the planet's biodiversity (Grenyer 2006: 93–96). Furthermore, economic growth threatens exhaustion of some natural resources, adversely affecting the opportunities of future generations. This is especially so in newly industrializing countries where the value system undergoes a sharp change resulting in, among other things, different expectations about the use of resources; this may even occur where industrialization is longstanding, as happened in central and eastern European countries with the change from a socialist to a market economy (Lütteken 1998: 347–358).[1]

The oil and gas industry, the major source of the Gulf region's income, is the main source of environmental pollution and destruction. Rapid population increase also places many stresses on the natural environment and Gulf society faces problems and challenges in protecting it. Preliminary data from the State of Qatar's 2010 census reports a 128 per cent increase in population on the 2004 census (Qatar Census 2004). This increase is the result of the demand for labour with the surge in spending on large infrastructure projects, notably extensive plans for urban development (see Rahman, chapter 3, this volume). Among the challenges facing Qatar are the environmentally unfriendly behaviours of some of the population that reveal a low level of environmental awareness. These include careless solid waste disposal, use of destructive fishing nets, reckless off-road driving (for example, hunting or searching for truffles) and insensitive camping that damages wilderness areas.

While the behaviour of individuals impacts on the environment, institutional attitudes may be more damaging. Government policies and private sector initiatives result in large-scale construction and industrial projects, such as building on land reclaimed from the sea, with enormous environmental impacts. Unless and until companies and others are encouraged to reinstate land damaged by their activities and support conservation measures, there would appear to be no end in sight to Qatar's irreparable ecological damage.

An example is the Al-Rwad (figure 20.1) area, which has largely disappeared due to reclamation and construction work. The demand of the construction industry for gravel means there are eighteen quarries covering an area of about 36 kilometres^2; the gravel crushers receive 18,669,750 tonnes of stone annually, producing 11,949,370 tonnes of gravel and 6,720,380 tonnes of waste. They impact on people's health with air pollution, noise and injuries, as well as wildlife due to habitat loss, dust covering vegetation near to quarries and solid and liquid waste thrown into holes excavated for gravel (Hussein and al-Din Abdou 2011).

Thus far, this chapter has catalogued an apparent lack of awareness about environmental issues among the population. Yet, formerly tribes lived in the peninsular in relative harmony with the environment, within the constraints that the desert imposed on them. The culture of the Gulf was well adapted to the harsh country, coping with lack of water and limited grazing opportunities. Much associated knowledge is being gradually lost with rapid social change. Is there a role for traditional ways and in-

Figure 20.1. Al-Rwad, Qatari countryside.

digenous knowledge in the future development of Qatar, and if so, what form might they take to promote again consideration of the natural environment at all levels in Qatari society?

It is thought that the transition from a subsistence to a market-based economy has a negative impact on traditional environment knowledge because market integration entails the specialized extraction or production of certain goods, the substitution of local natural products and manufactures for imported ones and the creation of greater socio-economic heterogeneity, undermining communal knowledge and resources (Zent 2008: 5). The forces of global development have resulted in many countries changing their economies to the Western market model without thinking about the viability of their traditional knowledge and practices with respect to environmental protection (Viriri 2009: 129–147). In the GCC countries these changes have occurred faster than any place in the world.

Today, with the focus in the Gulf on rapid economic development and 'modernization', the import of foreign technology and knowledge threatens the near extinction of valuable local knowledge that may better cope with environmental challenges. Communities have abandoned these ways with industrialization and new technology. The economic change based on extractive industry and reliance on consumer goods has completely crushed the traditional way of life based on the pearl trade, fishing, animal herding and hunting, and associated activities. These changes have led to the disintegration of the traditional relationship between the local population and its environment (Al Ghanim 2002: 93–100). While traditional knowledge accepted the constraints of the local environment and availability of resources, new technologies seek to override these, damaging ecosystems and giving rise to pollution.

Unfortunately, the Gulf people, no longer able to depend on their inventions and technologies honed through generations of experience, have turned to imported goods, evidencing insatiable consumer demand. Dependence is now the norm. A consequence is a changed relationship with the environment. There is an urgent need to document indigenous knowledge before those who hold it pass away. While there have been some efforts to do so by the Khalej Heritage Center (1982–2005), these data have yet to be organized. The Oral Heritage project (1990 and 2009) collected some further local knowledge data.

Local Knowledge and Sustainability

The question is how to have economic growth and protect the natural environment, how to have development that ensures sustainable use of resources? We are increasingly recognizing that a sustainable approach is necessary to achieve both development and conservation. The role of local communities in this and the key part that culture plays in shaping responses to environmental concerns are often overlooked (Millar 2007). There are two approaches to the role of culture in the conservation of natural resources and sustainability (Pretty et al. 2009). Firstly, there are those who look to the rediscovery and revival of traditional environmental knowledge to assist in the conservation of natural resources (Crespi 1987). By going beyond a narrow view of the environmental context to include socio-cultural issues, this approach advances more sustainable solutions that are more appropriate to the local historical context. Secondly, there are those who look at those aspects of human behaviour that are harmful to the environment and the role of raising awareness to change such behaviours (Gellerman et al. 2009). Many communities, including those in the Gulf, lack such programmes to encourage environmentally sustainable behaviour or necessary regulation to enforce it (see Al Othman and Clarke, chapter 5, this volume).

The lack of attention to traditional knowledge and skills in this context is surprising, given that typically these are tried and tested over a long period. Consideration of local culture and knowledge should help realize sustainable development and provide support to governmental programs and individual local efforts to conserve, improve and renew natural resources. Traditional environment knowledge can teach us lessons about environmental sustainability (Crespi 1987: 464–465). This approach goes beyond a narrow consideration of environmental issues to include wider social and cultural contexts. Until recently, local knowledge has not had the same weight as scientific knowledge in the analysis of problems of environmental sustainability, despite its importance and usefulness in many places in protecting the environment (Berkes, Colding and Folke 2000: 1251–1262). Since the 1980s efforts have grown to have such knowledge recognized, its value increasingly realized in respect to global environmental and social change as well as manifold threats to the survival and integrity of indigenous peoples and their cultural heritage around the world (Sillitoe 1998; Zent 2008: 2). Some studies seek to connect local knowledge with the natural sciences to improve environmental management and sustain ecosystems (Berkes, Colding and Folke 2000). Studies show that scientifically based ecological management could benefit from local knowledge, particularly by collaborating with community-based systems of resource management (Olsson and Folke 2001: 85–104; Sillitoe 2007).

This chapter argues for support of local Gulf communities' knowledge in a bid to support and promote moves towards a more sustainable future for the region. Knowledge and skills about the local desert and surrounding sea, formed over many generations, and traditional ways of living in this harsh environment may provide invaluable insights into how the region in general, and Qatar in particular, can develop in harmony with nature rather than against it. It has the potential to help conserve natural resources, protect biodiversity and restore natural environments.

The value of local Gulf heritage in promoting stewardship of the environment is apparent in ways of hunting and fishing that were common before the discovery of oil, which were less harmful to the environment than modern methods. It is also evident in building practices, as discussed earlier in this volume by Ali Alraouf and Sarah Clarke (chapter 13). For instance, the *al badjer* (wind tower) reduced the temperature inside buildings with ventilation holes top and bottom allowing cooler air to circulate in a house during the hottest months of the year. Buildings also had small, low windows designed to cool the interior. And *al-jhala* (clay pots) containing water cooled interiors through evaporation; water that leaked from the pots collected in utensils underneath. Craftwork was also in harmony with nature, with *saf al-khos* (wicker work) of palm fronds, used to make household items such as baskets, fans, mats and floor coverings. And *sadu* (woven work) used goat wool and camel hair to produce such items as bags, mats, camel harnesses and cushions.

Studies in the Middle East region, as elsewhere, show that development that involves local populations is more successful, as people are able to understand and contribute to the resolution of problems of their communities (Gahnem 2009).[2] An example is the Al-Ameid Reserve Project in Matruh, which aims to supply desalinated seawater in Egypt, Tunisia, Syria and Jordan.[3] According to Dr. Bushra Salem (project advisor): 'The beauty of this [initiative] is the participation of nomads in the project.… [We've] been able to win their confidence by [using them to] supply the project with local information and maps about the region.… [They] have helped and worked on the success of the project, which in the [final analysis] is for their benefit' (ibid. 2009). This example is a typical of development in the Arab region where government organizations play the main role (see Tan, Al-Khalaqi and Al-Khulaifi, chapter 2; Rahman, chapter 3; and Darwish, chapter 4, all this volume) and the participation of the local population and the integration of local knowledge in projects are unusual.

This chapter argues that including local knowledge in the development process will result in more appropriate management of resources with commensurate improvements in productivity, for example, in date palm cultivation and camel breeding. It catalogues some of these local techniques to raise awareness of, and create an interest in Qatari people's knowledge and experience of their desert environment and natural re-

486 | *Kaltham Al-Ghanim*

sources.[4] Until recently, this knowledge was inherited from father to son and mother to daughter. The chapter also aims to encourage policy makers to consider local ways and develop appropriate conservation strategies and education programmes to enable the population to protect and renew both its cultural and natural resources.

Local culture can inform conservationist attitudes in intriguing ways. For instance, people were reluctant to eat certain birds such as *um salem* (*Alaemon alaudipes*), *wargah* (*Lullula arborea*) or *khataf* (*Riparia paludicola*) even in periods of food scarcity. These prohibitions related to beliefs about *jin* (spirits), with stories warning people that individuals who captured or killed these species might disappear, go insane or, bird-like, climb mountains. People recited proverbs, poems, songs and tales about such things, inherited from parents and grandparents. This process enhanced knowledge, sentiments and values in children and encouraged and enforced Arabic and Islamic moral values and behaviour, for instance regarding custodianship of the land.

Environmental Protection in Qatar

There are habitats and species under threat that we have yet to research (GSDP 2009: 82). Some rare plants wait to be catalogued. We do not know why species grow in particular areas, what part they may play in the ecosystem and what benefits they may have to humans. This is due in part to the absence of a government or non-government organization with responsibility for documenting Qatar's biodiversity. Furthermore, we know little about the environmental impact of reduced vegetation cover that results from urbanization or what interventions are necessary to protect the land.

Until 1995 there was only one nature reserve in Qatar for the protection of marine and wildlife. That number is now eight, located in places where there are species of scientific interest and/or migratory birds. Generally, local knowledge and information does not feature in associated conservation programmes. The management of nature reserves depends primarily on Western scientific knowledge. Data are available regarding the number of wild animals in four of these reserves, which the Ministry of the Environment monitors (table 20.1). There are no data outside these areas. While initiatives are underway to preserve the environment, they are inhibited by lack of planning and management. For example, the Al-Reem Reserve, which covers 10 per cent of the country, is the largest protected area in Qatar, contains several villages and ranches and is affected by overgrazing and drought (see Sillitoe with Alshawi, chapter 10, this volume). Overgrazing due to increased herd size (camels, goats and sheep) has reduced vegetation across the region, particularly with camels that roam further. Other uncontrolled activities, such as in the night time *al-tnwar* (hunting rabbits) in four-wheel vehicles, further compromises Al-Reem's nature reserve status. Night hunting is particularly damaging; men using their car lights to disturb the animals will give chase when they run off, crushing vegetation in their path (men traditionally hunt with *al sager* [falcons] and *saluki* [dogs]).

Marine Environment

The majority of Qatar's listed endangered species are marine species, whereas globally terrestrial species are more endangered. From the limited information available, it is believed that twenty-seven marine species or 1.4 per cent of the acknowledged species present in Qatar's waters (table 20.2) are threatened with extinction. Endangered species include sea turtles and several species of shark but little is known of their population dynamics to facilitate local conservation (GDSP 2009: 82).

The marine environment of Qatar is distinctive for its diversity, with numerous species of fish and coral reefs (see James Howard, chapter 11, this volume). It includes the best-known pearl fisheries in the Gulf on the eastern coast. It is threatened by oil and gas fields and overfishing, combined with the degradation of coastal areas due to urban development, particularly real estate projects, such as West Bay, Pearl City and Lusail City, on or near the coast. The government's latest reports indicate the impact of overfishing in the last two decades, with total landings

Table 20.1. Number of species recorded in the State of Qatar in 2003. *Source:* Qatar Human Development First Report 2006: 57.

Organisms recorded	Total no.	Common	Rare	Threatened	Extinct
Wild plants	378	43	307	7	—
Fungi	153	56	108	—	—
Wild animals Non-chordates Chordates	230 280	51 85	179 194	—	—
Marine plants					
Marine animals Non-chordates Chordates	1,236 50	1,194 37	77 —	— 3	— —
Total	3,006	1,484	865	10	1

quadrupling since 1995 from 4,271 tonnes to 17,690 tonnes in 2008; the increase has been for all species (GSDP 2009: 76). Pearling was previously the main source of income for coastal dwellers, who traded pearls widely (Al-Ghanim 2002: 41–43). The diving community used methods that protected the marine environment; for example, collecting pearl molluscs by hand in baskets (figure 20.2). But the oil and gas industry has destroyed the *lulu heart* (pearl reservoirs).

The use of harmful and destructive fishing methods has increased pressure on the marine environment leading to the extinction or near extinction of some species. The *bakart bahr* (dugong) is one of the rarest marine creatures in the Gulf; it is now under threat and rarely sighted. Organisms such as molluscs and marine snails and some fish species have disappeared from some of the coastline. Species that lay their eggs on parts of the coast, such as turtles and some species of birds, are also under threat from loss of habitat. In 2003, the University of Qatar's Center for Environmental Studies monitored the marine turtles and their activities along the coast. The survey revealed that turtles are threatened with extinction due to changing ocean currents, the presence of garbage and changes in fishing methods. Marine debris such as plastic bags and bottles, fishing tackle, rope and other things constitute a danger to turtles feeding at sea (Al-Khayat and al-Ansi 2008). The hawksbill turtle is particularly under threat since most of its beach nesting areas are littered with waste washed ashore by the tide and wind. The centre calls for the protection of nesting sites at Ras Rekn and Foyrett (in the north of Qatar peninsula) and other areas necessary to protect other species, such as shrimp and hamur fish.

Some coastal areas have been declared protected regions, where fishing and development are prohibited. Various initiatives are currently underway in coastal areas, including planting of *qarm* trees. However, many marine areas have been affected by thoughtless development that has destroyed habitats. There

Figure 20.2. Pearl divers.

is no programme in place to reinstate these natural areas. Official efforts to enact further legislation have stalled (see Al Othman and Clarke, chapter 5, this volume).

Some traditional knowledge practices have the potential to assist marine conservation. There is the use of *al kerkor* (fish traps) made from organic materials that are biodegradable unlike today's metal fish traps anchored to the sea bed that harm many marine organisms which enter them and cannot exit, leading to their death. And *al msakr* (rock barriers) are built on the beach to trap fish entering on the tide. When the water rises above the barrier the fish swim freely in. This technique catches small numbers of fish, while not eliminating all that enter, as nets do. The local population used knowledge about the tides (weak in the winter and strong in the summer) to build *al msakr* at appropriate locations. Also, there are *hadra* (static nets) that fish enter and exit with the ebb and flow of the tide, which again do not kill all fish. Fishermen can collect large fish and release small ones. Formerly, *hadra* were made of fibre string which would decay and pollute the sea, but nowadays the new nets are made from nylon which does not decay, and does have that problem.

Terrestrial Environment

The desert of Qatar is home to some remarkable plant and animal species, some now extinct due to human activity. For example, *shomatri* (an aromatic plant) is no longer found anywhere on the peninsula. Similarly, *naïfl* (*Medicago orbicularis*), *ja'd* (*Teucrium polium*) and *taftaf* (*Chamomilla*) are endangered medicinal plants. Truffles (figure 20.3) that grow in the winter season after the rains in October and November, in association with the local plant called *regrog*, are also rare today (figure 20.4). The best places for truffles are now industrial zones, such as the Ras-Laffan liquid gas plant. Other locations are used for sewage

Figure 20.3. *Zubidey* truffle.

Figure 20.4. *Regrog.*

disposal or are irrigated farms. *Bent almatar* (daughter of rain) is a finger-nail-sized insect that has disappeared; it was seen, as the name suggests, after rainfall (figure 20.5). Locals looked for it after rain, believing that if they rubbed it on a young girl's forehead it increased her beauty.

Figure 20.5. *Bent almatar* insect.

The pastoral communities of Arabia have a wealth of knowledge about livestock management and well-being, including the availability of the best forage plants and those useful for animal health. They know how to manage vegetation to ensure adequate fodder, protecting new growth (unlike today, where people drive vehicles indiscriminately across the landscape, crushing vegetation). Among traditional knowledge practices that have the potential to help further conservation is the revival of *al hima* pasture areas, these comprised grazing reserved in the spring season to allow the propagation of seeds, distributed by dry season northwesterly winds (see Sillitoe with Alshawi, chapter 10, this volume). This ensured sufficient pasture for herds, with animals banned from grazing and trampling on the newly growing plants. Gulf communities have a diverse knowledge of the wind (seasonal direction, speed and duration), movement of stars, timing of rainfall and bird migration, all of which inform daily decisions about grazing and hunting; they historically determined the season for pearl diving too, as they do fishing today.

Table 20.2. Threatened and endangered fauna of Qatar (2006). *Source:* http://www.redlist.org. *Global Category: 2004 IUCN Red List of Threatened Species.*

Common name	Taxon Name	Breeder/ Visitor	Regional Category	Global Category
Desert hedgehog	*Hemiechinus aethiopicus*	B	EN	LC
Long-beaked common dolphin	*Elphinus capensis*	B	DD	LC
Indo-Pacific hump-back dolphin	*Sousa chinensis*	B	DD	DD
Finless porpoise	*Neophocaena phocaenoides*	B	DD	DD
Sand fox	*Vulpes rueppelli*	B	EN	DD
Sand cat	*Felis margarita*	B	EN	NT
Wildcat	*Felis silvestris*	B	EN	LC
Dugong/Sea cow	*Dugong dugon*	V/B	EN	VU-A1cd
Sand Gazelle/ Reem	*Gazella subgutturosa*	FB	RE/CB	NT
Arabian oryx	*Oryx leucoryx*	FB	RE/CB/RI	EN-D
Persian shearwater	*Puffinus persicus*	V	DD	NT

(continued on next page)

Table 20.2. continued

Socotra cormorant	*Phalacrocorax nigrogularis*	V/B	EN	VU- A1ce, B1+2acde
Ferruginous duck	*Aythya nyroca*	V	DD	NT
Marbled teal	*Marmaronetta angustirostris*	V	DD	VU-A2cd +3cd
Osprey	*Fandion haliaetus*	B	EN	LC
Greater spotted eagle	*Aquila clanga*	V	DD	VU-C1
Pallid harrier	*Circus macrourus*	V	DD	NT
Black kite	*Milvus migrans*	V	EN	LC
European honey buzzard	*Pernis apivorus*	V	EN	LC
Saker falcon	*Falco cherrug*	V	DD	EN-A2bcd +3bcd
Lesser kestrel	*Falco naumanni*	V	DD	VU-A2bce +3bce
Corncrake	*Crex crex*	V	DD	NT
Asian houbara	*Chlamydotis maqueenii*	FB/V	EN/CB	VU-A2bcd +3bcd
Black-winged pratincole	*Glareola nordmanni*	V	DD	DD
Sociable lapwing	*Vanellus gregarious*	V	DD	CR-A3bc
Slender-billed curlew	*Numenius tenuirostris*	V	DD	CR-C2a (ii); D
White-eyed gull	*Larus leucophthalmus*	V	DD	NT
European roller	*Coracias garrulus*	V	DD	NT
Semi-collared fly-catcher	*Ficedula semitorquata*	V	DD	NT
Cinerous bunting	*Emberiza cineracea*	V	DD	NT
Green turtle	*Chelonia mydas*	B/V	EN	EN-A1abd
Hawksbill turtle	*Eretmochelys imbricata*	B/V	EN	CR-A1abd +2bcd

CB: *Captive Breeding*, CD: *Conservation Dependent*, CR: *Critical*, DD: *Data Deficient*, EN: *Endangered*, EW: *Extinct in the Wild*, EX: *Extinct*, LC: *Least Concern*, NE: *Not Evaluated* NT: *Near Threatened*, RE: *Regionally Extinct*, RI: *Re-Introduced*, VU: *Vulnerable (Ministry of Environment, State of Qatar)*

Conclusion

Environmental degradation will continue in the Gulf unless there is urgent action to control certain activities. Action is needed at all levels of society, from the individual to institutional and international. Environmental laws and regulations should contribute to the country's ability to monitor and control activities and reduce the harmful effects of economic development. Undoubtedly, the development of new skills based on the local heritage can make a valuable contribution to environmental conservation. But, the rich local knowledge of, for example, nomadic grazing, fishing, hunting and nomadic stock-breeding is in danger of being lost to society. We need a mechanism to secure this cultural knowledge and heritage and where appropriate utilize it to help preserve the environment of the Gulf region.

We should beware however, of lionizing all aspects of traditional knowledge (see Sillitoe and Alshawi, chapter 10, this volume). Some long-held practices threaten certain organisms, such as eating turtle eggs and the belief that the *thab* (spiny-tailed agama) can treat certain diseases. There are no studies on the impact of local cultural practices: for example, the use of turtle eggs in folk medicine (while these activities adversely affect the turtles, they do not have the same impact as the destruction of the coastline through urban development on their annual migration along the coast). There is also a need for environmental awareness programmes to increase interest in environmental issues and promote moral responsibility for behaviour that is harmful to the environment. The use of nature reserves for environmental education, focusing on biodiversity, may help further the transfer of relevant local heritage and knowledge. It may also help change the negative behaviours of citizens and become more environmentally aware. It will require innovative training of those managing protected areas to create the necessary skills to deal with the local knowledge. In this way people may be encouraged to monitor their own activities that harm their environment within a legal framework designed to prevent abuses, rejecting products and services that increase environmental problems.

Acknowledgements

I am grateful to Jackie Sillitoe for invaluable help in preparing this chapter.

Notes

1. It should be noted that it is not only developing countries that harm the environment, major industrialized nations do so too.
2. The philosophy of inclusion is demonstrated by, for example, the Nunavut Research Institute's research protocol, which states that traditional ecological knowledge should feature in any research in the Nunavut region (Wenzel 1999: 74–79).
3. This initiative is managed by the International Centre for Agricultural Research in the Dry Area (ICARDA) in cooperation with the Belgian Government, under the auspices of the United Nations and UNESCO.
4. The data discussed come from field studies conducted in the early 1990s when I worked with the Gulf States' Heritage Center on an oral history project that included work on childhood songs, the life cycle, traditional dress and jewels of Qatari woman, collective celebrations, pearl diving culture, folk tales and Bedouin heritage. In addition, my research assistants Marim Hamad and Maha Al-Murkh interviewed some men and women, aged between fifty and eighty years, about their traditional knowledge.

References

Aba Hussein A. and S. al-Din A. Anwar. 2011. 'Integrated environmental assessment for the exploitation of gravel in the State of Qatar.' http://kenanaonline.com/users/hasan/topics/59097 (accessed 20 January 2011).

Al-Ghanim, K. 1991. *Anasheed Al-Tofoula fi Al-mojtama'aat Al-Khaleejeya* [Childhood songs in Gulf society]. Majallet Al-Maa'thourat Al-Shabeya. *Markaz Al-Torath Al-Shaabi Ledowal Al-Khaleej Al-Arabeya* 21.

———. 2002. *The Qatari Society: From Diving to Urbanization*. Doha: National Council for Culture and Heritage.

———. 2010. *Al-Ehtefalaat A-lJamaeya fi Al-Mojtamaa Al-Qatari* [Collective celebrations in Qatari society], 2nd ed. Doha: Al-Lajna Al-Monathem Lmahrajan Al-Bahr.

Al-Khayat, J. and M. al-Ansi. 2008. *Sea Turtles are Threatened With Extinction in Qatar*. Doha: National Council for Culture.

Berkes, F., J. Colding and C. Folke. 2000. 'Rediscovery of Traditional Ecological Knowledge as Adaptive Management.' *Ecological Applications* 10 (5): 1251–1262.

Crespi, M. 1987. 'Review of J. A. and D. Pitt, 1985, *Culture, and Conservation: The Human Dimension in Environmental Planning*.' *American Anthropologist* 89 (2): 464–465.

Gahnem, K. 2009. 'Install Sand and Range Land Protection and Management of Water Resources.' *Knowledge* 135. http://www.almarefh.org/news.php?action=show&id=1027 (accessed 25 January 2011).

Gellerman, J. P., et al. 2009. 'Understanding Sustainability: The Importance of Sustainable Development and Comprehensive Planning.' http://edis.ifas.ufl.edu/fy1104 (accessed 9 January 2011).

General Secretariat for Development Planning (GSDP). 2009. Qatar Second Human Development Report: Advancing Sustainable Development. Doha.

Grenyer, R., et al. 2006. 'Global Distribution and Conservation of Rare and Threatened Vertebrates.' *Nature* 444: 93–96. http://www.ncbi.nlm.nih.gov/pubmed/17080090 (accessed 1 January 2011).

Jackson, J. B. C. 2008. 'Ecological Extinction and Evolution in the Brave New Ocean.' *Proceedings of the National Academy of Sciences* 105: 11458–11465. http://www.pnas.org/content/105/suppl.1/11458 (accessed 1 January 2011).

Leff, E. 1985. 'Ethnobotany and anthropology as tools for a cultural conservation strategy.' *Culture and Conservation: The Human Dimension in Environmental Planning,* ed. J. A. McNeely and D. Pitt, 259–267. Dover, NH: Croom Helm.

Lütteken, A., and K. Hagedorn. 1996. 'Transformation, and Environment: Perspectives for Central and Eastern European Countries.' In *Economics of Agro-Chemicals,* eds. G. H. Peters, G. C. van Kooten and G. A. A. Wossink. Proceedings of a symposium of the International Association of Agricultural Economics, Wageningen, Netherlands.

Madhav Gadgil, M., F.Berkes and C. Folke. 1993. 'Indigenous Knowledge for Biodiversity Conservation.' *Ambio* 22 (2–3): 151–156.

Millar, H. 2007. 'Combining Community Development and Indigenous Cultureto Promote a Conservation Economy.' *The Journal of the Yale School of Forestry and Environmental Studies*. www.environment.yale.edu/magazine.

Olsson, P., and C. Folke. 2001. 'Local Ecological Knowledge and Institutional Dynamics for Ecosystem Management: A Study of Lake Racken Watershed, Sweden.' *Ecosystems* 4 (2): 85–104.

Planning Council. 2006. First Human Development Report. Doha: State of Qatar, Ministry of Environment. http://www.moe.gov.qa.22/1/2011.

———. 2006. Geographical Information Systems Unit, Qatar. http://www.qsa.gov.qa/QatarCensus/Ar/Populations.aspx.

Pretty, J., et al. 2009. 'How Do Biodiversity and Culture Intersect? Sustaining Cultural and Biological Diversity in a Rapidly Changing World: Lessons for Global Policy.' *Conservation and society* 7 (2): 100–112.

Sillitoe, P. 1998. 'The Development of Indigenous Knowledge: A New Applied Anthropology.' *Current Anthropology* 39 (2): 223–252.

——— (ed.). 2007. *Local Science vs. Global Science: Approaches to Indigenous Knowledge in International Development.* New York and Oxford: Berghahn Books.

Sillitoe, P., Ali Al-Shawi and A. K. Al-Amir Hassan. 2010. 'Challenges to Conservation: Land Use Change and Local Participation in the Al Reem Biosphere Reserve, West Qatar.' *Journal of Ethnobiology and Ethnomedicine* 6: 28 doi:10.1186/1746-4269-6-28.

Smith, B. R. 2009. 'Indigenous and Scientific Knowledge in Central Cape York Peninsula.' In *Local Science vs. Global Science: Approaches to Indigenous Knowledge in International Development,* ed. P. Sillitoe, 74–79. New York and Oxford: Berghahn Books.

Underwood, E. C., et al. 2008. 'Protecting Biodiversity When Money Matters: Maximizing Return on Investment.' *PLoS ONE* 3 (1): e1515. doi:10.1371/. http://www.plosone.org (accessed 1 January 2011).

Viriri, A. 2009. 'The Paradox of Africa's Poverty: The Role of Indigenous Knowledge in Zimbabwe's Environmental Management Issues.' *Journal of Sustainable Development in Africa* 10 (4): 129–147.

Wenzel, G. W. 1999. 'Traditional Ecological Knowledge and Inuit: Reflections on TEK Research and Ethics.' *Arctic* 52 (2): 113–124.

Zent, S. 2008. 'Global Indicators of the Status and Trends of Linguistic Diversity and Traditional Knowledge.' Centro de Antropología Instituto Venezolano de Investigaciones Científicas (IVIC), Caracas. http://www.terralingua.org/projects/vitek/ch4.htm (accessed 7 January 2011).

A Doha Undeclaration,
Puzzling over Sustainable Development
with Indigenous Knowledge

Paul Sillitoe

It is ironic that while the activities of 'overdeveloped' industrial nations are largely responsible for the current environmental crisis, much development amounts to the export of these very activities elsewhere, with many agencies promoting them globally in seeking to advance economic growth. There is a contradiction here, emblematic of why, as many of the previous chapters point out, we have problems with sustainable development, which I take up in this concluding chapter. To foreshadow my argument, it appears that talk of sustainability in development contexts implies undoing much of the change previously imposed on people to civilize and later develop them, for many subject to such interventions are heirs to cultural traditions that esteem sustainable ways of life highly (Jordan and O'Riordan 2000). The definition of one authority intimates this in emphasizing some key features of such cultural orders, talking of sustainable development requiring 'a move from an industrial (technical fix) approach … to a *holistic* approach, with *sustainable improvement* replacing profit as the implicit objective; from a technocratic and exclusive to a *participatory and inclusive* approach to development management; and from resource control by big organisations to *local resource management,* often with a strong *common property* aspect' (Shepherd 1998: 10, emphases added).

The undoing of development and heeding of the sustainability message challenges the current international political-economic order. The Doha Declaration that came out of the World Trade Organization's (WTO) 'Fourth Ministerial Conference', hosted by Qatar in 2001, epitomizes that order.[1] It amounts to a reaffirmation of the mandate for the capitalist economic approach to global relations, committing member governments, for instance, to improve market access, phase out export subsidies and reduce trade distorting domestic support; it also includes important resolutions on Trade-Related Aspects of Intellectual Property Rights (TRIPS) regarding public health (see WTO 2011). Our Doha conference was a modest contribution to the increasingly loud debate challenging such development's business-as-usual approach. In view of the pitifully slow progress made in the two decades since the 'UN Earth Summit' in Rio de Janeiro (which the 2012 ['Rio+20'] 'UN Conference on Environment and Development' did little to gee up, regardless of expectations), some rethinking is clearly necessary to kick-start meaningful movement towards sustainable development.

One thrust of the challenge to capitalist-informed unsustainable economic development contends that we should pay more attention to other, more sustainably rooted, cultural ways of being in the world. It offers a relatively novel contribution to the sustainability debate. A popular device in discussions of sustainable development is to talk about exploring links between the 'three pillars' that comprise such development, sometimes more memorably depicted – in good MBA sound-bite-flipchart style – as the 'three Es' (Baker 2006: 7; Robertson 2014: 4–6), which are the environmental, economic and equity (social) dimensions. This chapter, following on from several of this book's contributions, proposes the addition of a fourth E to the flipchart: the endogenous pillar, to advance not only the sustainability of development but also of development initiatives themselves. (In chapter 2, Trudy Tan, Aziza Al-Khalaqi and Najla Al-Khulaifi refer to four sustainable development 'pillars' – human, social, economic and environmental – in the *Qatar National Vision 2030,* of which the human incorporates the endogenous dimension.)

Sustainable Economics?

Any economic activity has environmental implications – i.e. the pursuit of material well-being modifies the environment to some degree – but the extent varies. Market regimes, notably capitalist but also socialist, and associated industrial technology have the most extensive repercussions in human history; whereas other orders are more in harmony with the environment, such as the Islamic one potentially, as Rodney Wilson points out, at least to the extent that the activities they support can continue for the foreseeable future without environmentally compromising their ability to do so.

The capitalist wealth-focused approach, promoting runaway industrialization and profligate use of non-renewable energy sources, has resulted, as Thomas Henfrey reminds us, in unprecedented damage to the planet (Meadows et al. 1972; Meadows, Meadows and Randers 1992; Meadows, Randers and Meadows 2004).[2] He points out that non-renewable energy not only fuels, and temporarily allows us to dodge the consequences of, inherently unsustainable patterns of development, resource use and economic growth, but that it is also likely to hasten the onset of future resource crises, probably increase their magnitude and undermine our capacity to cope with them (Heinberg 2011: 145). The environmental costs of the global market as currently organized are potentially unsupportable in the long term (Elliott 1994: 27–31). It is necessary to prioritize environmental considerations along with the bottom line if we are serious about sustainability. Under current commercial arrangements it pays entrepreneurs/companies in the short term to pollute and degrade resources to make a profit. So long as they are able to treat damage to our natural commons as something left off the balance sheet (i.e. it is something for which we all have to pay, as so-called externalities), sustainability will be a policy will-o'-the-wisp. The attempts by environmental economics to devise cost-benefit analyses to assess environmental damage may be a move in the right direction, albeit they are also a continued symptom of the problem, being framed according to economic assumptions and suggesting that we can put a price on such damage (Pearce, Barbier and Markandya 1990; Pearce and Barbier 2000; Redclift 1987: 38–39; Reid 1995: 111–125). Rather than perpetuate it, we need to come up with alternatives to the growth-based model (Harrison 2014). And Muslim nations, especially those emerging as significant economic global powers such as in the Gulf region, can help, as Rodney Wilson points out, by introducing some much-needed diversity of perspective.

The global community is seeking ways to ensure that those responsible for damaging the environment make good the harm, such as enforceable mechanisms that ensure they take necessary steps to maintain overall ecological stability (e.g. create CO_2 sinks equivalent to the CO_2 released by energy used in their economic activities; Martinez-Alier 1994). This assumes necessary technological advances (e.g. to make CO_2 sequestration possible; Fauset 2008), in addition to internationally agreed and binding regulations (which the snail-like progress at Earth Summits suggests is far off). The technological changes seen in the archaeological record, such as those in irrigation procedures described by Mark Manuel, Robin Coningham, Gavin Gillmore and Hassan Fazeli, are an early example of human technical ingenuity overcoming environmental constraints that many assume will continue to solve our problems. But such advances often bring unforeseen environmental problems – as evident for example in the so-called Green Revolution with its High Yielding Varieties – and we have to ask if there is a limit to our technological interference in the natural world and if we are reaching it or have even perhaps passed it, developing hi-tech capabilities (such as in-vitro conception and atomic technology) beyond our socio-political capacity to manage (Sillitoe 2007: 19).

Some business gurus are optimistic, arguing that the evidence points to capitalism possibly reinventing, even reinvigorating itself with the environmental crisis (Barbier 2010; Collier 2010; Dixon and Gorecki 2010; Moody and Nogrady 2010). When the environmental movement gained traction in the 1970s, the dominant assumption was that economic growth and ecological integrity were incompatible, but an alternative argument has subsequently emerged that seeks to reconcile a concern for profit with a concern for the planet. This 'eco-capitalist' view argues firstly that new technologies such as computers, biotechnology and nanotechnology will save capitalism from the environment, allowing growth to continue by sidestepping current natural constraints. Secondly, if economics accommodates environmental considerations – that is, costs the environment – then capitalism can save the environment, harnessing the operation of markets to protect rather than degrade it. Thirdly, problems such as climate change and peak oil will lead to innovation and a new wave of resource-efficient green technologies; the environmental crisis will save capitalism by reinvigorating economic growth, boosting profit rates and creating employment, overcoming current economic stagnation. Whatever the case, it is unlikely on current evidence that any technological breakthroughs will reduce poverty as planned through increased economic growth without further considerable destruction of natural resources and increasing numbers of unsustainable ecological footprints, until their trampling results in the planet's ecological collapse.

It seems that the market economics that informs development, notably the idea of growth (Redclift 1987: 52–55; Adams 2001: 104–110; Grainger 2004: 9–13), is at odds with the goal of sustainability. Various policy documents, such as the British Government's White Papers on international development, reveal the confusion, in advancing apparently opposed aims without comment, in seeking to stimulate economic growth while promoting sustainability. We can either go for growth, which implies increased exploitation of resources, or we can go for sustainability, which implies their conservation (Reid 1995: 24–29; Jackson 2009).[3] The idea of 'growth with equity', current development-speak for the imposition of capitalist market 'solutions', confuses things further. It is difficult to comprehend how these will advance sustainable development's third equity pillar given the profit philosophy that informs market economics. The promotion of economic growth to reduce global poverty implies encouraging entrepreneurs and companies to maximize profit-making activity above all else – that is, enrich themselves. The forces that drive such economic activity inevitably result in a few wealthy and many poor (witness the ever-growing gap in the United Kingdom with the imposition of market nostrums on the country over the past thirty years). It is further ironical that governments advocating and funding such economic development sometimes recoil for other reasons at the outcome of lauded market forces; such as opium-poppy cultivation in Central Asia, which is by far the most profitable crop (pomegranates and apricots cannot compete).

The issues of worrying environmental damage and widespread poverty relate to population growth, which has somewhat slipped off the agenda in recent decades but looks set to make a return. Again, talk of sustainable development makes little sense without reference to the 'population issue' (Redclift 1987: 29–32; Heinberg 2011 12–15). While many attribute the limited resources argument to a mid-twentieth century report for the Club of Rome (Meadows et al. 1972; Meadows, Meadows and Randers 1992; Meadows, Randers and Meadows 2004; Heinberg 2010), they date back at least to Thomas Malthus (1806) and beyond. The world has seen an almost threefold increase in the human population in half a century and projections show it reaching a staggering 8 billion or more in twenty year's time (Reid 1995: 10). The prospect of feeding so many people is daunting enough without talk of economic growth to raise standards of living globally. Population growth implies increased exploitation of resources, unless evermore people are to live in abject poverty with insufficient resources to go around or the affluent agree to consume less so that the poor can consume more, which is unlikely under the current global political order. Humankind cannot go on increasingly exploiting the planet's finite resources indefinitely as inferred by economic growth. From an environmental perspective, the growth recommendations to reduce poverty are reminiscent of those about ways to improve the décor of a room while the activities of those responsible for supplying the furnishings are making it uninhabitable. If we do not get a grip, nature will take us in hand, probably brutally in Malthusian ways that we should rather not imagine – as increasingly evident in the climate change predictions.

Participating for Sustainability

It is not only the potentially catastrophic environmental costs of industrial technology and market arrangements that are a concern but also the social changes that they bring. Here is an enduring source of confusion about development, which relates to the inadequacy of the widely held materialistic evolutionary-framed assumptions that I outlined in the book's introduction. These frame development as material progress, as exemplified in modernization approaches discussed by Trudy Tan, Aziza Al-Khalaqi and

Najla Al-Khulaifi (chapter 2), Khondker Rahman (chapter 3) and Bahaa Darwish (chapter 4), and sustainability as natural process, as exemplified in ecological perspectives discussed by Noboyuki Yamaguchi (chapter 12), James Howard (chapter 11), Ben Campbell (chapter 9) and Tom Henfrey (chapter 6). Thus development concerns phenomena 'out there' that we can detect with our senses, about which we can agree objective measures – i.e. rate of communications – and talk of progress with respect to these, which planners set 'milestone targets' to monitor. Similarly, we can measure the impact of resulting human activities on the environment.

But technology and market are not socially neutral; any change they bring will have social implications, often difficult to foresee. And these implications are beyond objective measurement, for well-being as it relates to our socio-cultural expectations is a subjective phenomenon that 'exists in' our minds and features abstract ideas that we use to make sense of our communal behaviour as human beings. After all, we cannot see or touch a social value and so we cannot assess any changes in values in terms of progress, except on subjective grounds that my culture and life experiences prompt me to think one is better than another. And seeking to change peoples' social arrangements is not as defensible as intervening to change their material conditions according to agreed measures of progress. Encouraging profit-seeking market arrangements because thought more efficient at utilizing available resources, or interfering in political structures because thought undemocratic, or meddling with family arrangements because thought to support unfair gender relations, is to engage in questionable social engineering. It is necessary to respect other people's rights to arrange their own socio-cultural organization and beliefs; anything less is not only morally questionable but also likely to prove counter-productive.

Those advocating development came to realize that it is not simply a case of transferring technology and economic arrangements from the top (or developed places) to the bottom (undeveloped places). It became apparent that the human element (i.e. those caught up in the process) figured large, as evident in peoples' responses to development interventions. It was naive to assume that communities would just adopt foreign technology and adjust to market demands, particularly where these conflicted with their way of life and values. Slowly, development agencies – like all institutions, notoriously sluggish to change – have sought to incorporate the human social dimension into development, as Gina Porter and Serena Heckler describe, with the flowering of participatory approaches in the past three decades (Shepherd 1998: 179–188), even if participatory programmes have not necessarily enjoyed the success anticipated by advocates (Cooke and Kothari 2001; Hickey and Mohan 2004; Mosse 2005).

Box 21.1. The Participatory (People-Centred) Approach

Participatory approaches to development vary widely but they all adhere to the same basic tenet, which is to include 'beneficiaries' in the planning and implementation of interventions. According to a prominent advocate of participation it comprises 'a growing family of approaches and methods to enable local people to share, enhance and analyse their knowledge of life and conditions, and to plan, act, monitor and evaluate ... [and consists of an] extensive and growing menu of methods' (Chambers 1997: 102). An early example of such an approach to development is the FAO's Small Farmer Development Programme that sought to organize small farmers and the landless in Nepal into local groups to formulate plans to undertake jointly some income-generating activity, on the basis of which they could apply for credit (Oakley and Marsden 1984: 39–43). Previously they had no access to formal credit, lacking the organization necessary for bureaucratic agencies to deliver it to them. Evaluations of the programme concluded that it benefited those who took part economically and also possibly helped them mobilize and change their relatively powerless place in society. The programme depended on 'group organizers' to bring the local groups into being and organize their structure and management. The aim was that they should become self-reliant, with the organizers described as 'initiators not the permanent crutches' of groups. Even at this early stage in the emergence of participatory development, problems were evident that would subsequently question its efficacy. The organization of poor people by outsiders to interface with development agencies limits their participation at the outset, but is perhaps unavoidable, not because they necessarily lack the ability to organize themselves, but because they are unlikely to do so in ways that such agencies can recognize or do business with. While intended to act as facilitators only, there was a danger of groups becoming dependent on 'group organizers' who might manipulate events to this end to secure some power. While the Small Farmer Development Programme has assisted some previously excluded people, it has not reached all such people; evaluations point to the need to involve more women in such interventions.

Similar problems have become increasingly evident with participatory development programmes. The Joint Forest Management approach seeks to involve local communities in the management of their forests (Shepherd 1998: 72–74). It became prominent in parts of India such as the Western Ghats (Hildyard et al. 2001) at the end of the twentieth century following mounting protests over resource degradation with commercial forestry and associated declining access to forest products, combined with pressure from international agencies on government forestry departments to adopt a participatory approach to forest management. The aim of participatory forest management is to give local communities a voice in the conservation and exploitation of their forest resources alongside state forest departments that have dictated forest use, often at the behest of commercial interests and frequently featuring corruption. In order to organize local participation, the UK-funded Western Ghats Forestry Project encouraged communities to form Village Forest Committees that would decide how to restore and conserve forest and share out the income from the exploitation of resources such as timber sales. They would liaise with the Karnataka State Forest Department, the management capacity of which the project set out to improve 'in particular to enable it to respond to the conflicting demands from different users for access to the forest' (ibid.: 63). While the project succeeded in formalizing village-level participation in forest management, it ironically reinforced local inequalities, undermining its development aims of alleviating poverty. The local communities are differentiated along caste lines and those with power predictably came to dominate the Village Forest Committees; there was also a marked gender imbalance in favour of men (Feeney 1998). The committees made decisions that favoured wealthy families, discriminating against low-caste families that depend on forest products to meet their basic needs and poorer tribal people who herd cattle and depend on access to common land for pasture. The committees have also legitimated the right of powerful persons to regulate others' access to the forest and the means to sanction those who ignore their directions, such as evicting landless families off common lands. But what else should we expect of participation than people acting according to their socio-political arrangements? It is surely unrealistic to expect a local revolution that puts the poorest in control of decisions, which is what some advocates of participation seem to want, coming perilously close to advocating social engineering when the revolution fails to occur.

While participatory approaches to development have encountered some problems, one aspect offers novel insights into sustainability and affords a promising way to address some of the challenges encountered by sustainable development. It is the so-called indigenous knowledge (IK) approach. The term, particularly the indigenous part, has been subject to politically correct debate ('how can one define *indigenous* in the modern cosmopolitan world?') and several alternatives have been proposed including local knowledge, traditional knowledge, people's knowledge, citizen science, even 'glocal' knowledge, to name a few. I use indigenous knowledge as the one largely heard in development discourse and, where acronyms abound, the inevitable IK shorthand.

The Cultural Relativity of Development

IK includes all knowledge held more or less collectively by a community that informs interpretation of the world, critically shaping peoples' views of environments and livelihood choices, health and illness, social behaviour and so on. In short, it is any understanding rooted in local culture, as discussed by Serena Heckler (chapter 18), Fadwa El Guindi (chapter 19) and Kaltham Al-Ghanim (chapter 20). It varies between regions, focusing on local interests and concerns, often communicated in (to outsiders) strange idioms and styles; which, as the postmodern critique affirms, outsiders understand to varying extents. IK is founded on experience, often tested by many generations, and is adapted to local conditions, and subject to ongoing revision in response to changes. It comes from a 'range of sources, is a dynamic mix of past "tradition" and present invention with a view to the future' (Sillitoe 2006: 1). While it is ever changing and modified by information from elsewhere – a process to which development aims to contribute, even hasten – it maintains its distinctive character, subject to ongoing local, regional and global negotiation.

The IK approach invites us to consider what people are already doing in any environment, or did in the past, to secure their livelihoods, for in all probability they will reveal sustainable ways if humans have occupied a region for any time, perhaps millennia. As Michael Redclift (1987: 171) comments, 'For those who recognise the importance of these cultures, sustainable development is not so much an invention of the future as a rediscovery of the past', which is the point that Al-Ghanim makes. While the assumptions of market economics may sit uncomfortably with the idea of sustainability, other socio-culturally informed views of human-environment relations intimate viable alternatives. The lesson that I draw from the experiences of development, as an anthropologist imbued with the ethic of cultural relativity, is the need to allow space for other views of the 'good life' (aka development) to achieve sustainable interventions. It is a tenet of IK that we have something to learn from such other views, however improbable at first sight, that those we presume to assist to develop can teach us a lot about sustainability (Redclift 1987: 150–157; Shepherd 1998: 45; Adams 2001: 337–341).[4]

Box 21.2. Hunter-Gatherer Sustainability

Many hunter-gatherers – who according to social evolutionists are the least developed of humankind – see themselves as related to the natural world, as part of it. The Australian Aborigines, for example, express this relationship in totemism, a belief that conceives a unity of substance between humans and the natural world. This belief informs their relations with nature and exploitation of its resources (Redclift 1987: 150), which depends not only on an intimate knowledge of the natural environment but also of the right ways to behave with respect to the spirit world and ensure well-being, such as performing appropriate rites. These two elements are intimately inter-connected, ritual knowledge informing ecological knowledge (Gammage 2011). Humans ensure their well-being by living according to the sacred lore established by the spirit beings that fashioned the world in the so-called Dreamtime[5] creation period – shaping the landscape and leaving some of their vital life essence to animate generations of humans, animals and plants – who accord life-giving power in return (Elkin 1979: 220–261). The need to behave properly, to guarantee the passage of this power from the spirit domain, is an integral aspect of land custodianship. It expresses concern for long-term environmental and social stability, such beliefs inherently pro-moting the sustainable exploitation and conservation of natural resources. In some senses the food quest is a religious act, not an economic one. They are not alone in their respectful behaviour. The Inuit of the Canadian Arctic perceive of the universe as a combination of natural and supernatural forces over which humans have limited control. They believe in spirit forces linked to an underworld that they could influence in their favour with appropri-ate taboos, magic and ritual, and today prayers, to ensure hunting success. All animals possess spirits related to those of the underworld and hunters treated their quarry with respect, only killing as subsistence needs demand (figure 21.1).

We can appreciate how these people might help us to reform our ideas about sustainability by considering their relationship with the land. Aus-tralian customary land custodianship stands in stark contrast with capital-ist property relations. The difference is nicely captured in an Australian musical where an Aboriginal retorts 'This land is me' to a rancher's asser-tion 'This land is mine' (Gibson 2007: 63). It is intriguing to consider the implications of accommodating such inclusive systems of custodianship and different resource attitudes and values into legal frameworks and their potential to revolutionize views of sustainability. We have further lessons to learn from the ways in which such people have prompted legislation to protect their rights when faced with encroachment by commercial interests. The outcomes of the 1971 Alaska Native Claims Settlement Act intimate how Inuit responses based on subsistence values spiritually tied to place might influence 'deracinated, competitive, short-sighted, and often corrupt' business corporations to prioritize sustainability (Thornton 2007: 42). It is possible that the 'seemingly paradoxical forces of subsistence and corporate economies might be reconciled in ways that could serve as a model for sus-tainability' (ibid.: 60).

The IK approach has the potential constructively to destabilize the idea of economic development, as Serena Heckler (chapter 18) and Fadwa El Guindi (chapter 19) point out, which is clearly relevant if we wish to pro-mote sustainability. Our view of development as progress – a process that improves peoples' standard of living, assessed largely in material terms – is culturally relative (Reid 1995: 129–130; Latouch 1995). In other

Figure 21.1. An Arctic hunter scrapping blubber off seal skin.

words, to imagine development at all, in the evolutionary-change sense, is to subscribe to a value-loaded Western concept derived from Enlightenment ideas about progress, which many Euro-Americans assume to be universal (Schech and Haggis 2000). There are other entirely different views. Indeed, we have ethnographic evidence of the antithesis, that is, of inherently conservative cultures that resist change from generation to generation. It is not that such people are unaware of change at the individual level; we all grow up and age and finally pass away (again biologically universal processes). But they resist change collectively as social beings, belonging to cultures that do not recognize the possibility of structural change or development (culturally relative processes).

The followers of the more conservative sects of Islam are an example. The imams with religious authority teach that the Koran lays down how to live a righteous life for all time according to Allah's will. It is the duty of believers to resist any challenges to these values and way of living, such as capitalist-informed economic development might pose, with its dependence for instance on usury, as Rod Wilson describes (chapter 8). The Dreamtime beliefs of Aborigines are another example; they prescribe a perpetual unchanging pattern of life, emphasizing the continuity of the past with the present and future. It is sacrilege to interfere with the supernaturally ordained relationship between humans and nature, to speak of Western-style development. The contrast between linear and circular ideas of time is pertinent here. Time is circular for the Aborigines with spirit power cycling between this world and the other. Our linear view of history is alien. Likewise the Hindus have sophisticated beliefs about reincarnation, depending upon one's behaviour in this life. The values of capitalism will earn you reincarnation as some decidedly lower life form, the profit motive promoting immoral behaviour. While we may foster evermore-rapid change, these people value an unchanging pattern of life; the distinction has been characterized as 'hot versus cold' societies (Lévi-Strauss 1966). Structural change is not possible and the idea of progress is alien. This is not to deny history or the occurrence of social change, only the assumption that people everywhere at all times have embraced the prospect of change, such as promoted by Western economic development.[6]

These culturally conservative beliefs belong to people who follow ways of life that they think acceptable for all time, which implies that they have achieved some sort of balance both environmentally and socially. In other words, these are remarkably sustainable cultural-environmental arrangements: with the rejection of change culturally, we have the embracement of sustainability. The Australian archaeological evidence, for example, underlines the extent of the unchanging Aboriginal worldview and further confirms a highly sustainable environmental adaptation, showing a remarkably stable cultural formation for extended periods of the 50,000 or more years that humans have occupied the continent. It is arrogant to think that the capitalist world – under the guise of sustainable development or whatever – has anything to tell such people about sustainability given its unsustainable trajectory, evidenced, as noted earlier, by the mounting environmental problems for which it is responsible.

Other Views of the 'Good Life'

The suggestion is not that all communities other than Western ones have circular development-inhibiting worldviews. Many want to see change but progress on their own terms, which is likely to differ from our economic development. What shape might such alternative views of development take? It is difficult for someone from a dominant or developed nation, who inevitably reflects capitalist-democratic values to some extent, fully to appreciate or represent such other views of development, other than to give a shadowy hint. The point of the participatory movement, echoing the postmodern critique, is that only those who subscribe to such alternative values can do so. Nonetheless the participatory agenda allows us to glimpse the possibility of such other ideas of development, illustrating the IK point about meaningfully involving people in development, however they may conceive of it. It accepts that development is a culturally relative idea, that there are entirely different views. And in pointing the way to possibly genuinely sustainable development (Reid 1995: 151–165), these other views demonstrate the significance of culture to sustainable life ways as discussed by Serena Heckler (chapter 18) and Fadwa El Guindi (chapter 19); to wit, how culture needs to mesh with sustainability (Raynaut et al. 2007: 23).

Box 21.3. Endogenous (IK) Approach

The NGOs that seek to work closely with local communities give us a glimpse of alternative views and approaches to development, such as those in the COMPAS endogenous development network (Haverkort and Heimstra 1999; Haverkort, van't Hooft and Heimstra 2003). The comments of some representatives of an NGO in South India called 'Green Foundation' give an idea of where they are coming from, pointing out that the people of the Thalli region of Tamil Nadu talk of *sowbagya* 'welfare' as including good health, adequate food, happy family, good neighbours, healthy environment and community harmony, whereas development is 'rooted in the market economy based on cash transactions, and includes unsustainable use of resources, often alien to the local cultural ethos.... Non-participation in the market economy is ... misconstrued as poverty' (Ramprasad, Krishnaprasad and Manasi 2003: 89). The Foundation seeks to support the farming regime against unsustainable market-led interventions, strengthening practices that maintain genetic diversity against the erosion of commercial seed imports, on the grounds that 'diversity in agriculture is the heart of sustainability' (ibid.: 100) – such conservation of variety is important in dryland regions to protect against environmental shocks, which are increasingly likely given the predictions of climate warming. The Foundation liaises closely with communities to strengthen farmers' networks, arranges fairs at which they exchange seeds and discuss problems, and distributes a quarterly newsletter in the local vernacular. Women are central to the farming system, being responsible for the selection, storage and propagation of seeds (figure 21.2), as they embody the female power of *shakti* 'reproduction'. They oversee certain rites that are equally a part of the farming regime as practical activities, so influencing selection of new crop varieties and seed conservation (the plough deity rite, for instance, tests seeds' germination potential and leaves used in the seed storage rite have insecticidal properties). The Foundation encourages women's cropping experiments without taking undue risks, a priority being the families' food security. The Foundation's work, seeking to build on what people know, intimates the destructive potential of uninformed outside interventions, such as well-intentioned plans to promote gender equality by sponsoring inappropriate formal education that could erode the knowledge and standing of women.[7]

The 'Integrated Development through Environmental Awakening' NGO in the nearby Eastern Ghats region of South India further illustrates such alternative views of development (Shankar 2003). The tribal population has a close affinity with place, necessary to well-being, but the forests in its hilly region have been logged in the last century or so, causing widespread concern that deforestation is undermining livelihoods. The NGO has helped people – for whom development should involve protection of their forested commons not their commercial destruction – to document the threat and make their findings and views known. It has drawn on their values, which readily lend themselves to a biodiversity conservation ethic, such as totemic-like beliefs about relations with animals and plants that look out for them supernaturally, which they will not harm. And it has drawn on their practices; for example, using a festival that involved a ceremonial hunt to conduct a survey of animal populations according to returns and agree on necessary conservation measures, 'transforming hunting into ecological protection' (ibid.: 126). It has established community committees that work with clan leaders to effect the implementation of resolutions and even punish those who flout them. The NGO links conservation work with interventions in natural resource management, notably shifting cultivation, which with an increasing population and diminishing forested land jeopardizes local livelihoods. It has coordinated the establishment of a network across the Eastern Ghats and periodic local knowledge *mela* fairs to facilitate the sharing of experiences and knowledge between communities. It campaigns for 'Tribal natural resource management practices and regulations, such the clan regulatory mechanisms to control deforestation, the totemic clan concepts, and the environment related festivals, [which] are not recognised as means for sustainable development' (ibid.: 127–128).

There is an intriguing parallel between the respective political orders of cultures that recognize the integrity of the natural environment and esteem sustainability and those that do not. Stateless political-economies characterize the former and states the latter. The distinction between nomadic Bedouin and sedentary Hadar in the Gulf region reflects these different political arrangements. Tensions between them have featured prominently in the history of the Arab world; for instance, they are central

Figure 21.2. A woman shakes rice grains off straw.

to Ibn Khaldun's cyclical social theory, where desert nomads with strong *asabiyyah* 'group feeling' conquer less-cohesive city dwellers, subsequently being conquered themselves after becoming socially enfeebled following some generations of sedentary *dawlah* 'state' life (Gellner 1975; Al-Azmeh 2003: 70–74). Where people perceive themselves living with nature, borrowing respectfully of resources and replenishing as necessary, we see an extension of egalitarian relations and philosophy to the natural world. On the other hand, where populations seek to dominate nature and exploit resources to further economic growth, there is a reflection of hierarchical relations of command and control. This correlation suggests that those who follow more sustainable ways of life have something to teach us not only about the environmental 'pillar' of sustainable development but also the equity 'pillar'. People who live in the world and recognize reciprocal relations with nature have an equal-winners outlook that makes development with equity conceivable as all share in its fruits, whereas those who exist on the world and support exploitative relations have winner-loser expectations that make such development improbable with only some profiting from it.

Politics of Sustainable Development

The issue of political relations brings us to the matter of power in development contexts, which concerns control of necessary resources. How realistic is it to expect nations, multinationals and international bodies to relinquish any authority, when they believe that they have the answer to the problems of developing nations, namely commercial democracy? A challenge facing the incorporation of IK into development is overcoming the assumption that industrial technology and market economic arrangements are the only ways forwards. The Doha Declaration is witness to the strength of this view: in responding to criticisms that the current global market is both damaging our global commons and inequitable to poorer nations, it reiterates unequivocally the WTO's conviction that free trade is the way to further development (Baker 2006: 173–175). The modern Gulf city, such as Doha with its high-rise 'supermodern' skyline, suggests the towering barrier of accepted wisdom that we have to get over.

Box 21.4. Towards Urban Sustainability

The cities of the Gulf are, as currently set up, unsustainable urban conurbations. Their air-conditioned buildings, with running water and electric power, depend heavily on non-renewable resources, not only fossil fuels but also other mined materials such as iron, copper, aluminium etc. used in their construction. We have surely to be apprehensive about such worldwide urban developments in the long term (Elliott 1994: 82–106; Baker 2006: 117–120), as discussed by Andrew Gardner (chapter 14) and Sarah Clarke and Salah Almannai (chapter 15). What to do about them? Until not so long ago the population of this arid region followed a sustainable way of life, which according to the archaeological evidence extends back over thousands of years. It was a nomadic existence herding camels, sheep and goats with irrigated horticulture around oases, and sedentary fishing and pearling on the coast. While it was an astonishing adaptation to a harsh environment, it is difficult to see how it might contribute to current development. It will probably strike most, if not all readers, as ridiculous to imagine Doha as an enormous mud-brick and tented community with camel transport around town. But it is incorporating such lateral thinking into high-tech architecture that may help break with unsustainable, environmentally damaging approaches to urban growth, as Ali Alraouf and Sarah Clarke (chapter 13) argue. Before you clap the book shut thinking that I am stupid, recall that archaeology shows that some of the world's first urban centres emerged in this region – as Mark Manuel, Robin Coningham, Gavin Gillmore and Hassan Fazeli (chapter 1) remind us. How were they able to sustain themselves? One feature that comes to mind is the sophisticated *qanat* or *falaj* system, an engineering triumph of underground waterways and linked well networks that exploited a region's water resources by tapping into the water table (Cressey 1958; Goblot 1979; Bonine 1996; Motiee et al. 2006). It was part of a highly developed system of irrigation that supported a sophisticated horticultural regime, providing for considerable populations in places where water is scarce (figure 21.3), the sustainable supply of which, as several contributors to this book point out, is a major sustainability challenge today.

In this respect, comparison of the present-day urban sprawl of Mexico City with the sixteenth-century Aztec settlement indicates further how we can learn from the way other communities manage urban environments (Redclift 1987: 105–112). The sustainable 'floating' *chinampas* gardens and canal system contrast markedly with today's land degradation and pollution. The Aztecs used sludge trawled from Lake Texcoc as fertilizer, building fertile islands in the shallows. The farming regime acted as a sewage treatment system too, a bacterium in the lake converting human waste in the sludge into slurry suitable as fertilizer. Although they almost entirely abandoned these practices after the Spanish conquest and imposition of European hacienda plantation-style agriculture, the *chinampas* still exist in places and recently an NGO working with farmers has revived the cultivation system to recycle organic waste, reducing pollution in the valley. Cooperation between farmers and GTA (*Grupo de Tecnologia Alternativa*) has lead to the development of the Integrated System for Recycling of Organic Wastes, a cheap and sustainable form of sanitation (see Ayres 2004 on current rehabilitation efforts).

But is the genuine empowerment of communities without participant manipulation, as the IK approach demands (Soussan 2004), likely with current global political arrangements?[8] The above examples are about IK influencing business-as-usual technologically framed development that does not challenge the hegemony of global powers; indeed, it reinforces their position as the suppliers of much of the know-how and materials. What about where people's ideas about development, if present, or their nearest equivalent, are at odds with market ideology and state regulation,

Figure 21.3. *Qanat* canal supplying the city of Nizwa in Oman with water.

which is possible if they relate to a more sustainable philosophy of life that may, as pointed out, conflict with them? In short, will nations with the resources to support development sponsor activities that they may not consider development? For example, it is improbable that Euro-American agencies would support a Muslim community that decided investment in *madrassa* schools was its development priority, not only because such schools put emphasis on conservative Koranic learning that is thought out of step with development but also because they have been implicated in radicalizing Islamic youth and even training terrorists. The forces at work are more complex than dependency theorists argue with multinational lobbied governments of dominant nations seeking to maintain their global hegemony. The realities of democratic politics make it quixotic to expect such governments to make resources, raised through taxes on their citizens, available to populations with radically different political-economic aspirations and ideas about development, for the taxpayer-voters would probably eject any government following such a strategy.

Even wealthy nations, such as the Gulf states, that can resource their own development have to proceed cautiously. The politics are tricky. If a nation fails to comply with what the powerful think is right, it may be invaded, as the Iraq debacle at the head of the Gulf reminds us, particularly if scarce natural resources such as oil are at stake. The hegemony issue raises a further intriguing paradox regarding development as material progress. Some nations dominate the globe because of their technological superiority, which when it comes down to it means better weaponry (Diamond 1997). While economic development envisages less technologically developed regions advancing materially, it is only in certain ways. If they seek genuinely to empower themselves by developing a matching armoury to 'participate' on equal terms and maybe resist uninvited incursions into their lives, the dominant nations are likely to sanction them and may attack, resorting to propaganda of the 'mad mullahs incite war' sort to carry a majority of citizens – witness the current tensions over Iran's uranium-enrichment programme that could supply weapons-grade nuclear material for missile warheads. Those who subscribe to the development-as-evolution view may see this as ensuring the survival of the fittest, albeit today's dominant nations' unsustainable ways and associated environmental squandering may result in their long-term demise as the unfittest.

Development becomes murky when politics enters the equation, as evident in the contributions here of Emma Gilberthorpe, Sarah Clarke, Wesam Al Othman and myself (chapters 5 and 7). Political realities seem to compromise the idea of sustainable development further in thwarting the emergence of alternatives to challenge the environmentally over-destructive commercial order (Redclift 1987: 36; Middleton and O'Keefe 2001). We find ourselves in a quandary if brought up to value democratic ideals, in seeming to question democracy (Reid 1995: 235) when our target is its current close association with the capitalist market, which exploits the value put on liberty to allow unsustainable ways harmful to the environment.

The Sustainability of Development

Politics feature prominently regarding the sustainability of development interventions themselves. Repeated project failures confirm that it is necessary to challenge current market-dominated political-economic assumptions to promote enduring development. When initiatives are over, whatever they have initiated often falters and fails to continue, as Gina Porter points out in chapter 17. They are not apparently sustainable for one reason or another, sometimes because people sense that they are unsound, environmentally or otherwise. In the top-down techno-economic approach that continues to dominate development – as in central planning discussed by Trudy Tan, AzizaAl-Khalaqi and Najla Al-Khulaifi (chapter 2), Khondker Rahman (chapter 3), Bahaa Darwish (chapter 4) and Wesam Al Othman and Sarah Clarke (chapter 5) – experts not only decide what needs to be done locally, that is, conceive of interventions to achieve some development, but the projects also depend on them for their implementation. The local population goes along with them so far as obliged by political coercion or by the economic goodies they receive for cooperating with the outsider's plans. When they leave, the development initiative often goes with them.

The cultural acceptability of any planned intervention is significant here, as Serena Heckler (chapter 18) indicates, but tends to be overlooked. The local response to any project will obviously affect its sustainability. It is necessary to allow people to genuinely make their own judgements about what is and is not acceptable change contingent upon any planned development. They will anyway, rejecting change that they find unacceptable, as evidenced by the catalogue of flopped projects. What they make of the possible implications of any development will vary from one region to another, communities not responding in a uniform way to any intervention, which presents further problems where agencies expect to apply generic solutions to problems after the manner of techno-economic fixes, not socio-culturally tailored ones.

Box 21.5. Cultural Dimensions of Sustainability

The reaction of communities to national parks intended to protect the environment illustrate issues of project sustainability from a cultural perspective, as Ali Alshawi and I discuss in chapter 10. There is a tendency to equate sustainable development, in the ecological sense, with conservation projects that aim to protect biodiversity, which is ironical given the unsustainable record of such projects in the cultural sense. Local populations regularly challenge such arrangements (Adams 2001: 270–277).

Some thirty years ago the government of Nepal established the Langtang National Park with scarcely any local consultation, prohibiting swidden cultivation, pasture management by firing, hunting animals and gathering forest products without a licence (Campbell 2004). It employs rangers to enforce these restrictions and prosecute offenders. The impact on local Tamang people's livelihoods has been considerable with limited access to needed raw materials such as bamboo and wood, restricted ability to control crop pests such as monkeys and deer, and reduced supply of forest products to trade for grain with lowland farmers. They regularly contravene the Park regulations and engage in illicit activities in the forest; in addition to having become dependent, as Ben Campbell describes in chapter 9, on migrant labour remittances. It is the Park authorities that act illegally from the Tamang perspective, who believe that it is necessary ritually to legitimate pasture and hunting rights through offerings to local deities, such as *shyibda*, Lord of the Soil, who guards wildlife (this is why official government hunters licensed to cull animals are so unsuccessful they say). Furthermore, it is ironic that the Park has undermined local mechanisms for regulating forest and pasture access where *mukhiya* 'headmen' declared when open and closed in summer and winter, and coordinated village livestock movements. The rangers were unable to police the park effectively and the Nepalese government decided to create buffer zones around it to which local people have some limited access (Redclift 1987: 139–141). Communities were obliged to organize committees and draw up 'development plans' to participate (Banjade, Luintel and Neupane 2008), which amounted to the imposition of alien bureaucracy, interpreted locally as an extension of government control. Confusion over land rights in the buffer zone made villagers chary of the plan and they were reluctant to work there except when an NGO offered payment, understandable in a region where participation is synonymous with exploitation of unpaid labour (Campbell 2004: 160).[9]

It is not only the inhabitants of such regions who may find such arrangements insupportable but also the ecology. Projects regularly underestimate the extent to which humans are responsible for today's environment, managing and modifying it; even hunter-gatherers do so to some extent. Excluding local people may result in significant changes to the ecology and even perversely decrease biodiversity (Saberwal, Rangharajan and Kothari 2001: 44–70). Sustainable resource use, as Noboyuki Yamaguchi (chapter 12) points out, is not about returning places to pristine nature but ensuring that livelihood regimes can continue for the foreseeable future in balance with the human-modified ecosystem.

The IK approach, in seeking to incorporate peoples' knowledge and aspirations more meaningfully in development, addresses the issue of the sustainability of interventions. They are more likely, as argued several times in this volume, to be relevant to people's needs, and hence successful, if implemented with an appreciation of cultural context and respect for local ways (Sillitoe, Dixon and Barr 2005: 12–18). The approach helps reconcile different and potentially conflicting cultural perspectives regarding development, and discourages the imposition of inappropriate foreign ideas that can result in costly mistakes with projects founded on false premises. It facilitates communication between development projects and local communities, raising awareness of possible alternatives. It promotes negotiated action by identifying locally perceived problems and effects more meaningful local participation in planning, decision making and so on. It also helps those involved in extension work address problems from the local perspective, and hence 'beneficiaries' to make more informed decisions. Furthermore, the IK approach facilitates interdisciplinary participatory research, as discussed by Gina Porter (chapter 17) and James Howard (chapter 11), necessary to overcome narrow sector biases (Adams 2001: 16; Sillitoe 2004), and creating opportunities for synergy between local and scientific knowledge (for examples, see Sillitoe 2007).

But the IK approach is not enjoying the success that some of us anticipated (Sillitoe and Marzano 2009). We encounter further double binds regarding sustainable development. In order to promote cultural sustainability – i.e. the relevance of any intervention to the local population – it is necessary to involve people from the start (i.e. from the planning stage) and throughout regarding any initiative that will affect them. This implies meaningful empowerment and not puppeteering as in much current participatory development (Cooke and Kothari 2001; Hickey and Mohan 2004; Mosse 2001, 2005). The heavy monitoring and evaluation characteristic of contemporary audit culture is partly responsible for the manipulation of participatory activities by agency staff, obliging them to manage projects to demonstrate achievement of funding agencies' objectives, not least to ensure continuity of employment. Corruption is also a factor here and of growing concern, particularly where, to further participation, resources go directly to government and non-government organizations that have weak accounting mechanisms. Political demands for control and 'results' (preferably quick), subject to relentless appraisal to show taxpayers' or investors' money well spent, obliges a blueprint approach that determines objectives before any project starts, subject to a series of 'milestone' markers to track progress. Sustainable, sustainable development, where projects continue to flourish when outside intervention stops, demands a flexible process approach and substantial participation allowing people to define *development* according to their own priorities and aspirations (Reid 1995: 231).

While agencies have made some positive noises about process approaches, it is difficult to break away from the objectives-milestone culture under current political arrangements and imperatives (Shepherd 1998: 123–127). In this event, for some cynics, sustainability becomes yet another subterfuge to maintain dominance, as evoked by a colleague's examination question that asked 'does sustainable development aim at developing sustainability or sustaining development'? Anyone who has tangled with the 'Sustainable Livelihoods Framework' of the UK's Department for International Development might have some sympathy with this view. It is a baffling bureaucratic invention that reduces livelihoods' analysis to five sorts of capital – financial, physical, social, human and natural – the terminology gives away the capitalist economic view. It arranges these 'capital assets' around a pentagon linked to a series of boxes dealing with such issues as 'transforming structures and processes', 'livelihood outcomes' and 'vulnerability context' (DFID n.d.; Carney 1998). Someone engaging with it might be forgiven for concluding that sustainable development aims to sustain the work of development agencies, the only bodies that can make sense of such Byzantine procedures, likely to meet the same fate as previous demised development 'solutions'.

The apparent wish to keep control is open to interpretations that it further undermines the advancement of sustainable development. It creates the impression that materially affluent nations intend to continue their insatiable consumerism with its giant ecological footprint at the expense of others, by impeding their further development in the name of sustainability, which apparently entails the imposition of restrictions to ameliorate the global environmental damage for which the 'developed' are largely responsible (Lee 2000). The concern to protect the world's forests is an instance; it appears that the West, having cleared large areas of forest previously, now wishes to stop others from doing likewise in their quest for similar material advancement. It is a sticking point in current international negotiations to promote the global cooperation necessary to tackle climate change, as evident at the 2012 Doha and other Climate World Summits (http://unfccc.int/meetings/doha_nov_2012/meeting/6815.php). From the viewpoint of emerging market economies such as China and India, it is the historical activities of affluent nations that have contributed largely to current problems and they cannot expect to make good the damage by inhibiting their economic growth because of concerns for the future of the planet. It is unfair to start from where we are currently and overlook the harm done by the culpable long-industrialized nations, which seem to be trying to shift the onus for dealing with it onto the rest of the world, instead of taking robust action to correct their activities.

The up-shot is that although top-down interventions have been thoroughly criticized, they continue to dominate development interventions (Adams 2001: 381–382), even where these are wrapped up in the rhetoric of participatory discourse. This is certainly so in the Gulf as the planning chapters show. Those with the political-economic power, namely the resources to finance development programmes, are reluctant, as noted, to give away any real control over decision making, particularly with respect to defining the goals of development (Middleton and O'Keefe 2001: 1–16). The left wing conspiracy view of Marxist-informed dependency theory argues that these powers seek to use development as a way of maintaining political-economic control and exploiting the world's resources unfairly, while the right wing more charitable liberal-capitalist view argues that these powers believe that their democratic-market approach to development is the only way to promote progress and prosperity. Whichever is your preferred ideology, current political realities pose several conundrums for sustainable development.

Participation for Sustainability?

In fairness to development agencies, the inclusion of people and their knowledge is not straightforward. Some may not expect to participate in any decision making; for instance, participation may not make much sense to the poor. In hierarchically organized societies where patron/client relationships occur, or specialists/non-specialists in state market contexts, many expect those above them to make decisions and perhaps solve problems on their behalf. Generations of outside interference, first in the colonial and now the development era, has also conditioned people to expect experts to come up with solutions to their problems, a tendency exacerbated by seeing the technology available to outsiders. The assumption is that they of all persons must know how to pass on these material benefits. Some communities may even appear clueless about how to further their development, especially if ideas about progress differ radically from the accepted development paradigm, such that they defer to those who claim to know; for instance the host of expatriate planners in the Gulf region. We have another contradiction. In these contexts participation on local terms may sideline many, with the patron or expert classes assuming control. To overcome this assumes interference to subvert local arrangements to reach the excluded, which is social engineering of the sort that the IK approach censures, arguing for change from within, whereas inertia looks the more likely outcome in many places.

There is a deep political division in development thought. On the one hand, those of a left wing persuasion argue that development is about improving the life chances of the excluded, notably the poor, through participation that promotes self-determination, albeit participation on their terms, namely that manipulates the local political order as necessary to empower the 'target beneficiaries'. On the other hand, those of a right wing persuasion argue that development is about getting the market to work, which may well mean working with, even reinforcing established hierarchies but to the benefit of all by increasing productivity overall, reaching the poorer through 'trickle down'. Neither side of the political divide will allow communities subject to their development attentions to freely associate on their terms with any intervention. The left believes some oversight is necessary to ensure that the powerful do not highjack development initiatives to their own ends, to consolidate their control of assets such as land and capital. And for the right some supervision is necessary to ensure that required technological and economic changes to improve peoples' standard of living are implemented appropriately. It is understandable that participation for canny 'beneficiaries' amounts to figuring out what the development agency or NGO thinks is necessary and parroting this back to ensure that it releases the resources that it has available to the community (Mosse 2001).

The sustainability challenge is to devise an approach that allows the knowledge and aspirations of the excluded in any community to feature equally, which assumes meaningful participation. The elusive part is seeing that the powerful do not high-jack the agenda, without interfering directly in local socio-political arrangements, which is likely to result in unsustainable outcomes as the powerful later seek to reassert their hegemony. It assumes a deep understanding of any community. The IK approach furthers such understanding and helps assess the social impact of interventions – such as with respect to relations between different interest groups, assessing local variation in knowledge (by gender, age, caste, occupation etc.) and accommodating different perspectives and agendas – and can help predict possible conflict through different groups manipulating interventions to their advantage. While it may further the empowerment of people through respect for their knowledge and practices, it is otherwise stymied, like other approaches, by the paradox of these political realities, balancing assistance against imposition.

To further complicate the picture, it is ironical that if people are free to participate on their own terms, thus ensuring from a cultural perspective the probable sustainability of any change because thoroughly informed by local values and aspirations – i.e. what they want – they may engage in activities that are not only socially unattractive from a liberal perspective but that are also not necessarily sustainable from an ecological one. Local communities, even those that live close to the land, are not always the innate conservationists that some environmental campaigners imagine, as Alshawi and I describe in chapter 10. The IK initiative is not arguing that we can expect all local populations to act as model environmental stewards. They can sometimes get it wrong too: IK is not perfect; if it were, development would be redundant and we should have no need to advocate each informing the other. It is particularly vulnerable where rapid change occurs, such as when populations migrate elsewhere (perhaps forced as refugees), or unheard of opportunities occur, the consequences of which they cannot imagine (such as industrial exploitation of their region's natural resources).

Box 21.6. Environmentally Unsustainable Participation

Ecologically unsustainable participation in development occurs in parts of Papua New Guinea where central government is weak and local communities engage directly with companies seeking to exploit their natural resources. The country is rich in valuable minerals, in addition to having the world's second largest area of tropical forest. The local view of economic development is the rentier one of the Gulf, namely to secure the maximum royalties for the exploitation of any natural resources, be they metalliferous ores or tropical hardwoods. They give scant regard to the environmental despoliation that may follow at the time of agreeing contracts, although they may subsequently come to rue the devastation of land following the excavation of large open-cast mines or the destruction of forest following the mechanized removal of commercially valuable timber (figure 21.4) (Sillitoe and Wilson 2003; Filer, Burton and Banks 2008; Filer et al. 2009). They are left with little more than a large environmental headache after the royalty party, as Emma Gilberthorpe, Sarah Clarke and I describe (chapter 7), with little in the way of enduring development. Neither national government nor local communities make other than minimal investments in enterprises that will continue after the exploitation of natural resources. It is possible that ignorance of the full implications of proposed extraction activities may sometimes lead people to conclude agreements that with fuller knowledge of the outcomes, notably the environmental costs, they might not enter into. Even so, the environmental damage occurs, inevitably the consequence of such exploitation of natural resources, which itself is unavoidably unsustainable – once an area is logged or mined that is an end of it, the resource is exhausted.

What are the implications of such green-untuned attitudes, which often correlate with recent lifestyle changes that distance people from the environment? Some suggest the addition of a fifth *E* pillar to the sustainable development flipchart: education. This book seeks to contribute to this pillar, informing people about the sustainability debate, particularly those living in the Gulf, who currently follow one of the world's least

Figure 21.4. Logging forest near Vanimo in Papua New Guinea.

sustainable lifestyles. Several contributors recommend raising awareness through education, informing people about the issues so that they appreciate the urgency of taking action and the majority supports it, so making sustainable development a reality. Any such program of formal education demands cultural sensitivity and respect for what local people think and know, in promoting awareness of, and discussion of environmental issues, so that they may conclude in their own way what action to take.

In short, participation needs again to be genuine. Otherwise there is a danger that people may see formal education as the ethnocentric imposition of foreign views, amounting to brainwashing about sustainability, which appears to be a particularly Western concern, hardening opposition, as noted, to advocacy of sustainable development and resistance to interventions thought necessary to counteract local activities considered responsible for environmental degradation, suspected by some as cover for continued Western economic hegemony. Furthermore, education is necessary in all directions – to inform international agencies and national governments and local populations about one another's views. But it takes time, arguably generations, to have an effect, when environmental problems are urgent and demand measures now. It is a further conundrum. It is not politically feasible to force people to agree, let alone comply with a global green mandate, inviting taunts about 'eco-fascism'. While the IK approach may assist us in both developing sustainably and sustaining development, it is not straightforward, for it has somehow to accommodate such contradictions that plague development.

Ecologically and Culturally Sustainable Endogenous Development

Sustainable development presents us with many puzzles. But we have to strive to solve them, however contrary the challenges may appear, not only to reduce global poverty, but also, it is not hyperbole to argue, to save the planet as we know it. Its flawed efforts to date notwithstanding, giving up on development is not an option, whatever some critics may seem to suggest (Escobar 1995; Crush 1995; Schech and Haggis 2000). The improvement of peoples' standard of living, however they conceive it, particularly the reduction of hunger and disease globally, is a noble aim. We have to learn from past mistakes and push on.

The export of industrial technology and capitalist market arrangements does not look wise from a sustainable perspective. We need to challenge the ethos of the Doha Declaration and think beyond economic growth to ways sustainably to improve people's life chances. But how can we do this and yet lift people out of poverty globally or indeed prevent us all sinking into it with despoliation of the globe? The proposed fourth endogenous *E* sustainable development 'pillar' offers one way forwards, not only to benefit the poor, but also, in seeking to promote more sustainable lifestyles, to benefit everyone. An appreciation of local ideas and practices should encourage more sustainable development interventions in both the ecological and cultural senses, as it often represents understanding rooted in highly sustainable adaptations (Jordan and O'Riordan 2000). Reviewing the philosophies and lifeways of others we have presumed to date to assist 'develop' may also help us achieve needed environmental balance. We have something to learn from them about sustainability in revising our values and relations with nature, without falling into the trap of over-romanticization (Ellen 2000).

While the IK approach offers opportunities, there are substantial obstacles to its meaningful incorporation into development. It does not suggest, as some mistakenly assume, turning the clock back and heading off on camels into the desert with tents and flocks, rather it advocates a coming together of industrial/scientific technology with more sustainable ways of being in the world (Sillitoe 2007), potentially to the benefit of all. But the approach has considerable implications for current political-economic arrangements, predictably if other views of what might constitute development diverge to the extent suggested from the orthodox one. Real politick indicates that there is not going to be any sudden revolution in the way the world's wealthy nations conduct business. They are unlikely to forgo any of their control, in the foreseeable future anyway, to the less powerful to determine the use of resources invested in development.

The IK approach consequently proceeds on two fronts. On one, it seeks in the short-term to work with organizations that are pursuing development in the business-as-usual, largely top-down centrally planned manner, with the aim of increasing awareness and consideration of local views and knowledge, to benefit those currently excluded. On the other front, it seeks in the long term to change the terms of the debate, to consider what other views of development to the currently dominant Western one might look like, and how these might be given the space to express themselves and communities a chance to act on them. This assumes that the so-called developed world does not despoil the planet irrevocably in the meantime with its unsustainable economic activities, which it seeks to export elsewhere in the name of development, for changing values takes time, even generations to have effect. In this event humanity will wish that we had allowed those following more sustainable life ways to have developed the so-called developed.

Notes

1. When I gave a lecture likewise entitled 'A Doha Undeclaration' at Qatar University, on which this chapter draws, the interpreter quizzed me anxiously as to its meaning because he could not translate it into Arabic, taking it literally and not appreciating its punning criticism of The Doha Declaration's reaffirmation of capitalist business as usual.

2. As Bob Monks, who pioneered shareholder activism in the United States, comments in *The Corporation,* an award-winning documentary, 'It's almost as if we have created a doom machine in our search for wealth and prosperity. We've created something that's going to destroy us' (Richards 2007: 10).

3. Some argue that we can achieve economic growth without further exploiting natural resources by advancing more resource-efficient technologies, but at present this seems utopian, particularly given the numbers of poor people in the world whose material standards of living development seeks to improve.

4. In an early discussion of these issues, O'Riordan (1981) labels as 'ecocentric' such views of nature that attribute her inherent value, contrasting with our 'anthropocentric' view of nature that sees her as a source of resources exploitable in our service.

5. This is a wholly inadequate word to convey the profundity of related Aboriginal beliefs, and you should not make the mistake of equating it with the whimsical European notion of dreams nor recent ideas of Freudian psychiatry.

6. As an aside, I might note that some have criticized anthropologists, particularly earlier generations, for writing about cultures at one instance in time as if unchanging (what in the jargon they call the ethnographic present, or worse, the synchronic frame of reference). Arguably they represented the views of those they studied who thought of tradition as unchanging, as some people still do. These critics are open to criticism as ethnocentric, in seeking to impose on such people our obsession with rapid social change and history as a linear series of events stretching back in time.
7. Calls for popular participation on the left often feature gender-focused interventions, with appropriate guidance, to socially engineer unwanted local arrangements out of existence.
8. Experience to date of various global intergovernmental meetings and the signing of agreements under the auspices of various international UN bodies do not make for optimism, including progress in implementing the UN Framework Convention on Climate Change and associated Kyoto Protocol, and the UN Convention on Biological Diversity (Reid 1995: 182–190; Adams 2001: 83–95; Baker 2006: 82–93).
9. Assessments of community forestry in Nepal are not invariably negative (e.g. see Soussan 2004: 92–96).

References

Adams, W. M. 2001. *Green Development: Environment and Sustainability in the Third World*. London: Routledge.
Al-Azmeh, A. 2003. *Ibn Khaldun: An Essay in Reinterpretation*. Budapest: Central European University Press.
Ayres, A. 2004. 'Xochimilco's Sunken Treasure.' *New Scientist* 192 (2442): 50–51.
Baker, S. 2006. *Sustainable Development*. London: Routledge.
Banjade, M. R., H. Luintel and H. Neupane. 2008. 'Action Research on Democratising Knowledge in Community Forestry in Nepal.' In *Knowledge Systems and Natural Resources: Management, Policy and Institutions in Nepal*, eds. H. R. Ojha, et al., 110–134. Delhi: Foundation Books.
Barbier, E. B. 2010. *A Global Green New Deal: Rethinking the Economic Recovery*. Cambridge: Cambridge University Press.
Barnett, T. 1977a *The Gezira Scheme: An Illusion of Development*. London: Frank Cass.
———. 1977b. 'The Gezira Scheme: Black Box or Pandora's box?' University of East Anglia Development Studies Discussion Paper No. 45.
Barnett, T., and A. Abdelkarim. 1991. *Sudan: The Gezira Scheme and Agricultural Transition*. London: Frank Cass.
Bonine, M. E. 1996. 'Qanats and Rural Societies: Sustainable Agriculture and Irrigation Cultures in Contemporary Iran.' In *Canals and Communities: Small-Scale Irrigation Systems*, ed. J. B. Mabry, 183–209. Tucson: University of Arizona Press.

Brundtland Commission (World Commission on Environment and Development). 1987. *Our Common Future*. Oxford: Oxford University Press.

Campbell, B. 2004. 'Indigenous Views on the Terms of Participation in the Development of Biodiversity Conservation in Nepal.' In *Investigating Local Knowledge: New Directions, New Approaches*, eds. A. Bicker, P. Sillitoe and J. Pottier, 149–167. Aldershot: Ashgate

Carney, D. (ed.). 1998. *Sustainable Rural Livelihoods: What Contribution Can We Make?* London: Department for International Development.

Collier, P. 2010. *The Plundered Planet: Why We Must – and How We Can – Manage Nature for Global Prosperity*. Oxford: Oxford University Press.

Cressey, G. B. 1958. 'Qanats, Karez and Foggaras.' *Geographical Review* 48 (1): 27–44.

Department for International Development (DFID). n.d. Sustainable Livelihoods Guidance Sheets. London.

Diamond, J. 1997. *Guns, Germs, and Steel: A Short History of Everybody for the Last 13,000 Years*. London: Jonathan Cape.

Dixon, P., and J. Gorecki. 2010. *Sustainagility: How Smart Innovation and Agile Companies will Help Protect our Future*. Philadelphia, PA: Kogan Page.

Elkin, A. P. 1979. *The Australian Aborigines*. Sydney: Angus and Robertson.

Ellen, R. 2000. 'Local Knowledge and Sustainable Development in Developing Countries.' In *Global Sustainable Development in the 21st Century*, eds. K. Lee, A. Holland and D. McNeill, 163–186. Edinburgh: Edinburgh University Press.

Elliot, J. A. 1994. *An Introduction to Sustainable Development: The Developing World*. London: Routledge.

Fauset, C. 2008. *Techno-Fixes: A Critical Guide to Climate Change Technologies*. London: Corporate Watch.

Feeney, P. 1998. *Accountable Aid: Local Participation in Major Projects*. Oxford: Oxfam Publications.

Filer, C., J. Burton and G. Banks. 2008. 'The Fragmentation of Responsibilities in the Melanesian Mining Sector.' In *Earth Matters: Indigenous Peoples, the Extractive Industry and Corporate Social Responsibility*, eds. C. O'Faircheallaigh and S. Ali, 163–179. London: Greenleaf Publishing.

Filer, C., et al. 2009. 'Deforestation and Forest Degradation in Papua New Guinea.' *Annals of Forest Science* 66: 813.

Gaitskell, A. 1959. *Gezira: A Story of Development in the Sudan*. London: Faber & Faber.

Gammage, B. 2011. *The Biggest Estate on Earth: How Aborigines Made Australia*. Sydney: Allen and Unwin.

Gellner, E. 1975. 'Cohesion and Identity: The Maghreb from Ibn Khaldun to Emile Durkheim.' *Government and Opposition* 10 (2): 203–218.

Gibson, J. 2007. 'Communities Out of Place.' In *Sustainability and Communities of Place*, ed. C. A. Maida, 63–81. Oxford: Berghahn Books.

Goblot, H. 1979. *Les qanats: une technique d'acqusition de l'eau*. Paris: Mouton.

Grainger, A. 2004. 'Introduction.' In *Exploring Sustainable Development: Geographical Perspectives*, eds. M. Purvis and A. Grainger, 1–32. London: Earthscan.

Gray, H. L. 1959. *English Field Systems*. London: Merlin Press.

Harrison, N. E. 2014. *Sustainable Capitalism and the Pursuit of Well-Being*. London: Routledge.

Haverkort, B., and W. Heimstra (eds.). 1999. *Food for Thought: Ancient Visions and New Experiments of Rural People*. London: Zed Books.

Haverkort, B., K. van't Hooft and W. Heimstra (eds.). 2003. *Ancient Roots, New Shoots: Endogenous Development in Practice*. Leusden: COMPAS; London: Zed Books.

Heinberg, R. 2010. 'Beyond the Limits to Growth.' In *The Post Carbon Reader*, eds. R. Heinberg and D. Lerch, 3–12. Healdsburg: Watershed Media.

———. 2011. *The End of Growth: Adapting to Our New Economic Reality*. Gabriola Island, BC: New Society Pubs.

Hildyard, N., et al. 2001. 'Pluralism, Participation and Power: Joint Forest Management in India.' In *Participation: The New Tyranny?* eds. B. Cooke and U. Kothari, 56–71. London: Zed Books.

Hinterberger, F. 1994. 'Biological, Cultural and Economic Evolution and the Economy-Ecology Relationship.' In *Toward Sustainable Development: Concepts, Methods, and Policy*, eds. J. C. J. M. van den Bergh and J. van der Straaten, 57–81. Washington, DC: Island Press.

Jackson, T. 2009. *Prosperity Without Growth*. London: Earthscan.

Jordan, A., and T. O'Riordan. 2000. 'Environmental Politics and Policy Processes.' In *Environmental Science for Environmental Management*, ed. T. O'Riordan, 63–92. Harlow: Prentice Hall.

Latouch, S. 1995. *La mégamachine. Raison scientifique, raison économique et mythe du progrès*. Paris: La Découverte.

Lee, K. 2000. 'Global Sustainable Development: Its Intellectual and Historical Roots.' In *Global Sustainable Development in the 21ˢᵗ Century*, eds. K. Lee, A. Holland and D. McNeill, 31–47. Edinburgh: Edinburgh University Press.

Lévi-Strauss, C. 1966. *The Savage Mind*. London: Weidenfeld and Nicolson.

Malthus, T. R. 1806. *An Essay on the Principle of Population*. 3rd edition. London: Printed for J. Johnson by T. Bensley.

Martinez-Alier, J. 1994. 'Distributional Conflicts and International Policy on Carbon Dioxide Emissions and Agricultural Diversity.' In *Toward Sustainable Development: Concepts, Methods, and Policy*, eds. J. C. J. M. van den Bergh and J. van der Straaten, 235–263. Washington, DC: Island Press.

Meadows, D. H., et al. 1972. *The Limits to Growth: A Report for the Club of Rome's Project on the Predicament of Mankind*. New York: Universe Books.

Meadows, D. H., D. L. Meadows and J. Randers. 1992. *Beyond the Limits: Global Collapse or a Sustainable Future*. London: Earthscan.

Meadows, D. H., J. Randers and D. L. Meadows. 2004. *Limits to Growth: The 30-Year Update*. White River Junction, VT: Chelsea Green Pub. Co.

Middleton, N., and P. O'Keefe. 2001. *Redefining Sustainable Development*. London: Pluto Press.

Moody, J. B., and B. Nogrady. 2010. *The Sixth Wave: How to Succeed in a Resource-Limited World*. Sydney: Vintage.

Mosse, D. 2001. '"People's Knowledge", Participation and Patronage: Operations and Representations in Rural Development.' In *Participation: The New Tyranny?* eds. B. Cooke and U. Kothari, 16–35. London: Zed Books.

————. 2005. *Cultivating Development: An Ethnography of Aid Policy and Practice*. London: Pluto.

Motiee, H., et al. 2006. 'Assessment of the Contributions of Traditional *Qanats* in Sustainable Water Resources Management.' *Journal of Water Resources Development* 22 (4): 575–588.

Nye, P. H., and D. J. Greenland. 1960. *The Soil Under Shifting Cultivation*. Harpenden: Commonwealth Bureau of Soils Technical Bulletin No. 51.

O'Riordan, T. 1981. *Environmentalism*. London: Pion Press.

Oakley, P., and D. Marsden. 1984. *Approaches to Participation in Rural Development*. Geneva: International Labour Office.

Pearce, D., and E. B. Barbier. 2000. *Blueprint for a sustainable economy*. London: Earthscan.

Pearce, D., E. B. Barbier and A. Markandya. 1990. *Sustainable development: economics and environment in the Third World*. Aldershot: Edward Elgar.

Pezzey, J. 1989. *Definitions of Sustainability*. London: C.E.E.D.

Ramprasad, V., G. Krishnaprasad and S. Manasi. 2003. 'The Path of Rediscovery.' In *Ancient Roots, New Shoots: Endogenous Development in Practice*, eds. B. Haverkort et al., 89–101. Leusden: COMPAS; London: Zed Books.

Raynaut, C., et al. 2007. 'Sustainability: Where, When, for Whom? Past, Present and Future of a Local Rural Population in a Protected Natural Area (Guaraqueçaba, Brazil).' In *Sustainability and Communities of Place*, ed. C. A. Maida, 21–40. Oxford: Berghahn Books.

Redclift, M. R. 1987. *Sustainable Development: Exploring the Contradictions*. London: Methuen.

————. 1999. 'Dancing With Wolves? Sustainability and the Social Sciences.' In *Sustainability and the Social Sciences: A Cross-Disciplinary Approach to Integrating Environmental Considerations into Theoretical Reorientation*, eds. E. Becker and T. Kahn, 267–273. London: Zed Books.

————. 2002. 'Discourses of Sustainable Development.' In *The Companion to Development Studies*, eds. V. Deasi and R. B. Potter, 275–278. London: Arnold.

Reid, D. 1995. *Sustainable Development: An Introductory Guide*. London: Earthscan.

Richards, P. 2007. 'Why Greed isn't Good.' *CAM Cambridge Alumni Magazine* 52 (Michaelmas Term): 10–13.

Robertson, M. 2014. *Sustainability principles and practice*. London: Earthscan from Routledge.

Saberwal, V., M. Rangharajan and A. Kothari. 2001. *People, Parks and Wildlife: Towards Coexistence*. New Delhi: Orient Longman.

Shankar, G. 2003. 'Building on Tribal Resources: Endogenous Development in the North Eastern Ghats.' In *Ancient Roots, New Shoots: Endogenous Development in Practice*, eds. B. Haverkort et al., 115–128. Leusden: COMPAS; London: Zed Books.

Shepherd, A. 1998. *Sustainable Rural Development*. London: Macmillan Press.

Sillitoe, P. 2004. 'Interdisciplinary Experiences: Working with Indigenous Knowledge in Development.' *Interdisciplinary Science Reviews* 29 (1): 6–23.

————. 2006. 'Introduction: Indigenous Knowledge in Development.' *Anthropology in Action* 13 (3): 1–12.

——— (ed.). 2007. *Local Science vs Global Science: Approaches To Indigenous Knowledge In International Development*. Oxford: Berghahn Books.

Sillitoe, P., P. Dixon and J. Barr. 2005. *Indigenous Knowledge Inquiries: A Methodologies Manual for Development*. London: Intermediate Technology Publications.

Sillitoe, P., and M. Marzano. 2009. 'Future of Indigenous Knowledge Research in Development.' *Futures* 41 (1): 13–23.

Sillitoe, P., and R. A. Wilson. 2003. 'Playing on the Pacific Ring of Fire: Negotiation and Knowledge in Mining in Papua New Guinea.' In *Negotiating Local Knowledge: Power and Identity in Development*, eds. J. Pottier, A. Bicker and P. Sillitoe, 241–272. London: Pluto.

Soussan, J. 2004. 'Linking the Local to the Global: Can Sustainable Development Work in Practice?' In *Exploring Sustainable Development: Geographical Perspectives*, eds. M. Purvis and A. Grainger, 85–98. London: Earthscan.

Thornton, T. F. 2007. 'Alaska Native Corporations and Subsistence: Paradoxical Forces in the Making of Sustainable Communities.' In *Sustainability and Communities of Place*, ed. C. A. Maida, 41–62. Oxford: Berghahn Books.

World Trade Organization (WTO). 2011. 'The Doha Declaration Explained.' http://www.wto.org/english/tratop_e/dda_e/dohaexplained_e.htm.

Notes on Contributors

Ali A. Alraouf is Development and Research Coordinator with the Qatar National Master Plan, and was previously professor of Architecture, Urban Design and Planning Theories in the College of Arts and Sciences at Qatar University. He is an architect and urban designer researching architectural, urban and environmental design. He holds a PhD in architecture (University of California at Berkeley 1996), a master's of Architecture (1991), and a bachelor's of Architecture (1986) from Cairo University. He was a visiting scholar at the Center for Environmental Design Research at U.C. Berkeley (1993–1995). Professor Alraouf has held teaching positions at Cairo University, U.C. Berkeley, 6th October University, Modern Sciences and Arts University (MSA) and the High Institute of Architecture and University of Bahrain. His current research interests are: contemporary architectural education, the role of sustainable architecture in preserving natural environments, traditional smart buildings; the impact of globalization on the built environment, and Gulf cities' urban development. He is the recipient of the award for Best Research Paper from the Sharjah Urban Planning International Symposium 2009. He is the author of more than fifty papers and three books, and writes extensively in newspapers, periodicals and architectural magazines locally and internationally.

Ali Alshawi is assistant professor of Sociology in the Department of Social Sciences, Qatar University. He received his doctorate in Sociology in 2002 from Mississippi State University. His area of specialization is political sociology. He has held a Fulbright scholarship at the University of Michigan to research the place of tribalism in historical and contemporary Gulf society. He made a presentation entitled 'Tribal Self: The Ethics of Tribalism and the Spirit of Modernity' at an International Conference on Indigenous Studies and Engaged Anthropology held at Durham University. He is currently working with Paul Sillitoe on a Qatar National Research Fund project, funded by a grant from the National Research Priorities Program, which is continuing the work on the Al Reem biosphere in west Qatar that is the subject of their chapter to this volume.

Ben Campbell is lecturer in the Anthropology Department, Durham University, and is director of the master's degree programme in anthropology and sustainable development. He earned his PhD at the School of Development Studies, University of East Anglia. He has acted as social advisor to the former Overseas Development Administration, and has lectured on the anthropology of development at the universities of Edinburgh, Keele, Manchester and Hull, before becoming degree director of the MSc in Development Anthropology at Durham. He received an ESRC research award for 'Himalayan Biodiversity and Human Interests' (1997–1998), and worked in a cross European project on Public Understanding of Genetics (2002–2004). He is currently reviewing the comparative effects of sustainable development projects among indigenous communities in South Asia.

Sarah F. Clarke is vice chairman, DSC Solutions Co. WLL, Budaiya, Kingdom of Bahrain. She is a graduate of Bath University, Manchester Business School and the Schulich School of Business, York University, Toronto, where she completed her PhD in sustainable technology management. She has over twenty years of international experience across academic and not-for-profit sectors in fields including disability awareness, environmental sustainability, inclusive education, animal welfare and tourism. She is committed to developing environmentally sustainable solutions to complex community-based problems through the development of knowledge-based networks. While in Qatar she worked on various sustainability projects for the Qatar Green Business Council. An accomplished writer, she most recently authored a book, *101 Things to See and Do in Istanbul.*

Robin Coningham is pro-vice chancellor of the Faculty of Social Sciences and Health at Durham University, and Professor of Medieval Archaeology within the Department of Archaeology. He has worked extensively throughout South Asia and Iran, including the World Heritage Sites of Lumbini in Nepal and Anuradhapura in Sri Lanka. In addition he has undertaken excavations at Charsadda in Pakistan and Tepe Pardis and Sialk in Iran. He has worked as a UNESCO Consultant to Pakistan and Nepal, and is a fellow of the Royal Asiatic Society and Trustee of the Ancient India and Iran Trust. He is a director of the Centre for Ethics and Cultural Heritage at Durham University. His research interests include: the archaeology of Buddhism; caste and the development of craft specialisation; Indian Ocean trade; international cultural resource management; South Asian archaeology; politics, identity and archaeology; urbanization; and the prehistory of Iran.

Bahaa Darwish is a professor at Minya University, Egypt, and founding member of the International Association of Education in Ethics at GE Healthcare. He was formerly an associate professor in Philosophy at the College of Arts and Sciences, Qatar University. His interests in philosophical issues are wide ranging: theory of knowledge, philosophy of mind, philosophy of language, logic, critical thinking bio-ethics and ethics of science and technology. He has participated in numerous local, regional and international conferences covering these philosophical issues. He has published several books and papers, his most recent published book being his translation of Alfred J. Ayer's book *Philosophy in the Twentieth Century* (2005) preceded by a study on 'Ayer's philosophical position in the 20th Century'; he has also written on the legitimacy and limits of gene therapy.

Mark Eggerman is a research scientist in Global Health and Area Studies at the Macmillan Center for Area and International Studies, Yale University. In his recent research on the 'Resilience and Mental Health in Afghanistan' project – a project designed to integrate cross-cultural psychiatric epidemiology with medical anthropology – he conducted the first longitudinal survey of child and adolescent mental health in Afghanistan. It provided evidence for the cluster of adversities that impact family well-being and the mental health across generations, and identified culturally-meaningful leverage points for building family-level resilience, relevant to the prevention and intervention agenda in global mental health.

Hassan Fazeli is professor of Archaeology at Tehran University in Iran. He is currently the Marie Curie International Fellow at the Archaeology Department at the University of Reading. He was Director of the Iranian Centre for Archaeological Research, the government organization responsible for overseeing all archaeological and heritage work in Iran. Hassan has conducted and facilitated many international archaeological projects in different parts of Iran, mainly on the Neolithic and Chalcolithic periods. Hassan is working on a book entitled *Ancient Iran: A Social Archaeology*, which presents a new interpretation of Iran's past from the Palaeolithic to the end of the Achaemenid Empire.

Andrew M. Gardner is associate professor of Anthropology at the University of Puget Sound in Tacoma, Washington. Between 2008 and 2010, he also served as an assistant professor of Anthropology at Qatar University. He is a socio-cultural anthropologist and ethnographer by training. For the past decade, his fieldwork has been focused on the peoples and societies of the petroleum-rich states of the Arabian peninsula. He has conducted extensive fieldwork in Saudi Arabia, the United Arab Emirates, Bahrain and Qatar. In addition to numerous journal articles and book chapters, he is the author of *City of Strangers: Gulf Migration and the Indian Community in Bahrain* (Cornell, 2010), which explores the experiences of Indian transnational migrants in Bahrain and the society that hosts them, and more recently, the co-editor of *Constructing Qatar: Migrant Narratives from the Margins of the Global System* (2012), an ebook that illuminates the experiences and perspectives of transnational labour migrants in Qatar.

Kaltham Al-Ghanim is associate professor in the Sociology Program in the Department of Social Sciences in Qatar University. She has a Ph.D. in sociology from Ain Shams University-Egypt (1995). She has carried out field survey research on topics relating to human and cultural development, social problems, domestic violence, gender and youth identity problems. She is author of three books and several government reports. She has been and is currently involved in several research projects in Qatar funded by grants from the National Research Priorities Program of the Qatar National Research Fund working on these sociological issues, notably gender and violence. Her interests cover a wide range of issues including woman studies, social problems, consanguineous marriages, sustainable development, local culture, folklore and heritage. She has published research articles, including *The hierarchy of authority based on kinship, age, and gender in the extended family in Arab Gulf States* and *The intellectual frameworks and theoretical limits of Arab feminist thought.*

Emma Gilberthorpe is a senior lecturer in Anthropology and International Development at the University of East Anglia and previously held a Royal Anthropological Insititute Urgent Anthropology Fellowship at Durham University. She has a PhD from the University of Queensland, Australia. She has conducted extensive research on the social, political and economic impacts of mineral extraction, focusing on issues of long-term sustainability, resource dependency, and protracted poverty. Her main area of expertise is Papua New Guinea where she has worked with the Fasu and Min ethnic groups since 2000. She is author of *Development and Industry: A Papua New Guinea Case Study* (2009) and joint editor of *Natural Resource Extraction and Indigenouis Livelihoods* (2014).

Gavin Gillmore is professor of Environmental Geoscience and Head of School of Geography, Geology and the Environment, Kingston University, United Kingdom. He has a PhD in Geology from University College, London (1990). His research concerns geohazards, notably of Radon, a naturally occurring radioactive gas that comes from the decay of uranium in rocks and soils, and he is Director of the Radon Council UK (the regulatory body for the radon remediation industry). His work currently includes health risk assessments for archaeologists and earth scientists working in confined spaces such as caves. He also has interests in palaeoenvironments, and is Research Associate at Exploro, Norway, where he works on palaeoenvironmental and palaeobathymetric analysis.

Fadwa El Guindi was formerly a distinguished professor and head of the Department of Social Sciences, at Qatar University, and is currently the program manager of Pillar of Social Sciences, Arts, and Humanities at Qatar National Research Fund, Qatar Foundation, Doha. She earned her bachelor's in Political Science from the American University in Cairo and her PhD in Anthropology from the University of Texas at Austin. She has taught at the University of California, Los Angeles, the University of Southern California and at Georgetown University. She is a noted anthropologist who has published widely and lectures internationally. Her expertise on the Middle East brought her to the Clinton White House for a meeting with the president. She is a past president of the Middle East Section of the American Anthropological Association and the Association's Society for Visual Anthropology. She has made a number of anthropological films on Arab society and is the author of many research articles and books, including *Veil: Modesty, Privacy and Resistance* and *By Noon Prayer: The Rhythm of Islam.*

Serena Heckler works in international development. She received her doctorate in Ethnobotany, Environmental Anthropology and Sustainable Development from Cornell University and was a Nuffield Early Career Development Fellow at Durham University. She has lived and worked with the Wõthɨ̃hã of the Venezuelan Amazon, studying the ways in which the market economy and demographic change have affected their environmental knowledge. She also undertook participatory research on similar themes with the Shuar of Ecuador, in collaboration with the Intercultural University of Indigenous Peoples and Nations-Amawtay Wasi based in Quito, Ecuador. She is editor of *Landscape, Power and Process: Reevaluating Traditional Environmental Knowledge* (Berghahn Books, 2009) and numerous journal articles.

Thomas Henfrey was formerly a teaching fellow and research fellow in the Anthropology Department at Durham University, and is now senior researcher and learning programmes coordinator at the Schumacher Institute for Sustainable Systems in Bristol, UK. He studied Biological Sciences at Oxford University and completed a PhD in Environmental Anthropology at Kent University, based on research on indigenous forest use in Guyana. His work on social and cultural dimensions of energy transition combine academic and practical interests; he is a professionally qualified designer of small-scale solar power installations, cofounded an eco-village in Spain, and is active in a range of grassroots environmental initiatives. He helped initiate and co-coordinates the Transition Research Network, that seeks to improve collaboration between researchers and community-based sustainability initiatives, and is a member of the UK Permaculture Association's Research Advisory Board..

James Howard is a postdoctoral research fellow at the Marine Research Institute of the University of Cape Town, where he is working on an international interdisciplinary project researching the vulnerability of coastal communities to climate change, having previously worked as a research assistant at the School of Marine Science and Technology, at Newcastle University and as a volunteer in Botswana with an NGO on a human-wildlife conflict project. He studied his MSc at the University of Cape Town in Applied Marine Sciences where he studied regime shifts in a large marine ecosystem off southern Africa working towards an ecosystem-based approach to fisheries management. He has a PhD from Durham University for interdisciplinary research focusing on the trade in marine ornamental reef fish in Sri Lanka, which looked at both the ecological impacts of this trade on the coral reefs and fish as well as the socio-economic and socio-cultural effects on fishing communities and alternative livelihoods for the ornamental fishers.

Aziza Al-Khalaqi is a researcher in the Social Development Department of the General Secretariat for Development Planning, Qatar and a graduate of the University of Qatar. She supports and contributes to research on social issues generally in the State of Qatar. She contributed to the preparation of Qatar's National Development Strategy, 2011–2016, which supports the Qatar National Vision 2030, which is a statement of Qatar's strategic goals and the challenges. She was a researcher for the 2012 Qatar Human Development Report.

Najla Al-Khulaifi has a bachelor's in Sociology from Qatar University and is a researcher in the Social Development Department of the General Secretariat for Development Planning. She supports and contributes to research related to the education and labour-market sectors. She has actively supported the preparation of Qatar's National Development Strategy, 2011–2016 and was a researcher for the 2012 Qatar Human Development Report. While at Qatar University she also played a key role in AIESEC, a global student organization.

Salah Almannai is director of services and consulting at the Qatar Foundation for Child and Woman Protection. He was formerly assistant professor of Social Work in the Department of Social Sciences, Qatar University. He earned his doctorate at the University of Leicester in 2006. He specializes in social welfare, women's rights, youth and social movements. He contributed a background paper entitled Youth Development through Education for the 2012 Qatar Human Development Report.

Mark Manuel is a postdoctoral research associate in the Department of Archaeology at Durham University. His PhD research focused upon the Indus civilization and argued that existing models are routed in ethnocentric interpretations of the archaeological record. He is currently working on projects at Anuradhapura in Sri Lanka, and Tepe Pardis, Sialk and Darabgerd in Iran. His research interests include: South Asian archaeology; the development of urban communities in South Asia; the relationship between urban and non-urban communities; the history of South Asian archaeology; and archaeological survey methodologies.

Sheikha Abdulla Al-Misnad is president (vice chancellor) of Qatar University and a minister of state in the Qatar government. She has a bachelor's and Diploma in Education from Qatar University (1977) and a PhD from the University of Durham. She has served on Qatar's Supreme Education Council, entrusted with the reform of publicly funded education. Under her leadership, the university has forged collaborative relations with leading universities and research centres around the world. She is involved with the Qatar Foundation for Education and the flagship Education City, a group of educational institutions that includes, among others, the Qatar Academy, an international school, where she has served ex-officio member of the Board of Governors. She is a passionate advocate for women's education in the Gulf region and the author of *The Development of Modern Education in the Gulf States with Special Reference to Women's Education* (Ithaca Press, 1985).

Wesam Al Othman is associate professor in the Department of Social Sciences, Qatar University. She earned a PhD in Medical Anthropology from Cairo University. Her research interests are on family, women, health issues, environmental issues and culture. She has written a textbook on cultural anthropology and is presently carrying out research and is co-authoring publications on Khaliji dress. She has worked with Fadwa El Guindi on Qatar National Research Fund projects, from the Undergraduate Research Experience Program, on Qatari milk kinship. She is currently working with Paul Sillitoe on a Qatar National Research Fund project, with a grant from the National Research Priorities Program, conducting research on the Al Reem biosphere in west Qatar.

Catherine Panter-Brick is professor of Anthropology at Yale University. Her research creates new interdisciplinary perspectives for evaluating human health, bridging the fields of biological, social and medical anthropology with the field of public health. She focuses her work on critical risks to health and well-being across key stages of human development, and has directed over twenty interdisciplinary projects in Afghanistan, Ethiopia, the Gambia, Nepal, Niger, Pakistan, Saudi Arabia, Tanzania and the United Kingdom. She has co-edited many books bridging research and teaching practice, and fostering interdisciplinary understanding on issues relevant to human biology and society. These include *Hunter Gatherers; Abandoned Children; Hormones, Health and Behaviour;* and *Biosocial Perspectives on Children,* all published by Cambridge University Press. Her most recent co-edited book is *Health, Risk and Adversity,* published by Berghahn Books. She serves on the editorial board of a number of journals, and is senior editor in Medical Anthropology for the interdisciplinary journal *Social Science & Medicine.*

Gina Porter is a senior research fellow in the Anthropology Department at Durham University. She has undertaken extensive research in sub-Saharan Africa (particularly South Africa, Ghana, Nigeria and Malawi), including studies of gendered mobility and transport, NGO-state relations, youth social networks, trade and market institutions and trade-related conflict. She has a particular interest in developing innovative methodologies for effective field research (action research, child-centred research, networked approaches). She currently directs an ESRC/DfID funded research project in various African nations entitled 'The impact of mobile phones on young people's lives and life chances in sub-Saharan Africa: a three-country study to inform policy and practice'. She is also transport services adviser to the DFID-funded Africa Community Access Programme [AFCAP] which supports transport research and knowledge sharing in a number of African countries.

Khondker Rahman is senior environmental planner and team leader for the Qatar National Master Plan (QNMP) Specialists' and Experts' Group responsible for developing the sustainability evaluation framework and undertaking environmental management strategies. He has over twenty-eight years of experience – working in Thailand, Bangladesh, India, Australia and now in Qatar – in the fields of strategic environmental and water-resources planning, project management, and most recently development and implementation of environmental and sustainability-related policies and regulatory tools. His work on policies reflects a strong focus on minimizing environmental impacts through sustainable planning and design considerations and taking into account climate change issues and minimizing ecological and carbon footprint. He has developed a number of related guidelines and presented at many international symposiums and conferences.

Mylène Riva, PhD, is assistant professor in the Département de Médecine sociale et préventive, Université Laval, Axe Santé des populations et pratiques optimales en santé, Centre de recherche du CHU de Québec, Qc, Canada. She was previously a postdoctoral researcher at the Department of Geography at Durham University, England. She holds a bachelor's degree in Geography and a PhD in Public Health and Health Promotion from Université de Montréal in Canada. Her research is interdisciplinary, applying theories and mixed methods from epidemiology, geography and social sciences to study the social and geographical distribution of health and of the determinants of health in societies. Her work focuses on investigating how the changing socio-economic and natural conditions of local areas impact on population health, health-related behaviours and well-being over the course of life.

Paul Sillitoe is professor of Anthropology at Durham University, England. His research interests focus on natural resource management strategies. A champion of local knowledge in development, he specializes in international development and social change, livelihood and technology, environment and conservation, political ecology and land issues, human ecology and ethno-science. He seeks to further the incorporation of indigenous knowledge in development, particularly in the context of sustainable livelihood initiatives and appropriate technologies, by furthering understanding of local knowledge and the sympathetic tailoring of development initiatives to it, and has experience of working with several international development agencies. He has conducted extensive fieldwork in the Southwest Pacific region, and South Asia researching local environmental knowledge, and is currently working in the Gulf region on sustainable development initiatives and conservation issues.

Trudy Tan was formerly a social development expert in the Social Development Department of the General Secretariat for Development Planning. She obtained her master's in Development Studies from the University of East Anglia and is a Chartered Financial Analyst Level II from the Association for Investment Management and Research. She was responsible for human development programmes, including technical support for the National Human Development Report, and for formulating new social and human development projects of priority to achieve the Qatar National

Vision 2030. She played a key role in the development of Qatar's Second Human Development Report, Advancing Sustainable Development, which was launched in July 2009. Ms Tan formerly served for three years as programme manager at the United Nations Development Programme, Malaysia. During her tenure at UNDP, she worked in the areas of trade and human development, HIV/AIDS policy, public-private partnerships and gender. She was also UNDP Malaysia's focal point for private sector partnerships and entrepreneurial development.

Rodney Wilson is an emeritus professor in the International Centre for Education in Islamic Finance (INCEIF), Malaysia and an emeritus professor of Economics at Durham University. He has been involved in research and teaching in Islamic economics and finance for over thirty years and he founded the Durham University Islamic Finance Programme. Before joining INCEIF he was a visiting professor at the Qatar Faculty of Islamic Studies. He has extensive consultancy experience including with the African Development Bank (2011 and 2012), the Qatar Central Bank (2010) and the Islamic Financial Services Board Working Group on *Shari'ah* Governance (2007–2009). He has authored twelve books and over fifty articles. His most recent books are *Legal, Regulatory and Governance Issues in Islamic Finance* (Edinburgh University Press, 2012) and *Economic Development in the Middle East* (Routledge, 2013).

Nobuyuki Yamaguchi is associate professor in the Department of Biological and Environmental Sciences at Qatar University. He earned an MSc in Eendocrinology from Waseda University, Tokyo (1992) and a DPhil in Wildlife Biology from the University of Oxford (2000) by researching the ecology and reproductive biology of American mink (*Neovison vison*). His interests cover evolution and conservation of large terrestrial carnivores, especially big cats, and his goal is to bring more science into conservation decision making. He is keenly interested in conservation issues, notably how to select reliable units for research (e.g. taxonomically, ecologically, and evolutionarily), and the soundness of monitoring parameters conservationists use to assess conservation 'success'. He currently directs a research programme on the behavioural ecology of the Ethiopian hedgehog (*Paraechinus aethiopicus*) in Qatar, funded by grants from the National Priorities Research Program and the Undergraduate Research Experience Program of the Qatar National Research Fund. He has published papers in a wide range of journals.

Index

CPSIA information can be obtained at www.ICGtesting.com
Printed in the USA
LVOW05*0854261114

415574LV00014B/189/P